— FIFTH EDITION —

TEN STEPS
to
IMPROVING
COLLEGE
READING SKILLS

John Langan

ATLANTIC CAPE COMMUNITY COLLEGE

INSTRUCTOR'S EDITION

Books in the Townsend Press Reading Series:
Groundwork for College Reading with Phonics
Groundwork for College Reading
Ten Steps to Building College Reading Skills
Ten Steps to Improving College Reading Skills
Ten Steps to Advancing College Reading Skills
Ten Steps to Advanced Reading

Books in the Townsend Press Vocabulary Series:
Vocabulary Basics
Groundwork for a Better Vocabulary
Building Vocabulary Skills
Building Vocabulary Skills, Short Version
Improving Vocabulary Skills
Improving Vocabulary Skills, Short Version
Advancing Vocabulary Skills
Advancing Vocabulary Skills, Short Version
Advanced Word Power

Supplements Available for Most Books:
Instructor's Edition
Instructor's Manual and Test Bank
Online Exercises

Copyright © 2008 by Townsend Press, Inc.
Printed in the United States of America
9 8 7 6 5 4 3 2 1

ISBN-13 (Student Edition): 978-1-59194-099-9
ISBN-10 (Student Edition): 1-59194-099-0
ISBN-13 (Instructor's Edition): 978-1-59194-100-2
ISBN-10 (Instructor's Edition): 1-59194-100-8

Send book orders and requests for desk copies or supplements to:

Townsend Press Book Center
439 Kelley Drive
West Berlin, New Jersey 08091

For even faster service, contact us in any of the following ways:

By telephone: 1-800-772-6410
By fax: 1-800-225-8894
By e-mail: cs@townsendpress.com
Through our website: www.townsendpress.com

Contents

Part Two

Part Three

Appendixes

Preface: To the Instructor

We all know that many students entering college today do not have the reading skills needed to do effective work in their courses. A related problem, apparent even in class discussions, is that students often lack the skills required to think in a clear and logical way.

The purpose of *Ten Steps to Improving College Reading Skills, Fifth Edition,* is to develop effective reading and clear thinking. To do so, **Part One** presents a sequence of ten reading skills that are widely recognized as essential for basic and advanced comprehension. The first six skills concern the more literal levels of comprehension:

- Understanding vocabulary in context
- Recognizing main ideas
- Identifying supporting details
- Recognizing implied main ideas
- Understanding relationships that involve addition and time
- Understanding relationships that involve examples, comparison and/or contrast, and cause and effect

The remaining skills cover the more advanced, critical levels of comprehension:

- Making inferences
- Identifying an author's purpose and tone
- Evaluating arguments
- Separating fact from opinion, detecting propaganda, and recognizing errors in reasoning

In every chapter in Part One, the key aspects of a skill are explained and illustrated clearly and simply. Explanations are accompanied by a series of practices, and each chapter ends with four review tests. The last review test consists of a reading selection so that students can apply the skill just learned to real-world reading materials, including newspaper and magazine articles and textbook selections. Together, the ten chapters provide students with the skills needed for both basic and more advanced reading comprehension.

Following each chapter in Part One are **at least six mastery tests for the skill in question.** The tests progress in difficulty, giving students the additional practice and challenge they may need for the solid learning of each skill. While designed for quick grading, the tests also require students to think carefully before answering each question.

Part Two is made up of ten additional readings that will improve both reading and thinking skills. Each reading is followed by *Basic Skill Questions* and *Advanced Skill Questions* so that students can practice all ten skills presented in Part One. In addition, an *Outlining, Mapping,* or *Summarizing* activity after each reading helps students think carefully about the basic content and organization of a selection. *Discussion Questions* then afford instructors a final opportunity to engage students in a variety of reading and thinking skills and thus deepen their understanding of a selection.

Part Three consists of a series of twenty combined-skills tests that review the skills in Part One and help students prepare for the standardized reading test that is often a requirement at the end of a semester. Appendixes then include a limited answer key as well as writing assignments for all twenty readings in the text. When time permits, asking students to write about a selection will help reinforce the reading and thinking skills they have practiced in the book.

Important Features of the Book

- Focus on the basics. The book is designed to explain, in a clear, step-by-step way, the essential elements of each skill. Many examples are provided to ensure that students understand each point. In general, the focus is on teaching the skills—not just on explaining or testing them.

- Frequent practice and feedback. Because abundant practice and careful feedback are essential to learning, this book includes numerous activities. Students can get immediate feedback on the practice exercises in Part One by turning to the limited answer key at the back of the book. The answers to the review and mastery tests in Part One, the reading questions in Part Two, and the combined-skills tests in Part Three are in the *Instructor's Manual*.

The limited answer key increases the active role that students take in their own learning. They are likely to use the answer key in an honest and positive way if they know they will be tested on the many activities and selections for

At Townsend Press, I thank Kathryn Bernstein, Bill Blauvelt, Denton Cairnes, Beth Johnson, Paul Langan, and Ruth A. Rouff for the help they provided along the way. And I owe special thanks to two TP editors who brought their exceptional talents to this revision. Barbara Solot is responsible for a layout and four-color text design that are as clear as they are inviting. The result of her artistry is a strikingly attractive book that both students and teachers will appreciate. Janet Goldstein has provided design input along with her usual superb editorial skills. Her insights, coupled with her many years of classroom teaching, have strengthened the clarity and pedagogy of the book.

It is always a special pleasure to work with people who aspire toward excellence. With help from my colleagues in the teaching profession and at Townsend Press, I have been able to create a much better book than I could have managed on my own.

John Langan

To summarize, *Ten Steps to Improving College Reading Skills,* Fifth Edition, teaches and reinforces ten essential reading skills. Through an appealing collection of readings and a carefully designed series of activities and tests, students receive extensive guided practice in the skills. The result is an integrated approach to learning that will, by the end of the course, produce better readers and stronger thinkers.

Changes in the Fifth Edition

Following are changes in this edition of the book:

- **A full-color design.** Color has been carefully used throughout, not as window dressing but to add clarity and readability to the different parts of the book.

- **Numerous cartoons and other graphics.** Because so many students today are visual learners, over thirty illustrations have been added to help introduce or reinforce points made in the book.

- **A new chapter on critical reading.** "Fact and Opinion," a separate chapter in previous editions, is now part of a new Chapter 10, "Critical Reading." It will give students practice in all of the following: separating fact from opinion, detecting propaganda, and recognizing errors in reasoning.

- **New practice materials and readings.** The book includes four new readings, and practice materials have been freshened throughout.

Acknowledgments

I am grateful for the many helpful suggestions provided by the following reviewers: Glenda Bell, University of Arkansas Community College at Batesville; Carol Brenner, Pellissippi State Technical Community College; Gwendolyne Bunch, Midlands Technical College; Donna Clack, Schoolcraft College; Joanne Ernst, Pfeiffer University; Rochelle Favale, College of DuPage; Kay Fell, Tarrant County College; Linda Gilmore, Carroll Community College; Marianne Friedell, College of the Mainland; Belinda C. Hauenstein, Burlington County College; Iris Hill, Wake Technical Community College; Mary Huffer, Lake Sumter Community College; Nancy Joseph, Southeast Community College; Ellen Kaiden, Ramapo College; Miriam Kinard, Trident Technical College; Evelyn Koperwas, Broward Community College; Jackie Lumsden, Greenville Technical College; Denise May, Bucks County Community College; Vashti Muse, Hinds Community College; Helen Sabin, El Camino College; Annis Shields, Catawba Valley Community College; Tonya Strickland, Bainbridge College; Eileen Suruda, Essex Community College; Mary Temerson, Richmond Community College; Posy Thurow, Fox Valley Technical College; José Rafael Trevino, Laredo Community College; B. Jean Van Meter, Montgomery College; Paula Wimbish, Hinds Community College; and Leta Wium, Florida Community College at Jacksonville.

● **Supplementary materials.** The two helpful supplements listed below are available at no charge to instructors who have adopted the text. They can be obtained quickly by writing or calling Townsend Press (439 Kelley Drive, West Berlin, New Jersey 08091; 1-800-772-6410), by sending a fax to 1-800-225-8894, or by e-mailing Customer Service at cs@townsendpress.com.

1 An *Instructor's Edition*—chances are that you are holding it in your hand—is identical to the student book except that it also provides hints for teachers (see the inside front cover of the book), answers to all the practices and tests, and comments on most items. *No other book on the market has such detailed and helpful annotations.*

2 A combined *Instructor's Manual and Test Bank* includes suggestions for teaching the course, a model syllabus, and readability levels for the text and the reading selections. The test bank contains four additional mastery tests for each of the ten skills and four additional combined-skills tests— all on letter-sized sheets so they can be copied easily for use with students.

● **One of a sequence of books.** This text is the fourth in a series of six books.

Groundwork for College Reading with Phonics and *Groundwork for College Reading* are the basic texts in the series. They are suitable for ESL students and basic adult learners.

Ten Steps to Building College Reading Skills is often the choice for a first college reading course.

Ten Steps to Improving College Reading Skills is an intermediate text appropriate for the core developmental reading course offered at most colleges.

Ten Steps to Advancing College Reading Skills is a higher-level developmental text than the *Improving* book. It can be used as the core book for a more advanced class, as a sequel to *Ten Steps to Improving,* or as a second-semester alternative to it.

Finally, *Ten Steps to Advanced Reading* is the most advanced text in the series. It can also be used as a sequel (or a second-semester alternative) to either the *Improving* or the *Advancing text.*

A companion set of vocabulary books, listed on the copyright page, has been designed to go with the *Ten Steps* books. Recommended to accompany this book is *Improving Vocabulary Skills* (300 words and word parts) or *Improving Vocabulary Skills, Short Version* (200 words).

Together, the books and all their supplements form a sequence that should be ideal for any college reading program.

which answers are not provided. (Answers not in the book can be easily copied from the *Instructor's Edition* or the *Instructor's Manual* and passed out at the teacher's discretion.)

- **High interest level.** Dull and unvaried readings and exercises work against learning. Students need to experience genuine interest and enjoyment in what they read. Teachers as well should be able to take pleasure in the selections, for their own good feeling can carry over favorably into class work. The readings in the book, then, have been chosen not only for the appropriateness of their reading level but also for their compelling content. They should engage teachers and students alike.

- **Ease of use.** The logical sequence in each chapter—from explanation to example to practice to review test to mastery test—helps make the skills easy to teach. The book's organization into distinct parts also makes for ease of use. Within a single class, for instance, teachers can work on a new skill in Part One, review other skills with one or more mastery tests, and provide variety by having students read one of the selections in Part Two. The limited answer key at the back of the text also makes for versatility: the teacher can assign some chapters for self-teaching. Finally, the mastery tests—each on its own tear-out page—and the combined-skills tests make it a simple matter for teachers to test and evaluate student progress.

- **Integration of skills.** Students do more than learn the skills individually in Part One. They also learn to apply the skills together through the reading selections in Parts One and Two as well as the combined-skills tests in Part Three. They become effective readers and thinkers through repeated practice in applying a combination of skills.

- **Online exercises.** As they complete each of the ten chapters, students are invited to go online to the Townsend Press website to work on two additional practice exercises for each skill—exercises that reinforce the skill taught in the chapter.

- **Thinking activities.** Thinking activities—in the form of outlining, mapping, and summarizing—are a distinctive feature of the book. While educators agree that such organizational abilities are important, these skills are all too seldom taught. From a practical standpoint, it is almost impossible for a teacher to respond in detail to entire collections of class outlines or summaries. This book, then, presents activities that truly involve students in outlining, mapping, and summarizing—in other words, that truly make students *think*—and yet enable a teacher to give immediate feedback. Again, it is through continued practice *and* feedback on challenging material that a student becomes a more effective reader and thinker.

Introduction

1 How to Become a Better Reader and Thinker

The chances are that you are not as good a reader as you should be to do well in college. If so, it's not surprising. You live in a culture where people watch an average of *over seven hours of television every day!!!* All that passive viewing does not allow much time for reading. Reading is a skill that must be actively practiced. The simple fact is that people who do not read very often are not likely to be strong readers.

Answers will vary.

● How much TV do you guess you watch on an average day? _____

Another reason besides TV for not reading much is that you may have a lot of responsibilities. You may be going to school and working at the same time, and you may have a lot of family duties as well. Given your hectic schedule, you're not going to have much time to read. When you have free time, you're exhausted, and it's easier to turn on the TV than to open up a book.

● Do you do any regular reading (for example, a daily newspaper, weekly

magazines, occasional novels)? _____

● When are you most likely to do your reading? _____

A third reason for not reading is that school may have caused you to associate reading with worksheets and drills and book reports and test scores. Experts agree that many schools have not done a good job of helping students discover the pleasures and rewards of reading. If reading was an unpleasant experience in school, you may have concluded that reading in general is not for you.

● Do you think that school made you dislike reading, rather than enjoy it?

_____

Here are three final questions to ask yourself:

- Do you feel that perhaps you don't need a reading course, since you "already know how to read"? _____

- If you had a choice, would you be taking a reading course? (It's okay to be honest.) _____

- Do you think that a bit of speed reading may be all you need? _____

Chances are that you don't need to read *faster* as much as you need to read *smarter*. And it's a safe bet that if you don't read much, you can benefit enormously from the reading course in which you are using this book.

One goal of the book is to help you become a better reader. You will learn and practice ten key reading comprehension skills. As a result, you'll be better able to read and understand the many materials in your other college courses. The skills in this book have direct and practical value: they can help you perform better and more quickly—giving you an edge for success—in all of your college work.

The book is also concerned with helping you become a stronger thinker, a person able not just to *understand* what you read but to *analyze* and *evaluate* it as well. In fact, reading and thinking are closely related skills, and practice in thoughtful reading will also strengthen your ability to think clearly and logically. To find out just how the book will help you achieve these goals, read the next several pages and do the brief activities as well. The activities are easily completed and will give you a quick, helpful overview of the book.

How the Book Is Organized

The book is organized into four main parts:

Introduction (pages 1–18)

In addition to this chapter, which will give you a good sense of the book, there are two other parts to the introduction. "Reading for Pleasure and Power" is a personal essay that describes my own experience in becoming a reader and suggests ways for you to develop the reading habit. Turn to page 13 and write, on the line below, the first of the suggestions:

Create a half hour or an hour of reading in your daily schedule.

"Some Quick Study Tips" presents four hints that can make you a better student. If I had time to say just four things to incoming college students based on my thirty years of teaching experience, these are the things I would say. Turn to page 17 and write, in the space below, the first of these tips:

Go to every class and take a lot of notes.

Part One: Ten Steps to Improving College Reading Skills (pages 19–442)

To help you become a more effective reader and thinker, this book presents a series of ten key reading skills. They are listed in the table of contents on pages v and vi. Turn to those pages to fill in the skills missing below:

1 Vocabulary in Context
2 *Main Ideas*
3 *Supporting Details*
4 Implied Main Ideas
5 Relationships I
6 Relationships II
7 *Inferences*
8 Purpose and Tone
9 *Argument*
10 Critical Reading

Each chapter is developed in the same way.

First of all, clear explanations and examples help you *understand* each skill. Practices then give you the "hands-on" experience needed to *learn* the skill.

- How many practices are there for the second chapter, "Main Ideas" (pages 57–90)? _____ *Seven*

Closing each chapter are four review tests. The first review test provides a check of the information presented in the chapter.

- On which page is the first review test for "Main Ideas"? _____ *81*

The second and third review tests consist of activities that help you practice the skill learned in the chapter.

- On which pages are Review Tests 2 and 3 for "Main Ideas"? *81–84*

The fourth review test consists of a story, essay, or textbook selection that both gets you reading and gives you practice in the skill learned in the chapter as well as skills learned in previous chapters.

- What is the title of the reading selection in the "Main Ideas" chapter?
  "Here's to Your Health"

Following each chapter are at least six mastery tests which gradually increase in difficulty.

● On what pages are the mastery tests for the "Main Ideas" chapter? <u>91–102</u>

The tests are on tear-out pages and so can be easily removed and handed in to your instructor. So that you can track your progress, there is a score box at the top of each test. Your score can also be entered into the "Reading Performance Chart" on the inside back cover of the book.

Part Two: Ten Reading Selections (pages 443–548)

The ten reading selections that make up Part Two are followed by activities that give you practice in all of the skills studied in Part One. Each reading begins in the same way. Look, for example, at "The Yellow Ribbon," which starts on page 445. What are the headings of the two sections that come before the reading itself?

● _____ Preview _____

● _____ Words to Watch _____

Note that the vocabulary words in "Words to Watch" are followed by the numbers of the paragraphs in which the words appear. Look at the first page of "The Yellow Ribbon" and explain how each vocabulary word is marked in the reading itself.

● _____ It has a small circle after it. _____

Activities Following Each Reading Selection

After each selection, there are four kinds of activities that will help you to improve the reading and thinking skills you learned in Part One of the book.

1 The first activity consists of **basic skill questions**—questions involving vocabulary in context, main ideas (including implied main ideas and central points), supporting details, and relationships.

● Look at the basic skill questions for "The Yellow Ribbon" on pages 447–449. Note that the questions are labeled so you know what skill you are practicing in each case. How many questions deal with understanding vocabulary in context? _____ Two _____

2 The second activity is made up of **advanced skill questions**—those involving inferences, purpose and tone, argument, and critical reading.

● Look at the advanced skill questions on pages 449–451. How many questions deal with making inferences? _____ Four _____

3 The third activity involves **outlining, mapping,** or **summarizing**. Each of these activities will sharpen your ability to get to the heart of a selection and to think logically and clearly about what you read.

- What kind of activity is provided for "The Yellow Ribbon" on page 451?

  <u>Summarizing</u>

- What kind of activity is provided for the reading titled "The Certainty of Fear" on page 461? <u>Mapping</u>

Note that a map, or diagram, is a highly visual way of organizing material. Like an outline, it shows at a glance the main parts of a selection.

4 The fourth activity consists of **discussion questions**. These questions provide a chance for you to deepen your understanding of each selection.

- How many discussion questions are there for "The Certainty of Fear" (page 462)—and indeed for nearly every other reading?

  <u>Four</u>

Part Three: Combined-Skills Tests (pages 549–591)

This part of the book is made up of short passages that give you practice in all the reading skills taught in the book.

- How many such tests are there in all? <u>Twenty</u>

Appendixes (pages 593–622)

Following Part Three are appendixes that include a pronunciation guide, a limited answer key, and writing assignments for all twenty of the reading selections in the book. Reading and writing are closely connected skills, and writing practice will improve your ability to read closely and to think carefully.

Helpful Features of the Book

1 The book centers on *what you really need to know* to become a better reader and thinker. It presents ten key comprehension skills and explains the most important points about each one.

2 The book gives you *lots of practice.* We seldom learn a skill only by hearing or reading about it; we make it part of us by repeated practice. There are, then, numerous activities in the text. They are not "busywork," but carefully designed materials that should help you truly learn each skill.

Notice that after you learn each skill in Part One, you progress to review tests and mastery tests that enable you to apply the skill. And as you move from one skill to the next, the reading selections help you practice and reinforce the skills already learned.

3 The selections throughout the book are *lively and appealing.* Dull and unvaried readings work against learning, so subjects have been carefully chosen for their high interest level. Almost all of the selections here are good examples of how what we read can capture our attention. For instance, begin "The Yellow Ribbon," which is about a repentant man just released from prison who is wondering if his wife will allow him to return home—and try to *stop* reading. Or read the textbook selection "Gender Inequality in Health Care and in the Workplace," which reveals surprising facts about the different ways that men and women are treated in our culture. Or look at the textbook selection on pages 515–524, which considers the question of whether Lizzie Borden really was an ax-murderer.

4 The readings include *six selections from college textbooks.* Therefore, you will be practicing on some materials very much like the ones in your other courses. Doing so will increase your chances of transferring what you learn in your reading class to your other college courses.

How to Use the Book

1 A good way to proceed is to read and review the explanations and examples in a given chapter in Part One until you feel you understand the ideas presented. Then carefully work through the practices. As you finish each one, check your answers with the "Limited Answer Key" that starts on page 615.

   For your own sake, *don't just copy in the answers without trying to do the practices!* The only way to learn a skill is to practice it first and then use the answer key to give yourself feedback. Also, take whatever time is needed to figure out just why you got some answers wrong. By using the answer key to help teach yourself the skills, you will prepare yourself for the review and mastery tests at the end of each chapter as well as the other reading tests in the book. Your instructor can supply you with answers to those tests.

   If you have trouble catching on to a particular skill, stick with it. In time, you will learn each of the ten skills.

2 Read the selections first with the intent of simply enjoying them. There will be time afterward for rereading each selection and using it to develop your comprehension skills.

3 Keep track of your progress. Fill in the charts at the end of each chapter in Part One and each reading in Part Two. And in the "Reading Performance Chart" on the inside back cover, enter your scores for all of the review and mastery tests as well as the reading selections. These scores can give you a good view of your overall performance as you work through the book.

In summary, *Ten Steps to Improving College Reading Skills* has been designed to interest and benefit you as much as possible. Its format is straightforward, its explanations are clear, its readings are appealing, and its many practices will help you learn through doing. *It is a book that has been created to reward effort,* and if you provide that effort, you will make yourself a better reader and a stronger thinker. I wish you success.

John Langan

2 Reading for Pleasure and Power

Why Read?

Recently I was at a conference where a panel of first-year college students were asked, "If you could give just one bit of advice to high-school kids, what would it be?" One student answered, "I can answer that in one word: **Read.** Read everything you can. The more you read, the better off you're going to be." Up and down the panel, heads nodded. No one disagreed with this advice.

All these students agreed because they had learned the truth about reading—that it is the very heart of education. They had been in college long enough to realize that the habit of regular reading is the best possible preparation for college and for success in life. Here are four specific reasons why you should become a regular reader:

1 **Real Pleasure.** Chances are that you have done little reading for pleasure in your life. You may be an unpracticed reader who has never gotten into the habit of regular reading.

Perhaps you grew up in a home like mine where a television set dominated the household. Perhaps you got off to a bad start in reading class and never seemed to catch up. Or maybe you were eager to learn about reading when you began school but then soured on it. If you were given uninteresting and irrelevant material to read in school, you may have decided (mistakenly) that reading cannot be rewarding for you.

The truth is that reading can open the door to a lifetime of pleasure and adventure. If you take the time to walk through that door, chances are you will learn that one of the great experiences of life is the joy of reading for its own sake.

2 **Language Power.** Research has shown beyond any question that frequent reading improves vocabulary, spelling, and reading speed and comprehension, as well as grammar and writing style. If you become a regular reader, all of these language and thinking abilities develop almost automatically!

3   **Job Power.**   Regular reading will increase your chances for job success. In today's world more than ever before, jobs involve the processing of information, with words being the tools of the trade. Studies have found that the better your command of words, the more success you are likely to have. *Nothing will give you a command of words like regular reading.*

4   **Human Power.** Reading enlarges the mind and the heart. It frees us from the narrow confines of our own experience. Knowing how other people view important matters helps us decide what we ourselves think and feel. Reading also helps us connect with others and realize our shared humanity. Someone once wrote, "We read in order to know that we are not alone." We become less isolated as we share the common experiences, emotions, and thoughts that make us human. We grow more sympathetic and understanding because we realize that others are like us.

A Personal Story about the Value of Reading

I did little reading as a boy, with one notable exception: I loved comic books. In particular, I can remember reading comics at lunchtime. Since I attended a grade school that was only several blocks away, I could walk home at noon. There I would drink chocolate milk and eat my favorite sandwich—baloney, mustard, and potato chips layered between two pieces of white bread. I would sit at the kitchen table with my two sisters, home from the same school, as well as my father, home for lunch from his job with a local insurance company. The four of us sat silently because we were all reading. My sisters and I read mostly Donald Duck, Scrooge McDuck, and Mickey Mouse comic books, while my father read *Reader's Digest, Life* magazine, or the morning newspaper. Coffee cup in hand, my mother hovered nearby, always a bit frustrated, I suspect. She was in the mood for conversation, but her family was too busy reading.

Even when I went on to high school, I was more likely to read a comic book than anything else. Each year my English teachers typically assigned two books for students to read and report on—books such as Sir Walter Scott's *Ivanhoe* and Charles Dickens's *A Tale of Two Cities.* I had no interest in reading such books, especially ones that seemed to be about, as I remember saying at the time, "old dead stuff." How, then, did I deal with these assignments? I was rescued by a series of classic comic books, which were illustrated stories of famous novels. Classic comics helped me pass tests and do book reports. They also kept me from actually having to sit down and read a book—an activity that I never imagined could be a source of enjoyment.

What did give me pleasure was watching television. I developed a routine after school: get my homework done, do any household chores, eat dinner, and then spend the whole evening watching the tube.

Fortunately, something happened in the summer before my junior year that changed my life. The country was in the middle of a recession, so I was not able to get a job. I felt too old to spend the summer playing back-alley baseball with neighborhood buddies, and there was not enough on daytime TV (this was before cable) to hold my interest. Except for a once-a-week job of cutting my aunt's grass, I had nothing to do and felt restless and empty.

Then, sitting on my front porch one day in early June, I saw a public service message on the side of a bus that was rumbling noisily down the street. I remember the exact words: "Open your mind—read a book." Such messages had always annoyed me. On general principle I never liked being told what I should do. I also resented the implication that my mind was closed just because I didn't read books. I thought to myself, "For the heck of it, I'm going to read a book just so I know for sure there's nothing there."

That afternoon I walked to the one bookstore in town, browsed around, and picked out a paperback book—*The Swiss Family Robinson*—about a family that had been shipwrecked on an island and had to find a way to survive until rescue came. I spent a couple of days reading the story. When I was done, I had to admit that I had enjoyed it and that I was proud of myself for actually having read an entire book.

But in the perverse frame of mind that was typical of me at age 15, I thought to myself, "I just happened to pick out the one story in the world that is actually interesting. Chances are there aren't any more." But the more reasonable part of me wondered, "What if there are other books that wouldn't waste my time?"

I remembered that upstairs in my closet were some books that my aunt had once given me but I had never read. I selected one that I had heard of and that seemed to have some promise. It was *The Adventures of Tom Sawyer*, by Mark Twain, and it was a hardbound book now so old that its binding cracked when I opened it. I began reading, and while the activities of Tom were interesting enough, it was his girlfriend Becky Thatcher who soon captured my complete attention. My adolescent heart raced when I thought of her, and for a while I thought about her night and day. For the first time in my life, I had fallen in love— incredibly enough, with a character in a book! The character of Becky helped show me what power a book can have.

Tom had a friend named Huck Finn, about whom Mark Twain had written another book. So when I finished Tom's story, I went to the library, got a library card, and checked out *The Adventures of Huckleberry Finn*. I figured this book might tell me more about Becky. As it turned out, it didn't, but by pure chance I wound up reading one of the great works of American literature.

If Becky had made my blood race, the story of Huck Finn and the trip that he and his friend Jim took on a raft down the Mississippi River caught me up in a different but equally compelling way. While I could not express what happened at the time, the book made me look at people in a new light. I saw a whole stage of characters who felt very human and whose stories seemed very real. Some of these characters were mean and stupid and cowardly and hateful, others were loyal and courageous and dignified and loving, and a few were a blend of good and evil. By the time I finished Huck's story, I knew that books could be a source of pleasure, and I sensed also that they could be a source of power—that they could help me learn important things about the world and the people around me. I was now hooked on books. By the end of the summer, I had read over twenty novels, and I have been reading ever since.

How to Become a Regular Reader

How, you might be wondering, does one become a regular reader? The key, as simple as it might sound, is to do a great deal of reading. The truth of the matter is that reading is like any other skill. The more you practice, the better you get. In his book *The Power of Reading: Insights from the Research*, the reading scholar Stephen Krashen surveys an extensive number of studies and concludes that reading itself is the "way that we become good readers." The value of regular reading is a point about which common sense and research are in complete agreement.

The following suggestions will help you make reading a part of your life. Remember, though: These suggestions are only words on a page. You must decide to become a regular reader, and you must follow through on that decision. Only then will reading become a source of pleasure and power.

- Create a half hour or an hour of reading in your daily schedule. That time might be during your lunch hour, or late afternoon before dinner, or the half hour or so before you turn off your light at night. Find a time that is possible for you, and make reading then a habit. The result will be both recreation time and personal growth.

- Subscribe to a daily newspaper and read the sections that interest you. Keep in mind that it is not *what* you read that matters—for example, you should not feel obliged to read the editorial section if opinion columns are not your interest. What does matter is *the very fact that you read*. Feel perfectly free to read whatever you like: the sports page, the fashion section, movie reviews, front-page stories—even the comics.

- Subscribe to one or more magazines. Browse in the magazine section of your library or a local bookstore; chances are you'll find some magazines that interest you. You may want to consider a weekly news magazine, such as *Newsweek* or *Time*; a weekly general-interest magazine such as *People*; or any number of special-interest monthly magazines such as *Glamour, Sports Illustrated, Essence,* or *Health and Fitness*.

  You'll find subscription cards within most magazines; and on many college bulletin boards, you'll see display cards offering a wide variety of magazines at discount rates for students.

● Read aloud to children in your family, whether younger brothers or sisters or sons or daughters or nephews or nieces. Alternatively, have a family reading time when you and the children take turns reading.

● Read books on your own. This is the most important step on the road to becoming a regular reader. Reading is most enjoyable when you get drawn into the special world created by a book. You can travel in that world for hours, unmindful for a while of everyday concerns. In that timeless zone, you will come to experience the joy of reading. Too many people are addicted to smoking or drugs or television; you should try, instead, to get hooked on books.

What should you read? Select anything that interests you. That might be comic books, fantasies or science fiction, horror and mystery stories, romances, adventure and sports stories, biographies and autobiographies, or how-to books. To select a book, browse in a bookstore, library, or reading center. Find something you like and begin reading. If you stick to it and become a regular reader, you may find that you have done nothing less than change your life.

Questions

1. Was reading a priority in the home where you grew up? If so, tell how reading was emphasized. If not, describe what seemed to be the attitude towards reading in your home. How did your family's attitude (positive or negative) about reading affect your development as a reader?

2. When you were growing up, what role did school play in encouraging or discouraging you to read? Describe experiences in school that made you feel positive or negative about reading.

3. What do you think that parents and schools could do to make reading a source of pleasure for children? Suggest some specific ideas that would have worked for you as a child.

4. Of the five suggestions that appear in the section in this chapter titled "How to Become a Regular Reader," which one or two seem the most appealing and realistic to you?

5. Read one of the books recommended on the Townsend Press website. Go to www.townsendpress.com and click on "TP Library and Bluford Series." Over seventy books are available, each at only $1 apiece plus shipping and handling.

A Special Offer

To promote your reading growth, Townsend Press will send you three books at no charge except for postage and handling. Here are the three books:

Great Stories of Suspense
and Adventure

Making the Most
of Your Life

Dracula

Use the order form below, enclosing five dollars to cover the cost of shipping and handling. You'll then be sent these three very readable books.

ORDER FORM

YES! Please send me copies of *Great Stories, Making the Most of Your Life,* and *Dracula.* Enclosed is five dollars to cover the shipping and handling of the books.

Please PRINT the following very clearly. It will be your shipping label.

Name _____

Address _____

City _____ State _____ Zip _____

MAIL TO: TP Book Center, 439 Kelley Drive, West Berlin, NJ 08091.

3 Some Quick Study Tips

While it's not my purpose in this book to teach study skills, I do want to give you four quick hints that can make you a better student. The hints are based on my thirty years of experience working with first-year college students and teaching reading and study skills.

 TIP 1 The most important steps you can take to succeed in school are to go to every class and take a lot of notes. If you don't go to class, or you go but just sit there without taking notes, chances are you're heading for a heap of trouble.

 TIP 2 Let me ask you a question: Which is more important—learning how to read a textbook or learning how to read your professor?

Write your answer here: _____ *Learning how to read your professor* _____

You may be surprised at the answer: What is far more important is learning how to read your professor—to understand what he or she expects you to learn in the course and to know for tests.

I remember becoming a good student in college only after I learned the truth of this statement. And I have interviewed hundreds of today's students who have said the same thing. Let me quote just one of them:

> *You absolutely have to be in class. Then you learn how to read the teacher and to know what he or she is going to want on tests. You could read an entire textbook, but that wouldn't be as good as being in class and writing down a teacher's understanding of ideas.*

 TIP 3 Many teachers base their tests mainly on the ideas they present in class. But when you have to learn a textbook chapter, do the following.

First, read the first and last few paragraphs of the chapter; they may give you a good overview of what the chapter is about.

Second, as you read the chapter, look for and mark off definitions of key terms and examples of those definitions.

Third, as you read the chapter, number any lists of items; if there are series of points and you number them *1, 2, 3,* and so on, it will be easier to understand and remember them.

Fourth, after you've read the chapter, take notes on the most important material and test yourself on those notes until you can say them to yourself without looking at them.

 TIP 4 Here's another question: Are you an organized person? Do you get out of bed on time, do you get to places on time, do you keep up with school work, do you allow time to study for tests and write papers?

If you are *not* an organized person, you're going to have trouble in school. Here are three steps to take to control your time:

First, pay close attention to the course outline, or *syllabus,* your instructors will probably pass out at the start of a semester. Chances are that syllabus will give you the dates of exams and tell you when papers or reports are due.

Second, move all those dates onto a *large monthly calendar*—a calendar that has a good-sized block of white space for each date. Hang the calendar in a place where you'll be sure to see it every day—perhaps above your desk or on a bedroom wall.

Third, buy a small notebook and write down every day a *"to do"* list of things that need to get done that day. Decide which items are most important and focus on them first. (If you have classes that day, going to those classes will be "A" priority items.) Carry your list with you during the day, referring to it every so often and checking off items as you complete them.

Questions

1. Of the four hints listed above, which is the most important one for you? Why?

2. Which hint is the second most important for you, and why?

3. A graph later in this book makes clear just how quickly we forget new material. For example, how much class material do you think most people forget in just two weeks? Check (✓) the answer you think is correct.

   _____ 20 percent is forgotten within two weeks

   _____ 40 percent is forgotten within two weeks

   _____ 60 percent is forgotten within two weeks

   __✓__ 80 percent is forgotten within two weeks

   The truth is that within two weeks most people forget almost 80% of what they have heard! Given that fact, what should you be sure to do in all your

   classes? _____ *Take lots of notes.* _____

Part One

Ten Steps to Improving College Reading Skills

1 Vocabulary in Context

To the Instructor:

1. Any material in this smaller type appears only in the *Instructor's Edition*.
2. Pronunciations are provided for the words in this chapter and for vocabulary questions that follow the readings in Parts I and II. You may want to review with students the brief guide to pronunciation on pages 595–596.

If you were asked to define the words *ambivalent, adverse,* and *incessant,* you might have some difficulty. On the other hand, if you saw these words in sentences, chances are you could come up with fairly accurate definitions. For example, see if you can define the words in *italics* in the three sentences below. Then, using a capital letter, write the letter of your choice on the answer line.

Do not use a dictionary for this work. Instead, in each sentence, try the word you think is the answer. For example, put *mixed* or *critical* or *approving* into the sentence in place of *ambivalent* to see which one makes the best sense.

_A_ Many of us have *ambivalent* (ăm-bĭv′ə-lənt) feelings about our politicians, admiring but also distrusting them.

Ambivalent means

A. mixed.   B. critical.   C. approving.

_C_ The *adverse* (ăd-vûrs′) effects of this drug, including dizziness, nausea, and headaches, have caused it to be withdrawn from the market.

Adverse means

A. artificial.   B. energetic.   C. harmful.

_C_ I prefer the occasional disturbance of ear-splitting thunder to the *incessant* (ĭn-sĕs′ənt) dripping of our kitchen sink.

Incessant means

A. harmless.   B. exciting.   C. nonstop.

In each sentence above, the **context**—the words surrounding the unfamiliar word—provides clues to the word's meaning. You may have guessed from the context that *ambivalent* means "mixed," that *adverse* means "harmful," and that *incessant* is "nonstop."

Using context clues to understand the meaning of unfamiliar words will help you in several ways:

- It will save you time when reading. You will not have to stop to look up words in the dictionary. (Of course, you won't always be able to understand a word from its context, so you should always have a dictionary nearby as you read.)

- After you figure out the meaning of the same word more than once through its context, it may become a part of your working vocabulary. You will therefore add to your vocabulary simply by reading thoughtfully.

- You will get a good sense of how a word is actually used, including any shades of meaning it might have.

Types of Context Clues

There are four common types of context clues:

1 Examples

2 Synonyms

3 Antonyms

4 General Sense of the Sentence or Passage

In the following sections, you will read about and practice using each type. The practices will sharpen your skills in recognizing and using context clues. They will also help you add new words to your vocabulary.

Remember not to use a dictionary for these practices. Their purpose is to help you develop the skill of figuring out what words mean without using a dictionary. Pronunciations are provided in parentheses for the words, and a brief guide to pronunciation is on pages 595–596.

1 Examples

Examples may suggest the meaning of an unknown word. To understand how this type of clue works, look again at the sentence on page 21: "The *adverse* effects of this drug, including dizziness, nausea, and headaches, have caused it to be withdrawn from the market." The examples—dizziness, nausea, and headaches—helped you figure out that the word *adverse* means "harmful."

Look also at the cartoon on the next page. What do you think the word *initiative* (ĭ-nĭsh′ə-tĭv′) means?

A. anger   B. willpower   C. ability to take charge

HERMAN®   by Jim Unger

"You told me to use my initiative if I needed
money, so I sold your car."

HERMAN: © Jim Unger/Dist. by Newspaper Enterprise Association, Inc.

Note that the example of the wife's using initiative—going out and selling her husband's car—helps you understand that *initiative* means "ability to take charge."

✓ Check Your Understanding

Now read the items that follow. An *italicized* word in each sentence is followed by examples that serve as context clues for that word. These examples, which are **boldfaced,** will help you figure out the meaning of each word. On each line, write the letter of the answer you think is correct. Then read the explanation that follows.

Note that examples are often introduced with signal words and phrases like *for example, for instance, including,* and *such as.*

_C_ 1. *Nocturnal* creatures, such as **bats and owls**, have highly developed senses that enable them to function in the dark.

Nocturnal (nŏk-tûr′nəl) means

A. feathery.   B. living.   C. active at night.

_C_ 2. *Mundane* activities such as **doing the laundry or dishes** or **going food shopping** or **reading the newspaper** all help me relax.

Mundane (mŭn-dān′) means

A. exciting.   B. painful.   C. ordinary.

_C_ 3. Instances of common *euphemisms* include **"final resting place"** (for *grave*), **"intoxicated"** (for *drunk*), and **"restroom"** (for *toilet*).

Euphemisms (yōo′fə-mĭz′əmz) means

A. unpleasant reactions.   B. answers.   C. substitutes for offensive terms.

Explanation

In each sentence, the examples probably helped you to figure out the meanings of the words in italics:

- In sentence 1, the examples given of nocturnal creatures—bats and owls—may have helped you to guess that nocturnal creatures are those that are "active at night," since bats and owls do come out at night.

- In sentence 2, the activities referred to are clues to the meaning of *mundane*, which is "ordinary."

- In sentence 3, as the examples indicate, *euphemisms* means "substitutes for offensive terms."

PRACTICE 1: Examples

For each item below, underline the examples that suggest the meaning of the italicized term. Then write the letter of the meaning of that term on the answer line. Note that the last five sentences have been taken from college textbooks.

_A_ 1. Today I had to deal with one *mishap* after another. I couldn't find my car keys, I dropped a bowl of soup at lunchtime, and my computer crashed twice.   Three examples of unlucky accidents are given.

Mishap (mĭs′hăp′) means

A. unlucky accident.   B. event.   C. unexpected question.

Hint: For this and all the exercises in this chapter, actually insert into the sentence the word you think is the answer. For example, substitute *unlucky accident* or *event* or *unexpected question* in the sentence in place of *mishap* to see which one fits.

Two examples of odd ideas, signaled by *For instance.*   _C_ 2. Some mentally ill people have *bizarre* ideas. For instance, they may think the TV is talking to them or that others can steal their thoughts.

Bizarre (bĭ-zär′) means

A. limited.   B. ordinary.   C. odd.

To the Instructor: Hints such as the one above appear throughout the student edition. Students should be encouraged to use these hints when working through a chapter.

_B_   3. Some animals have remarkable *longevity*. For example, the giant land tortoise can live several hundred years.

An example of length of life, signaled by *For example*.

Longevity (lŏn-jĕv′ĭ-tē) means

A. appearances.   B. length of life.   C. habits.

_A_   4. Before the invention of television, people spent more time on *diversions* such as going to town concerts and ball games, visiting neighborhood friends, and playing board games.

Three examples of amusements, signaled by *such as*.

Diversions (dĭ-vûr′zhənz) means

A. amusements.   B. differences.   C. chores.

_A_   5. Since my grandfather retired, he has developed several new *avocations*. For instance, he now enjoys gardening and chat groups on the Internet.

Avocations (ăv′ō-kā′shənz) means   Two examples of hobbies, signaled by

A. hobbies.   B. vacations.   C. jobs.   *For instance.*

_A_   6. Children who move to a foreign country *adapt* much more easily than their parents, soon picking up the language and customs of their new home.

Adapt (ə-dăpt′) means   An example of adjusting.

A. adjust.   B. struggle.   C. become bored.

_C_   7. The Chinese government provides *incentives* for married couples to have only one child. For example, couples with one child get financial help and free medical care.

Two examples of encouragements, signaled by *For example*.

Incentives (ĭn-sĕn′tĭvz) means

A. warnings.   B. penalties.   C. encouragements.

_B_   8. Changes in such abilities as learning, reasoning, thinking, and language are aspects of *cognitive* development.

Four examples of mental abilities, signaled by *such . . . as*.

Cognitive (kŏg′nĭ-tĭv) means

A. physical.   B. mental.   C. spiritual.

_B_   9. Today was a day of *turmoil* at work. The phones were constantly ringing, people were running back and forth, and several offices were being painted.

Three examples of confusion.

Turmoil (tûr′moil′) means

A. discussion.   B. confusion.   C. harmony.

_C_ 10. *White-collar crime*—for example, accepting a bribe from a customer or stealing from an employer—is more costly than "common" crime.

White-collar crime (hwīt-kŏl′ər krīm) means crime committed by

A. gang members.   B. strangers.   C. people in the workplace.

Two examples of crimes committed by people in the workplace, signaled by *for example*.

2 Synonyms

A context clue is often available in the form of a **synonym**: a word that means the same or almost the same as the unknown word. A synonym may appear anywhere in a passage to provide the same meaning as the unknown word.

Look at the cartoon below.

"My doctor said smoking could terminate my life. But I told him, 'Everybody's life has to end some time.'"

© Randy Glasbergen. www.glasbergen.com

Notice that the synonym that helps you understand the word *terminate* is "end."

✓ ### *Check Your Understanding*

In each of the following items, the word to be defined is italicized. Underline the synonym for the italicized word in each sentence.

1. Fresh garlic may not *enhance* (ĕn-hăns′) the breath, but it certainly does improve spaghetti sauce.

2. As soon as I made a *flippant* (flĭp′ənt) remark to my boss, I regretted sounding so disrespectful.

3. Although the salesperson tried to *assuage* (ə-swāj′) the angry customer, there was no way to soothe her.

Explanation

In each sentence, the synonym given should have helped you understand the meaning of the word in italics:

● *Enhance* means "improve."
● *Flippant* means "disrespectful."
● *Assuage* means "soothe."

PRACTICE 2: Synonyms

Each item below includes a word that is a synonym of the italicized word. Write the synonym of the italicized word in the space provided. Note that the last five sentences have been taken from college textbooks.

__embarrasses__

1. Speaking in front of a group *disconcerts* (dĭs′kən-sûrtz′) Alan. Even answering a question in class embarrasses him.

   Hint: How does Alan react when he has to speak in public?

__examine__

What should someone do to a lease before signing it?

2. Because my friends had advised me to *scrutinize* (skrōōt′n-īz′) the lease, I took time to examine all the fine print.

__practical__

What kind of answers would the American people want?

3. The presidential candidate vowed to discuss *pragmatic* (prăg-măt′ĭk) solutions. He said the American people want practical answers, not empty theory.

__confusing__

If she cannot explain it, it must be confusing to her, too.

4. I asked the instructor to explain a confusing passage in the textbook. She said, "I wish I could, but it's *obscure* (ŏb-skyŏor′) to me, too."

__overlook__

What would a teacher **not** do if someone walked into class half an hour late?

5. Teachers may overlook it when a student is two minutes late. But they are not going to *condone* (kən-dōn′) someone's walking into class a half hour late.

__necessary__

What did the people—who are now broke—previously think about the things they used to buy?

6. When people are broke, they find that many things which seem *indispensable* (ĭn′dĭ-spĕn′sə-bəl) are not so necessary after all.

__opponents__

What kind of people should managers **not** permit to work together?

7. Managers should beware of having *adversaries* (ăd′vər-sĕr′ēz) work together; opponents often do not cooperate well.

__arrival__

If the arrival of mechanical equipment took farm jobs, the arrival of the computer would take manufacturing jobs.

8. In the same way that the arrival of mechanical equipment meant fewer farm jobs, the *advent* (ăd′vĕnt′) of the computer has led to fewer manufacturing jobs.

__charitable__

How would big corporations like to be seen?

9. Many corporations like to be seen as *benevolent* (bə-nĕv′ə-lənt) and will actively seek publicity for their charitable donations.

__customary__

Males being in control would be what kind of family authority pattern, in general?

10. Throughout history, the *prevalent* (prĕv′ə-lənt) authority pattern in families has been patriarchy, in which males are in control. In only a few societies has matriarchy been the customary authority pattern.

To the Instructor: Another way to approach synonyms is to notice the parallel structure of the sentence. For example, parallel structure points to the synonym in Item 2: to *scrutinize* the lease . . . to **examine** all the fine print.

3 Antonyms

An **antonym**—a word that means the opposite of another word—is also a useful context clue. Antonyms are often signaled by words and phrases such as *however, but, yet, on the other hand*, and *in contrast*.

Look again at the sentence on page 21: "I prefer the occasional disturbance of ear-splitting thunder to the *incessant* dripping of our kitchen sink." Here the word *occasional* is an antonym that helps us realize that the word *incessant* means "nonstop."

Look also at the cartoon below.

Copyright 2001 by Randy Glasbergen.
www.glasbergen.com

GLASBERGEN

"It's a special hearing aid. It lowers criticism
and amplifies compliments."

Note that the antonym *lowers* help you figure out that *amplifies* must mean "increases."

✔ *Check Your Understanding*

In each sentence below, underline the word that means the opposite of the italicized word. Then, on the answer line, write the letter of the meaning of the italicized word.

___B___ 1. Many people have pointed out the <u>harmful</u> effects that a working mother may have on the family, yet there are many *salutary* effects as well.

Salutary (săl′yə-tĕr′ē) means
A. well-known.   B. beneficial.   C. hurtful.

_____A_____ 2. Trying to control everything your teens do can *impede* their growth. To advance their development, allow them to make some decisions on their own.

Impede (ĭm-pēd′) means
A. block.   B. predict.   C. improve.

_____A_____ 3. During their training, police officers must respond to *simulated* emergencies in preparation for dealing with real ones.

Simulated (sĭm′yə-lā′tĭd) means
A. made-up.   B. mild.   C. actual.

Explanation

In the first sentence, salutary effects are the opposite of "harmful effects," so *salutary* means "beneficial." In the second sentence, *impede* is the opposite of "advance," so *impede* means "block." Last, the opposite of "real" is "simulated"; *simulated* means "made-up."

PRACTICE 3: Antonyms

Each item below includes a word that is an antonym of the italicized word. Underline the antonym of each italicized word. Then, on the answer line, write the letter of the meaning of the italicized word. Note that the last five sentences have been taken from college textbooks.

_____A_____ 1. Many politicians do not give *succinct* answers. They prefer long ones that help them avoid the point.

> **Hint:** If politicians prefer to give long answers, what kind of answer do they usually *not* give?

Succinct (sək-sĭngkt′) means
A. brief.   B. accurate.   C. complete.

_____B_____ 2. Although investments in the stock market can be *lucrative,* they can also result in great financial loss.

What is the opposite of something that is a financial loss?

Lucrative (loo′krə-tĭv) means
A. required.   B. financially rewarding.   C. risky.

_____B_____ 3. "I've seen students *surreptitiously* check answer sheets during exams," said the professor. "However, until today I never saw one openly lay out a cheat sheet on his desk."

If most students do not openly lay out cheat sheets, in what manner do they look at them?

Surreptitiously (sûr′əp-tĭsh′əs-lē) means
A. legally.   B. secretly.   C. loudly.

To the Instructor: Here, too, it's helpful to look at the parallel structure of the sentence. For example, parallel structure points to the antonym in item 3: *surreptitiously* check…. **openly** lay out.

_B_   4. While Melba's apartment is decorated <u>plainly</u>, her clothing is very *flamboyant.*   Melba's clothing is the opposite of her apartment decoration.

Flamboyant (flăm-boi′ənt) means

A. inexpensive.   B. flashy.   C. washable.

_A_   5. To keep healthy, older people need to stay <u>active</u>. Remaining *stagnant* results in loss of strength and health.   If being active keeps one healthy, being inactive leads to loss of health.

Stagnant (stăg′nənt) means

A. inactive.   B. lively.   C. unhealthy.

_C_   6. In formal communication, be sure to avoid *ambiguous* language. <u>Clear</u> language prevents confusion.   If clear language prevents confusion, what kind of language should be avoided?

Ambiguous (ăm-bĭg′yōō-əs) means

A. wordy.   B. ineffective.   C. unclear.

_B_   7. Being raised with conflicting values can be a *detriment* to boys' and girls' relationships with each other. In contrast, shared values can be a <u>benefit</u>.   If shared values can be a benefit, what would conflicting values be?

Detriment (dĕt′rə-mənt) means

A. improvement.   B. drawback.   C. relationship.

_B_   8. While houses and antiques often <u>increase in value</u>, most things, such as cars and TVs, *depreciate.*   In contrast to the increase in value of houses and antiques, what do most things do?

Depreciate (dĭ-prē′shē-āt′) means

A. remain useful.   B. lose value.   C. break.

_C_   9. Reliable scientific theories are based not upon <u>careless</u> work, but rather upon *meticulous* research and experimentation.

If they are not based on careless work, what kind of work would they be based on?

Meticulous (mĭ-tĭk′yə-ləs) means

A. hasty.   B. expensive.   C. careful.

_C_ 10. In the early days of automobile manufacturing, *stringent* laws controlled motorists' speed. In contrast, the laws designed to protect consumers from faulty products were extremely <u>weak</u>.

Stringent (strĭn′jənt) means

A. informal.   B. not effective.   C. strict.

If the speed laws are the opposite of the weak consumer protection laws, they would be strict laws.

4   General Sense of the Sentence or Passage

Sometimes it takes a bit more detective work to puzzle out the meaning of an unfamiliar word. In such cases, you must draw conclusions based on the information given with the word. Asking yourself questions about the passage may help you make a fairly accurate guess about the meaning of the unfamiliar word.

Look at the cartoon below.

Copyright 2006 by Randy Glasbergen.
www.glasbergen.com

GLASBERGEN

"I'd like a prescription that will alleviate my aches and pains and also make me younger and thinner."

To figure out the meaning of *alleviate*, try asking this question: What would the patient want the prescription to do to his aches and pains? The patient's words to his doctor strongly suggest that *alleviate* means "lessen."

✔ Check Your Understanding

Each of the sentences below is followed by a question. Think about each question; then, on the answer line, write the letter of the answer you think is the correct meaning of the italicized word.

_B_ 1. A former employee, *irate* over having been fired, broke into the plant and deliberately wrecked several machines.

(What would be the employee's state of mind?)

Irate (ī-rāt′) means
A. relieved.   B. very angry.   C. undecided.

_B_   2. Despite the *proximity* of Ron's house to his sister's, he rarely sees her.

(What about Ron's house would make it surprising that he didn't see his sister more often?)

Proximity (prŏk-sĭm′ĭ-tē) means
A. similarity.   B. nearness.   C. superiority.

_C_   3. The car wash we organized to raise funds was a *fiasco*—it rained all day.

(How successful would a car wash be on a rainy day?)

Fiasco (fē-ăs′kō) means
A. great financial success.   B. welcome surprise.   C. complete disaster.

Explanation

The first sentence provides enough evidence for you to guess that *irate* means "very angry." *Proximity* in the second sentence means "nearness." And a *fiasco* is a "complete disaster." (You may not hit on the exact dictionary definition of a word by using context clues, but you will often be accurate enough to make good sense of what you are reading.)

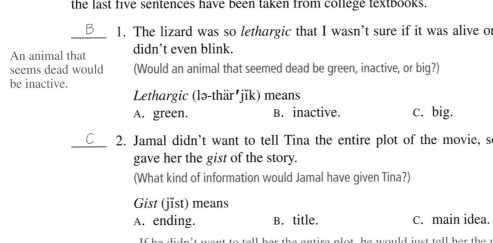

PRACTICE 4: General Sense of the Sentence or Passage

Try to answer the question that follows each item below. Then use the logic of each answer to help you write the letter of the meaning you think is correct. Note that the last five sentences have been taken from college textbooks.

_B_   1. The lizard was so *lethargic* that I wasn't sure if it was alive or dead. It didn't even blink.

An animal that seems dead would be inactive.

(Would an animal that seemed dead be green, inactive, or big?)

Lethargic (lə-thär′jĭk) means
A. green.   B. inactive.   C. big.

_C_   2. Jamal didn't want to tell Tina the entire plot of the movie, so he just gave her the *gist* of the story.

(What kind of information would Jamal have given Tina?)

Gist (jĭst) means
A. ending.   B. title.   C. main idea.

If he didn't want to tell her the entire plot, he would just tell her the main idea.

_A_   3. After the accident, I was angered when the other driver told the police officer a complete *fabrication* about what happened. He claimed that I was the person at fault.   The speaker would be angered if the other driver lied about the accident.

(How truthful was the other driver's information?)

Fabrication (făb′rĭ-kā′shən) means
A. lie.   B. description.   C. confession.

_B_   4. The public knows very little about the *covert* activities of CIA spies.

(What kind of activities would the CIA spies be involved in that the public wouldn't know much about?)   If the public knows little about the activities, they must be secret.

Covert (kŭv′ərt *or* kōv′ərt *or* kō-vûrt′) means
A. public.   B. secret.   C. family.

_C_   5. Whether or not there is life in outer space is an *enigma*. We may never know for sure until we are capable of space travel or aliens actually land on our planet.

If we may never know for sure, it must be a mystery.

(What would we call something to which we have no answer?)

Enigma (ĭ-nĭg′mə) means
A. reason.   B. certainty.   C. mystery.

_A_   6. Suicide rates tend to *fluctuate* with the seasons, with much higher rates in the winter than in the summer.

If the rates are higher in winter than in summer, the rates must go up and down with the seasons.

(What happens to the suicide rate from season to season?)

Fluctuate (flŭk′chōō-āt′) means
A. go up and down.   B. disappear.   C. stay the same.

_C_   7. Human beings are *resilient* creatures—they can often bounce back from negative experiences and adjust well to life.

(What point is the author making about the nature of human beings?)

If they bounce back, they must be able to recover.

Resilient (rĭ-zĭl′yənt) means
A. not flexible.   B. living.   C. able to recover.

_B_   8. A major accomplishment of sociology is *dispelling* the myths and prejudices that groups of people have about each other.

(What would a profession do to "myths and prejudices" that could be considered a "major accomplishment"?)

Dispelling (dĭ-spĕl′ĭng) means
A. ignoring.   B. making vanish.   C. creating again.

It would be a major accomplishment to make prejudices between groups vanish.

_C_ 9. Ten years of research *culminated* in a report explaining the mysterious behavior of the praying mantis, a large green or brownish insect.

It would be logical for ten years of research to conclude in a report.

(What would be the relationship of the report to the research?)

Culminated (kŭl′mə-nā′tĭd) means

A. failed.   B. began.   C. concluded.

_B_ 10. Despite complaints from parents, educators, and government officials, violence and sex on television seem to go on *unabated.*

(In spite of the complaints, does anything happen?)

Unabated (ŭn′ə-bā′tĭd) means

A. more slowly.   B. unstopped.   C. at great expense.

If the complaints have done no good, the violence and sex have not stopped.

An Important Point about Textbook Definitions

You don't always have to use context clues or the dictionary to find definitions. Very often, textbook authors define important terms. Also, after giving a definition, authors usually follow it with one or more examples to ensure that you understand the new term. For instance, here is a short textbook passage that includes a definition and an example:

[1]People do not always satisfy their needs directly; sometimes they use a substitute object. [2]Use of a substitute is known as **displacement.** [3]This is the process that takes place, for instance, when you control your impulse to yell at your boss and then go home and yell at the first member of your family who is unlucky enough to cross your path.

Textbook authors, then, often do more than provide context clues: they define a word, set it off in *italic* or **boldface** type, and provide examples as well. When they take the time to define and illustrate a word, you should assume that the term is important enough to learn.

More about textbook definitions and examples appears on pages 224–225 in the "Relationships II" chapter.

CHAPTER REVIEW

In this chapter, you learned the following:

- To save time when reading, you should try to figure out the meanings of unfamiliar words. You can do so by looking at their *context*—the words surrounding them.

- There are four kinds of context clues: **examples** (marked by words like *for example, for instance, including,* and *such as*); **synonyms** (words that mean the same as unknown words); **antonyms** (words that mean the opposite of unknown words); and **general sense of the sentence** (clues in the sentence or surrounding sentences about what words might mean).

- Textbook authors typically set off important words in *italic* or **boldface** and define those words for you, often providing examples as well.

The next chapter—Chapter 2—will introduce you to the most important of all comprehension skills, finding the main idea.

On the Web: If you are using this book in class, you can visit our website for additional practice in understanding vocabulary in context. Go to **www.townsendpress.com** and click on "Online Exercises."

REVIEW TEST 1

To review what you've learned in this chapter, answer the following questions by filling in the blank or writing the letter of the correct answer.

1. Often, a reader can figure out the meaning of a new word without using the dictionary—by paying attention to the word's _____*context*_____.

See page 21.

___A___ 2. In the sentence below, which type of context clue is used for the italicized word?   Spanish III is an example of a prerequisite.

   A. example   B. synonym   C. antonym

   You can't take certain courses unless you've taken a *prerequisite* (prĕ-rĕk′wĭ-zĭt); for instance, you can't take Spanish Literature I unless you've taken Spanish III.

___C___ 3. In the sentence below, which type of context clue is used for the italicized word?   *Thick* is the opposite of *sparse*.

   A. example   B. synonym   C. antonym

   There are thick pine forests at the foot of the mountain, but higher up, the trees become *sparse* (spärs).

___B___ 4. In the sentences below, which type of context clue is used for the italicized word?   *Talent* is a synonym for *aptitude*.

   A. example   B. synonym   C. antonym

   Talent may take years to surface. When Beethoven was a young child, his great *aptitude* (ăp′tĭ-tood′) in music was not at all apparent to his teachers.

5. Often when textbook authors introduce a new word, they provide you with a _____*definition*_____ and follow it with _____*examples*_____ that help make the meaning of the word clear.

See page 34.

REVIEW TEST 2

A. Look at the cartoon below, and then answer the questions which follow.

Copyright 2002 by Randy Glasbergen.
www.glasbergen.com

GLASBERGEN

"I'm trying to curtail my coffee drinking by cutting down to just one cup a day."

___B___ 1. Using the context clues in the cartoon, write the letter of the best meaning of *curtail* (kər-tāl′) in the space provided.
   A. improve   B. reduce   C. supplement
   Cutting down is a synonym clue.

___B___ 2. What kind of context clue helps you understand the meaning of the cartoon?
   A. Examples clue   B. Synonym clue   C. Antonym clue

B. Using context clues for help, write the letter of the best meaning for each italicized word. Use the space provided.

___B___ 3. *Nepotism* (nĕp′ə-tĭz′əm) is commonplace where I work: the boss's daughter is vice-president of the company, her husband runs the order department, and their son has just started working in the warehouse.
   A. good managerial practice   C. arguments among employees
   B. favoritism to relatives   D. confusion among management

___A___ 4. Because the professor's explanation was *nebulous* (nĕb′yə-ləs), several of the students asked him to make himself clear.
   A. vague   C. fascinating
   B. boring   D. brief
   Antonym clue: If the students ask him to make himself clear, the explanation must be vague.

_B_ 5. The bank robber was apparently *nondescript* (nŏn′dĭ-skrĭpt′)—none of the witnesses could think of any <u>special characteristics</u> that might identify him.   Antonym-like clue: If the witnesses cannot think

A. poorly disguised   C. memorable   of any special
                                                    characteristics,
B. lacking distinctive qualities   D. cruel   the robber must be lacking in
                                                    distinctive qualities.

C. Using context clues for help, write the definition for each italicized word. Then write the letter of the definition in the space provided. Choose from the definitions in the box below. Each definition will be used once.

| A. discouraged | B. doubtful | C. nag |
| D. overjoyed | E. provided | |

_D_ 6. I would not just be glad if I won the lottery; I'd be *ecstatic*.

Ecstatic (ĕk-stăt′ĭk) means ___overjoyed___.
                                        How would winning the lottery make one feel?

_E_ 7. Nature has *endowed* hummingbirds with the ability to fly backward.

Endowed (ĕn-doud′) means ___provided___.
        If hummingbirds have a special ability, it must have been provided by nature.

_A_ 8. Opponents of the death penalty say it has never actually *deterred* anyone from committing murder.

Deterred (dĭ-tûrd′) means ___discouraged___.
                            What is the death penalty supposed to do?

_C_ 9. Around the age of two or three, small children like to *badger* their parents with endless questions beginning with the word "why."

Badger (băj′ər) means ___nag___.
                    If they are asking endless questions, they are nagging.

_B_ 10. While four-year-old Mattie claimed she was going to stay up until midnight on New Year's Eve, her parents were *dubious* of her ability to remain awake that late.

Dubious (doo′bē-əs) means ___doubtful___.

How would a four-year-old's parents feel about her ability to stay up so late?

REVIEW TEST 3

A. Use context clues to figure out the meaning of the italicized word in each of the following sentences, and write your definition in the space provided.

Wording of answers may vary.

1. While it's often not *feasible* to work full-time while going to school, it may be practical to hold down a part-time job.

   Feasible (fē′zə-bəl) means _____practical_____

   Synonym clue: *practical.*

2. It's amazing that my neighbors always appear *immaculate*, yet their apartment is often quite dirty.

   Antonym clue: *dirty.*

   Immaculate (ĭ-măk′yə-lĭt) means _____clean_____.

3. It's against the law to ask people to *divulge* their ages at job interviews.

   Divulge (dĭ-vŭlj′) means _____reveal_____.

   What (regarding age) is it illegal to ask in a job interview?

4. Doctors should *alleviate* the pain of terminally ill patients so that their final days are as comfortable as possible.

   Alleviate (ə-lē′vē-āt′) means _____relieve_____.

   What would a doctor do to pain to make patients comfortable?

5. When rain and sunshine are *simultaneous*, the rain is often described as a sun shower.

   Simultaneous (sī′məl-tā′nē-əs) means _____at the same time_____.

   If the rain is described as a sun shower, it must be rainy and sunny at the same time.

B. Use context clues to figure out the meanings of the italicized words in the following textbook passages. Write your definitions in the spaces provided.

[1]Although mysteries and science fiction may seem like very different kinds of writing, the two forms share some basic similarities. [2]First of all, both are action-directed, emphasizing plot at the expense of character development. [3]Possibly for this reason, both types of literature have been *scorned* by critics as being merely "entertainment" rather than "literature." [4]But this attack is unjustified, for both mysteries and science fiction share a concern with moral issues. [5]Science fiction often raises the question of whether or not scientific advances are of benefit to humanity. [6]And a mystery story rarely ends without the *culpable* person being brought to justice.

Item 6:
If it is merely entertainment (rather than literature), how would critics feel about it?

6. *Scorned* (skôrnd) means _____looked down upon_____.

7. *Culpable* (kŭl′pə-bəl) means _____guilty_____.

What kind of person would need to be brought to justice?

¹Why did people begin to live in cities? ²To answer this question, we must start by looking back some ten thousand years ago. ³In certain parts of the world (probably those where the natural food supply was fairly unreliable), people *endeavored* to tame nature for their own purposes. ⁴They began weeding and watering groups of edible plants, adding organic matter to help fertilize the soil, and saving the seeds from the strongest, most desirable plants to sow the next spring. ⁵At the same time, they began protecting herds of small wild animals that were often hunted by larger animals. ⁶They would move them to more plentiful pastures during the dry months of summer. ⁷During the harshest periods of winter, they would *supplement* whatever fresh food was available with stored food. ⁸These changes, *coupled* with a few simple techniques for storing grain and meat, enabled people to abandon a wandering lifestyle in favor of settlement in small villages. ⁹These villages were the basic form of human social organization for the next several thousand years.

Item 8:
If the natural food supply is unreliable, people would try to tame nature (in order to increase the food supply).

8. *Endeavored* (ĕn-dĕv′ərd) means _____ tried _____ .

9. *Supplement* (sŭp′lə-mənt) means _____ add to _____ .
    If only limited fresh food is available, people would add to the supply with stored food.

10. *Coupled* (kŭp′əld) means _____ joined _____ .
    If the changes alone are not enough, they would have to be joined with the simple techniques.

REVIEW TEST 4

Here is a chance to apply the skill of understanding vocabulary in context to a full-length selection. Read the story below, a version of which appeared in *Reader's Digest*, and then answer the questions that follow.

Words to Watch

Below are some words in the reading that do not have strong context support. Each word is followed by the number of the paragraph in which it appears and its meaning there. These words are indicated in the article by a small circle (°).

smudged (2): dirty with streaks or stains
boondocks (3): a rural region
maneuvers (3): military exercises

NIGHT WATCH

Roy Popkin

1   The story began on a downtown Brooklyn street corner. An elderly man had collapsed while crossing the street, and an ambulance rushed him to Kings County Hospital. There, during his few returns to consciousness, the man repeatedly called for his son.

2   From a smudged°, often-read letter, an emergency-room nurse learned that the son was a Marine stationed in North Carolina. Apparently, there were no other relatives.

3   Someone at the hospital called the Red Cross office in Brooklyn, and a request for the boy to rush to Brooklyn was relayed to the Red Cross director of the North Carolina Marine Corps camp. Because time was short—the patient was dying—the Red Cross man and an officer set out in a jeep. They located the sought-after young man wading through marshy boondocks° on maneuvers°. He was rushed to the airport in time to catch the one plane that might enable him to reach his dying father.

4   It was mid-evening when the young Marine walked into the entrance lobby of Kings County Hospital. A nurse took the tired, anxious serviceman to the bedside.

5   "Your son is here," she said to the old man. She had to repeat the words several times before the patient's eyes opened. Heavily sedated because of the pain of his heart attack, he dimly saw the young man in the Marine Corps uniform standing outside the oxygen tent. He reached out his hand. The Marine wrapped his toughened fingers around the old man's limp ones, squeezing a message of love and encouragement. The nurse brought a chair, so the Marine could sit alongside the bed.

6   Nights are long in hospitals, but all through the night the young Marine sat there in the poorly lighted ward, holding the old man's hand and offering words of hope and strength. Occasionally, the nurse suggested that the Marine move away and rest a while. He refused.

7   Whenever the nurse came into the ward, the Marine was there. His full attention was on the dying man, and he was oblivious of her and of the night noises of the hospital—the clanking of an oxygen tank, the laughter of night-staff members exchanging greetings, the cries and moans and snores of other

patients. Now and then she heard him say a few gentle words. The dying man said nothing, only held tightly to his son through most of the night.

8   Along toward dawn, the patient died. The Marine placed on the bed the lifeless hand he had been holding, and went to tell the nurse. While she did what she had to do, he relaxed—for the first time since he got to the hospital.

9   Finally, she returned to the nurse's station, where he was waiting. She started to offer words of condolence for his loss, but the Marine interrupted her. "Who was that man?" he asked.

10   "He was your father," she answered, startled.

11   "No, he wasn't," the Marine replied. "I never saw him before in my life."

12   "Why didn't you say something when I took you to him?" the nurse asked.

13   "I knew right off there'd been a mistake, but I also knew he needed his son, and his son just wasn't here. When I realized he was too sick to tell whether or not I was his son, I figured he really needed me. So I stayed."

14   With that, the Marine turned and left the hospital. Two days later a routine message came in from the North Carolina Marine Corps base informing the Brooklyn Red Cross that the real son was on his way to Brooklyn for his father's funeral. It turned out there had been two Marines with the same name and similar serial numbers in the camp. Someone in the personnel office had pulled out the wrong record.

15   But the wrong Marine had become the right son at the right time. And he proved, in a uniquely human way, that there are people who care what happens to their fellow human beings.

Vocabulary Questions

Use context clues to help you decide on the best definition for each italicized word. Then, on the answer line, write the letter of each choice.

___B___ 1. In the sentence below, the word *relayed* (rē'lād) means
   A. hidden.
   B. passed along.
   C. made a gift.
   D. ignored.

How could one get the message from Brooklyn to North Carolina?

"Someone at the hospital called the Red Cross office in Brooklyn, and a request for the boy to rush to Brooklyn was relayed to the Red Cross director of the North Carolina Marine Corps camp." (Paragraph 3)

___D___ 2. In the sentence below, the words *enable him* (ĕ-nā'bəl hĭm) mean
   A. stop him.
   B. encourage him.
   C. know him.
   D. make him able.

By catching the plane, he might be able to reach his dying father.

"He was rushed to the airport in time to catch the one plane that might enable him to reach his dying father." (Paragraph 3)

_____D_____ 3. In the excerpt below, the word *sedated* (sĭ-dāt′ĭd) means

What might a hospital do to a person in pain?

A. spoken loudly.   C. armed.
B. wide awake.   D. drugged with a pain reliever.

"'Your son is here,' she said to the old man. She had to repeat the words several times before the patient's eyes opened. Heavily sedated because of the pain of his heart attack, he dimly saw the young man …" (Paragraph 5)

_____B_____ 4. In the excerpt below, the word *dimly* (dĭm′lē) means

If he is drugged and difficult to awaken, he would see the man unclearly.

A. clearly.   C. rarely.
B. unclearly.   D. often.

"She had to repeat the words several times before the patient's eyes opened. Heavily sedated because of the pain of his heart attack, he dimly saw the young man …" (Paragraph 5)

_____A_____ 5. In the sentence below, the word *limp* (lĭmp) means

Antonym clue: *toughened.* Also, if the old man is sedated and near death, his fingers would lack firmness and strength.

A. lacking firmness and strength.   C. long.
B. equally tough.   D. bleeding.

"The Marine wrapped his toughened fingers around the old man's limp ones, squeezing a message of love and encouragement." (Paragraph 5)

His toughened fingers … the old man's limp ones (fingers).

_____A_____ 6. A clue to the meaning of *limp* in the sentence above is the antonym

A. toughened.   C. message.
B. old.   D. love.

_____C_____ 7. In the excerpt below, the word *oblivious* (ə-blĭv′ē-əs) means

If his full attention is on the dying man, he would be unaware of other things around him.

A. mindful.   C. unaware.
B. bothered.   D. informed.

"Whenever the nurse came into the ward, the Marine was there. His full attention was on the dying man, and he was oblivious of her and of the night noises of the hospital …" (Paragraph 7)

_____D_____ 8. In the excerpt below, the word *condolence* (kən-dō′ləns) means

If she thinks he just lost his father, what kind of words would she offer?

A. excuse.   C. surprise.
B. bitterness.   D. sympathy.

"She started to offer words of condolence for his loss …" (Paragraph 9)

_____D_____ 9. In the excerpt below, the word *startled* (stär′tld) means

If she thinks the Marine is the man's father, she would be surprised by his question.

A. very pleased.   C. angry.
B. with admiration.   D. surprised.

"'Who was that man?' he asked. 'He was your father,' she answered, startled." (Paragraphs 9–10)

_C_ 10. In the sentence below, the words *uniquely human* (yoo-nĕk′lē hyoo′mən) mean

What animals besides human beings would do what the Marine did?

A. impossible for humans.
B. scary to humans.
C. done only by humans.
D. sudden by human standards.

"And he proved, in a uniquely human way, that there are people who care what happens to their fellow human beings." (Paragraph 15)

Discussion Questions

1. When do you think the Marine realized that calling him to the hospital was a mistake? Was it when he first saw the old man or before? What parts of the reading support your conclusion?

2. How do you think the dead man's real son felt about the other Marine being with his dying father? How would you feel?

3. The incident in the reading took place because of some surprising coincidences. What were they? Has a surprising or interesting coincidence ever taken place in your life? If so, what was it, and how did it affect you?

4. By going out of his way for a stranger, the Marine showed "in a uniquely human way that there are people who care what happens to others." Have you ever gone out of your way to help a stranger? Or have you seen someone else do so? Tell what the situation was and what happened.

Note: Writing assignments for this selection appear on page 599.

Check Your Performance   VOCABULARY IN CONTEXT

Activity	Number Right	Points	Score
Review Test 1 (5 items)	_____	× 2 =	_____
Review Test 2 (10 items)	_____	× 3 =	_____
Review Test 3 (10 items)	_____	× 3 =	_____
Review Test 4 (10 items)	_____	× 3 =	_____
		TOTAL SCORE =	_____ %

Enter your total score into the **Reading Performance Chart: Review Tests** on the inside back cover.

VOCABULARY IN CONTEXT: Mastery Test 1

A. Look at the cartoon below, and then answer the question that follows.

_A___ 1. Using the context clues in the cartoon, write the letter of the meaning of *gullibility* (gŭl′lə-bĭl′ĭ-tē) in the space provided.
   A. state of being easily fooled
   B. assertiveness   If the man believes the herbal stuff can do all
   C. irritability   the label says it can, he must be easily fooled.

B. For each item below, underline the **examples** that suggest the meaning of the italicized word. Then, on the answer line, write the letter of the meaning of that word.

_D___ 2. When I finally get around to cleaning out my refrigerator, I always find something *vile* (vīl) at the back of a shelf, such as moldy fruit or old smelly beans.
   A. tempting   C. false   Two examples of disgusting things
   B. recent   D. disgusting   found in the refrigerator.

_B___ 3. The Easter egg hunt featured *cryptic* (krĭp′tĭk) clues such as, "You'll find a prize somewhere narrow" and "Look for the pink."
   A. rhyming   C. clear
   B. puzzling   D. overused   Two examples (signaled by *such as*) of puzzling clues.

(Continues on next page)

45

_C_   4.   *Verbose* (vər-bōs′) writing can be hard to follow. For instance, "At this point in time, we have an urgently felt need for more and greater financial resources" is less clear than "We need money now."

     A. realistic   C. wordy   One example (signaled by *For*
     B. informal   D. ungrammatical   *instance*) of wordy writing.

C. Each item below includes a word or words that are a **synonym** of the italicized word. Write the synonym of the italicized word in the space provided.

search   5.   Americans spend millions each year on a *quest* (kwĕst) for the perfect weight-loss plan. Their search is for a pill or diet that will allow them to eat much and exercise little.   If people are searching for a pill or diet, they must be on a search for the perfect weight-loss plan.

false name   6.   Samuel Langhorne Clemens wasn't the first author to use the *pseudonym* (sōōd′n-ĭm′) Mark Twain. A newspaper writer of the time used the same false name.

Clemens and a newspaper writer both used the same assumed name: Mark Twain.

D. Each item below includes a word or words that are an **antonym** of the italicized word. Underline the antonym of each italicized word. Then, on the answer line, write the letter of the meaning of the italicized word.

_C_   7.   Computer manuals are often very hard to understand, so I was surprised to discover how *lucid* (lōō′sĭd) this one is.

     A. long   C. clear   If computer manuals are hard to
     B. expensive   D. new   understand and this one surprises
                                    the writer, it must be clear.

_B_   8.   When my sister first got her job at the recording studio, she was excited to go to work each day. Now, after ten years, she's *blasé* (blä-zā′) about her work and wants to change jobs.

     A. tardy   C. thrilled   Ten years ago, my sister was excited
     B. bored   D. curious   to go to work each day. But now
                                    she is bored with her work.

E. Use the **general sense of each sentence** to figure out the meaning of each italicized word. Then, on the answer line, write the letter of the meaning of the italicized word.

_A_   9.   A person can be very intelligent and yet be *deficient* (dĭ-fĭsh′ənt) in common sense.   The sentence contrasts having
                                                intelligence with

     A. lacking   C. overqualified   lacking common sense.
     B. well supplied   D. lucky   (*Yet* signals the contrast.)

_B_ 10.   The store detective faced the *dilemma* (dĭ-lĕm′ə) of either having an elderly, needy man arrested or ignoring store rules about shoplifters.

     A. memory   C. proof   *Either . . . or* tells us there is a choice.
     B. difficult choice   D. reason   The choice between having the
           elderly, needy man arrested and ignoring the store rules is a difficult one.

VOCABULARY IN CONTEXT: Mastery Test 2

A. Look at the cartoon below, and then answer the question that follows.

PEANUTS: © United Feature Syndicate, Inc.

_A_ 1. Using the context clues in the cartoon, write the letter of the meaning of
degraded (dĭ-grād′ĭd) in the space provided.

    A. treated with disrespect   The girl gives three examples of

    B. treated with care   being treated with disrespect.

    C. treated with fear

B. For each item below, underline the **examples** that suggest the meaning of the
italicized word. Then, on the answer line, write the letter of the meaning of that
word.

_B_ 2. Every *habitat* (hăb′ĭ-tăt′) in the world, from <u>volcano tops</u> to <u>icebergs</u>,
can support some sort of life.

    A. country   C. food source   Two examples of environments

    B. environment   D. practice   are given.

_A_ 3. Common *redundant* (rĭ-dŭn′dənt) phrases include "<u>cooperate together</u>"
(instead of simply "cooperate") and "<u>postponed until later</u>" (instead of
"postponed").

    A. repetitious   C. difficult   Two examples (signaled

    B. descriptive   D. useful   by *include*) of repetitious

                                                   phrases are given.

C. Each textbook item below includes a word that is a **synonym** of the italicized word.
Write the synonym of the italicized word in the space provided.

_____plain_____ 4. The Amish people prefer *austere* (ô-stîr′) styles—their
clothing and homes are plain.

                   Their plain clothing and homes reflect their preferred style.

_____conduct_____ 5. Airport security guards must observe people's
demeanor (dĭ-mē′nər) in order to notice any suspicious

The security guards have to   conduct.
observe people's conduct.

(Continues on next page)

47

_____modest_____   6. In business, it can be harmful to be too *unassuming*

If you are too modest about your achievements, the boss might not realize what you've accomplished.

(ŭn'ə-sōō'mĭng). If you're overly modest about your achievements, for example, you may be passed up for a promotion.

D. Each textbook item below includes a word that is an **antonym** of the italicized word. Underline the antonym of each italicized word. Then, on the answer line, write the letter of the meaning of the italicized word.

_____C_____   7. Even when textbooks are *standardized* (stăn'dər-dīzd') throughout a

Even though the textbooks are the same, the teaching methods may be quite different.

school system, methods of teaching with them may be greatly varied.
   A. different   C. made the same
   B. expensive   D. lacking

_____C_____   8. During the Middle Ages, everyone—from the rich landowner down to the most *impoverished* (ĭm-pŏv'ər-ĭsht) peasant—had a clear place in society.   The sentence contrasts the
   A. weak   C. poor   rich landowners with
   B. common   D. decent   the poor peasants.

E. Use the **general sense of each sentence** to figure out the meaning of each italicized word. Then, on the answer line, write the letter of the meaning of the italicized word.

_____D_____   9. It is odd how often public figures who loudly *espouse* (ĭ-spouz') "traditional family values" are later caught in some scandal concerning their own private lives.   What is odd about these
   A. recognize   C. reject   public figures who have been
   B. remember   D. argue for   caught in personal scandals?

_____B_____ 10. It is widely believed that Columbus sailed westward to *validate* (văl'ĭ-dāt') the theory that the world is round. In fact, it was already well known at that time that the world is round.
   A. think up   C. contradict   A theory is something that
   B. prove   D. foresee   has not yet been proved.

VOCABULARY IN CONTEXT: Mastery Test 3

Using context clues for help, write, in the space provided, the letter of the best meaning for each italicized word.

__A__ 1. It's a good idea for married couples to discuss their plans in case of each other's *demise* (dĭ-mīz'). For example, do they wish to be buried or cremated?
Burial and cremation are
A. death   C. desire to divorce   two ways of handling the
B. success   D. concern   body after a person dies.

__C__ 2. The press *assailed* (ə-sāld') the mayor for giving large city construction jobs to his brother-in-law's firm.
If the mayor is guilty of
A. searched for   C. attacked   corrupt behavior, the press
B. paid   D. fined   would attack him.

__C__ 3. One *tenet* (tĕn'ĭt) of Islam is that its followers should not drink alcohol.
An example of a tenet.
A. answer   C. teaching
B. prediction   D. guarantee

__C__ 4. Toddlers are naturally *inquisitive* (ĭn-kwĭz'ĭ-tĭv). Because they are so interested in their surroundings, they are eager to explore everything.
A. unreliable   C. curious   If they are eager to explore
B. clumsy   D. tired   everything, they must be curious.

__B__ 5. After x-rays were discovered in 1895, there were some *preposterous* (prĭ-pŏs'tər-əs) reactions. For example, London merchants sold x-ray-proof underwear.
The idea of selling people x-ray-proof
A. logical   C. dangerous   underwear is a ridiculous one.
B. ridiculous   D. delayed

__D__ 6. The foolish defendant *waived* (wāvd) his right to an attorney and instead spoke for himself in court.
If the defendant spoke for himself
A. depended upon C. wrote   in court, he must have given up his
B. greeted   D. gave up   right to an attorney.

(Continues on next page)

___D___ 7. Sexual standards in England during the 1800s were so strict that it was considered *sordid* (sôr′dĭd) for women to reveal their legs in public.

    A. proper   C. popular   If the sexual standards were very

    B. impossible   D. indecent   strict, then it would be indecent
                                          for women to reveal their legs.

___C___ 8. Young children believe their parents are perfect, until they become teenagers, when their parents suddenly become quite *fallible* (făl′ə-bəl).

    A. unhealthy   C. imperfect   Unlike young children, who

    B. dangerous   D. skilled   think their parents are perfect,
                                 teenagers consider their parents
                                              quite imperfect.

___D___ 9. America has often been called a "melting pot" into which people of many different cultures *assimilate* (ə-sĭm′ə-lāt′).

    A. learn   C. avoid each other   What would happen

    B. leave   D. blend   to things put into a
                                              pot to melt?

___B___ 10. The Englishman John Merrick's illness gave him such a *grotesque* (grō-tĕsk′) appearance that he was called "the Elephant Man." Despite people's reactions to his abnormally large head and twisted body, Merrick remained affectionate and gentle.

    A. strong   C. gray   How would you describe

    B. deformed   D. childlike   an abnormally large head
                                              and twisted body?

VOCABULARY IN CONTEXT: Mastery Test 4

Using context clues for help, write, in the space provided, the letter of the best meaning for each italicized word or words. Note that all of the sentences have been taken from college textbooks.

_C_ 1. After the Civil War, trolleys and streetcars greatly expanded workers' *mobility* (mō-bĭl′ĭ-tē), permitting them to move beyond walking distance from factories.

If streetcars permitted workers to live farther from their jobs, they must have increased the ability of the workers to move about.

A. pay   C. ability to move
B. skills   D. interests

_C_ 2. What people say may not reflect accurately what they are actually feeling. It is sometimes necessary to *resort to* (rĭ-zôrt′ tōō) clues other than their spoken words to understand them fully.

If people's words do not reflect what they are feeling, we have to make use of other clues to understand them fully.

A. remove from   C. make use of
B. make light of   D. ignore

_A_ 3. Individual political organizations often join together to form *coalitions* (kō′ə-lĭsh′ənz) to increase the support for their issues.

What would help an organization get more support for its issues? Synonym-like clue: *join together.*

A. partnerships   C. contests
B. lines   D. questions

_B_ 4. Surveys about people's sexual habits are often inaccurate because people may lie, and there is no way to *corroborate* (kə-rŏb′ə-rāt′) what they say.

If the surveys are often inaccurate, it must be because there is no way to prove the truth of what people say.

A. forget   C. change
B. prove the truth of   D. recall

_D_ 5. Everyone at the party was shocked by how *blatantly* (blāt′nt-lē) the woman insulted her former boss. She refused to shake his hand, saying, "I don't want to get my hand dirty."

The woman's refusal to shake hands and the words she speaks are an example of an obvious insult.

A. secretly   C. barely
B. accidentally   D. obviously

_C_ 6. Following the English principle that voters had to have a *stake* (stāk) in the community, the colonies generally required citizens to own a certain minimum amount of land in order to vote.

An example of an investment in the community.

A. job   C. investment
B. relative   D. employee

(Continues on next page)

_A_ 7. William Henry Harrison's 1840 campaign brought many *innovations* (ĭn'ə-vā'shənz) to the art of electioneering. For example, for the first time, a presidential candidate spoke out on his own behalf.

    A. new things   C. crimes   An example of a new thing.

    B. people   D. financial skills

_D_ 8. To fully *assess* (ə-sĕs') patients in order to place them in appropriate programs, mental health professionals need information on emotional adjustment and physical health.

                                  By studying information on

    A. find   C. hide   emotional adjustment and physical

                                   health, mental health professionals

    B. recognize   D. evaluate   are evaluating the patients.

_B_ 9. In the eating disorder known as bulimia nervosa, a person will go on huge eating binges and then will try to *nullify* (nŭl'ə-fī') the outrageous food intake by purposely vomiting or strictly dieting.

    A. increase   C. forget   Two examples of ways to undo the

    B. undo   D. delay   effects of the huge food intake.

_C_ 10. Adults who have both children of their own and elderly parents need to balance their commitments. They must look after their children and also *allocate* (ăl'ə-kāt') time and energy to care for their parents.

    A. recall   C. set aside

    B. pay for   D. view

                      Adults who are responsible for children and elderly parents cannot let the children take up all of their time and energy. They must set aside time and energy for the parents as well.

VOCABULARY IN CONTEXT: Mastery Test 5

A. Using context clues for help, write, in the space provided, the letter of the best meaning for each italicized word. Note that all of the sentences have been taken from college textbooks.

___C___ 1. The possibility of developing a top seller is so *alluring* (ə-loŏr′ĭng) that American companies spend billions of dollars a year trying to create new products or improve old ones.

If companies spend billions of dollars a year, the possibility of developing a top seller must be very attractive.

    A. dangerous   C. attractive
    B. final   D. unreasonable

___D___ 2. Using sign language, chimpanzees can *convey* (kən-vā′) such ideas as "Candy sweet" and "Give me hug."

    A. reject   C. think of
    B. accept   D. communicate

If the chimpanzees are using sign language, they are communicating.

___C___ 3. Smoking or chewing tobacco, wrote King James I, was "*loathsome* (lōth′səm) to the eye, hateful to the nose, harmful to the brain, and dangerous to the lungs."

    A. appealing   C. disgusting
    B. hidden   D. healthy

If a habit is hateful, harmful, and dangerous, it is logical that it would also be disgusting.

___A___ 4. The death of a spouse can cause *profound* (prə-found′) depression that, in some cases, can even lead to the death of the partner.

    A. deep   C. occasional
    B. accidental   D. mild

If the depression can lead even to death, it must be deep.

___C___ 5. The healthiest type of parents are those who guide and instruct their children, but also grant them a degree of *autonomy* (ô-tŏn′ə-mē), encouraging the children to make their own decisions and form their own opinions.

    A. financing   C. independence
    B. knowledge   D. guidance

Children who make their own decisions and form their own opinions are independent.

(Continues on next page)

B. Use context clues to figure out the meaning of the italicized word in each of the following items. Then write your definition in the space provided.

Wording of answers may vary.

6. A person giving first aid needs to make sure a body part that has been completely *severed* is sent to the hospital with the victim. Surgeons can often reattach the body part with microsurgery.

   Severed (sĕv′ərd) means _____ cut off _____

7. Tabloid newspapers often *distort* the news by reporting rumors as if they were true.

   Distort (dĭ-stôrt′) means ___ give a false account of; misrepresent ___

8. It's not always necessary for adults to *intervene* in children's fights; sometimes it's best to let children handle quarrels themselves.

   Intervene (ĭn′tər-vēn′) means ___ come between; get involved ___

9. Many companies once had retirement policies that made it *mandatory* for people to quit working as soon as they turned a certain age.

   Mandatory (măn′də-tôr′ē) means _____ required _____

10. After a heavy public relations campaign against the union, the hospital finally *relented* and allowed its workers to join.

    Relented (rĭ-lĕnt′ĭd) means ___ became more forgiving; gave in ___

Item 6: For surgeons to reattach the body part, it would first have to be cut off.
Item 7: An example of misrepresenting the news.
Item 8: If the children are handling the quarrel themselves, the adults are not getting involved.
Item 9: If it was company policy, then people must have been required to retire.
Item 10: If the hospital was against the unions but then let the workers join, the hospital must have given in.

VOCABULARY IN CONTEXT: Mastery Test 6

A. Five words are italicized in the textbook passage below. Write the definition for each italicized word, choosing from the definitions in the box. Also, write the letter of the definition in the space provided.

Be sure to read the entire passage before making your choices. Note that five definitions will be left over.

A. causing	B. deadly	C. delay	D. die
E. enjoyable	F. forced to experience	G. give credit for	H. helpful
I. pay for	J. reducing		

Item 1: Synonym-like clue: *dying*.

Item 2: If treatments led to many deaths (sentence 4), they were deadly.

Item 3: Patients are not likely to choose such unpleasant treatments. They must have been forced to experience them.

Item 4: Most remedies were not effective, but they gave relief. What can be given credit for the fair level of success?

Item 5: If patients' symptoms disappear, the placebos must reduce pain and discomfort.

¹In the early days of medicine, there were few drugs or treatments that gave any real physical benefit. ²As a result, patients were treated in a variety of strange, largely ineffective ways. ³For instance, Egyptian patients were medicated with "lizard's blood, crocodile dung, the teeth of swine, the hoof of an ass, rotten meat, and fly specks." ⁴If the disease itself didn't cause the patient to *succumb*, he or she had a good chance of dying instead from the treatment. ⁵Medical treatments of the Middle Ages were somewhat less *lethal*, but not much more effective. ⁶And as late as the eighteenth century, patients were *subjected to* bloodletting, freezing, and repeatedly induced vomiting to bring about a cure.

⁷Amazingly, people often seemed to get relief from such treatments. ⁸Physicians have, for centuries, been objects of great respect, and this was no less true when few remedies were actually effective. ⁹To what can one *attribute* the fair level of success that these treatments provided and the widespread faith in the effectiveness of physicians? ¹⁰The most likely answer is that these are examples of the tremendous power of the placebo effect—"any medical procedure that produces an effect in a patient because of its therapeutic intent and not its specific nature, whether chemical or physical." ¹¹Even today, the role of placebos in *curtailing* pain and discomfort is substantial. ¹²Many patients who swallow useless substances or who undergo useless procedures find that, as a result, their symptoms disappear and their health improves.

_D_ 1. In sentence 4, *succumb* (sə-kŭm′) means _____die_____ .

_B_ 2. In sentence 5, *lethal* (lē′thəl) means _____deadly_____ .

_F_ 3. In sentence 6, *subjected to* (səb-jĕk′tĭd tōō) means forced to experience .

_G_ 4. In sentence 9, *attribute* (ə-trĭb′yōōt) means _____give credit for_____ .

_J_ 5. In sentence 11, *curtailing* (kər-tāl′ĭng) means _____reducing_____ .

(Continues on next page)

B. Five words are italicized in the textbook passage below. Write the definition for each italicized word, choosing from the definitions in the box. Then write the letter of the definition in the space provided.

Be sure to read the entire passage before making your choices. Note that five definitions will be left over.

A. colorful	B. delayed	C. disappeared	D. increased
E. most common	F. passed	G. pray	H. punished
I. stir up interest	J. uncontrolled		

Item 6: If companies treated people so irresponsibly (sentences 3–8), their most common view must have been that their one responsibility was to make money.

Item 7: If the muckrakers' efforts led to new laws, they must have stirred up interest in the problem.

Item 8: What kind of capitalism would let businesses pursue profits above all else?

Item 9: If people lost faith in the current system, pressure would increase to fix it.

Item 10: The whole paragraph describes laws that Congress "voted in" or passed.

¹A century ago, the *prevailing* view among industrialists was that business had only one responsibility: to make a profit. ²By and large those were not good times to be a low-level worker or an incautious consumer. ³People worked sixty-hour weeks under harsh conditions for a dollar or two a day. ⁴The few people who tried to fight the system faced violence and unemployment. ⁵Consumers were not much better off. ⁶If you bought a product, you paid the price and took the consequences. ⁷There were no consumer groups or government agencies to come to your defense if the product was defective or caused harm. ⁸If you tried to sue the company, chances were you would lose.

⁹These conditions caught the attention of a few crusading journalists and novelists known as muckrakers. ¹⁰They used the power of the pen to create public anger and *agitate* for reform. ¹¹Largely through their efforts, a number of laws were passed to limit the power of monopolies and to establish safety standards for food and drugs.

¹²Despite these reforms, business continued to pursue profits above all else until the Great Depression. ¹³When the economic system collapsed in 1929 and 25 percent of the work force was unemployed, people lost their faith in *unbridled* capitalism. ¹⁴Pressure *mounted* for government to fix the system.

¹⁵At the urging of President Franklin Roosevelt, Congress voted in laws to protect workers, consumers, and investors. ¹⁶The Social Security system was set up, employees were given the right to join unions and bargain collectively, the minimum wage was established, and the length of the workweek was limited. ¹⁷Legislation was also *enacted* to prevent unfair competition and false advertising.

_____E_____ 6. In sentence 1, *prevailing* (prĭ-vā′lĭng) means ____most common____ .

_____I_____ 7. In sentence 10, *agitate* (ăj′ĭ-tāt′) means ____stir up interest____ .

_____J_____ 8. In sentence 13, *unbridled* (ŭn-brīd′ld) means ____uncontrolled____ .

_____D_____ 9. In sentence 14, *mounted* (moun′tĭd) means ____increased____ .

_____F_____ 10. In sentence 17, *enacted* (ĕn-ăk′tĭd) means ____passed____ .

2 Main Ideas

What Is the Main Idea?

"What's the point?" You've probably heard these words before. It's a question people ask when they want to know the main idea that someone is trying to express. The same question can guide you as you read. Recognizing the **main idea**, or point, is the most important key to good comprehension. Sometimes a main idea is immediately clear, as in the above cartoon. The point—that the marriage has problems—is well supported by the three differences between the couple.

To find the main idea of a reading selection, ask yourself, "What's the point the author is trying to make?" For instance, read the paragraph on the following page, asking yourself as you do, "What is the author's point?"

¹School bullies have been around as long as there have been schools. ²Studies reveal several reasons why some children become bullies. ³Research shows that a certain combination of size and personality may be one factor. ⁴Bigger, more aggressive children are more likely to try to dominate their smaller, quieter peers. ⁵Another factor linked to bullying is overexposure to violent TV programs. ⁶By the time the average American child is ten years old, he or she has watched thousands of acts of violence, including assault and murder. ⁷Such exposure can lead to aggression and violence. ⁸Finally, exposure to *real* violence is a factor in bullying. ⁹Studies indicate that victims of bullies often turn into bullies themselves. ¹⁰Whether abused by family members or tormented by other kids, bullies typically learn their behavior from others. ¹¹Look closely into the eyes of a bully, and you may be looking into the eyes of a former victim.

A good way to find an author's point, or main idea, is to look for a general statement. Then decide if that statement is supported by most of the other material in the paragraph. If it is, you have found the main idea.

Following are four statements from the passage. Pick out the one that is both a general statement *and* that is supported by the other material in the passage. Write the letter of that statement in the space provided. Then read the explanation that follows.

Four statements from the passage:

A. School bullies have been around as long as there have been schools.

B. Studies reveal several reasons why some children become bullies.

C. Research shows that a certain combination of size and personality may be one factor.

D. Studies indicate that victims of bullies often turn into bullies themselves.

The general statement that expresses the main idea of the passage is __B__.

Explanation

Sentence A: While this *is* a general statement, the paragraph does not go on to show how bullying has been a problem from when schools first began to the present day. Sentence A, then, is not the main idea.

Sentence B: The phrase "several reasons" is a general one. And in fact the rest of the passage goes on to describe a series of three supporting reasons why some children become bullies. Sentence B, then, is the sentence that expresses the main idea of the passage.

Sentence C: This sentence is about only one reason. It is not general enough to include the other reasons for bullying.

Sentence D: This sentence provides detailed support for the third reason for bullying—"exposure to *real* violence." It does not cover the other material in the paragraph.

The Main Idea as an "Umbrella" Idea

Think of the main idea as an "umbrella" idea. The main idea is the author's general point; all the other material of the paragraph fits under it. That other material is made up of **supporting details**—specific evidence such as examples, causes, reasons, or facts. The diagram below shows the relationship.

STUDIES REVEAL
REASONS SOME CHILDREN
BECOME BULLIES

Combination of size and personality
Overexposure to violent TV programs
Exposure to *real* violence

The explanations and activities on the following pages will deepen your understanding of the main idea.

Recognizing a Main Idea

As you read through a passage, you must **think as you read**. If you merely take in words, you will come to the end of the passage without understanding much of what you have read. Reading is an active process, as opposed to watching television, which is passive. You must actively engage your mind, and, as you read, keep asking yourself, "What's the point?" Here are three strategies that will help you find the main idea.

1 Look for general versus specific ideas.
2 Use the topic to lead you to the main idea.
3 Use key words to lead you to the main idea.

Each strategy is explained on the following pages.

1 Look for General versus Specific Ideas

You saw with the bullying paragraph that the main idea is a *general* idea supported by *specific* ideas. The following practices will improve your skill at separating general from specific ideas. Learning how to tell the difference between general and specific ideas will help you locate the main idea.

PRACTICE 1

Each group of words below has one general idea and three specific ideas. The general idea includes all the specific ideas. Identify each general idea with a **G** and the specific ideas with an **S**. Look first at the example.

Example

    S dogs
    S goldfish
    S hamsters
    G pets

To the Instructor: You might want to ask questions such as the following:
    Item 1: Which of the ideas are ways to eat dinner?
    Item 2: Which of the ideas are weather forecasts?
    Item 3: Which of the ideas are bad habits?
    Item 4: Which of the ideas are minor problems?
Similar questions can be asked for items 5 through 10.

(*Pets* is the general idea which includes three specific types of pets: dogs, goldfish, and hamsters.)

1. S home cooking
   S take-out
   G ways to eat dinner
   S frozen foods

2. S hot and humid
   S cold and rainy
   S cloudy with scattered showers
   G weather forecasts

3. S oversleeping
   G bad habits
   S overeating
   S smoking

4. S traffic delays
   S head cold
   S bad coffee
   G minor problems

5. S deadbolt locks
   S alarm system
   S barking dog
   G kinds of security

6. S divorce
   S failing grades
   G major problems
   S eviction

7. S not taking notes in class
   G poor study habits
   S missing classes
   S cramming for exams

8. S surprised
   G tone of voice
   S enthusiastic
   S bored

9. _G_ communicating
   _S_ writing
   _S_ reading
   _S_ speaking

10. _S_ hurry up
    _S_ get to bed
    _G_ commands
    _S_ clean up this mess

PRACTICE 2

Answers will vary.

1. Let's say you are describing a good friend. That he or she is a good friend is a general idea. List three *specific* reasons why he or she is a good friend.

   _____   _____   _____

2. All of us have certain valued material possessions in our lives. What are three *specific* objects that are very important to you?

   _____   _____   _____

3. Everyone has goals. What are three of the *specific* goals in your life?

   _____

   _____

   _____

4. Most students have had teachers whom they admire. Name one such teacher and three *specific* qualities or behaviors that made you like or respect that teacher.

   Name of teacher: _____

   Specific qualities or behaviors: _____
   Among qualities students might name: fair, enthusiastic, caring, appreciative,
   humorous, respectful.
   _____

5. At one time or another you had to do a really unpleasant chore or job. Write three *specific* reasons why that chore or job was so unpleasant.
   Among reasons students might list: poor pay, inconsiderate boss, long hours,
   few breaks, noisy or dirty or stressful environment.
   _____

PRACTICE 3

In the following groups, one statement is the general point, and the other statements are specific support for the point. Identify each point with a **P** and each statement of support with an **S**.

1. _P_ My family has real problems.

   _S_ My mother has cancer.

   _S_ My sister is pregnant.

   _S_ I lost my job.

   Three specific problems are stated.

2. _S_ Iris has a great smile.

   _S_ Iris asks you questions about yourself.

   _P_ Iris is a pleasure to be around.

   _S_ Iris really listens when you talk.

   Three specific reasons why Iris is a pleasure to be around.

3. _S_ I feel short of breath.

   _S_ I'm getting dizzy and sweating.

   _S_ There is a pain in my chest.

   _P_ I may be having a heart attack.

   Three symptoms of a heart attack.

4. _P_ My boss is hard to work for.

   _S_ He lacks a sense of humor.

   _S_ He never gives praise.

   _S_ He times all our breaks to the second.

   Three specific reasons the boss is hard to work for.

5. _S_ We had different political beliefs.

   _P_ The date was a nightmare.

   _S_ We were dressed completely differently.

   _S_ Both of us were too nervous to say much.

   Three specific reasons the date was a nightmare.

PRACTICE 4

In each of the following groups, one statement is the general point, and the other statements are specific support for the point. Identify each point with a **P** and each statement of support with an **S**.

1. _S_ A. Last night we could hear and smell a large animal prowling outside our tent.

   _S_ B. Green flies with stinging bites are in abundance around our campsite.

   _P_ C. The time has come to find a new campsite.   Three reasons for finding a new

   _S_ D. Nearby we came upon a nest of baby rattlesnakes.   campsite are given.

2. _P_ A. Children are at risk at the school.

   _S_ B. There are two active gangs in the school.   Three reasons why the children are at

   _S_ C. Knives and guns have been found in lockers.   risk are stated.

   _S_ D. Drug busts have been made at the school.

3. _S_ A. Cats are clean and do not require much attention.   Three advantages of cats. *Definite*

   _P_ B. There are definite advantages to having a cat as a pet.   *advantages*

   _S_ C. Cats like living indoors and are safe to have around children.   is a clue.

   _S_ D. Cats are inexpensive to feed and easy to keep healthy.

4. _S_ A. Communicating with family and friends using computer e-mail takes very little effort or time.

   _S_ B. Finding information is as easy as typing several key words.

   _S_ C. Shopping can be quickly handled online with a few clicks of the mouse and the use of a credit card.   Three examples of everyday matters that

   _P_ D. Computers make everyday matters much easier.   computers make easier.

5. _S_ A. Instead of working full-time, many of today's employees work part-time with little job security and few benefits.

   _P_ B. Job security and our ideas about work have changed dramatically in recent years.

   _S_ C. Unlike in years past, most people entering the workforce today will change jobs several times during their careers.

   _S_ D. Rather than work for someone else, many of today's workers hope to start their own businesses.

         Three examples of changes in job security and ideas about work.

2   Use the Topic to Lead You to the Main Idea

You already know that to find the main idea of a selection, you look first for a general statement, which is often at the beginning of a selection. You then check to see if that statement is supported by most of the other material in the paragraph. If it is, you've found the main idea. Another approach that can help you find the main idea is to decide on the topic of a given selection.

The **topic** is the general subject of a selection. It can often be expressed in one or more words. Knowing the topic can help you find a writer's main point about that topic. Paying close attention to the topic of a selection can lead you to the main idea.

Textbook authors use the title of each chapter to state the overall topic of that chapter. They also provide many topics and subtopics in boldface headings within the chapter. For example, here is the title of a chapter in a sociology textbook:

Aggression: Hurting Others (a 38-page chapter)

And here are the subtopics:

Theories of Aggression (a 12-page section)

Influences on Aggression (a 20-page section)

Reducing Aggression (a 6-page section)

If you were studying the above chapter, you could use the topics to help find the main ideas. (Pages 17–18 explain just how to do so, as well as other textbook study tips.)

But there are many times when you are not given topics—with standardized reading tests, for example, or with individual paragraphs in articles or textbooks. To find the topic of a selection when the topic is not given, ask this simple question:

Who or what is the selection about?

For example, look again at the beginning of the paragraph that started this chapter:

School bullies have been around as long as there have been schools. Studies reveal several reasons why some children become bullies.

What, in a single word, is the above paragraph about? On the line below, write what you think is the topic.

Topic: _____ Bullies _____

You probably answered that the topic is "Bullies." As you read the paragraph again, you saw that, in fact, every sentence in it is about bullying.

The next step after finding the topic is to decide what main point the author is making about the topic. Authors often present their main idea in a single sentence. (This sentence is also known as the **main idea sentence** or the **topic sentence**.) As we have already seen, the main point that is made about bullying is that "Studies reveal several reasons why some children become bullies."

✔ *Check Your Understanding*

Let's look now at another paragraph. Read it and then see if you can answer the questions that follow.

> ¹Though fun to watch, chimpanzees should not be kept as pets. ²They are dangerously stronger than any NFL lineman. ³Adult chimps weigh only 100 to 160 pounds, but have been measured pulling six to nine times their own weight—*with one hand.* ⁴Thus, to match the strength of an average chimp, a human being would have to be able to register a two-handed pull of about a ton; it takes a very strong man to pull a quarter of that. ⁵Combined with this strength is the fact that a chimp is capable of losing its temper—for reasons known only to the chimp. ⁶Chimps signal their feelings with subtle cues of behavior that aren't apparent to most humans. ⁷It's quite possible for a chimp to be on the verge of violence while its owner sits unaware or even unknowingly continues to provoke it. ⁸Furthermore, it's not wise to keep a cute young chimp and release it into the wild when it becomes dangerous. ⁹Wild-raised chimps will routinely gang up on and kill those raised in captivity.

1. What is the *topic* of the paragraph? In other words, what is the paragraph about? _____ *chimpanzees* _____

   Hint: It often helps to look for (and even circle) a word or idea that is repeated in the paragraph.

2. What is the *main idea* of the paragraph? In other words, what point is the author making about the topic? (Remember that the main idea will be supported by the other material in the paragraph.)

   Chimpanzees should not be kept as pets.
   _____

Explanation

As the first sentence of the paragraph suggests, the topic is "chimpanzees." Reading the paragraph, you see that, in fact, everything in it is about chimpanzees. And the main idea is clearly that "chimpanzees should not be kept as pets." This idea is a general one that sums up what the entire paragraph is about. It is an "umbrella" statement under which all the other material in the paragraph fits. The parts of the paragraph could be shown as follows:

Topic: Chimpanzees

Main idea: Chimpanzees should not be kept as pets.

Supporting details:
1. Dangerously strong
2. Capable of losing temper
3. Liable to be attacked if released in the wild

The following practices will sharpen your sense of the difference between a topic, the point about the topic (the main idea), and supporting details.

PRACTICE 5

Below are groups of four items. In each case, one item is the topic, one is the main idea, and two are details that support and develop the main idea. Label each item with one of the following:

> **T** — for the **topic** of the paragraph
> **MI** — for the **main idea**
> **SD** — for the **supporting details**

Note that an explanation is provided for the first group; reading it will help you do this practice.   *To the Instructor:* The topics are easy to spot because they are short phrases, not full sentences.

Group 1

____SD____ A. The creakings of a house settling may sound like a monster coming out of a grave.

____SD____ B. Gusts of wind rattling a bedroom window can sound like invaders about to break in.

____MI____ C. Nighttime noises can be frightening to children.

____T____ D. Noises at night.

Explanation

All of the statements in Group 1 are about noises at night, so item D must be the topic. Statements A and B each describe specific nighttime noises. Statement C, however, presents the general idea that nighttime noises can be frightening to children. It is the main idea about the topic "noises at night," and statements A and B are supporting details that illustrate that main idea.

Group 2

____MI____ A. People vary in the amount of daydreaming they do.

____SD____ B. Around 2 to 4 percent of the population spend at least half their free time fantasizing.

____SD____ C. Almost everyone daydreams about 10 percent of the time.

____T____ D. Daydreaming.   Statements B and C are specific examples of how people vary in their daydreaming.

Group 3

_T_ A. Global warming.

The words *destructive changes* are a clue to the main idea. Statements B and C are examples of destructive changes.

_SD_ B. Melting ice caps will raise ocean water levels and flood coastal areas.

_SD_ C. A warmer atmosphere may cause droughts that will turn farmlands to deserts.

_MI_ D. Global warming may cause destructive changes to life on Earth.

Group 4

The words *ways to remain healthy* point to the main idea. Statements B and C give examples of ways to remain healthy.

_MI_ A. There are ways to remain healthy in old age.

_SD_ B. One way for people to remain healthy as they age is to continue to find mental challenges.

_SD_ C. Sticking to a balanced, low-cholesterol diet and a reasonable exercise program helps keep people in good shape throughout their lives.

_T_ D. Health in old age.

Group 5

Identifying the topic—love at first sight—helps lead to the main idea. Statements B and D give two reasons love at first sight is a poor basis for marriage.

_MI_ A. Love at first sight is a poor basis for a happy marriage, according to a study of one thousand married and divorced couples.

_SD_ B. Couples who knew each other only slightly but fell instantly in love found that their feelings for each other grew weaker instead of stronger.

_T_ C. Love at first sight.

_SD_ D. The couples who considered themselves happily married reported that they were not powerfully attracted to their partners when they first met, but that they gradually found each other more attractive as they grew to know and understand each other.

PRACTICE 6

Following are five paragraphs. Read each paragraph and do the following:

1 Ask yourself, "What seems to be the topic of the paragraph?" (It often helps to look for and even circle a word or idea that is repeated in the paragraph.)

2 Next, ask yourself, "What is the writer's main point about this topic?" This will be the main idea. It is stated in one of the sentences in the paragraph.

3 Then test what you think is the main idea sentence by asking, "Is this statement supported by all or most of the other material in the paragraph?"

> *Hint:* When looking for the topic, make sure you do not pick one that is either **too broad** (covering a great deal more than is in the selection) or **too narrow** (covering only part of the selection). The topic and the main idea of a selection must include everything in that selection—no more and no less.
>
> For example, in Group 1 on page 66, the topic is "noises at night." "Noises" would be too broad, since there are many other types of noises that are not mentioned. "The creakings of a house" would be too narrow, since this is only one type of nighttime noise mentioned.

Paragraph 1

¹Stories have the magic to focus our attention and maintain our interest. ²The politician or preacher who says, "That reminds me of a story . . . " has an audience's attention immediately. ³Consider the success of television's *60 Minutes*, the longest-running and most profitable prime-time show in the history of television. ⁴The person behind its success, producer Don Hewitt, says, "The secret of our show is so simple I can't believe the formula hasn't been followed by others. ⁵It's four words that every kid knows: 'Tell me a story.' ⁶I look at things in screening rooms and I say, 'That's an interesting guy and those are some great scenes you've got, but what's the story?'" ⁷Without the "story," Hewitt knows the audience is leaving.

1. What is the *topic* of the paragraph? In other words, what (in one or more words) is the paragraph about? _____ Stories _____

___1___ 2. What point is the writer making about this topic? In other words, what is the *main idea* of the paragraph? In the space provided, write the number of the sentence containing the main idea. (Remember that the main idea will be supported by the other material in the paragraph.)

> The word *story* (or *stories*) appears five times in the paragraph. The example in sentence 2 and the long example in sentences 3–7 provide support for the main idea in sentence 1.

Paragraph 2

¹Extrasensory perception, or ESP, is an area that fascinates people. ²However, ESP is not documented by any convincing evidence. ³For instance, it would seem that ESP would be an excellent way of winning at games of chance, such as those played at gambling casinos. ⁴But casino owners in Las Vegas and Atlantic City report no problem with "psychics" winning great sums of money. ⁵Also, although great publicity is generated when a psychic seems to help police solve a crime, the value of such help has never been scientifically proven. ⁶Tips from psychics are usually worthless, and almost all cases are solved through traditional police work. ⁷And while audiences may be amazed at the feats of "mind readers," the fact is that mind readers use simple psychological tricks to exploit their audiences' willingness to believe.

1. What is the *topic* of the paragraph? _____ ESP _____

_2_ 2. What point is the writer making about this topic? In other words, what is the *main idea* of the paragraph? In the space provided, write the number of the sentence containing the main idea.

> Sentence 1 announces the topic. Sentences 3–9 are examples of the lack of convincing evidence for ESP.

Paragraph 3

¹Hospices are a special type of health-care institution. ²Hospices differ from hospitals and nursing homes in several ways. ³First of all, they treat patients suffering from incurable diseases who are not expected to live for more than a year. ⁴Hospitals, however, aim to help patients recover from disease, and nursing homes provide long-term care for the disabled and elderly. ⁵Also, the hospice's purpose is to help the dying and their families. ⁶In contrast, hospitals and nursing homes have limited resources for helping patients' families.

1. What is the *topic* of the paragraph? _____ Hospices vs. hospitals _____

_2_ 2. What point is the writer making about this topic? In other words, what is the *main idea* of the paragraph? In the space provided, write the number of the sentence containing the main idea.

> Sentence 1 introduces the topic of hospices. Sentences 3–6 describe two ways that hospices differ from hospitals and nursing homes.

Paragraph 4

[1]Some people persist in believing that they can drink and be alert drivers. [2]Yet alcohol is estimated to be a factor in at least half of all fatal highway accidents. [3]Another poor attitude about driving is the refusal to wear seat belts. [4]Statistics show that the chances of being seriously hurt or dying in a car accident are greater when a seat belt is not worn. [5]Also potentially deadly is the view that the best driving is fast driving. [6]Again, statistics contradict this attitude—fast driving is more likely to be deadly driving. [7]After speed limits are lowered, traffic fatalities fall significantly. [8]A final mistaken attitude is that speaking on a cell phone will not detract from a driver's attention and response time to unexpected traffic conditions. [9]Studies prove otherwise, with the result that many have called for a ban on cell phones while driving. [10]There is simply no question that poor attitudes about driving contribute to the high rate of traffic accidents and their brutal effects.

1. What is the *topic* of the paragraph? _____*Driving*_____

    _____*(or Poor attitudes about driving)*_____

_10_ 2. What point is the writer making about this topic? In other words, what is the *main idea* of the paragraph? In the space provided, write the number of the sentence containing the main idea.

> The word *attitude* appears four times in the paragraph, and the word *driving* appears seven times. They are clues to the topic. Sentences 1–9 provide examples of how poor attitudes about driving contribute to accidents.

Paragraph 5

[1]In some ways, dark chocolate is a health food. [2]Rich in iron, magnesium, and fiber, it's also loaded with flavonoids, compounds known to reduce cell damage. [3]Medical journals report that regularly eating a moderate amount of dark chocolate (about 3 ounces a day) reduces blood pressure both in healthy people and in patients with high blood pressure. [4]Lower blood pressure means less risk of irregular heartbeat, heart attack, and heart failure. [5]Continuous moderate consumption of dark chocolate also lowers bad cholesterol (the type that clogs arteries) and raises good cholesterol (the type that counters clogging). [6]In addition, dark chocolate helps prevent blood clots and arterial plaque, and so protects against stroke. [7]Dark chocolate even boosts the body's ability to metabolize sugar, thereby reducing the risk of diabetes.

1. What is the *topic* of the paragraph? _____*Dark chocolate*_____

    _____*(or Health benefits of dark chocolate)*_____

_1_ 2. What point is the writer making about this topic? In other words, what is the *main idea* of the paragraph? In the space provided, write the number of the sentence containing the main idea.

> Sentences 2–7 give evidence that dark chocolate is a health food.

3   Find and Use Key Words to Lead You to the Main Idea

Sometimes authors make it fairly easy to find their main idea. They announce it by using **key words**—verbal clues that are easy to recognize. First to note are **list words**, which tell you a list of items is to follow. For example, the main idea in the paragraph about bullies was stated like this: "Studies reveal several reasons why some children become bullies." The expression *several reasons* helps you zero in on your target: the main idea. You realize that the paragraph is going to be about specific reasons why some children become bullies.

Here are some common word groups that often announce a main idea. Note that each of them contains a word that ends in *s*—a plural that suggests the supporting details will be a list of items.

List Words

several kinds (or ways) of	several causes of	some factors in
three advantages of	five steps	among the results
various reasons for	a number of effects	a series of

When expressions like these appear in a sentence, look carefully to see if that sentence might be the main idea. Chances are a sentence with such clue words will be followed by a list of major supporting details.

 Check Your Understanding

Underline the list words in the following sentences.

> *Hint:* Remember that list words usually end in *s*.

Example   Certain kinds of behavior can quickly get you fired from a job.

1. American workers can be said to earn several types of income.

2. Water pollution takes two forms.

3. The purchase price of a house is only one of various costs that buyers must consider.

4. Problem solving usually involves a series of four steps.

5. The increasing flow of women into the labor force was caused by a number of economic factors.

Explanation

You should have underlined the following groups of words: *several types of, two forms, various costs, a series of four steps,* and *a number of economic factors.* Each of these phrases tells you that a list of details will follow.

In addition to list words, addition words can alert you to the main idea. **Addition words** are generally used right before a supporting detail. When you see this type of clue, you can assume that the detail it introduces fits under the umbrella of a main idea.

Here are some of the addition words that often introduce supporting details and help you discover the main idea.

Addition Words

one	to begin with	also	further
first (of all)	for one thing	in addition	furthermore
second(ly)	other	next	last (of all)
third(ly)	another	moreover	final(ly)

Check Your Understanding

Reread the paragraph about bullies, underlining the addition words that alert you to supporting details.

[1]School bullies have been around as long as there have been schools. [2]Studies reveal several reasons why some children become bullies. [3]Research shows that a certain combination of size and personality may be <u>one</u> factor. [4]Bigger, more aggressive children are more likely to try to dominate their smaller, quieter peers. [5]<u>Another</u> factor linked to bullying is overexposure to violent TV programs. [6]By the time the average American child is ten years old, he or she has watched thousands of acts of violence, including assault and murder. [7]Such exposure can lead to aggression and violence. [8]<u>Finally</u>, exposure to real violence is a factor in bullying. [9]Studies indicate that victims of bullies often turn into bullies themselves. [10]Whether abused by family members or tormented by other kids, bullies typically learn their behavior from others. [11]Look closely into the eyes of a bully, and you may be looking into the eyes of a former victim.

Explanation

The words that introduce each new supporting detail for the main idea are *one, Another*, and *Finally*. These addition words introduce each of the three reasons for bullying.

Note also that the main idea includes the list words *several reasons*, which signal that the supporting details will be a list of the reasons for bullying. In this and many paragraphs, list words and addition words often work hand in hand.

The following chapter, "Supporting Details," includes further information about words that alert you to the main idea and the details that support it. But what you have already learned here will help you find main ideas.

Locations of the Main Idea

Now you know how to recognize a main idea by 1) distinguishing between the general and the specific, 2) identifying the topic of a passage, and 3) using key words. You are ready to find the main idea no matter where it is located in a paragraph.

A main idea may appear at any point within a paragraph. Very commonly, it shows up at the beginning, as either the first or the second sentence. However, main ideas may also appear further within a paragraph or even at the very end.

Main Idea at the Beginning

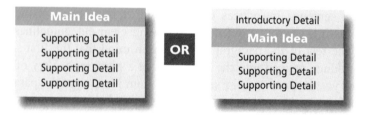

In textbooks, it is very common for the main idea to be either the first or the second sentence. See if you can underline the main idea in the paragraph on the following page.

¹Spanking is a poor way to shape a child's behavior. ²For one thing, spanking will result in feelings of anger and frustration. ³The child, then, will not learn anything positive from the punishment. ⁴In addition, spanking may actually lead to more bad behavior. ⁵Having learned that hitting is okay, the child may attack smaller children. ⁶Finally, spanking teaches children to hide certain actions from their parents. ⁷Once out of their parents' sight, however, children may feel they can get away with the bad behavior.

In this paragraph, the main idea is in the *first* sentence. All the following sentences in the paragraph provide details about the negative effects of spanking.

✔ ## Check Your Understanding

Now read the following paragraph and see if you can underline its main idea:

¹Tailgating—following too closely behind another vehicle—is a common cause of accidents. ²Yet tailgating accidents could be avoided if drivers followed some clear-cut guidelines. ³Any car that is less than two seconds behind the one ahead is definitely too close. ⁴Two car lengths is a safe following distance to maintain in local driving. ⁵Two-car accidents often become chain-reaction pileups when a number of drivers are all tailgating in a line. ⁶At freeway speeds, or in snowy, icy or foggy conditions, people should increase following distance well beyond what is normally safe. ⁷Finally, drivers who are impatient or aggressive need to develop the self-control not to express those feelings through dangerous behaviors like tailgating.

Explanation

In the preceding paragraph, the main idea is stated in the *second* sentence. The first sentence introduces the topic, but it is the idea in the second sentence—tailgating can be avoided by following clear-cut guidelines—that is supported in the rest of the paragraph. So keep in mind that the first sentence may simply introduce or lead into the main idea of a paragraph. Very often, a contrast word like *yet*, *but*, or *however* signals the main idea, as in the paragraph you have just read:

Tailgating—following too closely behind another vehicle—is a common cause of accidents. **Yet** tailgating accidents could be avoided if drivers followed some clear-cut guidelines.

To the Instructor: Main ideas in the paragraphs on this page and on page 75 have been underlined in this *Instructor's Edition.*

Main Idea in the Middle

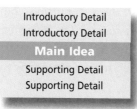

The main idea at times appears in the middle of a paragraph. Here is an example of a paragraph in which the main idea is somewhere in the middle. Try to find it and underline it. Then read the explanation that follows.

> [1]Many of us are annoyed by telemarketers who call us day and night, trying to sell us everything from magazine subscriptions to vacation homes. [2]These electronic intruders don't seem to care how much they are inconveniencing us and refuse to take "no" for an answer. [3]However, nuisance callers can be stopped if we take charge of the conversation. [4]As soon as one of them asks if we are Mr. or Ms. X, we should respond, "Yes, and are you a telephone solicitor?" [5]This technique puts them on the defensive. [6]We then have an opening to say that we don't accept solicitations over the phone, only through the mail. [7]This puts a quick end to the conversation.

If you thought the third sentence states the main idea, you were correct. The two sentences before the main idea introduce the topic: the problem of annoying telemarketers. Then the writer presents the main idea, which is that we can stop telemarketers from going on by taking charge of the conversation. The rest of the paragraph develops that idea by telling us how we can take charge of the conversation.

Main Idea at the End

Sometimes all the sentences in a paragraph will lead up to the main idea, which is presented at the end. On the next page is an example of such a paragraph.

[1]A study at one prison showed that owning a pet can change a hardened prison inmate into a more caring person. [2]Another study discovered that senior citizens, both those living alone and those in nursing homes, became more interested in life when they were given pets to care for. [3]Even emotionally disturbed children have been observed to smile and react with interest if there is a cuddly kitten or puppy to hold. **[4]Animals, then, can be a means of therapy for many kinds of individuals.**

Main Idea at the Beginning and the End

At times an author may choose to state the main idea near the beginning of the paragraph and then emphasize it by restating it later in the paragraph. In such cases, the main idea is at both the beginning and the end. Such is the case in the following paragraph.

[1]**People react strongly to red.** [2]The next time you go into a bookstore, notice which books catch your eye. [3]Those with red covers are likely to stand out. [4]The color of blood, red puts us on the alert. [5]Often it signals danger. [6]Red traffic lights and stop signs tell us to halt. [7]Red also flags problems. [8]Errors commonly are marked in red. Debts place us "in the red." [9]Red is the color of negative emotion. [10]We redden with overexertion or embarrassment. [11]When we're angry, we "see red." [12]But red also is associated with strong positive feelings. [13]The red hearts and roses of Valentine's Day speak of romance. [14]Red cheeks convey health; red lips and nails, sexuality. [15]Red can even confer a competitive advantage. [16]When the colors worn by Olympic athletes in sports such as boxing were analyzed, researchers found that athletes who wore red tended to outperform opponents in blue. [17]Apparently, red suggests power. [18]Physiologically, our eyes are more sensitive to red than to blue or green. [19]Asked to name any color, most adults respond, "Red." [20]**Red is the one color that humans simply cannot ignore.**

The main ideas of the following paragraphs appear at different locations—in the beginning, somewhere in the middle, or at the end. Identify each main idea by filling in its sentence number in the space provided.

_____1_____ 1. ¹Nearly every day, we all use expressions that have unusual and not commonly-known origins. ²For example, if you've ever said or heard that someone is the "spitting image" of someone else, here's some news: it has nothing to do with spit! ³The original phrase, "spirit and image," was used by slaves hundreds of years ago to describe a child who was so similar to another family member that it was believed that the same spirit occupied both people. ⁴Over the years, the words have run together to give us "spitting image." ⁵And everyone knows that to "live high on the hog" implies living well, but where did such a phrase come from? ⁶This expression originally referred to those who could afford the more expensive cuts of meat higher up on a hog, such as the shoulder roasts and the ribs, as opposed to the cheap "lower" parts, the pig's feet and the bacon from the belly. ⁷Finally, when we say that someone "takes the cake," we don't really mean that that person is going to receive a cake. ⁸However, originally, that's exactly what it meant! ⁹In the 1800s, a dance that made fun of stuffy ballroom dancing became so popular that eventually contests were held to see who could look the most ridiculous. ¹⁰Over time, this dance became known as the "Cakewalk" because winners were awarded cakes. ¹¹So those who really stood out in a comical and memorable way did, in fact, "take the cake."

Sentences 2–11 give three examples of expressions that do not have commonly-known origins: "spitting image" (sentences 2–4), "live high on the hog" (sentences 5–6), and "takes the cake" (sentences 7–11).

_____3_____ 2. ¹Recently while I was sitting in a small auditorium waiting for a play to begin, I saw three audience members chatting on cell phones. ²In fact, people converse on their cell phones while they drive, shop, walk down the street, use public transportation, eat in restaurants, or go to the bathroom. ³Let's face it: in the 21st century, cell phones are everywhere. ⁴In addition to using cell phones to talk, people use them to e-mail, text-message, surf the Web, organize their day, take photos, listen to music, watch videos, play games, and, by means of the phone's light, find something in the dark, such as a keyhole. ⁵More than 200 million Americans, including about half of those aged thirteen to sixteen, carry a cell phone. ⁶In a 2005 survey of U.S. cell-phone users, 26 percent said they would rather leave home without their wallet than without their cell phone. ⁷Almost three-fourths of U.S. households have at least one cell phone; many have three or more. ⁸In the United States, cell phones now far outnumber wired phones. ⁹Americans clearly love cell phones, right? ¹⁰Wrong. ¹¹A survey asked U.S. adults which invention they most hate. ¹²The most frequent reply? ¹³The cell phone.

Sentences 1–2 introduce the topic of cell phones and support the idea that cell phones are everywhere. Sentences 4–13 give statistics and further examples supporting the main idea.

To the Instructor: In these paragraphs and the tests that follow, addition words that signal supporting details are underlined in this *Instructor's Edition*.

_2_   3. [1]Caffeine is a natural ingredient in coffee, tea, colas, cocoa, and chocolate, and is added to some prescription and non-prescription drugs. [2]Despite being "natural," caffeine is also a powerful drug which greatly affects the body. [3]In healthy, rested people, a dose of 100 milligrams (about one cup of coffee) increases alertness, banishes drowsiness, quickens reaction time, enhances intellectual and muscular effort, and increases heart and respiratory rates. [4]Drinking one to two cups of coffee an hour before exercise encourages the body to preserve glycogen and burn fat—something that results in greater endurance. [5]In addition, caffeine masks fatigue. [6]In doses above 300 milligrams, caffeine can produce sleeplessness, nervousness, irritability, headaches, heart palpitations, and muscle twitches. [7]Caffeine is also habit-forming, and those who try to suddenly stop after heavy use may experience such withdrawal symptoms as headaches, lethargy, irritability, and difficulty in concentrating.

Sentence 1 introduces the topic of caffeine. Sentences 3–7 support the main idea—that caffeine is a powerful drug which greatly affects the body.

_5_   4. [1]Queen Isabella of Spain, who died in 1504, boasted that she'd had only two baths in her life—at birth and before her marriage. [2]In colonial America, leaders frowned on bathing, because it involved nudity, which, they feared, could lead to loose morals. [3]Indeed, laws in Virginia and Pennsylvania either limited or outright banned bathing—and for a time in Philadelphia, anyone who bathed more than once a month faced jail. [4]Furthermore, some of the early Christian churches discouraged sudsing up because of its association with the immorality common in the Roman baths. [5]Clearly, the notion that cleanliness is next to godliness has not always been a popular one.

Sentences 1–4 give examples that support the main idea—that the notion that cleanliness is next to godliness has not always been a popular one.

_1_   5. [1]Research has demonstrated our self-centered tendency to rate ourselves more favorably than others rate us. [2]In one study, members of a random sample of men were asked to rank themselves on their ability to get along with others. [3]Defying mathematical laws, all subjects—every last one—put themselves in the top half of the population. [4]Sixty percent rated themselves in the top 10 percent of the population, and an amazing 25 percent rated themselves in the top 1 percent. [5]In the same study, 70 percent of the men ranked their leadership in the top quarter of the population, whereas only 2 percent ranked their leadership as below average. [6]Sixty percent said they were in the top quarter in athletic abilities, whereas only 6 percent said they were below average.

Sentences 2–6 describe the results of a study that supports the main idea—that we tend to rate ourselves more favorably than others rate us.

A Note on the Central Point

Just as a paragraph may have a main idea, a longer selection may have a **central point**, also known as a **central idea** or **thesis**. The longer selection might be an essay, a reading, or a section of a textbook chapter. You can find a central point in the same way that you find a main idea—by identifying the topic (which is often suggested by the title of the selection) and then looking at the supporting material. The paragraphs within the longer reading will provide supporting details for the central point. You will see, for example, that the essay that ends this chapter has a central point.

A Final Thought

Whether we are readers, writers, listeners, or speakers, the "heart" of clear communication is the main idea, or point, and the support for the main idea. Look at the following diagram:

The diagram underscores the importance of the most important of all reading skills: the ability to identify main ideas. The diagram also shows that the ability to identify supporting details for the main idea is an almost equally important skill.

CHAPTER REVIEW

In this chapter, you learned the following:

- Recognizing the main idea is the most important key to good comprehension. The main idea is a general "umbrella" idea; all the specific supporting material of the passage fits under it.

- Three strategies that will help you find the main idea are to 1) look for general versus specific ideas; 2) use the topic (the general subject of a selection) to lead you to the main idea; 3) use key words—verbal clues that lead you to the main idea.

- The main idea often appears at the beginning of a paragraph, though it may appear elsewhere in a paragraph.

The next chapter—Chapter 3—will sharpen your understanding of the specific details that authors use to support and develop their main ideas.

On the Web: If you are using this book in class, you can visit our website for additional practice in recognizing main ideas. Go to **www.townsendpress.com** and click on "Online Exercises."

REVIEW TEST 1

To review what you've learned in this chapter, answer the following questions by filling in the blank or writing the letter of the correct answer.

See page 59. _B_ 1. The umbrella statement that covers all of the material in a paragraph is called the

   A. topic.   B. main idea.   C. supporting details.

See page 59. _B_ 2. Supporting details are always more (A. general; B. specific) than the main idea.

See page 64. _A_ 3. To locate the main idea of a selection, you may find it helpful to first decide on its

   A. topic.   B. structure.   C. length.

See page 73. _A_ 4. While a main idea may appear anywhere within a paragraph, in textbooks it very commonly appears

   A. at the beginning.   B. in the middle.   C. at the end.

5. To help you decide if a certain sentence is the main idea, ask yourself, "Is this statement supported by all or most of the _____ _____ other material in the paragraph _____?"

See pages 58, 64, and 68.

REVIEW TEST 2

A. In each of the following groups, one statement is the general point, and the other statements are specific support for the point. Identify each point with a **P** and each statement of support with an **S**.

1. _S_ A. Executives kept fake accounting records to hide the fact that the company was losing money.

   _S_ B. Employees were strongly encouraged to buy company stock, which is now worthless.

   _S_ C. Top company executives made millions of dollars while the company was failing.

   _P_ D. Officers of that failed energy company should be put in jail for a long time.

Sentences A, B, and C are all specific reasons why the officers should go to jail.

2. <u>S</u> A. Traditional Japanese culture emphasizes self-discipline and respect for authority.

   <u>S</u> B. No one in Japan, including police officers, may keep a handgun at home.

   <u>P</u> C. The crime rate in Tokyo is the lowest of any major city in the world for a number of reasons.

   <u>S</u> D. At least once a year, police officers visit every home in Japan to discuss neighborhood conditions.   Sentences A, B, and D are all specific reasons for the low crime rate in Tokyo.

B. Each group of statements below includes one topic, one main idea, and two supporting details. In the space provided, label each item with one of the following:

   T — for the **topic** of the paragraph
   MI — for the **main idea**
   SD — for the **supporting details**

Group 1

   <u>SD</u> A. Staying in the sun too long can cause sunstroke.

   <u>SD</u> B. People develop skin cancer after years of "working in the sun" or after years of exposure to direct sunlight.

   <u>T</u> C. Time in the sun.

   <u>MI</u> D. Spending time in the sun can be dangerous.

   Details in statements A and B support the idea that time spent in the sun can be dangerous.

Group 2

   <u>SD</u> A. Rubbing one's nose and eyes transfers viruses to the hands, which then contaminate whatever they touch, such as a doorknob, serving spoon, or telephone.

   <u>SD</u> B. Because the dried cold virus can live as long as three hours, you can pick it up from an object after the person with a cold is gone.

   <u>T</u> C. Catching a cold.

   <u>MI</u> D. The most likely way to catch a cold is by touching an object that someone suffering from a cold has handled.

   Details in statements A and B support the idea of catching a cold by touching an object handled by a person with a cold.

REVIEW TEST 3

The main idea appears at various places in the following paragraphs. Write the number of each main idea in the space provided.

_____1_____ 1. ¹Two unlikely heroes, the goose and the canary, have earned their places in history as protectors of humans. ²In 390 B.C., the Romans placed geese (and dogs) in lookout positions on castle towers to warn of approaching enemies. ³A goose, the Romans knew, has remarkable powers of perceiving motion and sound, even in the middle of the night. ⁴As a result, while the dogs slept right through the approach of the fierce Gaul army, the guard geese sensed the Gallic invasion and warned the Romans well in advance with their thunderous honking and frantic wing flapping. ⁵Fifteen hundred years later, the use of canaries in coal mines saved more than a few coal miners from suffocation. ⁶Miners, who were always threatened by pockets of poisonous gases in the mines, used to carry canaries in small cages, holding them in front of them as they descended deeper and deeper into new mines. ⁷Because a canary's lungs are significantly more sensitive than a human's, the canary would show the effects of bad air long before the miners could sense it. ⁸Therefore, when the canary either appeared to be sick or (unfortunately) suddenly died, the miners were warned of the deadly air ahead, and they retreated quickly to safety.

The list words *two . . . heroes* (sentence 1) point to the main idea. Sentences 2–8 present supporting details about the goose and the canary as protectors of humans.

_____3_____ 2. ¹Criticism is a valuable means of helping ourselves and others achieve personal growth. ²However, because it is often done carelessly or cruelly, criticism has a bad reputation. ³Here are some guidelines for offering criticism constructively. ⁴First, wait until the person asks for feedback on his or her performance or actions. ⁵Unasked-for criticism is not usually valuable. ⁶Second, describe the person's behavior as specifically as possible before you criticize it. ⁷Instead of just saying, "You were awful," tell the person exactly what you observed. ⁸And finally, try to balance your criticism with positive statements. ⁹Look for significant points in the other person's performance that you can honestly praise.

Sentences 1–2 introduce the idea of constructive criticism. The words *some guidelines* (sentence 3) indicate the main idea. Sentences 4–9 give supporting details in the form of three guidelines.

_____9_____ 3. ¹In Bulgaria, one nods one's head for "no" and shakes it back and forth for "yes." ²If you make the "A-OK" sign in Brazil, with the index finger and thumb making a circle, it's not only not okay, it's very impolite. ³To show the bottom of one's feet to a Turk is a serious insult, implying that "you are lower than the ground I walk on." ⁴Throughout the Middle East, to offer the left hand in a handshake—or to wave it at someone—will give deep offense. ⁵The Japanese consider it polite to bow to varying levels, depending on the message one is trying

Sentences 1–8
provide examples
that support the
main idea.

to convey. ⁶When a Frenchman wants to make a strong point, he waves his upraised index finger from side to side. ⁷In many Mediterranean cultures, men who are nonromantic friends walk hand in hand. ⁸And in America—especially out West—a firm handshake and a direct look in the eye are expected when men meet one another; in many cultures, this would be considered very rude. ⁹Clearly, body language that is perfectly normal or meaningless in one culture may mean something quite different in another.

_2_   4. ¹Some Americans believe that colonials cleverly won the Revolutionary War by hiding behind rocks and trees and sniping at the British, who marched and fought in bright red rows and didn't even aim their muskets. ²In fact, the British were worn down in the American colonies by a combination of factors. ³While the colonies never had a powerful army, they had a steady source of plentiful manpower and could easily replace their losses. ⁴The British regular soldiers (or German soldiers for hire), by contrast, took more time to train and generally had to be shipped across the Atlantic Ocean. ⁵Also, the colonies were not Britain's only worry; a much greater concern was France, with which the British were consistently at odds. ⁶If too much energy had been spent holding the colonies, France might well have invaded and conquered Britain. ⁷France was well aware of this, so it began sending supplies to the colonials early in the war and soon sent a fleet and an army. ⁸The French contributions proved decisive at Yorktown in 1781, where the French and American armies held Lord Cornwallis's army at bay in Virginia while the French fleet turned back the Royal Navy's rescue effort.

Sentence 1 introduces
the topic. The words
*a combination of
factors* (sentence
2) are a clue to the
main idea. Sentences
3–8 give supporting
details.

_2_   5. ¹People often think of shame as a strong form of embarrassment. ²A psychological study of 104 persons, however, suggests that shame and embarrassment are quite different experiences. ³In general, embarrassment results from a relatively minor event that occurs while others are around. ⁴It is more likely to cause a person to blush. ⁵Also, an embarrassing event is likely to include an element of surprise and to be remembered with smiles or jokes. ⁶Embarrassment generally does not lead to a feeling that one must correct a situation. ⁷Shame is felt when people reveal a personal flaw to themselves and perhaps to others. ⁸Unlike embarrassment, it is likely to make one feel that a situation needs repairing. ⁹In addition, while embarrassment is strongly related to how we believe others view us, shame is often felt when one is alone. ¹⁰And it is not generally looked upon later as humorous.

If sentence 1
were the main idea,
there would be
supporting
examples of how
shame is a strong
form of
embarrassment.
The details in
sentences 3–10 all
support the point
in sentence 2.

Here is a chance to apply your understanding of main ideas to a full-length selection. Read the article below about the popularity of alcohol in our culture, and then answer the questions on main ideas that follow. There are also questions to help you continue practicing the skill of understanding vocabulary in context.

Words to Watch

Below are some words in the reading that do not have strong context support. Each word is followed by the number of the paragraph in which it appears and its meaning there. These words are indicated in the reading by a small circle (°).

> *myth* (3): a false belief
> *irony* (11): a meaning that is the opposite of what is actually said

HERE'S TO YOUR HEALTH

Joan Dunayer

1   As the only freshman on his high school's varsity wrestling team, Tod was anxious to fit in with his older teammates. One night after a match, a teammate offered him a ride home. Several other teammates also were passengers. One of them took out a bottle of tequila and started passing it around. When the bottle reached Tod, he felt he had to drink, or he would seem like a "sissy." He took a swallow. Each time a teammate passed the bottle back to him, Tod took another swallow. After seven swallows he passed out. Terrified, his teammates carried him into his house. Tod's mother rushed him to the hospital, where his stomach was pumped. Tod recovered, but his blood alcohol level had been so high that he was lucky not to be in a coma or dead.

Although alcohol can cause rapid   2 poisoning, frequently leads to long-term addiction, and always threatens self-control, U.S. society encourages drinking. By their example, many parents give children like Tod the impression that alcohol is an essential ingredient of social gatherings. Peer pressure turns bachelor parties, fraternity initiations, and spring-semester beach vacations into competitions in "getting trashed." In soap operas, glamorous characters pour Scotch whisky from crystal decanters as readily as most people turn on the faucet for tap water. In movies and music videos, trendsetters party by drinking in nightclubs and bars. The worst culprit of all is advertising. Alcohol ads appear with pounding frequency in magazines, on billboards, in newspapers, and on television. Who can recall a televised baseball or basketball game without a beer commercial? In 2005 more than 300,000 alcohol commercials appeared on U.S. television. It is no surprise that 70 percent of 21- to 25-year-olds report using alcohol in the last month, and nearly 48 percent of 21-year-olds are binge drinkers, downing five or more drinks in one session.

3   This nonstop promotion of alcohol in the mass media has resulted in several harmful beliefs about drinking that have spread throughout U.S. society. One alcohol myth° is that liquor signals professional success. In a slick men's magazine, one full-page ad for Scotch whiskey shows two men seated in an elegant restaurant. Both are in their thirties, perfectly groomed, and wearing expensive-looking gray suits. The windows are draped with velvet, the table with spotless white linen. Each place setting consists of a long-stemmed water goblet, silver utensils, and thick silver plates. On each plate is a half-empty cocktail glass. The two men are grinning and shaking hands, as if they've just concluded a business deal. The caption reads, "The taste of success."

4   Contrary to what the liquor company would have us believe, drinking is more closely related to failure than to achievement. Among students, the heaviest drinkers generally have the lowest grades. In the work force, alcoholics are frequently late or absent, tend to perform poorly, and often get fired. Although alcohol abuse occurs in all economic classes, it remains most prevalent among the poor.

5   Another alcohol myth that non-stop advertising supports is that drinking makes a person more sexually attractive. "Hot, hot, hot," one commercial's sound-track begins, as the camera scans a crowd of college-age beachgoers. The camera then zooms in on one woman sitting amid the crowd. She is beautiful, wearing a bikini. The camera follows the shape of her leg up to her bare hip and lingers there. Carrying an ice chest, a man positions himself near the woman. He is handsome, tan, muscular. The woman doesn't show much interest—until the man opens the chest and takes out a beer. Now she smiles at him. He raises

his eyebrows and invitingly holds up another can. The woman joins him. The advertised beer "attracts like no other," the commercial's song concludes.

6   The truth, however, is that beer doesn't make anyone sexier. Like all alcohol, it lowers the levels of male hormones in men and of female hormones in women—even when drunk in small amounts. In substantial amounts, alcohol can cause infertility in women and impotence in men. Some alcoholic men even develop enlarged breasts.

7   Yet another myth is that alcohol and athletics are a good combination. One billboard features three high-action images: a sprinter running at top speed, a surfer riding a wave, and a basketball player leaping to make a dunk shot. A particular light beer, the billboard declares, "won't slow you down."

8   But "slow you down" is exactly what alcohol does. Even in small amounts, alcohol dulls the brain, reducing muscle coordination and slowing reaction time. It also interferes with the ability to focus the eyes and adjust to a sudden change in brightness, such as the flash of a car's headlights. The leading cause of death among U.S. teenagers, drinking and driving is responsible for about 40 percent of all U.S. traffic fatalities. Drinking also results in many home and workplace accidents, such as falls, that cause injury or death. Continued alcohol abuse can physically change the brain, permanently impairing learning and memory. Long-term drinking is related to malnutrition, weakening of the bones, and ulcers. It increases the risk of liver failure, heart disease, and stomach cancer. Drinking during pregnancy can lead to miscarriage and is a major cause of birth defects such as limb deformities and brain damage.

9   Finally, advertising creates the myth that alcohol fosters happy relationships. In one TV commercial, an overweight man sits alone in his drab living room. He reaches into a cooler, takes out a bottle of beer, and twists off the cap. Instantly, dance music plays, and dozens of attractive young adults appear in a shower of party streamers and confetti. "Where the party begins," a voice announces. The previously lonely man now is surrounded by male and female friends. The message: drinking solves social problems.

10   In reality, relationships in which alcohol plays a major role are unlikely to be happy. Heavy drinking destroys relationships and contributes to antisocial feelings and behavior. Alcoholics are about twenty-one times more likely than nonalcoholics to have antisocial personality disorder. In the United States, an estimated 30 percent of violent crimes are committed by people who had been drinking, and three-fourths of reported cases of spouse abuse involve alcohol. Parents with a drinking problem are more likely to neglect or abuse their children. Approximately 30 percent of Americans who commit suicide are alcoholics; the

suicide rate among alcoholics is fifty times the rate among nonalcoholics.

11   Alcohol, many would have us believe, is part of being successful, sexy, healthy, and happy. Those who have suffered from alcohol's destructive effects know otherwise. For alcohol's victims, "Here's to your health" rings with a terrible irony° when it is accompanied by the clink of liquor glasses.

Reading Comprehension Questions

Vocabulary in Context

__D__ 1. In the excerpt below, the word *caption* (kăp'shən) means
   A. man.
   B. menu.
   C. contract that seals the business deal.
   D. words accompanying the picture.

   "In a slick men's magazine, one full-page ad for Scotch whiskey shows two men seated in an elegant restaurant. . . . The caption reads, 'The taste of success.'" (Paragraph 3)   The word *reads* is a clue.

__C__ 2. In the sentence below, the word *prevalent* (prĕv'ə-lənt) means
   A. weak.
   B. colorful.
   C. widespread.
   D. inexpensive.

   General sense of the sentence: Although it happens everywhere, it is most widespread among the poor.

   "Although alcohol abuse occurs in all economic classes, it remains most prevalent among the poor." (Paragraph 4)

__A__ 3. In the excerpt below, the word *substantial* (səb-stăn'shəl) means
   A. large.
   B. reasonable.
   C. weak.
   D. pleasing.

   ". . . beer . . . lowers the levels of male hormones in men and of female hormones in women—even when drunk in small amounts. In substantial amounts, alcohol can cause infertility in women and impotence in men." (Paragraph 6)

   Antonym clue: *small.*

_____A_____ 4. In the sentence below, the word *impairing* (ĭm-pâr′ĭng) means

    A. damaging.

    B. doubling.

    C. postponing.

    D. teaching.

> If alcohol abuse changes the brain, it damages it.

> "Continued alcohol abuse can physically change the brain, permanently impairing learning and memory." (Paragraph 8)

_____C_____ 5. In the sentence below, the word *fosters* (fŏs′tərz) means

    A. removes.

    B. hides.

    C. produces.

    D. follows.

> The entire selection describes the negative effects of alcohol. Therefore, it is a myth—in other words, untrue—that alcohol produces happy relationships.

> "Finally, advertising creates the myth that alcohol fosters happy relationships." (Paragraph 9)

Central Point and Main Ideas

_____A_____ 6. The main idea of paragraph 2 is its

    A. first sentence.

    B. second sentence.

    C. third sentence.

    D. last sentence.

> The rest of the paragraph gives details and statistics that support the idea that U.S. society encourages drinking.

_____B_____ 7. The main idea of paragraph 3 is its

    A. first sentence.

    B. second sentence.

    C. third sentence.

    D. seventh sentence.

> The first sentence introduces the general idea of harmful beliefs. The details of the ad (described starting in the third sentence) support the mistaken idea that alcohol signals professional success.

_____D_____ 8. The topic of paragraph 4 is drinking and

    A. grades.

    B. work.

    C. the poor.

    D. lack of success.

> Answers A, B, and C are all too narrow. Each covers only one sentence of the paragraph.

_____B_____ 9. The main idea of paragraph 10 is its

    A. first sentence.

    B. second sentence.

    C. third sentence.

    D. fourth sentence.

> The first sentence introduces the idea that relationships involving alcohol are likely to be unhappy. The details and statistics given, starting in the third sentence, all support the idea that heavy drinking contributes to antisocial behavior.

_A_ 10. Which sentence best expresses the central point of this selection?

Statement B
covers only part
of paragraph 2.
Statement C covers
only paragraph 4.
Statement D covers
only paragraph 11.

A. Although U.S. society encourages drinking, alcohol consumption is harmful in a number of ways.

B. Alcohol ads appear very often in magazines, on billboards, in newspapers, and on television.

C. Contrary to what the liquor industry wants us to believe, drinking is more closely related to failure than to achievement.

D. Alcohol's victims know that alcohol is not part of being successful, sexy, healthy, and happy.

Discussion Questions

1. Unfortunately, Tod's experience with alcohol is not so rare. Do you know anyone who has had a negative experience because of drinking or because of drinking and driving? Where was that person drinking, and how much did he or she have? Explain what eventually happened.

2. If it's true that "beer doesn't make anyone sexier," why do you think so many young people drink so much beer in social situations?

3. Think about a wine, beer, or liquor ad you have seen in a magazine, in a newspaper, or on television. Which alcohol myth described in "Here's to Your Health" does that ad promote? What details of the ad contribute to that myth?

4. Cigarette advertising is no longer allowed on television. Do you think beer ads should also be outlawed on TV? In college newspapers? Explain your answers.

Note: Writing assignments for this selection appear on page 600.

Check Your Performance   MAIN IDEAS

Activity	Number Right	Points	Score
Review Test 1 (5 items)	_____	× 2 =	_____
Review Test 2 (16 items)	_____	× 2.5 =	_____
Review Test 3 (5 items)	_____	× 4 =	_____
Review Test 4 (10 items)	_____	× 3 =	_____
		TOTAL SCORE =	_____ %

Enter your total score into the **Reading Performance Chart: Review Tests** on the inside back cover.

MAIN IDEAS: Mastery Test 1

A. In each of the following groups, one statement is the general point, and the other statements are specific support for the point. Identify each point with a **P** and each statement of support with an **S**.

1. _P_ A. I'm a good example of someone who has "math anxiety."

   Statements B, C, and D are specific illustrations of the person's math anxiety.

   _S_ B. I feel dread every time I sit down to take our Friday math quiz.

   _S_ C. During the math midterm, I "froze" and didn't even try to answer most of the questions.

   _S_ D. I turned down a job as a salesclerk because I would have had to figure out how much change customers should get back.

2. _S_ A. Hungry bears searching for food often threaten hikers.

   In statement B, the word *dangerous* is a clue. Statements A, C, and D give specific supporting examples of the dangers.

   _P_ B. Hiking on that mountain trail can be very dangerous.

   _S_ C. Severe weather develops quickly, leaving hikers exposed to storms and cold.

   _S_ D. When it rains, the trail—which is very steep at some points—becomes slippery.

3. _S_ A. Terrorists hijacked and flew jetliners into the World Trade Center and the Pentagon, both on the same day.

   Statements A, B, and C are specific examples of "horrible acts of terrorism."

   _S_ B. Suicide bombers have killed themselves and thousands of others in Iraq and the Middle East.

   _S_ C. One hundred sixty-eight people died when an American terrorist blew up the federal building in Oklahoma City.

   _P_ D. Children have had to deal with the knowledge of many horrible acts of terrorism.

(Continues on next page)

B. Each group of statements below includes one topic, one main idea, and two supporting details. In the space provided, label each item with one of the following:

      T — for the **topic** of the paragraph
    MI — for the **main idea**
    SD — for the **supporting details**

Group 1

   _SD_ A. Some people knock on wood when talking about good luck.

   _T_ B. Everyday superstitions.

   _SD_ C. Some people believe they should leave a house through the same door they entered.

   _MI_ D. There are many superstitions that are practiced in everyday life.

> Statements A and C are examples of the "superstitions . . . practiced in everyday life" referred to in statement D.

Group 2

   _T_ A. Vegetarian diets.

   _SD_ B. The incidence of heart disease is much lower for vegetarians than for non-vegetarians.

   _MI_ C. People who eat vegetarian diets are generally healthier than non-vegetarians.

   _SD_ D. Vegetarians have a lower rate of cancer than non-vegetarians.

> Statements B and D describe two specific ways that vegetarians are healthier than non-vegetarians.

MAIN IDEAS: Mastery Test 2

A. In each of the following groups, one statement is the general point, and the other statements are specific support for the point. Identify each point with a **P** and each statement of support with an **S**.

Statements A, C, and D name specific advantages of limits on campaign spending.

1. _S_ A. Elected officials could spend more time on their jobs and less on raising money.

   _P_ B. There should be a limit on how much can be spent for political campaigns.

   _S_ C. Candidates with less money would have a fairer chance of competing.

   _S_ D. Elected officials would be less likely to be influenced by rich contributors to their campaigns.

Statements A, B, and C name three specific problems that show why it is wise to avoid the Route 27 bus.

2. _S_ A. Often you'll wait half an hour for a Route 27 bus, and then three will show up at once.

   _S_ B. Sometimes Route 27 buses will roar right past you at a bus stop, even though they aren't full.

   _S_ C. Route 27 seems to be assigned the oldest buses, ones that rattle and have broken seats.

   _P_ D. It is wise to avoid the Route 27 bus whenever possible.

Statements B, C, and D give three specific reasons Congress should enact a highway program.

3. _P_ A. Congress should enact a comprehensive highway program.

   _S_ B. Some of the numerous accidents, injuries, and fatalities on our nation's roads are the result of poor highway design.

   _S_ C. There is an urgent need for bridge construction and maintenance throughout this country.

   _S_ D. This nation needs programs to alleviate traffic jams.

(Continues on next page)

B. Each group of statements below includes one topic, one main idea, and two supporting details. In the space provided, label each item with one of the following:

  T — for the **topic** of the paragraph
  MI — for the **main idea**
  SD — for the **supporting details**

Group 1

  _SD_ A. School officials complain that students damage school property, and parents complain their children can't read or do math.

  _SD_ B. Teachers complain about the low salaries they get for their difficult and important jobs.

  _T_ c. Problems in our schools.

  _MI_ D. The problems within our school systems are varied and affect almost everyone involved.

  Statements A and B are specific examples of problems within the school system.

Group 2

  _MI_ A. Self-help groups based on the Alcoholics Anonymous model exist to serve people with a variety of problems.

  _T_ B. Self-help groups.

  _SD_ c. Narcotics Anonymous sponsors meetings where drug abusers and their loved ones can get support.

  _SD_ D. Overeaters Anonymous assists people whose eating has gotten out of control.

  The words *variety of problems* are a clue that statement A is the main idea. Statements C and D are specific examples of the variety of problems addressed by self-help groups.

MAIN IDEAS: Mastery Test 3

The main idea may appear at any place within each of the five paragraphs that follow. Write the number of each main idea sentence in the space provided.

_____1_____ 1.

Sentences 2–7 give three examples (birds, houseflies, and cats) of creatures that can "predict" a change in the weather.

[1]Creatures that are very sensitive to the changes in the air before a storm can "predict" a change in the weather. [2]Birds, for example, sense the pressure change and fly lower. [3]Low-flying birds, then, indicate that rain is coming. [4]Similarly, houseflies detect this change and move indoors to avoid the downpour. [5]And cats are known to groom themselves just before a storm. [6]In doing so, they are reacting to the static electricity that enters the air before a thunderstorm. [7]The electricity separates their fur and makes them feel dirty, so they lick themselves to make the fur smooth and "clean" again.

_____2_____ 2.

Sentence 1 introduces the topic with a statement that contrasts with the main idea. In sentence 2, the words *a number of health problems* (note the *s* word) are a clue to the main idea. Sentences 3–8 give specific examples of health problems of men.

[1]Men, we are reminded over and over, are the stronger sex. [2]Yet men are more likely than women to have a number of health problems at every age. [3]More males than females are miscarried, are stillborn, or die in their first year of life. [4]In all societies, men die earlier than women do. [5]American men are more likely than women to die from heart disease, lung disease, and cirrhosis of the liver. [6]They are more likely to suffer from stress-related diseases, such as hypertension, ulcers, and asthma. [7]They are hospitalized for mental illness more frequently. [8]Women attempt suicide more often than men, but men succeed in killing themselves three times as often (largely because they use violent means—guns rather than sleeping pills).

_____6_____ 3.

Sentence 1 introduces the topic with a statement that contrasts with the main idea. Sentences 2–5 give specific examples of benefits of volcanoes. In sentence 6, the words *various ways* (note the *s* word) are a clue to the main idea.

[1]The eruption of volcanoes has caused death and misery throughout the centuries. [2]But in parts of Italy, Iceland, Chile, and Bolivia, volcanic steam is used to run heat and power plants. [3]Pumice, which is made from volcanic lava, is used as a grinder and polisher. [4]Sulfur produced by volcanoes is useful to the chemical industry. [5]Hawaiian farmers grow crops on land made rich by decayed volcanic material. [6]Clearly, in spite of all the damage they cause, volcanoes do benefit us in various ways.

(Continues on next page)

_____1_____ 4.   ¹Adult children who move back home can avoid family conflicts by following some helpful tips. ²First, they should contribute what they can—and it doesn't necessarily have to be in terms of money. ³Being productive family members will help them earn their keep. ⁴This can involve tutoring or coaching younger sisters or brothers, or helping Mom and Dad with household chores and errands. ⁵Second, grown children at home should not expect their parents to rescue them from difficulties. ⁶As adults, they are responsible for getting out of their own scrapes—and for trying to avoid scrapes in the first place. ⁷Last, they must respect their parents' lifestyles and own needs for independence. ⁸It is unrealistic to expect parents' lives to revolve around the needs of a grown child, as they may have when the child was younger.

The words *helpful tips* (note the *s* word) in sentence 1 are a clue to the main idea. Each of the three specific tips in sentences 2–8 is introduced by an addition word: *First* (sentence 2), *Second* (sentence 5), and *Last* (sentence 7).

_____2_____ 5.   ¹Police estimate that only 1 to 2 percent of hitchhiking crimes are reported, so there are no accurate statistics on such events. ²But frequent horror stories indicate that hitchhiking can be dangerous to both hitchhiker and driver. ³There was the nineteen-year-old woman who accepted a lift from three young men in New Jersey, expecting a ride across the bridge to New York City. ⁴Instead they drove to a motel, where they repeatedly raped her. ⁵Luckily, she escaped with her life. ⁶Less fortunate was the eighteen-year-old woman student who disappeared from campus after accepting a ride with a stranger and whose decomposed body was found in a suburban sewage plant two years later. ⁷Male hitchhikers are less open to assault, but a number of incidents show that they are far from immune. ⁸Hitchhikers also face the hazards of riding with an intoxicated or stoned driver, not the least of which is an accident. ⁹They also risk assault or robbery by other hitchhikers and being stranded in out-of-the-way places. ¹⁰Drivers, too, are subject to assault and robbery. ¹¹And they risk an accident by stopping on a busy highway, or arrest if their passengers happen to be carrying drugs. ¹²Some male drivers have picked up young girls who threatened to call the police and cry rape unless the men handed over all their money.

Sentence 1 introduces the topic of hitchhiking crimes. In sentence 2, the words *frequent horror stories* (another *s* word) signal the main idea. Sentences 3–12 support the main idea by describing some of the specific horror stories.

MAIN IDEAS: Mastery Test 4

The main idea may appear at any place within each of the five paragraphs that follow. Write the number of each main idea sentence in the space provided.

___3___ 1.

Sentences 1 and 2 provide specific examples of the main idea, stated in sentence 3. Sentences 4–7 provide more evidence of the "many ways" in which fire has benefited us.

[1]Fire extended humans' geographical boundaries by allowing them to travel into regions that were previously too cold to explore. [2]It <u>also</u> kept predators away, allowing early humans to sleep securely. [3]Fire, in fact, has been a significant factor in human development and progress in many ways. [4]Other obvious benefits of fire are its uses in cooking and in hunting. [5]Probably even more important, however, is that learning to control fire allowed people to change the very rhythm of their lives. [6]Before fire, the human daily cycle coincided with the rising and setting of the sun. [7]With fire, though, humans gained time to think and talk about the day's events and to prepare strategies for coping with tomorrow.

___2___ 2.

Sentence 1 presents an idea in contrast to the main idea in sentence 2: that society shapes the way we think about life's stages. Sentences 3–8 provide evidence to support the main idea.

[1]The stages of life, from birth to death, may seem controlled by biology. [2]However, the way we think about life's stages is shaped by society. [3]During the Middle Ages, for example, children dressed—and were expected to act—just like little adults. [4]Adolescence became a distinct stage of life only fairly recently, when a separate teenage subculture began to appear. [5]But in the Middle Ages, young people were "children" until about age 16. [6]Then they went to work, married, and had their own children. [7]Today, "young adulthood" has become a new stage of life, stretching from about age 20 to 30. [8]As life expectancy becomes longer and people spend years in active retirement, older adulthood has also become a distinct life stage.

___1___ 3.

Sentence 1 presents the main idea. Sentences 2–5 give specific illustrations of ways in which new technologies have created problems.

[1]New technology often creates unanticipated problems. [2]Automobiles, for example, provide numerous benefits, but they also pollute the air and kill about fifty thousand Americans each year. [3]It is difficult to imagine life without electricity and heat, but power plants pollute the air, cause the thermal pollution of rivers, and contribute to global warming. [4]Insecticides and chemical fertilizers have performed miracles in agriculture but have polluted food and streams (and even "killed" some lakes). [5]Jet planes, while helping us in many ways, cause air pollution (one jet taking off emits the same amount of hydrocarbon as the exhausts from ten thousand automobiles) and noise pollution near busy airports.

(Continues on next page)

_____7_____ 4.   ¹By the end of the first series of Sherlock Holmes stories, the author, Sir Arthur Conan Doyle, had become tired of writing detective stories. ²So at the end of his second book of Holmes stories, he decided to have the detective die. ³The book ends with Holmes and his archenemy, Moriarty, plunging to their deaths from a high cliff overlooking a waterfall. ⁴After that, hundreds of letters poured in to Conan Doyle, begging him to bring Holmes back. ⁵Also, magazines offered him huge sums of money for additional Sherlock Holmes adventures. ⁶Finally, after nine years, Conan Doyle wrote a new story in which Holmes reappears and tells Dr. Watson that he did not die after all. ⁷Sometimes it is the reader, not the author, who determines how long fictional heroes will live.

Sentences 1–6 state the specific events in the "death" and reappearance of Sherlock Holmes. Sentence 7 expresses the main idea: sometimes readers decide how long fictional characters will live.

_____2_____ 5.   ¹With so many young, single people having babies, the question arises as to how happy they are being young parents. ²A national survey of young, single mothers and fathers reveals that most were happier before they became parents. ³Sixty-seven percent of the nine thousand new parents who responded to the survey said having a baby presented more problems than they envisioned. ⁴Fifty-six percent of the respondents said they had to drop out of school, despite their hopes that they could manage schoolwork while rearing a baby. ⁵A majority (73 percent) said they were forced to seek financial help from family, friends, and/or government agencies, and 37 percent said they accepted low-paying, unsatisfying jobs out of necessity. ⁶Also, 70 percent said they missed the "good times" with friends that they enjoyed before their babies were born.

Sentence 1 introduces the topic. Sentence 2 presents the main idea about the topic. Sentences 3–6 give details showing why young, single parents are less happy with their lives.

MAIN IDEAS: Mastery Test 5

The five paragraphs that follow are all taken from college textbooks. The main idea may appear at any place within each paragraph. Write the number of each main idea sentence in the space provided.

___6___ 1.

Sentence 1 introduces the topic: what Americans say makes them happy. Sentences 2–5 give specific examples of the main idea: most things that make us happy are simple and free or inexpensive.

¹An author doing research for a book asked thousands of Americans what made them happy. ²Among the popular responses she received were eating ice-cream sandwiches and candy, being offered a football ticket, and visiting city parks. ³Other specific responses included eating ravioli, feeling the cool underside of a pillow, and rereading old love letters. ⁴The most frequently cited response was simply spending time with family. ⁵Almost no one gave the answer of owning flashy jewelry, showy cars, or other fancy things. ⁶The author concluded that most of the things that put a smile on our face are simple and free or inexpensive.

___4___ 2.

Sentences 1–3 provide the background for the main idea in sentence 4: students who change answers they are unsure of usually improve their test scores. Specific reasons are given in sentences 5–7.

¹To erase or not to erase? ²That is the question in many students' minds after they've penciled in one of those small circles in multiple-choice tests. ³Folk wisdom has long held that when answering questions on such tests—or on any test—you should trust your first instincts. ⁴However, a research instructor has found that students who change answers they're unsure of usually improve their scores. ⁵The instructor spent three years compiling and analyzing college students' tests, watching for telltale erasure marks, which would indicate that the student had, indeed, revised his or her answer. ⁶What the instructor found was that revised answers were two and a half times as likely to go from wrong to right as vice-versa. ⁷This statistic held up even across such variables as sex, age, and race; the subject matter of the tests studied also proved not to be a factor.

___2___ 3.

Sentence 1 introduces the topic of garbage removal. Sentences 3–6 illustrate the problems communities have encountered in getting rid of garbage.

¹Finding a good way to get rid of garbage is a problem that faces many municipalities today. ²It may be of some consolation for them to know that getting rid of garbage has almost always involved problems. ³When settlements were very small, garbage was simply thrown outdoors, where it eventually decomposed. ⁴But as communities grew, pigs and other animals helped clear away garbage by eating it; of course, the animals, in turn, recycled that garbage and thus created an even less appealing waste problem. ⁵The first municipal effort to deal with garbage was begun in Philadelphia by Benjamin Franklin, whose solution was to have it dumped into the Delaware River. ⁶A century later, municipal incinerators, generally located in the most crowded part of town, burned garbage and produced the worst of odors as a by-product.

(Continues on next page)

_____1___ 4.

The main idea is that many people who get arrested do not receive appropriate punishment for their crimes. Sentences 2–7 give specific illustrations of how and why they fail to receive this punishment.

[1]In both Canada and the United States, many people arrested for a crime never receive appropriate punishment. [2]Prosecutors often drop charges because of flaws in the arrest procedures—officers didn't follow the rules with sufficient care or file their paperwork properly. [3]In many other cases, the charges are dismissed at preliminary hearings because of problems of evidence, such as key witnesses failing to appear. [4]Of cases surviving these barriers, many are resolved by a plea bargain. [5]That is, the charges are reduced in exchange for a plea of guilty. [6]This spares the government the expense of a trial, but it also makes punishment less severe. [7]And of those who do go to prison, very few will serve their full sentence. [8]Time off for good behavior often equals 25 percent of one's sentence, so most will be out on parole well before their time is up.

_____2___ 5.

Sentence 1 provides the background for the main idea. Sentences 3–8 give specific examples supporting the main idea—that humans have achieved remarkable things.

[1]If we compressed the entire history of life on the planet into a single year, the first modern human would not appear until December 31 at about 11:53 p.m., and the first civilizations would emerge only about a minute before the end of the year. [2]Yet humanity's achievements in its brief history on Earth have been remarkable. [3]Some 15,000 years ago, our ancestors practiced religious rituals and painted superb pictures on the walls of their caves. [4]Around 11,000 years ago, some human groups began to domesticate animals and plants, thereby freeing themselves from total dependence on hunting and gathering food. [5]About 6,000 years ago, people began to live in cities, to specialize in different forms of labor, to divide into social classes, and to create distinct political and economic institutions. [6]Within a few thousand years, empires were created, linking isolated groups and bringing millions under centralized rule. [7]Advanced agricultural practices improved farming, resulting in growing populations and the emergence of large nation-states. [8]A mere 250 years ago, the Industrial Revolution began, thrusting us into the modern world of factories and computers, jets and nuclear reactors, instantaneous global communications, and terrifying military technologies.

MAIN IDEAS: Mastery Test 6

The five paragraphs that follow are all taken from college textbooks. The main idea may appear at any place within each paragraph. Write the number of each main idea sentence in the space provided.

___2___ 1. ¹People may think that love and romantic feelings are enough of a basis for choosing a spouse. ²The chances of a marriage surviving, however, would improve if prospective marriage partners considered a few unromantic questions before deciding on matrimony. ³For example, do the two individuals involved share a common socioeconomic background? ⁴The more similar they are in their social, economic, religious, and cultural backgrounds, the more similar their expectations about married life will be. ⁵In addition, what are their goals? ⁶It's a big advantage to the marriage if they know and share one another's goals concerning career, lifestyle, and family. ⁷Finally, and maybe most important, how does the prospective spouse treat others in his or her life? ⁸During the courtship, the boyfriend or girlfriend may get special consideration, but in the long run, spouses will probably treat each other about the same way they treat their own family members.

Sentence 1 introduces the topic. In sentence 2, the words a few unromantic questions signal the main idea. Sentences 3–8 ask and explain three unromantic but important questions.

___1___ 2. ¹There is a tendency in our society to turn important decisions over to groups. ²In the business world, most important decisions are made around a conference table rather than behind one person's desk. ³In politics, major policy decisions are seldom made by just one person. ⁴Groups of advisers, cabinet officers, committee members, or aides meet to deliberate and decide. ⁵In the courts, a defendant may request a trial by jury, and for some serious crimes, a jury trial is required by law. ⁶And of course, the U.S. Supreme Court renders group decisions on issues of major importance.

Sentence 1 presents the main idea—groups make the important decisions. Sentences 2–6 provide specific evidence to support the main idea.

___2___ 3. ¹The American ideal of a lush green lawn is borrowed from England, where the cool, misty climate makes it easy to grow grass. ²In America, however, lawns are an energy-intensive, wasteful, and nonproductive form of landscaping. ³To begin with, achieving a picture-perfect lawn requires gallons of expensive fertilizer and hazardous pesticides that pollute groundwater and run off into lakes and rivers. ⁴In addition, lawn owners often exterminate the insects, moles, and gophers that play a part in the balance of nature. ⁵Equally destructive is the constant watering lawns require, often where water is a limited resource. ⁶Finally, the lawn must be mowed on a regular basis to give it that green carpet effect, requiring endless output of human and mechanical energy. ⁷After all the labor and expense, the final result is a flat covering that lacks interesting features, wildlife, or edible produce.

Sentence 1 introduces the topic of American lawns. Sentences 3–7 give examples of the main idea in sentence 2: the lawns are a waste of money and energy.

(Continues on next page)

_3_ 4. ¹Propaganda is information that is methodically spread in order to persuade audiences to adopt a certain opinion. ²Advertising is an ever-present form of propaganda in our lives. ³Four common propaganda techniques are present in the advertising we see and hear every day. ⁴One technique, the testimonial, involves having a well-known person appear on behalf of the product being sold. ⁵Advertisers assume, for example, that if we admire a sports star, we'll want to eat the cereal he or she endorses. ⁶Another common propaganda technique, the bandwagon, makes us want to be "one of the gang." ⁷"Everybody's switching to . . . " "Don't be left out . . . " and "All across America, people are discovering . . . " are phrases that signal a bandwagon approach. ⁸The plain-folks propaganda technique is especially popular on TV. ⁹In plain-folks commercials, we see and hear "regular" consumers talk about their experience using a certain phone company, headache remedy, or brand of coffee. ¹⁰The fourth common propaganda technique, the transfer, encourages us to link two unrelated objects in our mind. ¹¹When a powerful cougar prowls around a shiny new car, for example, advertisers hope we will transfer our sense of the wild cat's speed, strength, and beauty to our vision of their product.

Sentences 1–2 are background information leading up to the main idea: ads use four propaganda techniques. Sentences 4–11 explain the four techniques.

_11_ 5. ¹Stories of the mythical Camelot, the location in England of King Arthur's court, depict a world of dashing knights in shining armor and beautiful damsels in distress. ²In actuality, the real world of that time probably consisted of smelly men in rusty tin suits and damsels in a certain kind of distress—the distress of being constantly pregnant and of having no rights in a male-dominated society. ³Those same stories often glorified the brave men who fought to the death for king and country. ⁴However, most battle fatalities of the time resulted from medieval medicine. ⁵Letting the "bad blood" out of a sick person was a common medical practice, and cleanliness was not. ⁶Other stories of the fabled Camelot housed royalty in glittering palaces, clothed them in silks, and covered them in mystery and awe. ⁷But what is awesome about living in a cold, stone, rat-infested fortress with poor ventilation? ⁸As for silks, war-indebted kings could rarely afford such foreign commodities. ⁹Wool from home usually did the trick. ¹⁰And there's certainly nothing silky about the discomfort caused by coarse woolen undergarments. ¹¹It is obvious that the Camelot myth ignores the harsh realities of life in the Middle Ages in favor of a fantastic, unrealistic view of history.

Sentence 11 states the main idea, that the Camelot myth ignores the harsh realities of life in the Middle Ages. Sentence 1 introduces the topic with a statement that contrasts with the main idea. Sentences 2–10 provide specific evidence to support the main idea.

3 Supporting Details

In Chapter 2 you worked on the most important reading skill—finding the main idea. A closely related reading skill is locating *supporting details*—the added information that is needed for you to make sense of a main idea.

This chapter describes supporting details and presents three techniques to help you take study notes on main ideas and their supporting details: outlining, mapping, and summarizing.

What Are Supporting Details?

© 2001 Randy Glasbergen.
www.glasbergen.com

GLASBERGEN

"This morning I almost didn't get a doughnut,
later somebody put me on hold for three minutes,
and then I got a paper cut! *My job is unbearable!*"

Supporting details are reasons, examples, facts, steps, or other kinds of evidence that explain a main idea. In the cartoon shown above, the main idea is that "My job is unbearable." The joke in the cartoon is that the man's supporting examples are not very convincing!

On the next page is a paragraph with strong support for its point.

A Paragraph with Strong Support

In the paragraph below, three major details support the main idea that many people are strangely passive when they visit a doctor. As you read the paragraph, try to identify and check (✓) the three major details.

¹Many people are strangely passive when they visit a doctor. ²First of all, they often fail to provide the doctor with complete information about their medical problem. ³They may barely describe their symptoms, believing that a skilled doctor—like a master car mechanic—will somehow easily be able to diagnose what is wrong with them. ⁴Secondly, many people fail to ask their doctors for a full and clear explanation of their condition. ⁵They don't want to appear ignorant in front of their "all-knowing" doctor, and they don't want to take up too much of this Important Person's time, so they say little and ask almost nothing. ⁶Last of all, they often fail to understand a doctor's orders. ⁷Studies show that many patients don't understand why they should take a certain medication or for how long they should take it. ⁸Incredibly enough, some patients are not even sure, as they are about to be rolled into an operating room, why they are having surgery!

✓ *Check Your Understanding*

See if you can complete the basic outline below that shows the three major details supporting the main idea.   *Wording of answers may vary.*

Main idea: Many people are strangely passive when they visit a doctor.

Supporting detail 1: *Don't provide enough information about their problem*

Supporting detail 2: *Don't get a full explanation of their problem*

Supporting detail 3: *Don't understand a doctor's orders*

Explanation

You should have added that patients fail to 1) provide enough information about their problem, 2) get a full explanation of their problem, and 3) understand a doctor's orders. These major supporting details help you fully understand the main idea. To read effectively, you must often learn to recognize main ideas *and* the details that support those ideas.

Understanding Major and Minor Details

There are often two levels of supporting details—major and minor. The **major details** explain and develop the main idea. In turn, the **minor details** help fill out and make clear the major details.

In the paragraph below, the main idea is stated in the first sentence. Read the paragraph and put a check (✓) by the two major details that support the main idea. The major details are in turn supported by minor details, which are examples in this case. The first major detail is followed by three examples, and the second major detail is followed by one long example.

> ¹There are two ways to relate to people in our lives. ²One way is to see them ✓as *objects*: we get something from them, but we are not concerned with how they feel. ³They are there only for our use. ⁴For example, we might treat as an object the person who sells us items in a convenience store or waits on us in a restaurant or even teaches a class we are taking. ⁵The second way we can see people is ✓as *subjects*, letting ourselves be aware that they have feelings just as we do. ⁶There is a story about a British woman who was expecting important guests for tea one afternoon. ⁷She looked out from her front porch after lunch and was horrified to see that her gardener had not shown up for work. ⁸When he finally arrived, she tore into him. ⁹"Do you know who is coming here in an hour? ¹⁰I ought to fire you!" ¹¹Without looking up, the man quietly said, "I'm sorry. ¹²My little girl died during the night, and we had to bury her today." ¹³For the first time, the woman saw the man as a human being, not simply as a device for keeping her lawn attractive. ¹⁴He stopped being an object and became a subject, a possessor of feelings, needs, pains, and relationships to which she had never given a thought.

Explanation

The major details are the "two ways to relate to people in our lives" mentioned in the main idea. The first major detail is to see people as objects, and the second detail is to see them as subjects. The minor details are the examples the author has used to make those two major details clear. The relationships between the main idea and its major and minor details can be seen at a glance in this brief, informal outline:

Main idea: There are two ways to relate to people in our lives.

1. See them as objects
   Examples: convenience-store salesperson, waiter, teacher

2. See them as subjects
   Example: British woman and her gardener

Notice that just as the main idea is more general than its supporting details, the major details are more general than the minor ones. For example, to see people as subjects is more general than the specific example of the British woman and her gardener.

The purpose of the rest of this chapter is to sharpen your sense of the relationships between main ideas and their major and minor supporting details. You will practice three note-taking techniques that will make you a better reader: outlining, mapping, and summarizing.

Outlining

Preparing an outline of a passage will help you understand and see clearly the relationship between a main idea and its supporting details. Outlines start with a main idea (or a heading that summarizes the main idea), followed by major supporting details. Sometimes there will be a level of minor details as well.

Suppose you wanted to outline the paragraph on bullying that appeared in Chapter 2. Reread the paragraph, trying to identify and check (✓) the three major supporting details.

> [1]School bullies have been around as long as there have been schools. [2]Studies reveal several reasons why some children become bullies. [3]Research shows that a certain combination of size and personality may be one factor. [4]Bigger, more aggressive children are more likely to try to dominate their smaller, quieter peers. [5]Another factor linked to bullying is overexposure to violent TV programs. [6]By the time the average American child is ten years old, he or she has watched thousands of acts of violence, including assault and murder. [7]Such exposure can lead to aggression and violence. [8]Finally, exposure to *real* violence is a factor in bullying. [9]Studies indicate that victims of bullies often turn into bullies themselves. [10]Whether abused by family members or tormented by other kids, bullies typically learn their behavior from others. [11]Look closely into the eyes of a bully, and you may be looking into the eyes of a former victim.

✓ *Check Your Understanding*

Now see if you can fill in the missing items in the following outline of the paragraph, which shows both major and minor details.

Main idea: **Studies reveal several reasons why some children become bullies.**

Major detail: **1.** A certain combination of size and personality

  Minor details: Bigger, more aggressive children may dominate their smaller, quieter peers.

Major detail:	2.	*Overexposure to violent TV programs*

Minor details:	*By age 10, a child has watched thousands of acts of violence on TV, including assaults and murder.*

Major detail:	3.	*Exposure to <u>real</u> violence*

Minor details:	Kids abused by family members or bullied by other kids often become bullies.

Explanation

You should have added two major supporting details: (2) overexposure to violent TV programs; (3) exposure to *real* violence. And to the second major supporting detail, you should have added the minor detail that the average American ten-year-old has watched thousands of acts of violence on television.

Notice that just as the main idea is more general than its supporting details, so major details are more general than minor ones. For instance, the major detail that "overexposure to violent TV programs" is a factor in bullying is more general than the minor detail that the average American child of ten "has watched thousands of acts of violence."

Outlining Tips

The following tips will help you prepare outlines:

 TIP 1 Look for words that tell you a list of details is coming. Here are some common list words:

List Words

several kinds of	various causes	a few reasons
a number of	a series of	three factors
four steps	among the results	several advantages

For example, look again at the main ideas in two paragraphs already discussed and underline the list words:

- Studies reveal <u>several reasons</u> why some children become bullies.
- There are <u>two ways</u> to relate to people in our lives.

Here the words *several reasons* and *two ways* tell us that a list of major details is coming. You will not always be given such helpful signals that a list of details will follow. For example, there are no list words in the paragraph with this main idea, "Though fun to watch, chimpanzees should not be kept as pets." However, you will want to note such words when they are present. *Such list words help you to understand quickly the basic organization of a passage.*

 TIP 2   Look for words that signal major details. Such words are called **addition words**, and they will be explained further on page 182. Here are some common addition words:

Addition Words

one	first of all	in addition	furthermore
first	also	next	last of all
second	another	moreover	finally

 Check Your Understanding

Now look again at the paragraph on bullying on page 106:

1. The word *one* (in *one factor*) signals the first major supporting detail.

2. Which addition word introduces the second major supporting detail?
   Another

3. Which addition word introduces the third major supporting detail?
   Finally

And look again at the selection on two ways of relating to people on page 105:

1. Which word introduces the first major detail? _____ One _____

2. Which word introduces the second major detail? _____ second _____

Explanation

In the paragraph on bullying, the second major detail is introduced by the word *Another (factor)* and the third by the word *Finally*. In the selection on relating to people, the first major detail is introduced by the word *One* and the second by the word *second*.

TIP 3   When making an outline, put all supporting details of equal importance at the same distance from the left margin. In the outline on bullying on pages 106–107, the three major supporting details are all placed at the same point on the margin. Likewise, all of the minor supporting details are placed at their own fixed point from the margin. You can therefore see at a glance the main idea, the major details, and the minor details.

Check Your Understanding

Put appropriate numbers *(1, 2, 3)* and letters *(a, b)* in front of the items in the following outline.

> **Main idea**
> _1_ **Major detail**
>> _a_ Minor detail
>> _b_ Minor detail
> _2_ **Major detail**
>> _a_ Minor detail
>> _b_ Minor detail
> _3_ **Major detail**

Explanation

You should have put a *1*, *2*, and *3* in front of the major details and an *a* and *b* in front of the minor details. Note that an outline proceeds from the most general to the most specific, from main idea to major details to minor details.

The practice on the following pages will give you experience in finding major details, in separating major details from minor details, and in preparing outlines.

PRACTICE 1

Read and then outline each passage. Begin by writing in the main idea, and then fill in the supporting details. The first outline requires only major details; the second calls for you to add minor details as well.   *Wording of answers may vary.*

A. [1]Parents can take several steps to discourage TV watching and encourage reading. [2]For one thing, have only one television set, and place it in the family room. [3]Then if your child wants privacy, he or she will have to go elsewhere, away from the TV. [4]Secondly, connect reading with eating. [5]Put a bookcase rather than a television in the kitchen, and make sure it is filled with comics, magazines, local newspapers, and so on. [6]Explain that all snacks have to be eaten in the kitchen. [7]Given the fact that most kids can go only a short time without putting food in their mouths, your kids should get a lot of reading done while they're snacking. [8]Last of all, don't even dream of putting a television set in a child's bedroom. [9]You want your kids to fall asleep over books, not glued to a flickering screen.

The three major supporting details are introduced with the addition words For one thing (sentence 2), Secondly (sentence 4), and Last of all (sentence 8).

Main idea: _Parents can take several steps to discourage TV watching and encourage reading._

Major detail: 1. _Have only one TV set, and place it in the family room._

Major detail: 2. _Connect reading with eating._

Major detail: 3. _Don't put a TV set in a child's bedroom._

B. [1]Colleges of the early nineteenth century had distinct differences from today's schools. [2]First, the student body during this time was almost entirely white males. [3]Higher education was considered a final polishing for upper-class gentlemen—a privilege unnecessary for those who had lower social status. [4]In addition, no matter what their interests were, all students had to take the same courses. [5]They were required to study the ancient languages (Latin, Greek, sometimes Hebrew), literature, natural science, mathematics, and political and moral philosophy. [6]A third feature of nineteenth-century colleges was their small size. [7]Except for a few of the very oldest institutions, most colleges had a student body of only a few dozen students. [8]The typical faculty consisted of just three or four professors and an equal number of tutors. [9]A final difference was that student life in the early 1800s was much more regulated than today. [10]Strict curfews determined what times students had to turn the lamps out in their rooms, and most schools required students to attend religious services on campus.

Note: Don't write in *all* the minor details, but try to summarize them in a few words.

Main idea: Colleges of the early nineteenth century were distinctly different from today's schools.

The four major supporting details are introduced with the addition words *First* (sentence 2), *In addition* (sentence 4), *third* (sentence 6), and *final* (sentence 9).

Major detail: 1. Students were mostly white males.

  Minor details: College was considered a final polishing for upper-class gentlemen.

Major detail: 2. All students had to take the same courses.

  Minor details: They studied ancient languages, literature, natural science, mathematics, and political and moral philosophy.

Major detail: 3. Colleges were small.

  Minor details: Most had only a few dozen students, three or four professors, and three or four tutors.

Major detail: 4. Student life was more regulated.

  Minor details: Strict curfews determined when students had to turn off lights, and attendance at religious services was required.

Study Hint: At times you will want to include minor details in your study notes; at other times, it may not be necessary to do so. If you are taking notes on one or more textbook chapters, use your judgment. It is often best to be aware of minor details but to concentrate on writing down the main ideas and major details.

Mapping

Students sometimes find it helpful to use maps rather than outlines. **Maps,** or diagrams, are highly visual outlines in which circles, boxes, or other shapes show the relationships between main ideas and supporting details. Each major detail is connected to the main idea. If minor details are included, each is connected to the major detail it explains.

✓ *Check Your Understanding*

Read the following passage and then see if you can complete the map and the questions that follow.

> [1]Several factors can interfere with having a good memory. [2]One such factor is a lack of motivation. [3]Without a real desire to learn or remember something, you probably won't. [4]Another cause is a lack of practice. [5]To stay sharp, memory skills, like any other skill, must be used on a regular basis. [6]A third factor that can hurt memory is self-doubt. [7]If you're convinced you won't remember something, you probably won't. [8]A person with a positive attitude will do much better on a test than someone who is sure he or she won't remember the material. [9]Last, distraction can interfere with memory. [10]If you are being distracted by the sound of a television or a conversation nearby, try to find a quiet environment before you attempt to commit something to memory.

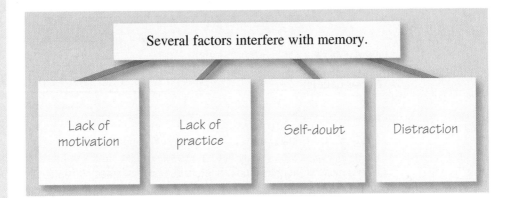

Which words introduce:

1. The first major detail? _____ *One* _____

2. The second major detail? _____ *Another* _____

3. The third major detail? _____ *A third (factor)* _____

4. The last major detail? _____ *Last* _____

Explanation

The map sets off the major details in a very visual way. You see at a glance the four factors that can interfere with memory: lack of motivation, lack of practice, self-doubt, and distraction. The words that introduce the major details are *One, Another, A third,* and *Last.*

PRACTICE 2

Read each passage, and then complete the maps that follow. The main ideas are given so that you can focus on finding the supporting details. The first passage requires only major details. The second passage calls for you to add both major and minor details.

A. ¹Many people become nearly tongue-tied when they want to meet other people. ²For those of us who find starting conversations with strangers difficult, the following four strategies may be useful. ³Notice that each is developed in question form, inviting the other person to respond. ⁴One approach is to introduce yourself, giving your name and asking the name of the other person. ⁵"Hi, I'm Shelby. And who are you?" ⁶A second approach is to refer to the physical setting in a question. ⁷You might, for example, make such a comment as, "This is awful weather for a game, isn't it?" ⁸Another approach is to give the other person a compliment and ask a question related to it. ⁹You might say, for instance, "Your braid looks great. Did it take long to do?" ¹⁰Finally, you can seek direct information from the other person. ¹¹At a work gathering, you can ask such a question as, "Which department do you work in?" ¹²At a party, you might say, "Walt and Jan give a really nice party. ¹³How do you happen to know them?"

Wording of answers may vary.

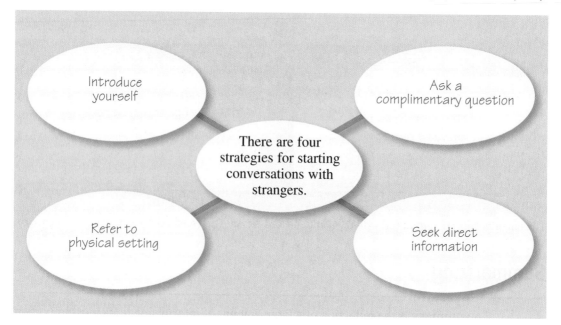

Introduce yourself

Ask a complimentary question

There are four strategies for starting conversations with strangers.

Refer to physical setting

Seek direct information

The major details are introduced with the addition words *One* (sentence 4), *second* (sentence 6), *Another* (sentence 8), and *Finally* (sentence 10).

B. [1]Industrialized dairy farming differs from old-fashioned dairy farming in two basic respects. [2]First of all, there is an immense saving of labor in industrial farming. [3]Industrial farms have milking machines installed on a huge carousel, and each revolution allows sufficient time for a cow to be milked. [4]Consequently, it takes only one operator to place and release cows as each milking station comes by the gateway. [5]In contrast, in many nations milking is still done by hand and takes about 10 minutes per cow. [6]The second major difference is the higher milk output per cow on industrial farms. [7]The average American cow gives 7.5 times more milk than does the average cow in Brazil, where farms are old-fashioned. [8]The productivity differences are so great that milk is far cheaper in the United States than in Brazil.

The major details are introduced with the addition words *First of all* (sentence 2) and *second* (sentence 6).

Summarizing

A **summary** is the reduction of a large amount of information to its most important points. The length and kind of summary will depend upon one's purpose as well as on the material in question. Often, a summary will consist of a main idea and its major supporting details. As a general guideline, a paragraph might be reduced to a sentence or two, an article might be reduced to a paragraph, and a textbook chapter might be reduced to about three pages of notes.

One of the most common types of summarizing occurs when you are taking study notes on textbook material. Very often you will find it helpful to summarize examples of key terms. For instance, look at the textbook passage below and the summary that follows.

> [1]In some circumstances, the most effective way of coping with stress is **withdrawal**—avoiding the situation. [2]A person at an amusement park who is overcome by anxiety when just looking at a roller coaster can walk on to a less threatening ride or even leave the park entirely. [3]A woman whose promotion depends on temporarily relocating might simply quit her job and join another company. [4]Or she might withdraw emotionally from the stressful situation by deciding that promotion no longer matters to her and that she has already advanced in her career as far as she wants to go.

Summary

> Withdrawal—coping with stress by avoiding the situation. For example, a person made anxious by being near a roller coaster can walk elsewhere.

Note that a textbook definition of a key term (such as *withdrawal*) should generally not be summarized, but should be worded in the language chosen by the author. On the other hand, it usually makes sense to summarize the supporting information. Summarizing often involves two steps:

1 *Select* one example from several that might be given. Which example you select is up to you, as long as it makes the term clear for you. In the summary above, the example about the roller coaster has been chosen to illustrate withdrawal.

2 *Condense* the example if it's not already very brief. Notice that the example about the roller coaster has been condensed from a very long sentence to a short one.

A definition of a key term followed by one condensed example is a very useful way to take notes—especially in introductory college courses, where many terms are defined and illustrated.

> *Study Hint:* If you have a textbook chapter to learn, very often you can get what you need by doing two things: 1) writing down the definitions in the chapter along with summarized examples of the definitions, and 2) writing down lists of major supporting details and any minor details that you think are important.

Summarizing a Passage

Read the selection below, taken from an introductory textbook for a college social science course. As is often the case in such introductory texts, a new term is presented and then followed by an extended example. Complete the study notes by circling the letter of the answer choice that best summarizes that example.

[1]Bureaucracies have become a part of modern life because they are a powerful form of social organization. [2]Once in existence, however, they tend to take on a life of their own. [3]In a process called **goal displacement**, an organization continues even after it achieves its goal and no longer has a reason to go on. [4]A classic example is the National Foundation for the March of Dimes, organized in the 1930s to fight polio. [5]At that time, the origin of polio was a mystery. [6]Parents lived in fear because no one knew whose child might be stricken next with this crippling disease. [7]To raise money to discover the cause and a cure, the March of Dimes placed posters of children on crutches near cash registers in almost every store in the United States. [8]The U.S. public took the campaign to heart and contributed heavily. [9]The organization raised money beyond its wildest dreams. [10]During the 1950s, Dr. Jonas Salk developed a vaccine for polio, and this threat was wiped out almost overnight.

[11]What then? [12]Did the organization fold? [13]After all, its purpose had been fulfilled. [14]But, of course, the March of Dimes is still around. [15]Faced with the loss of their jobs, the professional staff that ran the organization quickly found a way to keep its bureaucracy intact by pursuing a new enemy—birth defects. [16]Their choice of enemy is striking, for it is doubtful that we will ever run out of birth defects—and thus unlikely that these people will ever run out of jobs.

Study notes:

Goal displacement—An organization finds a way to continue even after it achieves its goal and no longer has a reason to go on.

Example—

A. A classic example is the National Foundation for the March of Dimes, organized in the 1930s to fight polio.

B. After the March of Dimes achieved its goal of wiping out polio, it found a way to continue by taking on a new enemy, birth defects.

C. The March of Dimes successfully raised money to discover a cause and cure for polio, and when Dr. Jonas Salk developed a vaccine for polio, the threat was wiped out almost overnight.

Explanation

Useful study notes should clearly show how an example illustrates a new term. In the case of the paragraph above, the notes should include the key point that an organization finds a way to continue even after reaching its goal. Neither answer A nor answer C explains how the organization in question, the March of Dimes, found a way to continue. Answer B does, so it is the correct answer. Remember, the purpose of an example is to make a definition clear.

PRACTICE 3

Read each textbook selection below. Then complete the study notes by circling the letter of the answer that best summarizes an example of the term being defined.

A. [1]People deceive themselves in various ways to cope better with problems. [2]One such way is **denial**, the unconscious refusal to recognize a painful or threatening reality. [3]One researcher cites the example of a woman who was near death from severe burns. [4]At first, she was depressed and frightened, but after a few days she began to feel sure that she would soon be able to return home and care for her children, although all her medical indications were to the contrary. [5]By denying the extent of her injuries, this woman was able to stay calm and cheerful. [6]She was not merely putting on an act for her relatives and friends; she actually believed she would recover. [7]In another situation, researchers interviewed the parents of children who were dying of leukemia. [8]Some parents denied their children's condition; others accepted it. [9]Physical examinations revealed that those who denied the illness did not have the physiological symptoms of stress, such as excessive stomach acid, found in those who accepted their children's illness.

Neither answer A nor answer B includes the "refusal to recognize a painful or threatening reality."

Study notes:

Denial—the unconscious refusal to recognize a painful or threatening reality.

Example—

A. Being near death from extreme burns depressed and frightened a woman.
B. According to all the medical indications, the woman who had suffered severe burns was near death.
C. By refusing to believe her burn injuries were deadly, a woman near death was able to stay calm and cheerful.

B. [1]Imagine a ball lying on a level table. [2]Left alone, the ball stays where it is. [3]Given a gentle push, the ball rolls a short way and then comes to a stop. [4]The smoother the ball and the tabletop, the farther the ball rolls before stopping. [5]Suppose that we have a perfectly round ball and a perfectly smooth and level tabletop, and that no air is present to slow down the ball. [6]If the table is infinitely long and we give the ball a push, will it ever stop rolling? [7]In fact, we can reasonably expect that under ideal conditions the ball would keep rolling forever. [8]This conclusion was first reached by Galileo and later stated by Newton as the first law of motion: An object will continue in its state of rest or of motion in a straight line at constant speed if the object does not interact with anything else.

Study notes:

Newton's first law of motion—an object will continue in its state of rest or of motion in a straight line at constant speed if the object does not interact with anything else.

Example—

A. If a ball lying on a level table is given a gentle push, it won't roll too far.
B. A perfectly round ball on an endless table won't move if left alone, but can roll forever if pushed.
C. Galileo first came to a conclusion which Newton later stated as his first law of motion.   Answer B illustrates Newton's first law of motion. Answer A describes what happens in the less-than-ideal conditions of our world. Answer C does not suggest what the law means.

PRACTICE 4

Read each textbook selection below. Then take study notes by 1) writing down the key term and its definition, 2) selecting an example that makes the definition clear, and 3) writing that example in your notes, condensing it if possible.

A. [1]**Passive listening** occurs when a listener tries to make sense out of a speaker's remarks without being able to interact with the speaker. [2]Probably the most familiar example of passive listening would be students hearing an instructor's lecture without having the opportunity to ask questions or otherwise interact with the speaker. [3]Passive listening also takes place in interpersonal settings, as when one person dominates a conversation while the others fall into the role of audience members, or when some parents lecture their children without allowing them to respond.

The paragraph gives three examples of passive listening—one in sentence 2 and two in sentence 3. Students may choose any one of the three examples.

Wording of answers may vary.

Study notes:

Passive listening _____ trying to make sense out of a
speaker's remarks without being able to interact with the speaker

Example—___Students listen to an instructor's lecture without having
the chance to ask questions.

B. [1]In an attempt to convince ourselves and others that the positive face we show to the world is true, we tend to judge ourselves in the most generous terms possible. [2]Social scientists have labeled this tendency the **self-serving bias**. [3]On one hand, when others suffer, we often blame the problem on their personal qualities. [4]On the other hand, when we suffer, we blame the problem on forces outside ourselves. [5]Consider a few examples. [6]When *they* botch a job, we might think they were not listening well or trying hard enough; when *we* botch a job, the problem was unclear directions or not enough time. [7]When *he* lashes out angrily, we say he's being moody; when *we* lash out angrily, it's because of the pressure we've been under. [8]When *she* gets caught speeding, we say she should have been more careful; when *we* get caught speeding, we deny that we were driving too fast, or we say, "Everybody does it."

Study notes:

Wording of answers may vary.

Self-serving bias _____ ___ the practice of judging ourselves leniently

Example— When _he_ lashes out angrily, we say he is moody. When _we_ lash out angrily, we say we're under pressure.

The paragraph gives three examples of self-serving bias—the first in sentence 6, the second in sentence 7, and the third in sentence 8. Students may choose any one of the three examples.

A Final Note

This chapter has centered on supporting details as they appear in well-organized paragraphs. But keep in mind that supporting details are part of readings of any length, including selections that may not have an easy-to-follow list of one major detail after another. Starting with the reading at the end of this chapter (page 125), you will be given practice in answering all kinds of questions about key supporting details. These questions will develop your ability to pay close attention to what you are reading.

CHAPTER REVIEW

In this chapter, you learned the following:

- Major and minor details provide the added information you need to make sense of a main idea.

- List words and addition words can help you to find major and minor supporting details.

- Outlining, mapping, and summarizing are useful note-taking strategies.

- Outlines show the relationship between the main idea, major details, and minor details of a passage.

- Maps are very visual outlines.

- Writing a definition and summarizing an example is a good way to take notes on a new term.

The next chapter—Chapter 4—will show you how to find implied main ideas and central points.

On the Web: If you are using this book in class, you can visit our website for additional practice in identifying supporting details. Go to **www.townsendpress.com** and click on "Online Exercises."

REVIEW TEST 1

To review what you've learned in this chapter, answer each of these questions about supporting details.

1. *Fill in the blanks:* Major supporting details are more *(general, specific)* _____*specific*_____ than main ideas. Minor supporting details are more *(general, specific)* _____*specific*_____ than major details.
   See page 107.

2. ___*T*___ TRUE OR FALSE? Supporting details can be reasons, examples, facts, or other specific information.
   See page 103.

3. Outlining is a way to show at a glance the relationship between a main idea and its _____*supporting details*_____.
   See page 106.

4. In _____*mapping*_____, you create a visual outline using circles, boxes, and other shapes to set off main ideas and supporting details.
   See page 111.

5. When taking notes on textbook material, you will often find it useful to write out each definition in full and then select and ___*condense*___ one example of that definition.
   See page 115.

REVIEW TEST 2

A. (1–7.) Complete the outline of the following paragraph by adding words to the main idea and filling in the missing major and minor details. Note that addition words introduce the major details and some of the minor details as well.

> ¹Several factors influence the justice system's treatment of criminals. ²For one thing, the sex of offenders affects the severity of sentences. ³A woman is less likely to receive the death penalty than a man. ⁴Also, the court is more reluctant to send a mother to prison than a father. ⁵Another factor in the treatment of offenders is their race. ⁶Nonwhites are awarded parole and probation less often. ⁷In addition, blacks are executed more often for capital crimes. ⁸Finally, the age of offenders is considered in sentencing. ⁹Young offenders are given special treatment. ¹⁰And the elderly are given more lenient sentences.

Main idea: _____ *Several factors* _____ **influence the justice system's treatment of criminals.**

Major detail: **1.** *Sex of offender affects severity of sentence*

Wording of answers may vary.

  Minor details: a. **Woman less likely to receive death penalty than a man**

  b. *Court more reluctant to send mother to prison than father*

Major detail: **2.** *Race is another factor*

  Minor details: a. *Nonwhites get parole and probation less often*

  b. *Blacks executed more often for capital crimes*

Major detail: **3. Age of offenders considered in sentencing**

  Minor details: a. *Young offenders given special treatment*

  b. **More lenient sentences for the elderly**

The major details are introduced with the addition words *For one thing* (sentence 2), *Another* (5), and *Finally* (sentence 8).

B. (8–10.) Answer the questions about supporting details that follow the passage. Note that the main idea is boldfaced.

> ¹More than one anthropologist has taken the time to explore old cemeteries in New England and look at the gravestones there. ²**The anthropologists discovered that over different time periods there were three different types of images carved on the gravestones.** ³The first, which appears on the oldest stones (from the 1600s into the mid-1700s), is the death's head: a grinning skull. ⁴The death's head corresponds with the pessimistic view of life and death held by the Puritans that populated New England at that time. ⁵But as more liberal thought took hold in New England in the mid-1700s, another image began to be seen on headstones. ⁶This was a cherub—a smiling, baby-faced angel. ⁷The cherub seemed to represent

To the Instructor: In Review Tests 2 and 3, the main ideas have been underlined in this *Instructor's Edition.*

a more hopeful view of death and a happy afterlife in heaven. [8]In the late 1700s, there was a preference for the classic-looking urn and willow. [9]This image indicates a turn to a more intellectual and less emotional attitude toward death.

___C___ 8. The addition word that signals the second major detail is
   A. *one.*   See sentence 5.
   B. *first.*
   C. *another.*
   D. *This.*

___C___ 9. The list words that tell what types of details will follow are
   A. "more than one anthropologist."   See sentence 2.
   B. "old cemeteries."
   C. "three different types of images."

___B___ 10. How many major supporting details are in the paragraph?
   A. Two   B. Three   C. Four

The major details are the "different time periods." Two of these are introduced with the addition words *first* (sentence 3) and *another* (sentence 5). The third time period is introduced with the phrase "In the late 1700s" (sentence 8).

REVIEW TEST 3

A. (1–5.) Outline the following passage by completing the main idea and filling in the major supporting details.   *Wording of answers may vary.*

[1]Serious depression, as opposed to the fleeting kind we all feel at times, has definite warning signs. [2]Some or all of these signs may be present within the affected individual. [3]One symptom of depression is a change in sleep patterns—either sleeplessness or sleeping too much. [4]Another sign is abnormal eating patterns, either eating too much or loss of appetite. [5]A third sign is trouble in thinking or concentrating—even to the point of finding it difficult to read a magazine or newspaper. [6]Finally, a general feeling of hopelessness may signal depression. [7]People feel indifferent to their families and jobs and may begin to think that life is not worth living.

Main idea: Serious depression has _____ *definite warning signs.*
   1. *Change in sleep patterns*
   2. *Abnormal eating patterns*
   3. *Trouble thinking or concentrating*
   4. *General feeling of hopelessness*

The major details are the warning signs of depression. The four major details are introduced with the addition words *One* (sentence 3), *Another* (sentence 4), *third* (sentence 5), and *Finally* (sentence 6).

B. (6–9.) Map the following paragraph by filling in the main idea and the major supporting details.

¹There are three common ways that people deal with their feelings. ²One way is to withhold them—to keep them inside without giving any verbal or nonverbal clues to their existence. ³Such people use "poker faces" in relationships, so that others have to guess about whether they are happy or sad inside. ⁴A second and often more appropriate way to deal with feelings is to display them—expressing them verbally or through facial or body language. ⁵For example, a person who displays feelings would cheer at a sporting event, laugh or cry at a moving scene in a movie, or openly admire an unexpected act of kindness. ⁶Displays must always be handled carefully if the feelings are negative. ⁷Often the best method of dealing with feelings is to describe them—put them into words in a calm, nonjudgmental way. ⁸If someone borrows one of your books without asking or otherwise takes advantage of you, tell him or her that makes you feel angry. ⁹If someone does you a favor, let him or her know how much you appreciate it. ¹⁰Describing feelings helps you keep open the clear lines of communication with other people.

Wording of answers may vary.

> **There are three common ways that people deal with their feelings.**
>
> | Withhold them | Display them | Describe them |

The major details are the three common ways of dealing with feelings. The three major details are introduced with the addition words *One* (sentence 2), *second* (sentence 4), and *best* (sentence 7). (Note that *best* acts as an addition word here. It introduces the third way of dealing with feelings.)

C. (10.) Read the textbook selection below. Then complete the study notes by circling the letter of the answer choice that best summarizes the example of the term being defined.

> [1]**Cultural lag** refers to a practice or belief that once made sense and still persists even though it is no longer useful. [2]You can see an example of cultural lag every time that you eat. [3]Americans, after they cut their meat, put down the knife and switch the fork from the left hand to the right. [4]Only then do they put the food in their mouths. [5]This differs from the European practice of simply raising the food to the mouth with the fork in the left hand after cutting the meat. [6]Why did Americans develop this habit? [7]Some experts guess that in the old days of the American frontier, Americans needed to keep a hand free in case they had to grab a weapon to fight an intruder. [8]Today the frontier is gone, and putting down the knife and switching the fork to the other hand is no longer of practical use. [9]Americans continue to do it anyway, and to eat in the European style is considered to be "bad manners."

Study notes:

Cultural lag—a practice or belief that once made sense and still persists even though it is no longer useful.

Example—

A. Europeans eat with a fork in the left hand, but Americans put the knife down after cutting and switch the fork to the right hand.
B. Americans consider the European style of eating with a fork in the left hand to be bad manners even though that method is more practical than switching the fork to the right hand.
C. Americans consider it correct to switch the fork to the right hand after cutting even though the supposed purpose—keeping the left hand free for a weapon—no longer exists.

> Answers A and B are incorrect because neither shows how the American practice "once made sense." Only answer C includes the idea of a practice continuing even after its original purpose is gone.

REVIEW TEST 4

Here is a chance to apply your understanding of supporting details to a passage from a college textbook: *Psychology*, Second Edition, by Diane E. Papalia and Sally Wendkos Olds. Read the passage and then answer the questions that follow.

To help you continue to strengthen your work on the skills taught in previous chapters, there are also questions on vocabulary in context and main ideas.

Words to Watch

Below are some words in the reading that do not have strong context support. Each word is followed by the number of the paragraph in which it appears and its meaning there. These words are indicated in the article by a small circle (°).

provocation (1): annoyance
loath (1): reluctant
temperament (1): emotional makeup
competence (2): skill
thrive (3): grow well
self-reliant (3): independent
assertive (3): positive and confident
detached (4): emotionally apart from others
withdrawn (4): shy

CHILD-REARING STYLES

Diane E. Papalia and Sally Wendkos Olds

1   What makes Mary burst into tears of frustration when she can't finish a jigsaw puzzle, while Gary will shrug and walk away from it, and Cary will sit with it for hours until he finishes? What makes Polly independent and Molly a clinger? What makes Tim ready to hit out at the slightest provocation° and Jim loath° to fight? One answer lies in the basic temperament° children are born with. A second very important influence on behavioral styles is the early emotional environment—how children are treated by their parents.

2   The psychologist Diana Baumrind set out to discover relationships between different styles of child rearing and the social competence° of children. She reviewed the research literature and conducted her own studies with ninety-five families of children in nursery school. Using a combination of long interviews, standardized testing, and observations at school and home, she identified three categories of parenting styles and linked them to children's behavior.

3   *Authoritative* parents exert firm control when necessary, but they explain why they take a stand and encourage children to express their opinions. They feel confident in their ability to guide their children, while respecting the children's interests, opinions, and unique personalities. They combine firm control with encouragement and love. Their children know that they

are expected to perform well, fulfill commitments, and carry out duties in the family. They know when they are meeting expectations and when it is worth risking their parents' displeasure to pursue some other goal. They seem to thrive° on their parents' reasonable expectations and realistic standards, and they are most self-reliant°, self-controlled, assertive°, exploratory, and content.

4   *Authoritarian* parents value unquestioning obedience and punish their children forcibly for not conforming to set and quite absolute standards. They are somewhat detached°, controlling, and distant. Their children tend to be discontented, withdrawn°, and distrustful of others.

5   *Permissive* parents make few demands on their children, set few rules, and hardly ever punish. As preschoolers,

their children are immature—the least self-reliant, the least self-controlled, the least exploratory.

On the basis of her research, 6 Baumrind has recommended that parents who want to raise competent, socially responsible, independent children should do several things:

- Teach by example; that is, behave the way you want your children to behave.

- Reward behaviors you want to encourage and punish behaviors you want to discourage, giving explanations in both cases.

- Show interest in children.

- Bestow approval only when the child has earned it.

- Demand achievement and the meeting of standards, while being open to hearing the child's point of view.

- Encourage original thinking.

Baumrind's work raises important 7 issues about child-rearing practices, but before we conclude that parenting is all that matters, we have to remember what children bring to the family. Through their own inborn temperaments, children influence their parents. It is possible, for example, that "easy" children will elicit an authoritative attitude from their parents, while "difficult" children may make tyrants out of theirs.

Reading Comprehension Questions

Vocabulary in Context

_____B_____ 1. In the sentence below, the word *bestow* (bĭ-stō′) means

Approval is given to someone—especially if it has been earned.

A. deny.   C. accept.
B. give.   D. risk.

"Bestow approval only when the child has earned it." (Paragraph 6)

_____A_____ 2. In the excerpt below, the word *elicit* (ĭ-lĭs′ĭt) means

"Easy" children would bring out encouragement and love that are part of an authoritative attitude.

A. draw out.   C. imitate.
B. dislike.   D. abuse.

"Through their own inborn temperaments, children influence their parents. It is possible, for example, that 'easy' children will elicit an authoritative attitude from their parents, while 'difficult' children may make tyrants out of theirs." (Paragraph 7)

Main Ideas

_____D_____ 3. The topic of paragraph 6 is
A. Diana Baumrind.
B. teaching by example.
C. giving approval.
D. raising children.

Each of the bulleted items suggests something parents should do to raise competent, socially responsible, independent children. Answers B and C each cover only one of the major details.

_____A_____ 4. Which sentence best expresses the main idea of paragraph 6?
A. "On the basis of her research, Baumrind has recommended that parents who want to raise competent, socially responsible, independent children should do several things:"

The words *several things* signal the main idea. Answers B, C, and D are major details that support the main idea.

B. "Teach by example, that is, behave the way you want your children to behave."
C. "Reward behaviors you want to encourage and punish behaviors you want to discourage, giving explanations in both cases."
D. "Demand achievement and the meeting of standards, while being open to hearing the child's point of view."

Supporting Details

5. Complete the sentence: To study the ninety-five families of children in nursery school, Baumrind used standardized tests, observations at school and at home, and _____ long interviews _____.

See the last sentence in paragraph 2.

6–10. Complete the following outline of parts of the reading by filling in the blanks.

A. Two influences on how a child behaves

1. _Basic temperament the child is born with_

2. _Early emotional environment_

B. Three parenting styles

1. _Authoritative_

2. _Authoritarian_

3. _Permissive_

For section A, see paragraph 1. For section B, see paragraphs 3, 4, and 5. Note that each of the three parenting styles is discussed in a separate paragraph and that each term is in italics.

Discussion Questions

1. What type of parenting style did you grow up with? Would you say this style was effective? Why or why not?

2. Why do you think Diana Baumrind feels that teaching by example is useful?

3. Baumrind encourages parents to show interest in children. What are some ways in which parents can show interest in children?

4. The authors feel that children are born with "their own inborn temperaments." Has your experience with children confirmed or contradicted their idea that children have different temperaments, starting from the time they are born? Give some examples.

Note: Writing assignments for this selection appear on pages 600–601.

Check Your Performance   SUPPORTING DETAILS

Activity	Number Right	Points	Score
Review Test 1 (5 items)	_____	× 2 =	_____
Review Test 2 (10 items)	_____	× 3 =	_____
Review Test 3 (10 items)	_____	× 3 =	_____
Review Test 4 (10 items)	_____	× 3 =	_____
		TOTAL SCORE =	_____%

Enter your total score into the **Reading Performance Chart: Review Tests** on the inside back cover.

SUPPORTING DETAILS: Mastery Test 1

A. (1–6.) Complete the outline of the following textbook passage by adding the main idea and the missing major or minor details. *Wording of answers may vary.*

[1]Divorce has serious negative consequences. [2]First, social adjustment after the divorce is a troublesome time. [3]The former couple often finds that starting to date again can be nerve-racking. [4]Also, married friends may exclude singles from social plans. [5]Secondly, emotional difficulties among the original family members are common. [6]Feelings of guilt and resentment may persist between the former husband and wife. [7]At the same time children may be confused and hurt; many also feel guilty, imagining that they were somehow to blame for the divorce. [8]A third consequence is that financial adjustments are necessary. [9]Alimony, child support, and property dispersal must be dealt with. [10]Also, the high fees that lawyers charge can be a burden.

Main idea: Divorce has serious negative consequences.

Major detail: 1. Social adjustment is troublesome.

Minor details: a. Starting to date again can be nerve-racking.

b. Married friends may exclude singles from social plans.

Major detail: 2. Emotional difficulties among original family members are common.

Minor details: a. Husband and wife feel guilt and resentment.

b. Children may be confused and hurt and feel guilty.

Major detail: 3. Financial adjustments are necessary.

Minor details: a. Alimony, child support, and property disposal must be dealt with.

b. High fees charged by lawyers can be a burden.

The major details are three negative consequences of divorce. The major details are introduced with the addition words *First* (sentence 2), *Secondly* (sentence 5), and *third* (sentence 8).

To the Instructor: In this mastery test and the five supporting-detail mastery tests that follow, the main ideas are underlined in this *Instructor's Edition*.

(Continues on next page)

B. (7–10.) Answer the questions about supporting details that follow the passage.

¹When we call someone "pig" or "swine," we do not mean it as a compliment. ²But pigs do not deserve to be used as a symbol for an insult. ³They are probably not as dirty as they are made out to be. ⁴According to one pig keeper, swine are very clean when allowed to live in a clean environment. ⁵He feels that pigs are usually dirty simply because their keepers don't clean their pens. ⁶In any case, no one has proven that the pig that wallows in mud prefers that to a cool bath. ⁷Furthermore, pigs are smarter than most people think. ⁸Many farmers, for example, have observed that pigs frequently undo complicated bolts on gates in search of adventure or romance. ⁹So the next time you call someone a pig, perhaps he or she ought to be someone you wish to praise.

_B__ 7. In general, the major details of this passage are
    A. reasons why pigs are dirty.
    B. reasons why pigs should not be used as symbols for insults.
    C. ways to insult or compliment people.

_A__ 8. Specifically, the major details are
    A. Pigs are probably not as dirty as people think; pigs are smarter than most people think.
    B. Pigs may be dirty because their pens are dirty; it hasn't been proved that pigs prefer mud to a cool bath; pigs have been seen undoing complicated bolts.
    C. People use "pig" and "swine" as insults; "pig" and "swine" should be considered praise.

_C__ 9. One pig keeper feels that pigs will stay clean if they are
    A. given baths.
    B. praised.
    C. kept in a clean environment.

10. What example is used to show that pigs are smarter than they are often thought to be? _They can undo complicated bolts on gates._

Item 7:   The first sentence introduces the topic of calling someone "pig" or "swine." The major details support the main idea (in sentence 2) by giving reasons why pigs should not be used as a symbol for an insult.

Item 8:   The first major supporting detail is stated in sentence 3; the second, in sentence 7.

Item 9:   See sentence 4.

Item 10: See sentence 8.

SUPPORTING DETAILS: Mastery Test 2

A. Answer the questions about supporting details that follow the textbook passage.

[1]A **social dilemma** is a situation in which the most rewarding short-term choice for an individual will ultimately lead to negative outcomes for all concerned. [2]For example, as you hike along a beautiful mountain trail, you stop for a snack. [3]You are tempted to throw away your empty water containers and granola bar wrappers, knowing that your backpack will be lighter if you don't have to carry your trash to the top of the mountain and back. [4]But you hesitate, knowing that if all hikers litter the trail, it will soon be unpleasant for all who use it. [5]Or consider the situation of many communities in the Southwest that have suffered severe drought for years, so that water conservation is essential. [6]Individuals living in such drought-stricken areas face personal decisions. [7]For instance, should I forgo the pleasure of a long shower today so that there will be more water for all in the future?

_____A____ 1. The main idea is expressed in sentence
    A. 1.   *The first sentence defines social dilemma.*
    B. 2.
    C. 7.

_____B____ 2. In general, the major supporting details of this paragraph are
    A. rewarding short-term choices.   *Sentences 2–7 give examples*
    B. examples of social dilemmas.   *that illustrate the term.*
    C. examples of negative outcomes.

_____A____ 3. How many major details are in this paragraph?
    A. Two   *The two major details are the examples: whether or not to*
    B. Three   *1) throw your trash on the trail and 2) take a long shower.*
    C. Four

_____C____ 4. The second major detail of the paragraph begins in sentence
    A. 1.   *The second major detail is presented in sentences 5–7.*
    B. 2.
    C. 5.

_____A____ 5. In the Southwest, the desire to take a long shower presents a social dilemma because
    A. a pleasant long shower could mean less water for others.
    B. the water is polluted.
    C. water costs more there, so long showers are expensive.

                                         See sentence 7.

(Continues on next page)

_____A_____ 6. Which summary best completes the study notes of the paragraph?

Answer A contains both parts of the definition. It states the short-term reward (convenience of littering) and the long-range negative outcome (making trail unpleasant).

Social dilemma—a situation in which the most rewarding short-term choice for an individual will ultimately lead to negative outcomes for all concerned.

Example—

A. Littering a beautiful trail is tempting, but would soon make for an unpleasant trail for all.

B. Littering a beautiful trail is convenient because then you wouldn't have to carry trash to the top of the mountain and back.

C. To avoid littering when hiking in public places, carry empty containers and wrappers until you get to a trash can.

B. (7–10.) Complete the outline of the textbook passage by filling in the missing main idea and major details, including a brief explanation of each. One explanation has been done for you.   *Wording of answers may vary.*

¹The three types of human memory allow a person to remove or retain information, as needed. ²Everything that we notice—see, smell, hear, or touch—forms a brief mental impression called a sensory memory. ³Information is stored in this sensory memory for only a few tenths of a second before it disappears forever. ⁴Information that is retained for slightly longer enters what's called short-term memory. ⁵This form of memory can store about seven items for about thirty seconds—about enough information to dial a telephone number. ⁶In order to be remembered for a long period, information must pass into long-term memory. ⁷No one knows just how much information can be stored in a person's long-term memory, but the capacity seems enormous.

Main idea: _Three types of human memory allow us to remove or keep_
information as needed.

1. _Sensory memory_____—stores memory for a few tenths of a second.

2. _Short-term memory—stores about 7 items for about 30 seconds_
   _____

3. _Long-term memory—stores enormous number of items for a long period_
   _____

The three supporting details are presented in sentences 2–3, sentences 4–5, and sentences 6–7, respectively.

SUPPORTING DETAILS: Mastery Test 3

A. Answer the questions about supporting details that follow the textbook passage.

> ¹Contemporary American society has a variety of markers of entrance into adulthood. ²There are legal definitions: at 17, young people may enlist in the armed forces; at age 18, in most states, they may marry without their parents' permission; at 18 to 21 (depending on the state), they may enter into binding contracts. ³Using sociological definitions, people may call themselves adults when they are self-supporting or have chosen a career, have married or formed a significant relationship, or have founded a family. ⁴There are also psychological definitions. ⁵Cognitive maturity is often considered to correspond with the capacity for abstract thought. ⁶Emotional maturity may depend on such achievements as discovering one's identity, becoming independent of parents, developing a system of values, and forming relationships. ⁷Some people never leave adolescence, no matter what their chronological age.

A   1. The main idea is expressed in sentence
    A. 1.   The words *a variety of markers* signal the main idea.
    B. 2.
    C. 3.

B   2. The paragraph is made up of a series of
    A. types of adults.   The three major details are three definitions
    B. definitions of adulthood.   of adulthood. The word *definitions*
    C. stages of adulthood.   (in sentences 2, 3, and 4) identifies each.

A   3. The second major detail of the paragraph is introduced in sentence
    A. 3.   The second major detail is "sociological definitions."
    B. 4.
    C. 5.

B   4. Sentence 4 contains
    A. the main idea.   Sentence 4 states the third major supporting
    B. a major supporting detail.   detail, psychological definitions.
    C. a minor supporting detail.

B   5. Sentences 5–7 contain
    A. major supporting details.   Sentences 5–7 give minor supporting details
    B. minor supporting details.   explaining the psychological definitions.

(Continues on next page)

_C_ 6. Which is the best outline of the paragraph?

A. Markers for adulthood
   1. Legal definitions
   2. Sociological definitions
   3. Psychological definitions
   4. Cognitive maturity
   5. Emotional maturity

Outline A mixes major details and minor details together. Outline B includes only minor details.

B. Markers for adulthood
   1. Age when entering the armed forces or marrying without parents' permission
   2. Age when self-supporting or when starting a family
   3. Age of discovering one's identity or learning to think abstractly

C. Markers for adulthood
   1. Legal definitions
   2. Sociological definitions
   3. Psychological definitions

B. (7–10.) Outline the following textbook passage by filling in the main idea and the major supporting details. Condense the major details.

¹Chimpanzees, skillful tool-users, use several objects found in their environment as tools. ²First of all, they use sticks. ³They have been seen inserting carefully trimmed sticks into termite mounds and then withdrawing the sticks and eating the termites that cling to them; they also are known to use sticks to steal honey from beehives. ⁴In addition, chimps use leaves in a variety of ingenious ways. ⁵For example, they have been seen rolling leaves into cones to use as drinking cups, dampening them and using them to clean their bodies, and chewing them until they can serve as sponges. ⁶Finally, chimpanzees have been observed using stones to crack open nuts.

Wording of answers may vary.

Main idea: _Chimpanzees use objects in their environment as tools._

1. _Sticks to catch termites and steal honey_

2. _Leaves as drinking cups, for cleaning, and as sponges_

3. _Stones to crack open nuts_

The three types of tools chimpanzees use are introduced with the addition words *First of all* (sentence 2), *In addition* (sentence 4), and *Finally* (sentence 6).

SUPPORTING DETAILS: Mastery Test 4

A. (1–5.) Outline the following textbook passage by filling in the main idea and a brief statement of each major supporting detail. *Wording of answers may vary.*

The four major details are introduced by addition words: *First of all* (sentence 3), *Another* (sentence 4), *also* (sentence 6), and *also* (sentence 8).

[1]After studying all night for an important exam, most college students find themselves wishing for one thing after their big test: sleep. [2]Although the exact reasons why people sleep are still being debated, researchers have come up with a number of theories to explain the functions of sleep. [3]First of all, sleep is believed to give the body time to repair burned-out brain cells and make more of the special chemical that makes it possible for the brain to think. [4]Another theory holds that sleep enables the body to save energy because when we sleep, the body temperature is lower, so less energy is needed to create heat. [5]This method of energy conservation may have helped people survive thousands of years ago when food was hard to find. [6]Sleep may also have helped humanity survive by keeping people out of trouble. [7]In prehistoric times, when many large predators like the saber-toothed tiger hunted in darkness, the habit of sleeping at night helped prevent people from being an animal's dinner. [8]Scientists also believe that sleep, in addition to being a survival tactic, is used to reduce memory. [9]It allows the brain to forget or unlearn things that are not necessary. [10]Otherwise, the mind would become cluttered and overwhelmed with unneeded information.

Main idea: Researchers have come up with a number of theories to explain the functions of sleep.

1. Gives the body time to repair brain cells and create chemical that makes brain think

2. Enables body to save energy

3. Keeps people out of trouble

4. Reduces memory

B. (6.) Read the textbook excerpt below. Then complete the study notes on the next page by circling the letter of the best summary of the supporting details.

[1]The **multiplier effect** refers to any change in one part of our economic system that creates changes elsewhere. [2]For example, if a university decides to build a new dormitory, some construction workers will have more income. [3]If some of these workers decide to spend the extra income on new boats, boat-builders will have more income. [4]The boat-builders, in turn, might spend this income in neighborhood restaurants, and the restaurant owners might spend it on cars. [5]Money never stays in one place, and every market decision has an impact on other markets.

(Continues on next page)

Study notes:

Answers A and B do not show the multiplier effect. Answer C shows how new work for construction workers "creates changes elsewhere."

Multiplier effect—Any change in one part of our economic system that creates changes elsewhere.

Example—

A. The decision to build a new university dormitory will lead to work for some construction workers.

B. Our economic system is very complicated.

C.) Building a dorm allows construction workers to buy boats, giving boat-builders money for restaurants, and so on.

C. Answer the questions about supporting details that follow the textbook passage.

[1]Studies done in the 1930s in New Guinea by the social scientist Margaret Mead show that not all cultures share our views of the differences between the sexes. [2]The mountain people called the Arapesh, for example, do not think men and women are different in temperament. [3]They expect both sexes to be equally gentle, home-loving, and what we would call "maternal" in their relations with others. [4]The neighboring Mundugumor people, by contrast, are as fierce as the Arapesh are gentle. [5]Men and women are equally "macho," paying less attention to their children than to plotting for power and position. [6]A third tribe, the Tchambuli, do believe the sexes are different in temperament, but their sex roles are the reverse of ours. [7]Tchambuli women are the practical, hard-headed providers, while the men of the tribe spend their days beautifying themselves and looking for approval from the women.

_____A___ 7. Sentence 1 provides
   A. the main idea.
   B. a major supporting detail.
   C. a minor supporting detail.

The main idea—that not all cultures share our views of the differences between the sexes—is stated in sentence 1.

_____B___ 8. In general, the major supporting details of this paragraph are
   A. differences between the sexes.
   B. examples of differing cultural views of the sexes.
   C. a series of stereotypes about Western culture.

The paragraph gives examples of the views of different tribes in New Guinea.

_____B___ 9. How many major details are in this paragraph?
   A. Two
   B. Three
   C. Four

The three major details are the examples of the views of the Arapesh (sentence 2), the Mundugumor (sentence 4), and the Tchambuli (sentence 6).

_____C___ 10. The Arapesh do not think that men and women are
   A. equally gentle.
   B. "maternal."
   C. different in temperament.

See sentence 2.

SUPPORTING DETAILS: Mastery Test 5

A. Answer the questions that follow the textbook passage.

[1]Suburbs arose out of a complex set of social factors. [2]One factor was the economic and technological developments that made it possible for people to live far from where they worked. [3]Early in this century, most people were limited in where they could live by the need to find transportation to work. [4]This meant that most had to live in the cities near where the jobs were. [5]Because there were relatively few automobiles and highways, people walked or used public transportation to get to work and go shopping. [6]This encouraged the concentration of population, and central cities served as the commercial and cultural core of urban areas. [7]By the 1940s and 1950s, the increasing prosperity of many Americans, along with the automobile, made it possible for them to live farther from work and opened up suburban life to middle-class Americans.

[8]In addition, government policy was also a factor contributing to suburbanization. [9]First of all, the government paid 80 percent of the cost of developing the interstate highway system. [10]With cars and high-speed highways, people can now live far from where they work and shop. [11]In sprawling cities such as Los Angeles, for example, it is common to live fifty or more miles from where you work. [12]Also, government agencies made available federally guaranteed mortgage loans for the purchase of new homes. [13]Because land outside of the cities was both inexpensive and available, this is where much of the construction took place.

_B_ 1. In general, the major details of this passage are
    A. economic developments that led to the growth of suburbs.
    B. factors that contributed to suburbanization.
    C. ways the government helped suburbs to develop.

_C_ 2. Specifically, the major details of the passage are
    A. suburbs; cities.
    B. central cities; federally guaranteed mortgage loans for new homes.
    C. economic and technological developments; government policy.

_A_ 3. Sentence 1 provides
    A. the main idea of the passage.
    B. a major detail of the passage.
    C. a minor detail of the passage.

Item 1: Answers A and C are too limited because each takes only one of the factors into account.

Item 2: The first paragraph is about economic and technological developments (introduced in sentence 2). The second paragraph is about government policy (introduced in sentence 8).

Item 3: Sentence 1 states the main idea of the passage—that the suburbs arose out of a combination of social factors.

(Continues on next page)

_____B_____ 4. Sentence 8 provides
    A. the main idea of the passage.
    B. a major detail of the passage.
    C. a minor detail of the passage.

Sentence 8 introduces the second major detail—the role of government policy in suburbanization.

_____C_____ 5. Sentence 12 provides
    A. the main idea of the passage.
    B. a major detail of the passage.
    C. a minor detail of the passage.

Sentence 12 provides a minor detail about government policy's role in suburbanization—that the government made guaranteed mortgage loans available for the purchase of new homes.

B. (6–10.) Complete the map of the following textbook passage by filling in the main idea and the four major supporting details.   *Wording of answers may vary.*

¹Through the years, experts in our country have suggested various purposes of imprisonment. ²Prior to 1800 it was widely assumed that the punishment of those who did not follow society's rules was necessary if the community was to feel morally satisfied. ³In recent years there has been a renewed interest in punishment—not for the sake of vengeance, but to restore a sense of moral order. ⁴During the last century and a half, a second purpose of imprisonment has been rehabilitation. ⁵In this view, crime resembles "disease," something foreign and abnormal to most people. ⁶It is presumed that individuals are not to blame for the disease, and that we should focus on curing them. ⁷Another purpose of imprisonment has been to deter crime. ⁸Some studies suggest that the certainty of arrest and punishment does tend to lower crime rates. ⁹Last, some argue that neither rehabilitation nor deterrence really works, so that it is useless to send people to prison with these goals in mind. ¹⁰Instead, imprisonment should be used as selective confinement, reducing crime rates by keeping "hard-core" criminals off the streets. ¹¹One study of young men in Philadelphia showed that 6 percent of the men were responsible for over half the crimes committed by the entire group.

Experts in our country have suggested various purposes of imprisonment.

Punishment   Rehabilitation   Deter crime   Keep criminals off streets

The main idea is signaled by the list words *various purposes of imprisonment.*
The major details are four purposes of imprisonment.

SUPPORTING DETAILS: Mastery Test 6

A. (1–6.) Outline the following textbook passage by filling in the missing major and minor details. *Wording of answers may vary.*

¹Certain significant differences exist between the House and the Senate. ²The most obvious difference, of course, is size—the House has 435 members and the Senate 100. ³This factor leads to differences in style. ⁴Perhaps, as one author has stated, "the most striking difference noticed by most visitors to the Capitol is the apparent formality and impersonality in the House chamber as contrasted to the relatively informal and friendly atmosphere in the Senate." ⁵Size also influences the procedures followed by the House and the Senate. ⁶House rules are many and complex; Senate rules are short and relatively simple. ⁷House rules, for example, sharply limit the time in which a member may speak during a debate, whereas senators are subject to few limits.

⁸Another difference between the two houses of Congress is the political outlook of their members. ⁹Most representatives have smaller constituencies; each speaks for the residents of a particular district. ¹⁰The representative's concerns, therefore, are often limited to local issues that are of interest to fewer groups. ¹¹Senators have statewide constituencies. ¹²As a result, they must keep in mind the interests of a variety of groups.

¹³A further major difference between the two houses of Congress derives from the different terms of office of their members (two years in the House, six years in the Senate). ¹⁴This means that most representatives are campaigning almost all the time, whereas senators have more time before they must seek reelection. ¹⁵As a result, senators can pay more attention to aspects of legislation that do not directly affect their chances of winning or losing voters' support.

Main idea: Significant differences exist between the House and the Senate.

A. Differences in size: 435 in House vs. 100 in Senate

　1. Style differences

　　a. Formal style in the House

　　b. _Informal and friendly atmosphere in the Senate_

　2. _Procedural differences_

　　a. _House rules—many and complex_

　　b. _Senate rules—short and simple_

B. _Political outlook of members_

　1. _Representatives concerned with local issues_

　2. Statewide outlook of senators

C. Differences in terms of office: 2 years in House vs. 6 years in Senate

　1. Constant campaigning of representatives

　2. More time for senators to spend on legislation not affecting their campaigns

The main idea is signaled by the list words Certain significant differences. For A.1.b.—see sentence 4. For A.2.—see sentence 5. For A.2.a. and b.— see sentence 6. For B.—see sentence 8. For B.1.—see sentence 10.

(Continues on next page)

B. (7–10.) Complete the map of the following textbook passage by filling in the main idea and the missing major supporting details.   *Wording of answers may vary.*

¹To a greater or lesser extent, all of us have learned aggressive responses. ²We are each a potential aggressor. ³A number of conditions have been found to stimulate aggression. ⁴For one thing, pain—both mental and physical— heightens aggressiveness. ⁵Any decidedly hurtful event, whether a big disappointment, a personal insult, or a physical pain, can incite an emotional outburst. ⁶Environmental irritants can also stimulate aggression. ⁷The most-studied is heat. ⁸Studies have found that, compared with students who answered questionnaires in a room with a normal temperature, those who did so in an uncomfortably hot room (over 90° F) reported feeling more tired and aggressive and expressed more hostility toward a stranger they were asked to rate. ⁹A third condition, one that especially provokes aggression, is attacks by another. ¹⁰Experiments confirm that attacks bring counterattacks, especially when the victim perceives the attack as intentional. ¹¹Finally, crowding—the feeling of not having enough space—can be stressful. ¹²The stress experienced by animals allowed to overpopulate a confined environment produces heightened aggressiveness. ¹³And it is undeniably true that dense urban areas suffer higher rates of crime and emotional distress.

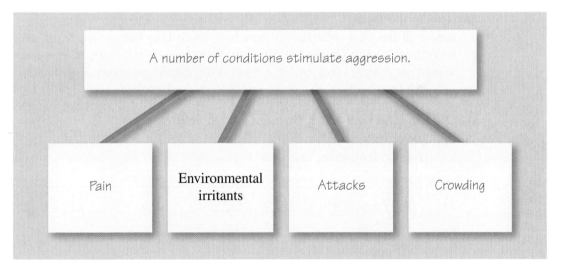

A number of conditions stimulate aggression.

| Pain | Environmental irritants | Attacks | Crowding |

The main idea is signaled by the list words *A number of conditions*. The four conditions are introduced with the addition words *For one thing* (sentence 4), *also* (sentence 6), *third* (sentence 9), and *Finally* (sentence 11).

4 Implied Main Ideas

Copyright 1997 by Randy Glasbergen.   www.glasbergen.com

GLASBERGEN

"The others are complaining that you don't
leave any coffee for everyone else."

In Chapters 2 and 3, you learned the two basic parts of anything you read: a *main idea* and the *supporting details* that explain and develop that idea. As you have seen, the main idea may be clearly stated in one sentence of a selection.

However, the main idea may be **implied**—only suggested by the supporting details and not clearly stated in one sentence. The reader must figure out such an implied main idea by considering the supporting details. In the above cartoon, you can figure out the implied main idea by noting the details: the man's coworkers are complaining that he doesn't leave coffee for anyone else; also, he has such a caffeine high that he is flying! The clearly implied idea is that he is drinking too much coffee.

This chapter offers practice in finding implied main ideas, whether in paragraphs or in longer selections.

Implied Main Ideas

Sometimes a selection lacks a sentence that directly states the main idea. In such cases, the author has simply decided to let the details of the selection suggest the main idea. You must figure out what that implied idea is by deciding upon the point all the details support. For example, read the following paragraph.

> [1]All people are concerned about a few great questions: the existence of God, the purpose of life, the existence of an afterlife, and morality. [2]About the first, science has nothing to say: no test tube has either proved or disproved God's existence. [3]As to the purpose of life, although science can provide a definition of life and describe the characteristics of living organisms, it has nothing to say about ultimate purpose. [4]Regarding an afterlife, science can offer no information, for it has no tests that it can use to detect a "hereafter." [5]As for the question of morality, science can demonstrate the consequences of behavior but not the *moral* superiority of one action compared with another. [6]Science cannot even prove that loving your family and neighbor is superior to hurting and killing them.

The above paragraph has no good "umbrella" statement that covers all of the other sentences. To decide on the main idea, we must ask the same three questions we've already used to find main ideas:

- "Who or what is this paragraph about?"
- "What is the main point the author is trying to make about that topic?"
- And when we think we know the main point, we can test it by asking, "Does *all or most* of the material in the paragraph support this idea?"

In the paragraph above, all of the details are about science and great human concerns, so that must be the topic. Which of the following statements expresses the general point that the author is trying to make about the topic? Check (✓) the answer you think is correct.

___✓___ A. Science alone cannot tell us about the four main concerns that all people have.

_____ B. Science alone has not contributed any answer to the question of whether God exists.

_____ C. There is no scientific data on whether there is life after death.

_____ D. Science alone cannot provide us with any guidance on whether we should love our neighbor as ourselves.

The details reveal the author's general point to be answer A: science alone cannot tell us about the four main concerns that all people have. All the other statements on the previous page are supporting details for this main idea. Although the main idea is not directly stated, it is clearly implied by all the material in the paragraph.

Figuring Out Implied Main Ideas in Paragraphs

To find implied main ideas, it often helps to decide on the topic first. Do so by asking yourself, "Who or what is the selection about?" After you find the topic, then ask yourself, "What is the author's main point about the topic?"

✔ *Check Your Understanding*

Read the following selection and try to answer the questions that follow.

[1]The original intention of a school worksheet was intelligent: to discover which students didn't understand the reading lesson, so the teacher could work with them individually. [2]Unfortunately, the teacher had to keep the rest of the class busy while doing that, so more worksheets were passed out. [3]The assessment tool soon turned into a crowd control device. [4]To make matters worse, the worksheets multiplied faster than the loaves and fishes, often reaching 1,000 per child per school year. [5]But research shows no connection between the number of worksheets a student does and how good a reader the child eventually becomes. [6]If you're fed reading as six worksheets a day, 1,000 sheets a year, under the pronouncement, "Boys and girls, it's time for reading," by the time you reach fourth grade you think worksheets *are* reading, and you mistakenly think you hate reading.

___A___ 1. What is the topic of the above paragraph?
    A. School worksheets
    B. Books
    C. Teaching tools
    D. Crowd control devices

___A___ 2. Which statement best expresses the unstated main idea of these sentences?
    A. School worksheets may do more harm than good.
    B. Reading is one of the most difficult skills for teachers to teach and students to learn.
    C. Over the years, school worksheets have served as both an assessment tool and a crowd control device.
    D. Teachers have a variety of teaching tools to choose from.

Explanation

The topic, referred to in a number of sentences in the paragraph, is school worksheets. The implied main idea about worksheets is that they may do more harm than good.

When you think you have determined an implied main idea, test yourself by asking, "Does all or most of the material in the paragraph support this idea?" In this paragraph, the author (Jim Trelease, in his book *The Read-Aloud Handbook*) describes how worksheets turned into a student control device and multiplied out of control. He also notes that research has showed no benefit from worksheets and that students given too many worksheets may wind up thinking they "hate reading." So the paragraph clearly supports the idea that worksheets may do more harm than good.

PRACTICE 1

Read each paragraph and then answer the questions that follow. Remember to find a topic by asking "Who or what is the selection about?" and to find an implied main idea by asking "What is the author's point about the topic?"

> *Hint:* Noticing addition words (such as *first, another, also, moreover,* and *finally*) will help you identify the major supporting details that can suggest the main idea.

Paragraph 1

¹Are you one of the millions of people who are terrified of going to the dentist? ²You should know that some dentists actually specialize in treating people who are very fearful of dental work. ³These dentists encourage patients to discuss their fears and will answer questions in an honest, understanding manner. ⁴Even if your dentist does not have such a specialty, you can arrange with him or her to use a signal, such as raising your right hand, if you experience too much pain. ⁵This will give you a feeling of control and the assurance that the pain—if any—will not go beyond what you can tolerate. ⁶You can also try the relaxation technique of breathing deeply, before and during appointments. ⁷A last good idea is to bring headphones and listen to your favorite music in the dental chair. ⁸It's hard for the brain to register pain when your favorite rap group, or classical musician, is filling your head.

_D_ 1. What is the topic of the above paragraph?
   A. Dentists
   B. Ways to relax
   C. Better communication with your dentist
   D. Less scary dental visits

All the details are about how to make dental visits less scary. Answers A and B are too broad. Answer C covers only sentences 4–5.

To the Instructor: In the practices and tests that follow, the addition words that introduce major details are underlined in this *Instructor's Edition.*

_B_   2. Which statement best expresses the unstated main idea?
  A. Millions of people are frightened of visits to the dentist.
  B. There are ways to make visits to the dentist less painful and frightening.
  C. There are dentists who specialize in treating patients who are very fearful of dental work.
  D. If you are frightened of going to the dentist, try the relaxation technique of breathing deeply before and during appointments.

Statement A is an introductory detail. Statement C covers only sentence 2. Statement D covers only sentence 6.

Paragraph 2

¹Mining coal is dangerous to the miner and usually leaves large areas of land unfit for further use. ²Acid rain from the burning of coal harms plant and animal life on a large scale. ³Also, the air pollution from the same source damages the health of millions of people. ⁴Moreover, coal-burning power plants expose the people living around them to more radioactivity, from traces of uranium, thorium, and radon in their smoke, than nuclear plants do. ⁵Most estimates put the number of deaths in the United States from cancer and respiratory diseases caused by burning coal at over ten thousand per year.

_D_   3. What is the topic of the above paragraph?
  A. Air pollution
  B. Mining
  C. Effects of acid rain
  D. Drawbacks of coal

All of the details describe drawbacks of coal. Answers A and B are too broad, covering more than the content of the paragraph. Answer C is too narrow, covering only sentence 2.

_A_   4. Which statement best expresses the unstated main idea?
  A. Coal is far from being a desirable fuel.
  B. Acid rain is a major environmental problem.
  C. More people are dying from cancer and respiratory diseases than at any time in the past.
  D. Air pollution has become our largest single environmental problem today.

Also and *Moreover* signal supporting details, hinting at the main idea. Statement B covers only sentence 2. Statements C and D are not supported.

Paragraph 3

¹Scientists count such animals as elephants, timber wolves, ducks, and whistling swans by flying over them and counting them. ²Small animals such as field mice are counted by trapping every single one in a given area and then counting them. ³Microscopic creatures are gathered in a sample and counted little by little under a microscope. ⁴Songbirds are counted by people walking through every part of a certain area at the same time, with each person counting every single songbird seen in his or her assigned space.

_C_   5. What is the topic of the above paragraph?
   A. Counting microscopic creatures
   B. Counting
   C. Methods of counting animals
   D. Scientists who count animals

Answer A covers only sentence 3. Answer B is too broad. Answer D is incorrect because the focus of the paragraph is not on scientists.

_B_   6. Which statement best expresses the unstated main idea?

Answer A is not supported; nothing is said about the reasons for counting populations.
Answer C covers only sentence 3.
Answer D is too broad.

   A. There are various reasons for counting the population of certain types of animals.
   B. The methods scientists use to count animals vary according to the species.
   C. The microscope is one of the tools used by biologists in counting the populations of species.
   D. Biologists face many difficult tasks in studying the large variety of animal life on Earth.

PRACTICE 2

The main idea of each of the following paragraphs is unstated, and each paragraph is followed by four sentences. In the space provided, write the letter of the sentence that best expresses each unstated main idea.

Remember to consider carefully all of the information given and to ask yourself the following two questions:

● Who or what is the selection about? (In other words, what is the topic?)

● What is the author's main point about that topic? (In other words, what is the implied main idea?)

Then test your answer by asking:

● Does *all or most* of the material in the paragraph support this idea?

Paragraph 1

¹The work homemakers do is essential to the economy. ²The estimated value of the cleaning, cooking, nursing, shopping, child care, home maintenance, money management, errands, entertaining, and other services homemakers perform has been estimated at equal to roughly one-fourth of the gross national product. ³In fact, the Commerce Department's Bureau of Economic Analysis has proposed a revision of the gross national product that would take into account the value of the homemaker's services. ⁴But homemaking is not formal employment that brings money or prestige. ⁵No financial compensation is associated with this position, and the *Dictionary of Occupational Titles* places mothering and homemaking skills in the lowest category of skills, lower than the occupation of "dog trainer."

Sentences 1–3 show homemaking is essential to the economy; sentences 4–5 show it brings no money or prestige. Answer A is incorrect because there is no comparison with past views of homemaking. Answers B and D are not supported.

_C_ Which statement best expresses the unstated main idea of the paragraph?

A. We no longer value the work done by homemakers.

B. Homemakers should receive salaries for their work.

C. Although homemaking is essential to the economy, it brings no money or prestige.

D. It's better to be a dog trainer than a homemaker.

Paragraph 2

[1]Albanian legend adheres to the traditional method for killing a vampire—a stake through the heart as the proper method. [2]According to legend, the Hungarian method of killing a vampire advised a stake through the heart, but insisted that a nail be driven through the temples as well. [3]The Irish way is less colorful; one simply piled rocks on the vampire's grave. [4]Macedonians were supposed to pour boiling oil on the vampire and then hammer a nail through its navel. [5]Their neighbors, the Serbs, held to a variant of that method: they proposed cutting off the undead creature's toes and pounding a nail through its neck. [6]Saxon legend says that a lemon in the mouth will do the trick, but in Prussian legend, you should instead put poppy seeds in the grave. [7]In Poland, it was believed that just burying the vampire face downward would kill it. [8]And from Romania itself—the home of the original Dracula—comes one of the most complicated methods: cut out the heart and slice it in two, put garlic in the monster's mouth, and pound a nail into its head.

_D_ Which statement best expresses the unstated main idea of the paragraph?

All of the major details describe ways to kill a vampire. Answer A is too narrow; it ignores other objects used. Answer B covers only sentences 4–5. Answer C is too broad because it does not focus on killing.

A. Nails play an important role in many European legends about killing vampires.

B. Macedonia and Serbia, two neighboring nations, share similar legends about how to kill vampires.

C. Vampires are popular legendary creatures in many European countries.

D. Although many European countries have legends about vampires, those countries vary wildly on the best way to kill a vampire.

Paragraph 3

[1]During the Civil War, soldiers first gathered into companies of a hundred men and then formed into regiments (ten companies). [2]When two or three regiments were assembled—2,000 to 3,000 men—they were called a brigade and then sent off to battle. [3]Under the command of a brigadier general, the soldiers formed double lines that advanced over a front of a thousand yards. [4]From there, junior officers led the army's charge through clouds of grapeshot, bullets, and thick black gunpowder smoke. [5]Men who panicked or broke from ranks were often shot by their own officers, who remained behind the advancing line. [6]Once the advancing army neared the enemy, they had to scramble through fortifications of earth and timber. [7]Finally, if they made it this far, the soldiers had to engage in hand-to-hand combat. [8]The attackers and defenders fought until everyone was killed or wounded or one side gave up and ran away.

All the major details describe a clear plan for battle. Answer A covers only sentence 7. Answer C covers only sentence 5. Answer D is not supported; nothing is said about the ease of defense or difficulty of attack.

_B_   Which statement best expresses the unstated main idea of the paragraph?

A. Hand-to-hand combat played an important role in most Civil War battles.

B. A battle during the Civil War followed a clear plan.

C. Officers in the Civil War had no sympathy for frightened soldiers.

D. Earth and timber fortifications were easy to defend and difficult to attack.

Putting Implied Main Ideas into Your Own Words

When you read, you often have to **infer**—figure out on your own—an author's unstated main idea. The implied main idea that you come up with should cover all or most of the details in the paragraph.

See if you can find and write the topic of the paragraph below. Then write the implied main idea in your own words. Finally, read the explanation that follows.

Hints: Remember that you can help yourself identify the topic and main idea if you 1) look for repeated words as you read and 2) try to mark major supporting details. Major details are often signaled by such common addition words as the following:

Addition Words

one	to begin with	in addition	last
first	another	next	last of all
first of all	second	moreover	finally
for one thing	also	furthermore	

¹A mistaken belief about sleepwalking is that sleepwalkers drift about in a ghost-like way, with arms extended. ²The fact is most sleepwalkers walk around quite normally, though their eyes are usually closed or glazed. ³It is also commonly believed that one should never wake a sleepwalker. ⁴But it is advisable to do so if the walker seems in immediate danger—for example, if he or she is going toward an open window or handling a sharp object. ⁵Another popular misconception is that sleepwalkers are not "really" sleeping or are only half-asleep. ⁶In fact, they are in a very deep state of sleep. ⁷A last commonly held belief is that sleepwalkers are easy to spot because they're in nighties or pajamas. ⁸Often this isn't true because sleepwalkers can do routine tasks, including getting completely dressed.

What is the topic of this paragraph? _Beliefs about sleepwalkers_

What is the implied main idea of this paragraph? _There are several mistaken beliefs about sleepwalkers._

Explanation

One key to the topic here is the word *sleepwalkers*, which is repeated through-out the paragraph. The other key to the topic is major details in the paragraph. Three of the details are signaled by addition words (*also* in "It is also commonly believed," *Another* in "Another popular misconception," and *last* in "A last commonly held belief"). Here are the four major details in the paragraph:

- Sleepwalkers drift in a ghost-like way.
- One should never wake a sleepwalker.
- Sleepwalkers are not really sleeping.
- Sleepwalkers are easy to spot.

What do those four major details have in common? They're all *beliefs about sleepwalkers,* so that phrase can be considered the topic. And the author's main point about the topic could be stated like this: *There are several mistaken beliefs about sleepwalkers.*

PRACTICE 3

In the spaces provided, fill in the topic of each paragraph. Then write the implied main ideas of the paragraphs in your own words.

Wording of answers may vary.

Hints:

1. Remember that to find the topic, it often helps to look for repeated words in a paragraph.
2. Remember that you can help yourself identify the topic and main idea if you mark major supporting details as you read. These major details are often signaled by such common addition words as the ones shown in the box on the previous page.

1.   ¹One of the reasons for lying is to save face. ²For example, you might pretend to remember someone at a party in order to save that person from the embarrassment of being forgotten. ³A second reason for lying is to avoid tension or conflict. ⁴You might, for instance, say you really like a friend's new hairstyle or a new outfit in order to prevent the hassle that would result if you expressed your real feelings. ⁵Lies are also told in order to make everyday relationships run smoothly. ⁶You might pretend to be glad to see someone you dislike, or you might fake interest in a person's boring stories just to make a social event pass quickly. ⁷An additional reason for lying is to expand or reduce relationships. ⁸In one study, a majority of college students willingly lied to improve their chances of getting a date with an attractive partner. ⁹Sometimes people lie to reduce interaction with others: "I really have to go. ¹⁰I should be studying for a test tomorrow." ¹¹A final reason for lying is to gain power. ¹²A person might turn down a last-minute request for a date by claiming to be busy, saying in effect, "Don't expect me to sit around waiting for you to call."

The word *lying* (or *lies* or *lied*) is used six times. The five major details— reasons for lying— are signaled by the underlined addition words.

Topic: ___Reasons for lying___

Implied main idea: ___People tell lies for several reasons.___

_____

2.

The paragraph describes three drawbacks of being an only child: no privacy, lack of certain advantages, and lack of companionship.

¹Many people think that children without brothers or sisters are lucky because of the material goods and attention they receive. ²But consider that an only child has no privacy—parents always feel entitled to know everything that's going on in his or her life. ³A <u>second</u> drawback of being an only child is the lack of certain advantages that children with brothers and sisters have. ⁴An only child can never blame a sibling for something that goes wrong or ask for a privilege that an older brother or sister was given earlier. ⁵<u>In addition</u>, only children miss the companionship of siblings. ⁶The result can be loneliness as well as trouble making friends later in life because they never learned to get along with a brother or sister.

Topic: _Being an only child_

Implied main idea: _Being an only child has its drawbacks._

_____

3.

The passage gives four reasons people oppose the death penalty: religious beliefs, racist overtones, brutalizing effect, and failure to deter murder.

¹Some people have opposed the death penalty for religious reasons. ²The Quakers, for instance, were the first to institute prison sentences in an effort to eliminate torture and execution. ³Others have opposed capital punishment on grounds of racism because African Americans were executed more often than whites. ⁴Some have even argued that executions actually increase murders by brutalizing the public sense of the value of life. ⁵Still others point to social-science research that seems to show capital punishment does not deter murder. ⁶If that's true, they say, there is no good reason for risking the execution of an innocent person.

Topic: _Opposition to capital punishment_

Implied main idea: _People oppose the death penalty for different reasons._

_____

Figuring Out Implied Central Ideas in Longer Passages

When you read, you may have to infer an author's unstated central idea (also called a **central point** or **thesis**) in a longer passage. As you learned in Chapter 2, you can find a central point in the same way that you find a main idea—by looking for a topic and considering the supporting material. The implied central idea that you come up with should cover all or most of the details in the passage. For example, read the following passage:

[1]Ben Franklin said that the only sure things in life are death and taxes. [2]He left something out, however: disappointment. [3]No one gets through life without experiencing many disappointments.

[4]Depression is a common negative response to disappointment. [5]Yvonne, for example, works hard for over a year in her department, trying to win a promotion. [6]She is so sure she will get it, in fact, that she has already picked out the car she will buy when her salary increase comes through.[7]However, the boss names one of her coworkers to the spot. [8]The fact that all the other department employees tell Yvonne she really deserved the promotion doesn't help her deal with the crushing disappointment. [9]Deeply depressed, Yvonne decides that all her goals are doomed to defeat. [10]She loses her enthusiasm for her job and can barely force herself to show up every day. [11]She tells herself that she is a failure and that doing a good job just isn't worth the work.

[12]Another negative reaction to disappointment is escape. [13]Kevin fails to get into the college his brother is attending, the college that was the focus of all his dreams, and reacts to his disappointment by escaping his circumstances. [14]Why worry about college at all? [15]Instead, he covers up his real feelings by giving up on his schoolwork and getting completely involved with friends, parties, and "good times." [16]Or Linda doesn't make the varsity basketball team—something she wanted very badly—and so refuses to play sports at all. [17]She decides to hang around with a new set of friends who get high every day; then she won't have to confront her disappointment and learn to live with it.

[18]The positive way to react to disappointment is to use it as a chance for growth. [19]This isn't easy, but it's the only useful way to deal with an inevitable part of life. [20]Yvonne, the woman who wasn't promoted, could have handled her disappointment by looking at other options. [21]If her boss doesn't recognize talent and hard work, perhaps she could transfer to another department. [22]Or she could ask the boss how she could improve her performance so that she would be a shoo-in for the next promotion. [23]Kevin, the young man who didn't get into the college of his choice, should look into other schools. [24]Going to another college may encourage him to be his own person, step out of his brother's shadow, and realize that being turned down by one college isn't a final judgment on his abilities or potential. [25]Rather than escape into drugs, Linda could improve her basketball skills for a year or pick up another sport, like swimming or tennis, that might turn out to be more useful to her as an adult.

[26]Disappointments are unwelcome but regular visitors to everyone's life. [27]The best response is to step over the unwelcome visitor on the doorstep and get on with life.

You can see that no sentence in the passage is a good "umbrella" statement that covers all of the other sentences. To decide on the implied central idea, we must ask the same three questions we've already used to find main ideas:

- "Who or what is this passage about?" That will be the topic.

- "What is the point the author is trying to make about that topic?"

- And when we think we know the central idea, we can test it by asking, "Does all or most of the material in the passage support this idea?"

✓ Check Your Understanding

In the passage on the previous page, all of the details concern disappointment, so that must be the topic. Which of the following statements expresses the central point that the author is trying to make about the topic? Check (✓) the answer you think is correct.

_____ A. Death, taxes, and disappointment are three inevitable parts of daily living.

_____ B. Many people react to disappointment in a negative way.

_____ C. One of the challenges of life is to react to disappointment in a positive way.

_✓_ D. Many people react to disappointment with depression or escape, rather than using it as an opportunity for growth.

Explanation

The details reveal the author's central idea to be answer D: Many people react to disappointment with depression or escape, rather than using it as an opportunity for growth. Answer A implies that the passage will deal equally with death and taxes, rather than simply disappointment. Answers B and C are both supporting details for the implied main idea, but neither in itself is the "umbrella" idea that covers all of the material in the passage.

The central idea of each of the following two passages is unstated, and each passage is followed by four sentences. In the space provided, write the letter of the sentence that best expresses each unstated central idea.

Remember to first ask yourself, "What is the implied central idea?" Then test your answer by asking, "Does all or most of the material in the passage support this idea?"

Passage 1

¹For many people, the image of the woman in movies about the old West is a gentle one of a mother quietly tending to her kitchen, shopping at the general store, and raising her children.

²But preparing even a simple meal was a time- and energy-consuming chore. ³Prior to the twentieth century, cooking was performed on a coal- or wood-burning stove. ⁴Unlike an electric or a gas range, which can be turned on with the flick of a single switch, cast-iron and steel stoves were especially difficult to use. ⁵Housewives would first have to clean out the ashes left from previous fires. ⁶Then, paper and kindling had to be set inside the stove, dampers and flues had to be carefully adjusted, and a fire had to be lit. ⁷Since there were no thermostats to regulate the stove's temperature, a woman had to keep an eye on the contraption all day long. ⁸Any time the fire slackened, she had to adjust a flue or add more fuel. ⁹All day long, the stove had to be fed with new supplies of coal or wood—an average of fifty pounds or more. ¹⁰At least twice a day, the ash box under the fire had to be emptied. ¹¹All together, a housewife spent four hours every day rubbing the stove with thick black wax to keep it from rusting, lighting the fire, adjusting dampers, sifting ashes, and carrying wood or coal.

¹²It was not enough for a housewife to know how to use a cast-iron stove. ¹³She also had to know how to prepare unprocessed foods for consumption. ¹⁴Prior to the 1890s, there were few factory-prepared foods. ¹⁵Shoppers bought poultry that was still alive and then had to kill and pluck the birds. ¹⁶Fish had to have scales removed. ¹⁷Green coffee had to be roasted and ground. ¹⁸Loaves of sugar had to be pounded, flour sifted, nuts shelled, and raisins seeded.

¹⁹Cleaning was an even more arduous task than cooking. ²⁰The soot and smoke from coal- and wood-burning stoves blackened walls and dirtied drapes and carpets. ²¹Gas and kerosene lamps left smelly deposits of black soot on furniture and curtains. ²²Each day, the lamps' glass chimneys had to be wiped and the wicks trimmed or replaced. ²³And periodically floors had to be scrubbed, rugs beaten, and windows washed.

²⁴Since indoor plumbing was available only to the wealthy, chores that involved the use of water were especially demanding. ²⁵The mere job of bringing water into the house was a challenge. ²⁶According to calculations made in 1886, a typical North Carolina housewife had to carry water from a pump or well or a

spring eight to ten times each day. [27]Washing, boiling, and rinsing a single load of laundry used about fifty gallons of water. [28]Over the course of a year, she walked 148 miles toting over 36 tons of water! [29]Homes without running water also lacked the simplest way to dispose of dirty water: sinks with drains. [30]That meant that women had to remove dirty dishwater, kitchen slops, and, worst of all, the contents of chamber pots from their house by hand.

_____C_____   Which sentence best expresses the implied central idea of the entire selection?

All of the details in the passage describe harsh physical labor. Answers A and D cover only sentences 2–18. Answer B covers only sentences 24–28.

    A. For nineteenth-century housewives, preparing even a simple meal was a time- and energy-consuming chore.

    B. During the nineteenth century, indoor plumbing was available only to the wealthy, so a typical housewife walked 148 miles, carrying over 36 tons of water, during the course of a year.

    C. In nineteenth-century America, a housewife's days were spent in harsh physical labor.

    D. Because coal-and wood-burning stoves were especially difficult to use and because most foods required intensive preparation, most nineteenth-century housewives were tied to their kitchens.

Passage 2

[1]Moderate drinking can bring social benefits, such as relaxation and recreation with others. [2]However, excessive use of alcohol is a factor in the relatively high rate of *automobile accidents*, the leading cause of death among young people in the United States. [3]Over half of each year's automobile deaths and injuries can be traced to excessive drinking. [4]As the National Institute on Alcohol Abuse and Alcoholism has found, "Most people killed in traffic accidents after drinking . . . have very high blood-alcohol concentration, averaging twice the level of alcohol considered legally impairing." [5]Those young people most likely to have auto accidents, including deadly ones, are more likely to drink excessively, use illicit drugs, violate various traffic laws, enjoy taking risks, and exhibit aggressiveness or hostility toward others.

[6]Excessive drinking also leads to a high rate of *other criminal offenses*. [7]The offenses include public drunkenness, disorderly conduct, and vagrancy. [8]Such crimes result in so many arrests that they put a severe strain on the operation of the criminal justice system. [9]Since 1970 many treatment programs for problem drinkers have helped reduce the number of arrests for alcohol-related offenses, but they still constitute the largest arrest category today. [10]The majority (over 90 percent) of the crimes committed by students on college campuses are also alcohol-related. [11]The perpetrators usually commit multiple crimes, including vandalism, fighting, theft, and alcohol violations.

[12]Heavy drinking further plays a significant part, albeit indirectly, in the commission of more serious *violent crimes*, such as homicide, aggravated assault, and forcible rape. [13]In fact, alcohol is implicated in 42 percent of all violent crimes

in the United States. [14]Those who commit these crimes seem to use alcohol as an excuse for expressing their aggression. [15]Alcohol can thus become dynamite in the hands of an aggressive person. [16]According to one study, subjects with a history of arguments and other aggressive acts were more likely to get involved in interpersonal aggression after they had done some heavy drinking.

The words in *italics* emphasize the major details (negative social consequences). Answer A covers only paragraph 1. Answer C covers only paragraph 3. Answer D covers only paragraphs 1 and 3.

_B__ Which sentence best expresses the implied central idea of the entire selection?

  A. If many people didn't abuse alcohol, the United States would have far fewer deadly automobile accidents.

  B. Excessive use of alcohol contributes to a number of negative social consequences.

  C. While moderate drinking can bring social benefits, excessive use of alcohol plays a significant part in the commission of violent crimes.

  D. Alcohol can become dynamite in the hands of an aggressive person, or a person who drinks and drives.

CHAPTER REVIEW

In this chapter, you learned the following:

- At times authors imply, or suggest, a main idea without stating it clearly in one sentence. In such cases, you must figure out that main idea by considering the supporting details.

- To find implied central points in longer reading selections, you must again look closely at the supporting material.

The next chapters—Chapters 5 and 6—will explain common ways that authors organize their material.

On the Web: If you are using this book in class, you can visit our website for additional practice in recognizing implied main and central ideas. Go to **www.townsendpress.com** and click on "Online Exercises."

REVIEW TEST 1

To review what you've learned in this chapter, complete each of the following sentences.

1. When a paragraph has no sentence that states the main idea, we say the main idea is *(central, general, implied)* _____*implied*_____.
   See page 141.

2. If you have trouble finding an implied main idea, it may help to first determine the *(topic, central point)* _____*topic*_____ of the paragraph.
   See page 142.

3. After you figure out what you think is the implied main idea of a paragraph, test yourself by asking, "Does all or most of the material in the paragraph _____*support*_____ this idea?" See page 142.

4. The "main idea" of a selection that is longer than several paragraphs is called the *(topic, central point)* _____*central point*_____ See page 150.

5. The central point is *(never, sometimes, always)* _____*sometimes*_____ implied.
   See page 150.

REVIEW TEST 2

A. In the space provided, write the letter of the sentence that best expresses the implied main idea of each of the following paragraphs.

_____*B*_____ 1. [1]Lean against a tree almost anywhere, and the first creature that crawls on you will probably be an ant. [2]Stroll down a suburban sidewalk—or anywhere else—with your eyes fixed on the ground, counting the different kinds of animals you see. [3]The ants will win hands down. [4]The British entomologist C.B. Williams once calculated that the number of insects alive on Earth at a given moment is one million trillion. [5]If, to take a conservative figure, 1 percent of those insects are ants, their total population is ten thousand trillion. [6]Individual workers weigh on average between one and five milligrams, according to the species. [7]When combined, all ants in the world taken together weigh about as much as all human beings.

All of the major details emphasize the large number of ants on Earth. Answer A covers only sentences 2–3. Answer C is not supported; the passage does not give an opinion. Answer D covers only sentence 4.

    A. Ants are commonplace in the suburbs.
    B. There are huge numbers of ants on Earth.
    C. There are too many ants in the world.
    D. C.B. Williams, the British entomologist, calculated the number of insects alive on Earth at any one time.

_____A_____   2.   ¹Some actors and rock stars are paid more than a hundred times as much per year as schoolteachers are. ²We enjoy such performers, but certainly they do not do work that is many times more important than those who teach and guide our nation's students. ³Indeed, the reverse is true. ⁴Also, professional athletes earn vastly more than firefighters. ⁵The first group may bring enjoyable diversion to our lives, but the latter literally save lives. ⁶Again, there can be little doubt that the lower-paid group, firefighters, makes the more important, indeed essential, contribution to society. ⁷Similarly, most high-fashion designers, who can make up to $50,000 for a single gown, far outearn police officers. ⁸Now, we can easily live without sophisticated clothes (and probably about 99.9 percent of us do), but a society without law-enforcement officers would be unlivable for all of us.

Three examples of workers not paid according to importance of work: teachers, firefighters, police officers. Answer B covers only sentences 1–3. The opinions in answers C and D are not supported.

   A. Workers in our society are not necessarily paid according to how important their work is.
   B. Teachers deserve to be paid as much as actors and rock stars.
   C. High-fashion designers should be paid less money for their work.
   D. Entertainment is a valuable and needed diversion in our society—one which commands a high salary.

B. Write out the implied main idea of the following paragraphs.

Wording of answers may vary.

The passage lists four benefits of TV: relaxation, entertainment, information, and education.

3.   ¹TV is our favorite way of relaxing. ²After a stressful day it's restful to just put our feet up and enjoy a favorite program. ³And, of course, TV is entertaining for all ages. ⁴Movies, video games, and special cable offerings, as well as regular network programming, provide a choice of amusements for the whole family. ⁵TV is also deservedly popular for being informative. ⁶When history is being made—for example, during the terrorist attacks on September 11, 2001—we are often there, thanks to TV. ⁷Perhaps the most important benefit of television is that it is a real educational tool. ⁸From *Sesame Street* to public television's nature programs, it teaches in a colorful and interesting fashion.

Implied main idea: _Watching television has several benefits._

_____

The passage contrasts ways that lower- and higher-class criminals are treated.

4.   ¹Lower-class criminals are more likely to be caught than wealthy criminals. ²And once caught, they are less likely to be able to afford highly skilled legal representation. ³When they appear in court, their life history—which often includes quitting school, unemployment, divorce, and an apparent lack of responsibility when judged by middle-class standards—may work against them. ⁴As a result, lower-income criminals are likely to receive heavier penalties than higher-income criminals for the same crime. ⁵And because they often cannot afford bail, lower-income criminals often have to wait for trial in jail cells rather than in the comfort of their own homes.

Implied main idea: _Lower-class criminals are not treated as well as_ _higher-class criminals._

REVIEW TEST 3

A. In the space provided, write the letter of the sentence that best expresses the implied main idea of each of the following paragraphs.

_____B_____ 1. ¹After anti-smoking campaigns made teens aware of the risk of smoking, the percentage of teens smoking dropped from 28 to 20 percent in 10 years. ²Additionally, in schools where students have access to health clinics which provide birth control information and devices, pregnancy rates have declined by 30 percent. ³Furthermore, another study demonstrated that students in schools with comprehensive health education were less likely to use alcohol, to try drugs, or to attempt suicide.

The passage gives three examples of programs that have a favorable effect: anti-smoking campaigns, health clinics, and comprehensive health education. Answer A covers only sentence 1. Answer C is not supported. Answer D covers only sentence 3.

A. If more schools would conduct anti-smoking campaigns, the number of teens who smoke would greatly decline.

B. Evidence suggests that health education programs have a favorable effect on teenagers' behavior.

C. Health education clinics are a positive influence on how people of all ages take care of themselves.

D. One study found that students in schools with comprehensive health education were less likely to use drugs or to attempt suicide.

_____D_____ 2. ¹President John Adams's wife, Abigail, helped him with speeches, public relations, and policy decisions. ²Abraham Lincoln's wife, Mary, and Ulysses S. Grant's wife, Julia, both advised their husbands on political appointments. ³When Woodrow Wilson suffered a paralyzing stroke, his wife, Edith, became his intermediary; she determined what papers he saw and when, kept high officials out of his bedroom, and relayed his instructions. ⁴Eleanor Roosevelt actively advised her husband, Franklin, on the New Deal and championed the cause of black people at a time when it was politically inconvenient for him to do so. ⁵With her husband confined to a wheelchair, she traveled widely to observe and report back to him on social and economic conditions and New Deal projects. ⁶Nancy Reagan protected her husband, Ronald, from those advisors she judged unfit, pushed him hard toward arms-control talks, and rewrote his speeches. ⁷More recently, Hillary Clinton acted as one of her husband Bill's chief advisors. ⁸Her strong behind-the-scenes role led to her own successful campaign for political office.

The passage gives examples of seven presidential wives who have been influential. Answer A covers only sentence 2. Answer B is not supported because social causes are mentioned only in connection with Eleanor Roosevelt. Answer C covers only sentences 3–5.

A. Presidents' wives have played a major role in shaping U.S. political appointments.

B. Many presidential wives have served as champions for important social causes.

C. Certain presidential wives have had great political power—especially when their husbands were ill.

D. Many presidential wives have been quite influential in government during their husbands' administrations.

B. Write out the implied main idea of the following paragraph.

Wording of answers may vary.

3. ¹If you have trouble getting a good night's sleep, don't have an alcoholic drink before bedtime. ²While alcohol can certainly knock you out, it also damages the quality of sleep you'll get. ³That's because it chemically interferes with dreaming, an important part of restful sleep. ⁴Also, avoid beverages and foods that contain caffeine, such as coffee, most teas, colas, and chocolate. ⁵Caffeine can stimulate you, making sleep difficult or impossible. ⁶A better before-bed choice is milk, which contains a mild, sleep-inducing type of protein. ⁷Another piece of good advice is to exercise during the day; this can leave you tuckered out enough at night to fall promptly and soundly asleep. ⁸But do avoid exercise right before bedtime, as its immediate effects are more stimulating than relaxing. ⁹Last, try to get up at about the same time every day; this practice will help your body establish a solid sleep and wake cycle. ¹⁰Varying your hours too much can confuse your body's "inner clock."

The passage lists four techniques to help one sleep: avoid alcohol, avoid caffeine, exercise during the day, and get up at the same time every day.

Implied main idea: Several techniques can help you get a good night's sleep.

C. In the space provided, write the letter of the sentence that best expresses the implied central idea of the following selection from a sociology textbook.

4. ¹Compared to middle-income people, the poor are ill more often, receive poorer and more limited medical care, and live shorter lives. ²The poor have a higher rate of mental illness, particularly for the more serious illnesses such as depression, schizophrenia, and personality disorders. ³They also report lower levels of personal happiness than the nonpoor.

⁴The children of the poor are at greater risk of dying in infancy, and if they survive, they have a greater risk than nonpoor children of getting into trouble with the law or becoming pregnant as teenagers. ⁵Their education is inferior to that of nonpoor children, and they are far less likely to complete high school. ⁶One study showed that in Chicago's public schools, where a large proportion of the students are from poverty-stricken families, fewer than half graduated on time, and of those who did graduate, only one out of three could read at a twelfth-grade level.

⁷Poor people spend more of their income on food and housing than the nonpoor, but they are still worse fed and worse housed. ⁸A study of housing in southern Illinois revealed that poor people were several times as likely as the general public to live in overcrowded housing, yet 80 to 90 percent of these poor people were paying more than the government standard of 25 percent of their incomes for rent.

[9]Poor people are more likely to commit street crimes and to be the victims of such crimes. [10]Crime rates are highest in poor neighborhoods, for criminals tend to victimize those who are close by and available. [11]As a result, a highly disproportionate number of victims of robbery, assault, and homicide are poor. [12]So high is the incidence of crimes in some poor neighborhoods that poor people are afraid to venture outside their homes. [13]Summer after summer in major cities, elderly poor people have died from heat-related illnesses because they could not afford air conditioning and were afraid to open their windows because of crime.

_____C_____

The passage lists numerous ways in which life is more difficult for poor people. Answer A covers only sentences 4–6. Answer B covers only sentences 10–12. Answer D covers only sentences 7–8.

Which sentence best expresses the implied central idea of the entire selection?

A. Children of the poor are at a greater risk of dying in infancy, of teenage pregnancies, and of not completing high school.

B. The victims of crime are more likely to be the poor than the nonpoor.

C. In virtually every way imaginable, life is more difficult for people living in poverty.

D. Poor people pay more of their income for food and housing than the nonpoor and at the same time are worse fed and worse housed.

REVIEW TEST 4

Here is a chance to apply your understanding of implied and central ideas to a reading about childhood cruelty.

To help you continue to strengthen your skills, the reading is followed by questions not only on what you've learned in this chapter but also on what you've learned in previous chapters.

Words to Watch

Below are some words in the reading that do not have strong context support. Each word is followed by the number of the paragraph in which it appears and its meaning there. These words are indicated in the article by a small circle (°).

simulate (1): imitate
musty (3): stale or moldy in odor
trudge (5): walk in a heavy, tired way
brunt (6): greatest part
taunted (6): mocked and insulted
gait (7): manner of moving
sinister (7): evil
distracted (9): interested in something else
stoic (13): emotionless
vulnerable (25): defenseless

ROWING THE BUS

Paul Logan

1   When I was in elementary school, some older kids made me row the bus. Rowing meant that on the way to school I had to sit in the dirty bus aisle littered with paper, gum wads, and spitballs. Then I had to simulate° the motion of rowing while the kids around me laughed and chanted, "Row, row, row the bus." I was forced to do this by a group of bullies who spent most of their time picking on me.

I was the perfect target for them. 2 I was small. I had no father. And my mother, though she worked hard to support me, was unable to afford clothes and sneakers that were "cool." Instead she dressed me in outfits that we got from "the bags"—hand-me-downs given as donations to a local church.

Each Wednesday, she'd bring 3 several bags of clothes to the house and pull out musty°, wrinkled shirts and worn bell-bottom pants that other families no longer wanted. I knew that people were kind to give things to us, but I hated wearing clothes that might have been donated by my classmates. Each time I wore something from the bags, I feared that the other kids might recognize something that was once theirs.

4   Besides my outdated clothes, I wore thick glasses, had crossed eyes, and spoke with a persistent lisp. For whatever reason, I had never learned to say the "s" sound properly, and I pronounced words that began with "th" as if they began with a "d." In addition, because of my severely crossed eyes, I lacked the hand and eye coordination necessary to hit or catch flying objects.

5   As a result, footballs, baseballs, soccer balls and basketballs became my enemies. I knew, before I stepped on the field or court, that I would do something clumsy or foolish and that everyone would laugh at me. I feared humiliation so much that I became skillful at feigning illnesses to get out of gym class. Eventually I learned how to give myself low-grade fevers so the nurse would write me an excuse. It worked for a while, until the gym teachers caught on. When I did have to play, I was always the last one chosen to be on any team. In fact, team captains did everything in their power to make their opponents get stuck with me. When the unlucky team captain was forced to call my name, I would trudge° over to the team, knowing that no one there liked or wanted me. For four years, from second through fifth grade, I prayed nightly for God to give me school days in which I

would not be insulted, embarrassed, or made to feel ashamed.

6   I thought my prayers were answered when my mother decided to move during the summer before sixth grade. The move meant that I got to start sixth grade in a different school, a place where I had no reputation. Although the older kids laughed and snorted at me as soon as I got on my new bus— they couldn't miss my thick glasses and strange clothes—I soon discovered that there was another kid who received the brunt° of their insults. His name was George, and everyone made fun of him. The kids taunted° him because he was skinny; they belittled him because he had acne that pocked and blotched his face, and they teased him because his voice was squeaky. During my first gym class at my new school, I wasn't the last one chosen for kickball; George was.

7   George tried hard to be friends with me, coming up to me in the cafeteria on the first day of school. "Hi. My name's George. Can I sit with you?" he asked

with a peculiar squeakiness that made each word high-pitched and raspy. As I nodded for him to sit down, I noticed an uncomfortable silence in the cafeteria as many of the students who had mocked George's clumsy gait° during gym class began watching the two of us and whispering among themselves. By letting him sit with me, I had violated an unspoken law of school, a sinister° code of childhood that demands there must always be someone to pick on. I began to realize two things. If I befriended George, I would soon receive the same treatment that I had gotten at my old school. If I stayed away from him, I might actually have a chance to escape being at the bottom.

8   Within days, the kids started taunting us whenever we were together. "Who's your new little buddy, Georgie?" In the hallways, groups of students began mumbling about me just loud enough for me to hear, "Look, it's George's ugly boyfriend." On the bus rides to and from school, wads of paper and wet chewing gum were tossed at me by the bigger, older kids in the back of the bus.

9   It became clear that my friendship with George was going to cause me several more years of misery at my new school. I decided to stop being friends with George. In class and at lunch, I spent less and less time with him. Sometimes I told him I was too busy to talk; other times I acted distracted° and gave one-word responses to whatever he said. Our classmates, sensing that they had created a rift between George and me, intensified their attacks on him. Each day, George grew more desperate as he

realized that the one person who could prevent him from being completely isolated was closing him off. I knew that I shouldn't avoid him, that he was feeling the same way I felt for so long, but I was so afraid that my life would become the hell it had been in my old school that I continued to ignore him.

10   Then, at recess one day, the meanest kid in the school, Chris, decided he had had enough of George. He vowed that he was going to beat up George and anyone else who claimed to be his friend. A mob of kids formed and came after me. Chris led the way and cornered me near our school's swing sets. He grabbed me by my shirt and raised his fist over my head. A huge gathering of kids surrounded us, urging him to beat me up, chanting "Go, Chris, go!"

11   "You're Georgie's new little boyfriend, aren't you?" he yelled. The hot blast of his breath carried droplets of his spit into my face. In a complete betrayal of the only kid who was nice to me, I denied George's friendship.

12   "No, I'm not George's friend. I don't like him. He's stupid," I blurted out. Several kids snickered and mumbled under their breath. Chris stared at me for a few seconds and then threw me to the ground.

13   "Wimp. Where's George?" he demanded, standing over me. Someone pointed to George sitting alone on top of the monkey bars about thirty yards from where we were. He was watching me. Chris and his followers sprinted over to George and yanked him off the bars to the ground. Although the mob quickly encircled them, I could still see

the two of them at the center of the crowd, looking at each other. George seemed stoic°, staring straight through Chris. I heard the familiar chant of "Go, Chris, go!" and watched as his fists began slamming into George's head and body. His face bloodied and his nose broken, George crumpled to the ground and sobbed without even throwing a punch. The mob cheered with pleasure and darted off into the playground to avoid an approaching teacher.

14   Chris was suspended, and after a few days, George came back to school. I wanted to talk to him, to ask him how he was, to apologize for leaving him alone and for not trying to stop him from getting hurt. But I couldn't go near him. Filled with shame for denying George and angered by my own cowardice, I never spoke to him again.

15   Several months later, without telling any students, George transferred to another school. Once in a while, in those last weeks before he left, I caught him watching me as I sat with the rest of the kids in the cafeteria. He never yelled at me or expressed anger, disappointment, or even sadness. Instead he just looked at me.

16   In the years that followed, George's silent stare remained with me. It was there in eighth grade when I saw a gang of popular kids beat up a sixth-grader because, they said, he was "ugly and stupid." It was there my first year in high school, when I saw a group of older kids steal another freshman's clothes and throw them into the showers. It was there a year later, when I watched several seniors press a wad of chewing gum into the hair of a new girl

on the bus. Each time that I witnessed another awkward, uncomfortable, scared kid being tormented, I thought of George, and gradually his haunting stare began to speak to me. No longer silent, it told me that every child who is picked on and taunted deserves better, that no one—no matter how big, strong, attractive or popular— has the right to abuse another person.

17   Finally, in my junior year when a loudmouthed, pink-skinned bully named Donald began picking on two freshmen on the bus, I could no longer deny George. Donald was crumpling a large wad of paper and preparing to bounce it off the back of the head of one of the young students when I interrupted him.

18   "Leave them alone, Don," I said. By then I was six inches taller and, after two years of high-school wrestling, thirty pounds heavier than I had been in my freshman year. Though Donald was still two years older than me, he wasn't much bigger. He stopped what he was doing, squinted, and stared at me.

19   "What's your problem, Paul?"

20   I felt the way I had many years earlier on the playground when I watched the mob of kids begin to surround George.

21   "Just leave them alone. They aren't bothering you," I responded quietly.

22   "What's it to you?" he challenged. A glimpse of my own past, of rowing the bus, of being mocked for my clothes, my lisp, my glasses, and my absent father flashed in my mind.

23   "Just don't mess with them. That's all I am saying, Don." My fingertips were tingling. The bus was silent. He got up from his seat and leaned over me, and

I rose from my seat to face him. For a minute, both of us just stood there, without a word, staring.

24   "I'm just playing with them, Paul," he said, chuckling. "You don't have to go psycho on me or anything." Then he shook his head, slapped me firmly on the chest with the back of his hand, and sat down. But he never threw that wad of paper. For the rest of the year, whenever I was on the bus, Don and the other troublemakers were noticeably quiet.

25   Although it has been years since my days on the playground and the school bus, George's look still haunts me. Today, I see it on the faces of a few scared kids at my sister's school—she is in fifth grade. Or once in a while I'll catch a glimpse of someone like George on the evening news, in a story about a child who brought a gun to school to stop the kids from picking on him, or in a feature about a teenager who killed herself because everyone teased her. In each school, in almost every classroom, there is a George with a stricken face, hoping that someone nearby will be strong enough to be kind—despite what the crowd says—and brave enough to stand up against people who attack, tease or hurt those who are vulnerable°.

26   If asked about their behavior, I'm sure the bullies would say, "What's it to you? It's just a joke. It's nothing." But to George and me, and everyone else who has been humiliated or laughed at or spat on, it is everything. No one should have to row the bus.

Reading Comprehension Questions

Vocabulary in Context

_B_   1. In the sentence below, the word *feigning* (fān′ĭng) means
   A. escaping.
   B. faking.
   C. recognizing.
   D. curing.

   If he wanted to get out of gym class, he would have faked an illness.

   "I feared humiliation so much that I became skillful at feigning illnesses to get out of gym class." (Paragraph 5)

_____C_____ 2. In the excerpt below, the word *rift* (rĭft) means

    A. friendship.

    B. agreement.

    C. break.

    D. joke.

> If he has stopped being friends with George, there would be a break between him and George.

"I decided to stop being friends with George. . . . Our classmates, sensing that they had created a rift between George and me, intensified their attacks on him." (Paragraph 9)

Central Point and Main Ideas

Answers A, B, and D are too narrow. Answer A omits all the details about George as well as the story of Paul's eventually standing up to a bully. Answer B covers only paragraphs 6–7. Answer D covers only paragraphs 14–17 and 25–26.

_____C_____ 3. Which sentence best expresses the central point of the selection?

    A. Although Paul Logan was a target of other students' abuse when he was a young boy, their attacks stopped as he grew taller and stronger.

    B. When Logan moved to a different school, he discovered that another student, George, was the target of more bullying than he was.

    C. Logan's experience of being bullied and his shame at how he treated George eventually made him speak up for someone else who was teased.

    D. Logan is ashamed that he did not stand up for George when George was being attacked by a bully on the playground.

_____A_____ 4. At times, a main idea may cover more than one paragraph. Which sentence best expresses the main idea of paragraphs 2–4?

    A. The first sentence of paragraph 2

    B. The first sentence of paragraph 3

    C. The first sentence of paragraph 4

    D. The first sentence of paragraph 5

> All three paragraphs give details that show Paul was the perfect target. Paragraph 5 begins a new topic.

_____A_____ 5. The topic sentence of paragraph 8 is its

    A. first sentence.

    B. second sentence.

    C. third sentence.

    D. final sentence.

> All of the sentences after the first give examples of how the kids taunted them.

Supporting Details

_D_   6. When Chris attacked George, George reacted by
   A. fighting back hard.
   B. shouting for Logan to help him.
   C. running away.
   D. accepting the beating.

See paragraph 13.

_A_   7. Logan finally found the courage to stand up for abused students when he saw
   A. Donald throwing paper at a younger student.
   B. older kids throwing a freshman's clothes into the showers.
   C. seniors putting bubble gum in a new student's hair.
   D. a gang beating up a sixth-grader whom they disliked.

See paragraph 17.

Implied Main Ideas

_A_   8. Which sentence best expresses the implied main idea of paragraph 5?
   A. Because of Logan's clumsiness, gym was a miserable experience for him in elementary school.
   B. Because Logan hated gym so much, he made up excuses to avoid it.
   C. The gym teacher caught on to Logan's excuses.
   D. Logan knew that other students did not want him to be a member of their team when games were played.

Answers B, C, and D each cover only one or two sentences of the paragraph.

_D_   9. Which sentence best expresses the implied main idea of paragraph 6?
   A. Logan's mother moved so that Logan could get a fresh start in a new school.
   B. Even at the new school, students laughed at Logan's appearance.
   C. Riding on the bus was the worst part of Logan's school experience.
   D. When Logan started at his new school, he realized that a student named George was more unpopular than he was.

There is no evidence to support answers A, B, and C.

_B_   10. Which sentence best expresses the implied main idea of paragraph 16?
   A. Older kids were often cruel to younger students at Logan's schools.
   B. Because of what happened to George, Logan became increasingly bothered by students' picking on others.
   C. In Logan's first year in high school, some students threw a freshman's clothes into the showers.
   D. In school, Logan learned a great deal about how people behave in various situations throughout life.

Answer A leaves out Paul's growing awareness that no one has the right to abuse another person. Answer C covers only one sentence. Answer D is too broad—the paragraph focuses on bullying, not on various situations.

Discussion Questions

1. Paul Logan titled his selection "Rowing the Bus." Yet very little of the reading actually deals with the incident the title describes—only the first and last paragraphs. Why do you think Logan chose that title?

2. Logan wanted to be kind to George, but he wanted even more to be accepted by the other students. Have you ever found yourself in a similar situation—where you wanted to do the right thing but felt that it had too high a price? Explain what happened.

3. Logan refers to "a sinister code of childhood that demands there must always be someone to pick on." Why do children need someone to pick on?

4. The novelist Henry James once said, "Three things in human life are important. The first is to be kind. The second is to be kind. And the third is to be kind." What do you think schools or concerned adults could do to encourage young people to treat one another with kindness, rather than with cruelty?

Note: Writing assignments for this selection appear on pages 601–602.

Check Your Performance   **IMPLIED MAIN IDEAS**

Activity		Number Right	Points		Score
Review Test 1	(5 items)	_____	× 2	=	_____
Review Test 2	(4 items)	_____	× 7.5	=	_____
Review Test 3	(4 items)	_____	× 7.5	=	_____
Review Test 4	(10 items)	_____	× 3	=	_____
		TOTAL SCORE		=	_____ %

Enter your total score into the **Reading Performance Chart: Review Tests** on the inside back cover.

IMPLIED MAIN IDEAS: Mastery Test 1

In the space provided, write the letter of the sentence that best expresses the implied main idea of each of the following paragraphs.

_____D_____ 1. ¹Children in Finland are the highest-scoring young readers in the world, but they also spend more time watching TV than reading. ²A Finnish national research coordinator has pointed out a key relationship between reading and Finnish TV: "Many programs have captions, and watching these programs seems to motivate and enhance reading among young students." ³In fact, almost 50 percent of Finnish television consists of foreign TV programs and movies whose subtitles must be read—and read quickly—for the shows to be understood. ⁴Finnish nine-year-olds want to learn to read in order to understand TV and therefore watch a moderately heavy amount.

Answer A covers only sentence 1. B appears to be true but ignores the idea that TV helps Finnish children read. C is not discussed.

  A. Children in Finland are the best young readers in the world.
  B. Finnish television is very different from television in the United States.
  C. Finnish teenagers watch less TV than younger children do.
  D. Captioned television appears to help children learn to read.

_____A_____ 2. ¹Intellectual curiosity is a desire for knowledge simply for its own sake—not to get a good grade, pass a test, get a diploma, or get a job. ²Intellectual curiosity prevents boredom and apathy—and bored, apathetic people are dreary people, to themselves and to others. ³Such curiosity also broadens our horizons. ⁴If we pursue only the knowledge that we think we need for "success," our possibilities will be limited. ⁵Moreover, curiosity of the mind makes us versatile. ⁶People with broad knowledge and wide interests can change the course of their work and activities if they need to—as they well might, given the rapid pace of change in our world—or simply if they want to. ⁷Last, although practicality is not its aim, intellectual curiosity can have practical advantages; at any time, any kind of knowledge may turn out to be useful to our happiness and growth in life.

Four benefits of intellectual curiosity are listed: prevents boredom, broadens horizons, makes us versatile, and has practical advantages. Answer B covers only sentence 2. C covers only sentence 6. D covers only sentence 7.

  A. Intellectual curiosity has many benefits.
  B. Intellectual curiosity prevents boredom and apathy.
  C. People with intellectual curiosity can change their jobs if they want or need to.
  D. Intellectual curiosity has practical advantages.

To the Instructor: In the mastery tests for this chapter, the addition words that introduce major details are underlined in this *Instructor's Edition.*

(Continues on next page)

_C_ 3. [1]Many people think there is no difference between an alligator and a crocodile. [2]However, the alligator's snout is shorter and broader than that of a crocodile. [3]A more dramatic difference between the two creatures lies in how dangerous they are to humans. [4]There are very few documented instances in which alligators have killed a person. [5]On the other hand, crocodiles, particularly those along the Nile River, are quite dangerous to humans. [6]It is said, in fact, that as far as killing people is concerned, crocodiles are second only to poisonous snakes.

    A. Poisonous snakes are more dangerous to humans than crocodiles.
    B. Many people believe that alligators and crocodiles are the same.
    C. There are clear differences between alligators and crocodiles.
    D. Alligators aren't particularly dangerous to humans.

> Answer A covers only sentence 6. Answer B covers only sentence 1.
> Answer D covers only sentence 4.

_D_ 4. [1]Adolescents and old people are both often segregated from the rest of society: young people are isolated in schools, and many old people live in retirement communities, assisted-living facilities, and nursing homes. [2]Also, both groups tend to be poorer than young adults or middle-aged people: adolescents because they do not yet have the education or experience to command high salaries, and old people because they are retired and living on their savings and social security. [3]Third, independence is important for both groups—they are conscious of wanting it, whereas young adults and middle-aged people take it for granted. [4]Adolescents want to become independent of their parents; old people want to keep their independence and not have to rely on their children or on social institutions. [5]Fourth, they both tend to have a relatively large amount of leisure time or, at least, time that they can choose or not choose to fill with study or work. [6]By contrast, young and middle-aged adults typically spend most of their time at their jobs or taking care of home duties such as child-rearing.

    A. Adolescents and old people, more than other social groups, strongly value their independence.
    B. Both adolescents and old people have different economic conditions from young and middle-aged adults.
    C. Young and middle-aged adults spend much of their time taking care of home duties such as child-rearing.
    D. Adolescents and old people, as groups in our culture, are very similar in certain ways.

> The major details are four similarities between adolescents
> and old people. Answer A covers only sentences 3–4.
> B covers only sentence 2. C covers only sentence 6.

IMPLIED MAIN IDEAS: Mastery Test 2

In the space provided, write the letter of the sentence that best expresses the implied main idea of each of the following paragraphs.

_B_ 1. ¹Many people dream of being celebrities, but do they consider what celebrities' lives are really like? ²For one thing, celebrities have to look perfect all the time. ³There's always a photographer ready to take an unflattering picture of a famous person looking dumpy in old clothes. ⁴Celebrities also sacrifice their private lives. ⁵Their personal struggles, divorces, or family tragedies all end up as front-page news. ⁶Most frighteningly, celebrities are in constant danger of the wrong kind of attention. ⁷Threatening letters and even physical attacks from crazy fans are things the celebrity must contend with.

Three difficulties of being a celebrity are listed: always looking perfect, no private life, and constant danger. Answer A covers only sentence 1. C covers only sentence 2–3. D covers only sentences 6–7.

A. Many people dream of being celebrities.
B. Being a celebrity is often difficult.
C. Being a celebrity means having to look good all the time.
D. Celebrities face dangers.

_C_ 2. ¹As you speak with someone, you can easily gather clues about how much he or she understands or agrees with you and adjust your conversation accordingly. ²But when you write, you must try to anticipate the reader's reactions without such clues. ³You also have to provide stronger evidence in writing than in conversation. ⁴A friend may accept an unsupported statement such as "He's a lousy boss." ⁵But in writing, the reader expects you to back up such a statement with proof.

A. There are special techniques for communicating verbally with others.
B. Speaking and writing are both challenging ways of communicating.
C. Communicating effectively in writing is more demanding than communicating verbally.
D. When speaking, you get feedback about a person's reaction that helps you to make your conversation more effective.

Two ways that effective written communication is more difficult are listed. Answers A and D ignore the information on written communication (sentences 2, 3, and 5). Answer B contradicts the main idea, that writing is more challenging than speaking.

(Continues on next page)

_____D_____ 3. [1]In murders investigated by the FBI, more than one-third have been committed by one family member against another. [2]Three percent of them involve the murder of a child by a parent. [3]Aggression by parents toward children also takes a less drastic form. [4]Each year two million children are kicked, beaten, or punched by their parents. [5]Aggression is evident in marriages as well. [6]Each year, four million husbands and wives violently attack each other. [7]These attacks result in severe injuries in a quarter of a million cases.

The major details describe two examples of aggression toward one's family: toward one's children and toward one's spouse. Answer A covers only sentences 2–4. Answer B covers only sentences 5–7. Answer C is not supported because there is no information about whether or not violence is increasing.

A. Abuse of children by parents is widespread in the United States.
B. Aggression is part of many marriages in this country.
C. In the United States, family violence is increasing steadily.
D. In the United States, aggression is often directed toward members of one's own family.

_____A_____ 4. [1]A baby's most basic cry consists of a rhythmic pattern which begins with a cry followed by a brief silence and then a shorter higher-pitched whistling sound. [2]Experts believe the basic cry is triggered by hunger, tiredness, or mild discomfort. [3]Researchers have also identified an anger cry. [4]A bit more forceful than the basic cry, the anger cry involves larger volumes of air passing over the baby's vocal chords. [5]Such a sound might be made when a baby wants to be picked up and is not, or when a baby is put in a crib when it wants to be held. [6]A third type of cry that babies use is the pain cry. [7]A sudden loud wail followed by an extended period of breath-holding, the pain cry is the loudest sound a baby can make.

A. Babies have three distinct cries to communicate what they are feeling.
B. The pain cry is the loudest sound a baby can make.
C. Babies communicate differently at different ages.
D. Experts believe that hunger, tiredness, or mild discomfort may cause the basic cry.

The major details describe three types of baby cries. Answer B covers only sentence 7. C is not supported because there is no information about communication at different ages. D covers only sentence 2.

IMPLIED MAIN IDEAS: Mastery Test 3

A. In the space provided, write the letter of the sentence that best expresses the implied main idea of each of the following paragraphs.

_____A_____ 1. ¹The earliest humans probably used the lengthening and shortening of shadows on the ground to measure the passage of time. ²Later, the sundial was invented to tell time more precisely, but still by using the shadow principle. ³The hourglass, a slightly more recent invention, measured time by allowing grains of sand to fall from one container to another. ⁴In about the year 1300, a primitive clock was invented. ⁵It had only an hour hand, but it became the most exact way yet to tell the time. ⁶Since then, clocks have been so improved technically that today's clocks and watches can be depended upon to be quite precise.

The major details describe various improved methods of measuring time that have been used. Answer B covers only sentence 3. C covers only sentences 1–2. D covers only sentences 4–5.

A. Throughout history, people have found better and better ways to measure the passing of time.
B. The hourglass is a slightly more recent invention than the sundial.
C. The first methods of measuring the passing of time took advantage of the changing shadows cast by the sun throughout a day.
D. A primitive clock invented in about 1300 was the most exact way to tell time up to that point.

_____D_____ 2. ¹Earth is surrounded by a thick gaseous envelope called the atmosphere. ²The atmosphere provides the air that we breathe and protects us from the sun's intense heat and dangerous radiation. ³The energy exchanges that continually occur between the atmosphere and space produce the effects we call weather. ⁴If, like the moon, Earth had no atmosphere, our planet would be lifeless, and many of the processes and interactions that make the surface such an energetic place could not operate. ⁵Without weathering and friction, the face of our planet might more closely resemble the lunar surface, which has not changed much in nearly three billion years.

A. The atmosphere is a thick gaseous layer covering the entire Earth.
B. The moon, unlike Earth, has no atmosphere and has therefore not changed much in almost three billion years.
C. There are many influences on Earth's development.
D. The atmosphere is a key part of our environment and of Earth's processes.

Answer A covers only sentence 1. B covers only sentences 4–5. Answer C is too broad because the paragraph discusses information on the effects of the atmosphere, not on other influences.

(Continues on next page)

B. Write out the implied main idea of the following paragraph:

3. ¹You don't have to scare your family with statistics about heart attacks. ²To get them to exercise more often, emphasize instead how good they'll feel and how much better they'll look if they work out daily. ³<u>Another</u> method you can use is to set an example. ⁴If they see you walking to the convenience store instead of driving, they might be encouraged to do likewise the next time they have errands in the neighborhood. ⁵<u>Finally</u>, make exercise a family activity. ⁶Suggest that the whole family go swimming together, take up early morning jogging, or join the Y at the group rate.

Wording of answers may vary.

The words To get them to exercise more often are a clue to the

Implied main idea: There are several positive ways to encourage your
family to exercise more often.

main idea. All three of the major details are positive ways to encourage exercise. Addition words signal two of the three ways listed.

C. In the space provided, write the letter of the item below that best expresses the implied central idea of the following textbook passage.

___D___ 4. ¹A researcher at Johns Hopkins University has repeatedly done a simple experiment with two rats. ²He holds one rat firmly in hand so that, no matter how much the rat struggles, he cannot escape. ³The rat will finally give up. ⁴The researcher then throws that unmoving rat into a tank of warm water, and the rat sinks, not swims. ⁵He has "learned" that there is nothing he can do, that there is no point in struggling. ⁶The researcher then throws another rat into the water—one that doesn't "know" that his situation is hopeless and that he is therefore helpless. ⁷This rat will swim to safety.

⁸A comparable experiment involving people has been conducted by Martin E.P. Seligman of the University of Pennsylvania. ⁹Two groups of college students are put in rooms where they are blasted with noise turned up to almost intolerable levels. ¹⁰In one room there is a button that turns off the noise. ¹¹The students quickly notice it, push it, and are rewarded with blissful silence. ¹²In the other room, however, there is no turn-off button. ¹³The students look for one, find nothing, and finally give up. ¹⁴There is no way to escape the noise (except to leave the room before a previously agreed-upon time period has elapsed), so they simply endure the noise.

¹⁵Later, the same two groups are put in two other rooms. ¹⁶This time, both rooms contain a switch-off mechanism—though not a simple button this time and not as easy to find. ¹⁷Nevertheless, the group that found the button the first time succeeds in finding the "off" switch the second time, too. ¹⁸But the second group, already schooled in the hopelessness of their circumstances, doesn't even search; its members just sit it out again.

Answers A and B do not include the outcome of the experiments. Answer C does not include the experiments.

A. Experiments suggest that humans and rats have similar reactions to unpleasant situations.

B. Experimenters at two leading universities have subjected both humans and rats to frustrating situations.

C. As strange as it may seem, both rats and humans give up trying in certain situations.

D. Experiments have revealed that past failures can teach both rats and humans to feel helpless and, as a result, to give up trying.

IMPLIED MAIN IDEAS: Mastery Test 4

A. In the space provided, write the letter of the sentence that best expresses the implied main idea of each of the following paragraphs.

_____D_____ 1. ¹There is no doubt that businesses can improve their productivity. ²If every person and machine did things right the first time, the same number of people could handle much larger volumes of work. ³High costs of inspection could be channeled into productive activities, and managers could take all the time they spend checking and devote it to productive tasks. ⁴Wasted materials would become a thing of the past. ⁵In fact, it's been estimated that attention to quality can reduce the total cost of operations anywhere from 10 to 50 percent. ⁶As Philip Crosby said: "Quality is free. ⁷What costs money are the unquality things—all the actions that involve not doing jobs right the first time."

The details describe ways that improved quality can lead to improved productivity. Answer A is not supported because nothing is said about Crosby's qualifications. Answer B covers only sentence 3. Answer C is not supported because nothing is said about sales.

A. Philip Crosby is an expert in quality in business.
B. It is wasteful to spend so much money on plant inspections.
C. Businesses can improve their sales in several ways.
D. If quality is improved, productivity improves.

_____D_____ 2. ¹In nineteenth-century America, people shared beds, both at homes with relatives and in hotels with strangers, without inquiring about their bed partner's health. ²They exchanged combs, hairbrushes, and even toothbrushes; and they fed babies from their mouths and spoons, with no sense of danger. ³They coughed, sneezed, and spat without concern for their own health or the health of those around them. ⁴They cooked and stored their meals with little worry about food-borne illness. ⁵They drank unfiltered water from wells and streams, often using a common dipper or drinking cup. ⁶Last but not least, they used chamber pots and outhouses with little regard for where the contents ended up in relation to the community water supply.

A. Nineteenth-century Americans were friendlier than modern Americans.
B. There was less water pollution in nineteenth-century America than there is today.
C. In nineteenth-century America, people were probably as concerned about health as they were about survival.
D. Nineteenth-century Americans engaged in behaviors that could easily spread disease.

Each detail describes a behavior that could easily spread disease. Answers A and B are not supported because nothing is said about friendliness or water pollution. All of the details contradict answer C.

(Continues on next page)

B. In the space provided, write the letter of the sentence that best expresses the implied main idea of each of the following paragraphs.

_____B_____ 3.   ¹Some baby animals are born nearly helpless. ²They cannot survive if they are not cared for, usually by older members of their species. ³Food and shelter are the most obvious needs of a baby animal. ⁴But scientists have also observed another, less obvious need. ⁵Monkeys who are raised alone, with no physical contact with other animals, develop strange habits such as constantly rocking or moving in circles. ⁶In addition, they cannot relate normally to other monkeys. ⁷The males can rarely breed with females. ⁸The females who do bear young ignore or abuse their babies. ⁹When monkeys who were raised alone are put in contact with friendly, "motherly" monkeys who touch and cuddle them, they eventually develop normal monkey behaviors.

Answer A covers only sentence 3. C is not supported, because the passage describes only monkeys, not all animals. D covers only sentences 4–5.

A. Baby animals need to be given food and shelter.
B. Studies suggest that for certain animals, touching, like food and shelter, is essential for normal development.
C. All animals that are raised without physical contact with other animals develop strange habits.
D. Scientists have done studies of monkeys raised without physical contact with other animals.

_____A_____ 4.   ¹As an alternative to marriage, a marriage contract would be valid for three years, at which time the partners would decide whether or not to renew the agreement. ²If they did not choose to stay together, no divorce would be necessary. ³They would simply file a paper stating that they would not be renewing their contract. ⁴One advantage of the marriage contract system is that it would force couples to think in practical terms about their marriages. ⁵They would have to talk ahead of time about such questions as the handling of money, the dividing of household chores, and the matter of children. ⁶In addition, a contract would encourage couples to work harder at their marriages. ⁷If they knew their contract was coming up for renewal at a certain point, they would closely consider the reasons why it should or should not be extended. ⁸Finally, a renewable marriage contract would make ending a marriage far easier than it is today. ⁹A couple would not have to hire expensive lawyers and endure long waits in divorce courts. ¹⁰The simple filing of a paper in the courthouse would close out the contract and end a marriage. ¹¹The couple would then go their separate ways.

A. People who want to marry would be better off if, instead, they signed a renewable marriage contract.
B. A marriage contract is an alternative to marriage.
C. A marriage contract would be a far easier and less costly way than divorce of ending a marriage.
D. A marriage contract would encourage a couple to think carefully in advance about what it would mean to live together.

The major details list advantages of renewable marriage contracts. Answer B covers only sentence 1. Answer C covers only sentences 8–11. Answer D covers only sentence 5.

IMPLIED MAIN IDEAS: Mastery Test 5

A. In the space provided, write the letter of the sentence that best expresses the implied main idea of each of the following paragraphs.

_____B_____ 1.

All the major details demonstrate that solitary confinement is cruel. Answers A, C, and D are not supported because nothing is said about its being necessary, widespread, or no longer preferred.

[1]In one Ohio prison each maximum-security inmate is confined, alone, for up to 23 hours a day, in a cell that has a solid metal door and is 7 by 14 feet. [2]Some cells in other U.S. prisons are even smaller. [3]Alfred McCoy, the author of *A Question of Torture*, says that solitary confinement can cause rage, stupor, and insanity. [4]Psychiatrist Stuart Grassian agrees that solitary confinement can drive prisoners "crazy." [5]After only a few days in solitary confinement, prisoners show altered brain waves typical of stupor and delirium. [6]Most U.S. prisoners placed in solitary confinement stay there for more than five years; many stay there for more than twenty. [7]In California and Texas prisons, most suicides occur among inmates in solitary confinement.

A. Solitary confinement is necessary for certain prisoners.
B. Solitary confinement is cruel.
C. Solitary confinement is widespread in American prisons.
D. Solitary confinement is no longer a preferred treatment.

_____B_____ 2.

All of the major details show that functional illiteracy is costly. Answer A is not supported because Americans are not compared to others. Answer C covers only sentences 6–7. Answer D covers only sentence 5.

[1]A Senate committee estimates the loss of earnings of men ages 25 to 34 who have less than high school-level skills at $236 billion. [2]Half of the heads of households classified below the federal poverty line cannot read an eighth-grade book. [3]More than a third of mothers on welfare are also functionally illiterate. [4](Functional illiteracy is the inability to read and write well enough for everyday practical needs.) [5]So are 60 percent of the adult prison population and 84 percent of juveniles who come before the courts. [6]Businesses have difficulty filling such entry-level jobs as clerk, bank teller, and paralegal assistant. [7]A major insurance firm reports that 70 percent of dictated letters must be retyped "at least once" because secretaries cannot spell and punctuate correctly. [8]The military, too, pays a price for functional illiteracy. [9]The navy has stated that 30 percent of new recruits are "a danger to themselves and costly to naval equipment" because they cannot read very well or understand simple instructions.

A. Americans are among the most poorly educated people in the world.
B. Functional illiteracy, widespread among Americans, is costly for individuals and society.
C. Businesses must face the problem of poorly prepared workers.
D. Our prisons and courts are filled with adults and juveniles who are functionally illiterate.

B. Write out the implied main idea of the following paragraph:

3. [1]According to study experts, one tip for exam success is regular daily and weekly study. [2]Another tip is to focus on, in your study sessions, ideas that the instructor has emphasized in class. [3]In addition, use the night before an exam for a careful review rather than a stressful cramming. [4]Then get up a bit early the next morning and review your notes one more time. [5]Arriving early for an exam is another helpful tip that experts suggest. [6]Sit in a quiet spot and go through a final reading of notes. [7]Last, once the test begins, the advice of experts is to answer

(Continues on next page)

Each major detail, introduced by an addition word, is a tip for doing better on exams.

the easier questions first; then go back and tackle the hard ones. [8]And on essay questions, it's most productive to think a few minutes and make a brief outline before beginning to write.

Implied main idea: Several tips will help you do better on exams.

_____

_____

Wording of answers may vary.

C. Read the following textbook passage and in the space provided, write the letter of the sentence that best expresses the implied main idea.

_C_ 4. [1]In the nineteenth century, reformers wanted to persuade Americans to adopt more godly personal habits. [2]They set up associations to battle profanity and Sabbath-breaking, to place a Bible in every American home, and to provide religious education for the children of the poor.

[3]At the start of the century, heavy drinking was an integral part of American life. [4]Many people believed that downing a glass of whiskey before breakfast was healthful. [5]Instead of taking coffee breaks, people took a dram of liquor at eleven and again at four o'clock as well as drinks after meals "to aid digestion" and a nightcap before going to sleep. [6]Campaigning politicians offered voters generous amounts of liquor during campaigns and as rewards for "voting right" on Election Day.

[7]By 1820 the typical adult American consumed more than 7 gallons of absolute alcohol a year (compared with 2.6 gallons today). [8]Consumption had risen markedly in two decades, fueled by the growing amounts of corn distilled by farmers into cheap whiskey, which could be transported more easily than bulk corn. [9]In the 1820s, a gallon of whiskey cost just a quarter.

[10]In their campaign, reformers identified liquor as the cause of a wide range of social, family, and personal problems. [11]Alcohol was blamed for the abuse of wives and children and the squandering of family resources. [12]Many businesspeople linked drinking with crime, poverty, and inefficient and unproductive employees.

[13]The stage was clearly set for the appearance of an organized movement against liquor. [14]In 1826 the nation's first formal national temperance organization was born: the American Society for the Promotion of Temperance. [15]Led by socially prominent clergy and laypeople, the new organization called for total abstinence from distilled liquor. [16]Within three years, 222 state and local anti-liquor groups were laboring to spread this message.

A. At the start of the 1800s, many Americans were heavy drinkers, but as the century wore on, the consumption of alcohol became less socially acceptable.

B. The American Society for the Promotion of Temperance helped reduce per capita consumption of alcohol and forced thousands of distillers to close.

C. In the early 1800s, an organized movement against liquor began as part of a larger moral reform campaign.

D. Although alcohol abuse is still a problem, it appears that Americans in the early 1800s drank much more than they do today.

Answer A is not supported because nothing is said about alcohol consumption becoming less acceptable. B is not supported because nothing is said about reduced consumption or the closing of distilleries. D covers only sentence 7.

IMPLIED MAIN IDEAS: Mastery Test 6

A. Read the following textbook passage and then follow the instructions to select the implied main idea.

> ¹Today's world puts a lot of pressure on teenagers to work. ²By working, they gain more independence from their families, and they also get the spending money needed to keep up with their peers. ³Many people argue that working can be a valuable experience for the young.
>
> ⁴However, schoolwork and the benefits of extracurricular activities tend to go by the wayside when adolescents work more than fifteen hours a week. ⁵Teachers are then faced with the problems of keeping the attention of tired pupils and of giving homework to students who simply don't have the time to do it. ⁶In addition, educators have noticed less involvement in the extracurricular events many consider healthy influences on young people. ⁷School bands and athletic teams are losing players to work, and sports events are poorly attended by working students. ⁸Those teenagers who try to do it all—homework, extracurricular activities, and work—may find themselves exhausted and prone to illness.
>
> ⁹Another drawback of too much work is that it may promote materialism and an unrealistic lifestyle. ¹⁰Some parents say that work teaches adolescents the value of a dollar. ¹¹Undoubtedly, it can, and it's true that some teenagers work to help out with the family budget or save for college. ¹²But surveys have shown that the majority of working teens use their earnings to buy luxuries—stereos, tape decks, clothing, even cars. ¹³These young people, some of whom earn $300 and more a month, don't worry about spending wisely—they can just about have it all. ¹⁴In many cases, experts point out, they are becoming accustomed to a lifestyle they won't be able to afford several years down the road, when they'll no longer have parents to pay for car insurance, food and lodging, and so on. ¹⁵At that point, they'll be hard pressed to pay for necessities as well as luxuries.

___D___ 1. Write the letter of the sentence that best expresses the implied main idea.

    A. Teenagers who work more than fifteen hours a week find that they have little or no time for homework and extracurricular activities.

    B. Some people believe that work teaches teenagers the value of a dollar, but others believe that it leads to materialism.

    C. These days, students who work often use their earnings to buy luxuries that they will no longer be able to afford when they're no longer living at home.

    D. By limiting their working hours, teenagers can benefit from both work *and* school—and also avoid an unrealistic lifestyle.

Answer A covers only sentences 4–7. B covers only sentences 9–15.
C covers only sentences 12–15.

(Continues on next page)

B. Read the following textbook passage and then follow the instructions to select the implied main idea.

¹Many of the world's girls and women are missing from schools. ²In sub-Saharan Africa, for every ten boys, only six girls are enrolled in secondary school, and in southern Asia, only four. ³In these regions, three-quarters of women aged 25 and over are still illiterate. ⁴A major reason why girls leave school is that they are married off, often to older men, and begin bearing children in their teens. ⁵Some are sold by their parents to prostitution rings, where young girls are in demand because they are considered less likely to carry the AIDS virus.

⁶Women are missing from the paid labor force. ⁷Women work as hard as or harder than men (on average, thirteen more hours a week worldwide). ⁸But the work women do—caring for children; providing food and health care to their families; tending gardens and livestock; processing crops; gathering firewood and hauling water; weaving cloth, carpets, and baskets; and selling home-grown food and home-made crafts at local markets—is not considered "real" work. ⁹When women do work for wages, they are usually employed in clerical, sales, and service occupations, and they are excluded from higher-paying jobs in manufacturing, transportation, and management. ¹⁰Even when women do the same work as men, they earn—on average worldwide—30 to 40 percent less.

¹¹Women are missing in the halls of power, policy, and decision making. ¹²Although women make up more than half the world's population, less than 5 percent of heads of state, heads of corporations, and directors of international organizations are female.

¹³Until recently, women were missing from the battlefield; however, they have never been missing from the ranks of the dead and wounded. ¹⁴In the many ethnic and civil wars in the world today, hostile groups are fighting for towns and cities, and civilians are caught in the crossfire. ¹⁵Hundreds of thousands of women and children have become widows, orphans, and refugees.

¹⁶War or not, women the world over are regularly abused sexually, physically injured, and even killed simply because they are women. ¹⁷In 1987 in India, 1,786 "dowry deaths"—in which the husband and/or his family kill a woman because her dowry was insufficient—were recorded. ¹⁸In Thailand, more than 50 percent of married women living in Bangkok's largest squatter settlement said they were regularly beaten by their husbands. ¹⁹Not until 1991 did the Brazilian Supreme Court outlaw the "honor" defense, which excused a man who murdered an adulterous wife on the grounds that he was defending his honor.

Each of the details describes a way in which females are second-class citizens or worse. Answer A covers only sentences 6–10. B covers only sentences 4–5 and 16–19. C is not supported because the passage does not connect educational opportunities with opportunities to become decision-makers.

_D_ 2. Write the letter of the sentence that best expresses the implied main idea.

A. Throughout the world, women's work is usually undervalued, even though women work as hard or harder than men.

B. All over the world, women and girls are sexually exploited and murdered by men simply because they are female.

C. Because girls and women receive far fewer educational opportunities than men throughout the world, they have far fewer opportunities to become decision-makers.

D. Throughout the world, females are clearly second-class citizens or worse.

5 Relationships I

Authors use two common methods to show relationships and make their ideas clear. The two methods—**transitions** and **patterns of organization**—are explained in turn in this chapter. The chapter also explains two common types of relationships:

- Relationships that involve **addition**
- Relationships that involve **time**

Transitions

Look at the following items and put a check (✓) by the one that is easier to read and understand:

____ One way to lose friends is to talk but not listen. A way to end friendships is to borrow money and not pay it back.

✓ One way to lose friends is to talk but not listen. Another way to end friendships is to borrow money and not pay it back.

You probably found the second item easier to understand. The word *another* makes it clear that the writer is adding a second way to lose friends. **Transitions** are words or phrases (like *another*) that show relationships between ideas. They are like signs on the road that guide travelers. Or they can be seen as "bridge" words, carrying the reader across from one idea to the next:

One way to lose friends
is to talk but not listen.
ANOTHER way to end friendships is to
borrow money and not pay it back.

Two major types of transitions are words that show addition and words that show time.

Words That Show Addition

Once again, put a check (✓) beside the item that is easier to read and understand.

_____ Many people rent DVDs because rental is cheaper than tickets to a movie theater. DVDs are now available online as well as in stores.

✓ Many people rent DVDs because rental is cheaper than tickets to a movie theater. Also, DVDs are now available online as well as in stores.

The word *also* in the second item makes the relationship between the sentences clearer. The author is providing reasons why renting movies is popular. The first reason is that renting DVDs is cheaper than buying tickets to the movies. A *second* reason is that the movies are so readily available. The word *also* makes it clear that another reason is being given. *Also* is an addition word.

Addition words signal added ideas. These words tell you a writer is presenting one or more ideas that continue along the same line of thought as a previous idea. Like all transitions, addition words help writers organize their information and present it clearly to readers. Here are some common words that show addition:

Addition Words

one	to begin with	also	further
first (of all)	for one thing	in addition	furthermore
second(ly)	other	next	last (of all)
third(ly)	another	moreover	final(ly)

Examples

The following examples contain addition words. Notice how these words introduce ideas that *add to* what has already been said.

- Garlic improves the flavor of many dishes. *In addition*, it lowers cholesterol, fights heart disease, and kills certain viruses.

- Rivers serve as highways for migrating birds. *Also*, the nearby wetlands provide the birds with places in which to rest and refuel.

- My neighbors are so safety-conscious that they had the wooden front door of their apartment replaced with a steel one. *Moreover*, they had iron bars installed on all their apartment windows.

PRACTICE 1

Complete each sentence with a suitable addition word from the box on the previous page. Try to use a variety of transitions.   *Answers may vary.*

> *Hint:* Make sure that each addition word or phrase that you choose fits smoothly into the flow of the sentence. Test each choice by reading the sentence aloud.

1. To avoid car thieves, lock valuables in the trunk or glove compartment. You should _____ also _____ try to park in a the middle of a block on a busy, well-lit street.

2. There are several ways to use old jeans. _____ For one thing _____, you can use them for patching other jeans.

3. One million stray dogs live in the New York City metropolitan area. _____ In addition _____, there are more than 500,000 stray cats in the same area.

4. "_____ First _____, and most important," said my adviser, "you've got to complete that term paper or you won't graduate on time."

5. Part-time workers have second-class status. For one thing, they are easily laid off. Second, they get no fringe benefits. _____ Third _____, they are often paid less than half the hourly rate of a full-timer.

Words That Show Time

Put a check (✓) beside the item that is easier to read and understand:

_____ The two neighboring families used to get along well. They are not on speaking terms.

✓ Previously, the two neighboring families got along well. Now they are not on speaking terms.

The words *previously* and *now* in the second item clarify the relationship between the sentences: *Before*, the families got along well; and *now* they don't speak to each other. *Previously* and *now* and words like them are time words.

These transitions indicate a time relationship. **Time words** tell us *when* something happened in relation to when something else happened. Below are some common words that show time:

Time Words

before	immediately	when	until
previously	next	whenever	often
first (of all)	then	while	frequently
second (ly)	following	during	eventually
third (ly)	later	as (soon as)	final(ly)
now	after	by	last (of all)

Note: Some additional ways of showing time are dates ("In 1890 . . . ," "Throughout the 20th century . . . ," "By 2012 . . .") and other time references ("Within a week . . . ," "by the end of the month . . . ," "in two years . . .").

Examples

The following examples contain time words. Notice how these words show us *when* something takes place.

● *While* the nurse prepared the needle, I rolled up my sleeve. *Then* I looked away.

● Many people get sleepy *after* eating a heavy meal.

● *During* my last semester in college, I spent more time job hunting than I did studying.

Helpful Tips about Transitions

Here are two points to keep in mind about transitions.

 TIP 1 Some transition words have the same meaning. For example, *also, moreover,* and *furthermore* all mean "in addition." Authors typically use a variety of transitions to avoid repetition.

 TIP 2 In some cases the same word can serve as two different types of transitions, depending on how it is used. For example, the word *first* may be used as an addition word to show that the author is presenting a series of points, as in the following sentences:

> For many athletes, life after a sports career is a letdown. *First,* they are often not prepared for nonathletic careers. In addition, they . . .

First may also may be used to signal a time sequence, as in these sentences:

> A trip to a giant supermarket can be quite frustrating. *First,* you have trouble finding a parking space close to the store. Then, . . .

PRACTICE 2

Complete each sentence with a suitable time word from the box on the previous page. Try to use a variety of transitions.   *Answers may vary.*

> *Hint:* Make sure that each time word or phrase that you choose fits smoothly into the flow of the sentence. Test each choice by reading the sentence aloud.

1. _____After_____ my cousin took a long shower, there was no hot water left for anyone else in the house.

2. To make chicken stock, begin by putting a pot of water on the stove to boil. _____Then_____ drop in a chicken and some diced celery and onions.

3. Gerald waited impatiently all day for the Monday night football game to begin on TV, but _____during_____ the first half, he fell asleep.

4. Recent advances in medicine make it possible to treat babies even _____before_____ they are born.

5. Some students listen to their iPods, eat snacks, and talk on their cell phones _____while_____ doing their homework.

Patterns of Organization

You have learned that transitions show the relationships between ideas in sentences. In the same way, **patterns of organization** show the relationships between supporting details in paragraphs, essays, and chapters. It helps to recognize the common patterns in which authors arrange information. You will then be better able to understand and remember what you read.

The rest of this chapter discusses two major patterns of organization:

● The **list of items pattern**
   (Addition words are often used in this pattern of organization.)

● The **time order pattern**
   (Time words are often used in this pattern of organization.)

Noticing the transitions in a passage can often help you become aware of its pattern of organization. Transitions can also help you locate the major supporting details.

1 The List of Items Pattern

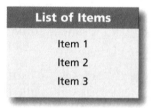

To get a sense of the list of items pattern, try to arrange the following sentences in a logical order. Put a *1* in front of the sentence that should come first, a *2* in front of the sentence that comes next, a *3* in front of the third sentence, and a *4* in front of the sentence that should come last. The result will be a short paragraph. Use the addition words as a guide.

_2_ One common strategy is to consume massive quantities of junk food, which is easily done thanks to all the ever-present convenience stores and fast-food restaurants.

_1_ There are some widely popular, inappropriate methods that people use to combat stress.

_4_ Finally, watching hours of nonstop TV can put people in a stupor that helps them forget the problems of everyday life.

_3_ Another way to deal with stress is to doze or sleep for hours and hours, even during the day.

This paragraph begins with the main idea: "There are some widely popular, inappropriate methods that people have to combat stress." The next three sentences go on to list three of those methods, resulting in the pattern of organization known as a list of items. The transitions *One, Another,* and *Finally* introduce the points being listed and indicate their order:

> ¹There are some widely popular, inappropriate methods that people use to combat stress. ²One common strategy is to consume massive quantities of junk food, which is easily done thanks to all the ever-present convenience stores and fast-food restaurants. ³Another way to deal with stress is to doze or sleep for hours and hours, even during the day. ⁴Finally, watching hours of nonstop TV can put people in a stupor that helps them forget the problems of everyday life.

A **list of items** refers to a series of reasons, examples, or other points that support an idea. The items have no time order, but are listed in whatever order the author prefers. Addition words, such as those in the box below, are often used in a list of items to tell us that other supporting points are being added to a point already mentioned. Textbook authors frequently organize material into lists of items, such as a list of types of economic systems, symptoms of heart disease, or reasons for teenage drinking.

Addition Words Used in the List of Items Pattern

one	to begin with	also	further
first (of all)	for one thing	in addition	furthermore
second (ly)	other	next	last (of all)
third (ly)	another	moreover	final (ly)

Check Your Understanding

The paragraph below is organized as a list of items. Complete the outline of the paragraph by first filling in the missing part of the main idea. Then add to the outline the three major details listed in the paragraph.

To help you find the major details, do two things to the paragraph:

● Underline the addition words that introduce the major details in the list;

● Number (*1, 2, . . .*) each item in the list.

> ¹Like all social institutions, sports serve various purposes. ²First, they provide the leisure-time exercise so necessary in a society in which most jobs provide little or no physical activity. ³Second, sports supply an outlet for energies that might otherwise strain the social order. ⁴Emotions such as anger and frustration can be expressed in ways that are acceptable to society—through both watching

To the Instructor: In this exercise and the practices and tests that follow, the transition words that introduce major details are underlined in this *Instructor's Edition.*

and participating in sports. ⁵Finally, sports give society role models. ⁶At their best, athletes, especially famous ones, are examples of dedication, hard work, and conduct for others to imitate.

Main idea: Sports serve *various purposes.*

1. *They provide leisure-time exercise.*

2. *They provide an outlet for energies that might strain the social order.*

3. *They give society role models.*

Explanation

The main idea is that sports serve various purposes. (You may also express main ideas at times in a short heading; the heading here could be "Purposes of sports.") Following are the three purposes you should have added to the outline:

1. They provide leisure-time exercise. (This point is signaled with the addition transition *First*.)

2. They supply an outlet for energies that might otherwise strain the social order. (This point is signaled with the addition transition *Second*.)

3. They give society role models. (This point is signaled with the addition transition *Finally*.)

PRACTICE 3

A. The following passage uses a listing pattern. Outline the passage by filling in the main idea and the major details.

> *Hint:* Underline the addition words that introduce the items in the list, and number the items.

> ¹Today, beef is America's favorite meat. ²But, for several reasons, America's most popular meat a hundred years ago was pork. ³First of all, pigs grew quickly. ⁴They could multiply their weight 150 times in just eight months by eating nuts, roots, fallen orchard fruit, spoiled food, and garbage. ⁵Another reason for the popularity of pork was that pigs required almost no attention. ⁶In a nation with lots of land and not enough workers, pigs were perfect because they could take care of themselves. ⁷Indeed, wild pigs, such as the American razorback, were so fierce that they didn't need a farmer's protection. ⁸A third reason for the preference for pigs was that they could be cheaply preserved. ⁹A butchered pig could be packed into barrels filled with heavily salted water and saved for up to a year. ¹⁰Indeed, it was salted pork—not hamburger—that fed most people in the first century and a half of the growing United States.

*Wording
of answers
here and below
may vary.*

Main idea: For several reasons, pork was America's most popular meat a hundred years ago.

1. Pigs grew quickly.

2. Pigs required little attention.

3. Pigs could be preserved cheaply.

The words *several reasons* (sentence 2) suggest a list will follow.
The addition words in sentences 3, 5, and 8 signal the major details.

B. The following passage uses a listing pattern. Complete the map of the passage by completing the main idea and filling in the missing major details.

¹Various theories explain the aging process. ²The most obvious is that our bodies simply wear out. ³Yet since many bodily systems are able to replace or repair their worn components (wounds heal, for example, and skin cells are constantly being generated), this version cannot be the whole story. ⁴A related theory is that as cells repeatedly divide, more and more contain genetic errors and stop working properly. ⁵A third theory holds that our body chemistry loses its delicate balance over the years. ⁶For example, our excretory system, after years of filtering pollutants from our bloodstream, becomes less efficient. ⁷The resulting change in our blood chemistry can produce a variety of other malfunctions. ⁸Finally, according to another theory, our bodies tend with age to reject some of their own tissues.

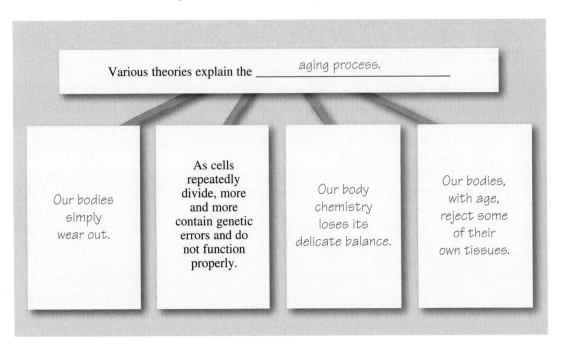

Various theories explain the ___aging process.___

| Our bodies simply wear out. | As cells repeatedly divide, more and more contain genetic errors and do not function properly. | Our body chemistry loses its delicate balance. | Our bodies, with age, reject some of their own tissues. |

The words *Various theories* (sentence 1) suggest a list will follow. The four major details (four theories) are stated in sentences 2, 4, 5, and 8. The last two are signaled by addition words.

2 The Time Order Pattern

To get a sense of the time order pattern, try to arrange the following sentences in a logical order. Put a *1* in front of the sentence that should come first, a *2* in front of the sentence that comes next, a *3* in front of the third sentence, and a *4* in front of the sentence that should come last. The result will be a short paragraph. Use the time words as a guide.

___3___ Next, the two people declare themselves a couple, telling friends and relatives about the new person in their lives.

___2___ The two people then make a commitment to have an exclusive relationship with each other.

___1___ A relationship begins when two people show interest in each other and choose to spend time together.

___4___ Last, the two people formalize the relationship by cohabitation or marriage.

Authors usually present events in the order in which they happen, resulting in the time order pattern of organization. Clues to the order of the above sentences are time transitions (*Next, when,* and *Last*). The paragraph should read as follows:

> [1]A relationship begins when two people show interest in each other and choose to spend time together. [2]The two people then make a commitment to have an exclusive relationship with each other. [3]Next, the two people declare themselves a couple, telling friends and relatives about the new person in their lives. [4]Last, the two people formalize the relationship by cohabitation or marriage.

As a student, you will see time order used frequently. Textbooks in all fields describe events and processes, such as the events leading to the Boston Tea Party, the important incidents in Abraham Lincoln's life, the steps involved for a bill to travel through Congress, the process involved in writing a paper, or the stages in the development of a cell.

In addition to the time transitions listed on page 184, as well as dates and other time references, signals for the time order pattern include such words as *stages, series, steps,* and *process*.

The two most common kinds of time order are 1) a series of events or stages and 2) a series of steps (directions for how to do something). Each is discussed on the following pages.

Series of Events or Stages

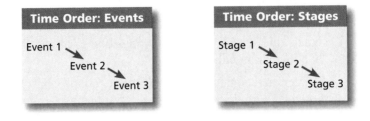

✔ *Check Your Understanding*

Following is a paragraph that is organized according to time order. Complete the outline of the paragraph by listing the missing stages in the order in which they happen.

To help you find the stages, do two things:

● Underline the words that introduce each stage;
● Number (*1, 2, . . .*) each stage.

> ¹Children master language in predictable stages. ²First, at about six months, babies start to repeat simple sounds, such as "ma-ma-me-me." ³About three or four months later, they can repeat sounds that others make and carry on little conversations. ⁴These interchanges are rich in emotional meaning, although the sounds themselves are meaningless. ⁵At the next stage, toddlers learn the meanings of many words, but they cannot yet talk. ⁶A toddler might understand a sentence such as "Bring me your sock" but be unable to say any of the words. ⁷Finally, the child begins to talk in single words and in two-word sentences.

Main idea: Children master language in predictable stages.

1. At about six months, babies begin to repeat simple sounds.

2. Three or four months later, babies can repeat sounds and carry on little "conversations."

3. Toddlers understand many words but cannot talk.

4. Finally, the child talks in single words and two-word sentences.

Explanation

You should have added these points to the outline:

1. At about six months, babies begin to repeat simple sounds. (The author signals this stage with the time transition *First* and the mention of age: "at about six months.")

3. Toddlers understand many words but cannot talk. (The author signals this stage with the time word *next:* "At the next stage. . . .")

4. Finally, the child talks in single words and two-word sentences. (The author signals this stage with the time word *Finally.*)

As emphasized by the transitions used, the relationship between the points is one of time: The second stage happens *after* the first, and so on.

PRACTICE 4

The following passage describes a sequence of events. Outline the paragraph by filling in the main idea and major details. Note that the major details are signaled by time words and dates.   *Wording of answers may vary.*

> **Hint:** Underline the time word or words that introduce each major detail, and number each major detail.

[1]The 1960s were a time of profound events in America. [2]The first thunderclap occurred in 1963, with the bullets that assassinated President John Kennedy, depressing the spirit of the country. [3]Then in 1965, urban riots moved the long-simmering issue of racial equality onto center stage. [4]A minor summer incident involving police in Watts, a black section of Los Angeles, set off five days of looting and rioting that left thirty-four people dead. [5]Over a hundred major urban riots, all centered in black ghettos in cities like Newark and Detroit, were to follow. [6]The next profound explosion was a series of protests against the increasing American presence in Vietnam. [7]The protests began in 1968 and spread across the country, centering on college campuses. [8]Soon almost every major campus in the United States was torn by rallies, teach-ins, and riots.

The words *profound events* (sentence 1) suggest that events will be described in time order.

Main idea: _The 1960s were a time of profound events in America._

1. _1963—assassination of President John Kennedy_

2. _1965—urban riots in black ghettos_

3. _1968—protests against increasing American presence in Vietnam_

PRACTICE 5

Wording of answers may vary.

The following passage describes a series of stages. Complete the map by writing the main idea in the top box and filling in the three major details (the stages).

¹Many people pass through three stages in reacting to their unemployment. ²At first they experience shock followed by relief. ³In many cases they had anticipated that they were about to lose their jobs, so when the dismissal comes, they may feel a sense of relief that at last the suspense is over. ⁴On the whole, they remain confident and hopeful that they will find a new job when they are ready. ⁵During this time, they maintain normal relationships with their family and friends. ⁶The first stage lasts for about a month or two. ⁷The second stage centers on a strong effort to find a new job. ⁸If workers have been upset or angry about losing their jobs, the feeling tends to evaporate as they marshal their resources and concentrate on finding a new job. ⁹This stage may last for up to four months. ¹⁰But if another job is not found during this time, people move into a third stage, one of self-doubt and anxiety, which lasts about six weeks. ¹¹They must struggle to maintain their self-esteem as they question their own personal power and worth.

The words *three stages* (sentence 1) suggest that the events happen in a particular time order.

People pass through three stages in reacting to unemployment.

| Shock followed by relief | → | Strong effort to find a new job | → | Self-doubt and anxiety if no job is found |

Series of Steps (Directions)

When authors give directions, they use time order. They explain step 1, then step 2, and so on through the entire sequence of steps that must be taken toward a specific goal.

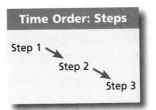

Time Order: Steps

Step 1
   Step 2
      Step 3

✓ *Check Your Understanding*

Below is a paragraph that gives directions. Complete the outline of the paragraph by listing the missing steps in the correct sequence. To help yourself identify each step, do two things:

- Underline the time words that introduce each item in the sequence;
- Number (*1, 2, . . .*) each step in the sequence.

[1]Here is a six-step technique that will help you relax quickly. [2]First, lie down with your arms at your sides and your fingers open. [3]When you are comfortable, close your eyes and put all distracting thoughts out of your mind. [4]Next, tighten all the muscles of your body at once. [5]Do this by pushing your toes together, tightening your buttocks and abdomen, clenching your fists, and squeezing your eyes shut. [6]Then, let everything relax, and feel the tension flow out of your body. [7]After that, take a deep breath through your mouth, hold it for twenty seconds, and then let it out slowly, breathing slowly and easily, as you do when you are sleeping. [8]Finally, think of a pleasant scene as you feel your whole body becoming calm and relaxed.

Main idea: Here is a six-step technique that will help you relax quickly.

1. Lie down, arms at your sides and fingers open.

2. When you are comfortable, close your eyes and clear your mind.

3. Tighten all muscles at once.

4. Let everything relax, and feel the tension flow out of your body.

5. Take a deep breath, hold it, let it out, and breathe slowly and easily.

6. Think of a pleasant scene as you feel yourself relax.

Explanation

You should have added these steps to the outline:

1. Lie down, arms at your sides and fingers open. (The author signals this stage with the time word *First*.)

2. When you are comfortable, close your eyes and clear your mind. (The author signals this stage with the time word *When*.)

4. Let everything relax, and feel the tension flow out of your body. (The author signals this stage with the time word *Then*.)

5. Take a deep breath, hold it, let it out, and breathe slowly and easily. (The author's signal is the time word *After*.)

6. Think of a pleasant scene as you feel yourself relax. (The author signals this last step with the time word *Finally*.)

As indicated by the transitions used, the relationship between the steps is one of time: The second step happens *after* the first, and so on.

PRACTICE 6

The following passage gives directions involving several steps that must be done in order. Complete the map below by writing the main idea in the top box and filling in the three missing steps. To help yourself identify each step, you may want to underline the time words.   *Wording of answers may vary.*

> *Hint:* Underline the time words that introduce each step in the sequence, and number each step.

¹There are several steps to remembering your dreams. ²To begin with, you must make up your mind to do so, for consciously deciding that you want to remember increases the likelihood that it will happen. ³Then put a pen and a notebook near your bed, so that you can write down what you remember as soon as you wake up. ⁴When possible, turn off your alarm before you go to sleep so that you can wake up gradually; this will increase the likelihood of remembering your dreams. ⁵Finally, when you wake up in the morning and remember a dream, write it down immediately, even before getting out of bed.

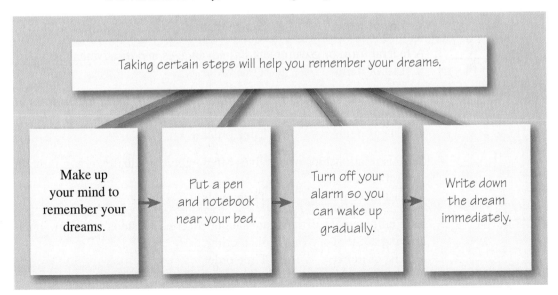

Taking certain steps will help you remember your dreams.

| Make up your mind to remember your dreams. | Put a pen and notebook near your bed. | Turn off your alarm so you can wake up gradually. | Write down the dream immediately. |

The words *several steps* (sentence 1) signal that a series of directions will be given in time order. Each of the four major details (four steps) is signaled by a time word.

A Note on Main Ideas and Patterns of Organization

A paragraph's main idea often indicates its pattern of organization. For example, here's the main idea of the paragraph you just read: "There are several steps to remembering your dreams." The words *several steps* suggest that this paragraph will be organized according to time order. Another good example is the main idea of the earlier paragraph on aging: "Various theories explain the aging process." The words *various theories* suggest that this paragraph will be a list of items.

Paying close attention to the main idea, then, can give you a quick sense of a paragraph's pattern of organization. Try, for instance, to guess the pattern of the paragraph with this main idea:

> While there are thousands of self-help groups, they all fall into three basic categories.

The phrase "three basic categories" is a strong indication that the paragraph will list those categories. The main idea helps us guess that the paragraph will be a list of three items.

PRACTICE 7

Most of the main ideas below have been taken from college textbooks. In the space provided, write the letter of the pattern of organization that each main idea suggests.

___B___ 1. The process of digestion can be divided into <u>four stages</u>.
        A. List of items   B. Time order

___A___ 2. A federal form of government has <u>advantages and disadvantages</u>.
        A. List of items   B. Time order

___A___ 3. The stock market crash resulted from <u>a number of basic weaknesses</u> in the economy.
        A. List of items   B. Time order

___B___ 4. Serious relationships in our lives often evolve gradually, going through <u>several phases</u>.
        A. List of items   B. Time order

___B___ 5. Law enforcement officers are taught <u>a series of steps</u> to follow upon arriving at the scene of a violent crime.
        A. List of items   B. Time order

To the Instructor: In Practice 7 and the tests that follow, list words and transitions that indicate each pattern of organization are underlined in this *Instructor's Edition*.

_A_ 6. There are several search aids that can be of great help when you are looking for information online.
   A. List of items   B. Time order

_A_ 7. Educational opportunities vary greatly in different regions of the United States.
   A. List of items   B. Time order

_B_ 8. Treating the allergic patient often involves a three-stage process.
   A. List of items   B. Time order

_A_ 9. Convenience products can be subdivided into four groups on the basis of how people buy them.
   A. List of items   B. Time order

_B_ 10. The worldwide fall of communism was marked by a series of dramatic events.
   A. List of items   B. Time order

Three Final Points

1 While many passages have just one pattern of organization, often the patterns are mixed. For example, you may find that part of a passage uses a list of items pattern, and another part of the same passage uses a time pattern.

2 You may have noted that when an author presents a series of events or stages or steps, that series is itself a list of items. For example, here's a time order passage:

> [1]To read and study a textbook more effectively, follow a few helpful steps. [2]**First**, preview the reading, taking a couple of minutes to get a quick sense of what the selection is about. [3]**Next**, read and mark the selection, using a highlighter pen to set off important points. [4]**Then** write up a set of study notes that summarize the most important ideas in the selection. [5]**Last**, go over and over the ideas in your notes until you know the material.

The above passage is indeed made up of a list of items. But what makes it a time order passage is that the list of items appears not at random but in a *time sequence*. Realizing that there is a time sequence will help you achieve your study purpose, which is probably to take effective notes on the material.

3 Remember that not all relationships between ideas are signaled by transitions. An author may present a list of items, for example, without using addition words. So as you read, watch for the relationships themselves, not just the transitions.

CHAPTER REVIEW

In this chapter, you learned how authors use transitions and patterns of organization to make their ideas clear. Just as transitions show relationships between ideas in sentences, patterns of organization show relationships between supporting details in paragraphs and longer pieces of writing.

You also learned two common kinds of relationships that authors use to make their ideas clear:

- **Addition relationships**

  — Authors often present a list or series of reasons, examples, or other details that support an idea. The items have no time order, but are listed in whatever order the author prefers.
  — Transition words that signal such addition relationships include *for one thing, second, also, in addition,* and *finally.*

- **Time relationships**

  — Authors usually discuss a series of events or steps in the order in which they happen, resulting in a time order.
  — Transition words that signal such time relationships include *first, next, then, after,* and *last.*

The next chapter—Chapter 6—will help you learn three other important kinds of relationships: definition-example, comparison and/or contrast, and cause-effect.

 On the Web: If you are using this book in class, you can visit our website for additional practice in understanding relationships that involve addition and time. Go to **www.townsendpress.com** and click on "Online Exercises."

REVIEW TEST 1

To review what you've learned in this chapter, fill in the blanks in the following items.

1. Transitions are words that signal *(parts of, the relationships between, the importance of)* _____the relationships between_____ ideas.
See page 182.

2. A(n) *(addition, time)* _____addition_____ transition signals that the writer is adding to an idea or ideas already mentioned. See page 182.

3. When a passage provides a series of directions or steps, or a sequence of events, it is likely to use *(addition, time)* _____time_____ transitions.
See page 190.

4. ___T___ TRUE OR FALSE? A main idea often suggests a paragraph's pattern of organization.
See page 196.

5. A passage's pattern of organization is the pattern in which its *(supporting details, main ideas, causes and effects)* _____supporting details_____ are organized.
See page 186.

REVIEW TEST 2

A. Fill in each blank with one of the words in the box. Use each transition once. Then write the letter of the transition in the space provided.

A. also	B. before	C. final
D. one	E. second	F. then

The statement explains when rubber tires were invented.

___B___ 1. Rubber tires were invented in 1845, _____before_____ cars existed. At that time, the tires were meant for bicycles.

The second sentence adds more facts about skin.

___A___ 2. The average square inch of human skin includes 19 million cells. It _____also_____ includes 625 sweat glands and 60 hairs.

___D___ 3. There are two main kinds of fats: _____one_____ is saturated fats; the other is unsaturated fats.

The sentence lists the two kinds of fats.

___F___ 4. Read the paragraph carefully and _____*then*_____ answer the questions that follow.   The sentence explains when to answer the questions.

___C___ 5. First dig a hole and work peat moss into the soil. Then put the plant in and pile in enough dirt to refill the hole. The _____*final*_____ step is to water the plant liberally.
The statements describe a series of steps in time order.

___E___ 6. The first type of small business is often called the "mom-and-pop operation." The majority of small businesses fall into this category. The _____*second*_____ type is the high-growth enterprise. This type of business aims to outgrow its small-business status as quickly as possible.   The sentences list two types of small business.

B. Read the textbook paragraph below, and then answer the questions that follow.

[1]The first professional baseball team, the Cincinnati Red Stockings, was founded in 1869. [2]After only a short time, there were teams in all the major Eastern and Midwestern cities. [3]The ballpark brought together crowds of strangers who could experience a sense of community within the big city as they watched a baseball game. [4]Immigrants were able to shake loose their ethnic ties and become absorbed in the new national game. [5]The green fields and fresh air of the ballpark were a welcome change from the sea of bricks and stone that dominated the city scene. [6]Workers could temporarily escape the routine of their daily lives. [7]They loved indirectly participating in the competition and accomplishment that baseball games symbolized. [8]The ballpark also provided a means for spectators to release their frustrations against authority figures. [9]The umpire became a symbol of scorn, and frequent cries of "kill the umpire" were heard.

___B___ 7. The relationship of sentence 2 to the sentence before it is one of
A. addition.   B. time.

8. The key transition word in sentence 2 is _____*After*_____.

___A___ 9. Sentences 3–9 present a
A. list of benefits people found in attending baseball games.
B. series of events in baseball's history.
C. series of stages in the history of baseball.

10. The relationship of sentence 8 to the sentences before it is signaled by the transition _____*also*_____.

The paragraph contains both a time pattern and a list pattern. The first two sentences tell us when the benefits developed (time order pattern). The benefits (sentences 3–9) are arranged in a list of items pattern.

REVIEW TEST 3

A. (1–5.) Fill in each blank with the appropriate transition from the box. Use each transition once.

A. after	B. as	C. first
D. later	E. then	

¹In one of the most terrifying scenes in all of literature, George Orwell in his classic novel *1984* describes how a government known as Big Brother destroys a couple's love. ²The couple, Winston and Julia, fall in love and meet secretly, knowing the government would not approve. ³(1) _____After_____ informers turn them in, a government agent named O'Brien takes steps to end their love. ⁴(2) _____First_____ he straps Winston down and explains that he has discovered Winston's worst fear. ⁵(3) _____Then_____ he sets a cage with two giant, starving sewer rats on the table next to Winston. ⁶He says that when he presses a lever, the door of the cage will slide up, and the rats will shoot out like bullets and bore straight into Winston's face. ⁷(4) _____As_____ Winston's eyes dart back and forth, revealing his terror, O'Brien places his hand on the lever. ⁸Winston realizes that the only way out is for Julia to take his place. ⁹Suddenly, he hears his own voice screaming, "Do it to Julia! Not me! Julia!" ¹⁰Orwell does not describe Julia's interrogation, but (5) _____later_____, when Julia and Winston see each other, they realize that each has betrayed the other. ¹¹Their love is gone. ¹²Big Brother has won.

___B___ 6. The pattern of organization for the above selection is
   A. list of items.   B. time order.

The paragraph describes what happens in the novel.
The events are presented in the order in which they occur.

B. Below are the beginnings of four passages. Label each one with the letter of its pattern of organization. (You may find it helpful to underline the transition or transitions in each item.)

The words that suggest a list pattern or time order pattern are underlined.

    A List of items
    B Time order

_B_ 7. ¹The process of labor during childbirth takes place in three overlapping phases. ²The <u>first</u> stage is the longest, lasting an average twelve to twenty-four hours for a woman having her first child. ³The <u>second</u> stage typically lasts about one and a half hours. . . .

        The passage presents the stages in time order.
        List words: three overlapping phases.

_A_ 8. ¹There are various ways to combat fatigue. ²<u>One</u> excellent way is exercise—walking, running, or lifting weights several times a week. ³<u>Another</u> useful strategy is to take a daily nap of twenty minutes or less, preferably in mid-afternoon, a low-energy period for many people. . . .

        The passage lists ways to combat fatigue.
        List words: various ways.

_B_ 9. ¹Even <u>before</u> he meets the three witches, Macbeth dreams of becoming king of Scotland. ²<u>Then</u> the witches predict he will be king, intensifying his ambition. ³<u>Finally,</u> his wife persuades him to murder King Duncan and take over the country. . . .

        The passage presents the sequence of events in the story.

_A_ 10. ¹Today's cell phones offer many convenient features. ²Voice mail allows you to leave and receive messages. ³<u>Another</u> helpful feature is automatic dialing, which allows you to make a call by pressing just one or two buttons. ⁴<u>Also,</u> a camera may be built in so you can take photos on the spur of the moment. . . .

        The passage lists three of the features of cell phones.
        List words: many convenient features.

REVIEW TEST 4

Here is a chance to apply your understanding of addition and time relationships to a full-length reading. The following story tells about a loving father who decides never to lie to his child—and then has to deal with Santa Claus. Read it and then answer the relationships questions that follow. There are also questions on understanding vocabulary in context, finding main ideas, and identifying supporting details.

Words to Watch

innumerable (3): too many to count
leprechauns (5): Irish elves
by osmosis (7): like a sponge
allegedly and *purportedly* (7): supposedly
deceived (8): misled
literal (9): factual
weasel words (9): deliberately misleading language
prevalent (14): widely held
stark (17): plain
ponder (23): think over
subtleties (24): details

WONDER IN THE AIR

Jeff Gammage

1   When my wife and I had our first child, we established one firm parental rule:

2   No lies.

3   Our daughter, Jin Yu, spent her first two years in an orphanage in China, and we knew that as she grew, she would ask innumerable° questions about her life there. We wanted to be able to answer from an established position of truth-telling.

4   For me, the "All the truth, all the time" policy extended onto the symbols and myths of the holidays.

5   Every April, I gladly helped fill a basket with candy rabbits and colored eggs for our daughter, and then for her new sister, but skipped the story of the Easter bunny. I avoided any mention of leprechauns°, tried to ignore the tooth fairy.

6   Most of all, I was adamant about not telling Jin Yu tales about a certain red-suited fat man who spends every

December 24 breaking into people's homes.

7   Of course, like the Grinch, I couldn't stop Christmas—or Santa Claus—from coming. Jin Yu absorbed a belief in Santa as if by osmosis°. By age 4 she knew who he (allegedly°) was, how he (purportedly°) looked, and what he (supposedly) did.

8   I didn't want to ruin her fun, but also didn't want her to feel deceived° later on.

9   So, I responded to her questions about the big man with what I liked to think of as precise and technically accurate versions of the literal° truth—and what she would no doubt characterize as weasel words°.

10   At the mall, we'd walk past a jolly Santa sitting upon a velvet throne.

11   "Is that really Santa?" my daughter would ask.

12   I'd reply with a lawyerly, "The people in line must think so."

13   The worst was when she wondered if Santa truly kept lists of children who behaved and misbehaved.

14   "That's the prevalent° belief," I said.

15   By last Christmas Eve, I had done such an expert job of parenting, made such a successful effort to be truthful, that as I tucked my daughter into bed, she was confused and near tears.

16   "Daddy, will Santa"—here her voice almost broke—"bring me any presents?"

17   This was it, the question squarely placed, a moment that offered a stark° choice between fable and fact, that demanded a reasoned response from a father grounded in principle. I looked at my adored child, her dark brown eyes threatening to overflow, knowing there was but one choice, and I made it:

18   I lied.

19   On Christmas Eve, the holy of holy nights, I lied to my 5-year-old daughter so fully, so deliberately and in such compelling detail that I nearly believed it myself.

20   "Darling, of course Santa is going to bring you presents. He would never overlook you. You're such a good girl [that part was true] that I know Santa will stop here. Listen, do you hear that sound outside? I think it's jingle bells! It must be his sleigh!"

21   Jin Yu turned to the window, hoping to glimpse a team of reindeer in flight, then lay back and drifted off, content, or at least relieved.

22   The next morning, she awoke to find that, sure enough, Santa had visited her home, proving his existence by magically delivering a wardrobe of princess gowns and dress-up shoes in exactly her size.

23   I think he left something for me as well: The power of a child's belief. A reminder that the best things in life cannot be seen with the naked eye. And that while there will be plenty of time for my daughter to ponder° cold and painful truths, her time of wonder should be savored.

24   This year, fully 6, Jin Yu is happily preparing for Santa by drawing crayon snowscapes and discussing his impending arrival with friends. She counsels her 3-year-old sister, Zhao Gu, on the subtleties° of naughty and nice.

25   Last week Jin Yu came to me with a very specific Christmas question, the sort that once again required a father's sure guidance: What kind of cookies should she leave for Santa on Christmas Eve?

26   I was firm in my response: Chocolate chip. Definitely, I told her, Santa likes chocolate chip.

Reading Comprehension Questions

Vocabulary in Context

_B_ 1. In the sentence below, the word *adamant* (ăd′ə-mənt) means
   A. undecided.
   B. determined.
   C. flexible.
   D. angry.

   "Most of all, I was adamant about not telling Jin Yu tales about a certain red-suited fat man who spends every December 24 breaking into people's homes." (Paragraph 6)

   If he has a strict "no lies" rule, he would be determined not to tell Jin Yu that Santa will come to visit.

_____C_____ 2. In the sentence below, the word *savored* (sā'vərd) means

    A. unnoticed.

    B. discouraged.   Because there will be time to face painful truths,

    C. fully enjoyed.   her time of wonder should be fully enjoyed.

    D. explained.

> "And that while there will be plenty of time for my daughter to ponder cold and painful truths, her time of wonder should be savored." (Paragraph 23)

_____B_____ 3. In the sentence below, the word *impending* (ĭm-pĕnd'ĭng) means

    A. late.

    B. soon to take place.   If Jin Yu is preparing for Santa,

    C. surprising.   he must be arriving soon.

    D. possible.

> "This year, fully 6, Jin Yu is happily preparing for Santa by drawing crayon snowscapes and discussing his impending arrival with friends." (Paragraph 24)

Central Point and Main Ideas

_____D_____ 4. Which sentence best expresses the central point of the selection?

    A. Holiday myths are so common in our culture that it is impossible to always tell the truth to children.

Answer A does not include the reason he lies to his daughter. Answer B ignores paragraphs 23 to 26. Answer C ignores paragraph 17.

    B. If a child wants to believe in Santa Claus, there is little a parent can do to stop her.

    C. The author reluctantly goes along with his daughter's belief in Santa Claus.

    D. When he sees how important a belief in Santa Claus is to his daughter, the author comes to understand that all children should be permitted their time of wonder.

_____C_____ 5. The main idea of paragraphs 1–5 is that

    A. the author's daughter was adopted from an orphanage in China as a two-year-old.

Answers A and B each cover only paragraph 3. Answer D covers only paragraph 5.

    B. the author knew that his adopted daughter would ask questions about her first two years in China.

    C. the author and his wife vowed never to lie to their adopted daughter, even about holiday symbols and myths.

    D. the author allowed his daughter to celebrate holidays, but skipped telling her holiday myths.

Supporting Details

_C_ 6. The author breaks his vow never to lie to his daughter
   A. when they see a Santa at the shopping mall.
   B. a few days before Easter.   See paragraphs 15 to 18.
   C. on Christmas Eve.
   D. when she asks him what kind of cookies she should leave for Santa on Christmas Eve.

_C_ 7. For Jin Yu, Santa's existence is proven when
   A. she sees him at the shopping mall.
   B. she finds that he has eaten all the chocolate chip cookies she left him on Christmas Eve.
   C. she finds that he has magically delivered princess gowns and dress-up shoes in exactly her size.
   D. all her friends tell her that he exists.   See paragraph 22.

Transitions

_B_ 8. Read the two sentences below and then answer the question that follows.

The words *The next morning* signal the time order relationship.

   "Jin Yu turned to the window, hoping to glimpse a team of reindeer in flight, then lay back and drifted off, content, or at least relieved.
   "The next morning, she awoke to find that, sure enough, Santa had visited her home . . . ." (Paragraphs 21–22)

   What does the second sentence do?
   A. It adds more detail to the first sentence.
   B. It shows a time order relationship.

Patterns of Organization

_A_ 9. Paragraph 23 mainly

The paragraph lists the benefits the author received.

   A. lists ways that the author benefited from his daughter's belief in Santa Claus.
   B. presents a series of events in time order.

_B_ 10. The main pattern of organization of this selection is
   A. a list of items.
   B. time order.

   The selection describes a series of events in the order in which they took place.

Discussion Questions

1. Was the author right to lie to his daughter? Why or why not?

2. When you were a child, did you believe in Santa Claus? How did you find out that he doesn't really exist?

3. When or if you have children, will you encourage them to believe in Santa, the Easter Bunny, and the tooth fairy? Why or why not?

4. The author and his wife decided that "no lies" would be their "one firm parental rule." What do you think are some other good parental rules?

Note: Writing assignments for this selection appear on page 602.

Check Your Performance   **RELATIONSHIPS I**

Activity	Number Right	Points		Score
Review Test 1 (5 items)	_____	× 2	=	_____
Review Test 2 (10 items)	_____	× 3	=	_____
Review Test 3 (10 items)	_____	× 3	=	_____
Review Test 4 (10 items)	_____	× 3	=	_____
		TOTAL SCORE	=	_____%

Enter your total score into the **Reading Performance Chart: Review Tests** on the inside back cover.

RELATIONSHIPS I: Mastery Test 1

A. Fill in each blank with an appropriate transition from the box. Use each transition once. Then, in the spaces provided, write the letter of the transition you have chosen.

A. after	B. also	C. another
D. moreover	E. then	

Hint: Make sure that each word or phrase that you choose fits smoothly into the flow of the sentence. Test your choices by reading each sentence to yourself.

___A___ 1. ¹If you're used to e-mail, sending an actual letter can seem like a long, drawn-out process. ²First you have to get a pen and paper, an envelope, and stamps. ³_____After_____ you write the letter, you have to fold it, place it in the envelope, and attach a stamp. ⁴Finally you find a place to mail the letter. ⁵No wonder people mail so few real letters these days!

The passage describes in sequence the steps in sending an actual letter. The word *process* in sentence 1 suggests the time order pattern.

___C___ 2. ¹I have a limited interest in people whose main topic of conversation is themselves and who never show any interest in what is happening to me. ²_____Another_____ group I avoid is people who never allow facts to interfere with their opinions.

The passage lists two groups avoided by the writer.

___B___ 3. ¹The world of business is one area in which technology has isolated us. ²Many people now work alone at a display terminal that connects to a large central computer. ³Personal banking has _____also_____ become a detached process. ⁴To deposit or withdraw money from their accounts, customers often interact with machines rather than people.

The passages lists two areas where technology has isolated us.

___D___ 4. ¹By today's standards, early automobiles were difficult to operate and uncomfortable to drive. ²A driver had to start the car's engine by cranking it by hand, and the crank sometimes sprang back and broke the driver's thumb. ³_____Moreover_____, early cars were open on top, so driving on unpaved roads left riders choking on dust and dirt.

The passage lists two examples of problems with early cars.

___E___ 5. ¹Many television ads proceed in three stages: the problem, the advice, and the resolution. ²For example, a mouthwash commercial will first establish the problem—that someone has bad breath. ³_____Then_____ it will suggest that the person try the advertised mouthwash. ⁴This is followed by an obvious resolution of the problem: the person's being chased by attractive members of the opposite sex.

The passage describes in sequence the three stages of TV ads.

To the Instructor: In these mastery tests, list words and transitions that indicate each pattern of organization are underlined in this *Instructor's Edition*. Remind students that sentence structure and punctuation are useful in placing the transition words.

(Continues on next page)

B. (6–9.) Fill in each blank with an appropriate transition word from the box. Use each transition once.

> A. after   B. last   C. next
> D. then

¹Two Minnesota brothers, Ed and Norman, are engaged in a war. ²It all started (6)_____*after*_____ Ed's wife gave him a pair of pants that didn't fit. ³Ed wrapped up the pants and put them under Norman's Christmas tree. ⁴As soon as Norman opened the box, he recognized the unwanted pants. ⁵The (7)_____*next*_____ year, he gave them back to Ed, sealed in a heavy carton tied with knotted ropes. ⁶The War of the Pants was on. ⁷Each year, on one of the brothers' birthdays, or on Christmas, the dreaded pants reappear. ⁸Two years ago, Norman bought an old safe, put the pants in it, welded it shut, and delivered it to Ed's house. ⁹Somehow, Ed retrieved the pants. ¹⁰(One of the rules of the war is that the pants must not be damaged.) ¹¹(8)_____*Last*_____ year Ed took the pants to an auto junkyard. ¹²The pants were placed in an ancient Ford's backseat, and the car (9)_____*then*_____ went through the auto crusher. ¹³On his birthday, Norman found a four-foot square of smashed metal on his doorstep. ¹⁴He knew it could only be Ed's doing, and the pants must be inside. ¹⁵Norman is still trying to get at the pants and prepare next year's "topper."

_B_ 10. The pattern of organization of the above selection is
     A. list of items.
     B. time order.

> The passage tells, in time order, the story of the War of the Pants.

RELATIONSHIPS I: Mastery Test 2

A. Fill in each blank with an appropriate transition from the box. Use each transition once. Then, in the spaces provided, write the letter of the transition you have chosen.

A. also	B. before	C. first
D. then	E. when	

_____E_____ 1.

The passage describes in time order the steps a snapping turtle goes through to get a meal.

¹Big snapping turtles don't get to weigh so much without eating a lot of food. ²Here's how they do it: ³Most snapping turtles float, or lie motion-less on the bottom of a pond or river. ⁴____When____ a fish, frog, or other prey swims close enough, the turtle snaps very fast with powerful jaws.

_____C_____ 2.

The passage lists two of the reasons for Japan's low crime rate.

¹Experts cite several reasons for Japan's low crime rate. ²____First____, Japan has had strict gun control for four hundred years. ³In addition, the country relies on some fifteen thousand small neighborhood police stations known as *koban*. ⁴Police officers and their families actually live as part of the neighborhood, helping prevent the growth of conditions that might lead to crime.

_____D_____ 3.

The passage describes the sequence of events in the writer's dreams.

¹For much of my life, I have been haunted by dreams of falling. ²In a typical dream, I have fallen off a tall building or over the edge of a cliff or out of a plane, and I am plunging at a breathtaking speed toward the ground. ³____Then____, just as I am about to crash into the ground, I wake up in a cold sweat, my heart racing.

_____B_____ 4.

The passage tells in time order the story of the discovery of tea.

¹According to legend, tea was discovered quite by accident. ²One day about 4,000 years ago, a Chinese emperor was boiling water outside when leaves from a bush fell into the open pot. ³____Before____ the emperor could remove the leaves, they began to brew. ⁴He smelled the sweet aroma of the mixture, and once he tasted it, tea was born.

_____A_____ 5.

The passage lists two message carriers: television and magazine ads.

¹Whoever you are, whatever you look like, chances are you're not happy with your appearance. ²Our culture constantly sends out the message that you're not attractive enough. ³Television is one of the most powerful message-carriers, showing you an endless parade of impossibly thin, beautiful people. ⁴Magazines are ____also____ designed to make you feel ugly, with glossy airbrushed models on every page providing an impossible ideal of thin, ageless beauty.

(Continues on next page)

B. Read the passage and answer the question that follows.

> ¹Probably every child remembers digging a hole in his or her backyard and being told, "If you dig deep enough, you'll go to China." ²What would really happen if a man dug a hole through the center of the Earth and then jumped into it? ³The traveler entering the tunnel would <u>first</u> fall rapidly under the force of gravity. ⁴<u>Eventually</u>, as he approached the Earth's center, the jumper's weight would decrease. ⁵<u>By the time</u> he reached the center of the Earth, he would be weightless. ⁶An equal <u>amount</u> of the Earth's mass on all sides of him would cancel out the forces of gravity. ⁷Still, the traveler's original momentum would carry him past the center toward the opening on the far side of the world. ⁸<u>After</u> almost reaching that point, he would fall back up the hole toward his starting point. ⁹Back and forth he would <u>then</u> go, like a yo-yo, gradually slowing down until coming to a stop at the very center of the Earth.

   B   6. The main pattern of organization of the passage is

     A. list of items.   The passage describes the sequence of events

     B. time order.   in the order in which they would occur.

C. (7–9.) Fill in each blank with an appropriate transition word from the box. Use each transition once. Then answer the question that follows.

A. also	B. finally	c. first

> ¹The microbes that cause infection are transmitted to people in <u>several ways</u>. ²(7)_____First_____, there is direct transmission, which involves bodily contact with an infected person. ³Examples are passing along a cold through handshaking or herpes through sexual relations. ⁴There is (8)_____also_____ indirect transmission, which occurs when microbes are passed from an infected person to an individual via airborne particles, water, food, or anything else the infected person touches. ⁵For example, someone might catch the flu by drinking from a glass that has been used by a person with the flu. ⁶(9)_____Finally_____, animals and insects can transmit microbes. ⁷Flies, for instance, carry harmful microbes on their feet, and can transmit them to people by landing on their food.

   A 10. The pattern of organization of the above selection is

     A. list of items.   The paragraph lists three ways that microbes

     B. time order.   can be transmitted to people. The words *several*

                         ways suggest that a list of items will follow.

RELATIONSHIPS I: Mastery Test 3

A. (1–4.) Arrange the scrambled sentences below into a logical paragraph by numbering them *1, 2, 3,* and *4* in an order that makes sense. Then, in the space provided, write the letter of the pattern of organization used.

Note that transitions will help you by clarifying the relationships between sentences.

___3___ In addition, check the puppy's personality by watching how it plays with other puppies.

___1___ There are some important points to keep in mind when choosing a puppy.

___4___ Last, since curiosity is a sign of intelligence, clap your hands to see if the puppy is curious and interested.

___2___ For one thing, look for signs of good health, including clear, bright eyes and firm, pink gums.

___A___ 5. The pattern of organization of the above selection is
    A. list of items.
    B. time order.

> The paragraph lists important points for choosing a puppy. The addition transitions suggest the correct order for the sentences.

B. Read the passage and answer the question that follows. You may find it helpful to underline transitions as you read.

¹In January of 1954, Ernest and Mary Hemingway left Nairobi on a vacation trip on which they flew over grazing elephants, hippos bathing in the lakes, and huge flocks of feeding flamingos. ²As they were circling a spectacular waterfall, a flock of ibises flew in front of the plane. ³When the pilot dived to avoid the birds, he struck an abandoned telegraph wire that crossed the gorge. ⁴In the crash that followed, Ernest sprained his shoulder; Mary was only slightly injured. ⁵Luckily, a boat came down the river the next morning, and its crew rescued them. ⁶By that evening, they were on board a small plane bound for Entebbe. ⁷The plane lifted from the plowed field that served as a runway, then crashed and burst into flames. ⁸Ernest escaped by breaking through a window with his head and injured shoulder, and Mary got out through another window. ⁹Twice in two days they had crashed and come out alive, but Ernest had injured his head, his backbone, and a kidney. ¹⁰After this, even writing a letter was difficult for him.

___B___ 6. The pattern of organization of the above selection is
    A. list of items.
    B. time order.

> The paragraph tells about the events in the order they happened. Most of the major details are signaled by time transitions.

(Continues on next page)

C. Read the textbook passage below, and then answer the question and complete the outline.

> [1]Prevention against injury involves a combination of two types of preventive measures. [2]First is active prevention, which refers to methods that require people to do something to reduce the risk of being injured. [3]Examples include the use of nonautomatic seat belts, the use of bicycle and motorcycle helmets, following drunk driving laws, and obeying gun laws. [4]The second type of preventive measure is passive prevention. [5]Passive prevention refers to methods requiring little or no action on the part of those being protected. [6]These measures include seat belts that automatically engage when a person enters a car, automobile air bags, better street lighting, and built-in safety switches on power tools and electrical equipment.

___A___ 7. The pattern of organization of the above selection is

    A. list of items.

    B. time order.

The selection lists two types of prevention: active and passive.

8–10. Complete the outline of the passage.

Wording of answers may vary.

Main idea: _Prevention against injury involves a combination of two types of preventive measures._

Major supporting details:

1. _Active prevention—methods that require people to do something to reduce the risk of injury_

    Examples—use of nonautomatic seat belts; bike helmets

2. _Passive prevention—methods requiring little or no action on the part of those being protected_

    Examples—automatic seat belts; air bags

RELATIONSHIPS I: Mastery Test 4

A. (1–5.) Arrange the scrambled sentences below into a logical paragraph by numbering them *1, 2, 3,* and *4* in an order that makes sense. Then, in the space provided, write the letter of the pattern of organization used.

Note that transitions will help you by clarifying the relationships between sentences.

___4___ When you have chosen your apartment, have a lawyer or another person knowledgeable about leases examine your lease before you sign it.

___1___ If you're looking for an apartment, <u>begin</u> by making a list of promising openings. Check the classified ads and two or three real estate offices for apartments within your price range and desired locale.

___3___ As you inspect each apartment, make sure that faucets, toilets, stoves, and electrical wiring and outlets are functioning efficiently and safely.

___2___ After you have made a solid list, visit at least five of the most promising available apartments.

___B___ 5. The pattern of organization of the above selection is
    A. list of items.   The paragraph describes, in order, a series
    B. time order.   of steps to take to find an apartment.

B. Read the textbook passage below and answer the question that follows.

[1]Did you ever wonder how trainers get porpoises to do all those tricks, like leaping over a high bar or jumping through a hoop? [2]Wild porpoises are <u>first</u> taught to eat fish from their trainer's hand. [3]<u>When</u> the animal accepts a fish, the trainer blows a whistle. [4]The porpoise associates the whistle with "correct" behavior. [5]<u>Once</u> the porpoise touches a human hand to get a fish, it will touch other things, like a red target ball. [6]For example, the trainer will hold the ball high above the water while leaning over a kind of pulpit. [7]Seeing the ball, the porpoise leaps out of the water; it knows it will be rewarded with a fish. [8]A hoop can <u>then</u> be substituted for a ball, and the porpoise's behavior can be "shaped" so it will jump through the hoop. [9]If the porpoise misses by jumping too low, the fish reward is withheld. [10]The intelligent animal will associate "no fish" with "wrong" behavior; very quickly, the porpoise will be leaping gracefully through the center of the hoop.

___B___ 6. The pattern of organization of the above selection is
    A. list of items.   The passage describes a logical sequence of steps
    B. time order.   to follow in teaching porpoises to do tricks.

(Continues on next page)

C. (7–10.) Complete the map of the following textbook passage.

¹Work shapes human lives in <u>fundamental ways</u>. ²First, work consumes enormous amounts of people's time. ³Most people spend about one-third of their adult lives working. ⁴According to a recent survey, almost half of all employed people spend 40 hours or more per week at work; only 10 percent work less than 30 hours a week. ⁵Work <u>also</u> gives life a structure and rhythm. ⁶The traditional eight-hour "shift" allows people to balance their days with productive time and recreational time. ⁷This daily pattern promotes mental health. ⁸In fact, many studies show that when people are unable to work, they experience emotional distress and low self-esteem. ⁹A <u>third</u> way work shapes life is that it causes stress. ¹⁰For some this stress can be positive—resulting in increased performance and professional success. ¹¹For others, however, the stress can be extreme and lead to health problems and illness.

The words *fundamental ways* suggest a list pattern.
Each way is signaled by an addition word.

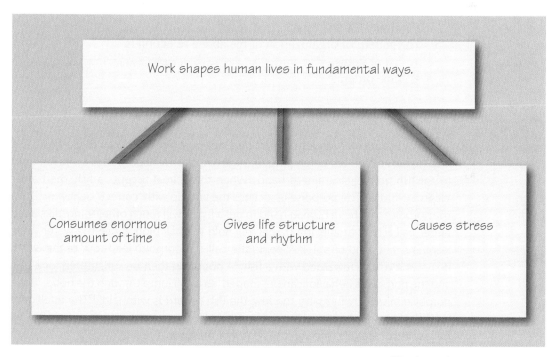

Wording of answers may vary.

RELATIONSHIPS I: Mastery Test 5

Read each textbook passage and answer the questions or follow the directions provided.

A. ¹Scoundrels have cheated their victims throughout history, but the term "confidence man" was apparently coined only in 1849, and it immediately achieved widespread currency. ²It originated in the story of a swindler of gentlemanly appearance and remarkable boldness named Samuel Thompson. ³He would approach a well-dressed stranger on the streets of a city and greet him as if he were an old acquaintance. ⁴After a brief conversation, Thompson would ask, "Have you confidence in me to trust me with your watch until tomorrow?" ⁵The victim, embarrassed to have forgotten this courtous and friendly gentleman and reluctant to deny such a direct request, would lend his watch. ⁶Then the "confidence man" would walk off laughing, never to return. ⁷He was finally caught by the police only after he was spotted by a previous victim.

The passage describes both the sequence of actions in Thompson's scam and the sequence of events that led to his capture.

_____B_____ 1. The pattern of organization of the above selection is
   A. list of items.
   B. time order.

2. One of the transitions that signals the pattern of organization is

   _____*Any of the following:* in 1849, After, Then, finally_____.

B. ¹Many food products are stamped with dates that tell consumers when the product is still fresh. ²Products are dated in one of three ways. ³Some food products contain the words "sell by" followed by the date. ⁴These foods remain fresh for about one week after the date on the label. ⁵Other foods list the date after the words "best if used by." ⁶Products with this label can still be used for a few weeks after the date on the label, but they might not have the same quality.

⁷_____, certain products, such as baby formulas, have an expiration date. ⁸These products should not be used after the date on the label.

_____A_____ 3. The paragraph
   A. lists ways in which food products are dated.
   B. describes stages in dating food products.

_____C_____ 4. The transition that would best fit the blank space in sentence 7 is
   A. *After.*   The words *three ways* suggests a list will follow. *After*
   B. *Eventually.*   and *Eventually* are not logical because the sentence
   C. *Third.*   requires an addition word, and they are time words.

(Continues on next page)

C. ¹Dr. Elisabeth Kübler-Ross has identified <u>five stages</u> in the reactions of dying patients. ²The <u>first</u> stage, she says, is denial. ³Patients will at first deny the seriousness of their illness, claiming that some error has been made. ⁴<u>Then</u> patients become angry. ⁵They ask, "Why me?" ⁶Their anger may be directed against God, fate, or even their doctors. ⁷<u>Next</u> comes depression. ⁸During this stage, patients feel hopeless and lose interest in life. ⁹<u>After</u> depression comes bargaining—patients try to bargain for their lives. ¹⁰They may promise God or their doctors that they'll be good, stop smoking, give up alcohol, or do whatever is necessary if only they can survive. ¹¹The <u>fifth</u> stage is that of acceptance. ¹²Patients finally resign themselves to the inevitable. ¹³They are not joyful, but they gain a sense of inner peace. ¹⁴While there has been some criticism of Kübler-Ross's stages, her work has contributed much to making death a more comfortable and better-understood subject.

_____B_____ 5. The pattern of organization of the above selection is
         A. list of items.   The passage describes in sequence the *five*
         B. time order.   *stages* (note the list words) of reactions of dying
                                        patients. Each stage is introduced by a time word.

6–10. Complete the map of the paragraph.

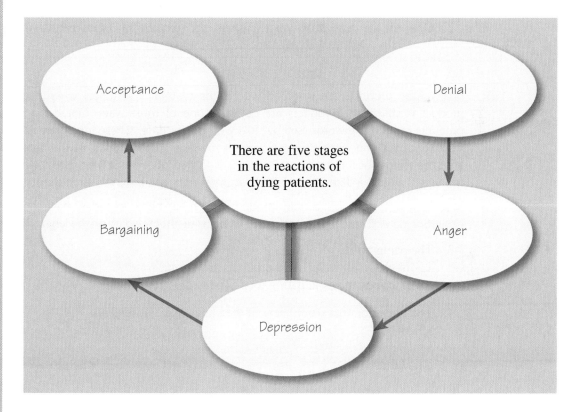

RELATIONSHIPS I: Mastery Test 6

Read each textbook passage and answer the questions or follow the directions provided.

A. ¹According to the National Institute on Drug Abuse, thirty million Americans—one out of eight people—suffer from a drug or alcohol dependency. ²The development of an addiction typically unfolds in <u>four stages</u>. ³<u>First</u>, some stimulus—drugs, alcohol, sex, chocolate—holds out the promise of short-lived pleasure or excitement. ⁴<u>Next</u>, a person discovers that indulging in one of these activities temporarily satisfies some psychological need, making him or her feel good, if only for a short time. ⁵<u>Third</u>, certain recurring situations start to trigger the addictive behavior, and the pattern repeats itself. ⁶<u>Finally</u>, the habit takes control, and the individual loses self-control. ⁷Often, by this stage, a physical dependency will have been added to a psychological one, thereby making the addictive behavior pattern even more difficult to break.

   _B__ 1. The pattern of organization of the above selection is
      A. list of items.   *The words* four stages *suggest a time pattern.*
      B. time order.   *Each of the stages of the development of an*
                            addiction is introduced by a time word.

   2–3. Two of the transitions that introduce the major details of the paragraph are
        Any two of the following: First, Next, Third, Finally

B. ¹After World War II began, women's roles changed. ²The most visible change was the sudden appearance of large numbers of women in uniform. ³The military organized them into auxiliary units with special uniforms, their own officers, and, amazingly, equal pay. ⁴Most either filled traditional women's roles, such as nursing, or replaced men in noncombat situations.

     ⁵Women <u>also</u> substituted for men on the home front. ⁶During the war, three million women entered the labor force, and for the first time in history, married working women outnumbered single working women. ⁷The war challenged the public's image of proper female behavior, as "Rosie the Riveter" became the popular symbol of women who abandoned traditional jobs as domestic servants and store clerks to work in construction and heavy industry.

   _A__ 4. The pattern of organization of the above selection is
      A. list of items.
      B. time order.

      5. The second major detail is signaled with the transition _____also_____.

   _A__ 6. The total number of major details is
      A. two.   *The passage lists two major ways that women's roles*
      B. three.   *changed after World War II began: they joined the military,*
      C. four.   *and they substituted in men's jobs on the home front.*
                                (Continues on next page)

C. ¹There are <u>three main ways</u> that children learn their gender roles. ²<u>One</u> is conditioning through rewards and punishments. ³For example, boys who play with model airplanes and girls who play with dolls will usually be encouraged by their parents. ⁴On the other hand, boys who prefer dolls and girls who prefer airplanes will often be criticized or even punished. ⁵<u>Another</u> element is imitation. ⁶Young children will usually imitate adults who they think are like themselves. ⁷This means that boys will usually imitate their fathers and girls their mothers. ⁸The <u>third</u> and perhaps most important element is self-definition. ⁹Children quickly learn that all people are either male or female and define themselves as belonging to one sex rather than the other. ¹⁰They then use this self-definition to choose their future interests and to develop their personalities and social roles.

_____A___ 7. The pattern of organization of the above selection is
   A. list of items.   The words *three main ways* suggest that a
   B. time order.   list will follow. Each of the major details
                                                            is introduced by an addition word.

8–10. Complete the outline of the paragraph.

Wording of answers may vary.

Main idea: _____Children learn their gender rules in three main ways._____

Major supporting details:

1. Conditioning through rewards and punishments
2. _Imitation_____
3. _Self-definition_____

6 Relationships II

In the previous chapter, you learned how authors use transitions and patterns of organization to show relationships and make their ideas clear. You also learned about two common types of relationships:

- Relationships that involve **addition**
- Relationships that involve **time**

In this chapter, you will learn about three other types of relationships:

- Relationships that involve **illustration**
- Relationships that involve **comparison and contrast**
- Relationships that involve **cause and effect**

1 Illustration

Words That Show Illustration

Put a check (✓) beside the item that is easier to understand:

_____ I've become very absent-minded. Last week I went to work on my day off.

__✓__ I've become very absent-minded. Last week, for instance, I went to work on my day off.

The second item is easier to understand. The words *for instance* make it clear that what happened on that day off is just one example of the absent-mindedness. *For instance* and other words and phrases like it are illustration words.

"I do share my deepest emotions with you. For instance, I am hungry and tired. Those are both deep emotions."

Illustration words indicate that an author will provide one or more *examples* to develop and clarify a given idea. In the cartoon above, the husband gives examples of what, to him, are deep emotions.

Here are some common words that introduce examples:

Illustration Words

(for) example	including	(as an) illustration	one
(for) instance	specifically	to illustrate	once
such as	to be specific		

Examples

The following items contain illustration words. Notice how these words signal that one or more *examples* are coming.

● Certain colors are associated with particular emotions. *For instance*, green represents jealousy, red stands for anger, and blue means "gloomy."

● My grandmother doesn't hear well anymore. *For example,* whenever I say, "Hi, Granny," she answers, "Fine, just fine."

● A cat's curiosity can get it into ridiculous situations. *Once,* a neighbor's cat got its head stuck in the garbage disposal.

PRACTICE 1

Complete each item with a suitable illustration word or phrase from the box on the previous page. Try to use a variety of transitions.   *Answers may vary.*

> *Hint:* Make sure that each word or phrase that you choose fits smoothly into the flow of the sentence. Test each choice by reading the sentence aloud.

1. Animals were once tried for crimes. _____For instance_____, in 1740 a cow convicted of witchcraft was hanged by the neck until dead.

2. Some soap opera fans take the shows too seriously. There are viewers, _____for example_____, who actually send threats to soap opera "villains."

3. My mother believes in various superstitions, _____such as_____ the idea that if you drop a fork, it means company's coming.

4. When a couple divorces, the partners often experience a wide range of emotions, _____including_____ anger, regret, depression, and relief.

5. People have chosen to end their lives in a variety of unusual ways. As an _____illustration_____, in ancient China, people committed suicide by eating a pound of salt.

The Definition and Example Pattern

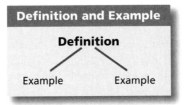

To get a sense of the definition and example pattern, try to arrange the following sentences in an order that makes sense. Put a *1* in front of the sentence that should come first, a *2* in front of the sentence that comes next, and a *3* in front of the sentence that should be last. The result will be a short paragraph.

_2_ Someone might, for instance, sit calmly through a friend's criticism and act as if it didn't bother him or her.

_1_ Apathy is an avoidance response in which a person acknowledges unpleasant information but pretends he or she does not care about it.

_3_ Another example is responding to the loss of a job by acting indifferent: "Who cares? It was a dumb job anyhow."

This paragraph begins with a definition: "Apathy is an avoidance response in which a person acknowledges unpleasant information but pretends he or she does not care about it." The second sentence makes clear this meaning of *apathy* with an example: "Someone might, for instance, sit calmly through a friend's criticism and act as if it didn't bother him or her." The third sentence then provides an added example: "Another example is responding to the loss of a job by acting indifferent: 'Who cares? It was a dumb job anyhow.'" The second and third sentences include the illustration words *for instance* and *example*. As you can see, the definition and example pattern of organization includes just what its name suggests: a definition and one or more examples.

> *An Important Study Hint:* Good textbook authors want to help readers understand the important ideas and terms in a subject—whether it is psychology, sociology, business, biology, or any other field. Such authors often take time, then, to include key definitions. These ideas and terms are usually set off in *italic* or **boldface** type, and the definitions are signaled by such words as *is, are, is called, termed,* and *refers to.* Here are some definitions from a variety of textbooks:
>
> - An **instinct** is a form of behavior that occurs in all normal members of a species without having been learned.
>
> - **Phobias** are fears that are out of proportion to the actual danger involved in a situation.
>
> - **Divergent thinking** refers to the ability to generate unusual, yet nonetheless appropriate, responses to problems or questions.
>
> - Once a tumor has been detected, cells can be removed from it in a procedure called a **biopsy**; the cells are then examined under the microscope by a pathologist.
>
> - Party funding, along with the money a candidate receives from individual contributors and interest groups, is termed **hard money** since it goes directly to the candidate and can be spent as he or she chooses.
>
> - Both rapidly growing countries and slowly growing countries can have a problem with their **dependency ratio**—the number of nonworking compared to working individuals in a population.

Sometimes a dash is used to signal a definition.

If an author defines a term, you can assume that it is important enough to learn. So when reading and taking notes on a textbook, always do two things:

1) Write down key definitions.

2) Write down helpful examples of definitions. When definitions are general and abstract, examples are often essential to help make an idea clear.

✔ Check Your Understanding

The following paragraph defines a word, explains it a bit, and then gives an example of it. After reading the paragraph, see if you can answer the questions that follow.

¹Acrophobia is an intense, unreasonable fear of high places. ²People with acrophobia exhibit emotional and physical symptoms in response to being at great heights. ³For instance, one sufferer of extreme acrophobia, Sally Maxwell, is unable to go above the third floor of any building without feeling enormous anxiety. ⁴Her acrophobia began one evening when she was working alone in her office on the eighth floor of a large building. ⁵Suddenly she was struck with terror by the idea that she might jump or fall out the open window. ⁶She crouched behind a steel filing cabinet, trembling, unable to move. ⁷When she finally gathered her belongings and left the building, she was sweating, her breathing was rapid, and her heart was pounding. ⁸Yet she had no rational explanation for her fears.

What word is being defined? _____ acrophobia _____

What is the definition? _____ An intense, unreasonable fear of high places _____

Which sentence explains more about the word? _____ Sentence 2 _____

In which sentence does the example begin? _____ Sentence 3 _____

Explanation

The word *acrophobia* is defined in the first sentence—"an intense, unreasonable fear of high places." The second sentence explains a bit more about acrophobia. The story about Sally Maxwell, which begins in the third sentence, provides an example of how acrophobia affects one sufferer. The example helps make the new term clear to the reader. The author introduces that illustration with the transition *For instance*.

To the Instructor: On pages 225–226, words being defined and transitions that signal examples are underlined in this *Instructor's Edition*.

PRACTICE 2

A. The following passage includes a definition and two examples. Underline the term being defined. Then, in the spaces provided, write the number of the definition sentence and the number of the sentence where each example begins.

[1]Shaping is a way to teach a new behavior by encouraging a series of small bits of the whole behavior. [2]This approach, for instance, was used to teach a disturbed little boy named Dickey to wear eyeglasses after cataract surgery. [3]His physician feared that without glasses, his vision would deteriorate permanently. [4]At the mere mention of eyeglasses, however, Dickey threw terrible temper tantrums. [5]So researchers used shaping to ease him into the idea of wearing his glasses. [6]Dickey was deprived of his breakfast so that food could be used as a reward. [7]He received a bit of food each time he picked up some glasses frames. [8]Later in the procedure, he had to put glasses on in order to receive a reward. [9]Within eighteen days, Dickey had learned through gradual steps to wear his glasses for twelve hours a day.

In sentence 2, for instance signals the first example. In sentence 10, example signals the second example.

[10]Another example is teaching a circus tiger to jump through a flaming hoop. [11]The tiger might first be rewarded for jumping up on a pedestal and then for leaping from that pedestal to another. [12]Eventually, the hoop would be set on fire, and the tiger would have to leap through the burning hoop to be rewarded.

Definition ____1____ Example 1 ____2____ Example 2 ____10____

B. The following passage includes a definition and one example. Underline the term being defined. Then outline the selection by doing two things: 1) filling in the word being defined and its definition; 2) in a few words, summarizing the example.

[1]Jonathan Swift (1667–1745), author of *Gulliver's Travels,* often used irony—saying one thing but meaning another—in his writing. [2]For example, in his famous essay "A Modest Proposal," he makes this suggestion for ending the famine in Ireland: the Irish should raise babies to be eaten. [3]Swift did not mean his suggestion to be taken seriously. [4]His actual goal was to shock his British audience into facing the mass starvation and misery in Ireland that British policies had produced at that time.

Wording of answers may vary.

_____Irony_____ — saying one thing but meaning another

Example— To end the famine in Ireland, Swift suggests the Irish should raise babies to be eaten.

Sentence 1 defines the term *irony.* The words *For example* (sentence 2) introduce the example.

2 Comparison and Contrast

Words That Show Comparison

Put a check (✓) beside the item that is easier to understand:

___ Driving a car is a skill that we learn through practice. Writing a paper is a skill that we learn through hands-on experience.

_✓_ Driving a car is a skill that we learn through practice. Similarly, writing a paper is a skill that we learn through hands-on experience.

The first item makes us wonder, "What has learning to drive a car got to do with writing a paper?" The word *similarly* makes it clear that the author intends to compare learning to write a paper with learning to drive a car. *Similarly* and words like it are comparison words.

DRABBLE: © Kevin Fagin/Dist. by United Feature Syndicate, Inc.

Comparison words signal similarities. Authors use a comparison transition to show that a second idea is *like* the first one in some way. In the cartoon above, the word *resemble* helps show a comparison is being made.

Here are some common words that show comparison:

Comparison Words

(just) as	likewise	in a similar manner
(just) like	in like manner	in the same way
alike	similar(ly)	resemble

Examples

The sentences below contain comparison words. Notice how these words show that things are *alike* in some way.

- When buying milk, my mother always takes a bottle from the back of the shelf. *Similarly,* when my father buys a newspaper, he usually grabs one from the middle of the pile.

- Moviemakers with a big hit tend to repeat the winning idea in their next film, *just like* authors who use a successful plot over and over.

- The printing press greatly changed the way people learned news and ideas. *In a similar manner,* the Internet has revolutionized the way in which people obtain information.

PRACTICE 3

Complete each sentence with a suitable comparison word or phrase from the box on the previous page. Try to use a variety of transitions.   *Answers may vary.*

1. Lighting a cigarette in a darkened theater will not win you any friends. _____Similarly_____, talking out loud with your movie partner will soon make people scowl in your direction.

2. _____Just like_____ an athlete in training, the mind of a reader grows stronger with practice.

3. Spicy foods make me very thirsty. Believe it or not, ice cream affects me _____in the same way_____.

4. The Amish people farm their land _____as_____ their 18th-century relatives did, without benefit of gasoline-powered tractors or other modern equipment.

5. _____Just as_____ rats become hostile when they live in a crowded cage, humans become aggressive in crowded conditions.

Words That Show Contrast

Put a check (✓) beside the item that is easier to understand:

____   A roller coaster scares many people. They love riding on it.

_✓_   Even though a roller coaster scares many people, they love riding on it.

In the first item, the two sentences seem to contradict each other. We want to ask, "Do people like a roller coaster, or don't they?" In the second item, the phrase *even though* makes clear the relationship between the two ideas: In spite of the fact that a roller coaster is scary, people still love riding on it. *Even though* and other words and phrases like it are contrast words.

"Smoking may kill me. On the other hand, the non-smokers
are inside working themselves to death."

Contrast words show that things *differ* in one or more ways. In the above cartoon, the speaker is contrasting two possible ways to die.

Here are some common words that show contrast:

Contrast Words

but	instead	still	even though
yet	in contrast	as opposed to	different (ly)
however	on the other hand	in spite of	differs from
although	on the contrary	despite	unlike
nevertheless	converse (ly)	rather than	while

Examples

The above cartoon and the sentences that follow contain contrast words. Notice how these words signal that one idea is *different from* another idea.

- People used to think that getting chilled would lead to catching a cold. *However,* getting chilled has nothing to do with getting sick.

- Skunks are unpopular creatures, *yet* they eat lots of mice and bugs and don't spray unless they feel threatened.

- Some people look upon eating as something to be done quickly so they can get on to better things. *In contrast,* others think eating *is* one of the better things.

PRACTICE 4

Complete each sentence with a suitable contrast word or phrase from the box on the previous page. Try to use a variety of transitions.   *Answers may vary.*

1. Most of us could live without food for a month; _____however_____, we need two quarts of water a day to survive.

2. _____Although_____ going up a ladder is easy, looking down from the top step can be difficult.

3. At first we were planning on spending our vacation at a campground, _____but_____ now we've decided to save money by relaxing at home.

4. Paula was not satisfied with her paper _____despite_____ the fact that she had already written five drafts.

5. We use seventeen muscles to smile. _____In contrast_____, we have to use forty-three muscles to frown.

Comparison and contrast transitions are often used in paragraphs organized in the comparison and/or contrast pattern.

The Comparison and/or Contrast Pattern

To get a sense of the comparison and/or contrast pattern, try to arrange the following sentences in an order that makes sense. Put a *1* in front of the sentence that should come first, a *2* in front of the sentence that comes next, and a *3* in front of the sentence that should be last. The result will be a short paragraph.

_3_ Yet the large, hairy tarantula is relatively harmless, while the small brown recluse is dangerously poisonous.

_1_ The tarantula and the brown recluse are more different than they are similar.

_2_ It's true that both spiders are alike in inspiring a great deal of fear.

The first sentence of this paragraph is the general one, the one with the main idea: "The tarantula and the brown recluse are more different than they are similar." The words *similar* and *different* suggest a comparison and/or contrast pattern of organization. The comparison word *alike* and the contrast words *yet* and *while* in the other two sentences show that the spiders are indeed being compared *and* contrasted: "It's true that both spiders are alike in inspiring a great deal of fear. Yet the large, hairy tarantula is relatively harmless, while the small brown recluse is dangerously poisonous."

The comparison-contrast pattern shows how two things are alike or how they are different, or both. When things are compared, their similarities are pointed out; when they are contrasted, their differences are discussed. (The tarantula and the brown recluse spider are alike in the fear they inspire; they are different in the effects of their bites, as well as in their appearance.)

You will find authors using a **comparison** pattern to show how two things are alike and a **contrast** pattern to show how they are different. Sometimes an author will compare and contrast in the same paragraph, pointing out both similarities and differences between two things. Comparison or contrast transitions will signal what an author is doing.

✔ *Check Your Understanding*

In the following paragraph, the main idea is stated in the first sentence. As is often the case, the main idea suggests a paragraph's pattern of organization. Here the transition *differently* is a hint that the paragraph may be organized in a comparison and/or contrast pattern. Read the paragraph and answer the questions below. Then read the explanation that follows.

> ¹In middle age, men and women often view life very differently, especially if they are couples who have led traditional lives. ²By middle age, the husband is often comfortable in his position at work and has given up any dreams of advancing further. ³He may then become more family-oriented. ⁴In contrast, once the children are grown, the wife may find herself free to explore interests and develop abilities she has had no time for in the previous fifteen or twenty years. ⁵Unlike her husband, she may be more interested in non-family activities than she was before.

1. Is this paragraph comparing, contrasting, or both? ___Contrasting___

2. What two things are being compared and/or contrasted? _Views of_
   ___traditional middle-aged men and women___

3. What three comparison or contrast transition words or phrases are used in the paragraph? _____differently, In contrast, Unlike_____

To the Instructor: In this exercise and the practices and tests that follow, the transition words that introduce major details are underlined in this *Instructor's Edition.*

Explanation

This paragraph is only contrasting, not comparing—it discusses only differences, not similarities. The two things being contrasted are the views of traditional middle-aged men and women. The transition words or phrases that show contrast are *differently, In contrast,* and *Unlike.*

PRACTICE 5

A. The following passage uses the pattern of either comparison or contrast. Read the passage and answer the questions that follow.

> [1]Employment policies are quite <u>different</u> in Japan and the United States. [2]In Japan, teamwork is an essential part of hiring and promotion. [3]College graduates who join a corporation are all paid about the same starting salary. [4]To learn about the company's various departments, they are rotated as a team through the organization. [5]They are also promoted as a team. [6]Only in later years are individuals singled out for recognition. [7]When there is an opening in the firm, outsiders are not even considered.
>
> [8]In the United States, <u>on the other hand</u>, an employee is hired on the basis of what the firm thinks that individual can contribute. [9]Employees try to outperform others, and they strive for raises and promotions as signs of personal success. [10]The individual's loyalty is to himself or herself, not to the company. [11]Outsiders are considered for openings in U.S. firms.   *Wording of answers may vary.*

Check (✓) the pattern which is used in this passage:

___ Comparison   The first paragraph introduces the topic and describes Japanese employment policies. The second paragraph

✓ Contrast   describes the contrasting U.S. practices.

What two things are being compared or contrasted?

1. Japanese employment practices   2. U.S. employment practices

B. The following paragraph uses the pattern of either comparison or contrast. Read the passage and then answer the questions and complete the outline that follows.

> [1]Among the school experiences new to young children is the regimented environment. [2]At home, children may have been able to do what they wanted when they wanted to do it. [3]<u>But</u> in school, they are given a set time for talking, working, playing, eating, and even going to the toilet. [4]Another source of anxiety may be the public method of discipline that some teachers use. [5]<u>Whereas</u> at home children are scolded in private, in school they may be held up to embarrassment in front of their peers. [6]"Mandy," the teacher may say, "why are you the only one in

the class who didn't do your homework?" ⁷Or, "Scott, why are you the only one who can't work quietly at your seat?" ⁸Last, a child may be scared by the competitive atmosphere of the school. ⁹At home, one hopes, such competition for attention is minimal. ¹⁰In school, <u>however</u>, children may vie for the teacher's approving glance or tone of voice, or for stars on a paper, or for favored seats in the front row.

Check (✓) the pattern which is used in this passage:

___   Comparison

_✓_   Contrast

Complete the following map of the paragraph:

There are three differences between _school_ and _home_.

1. Regimentation in school	Free movement at home
2. Public discipline in school	Private scolding at home
3. Much competition in school	Minimal competition at home

Sentences 1–3 contrast regimented school environment with the less regimented home setting.
Sentences 4–7 contrast school discipline with home discipline.
Sentences 8–10 contrast school competition with home competition.

3 Cause and Effect

Words That Show Cause and Effect

Put a check (✓) beside the item that is easier to understand:

____   The paint has worn off the wooden siding. Fungus has begun to grow on it.

_✓_   Because the paint has worn off the wooden siding, fungus has begun to grow on it.

In the first item, it seems the author is simply listing two things that have happened to the wooden siding. The word *because* in the second item makes clear the relationship between the two ideas—the protective paint wore off, and for this reason, the fungus was able to grow. *Because* and words like it are cause and effect words.

© 2007 by Randy Glasbergen.
www.glasbergen.com

GLASBERGEN

"It's an adjustable mortgage. If interest rates go up,
then your payment increases. If interest rates go down,
then your payment increases."

Cause and effect words signal that the author is explaining *the reason why* something happened or *the result* of something happening. In the cartoon above, the applicant is told that the result of interest rates going up or down will, unfortunately for him, be the same: Either way, his mortgage payment will go up!

Here are some common words that show cause and effect:

Cause and Effect Words

therefore	so	result	because (of)
thus	as a result	effect	reason
as a consequence	results in	cause	explanation
consequently	leads to	if . . . then	accordingly
due to	since	affect	

Examples

The above cartoon and the sentences that follow contain cause and effect words. Notice how these words introduce a *reason* for something or the *result* of something.

- My sister became a vegetarian *because* she doesn't want to eat anything that had a mother.

- *If* the weather gets too humid, *then* the wooden doors in our house swell up and begin to stick.

- At one time in history, birth records were not kept for ordinary people. *As a result,* the only birthday parties given were for kings, queens, and other royalty.

PRACTICE 6

Complete each sentence with a suitable cause and effect word or phrase from the box on the previous page. Try to use a variety of transitions.   *Answers may vary.*

1. _____*Because*_____ property taxes in the city have gone sky-high, many corporations are moving to the suburbs.

2. Maria's resumé is impressive; _____*as a result*_____, she has already had several job interviews.

3. My family is full of great Italian cooks, _____*so*_____ canned ravioli tastes like cardboard to me.

4. _____*Since*_____ car dealers have a monthly quota of cars to sell, they are more likely to offer good deals near the end of a month.

5. Some zoo animals have not learned how to be good parents. _____*Therefore*_____, baby animals are sometimes brought up in zoo nurseries and even in private homes.

Cause and effect transitions often signal the cause and effect pattern of organization.

The Cause and Effect Pattern

To get a sense of the cause and effect pattern, try to arrange the following sentences in an order that makes sense. Put a *1* in front of the sentence that should come first, a *2* in front of the sentence that comes next, and a *3* in front of the sentence that should be last. The result will be a short paragraph.

_2_ Growing up without parents around resulted in the monkeys drinking enormous amounts of alcohol.

_1_ A study of monkeys suggests two factors may lead to alcoholism.

_3_ Low levels of serotonin in the brain also caused the monkeys to drink more.

As the words *resulted in, lead to,* and *caused* suggest, this paragraph is organized in a cause and effect pattern. The paragraph begins with the general idea: "A study of monkeys suggests two factors may lead to alcoholism." Next come two causes: "Growing up without parents around resulted in the monkeys drinking enormous amounts of alcohol. Low levels of serotonin in the brain also caused the monkeys to drink more."

Note that even in the cause and effect pattern—or any other pattern—addition words may be used to introduce points and show their order. The last sentence of the above paragraph, for example, includes the word *also,* showing that a second point is being added to the first: "Low levels of serotonin in the brain also caused the monkeys to drink more."

Information in a cause and effect pattern addresses the questions "Why does a behavior or event happen?" and/or "What are the results of a behavior or event?" An author may then discuss causes, or effects, or both causes and effects.

Authors usually don't just tell what happened; they try to explain both what happened and why. A textbook section on the sinking of the ship *Titanic,* for example, would be incomplete if it did not include the cause of the disaster—going at a high speed, the ship collided with an iceberg. Or if the number of homeless families in the country increases, journalists will not simply report the increase. They would also explore the reasons for and effects of that increase.

✓ Check Your Understanding

Read the paragraph below and see if you can answer the questions about cause and effect that follow. Then read the explanation to see how you did.

¹Even the best listeners are unable to listen carefully to everything they hear. ²One reason is the overload of messages we encounter each day. ³Besides the numerous hours we spend hearing others speak, we may spend several more hours listening to the radio or television. ⁴It just isn't possible to avoid having our attention wander at least part of this time. ⁵Another cause of poor listening is a preoccupation with personal concerns. ⁶A romance gone sour or a good grade on a test may take prominence in our mind even as someone is speaking to us. ⁷In addition, being surrounded by noise may result in poor listening. ⁸For example, many voices at a noisy party or the sound of traffic may make it difficult for us to hear everything that is being said.

1. What are the three causes described in this paragraph?
   A. Message overload
   B. Preoccupation with personal concerns
   C. Being surrounded by noise

2. The three causes lead to what result or effect? _____
    Poor listening
    _____

3. What three cause and effect signal words or phrases are used?
    reason, cause, result in
    _____

Explanation

The paragraph begins with the main idea: "The best listeners are unable to listen carefully to everything they hear." That point is then supported by three reasons, or causes. The first is the overload of messages we hear each day. The second reason is our preoccupation with personal concerns. The third cause given is that we are at times surrounded by interfering noise. The effect is stated in the main idea—our inability to listen carefully to everything we hear. The cause and effect signals used are *reason, cause,* and *result in.*

PRACTICE 7

A. Read the paragraph below, looking for one cause and three main effects (the three major details). Then complete the diagram that follows.   *Wording of answers may vary.*

The paragraph describes three health problems caused by stress. Each is signaled by a cause and effect word.

¹Chronic stress can lead to many serious health problems. ²One effect of stress is painful muscle tension. ³Headaches, backaches and sore shoulders are direct consequences of this tension. ⁴Another result of long-term exposure to stress is a weakening of the body's immune system. ⁵The body is then more vulnerable to infection and diseases, and normal colds or minor infections are more likely to develop into serious illnesses. ⁶Third, stress can result in psychological disorders, including depression, anxiety, phobias, and addictions. ⁷In one way or another, our bodies will eventually protest a prolonged exposure to stressful situations.

(Cause)

Chronic stress

(Effect)
Painful muscle tension

(Effect)
Weakening of body's immune system

(Effect)
Psychological disorders

B. Read the paragraph below, looking for the one effect and the four causes. Then complete the outline that follows.   *Wording of answers may vary.*

¹Why do people daydream? ²One <u>reason</u> is boring jobs that are tolerable only when workers imagine themselves doing something else. ³Deprivation also <u>leads to</u> daydreaming. ⁴During World War II, conscientious objectors who volunteered to go on semistarvation diets for six months fantasized about food. ⁵Some even hung enticing pictures of foods on their walls to give themselves something to dream about. ⁶Another <u>reason</u> people daydream is to discharge hostile feelings. ⁷For example, an angry student may imagine dropping his instructor out of a classroom window, helping him to laugh at and dismiss his annoyance with her. ⁸Last, some people fantasize as a way to plan for the future so that by the time they face future situations, they will know what to say and how to act.

The first three causes of daydreaming are each signaled by a cause and effect word.

Main idea *(the effect):* ____There are several reasons people daydream.____

Major supporting details *(the causes):*

1. ___To tolerate boring jobs___

2. ___To endure deprivation___

3. ___To discharge hostile feelings___

4. ___To plan for the future___

A Note on Main Ideas and Patterns of Organization

Remember that a paragraph's main idea often indicates its pattern of organization. For example, here is the main idea of a paragraph you worked on earlier:

In middle age, men and women often view life very differently, especially if they are couples who have led traditional lives.

This sentence may have made you expect that the paragraph would go on to contrast the views of middle-aged men and women. If so, the paragraph would be organized according to the comparison and/or contrast pattern.

✓ Check Your Understanding

Finding the main idea of a paragraph may help you decide on its pattern of organization. Try, for instance, to guess the pattern of paragraphs with these main ideas:

The development of the automobile in the early twentieth century <u>resulted in</u> a number of changes in U.S. society.

Pattern: ____cause and effect____

A franchise is a business arrangement in which an individual obtains rights from a larger company to sell a well-known product or service.

Pattern: _definition and example_

Explanation

In the first sentence, the words *resulted in* suggest that the paragraph will have a cause and effect pattern, discussing the social effects of the introduction of the automobile. In the second sentence, the word *franchise* is defined, suggesting that the paragraph will follow a definition and example pattern, with examples of various franchises to follow.

PRACTICE 8

Most of the main ideas below come from college textbooks. In the space provided, write the letter of the pattern of organization that each suggests.

__A__ 1. A communicable disease is one in which an infectious organism is usually passed from person to person.
   A. Definition and example   B. Comparison and/or contrast   C. Cause and effect

   Term defined: communicable disease.

__C__ 2. Following are three reasons for the existence of stereotypes.
   A. Definition and example   B. Comparison and/or contrast   C. Cause and effect

   Cause and effect word: reasons.
   Stereotypes are the effect; three causes will be given.

__B__ 3. College students in their thirties and forties face many of the same pressures as younger students, but they are often better equipped to withstand these pressures.
   A. Definition and example   B. Comparison and/or contrast   C. Cause and effect

   Contrast word: *but.* Older and younger college students will be contrasted.

__C__ 4. A growing concern with health has affected the way that many Americans eat.
   A. Definition and example   B. Comparison and/or contrast   C. Cause and effect

   Cause and effect word: affected.
   Cause: growing health concern. *Effect:* Americans' eating habits.

__A__ 5. A mission statement is an organization's declaration of how it will achieve its purpose.
   A. Definition and example   B. Comparison and/or contrast   C. Cause and effect

   Term defined: mission statement.

_B_ 6. Americans typically think of men as naturally better suited to perform the most strenuous physical labor, but not all peoples of the world hold the same view.

Contrast word: *but.* Americans' and other peoples' views will be contrasted.

A. Definition and example
B. Comparison and/or contrast
C. Cause and effect

_C_ 7. Because of economic pressures, increasing numbers of people are seeking housing assistance.

A. Definition and example
B. Comparison and/or contrast
C. Cause and effect

Cause and effect word: *because of.* *Cause:* economic pressures. *Effect:* more people seek housing assistance.

_A_ 8. Nonverbal communication behaviors are those bodily actions and vocal qualities that accompany a verbal message and have agreed-upon interpretations within a culture.   Term defined: *Nonverbal communication.*

A. Definition and example
B. Comparison and/or contrast
C. Cause and effect

_C_ 9. There are several possible explanations for why retail prices often end on certain numbers.

Cause and effect word: *explanations.* Ending numbers in retail prices are the effect; several causes will be given.

A. Definition and example
B. Comparison and/or contrast
C. Cause and effect

_B_ 10. First-year college students who expect to do well in school need to learn quickly the right and wrong ways of preparing for exams.

A. Definition and example
B. Comparison and/or contrast
C. Cause and effect

The right way to prepare for exams and the wrong way will be contrasted.

A Final Point

Keep in mind that a passage may often be made up of more than one pattern of organization. For instance, the paragraph in this chapter about acrophobia (the unreasonable fear of high places) uses the definition and example pattern. But the example itself—a series of events on one evening in Sally Maxwell's life—uses a time order pattern.

Or consider the following passage:

[1]Have you ever had the experience of recognizing someone's face but not being able to recall his or her name? [2]The reason is that the information about that person is split up and stored in the two different sides of your brain, and each side has its own way of thinking and remembering. [3]Recalling someone's face is the task of the right side of your brain, which understands whole things at once and is responsible for visualizing, recognizing similarities, and supplying intuitions. [4]This side of your brain provides insights that are hard to put into words. [5]The left side of your brain deals with language and stores words themselves, including the person's name that you have temporarily forgotten. [6]This is the side responsible for speaking, reading, writing, and listening.

The paragraph uses, in part, a cause and effect pattern, explaining the reason why we may recognize a face but not recall a name. It also uses a contrast pattern, explaining the different functions of the two sides of the brain. Pages 265–272 offer practice on passages with more than one pattern of organization.

CHAPTER REVIEW

In this chapter, you learned about three kinds of relationships that authors use to make their ideas clear:

- ● **Definitions and examples**
  - — To help readers understand the important ideas and terms in a subject, textbook authors often take time to include key definitions (often setting them off in *italic* or **boldface**) and examples of those definitions. When reading a textbook, it is usually a good idea to mark off both definitions and examples.
  - — Transition words that signal the definition and example pattern include *for example, for instance, to illustrate,* and *such as.*

- ● **Comparison and/or contrast**
  - — Authors often discuss how two things are alike or how they are different, or both.
  - — Transition words that signal comparisons include *alike* and *similar.*
  - — Transition words that signal contrasts include *but, however,* and *in contrast.*

- ● **Cause and effect**
  - — Authors often discuss the reasons why something happens or the effects of something that has happened.
  - — Transition words that signal causes include *reason* and *because.*
  - — Transition words that signal effects include *therefore, consequently,* and *as a result.*

Note that pages 265–272 list and offer practice in all the transitions and patterns of organization you have studied in "Relationships I" and "Relationships II."

The next chapter—Chapter 7—will sharpen your ability to make inferences in reading.

On the Web: If you are using this book in class, you can visit our website for additional practice in in understanding relationships that involve examples, comparison or contrast, and cause and effect. Go to **www.townsendpress.com** and click on "Online Exercises."

 REVIEW TEST 1

To review what you've learned in this chapter, fill in the blanks or choose the best answer for the following items.

1. When textbook authors provide a definition of a term, they are also likely to provide one or more _____*examples*_____ to help make that definition clear.

   See page 224.

2. A(n) _____*comparison*_____ transition signals that two things are alike in some way.

   See page 227.

3. A(n) _____*contrast*_____ transition signals that two things are different in some way.

   See page 229.

___C___ 4. A cause and effect paragraph might be about

   A. reasons.
   B. results.
   C. reasons and/or results.

   See page 234.

___C___ 5. The pattern of organization of a paragraph may be suggested by

   A. the transitions it contains.
   B. its topic sentence.
   C. both A and B.

   See page 238 and 241.

REVIEW TEST 2

A. Fill in each blank with one of the words or phrases in the box. Use each transition once. Then write the letter of the transition in the space provided.

A. because	B. effects	C. however
D. just like	E. such as	

___B___ 1. Strong emotions can have negative _____*effects*_____ on digestion.

___D___ 2. Mariah claims her teenage brother is _____*just like*_____ a cockroach—he enjoys going out at night and eating junk food.

_C_ 3. An adult elephant weighs about 12,000 pounds. _____However_____, its eyes are almost exactly the size of a human's.

_A_ 4. _____Because_____ Ray's father and grandfather have both become bald, Ray expects to lose his hair, too.

_E_ 5. For people who wish to work with children, there are many career choices, _____such as_____ teaching, school counseling, and working at a day-care center.

B. Below are the beginnings of five passages. Label each one with the letter of its pattern of organization. (You may find it helpful to underline the transition or transitions in each item.)

> **A** Definition and example
> **B** Comparison and/or contrast
> **C** Cause and effect

_B_ 6. ¹Television news stories resemble newspaper articles in being timely and appealing to a wide audience. ²However, TV coverage tends to be more superficial, emphasizing the visual aspects of a story rather than important background issues. . . .   Compares and contrasts television news stories with newspaper articles.

_C_ 7. ¹Many drivers take to the roads in July and August, when families traditionally go on vacation. ²As a result, oil companies often raise the price of gasoline during the summer months. . . .
> *Cause:* drivers take to roads. *Effect:* oil companies raise gasoline prices.

_A_ 8. ¹In a mystery story, the term *red herring* refers to a false or misleading clue meant to deceive the reader. ²One famous red herring is Sherlock Holmes's farewell note to Dr. Watson in "The Final Problem," which leads the reader to believe Holmes has fallen to his death. . . .
> Sentence 1 defines the term *red herring.* Sentence 2 gives an example.

_C_ 9. ¹One type of hearing loss is caused by damage to the nerve cells in the inner ear. ²The damage may be the result of loud noises, allergic reactions to medicines, or a hard blow to the ear or skull. ³Certain diseases can also cause damage to the nerve cells of the inner ear. . . .
> *Cause 1:* damage to nerve cells. *Effect 1:* hearing loss. *Cause 2a:* loud noises, etc. *Cause 2b:* diseases. *Effect 2:* damage to nerve cells.

_A_ 10. ¹A complementary relationship is one in which the distribution of power is unequal. ²One partner says, "Let's go to a movie tonight," and the other says, "Sure." ³The boss asks several employees to work overtime, and they all agree. . . .
> Sentence 1 defines the term *complementary relationship.* Sentences 2 and 3 give examples.

REVIEW TEST 3

Read each paragraph and answer the questions that follow.

A.   ¹Pessimists have long had a poor image as sourpusses and doomsayers, but a concept called "defensive pessimism" is beginning to be recognized as a useful, helpful attitude. ²Defensive pessimism means acting positively—taking specific steps—to reduce the anxiety and stress of expecting the worst. ³For instance, taking the time to back up important files eliminates worries about computer crashes, viruses, and mistakes that can wipe out days or months of work. ⁴Diversifying one's savings and investments eliminates the fear of being financially ruined if a company in which one holds too much stock goes bankrupt. ⁵And rather than worry about being arrested for speeding or jailed for tax evasion, for example, the defensive pessimist drives within the speed limit and pays taxes honestly.

_A_   1. The main pattern of organization of the paragraph is
        A. definition and example.
        B. cause and effect.
        C. comparison and/or contrast.

        2. One transition that signals the pattern of organization of this paragraph
            is _____ *Either of the following:* For instance, for example _____.

            > The term *defensive pessimism* is defined in sentence 2. Sentences 3–5 give three examples of the term, two of which are signaled by illustration words.

B.   ¹The three most common non-prescription pain relievers are aspirin, acetaminophen, and ibuprofen. ²They are alike in inhibiting the production of prostaglandins in the body, which are hormone-like substances that trigger pain, inflammation, and fever. ³But while aspirin and ibuprofen can reduce all three symptoms, acetaminophen does not reduce inflammation. ⁴Aspirin is considered to have the greatest number of uses but also has the greatest number of side effects, including allergic reactions, stomach upset, and bleeding. ⁵In contrast, ibuprofen generally has fewer side effects than aspirin. ⁶Acetaminophen has the fewest side effects; its only drawback is that it is probably the least effective of the three pain killers.

_C_   3. The main pattern of organization of the paragraph is
        A. definition and example.
        B. cause and effect.
        C. comparison and/or contrast.

        4. One transition that signals the pattern of organization of this paragraph
            is _____ *Any of the following:* alike, But, while, In contrast _____.

            > The paragraph compares the three pain relievers in sentence 2 and contrasts them in sentences 3–6.

C.   ¹Alternate freezing and thawing is one of the most important processes of mechanical weathering. ²Water has the unique property of expanding about 9 percent as it freezes. ³This increase in volume occurs <u>because</u> as water solidifies, the water molecules arrange themselves into a very open crystalline structure. ⁴<u>As a result</u>, when water freezes, it exerts a tremendous outward force. ⁵In nature, water works its way into cracks or voids in rock. ⁶When the water then freezes and expands, the <u>effect</u> is to break the rock into angular fragments.

_B_   5. The main pattern of organization of the paragraph is
    A. definition and example.
    B. cause and effect.
    C. comparison and/or contrast.

   6. One transition that signals the pattern of organization of this paragraph
       is _____Any of the following: because, As a result, effect_____.

                    The paragraph describes three causes and three effects.

D.   ¹Corporate welfare refers to financial aid given by the government to corporations, especially when the handout is considered unjust. ²The government aid to Borden Chemicals in Louisiana is a good <u>example</u>. ³The company buried hazardous wastes without a permit and released hazardous chemicals so thick that to protect drivers, the police sometimes shut down the highway that runs near the plant. ⁴Borden even contaminated the groundwater beneath its plant, threatening the aquifer that provides drinking water for residents of Louisiana and Texas. ⁵Borden's pollution has cost the company a hefty $7 million, but thanks to corporate welfare, the company didn't make out so badly. ⁶With $15 million in reduced and canceled property taxes, Borden has enjoyed a net gain of $8 million.

_A_   7. The main pattern of organization of the paragraph is
    A. definition and example.
    B. cause and effect.
    C. comparison and/or contrast.

   8. The transition that signals the pattern of organization of this paragraph
       is _____example_____.

                    Sentence 1 defines *corporate welfare*. Sentences 2–6 give an example.

E.   ¹The use of fire by prehistoric people probably <u>affected</u> wildlife both intentionally and unintentionally. ²In all likelihood, early people used fire to drive game toward waiting hunters. ³Later, new plant growth in the burned areas would attract more wild animals. ⁴In addition, accidental fires must have occurred frequently. ⁵<u>Because</u> prehistoric people had trouble starting fires, they would have kept burning embers on hand. ⁶The <u>result</u> must have been widespread accidental fires, especially in dry areas. ⁷Certainly, these fires also would have greatly altered the habitat for wildlife.

_B_   9.   The main pattern of organization of the paragraph is
      A. definition and example.
      B. cause and effect.
      C. comparison and/or contrast.

    10.   One transition that signals the pattern of organization of this paragraph
        is _____ *Any of the following: affected, Because, result* _____.

> *Cause:* prehistoric people's use of fire. *Effect 1:* new plant growth attracted more animals. *Effect 2:* habitat for wildlife altered.

REVIEW TEST 4

Here is a chance to apply your understanding of relationships to a full-length reading—an article about stress in college.

To help you continue to strengthen your skills, the reading is followed by questions not only on what you've learned in this chapter but also on what you've learned in previous chapters.

Words to Watch

Below are some words in the reading that do not have strong context support. Each word is followed by the number of the paragraph in which it appears and its meaning there. These words are indicated in the article by a small circle (°).

aptitude (4): natural ability
anorexia (6): an abnormal lack of appetite which can result in serious
        illness or death
bulimia (6): an abnormal craving for food that leads to heavy eating and
        then intentional vomiting
stability (9): steadiness
bombarded (9): attacked
devastating (9): very destructive
magnitude (11): great importance
meditation (13): a relaxation technique involving mental concentration
relevant (14): related to the issue at hand

STUDENTS IN SHOCK

John Kellmayer

1   If you feel overwhelmed by your college experiences, you are not alone— many of today's college students are suffering from a form of shock. Going to college has always had its ups and downs, but today the "downs" of the college experience are more numerous and difficult, a fact that the schools are responding to with increased support services.

2   Lisa is a good example of a student in shock. She is an attractive, intelligent twenty-year-old college junior at a state university. Having been a straight-A student in high school and a member of the basketball and softball teams there, she remembers her high school days with fondness. Lisa was popular then and had a steady boyfriend for the last two years of school.

3   Now, only three years later, Lisa is miserable. She has changed her major four times already and is forced to hold down two part-time jobs in order to pay her tuition. She suffers from sleeping and eating disorders and believes she has no close friends. Sometimes she bursts out crying for no apparent reason. On more than one occasion, she has considered taking her own life.

4   Dan, too, suffers from student shock. He is nineteen and a freshman at a local community college. He began college as an accounting major but hated that field. So he switched to computer programming because he heard the job prospects were excellent in that area. Unfortunately, he discovered that he had little aptitude° for programming and changed majors again, this time to psychology. He likes psychology but has heard horror stories about the difficulty of finding a job in that field without a graduate degree. Now he's considering switching majors again. To help pay for school, Dan works nights and weekends as a sales clerk at K-Mart. He doesn't get along with his boss, but since he needs the money, Dan feels he has no choice except to stay on the job. A few months ago, his girlfriend of a year and a half broke up with him.

5   Not surprisingly, Dan has started to suffer from depression and migraine headaches. He believes that in spite of all his hard work, he just isn't getting anywhere. He can't remember ever being this unhappy. A few times he considered talking to somebody in the college psychological counseling center. He rejected that idea, though, because he doesn't want people to think there's something wrong with him.

6   What is happening to Lisa and Dan happens to millions of college students each year. That means roughly one-quarter of the student population at any time will suffer from symptoms of student shock. Of that group, almost half will experience depression intense enough to warrant professional help. At schools across the country, psychological counselors are booked up months in advance. Stress-related problems

such as anxiety, migraine headaches, insomnia, anorexia°, and bulimia° are epidemic on college campuses.

7   Suicide rates and self-inflicted injuries among college students are higher now than at any other time in history. The suicide rate among college youth is 50 percent higher than among nonstudents of the same age. It is estimated that each year more than 500 college students take their own lives.

8   College health officials believe that these reported problems represent only the tip of the iceberg. They fear that most students, like Lisa and Dan, suffer in silence.

9   There are three reasons today's college students are suffering more than those in earlier generations. First is a weakening family support structure. The transition from high school to college has always been difficult, but in the past there was more family support to help students get through it. Today, with divorce rates at a historical high and many parents experiencing their own psychological difficulties, the traditional family is not always available for guidance and support. And when students who do not find stability° at home are bombarded° with numerous new and stressful experiences, the results can be devastating°.

10   Another problem college students face is financial pressure. In the last decade tuition costs have skyrocketed—up about 66 percent at public colleges and 90 percent at private schools. For students living away from home, costs range from eight thousand dollars to as much as twenty thousand a year and more. And at the same time that tuition costs have been rising dramatically, there has been a cutback in federal aid to students. College loans are now much harder to obtain and are available only at near-market interest rates. Consequently, most college students must work at least part-time. And for some students, the pressure to do well in school while holding down a job is too much to handle.

11   A final cause of student shock is the large selection of majors available. Because of the magnitude° and difficulty of choosing a major, college can prove a time of great indecision. Many students switch majors, some a number of times. As a result, it is becoming commonplace to take five or six years to get a degree. It can be depressing to students not only to have taken courses that don't count toward a degree but also to be faced with

the added tuition costs. In some cases these costs become so high that they force students to drop out of college.

12   While there is no magic cure-all for student shock, colleges have begun to recognize the problem and are trying in a number of ways to help students cope with the pressures they face. For one thing, many colleges are upgrading their psychological counseling centers to handle the greater demand for services. Additional staff is being hired, and experts are doing research to learn more about the psychological problems of college students. Some schools even advertise these services in student newspapers and on campus radio stations. Also, juniors and seniors are being trained as peer counselors. These peer counselors may be able to act as a first line of defense in the battle for students' well-being by spotting and helping to solve problems before they become too big for students to handle.

13   In addition, stress-management workshops have become common on college campuses. At these workshops, instructors teach students various techniques they can use to deal with stress, including biofeedback, meditation°, and exercise.

14   Finally, many schools are improving their vocational counseling services. By giving students more relevant° information about possible majors and career choices, colleges can lessen the anxiety and indecision often associated with choosing a major.

15   If you ever feel that you're "in shock," remember that your experience is not unique. Try to put things in perspective. Certainly, the end of a romance or failing an exam is not an event to look forward to. But realize that rejection and failure happen to everyone sooner or later. And don't be reluctant to talk to somebody about your problems. The useful services available on campus won't help you if you don't take advantage of them.

Reading Comprehension Questions

Vocabulary in Context

_B_   1. In the sentence below, the word *prospects* (prŏs′pĕkts′) means
    A. failures.
    B. possibilities.
    C. candidates.
    D. limitations.

If he switched into the field, it must have been because of the possibilities of getting a good job.

> "So he switched to computer programming because he heard the job prospects were excellent in that area." (Paragraph 4)

_D_   2. In the excerpt below, the word *warrant* (wôr′ənt) means
    A. fight.
    B. have no need for.
    C. get degrees in.
    D. justify.

If the depressions are intense, they would justify seeking professional help.

> "Of that group, almost half will experience depressions intense enough to warrant professional help. At schools across the country, psychological counselors are booked up months in advance." (Paragraph 6)

Central Point and Main Ideas

_B_   3. Which sentence best expresses the central point of the selection?
    A. Going to college is a depressing experience for many students.
    B. College life has become more stressful, so schools are increasing support services.
    C. Lisa and Dan have experienced too much stress at school to enjoy college life.
    D. Colleges should increase their counseling services.

Answer A ignores paragraphs 12–14. C covers only paragraphs 2–5. D is not supported because paragraphs 12–14 say they already are increasing their services.

_A_   4. At times, a main idea may cover more than one paragraph. The main idea of paragraphs 2 and 3 is stated in
    A. the first sentence of paragraph 2.
    B. the second sentence of paragraph 2.
    C. the first sentence of paragraph 3.
    D. the last sentence of paragraph 3.

Answers B, C, and D are supporting details showing that Lisa is in shock.

_A_   5. The main idea of paragraphs 9, 10, and 11 is
    A. stated in the first sentence of paragraph 9.
    B. stated in the first sentence of paragraph 10.
    C. stated in the first sentence of paragraph 11.
    D. unstated.

Paragraphs 9, 10, and 11 each explain one of the three reasons today's students are suffering more.

Supporting Details

_C_ 6. According to the author, the large selection of majors now available
   A. makes for less stability in students' home lives.
   B. helps students get through school more quickly.
   C. makes many students' career choices more difficult.
   D. allows students to end up in careers for which they are especially well suited.

   See paragraph 11.

Transitions

_C_ 7. The sentence below expresses a relationship of
   A. contrast.
   B. cause and effect.
   C. illustration.
   D. addition.

   The words *such as* indicate that examples of stress-related problems will follow.

   "Stress-related problems <u>such as</u> anxiety, migraine headaches, insomnia, anorexia, and bulimia are epidemic on college campuses." (Paragraph 6)

_C_ 8. Read the two sentences below and then answer the question that follows.

   "College loans are now much harder to obtain and are available only at near-market interest rates. <u>Consequently</u>, most college students must work at least part-time." (Paragraph 10)

   Causes: college loans hard to get and expensive. *Effect:* students must work.

   What does the second sentence do?
   A. It adds more detail to the first sentence.
   B. It establishes a time order relationship.
   C. It establishes a cause and effect relationship with the first sentence.
   D. It contrasts how hard it is to obtain college loans now with how easy it used to be to get them.

Patterns of Organization

_B_ 9. Paragraphs 9–11
   A. compare college life as it used to be with college life today.
   B. list reasons that students today are suffering more than those in earlier generations.
   C. contrast college life today with what it used to be like.
   D. provide examples of students who are in shock.

   The words *three reasons* (paragraph 9, first sentence) suggest a list will follow.

_A_ 10. The main pattern of organization of paragraphs 12–14 is
   A. list of items.
   B. comparison and/or contrast.
   C. definition and example.
   D. cause and effect.   The words *a number of ways* (paragraph 12, first sentence) suggest a list will follow. Addition transitions such as *For one thing, Also, In addition,* and *Finally* signal some of the ways listed.

Discussion Questions

1. If you were a peer counselor for Lisa or Dan, what advice might you give her or him?

2. What were—or are—the most stressful parts of college life for you? Explain why. What ways have you found for dealing with that stress?

3. Kellmayer writes that "colleges . . . are trying in a number of ways to help students cope with the pressures they face." What resources does your college offer? Have you tried any of them? How do you think your school could improve the services it offers to help students deal with "student shock"?

4. On the basis of your college experience so far, what one piece of advice would you give to an incoming freshman?

Note: Writing assignments for this selection appear on page 603.

Check Your Performance   **RELATIONSHIPS II**

Activity	Number Right	Points	Score
Review Test 1 (5 items)	_____	× 2 =	_____
Review Test 2 (10 items)	_____	× 3 =	_____
Review Test 3 (10 items)	_____	× 3 =	_____
Review Test 4 (10 items)	_____	× 3 =	_____
		TOTAL SCORE =	_____%

Enter your total score into the **Reading Performance Chart: Review Tests** on the inside back cover.

RELATIONSHIPS II: Mastery Test 1

A. Fill in each blank with an appropriate transition from the box. Use each transition once. Then, in the spaces provided, write the letter of the transition you have chosen.

A. because	B. for example	C. in contrast
D. just as	E. therefore	

Hint: Make sure that each word or phrase that you choose fits smoothly into the flow of the sentence. Test your choices by reading each sentence to yourself.

___B___ 1. ¹Some thieves read the newspapers to find out good times to rob houses. ² _____For example_____ , after reading the obituaries, such thieves may "clean out" a home while the family is at a loved one's funeral.

An example of how thieves use newspapers to find a good time to rob a house.

___D___ 2. ¹Whenever something bad happens to me, my grandmother tries to help me through it. ²When I was depressed after breaking up with my boyfriend, she told me, "_____Just as_____ we must go through the storm before seeing the rainbow, we often must experience sorrow before joy."

Compares experiencing sorrow before feeling joy to going through a storm before seeing the rainbow.

___E___ 3. ¹Honeybees attack just to protect their hives. ² _____Therefore_____ , if you run away from the hive when attacked, the bees will eventually lose interest in you.

Cause: bees want to protect their hive.
Effect: they lose interest if you run away.

___A___ 4. ¹ _____Because_____ there are no clocks in gambling casinos, gamblers can easily lose all sense of time. ²That is clearly what the casino management wants to happen. ³The longer people stay at the tables or in front of the slot machines, the better.

Cause: No clocks in casinos. *Effect:* gamblers lose track of time and continue to gamble.

___C___ 5. ¹Most birds are born in either of two very different states. ²Some are born weak, blind, and usually naked. ³About all they can do for themselves is open their mouths for food. ⁴ _____In contrast_____ , other newborn baby birds are bright-eyed and covered with down. ⁵As soon as their down is dry, they are able to peck at things and run after their parents.

The passage contrasts the two types of newborn birds.

(Continues on next page)

B. Label each item with the letter of its main pattern of organization.

> **A** Definition and example
> **B** Comparison and/or contrast
> **C** Cause and effect

_A_ 6. [1]Phobias are intense, irrational fears that are out of proportion to the actual danger in a situation. [2]For example, people with the fear of open places (agoraphobia) are often reluctant to leave their homes.

> Defines *phobia* (sentence 1) and gives an example (sentence 2).

_C_ 7. [1]Bread made with whole-wheat flour is brown, but not all brown bread is whole-wheat bread. [2]Some manufacturers add molasses or honey to white-flour dough to give it a brown color, and they are allowed to label the product "wheat bread." [3]For this reason, it is important to read the package label before buying.

Cause: the fact that not all brown bread is whole-wheat bread.
Effect: the need to read the package label.

_C_ 8. [1]Prison overcrowding is dangerous because it increases unrest among inmates and produces a climate in which violence is more likely. [2]Riots, escapes, and hostage taking become more of a problem. [3]Prison overcrowding also makes it more difficult for correctional officers and prison administrators to manage the prison. [4]The result is that prisons are more costly to run.

Cause: prison overcrowding.
Effect: Violence is more likely; prisons are more costly to run.

_B_ 9. [1]In the 1890s, most Americans were struggling to reach a middle-class lifestyle. [2]By the 1990s, in contrast, an overwhelming majority had achieved the middle class but were either losing it or struggling to hold on to it. [3]In the 1890s, government responded to the prodding of reform-minded citizens and began to create a framework of rules to control the excesses of giant businesses and to protect the interests of the average citizen. [4]But in the 1990s, that framework of controls on large corporations was steadily dismantled.

> Contrasts the 1890s with the 1990s.

_A_ 10. [1]What sociologist George Ritzer has termed the "McDonaldization of society"—the standardization of everyday life—does not refer just to the robotlike assembly of food. [2]As Ritzer points out, this process is occurring throughout our society—and it is transforming our lives. [3]For instance, shopping malls offer one-stop shopping in controlled environments. [4]Travel agencies offer "package" tours. [5]They will transport middle-class Americans to ten European capitals in fourteen days. [6]All visitors experience the same hotels, restaurants, and other scheduled sites—and no one need fear meeting a "real" native. [7]The newspaper *USA Today* spews out McNews—short, blank, unanalytical pieces that can be digested between gulps of the McShake or the McBurger.

The term *McDonaldization of society* is defined in sentence 1. Sentences 3–7 give three examples.

To the Instructor: In this mastery test and the five mastery tests that follow, the transition words that signal the pattern of organization are underlined in this *Instructor's Edition.*

RELATIONSHIPS II: Mastery Test 2

Read each textbook passage and answer the questions or follow the directions provided.

A. ¹The incomes of middle- and working-class Americans were dealt a severe blow during the 1980s. ²A major reason was a decline in industrial jobs. ³The economy became less devoted to manufacturing goods and more focused on providing services. ⁴Many manufacturing jobs, especially in the steel and auto industries, were transferred from the United States to Third World countries. ⁵As a result, millions of blue-collar workers in the Midwest and Northeast were stranded. ⁶They were forced into much lower-paying jobs with fewer benefits and opportunities for advancement.

_B_ 1. The main pattern of organization of the paragraph is
   A. definition and example.
   B. cause and effect.
   C. comparison and/or contrast.

Cause: the decline in industrial jobs (sentence 2). *Effect:* millions of blue-collar workers forced into low-paying jobs (sentences 5–6).

2. One transition that signals the pattern of organization of this paragraph is _____ *Either of the following: reason, As a result* _____.

B. ¹Boys who mature early physically have a decided advantage over their more slowly maturing peers. ²Early maturers become heroes in sports and leaders in both formal and informal activities. ³Other boys look up to them; girls have crushes on them. ⁴Even adults tend to trust them. ⁵They are more self-confident and independent than other boys. ⁶In contrast, their less mature male peers, with their high-pitched voices and underdeveloped physiques, feel inadequate. ⁷They are weaker at sports and more awkward with girls.

_C_ 3. The main pattern of organization of the paragraph is
   A. definition and example.
   B. cause and effect.
   C. comparison and/or contrast.

Contrasts boys who physically mature earlier with more slowly maturing boys.

4. The transition that signals the pattern of organization of this paragraph is _____ *In contrast* _____.

C. ¹There are often more than two sides to a question, and offering only two choices when more actually exist is called an either-or fallacy. ²For example, the statement "You are either with us or against us" assumes that there is no middle ground. ³Or consider the following conclusion: People opposed to total freedom of speech are really in favor of censorship. ⁴This argument ignores the fact that a person could believe in free speech as well as in laws that prohibit slander or that punish someone for falsely yelling "Fire!" in a crowded theater.

(Continues on next page)

_____A_____ 5. The main pattern of organization of the paragraph is
       A. definition and example.   Defines the term *either-or fallacy*
       B. cause and effect.   and gives two examples.
       C. comparison and/or contrast.

      6. The transition that signals the pattern of organization of this paragraph
        is _____ For example _____.

D. ¹Why does lightning make such a loud sound? ²The answer has to do with the electrical energy it gives off. ³A single bolt may produce as much as 3,750 million kilowatts of electrical energy. ⁴Most of this energy—75 percent—turns into heat, causing the temperature of the surrounding air to rise greatly. ⁵Since heated air expands, the sudden increase in temperature leads to a rapid expansion of the air around the lightning. ⁶And that air expansion causes sound waves—thunder—which can be heard up to eighteen miles away.

_____B_____ 7. The main pattern of organization of the paragraph is
       A. definition and example.   The paragraph describes how
       B. cause and effect.   lightning (the cause) leads to
       C. comparison and/or contrast.   thunder (the effect).

      8. One transition that signals the pattern of organization of this paragraph
        is _____ *Any of the following:* causing, Since, leads to, causes _____.

E. ¹People are different from other primates, but not as different as they might like to think. ²It's true that that there are significant contrasts in size and proportion between humans and other primates. ³And, of course, humans are by far the more intelligent. ⁴Nevertheless, to use chimpanzees as an example, both they and humans have the same muscles and bones, located in almost the same places and working in nearly the same ways. ⁵The internal organs of both animals are also very much alike, as are their blood and other body fluids. ⁶Seen under a microscope, even their genes are strikingly similar.

_____C_____ 9. The main pattern of organization of the paragraph is
       A. definition and example.   The paragraph compares
       B. cause and effect.   and contrasts humans
       C. comparison and/or contrast.   with other primates.

    10. One transition that signals the pattern of organization of this paragraph
       is _____ *Any of the following:* different, not . . . different, contrasts, _____.
                Nevertheless, same, alike, similar

RELATIONSHIPS II: Mastery Test 3

A. (1–4.) Arrange the scrambled sentences below into a logical paragraph by numbering them *1, 2, 3,* and *4* in an order that makes sense. Then, in the space provided, write the letter of the pattern of organization used.

Note that transitions will help you by clarifying the relationships between sentences.

_3_ Also, high tuitions affect the amount of time available for studying; because loans and scholarships are hard to get, many students have to put in numerous hours at work in order to afford school.

_2_ For one thing, it undoubtedly prevents some students from attending college in the first place.

_4_ Finally, those who do manage to get loans know that they must begin their careers with large debts.

_1_ The high cost of college today causes problems for many students in more ways than one.

_C_ 5. The main pattern of organization is
   A. contrast.
   B. comparison.
   C. cause and effect.
   D. definition and example.

Cause: high cost of college. *Effects:* problems for many students. Note that the paragraph presents the problems as a list. The addition words *Also, For one thing,* and *Finally* signal the proper order for the sentences.

B. Read the passages and answer the questions that follow. You may find it helpful to underline transitions as you read.

¹Men and women may interpret women's actions on a date very differently. ²One study found that acts such as speaking in a low voice or smiling were interpreted by men as indicating that the woman was interested in sex. ³Women, in contrast, tended to see the same behaviors as simply friendly. ⁴Drinking with a man, going to the man's apartment, or wearing sexy clothes were all seen by men as indicating a desire for sex, while women regarded these behaviors as appropriate or fashionable.

_C_ 6. The main pattern of organization of the paragraph is
   A. definition and example.
   B. cause and effect.
   C. comparison and/or contrast.

Contrasts men's and women's interpretations of women's actions on a date.

7. One transition that signals the main pattern of organization of this paragraph is _Any of the following: differently, in contrast, while_.

(Continues on next page)

257

¹Mass hysteria is a type of group behavior that involves a widely held and contagious anxiety, usually as a result of a false belief. ²The reaction in part of the country to the 1938 radio broadcast of *The War of the Worlds* is one <u>example</u>. ³This dramatization of Martians landing on Earth was so realistic that people began to panic and flee before the realization set in that they were reacting to a radio play. ⁴The medieval witch-hunts are another good <u>example</u> of mass hysteria. ⁵They were based on the belief that witches were the cause of many problems in late medieval society, including natural disasters and illness. ⁶Those accused of being witches (mainly old women) were tortured until they confessed or they died. ⁷As many as 500,000 people were burned to death by the clergy between the fifteenth and seventeenth centuries.

_D_ 8. The major supporting details of the selection are
   A. definitions.
   B. causes.
   C. comparisons.
   D. examples.

_A_ 9. The main pattern of organization of the paragraph is
   A. definition and example.
   B. cause and effect.
   C. comparison and/or contrast.

10. The transition that signals the main pattern of organization of this paragraph is _____ *example* _____.

> The paragraph defines *mass hysteria* (sentence 1) and gives two examples (sentences 2–3 and 4–7).

RELATIONSHIPS II: Mastery Test 4

A. (1–4.) Arrange the scrambled sentences below into a logical paragraph by numbering them *1, 2, 3,* and *4* in an order that makes sense. Then, in the space provided, write the letter of the main pattern of organization used.

Note that transitions will help you by clarifying the relationships between sentences.

___4___ In contrast, the original Italian story is the gruesome tale of the Princess Talia, who falls into a deep magical sleep in the woods, where she is raped by a nobleman and, later on, gives birth to twins, whom the nobleman's wife tries to have killed and cooked for dinner.

___1___ It is often said that fairy tales, with their heavy doses of terror and violence, are too scary for young children.

___3___ Consider the story of Sleeping Beauty that today's children know, which involves a princess who is put to sleep by a wicked witch and then awakened by the kiss of her true love.

___2___ But today's versions of fairy tales are actually less frightening than the original stories.

___A___ 5. The main pattern of organization is
    A. contrast.
    B. comparison.
    C. cause and effect.
    D. definition and example.

The paragraph contrasts today's versions of fairy tales with the original stories.

B. Read each paragraph and answer the questions that follow.

[1]A small sausage in a bun received the name "hot dog" in 1906 as the result of a cartoonist's poor spelling ability. [2]A sausage vendor, Harry Stevens, sold what he called "dachshund sausages" (named after the short-legged dog) at New York City baseball games. [3]During one of those games, newspaper cartoonist Tad Dorgan was in the audience. [4]He sketched a cartoon of a live dachshund, smeared with mustard and folded into a bun. [5]Not knowing how to spell "dachshund," however, he settled on "dog," giving the cartoon the caption "Get your hot dogs!" [6]Once the cartoon was published in newspapers, readers began demanding their own "hot dogs."

___A___ 6. The main idea is expressed in the
    A. first sentence.
    B. second sentence.
    C. last sentence.

Sentence 1 states the main cause and effect. Sentences 2–6 give the details of the story.

(Continues on next page)

_B_   7. The selection mainly

Cause: cartoonist's
poor spelling ability.
Effect: sausages on
buns came to be
called "hot dogs."

A. defines and illustrates the term "hot dog."

B. gives the reason small sausages are now called hot dogs.

C. contrasts "dachshund sausage" with "hot dog."

8. The transition that signals the main pattern of organization of this
paragraph is _____ result _____.

[1]When a crowd is watching as someone threatens to jump from a building, its behavior seems <u>affected</u> by the time of day. [2]In daylight, the crowd is usually quite quiet, <u>but</u> under the cover of darkness, many individual members will shout encouragement to the person to kill himself or herself. [3]A <u>similar</u> reaction was seen when women college students took part in an experiment where they were asked to press a button to shock other volunteers. [4]When the women pushing the buttons were visible to the victims, they administered only brief shocks. [5]<u>However</u>, when they were allowed to wear gowns and masks that hid their identity, they shocked the volunteers twice as much. [6]Clearly the feeling of being anonymous <u>causes</u> people to engage in antisocial behavior.

_B or C_ 9. One pattern of organization of the selection is

A. definition and example.

B. cause and effect.

C. comparison and/or contrast.

_B or C_ 10. Another pattern of organization of the selection is

A. definition and example.

B. cause and effect.

C. comparison and/or contrast.

> The paragraph discusses the effects of anonymity on people's behavior. It also contrasts the way people behave when they are not anonymous with the way they behave when they are. Cause and effect words—*affected, causes.* Comparison-contrast words—*but, similar, However.*

RELATIONSHIPS II: Mastery Test 5

A. Read the textbook paragraph below. Then answer the question and complete the outline that follows.

> ¹There are several reasons why middle-aged adults are returning to school. ²Some want to learn to do their jobs better. ³College courses can help them improve their job skills and keep up in their fields. ⁴Others return to school because more credits may mean a raise or promotion. ⁵Teachers, for instance, get raises for reaching certain levels of education. ⁶Also, some adults return to the classroom because of interest in a new field, such as telecommunications or computer programming. ⁷Finally, others want to study subjects such as foreign languages, history, or literature for the sake of learning. ⁸Such classes help adults spend their time in more productive and interesting ways and deepen their understanding of themselves and their world.

_____B_____ 1. The organizational patterns of the paragraph are list of items and
- A. definition and example.
- B. cause and effect.
- C. comparison and/or contrast.

2–5. Complete the outline of the paragraph by writing in the four major supporting details.

Main idea: There are several reasons why middle-aged adults are returning to school.

Major supporting details:

Wording of answers may vary.

1. To learn to do their jobs better

2. To earn credits for a raise or promotion

3. To learn a new field

4. To learn for the sake of learning

> The paragraph lists four reasons (causes) that middle-aged adults return to school (the effect). List words: *several reasons*. Addition words: *Others, Also, Finally*. Cause and effect words: *reasons, because,* and *because of.*

(Continues on next page)

B. Read the textbook paragraph below. Then answer the question and complete the map that follows.

> [1]While management styles vary, there are certain factors that separate the good administrator from the poor one. [2]A good manager anticipates problems and prepares for them, but a poor manager is often taken by surprise. [3]The effective administrator makes changes to eliminate repeated problems; the less effective boss deals with one crisis at a time, never seeing patterns of problems. [4]In addition, a good boss delegates work to others, while the poor one prefers to take on one extra task after another rather than train employees to do the work right. [5]The effective administrator is also flexible enough to adapt to changing situations. [6]In contrast, the poor one often clings to the old rules whether or not they apply.

_B_ 6. The organizational patterns of the paragraph are list of items and
    A. definition and example.
    B. comparison and/or contrast.
    C. cause and effect.

7–10. Complete the map of the paragraph by writing in the missing supporting details. *Wording of answers may vary.*

Certain factors separate the good administrator from the poor one.

Good manager	**Poor manager**
1. Anticipates problems	1. Is surprised by problems
2. Eliminates repeat problems	2. Deals with one problem at a time, not noticing repetition
3. Delegates work	3. Takes on extra tasks
4. Is flexible	4. Clings to old rules

The paragraph lists the contrasting factors that separate the good administrator from the poor one. List words: *certain factors*. Addition words: *In addition* and *also*. Contrast words: *While*, *but*, and *In contrast*.

RELATIONSHIPS II: Mastery Test 6

A. Read the textbook paragraph below. Then answer the question and complete the outline that follows.

> ¹One researcher has identified <u>five basic causes</u> of frustration above and beyond daily hassles. ²<u>To begin with</u>, delays are hard for us to accept <u>because</u> our culture stresses the value of time. ³Anyone who has been caught in a traffic jam is familiar with the frustration of delay. ⁴Lack of resources is <u>another</u> <u>cause</u> of frustration, especially to low-income Americans, who cannot afford the new cars or vacations that TV programs and magazine articles would have us believe everyone must have. ⁵Losses, such as the end of a love affair or a cherished friendship, are frustrating <u>because</u> they often make us feel helpless, unimportant, and worthless. ⁶Failure is a frequent source of frustration in our competitive society. ⁷The aspect of failure that is hardest to cope with is guilt. ⁸We imagine that if we had done certain things differently, we might have succeeded, and so we feel responsible for our own or someone else's pain and disappointment. ⁹Discrimination can <u>also</u> be a source of frustration. ¹⁰Being denied opportunities or recognition simply because of one's sex, age, religion, or skin color, regardless of one's personal qualifications or accomplishments, is immensely frustrating.

_C_ 1. The organizational patterns of the paragraph are list of items and
    A. definition and example.
    B. comparison and/or contrast.
    C. cause and effect.

2–6. Complete the outline of the paragraph by writing in the five major supporting details.

Main idea: There are five causes of frustration above and beyond daily hassles.

Major supporting details:
1. Delays
2. Lack of resources
3. Losses
4. Failure
5. Discrimination

The paragraph lists five basic causes of frustration above and beyond daily hassles. List words: *five basic causes*. Addition words: *To begin with, another,* and *also.* Cause and effect words: *causes, cause,* and *because.*

(Continues on next page)

B. Read the textbook paragraph below. Then answer the question and complete the map that follows.

¹Role conflict is a situation in which the different roles an individual is expected to play make incompatible demands. ²A working mother provides one example. ³In meeting the requirements of a full-time job, she automatically violates the expectation that a mother will put her children's needs before everything else. ⁴In meeting the cultural demands of motherhood (staying home if the child is sick, attending school plays), she automatically violates the requirements of a nine-to-five job. ⁵A priest provides another example. ⁶He is expected to treat confessions as strictly confidential. ⁷But a priest, like any other citizen, has responsibilities toward the community. ⁸What should he do if a parishioner confesses that he has committed several rapes and cannot control his behavior? ⁹In living up to one role expectation (confidentiality), the priest violates another (community responsibility). ¹⁰The key point here is that the difficulties the individuals in these positions experience—the feelings of conflict, inadequacy, and anguish—are not of their own making. ¹¹They are built into their roles.

_B_ 7. The main pattern of organization of the passage is
    A. cause and effect.
    B. definition and example.
    C. comparison.
    D. contrast.

8–10. Complete the map of the passage. In doing so, you will need to summarize the main idea and the two supporting details.

Wording of answers may vary.

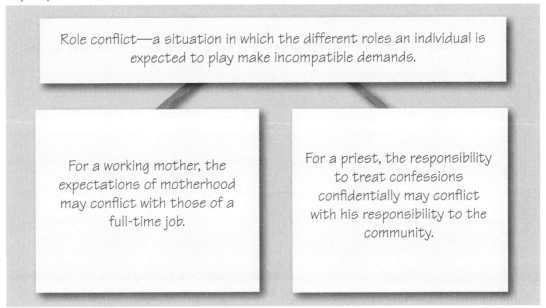

Role conflict—a situation in which the different roles an individual is expected to play make incompatible demands.

For a working mother, the expectations of motherhood may conflict with those of a full-time job.

For a priest, the responsibility to treat confessions confidentially may conflict with his responsibility to the community.

The paragraph defines *role conflict* (sentence 1) and gives two examples (sentences 2–4 and 5–9).

TO THE STUDENT

The pages that follow contain three mastery tests that offer additional practice in the skills covered in Chapters 5 and 6:

- Relationships that involve **addition**
- Relationships that involve **time**
- Relationships that involve **illustration**
- Relationships that involve **comparison and/or contrast**
- Relationships that involve **cause and effect**

For ease in reference, the lists of words that show these relationships have been reprinted on the next page.

Addition Words

one	to begin with	also	further
first (of all)	for one thing	in addition	furthermore
second(ly)	other	next	last (of all)
third(ly)	another	moreover	final(ly)

Time Words

before	immediately	when	until
previously	next	whenever	often
first (of all)	then	while	frequently
second (ly)	following	during	eventually
third (ly)	later	as (soon as)	final(ly)
now	after	by	last (of all)

Illustration Words

(for) example	including	(as an) illustration	one
(for) instance	specifically	to illustrate	once
such as	to be specific		

Comparison Words

(just) as	likewise	in a similar manner
(just) like	in like manner	in the same way
alike	similar(ly)	resemble

Contrast Words

but	instead	still	even though
yet	in contrast	as opposed to	different(ly)
however	on the other hand	in spite of	differs from
although	on the contrary	despite	unlike
nevertheless	converse(ly)	rather than	while

Cause and Effect Words

therefore	so	result	because (of)
thus	as a result	effect	reason
as a consequence	results in	cause	explanation
consequently	leads to	if . . . then	accordingly
due to	since	affect	

RELATIONSHIPS I & II: Mastery Test 1

A. Fill in each blank with an appropriate transition from the box. Use each transition once. Then, in the spaces provided, write the letter of the transition you have chosen.

A. cause	B. first	C. for example
D. then	E. unlike	

_____D_____ 1.

A sequence of steps to take to avoid being bitten by a dog.

[1]If you are approached by a vicious neighborhood or stray dog, you have a good chance of avoiding being attacked or bitten if you do the following. [2]First of all, stand still. [3]Secondly, do not look the dog directly in the eyes; instead, look just over the top of its head. [4]Next, talk in as soft and unconcerned a way as you can to the dog, saying, "Hey, what's up, pal?" [5]___Then___ slowly back away while facing the dog.

_____C_____ 2.

Defines the term *public opinion* (sentence 1) and gives two examples (sentence 3).

[1]Public opinion can be defined as those opinions held by ordinary citizens that they are willing to express openly. [2]This expression need not be verbal. [3]It could also take the form, ___for example___, of a protest demonstration or a vote for one candidate rather than another.

_____B_____ 3.

The words *several ways* suggest a list pattern. The passage lists three ways the opossum reacts to danger.

[1]The opossum reacts to danger in one of several ways. [2]___First___, some varieties of opossum can spray an unpleasant odor. [3]A second reaction to danger used by opossums is to bluff their way out of a tight spot by hissing and baring their teeth. [4]Finally, the best-known of opossum defenses is to "play dead" by entering into a coma-like state brought on by fear.

_____A_____ 4.

Cause: a blocked duct in a salivary gland.
Effect: swollen gland.

[1]Swollen glands can be uncomfortable, but they are a welcome sign that your body is working to defend itself. [2]They are often associated with an illness such as mumps, German measles, a cold, or flu; but an insect bite or infected cut can also result in swelling. [3]A blocked duct in a salivary gland is another possible ___cause___ of a swollen gland. [4]Still, if swollen glands last more than a few days, they can be a sign of a serious illness, such as Hodgkin's disease.

_____E_____ 5.

Compares and contrasts fear and awe.

[1]The feeling of awe is similar to fear in some ways. [2]With both, we have a sense of being overwhelmed, of confronting someone or something much more powerful than we are. [3]But ___unlike___ fear, awe is a positive feeling, an expansive feeling. [4]While fear makes us want to run away, awe makes us want to draw closer even as we hesitate to get too close.

(Continues on next page)

B. Fill in each blank with an appropriate transition from the box. Use each transition once. Then, in the spaces provided, write the letter of the transition you have chosen.

A. after	B. as a result	C. for instance
D. however	E. next	

_____D_____ 6.

Contrasts ancient Egyptian beliefs about death to beliefs today.

[1]There are more than a few similarities between the ancient Egyptian religion and our modern religions of today. [2]___However___, a belief that you "could take it with you" is a prime difference. [3]In fact, the Egyptians thought the dead could take a considerable number of items with them. [4]In many cases, Egyptian royalty and high officials began stocking their tombs with goods long before their death.

_____A_____ 7.

A series of steps in the process of manufacturing Scotch tape.

[1]Scotch tape is not wound up in the factory in the little rolls found in stores. [2]During the manufacturing process, sheets of cellophane several feet wide are first run through a machine that coats them with adhesive. [3]___After___ that, a machine winds the sticky film around tubes that are also several feet wide. [4]Next, this wide roll of Scotch tape is fed through a slicing machine, which produces the thin rolls of tape sold to consumers.

_____B_____ 8.

Causes: families limited to one child, boys prized in rural areas. *Effect:* Many girls died; China being short 50 million females.

[1]For two decades, the Chinese government tried to control population by limiting most rural families to one child. [2]Because boys are prized in rural areas—they can work the land and give more support to their families—many couples aborted female fetuses, killed newborn daughters, or neglected them to death. [3]___As a result___, China in 2002 was short 50 million females. [4]With so few brides to go around, desperate bachelors have taken to marrying relatives.

_____C_____ 9.

Defines communicators who want to keep themselves apart (sentence 1) and gives an example (sentences 2–3).

[1]Communicators who want to set themselves apart from others adopt the strategy of divergence, speaking in a way that emphasizes their differences from others. [2]___For instance___, an attorney who wants to impress a client might speak formally and use professional jargon to create a sense of distance. [3]The implicit message here is, "I'm different (and more knowledgeable) than you."

_____E_____ 10.

Describes the sequence of drafts that leads to a good piece of writing.

[1]Almost all good writing begins with terrible first efforts. [2]You need to start somewhere. [3]Start by getting something—anything—down on paper. [4]A friend of mine says that the first draft is the down draft—you just get it down. [5]The ___next___ draft is the up draft—you fix it up. [6]You try to say what you have to say more accurately. [7]And the third draft is the dental draft, where you check every tooth, to see if it's loose or cramped or decayed, or even, God help us, healthy.

RELATIONSHIPS I & II: Mastery Test 2

A. ¹Americans have mixed feelings about government. ²We complain about highway and bridge tolls, but we insist that every road be in good repair and wide enough to get us quickly to wherever we are going. ³Our consumption of tobacco and alcohol is among the highest in the world, yet we insist on strict regulations on who can buy them and where they can be sold and consumed. ⁴We complain without fail about our taxes; at the same time, however, we demand that government spend more on everything from cleaner air and higher-quality schools to safer streets and more jobs. ⁵We dislike "welfare" programs and those who use them. ⁶Still, we want government to provide all Americans with an economic "safety net" to protect them during hard times.

The passage describes the contrasting feelings Americans have about government.

_____C_____ 1. The main pattern of organization of the selection is
    A. time order.   B. list of items.   C. comparison and/or contrast.

2. One transition that signals the pattern of organization of this paragraph is _____*Any of the following:* but, yet, however, Still_____.

B. ¹Pictures of starving Africans leave the impression that Africa is overpopulated. ²Why else would all those people be starving? ³But the truth is far different. ⁴Africa has 22 percent of the earth's land, but only 10.5 percent of the earth's population. ⁵The reason for famines in Africa, then, cannot be too many people living on too little land. ⁶In fact, Africa contains some of the world's largest untapped lands suitable for agriculture. ⁷The reality is that famines are due to three primary causes: drought, inefficient farming techniques, and wars that disrupt harvests and food distribution.

Causes: drought, inefficient farming techniques, and wars. Effect: famine in Africa.

_____C_____ 3. The main pattern of organization of the selection is
    A. time order.   B. definition and example.   C. cause and effect.

4. One transition that signals the pattern of organization of this paragraph is _____*Any of the following:* reason, due to, causes_____.

C. ¹Sawing a woman in half is an easy illusion for magicians. ²The trick begins when a table holding a coffin-like box is rolled onstage. ³A female assistant is hiding inside that table. ⁴When the magician displays the box to the audience, it is, of course, empty. ⁵Then the magician asks a female assistant on stage to climb into the box. ⁶As she does this, the hidden woman enters the box through a trapdoor in the table, sticks her feet out one end, and curls up with her head between her knees. ⁷The other woman, drawing her knees up to her chin, puts her head out the other end of the box. ⁸Now the box appears to be holding one woman, and the magician can saw

(Continues on next page)

right through. [9]After he does so, the woman at the foot end slides back into the table as the magician reopens the box.

_____A_____ 5. The main pattern of organization of the selection is
The paragraph
describes the sequence
A. time order.   B. definition-example.   C. comparison and/or contrast.

of steps involved
in performing the   6. One transition that signals the pattern of organization of this paragraph
magic trick of sawing   is _____*Any of the following:* When, Then, As, Now, After_____.
a woman in half.

D. [1]A conflict of interest exists when a businessperson is faced with a situation in which an action benefiting one person or group has the potential to harm another. [2]For instance, lawyers, business consultants, or advertising agencies would face a conflict of interest if they represented two competing companies; a strategy that would most benefit one of the client companies might harm the other client. [3]Another example would be a real estate agent who faces an ethical conflict if he or she represents both the buyer and seller in a transaction. [4]In general, the buyer benefits from a low price, and the seller benefits from a high price. [5]Handling the situation responsibly may be possible, but it would also be difficult.

_____B_____ 7. The main pattern of organization of the selection is
A. time order.   B. definition and example.   C. list of items.

8. One transition that signals the pattern of organization of this paragraph
is _____*Either of the following:* For instance, example_____.

The paragraph defines the term *conflict of interest* (sentence 1) and gives two illustrations of it (sentence 2 and sentences 3–5).

E. [1]Three musical instruments played an important role in eighteenth-century warfare. [2]One of the most important was the snare drum. [3]Often played by boys between 12 and 16 years old, snare drums were used to set the marching rhythm for soldiers. [4]With a skilled drummer playing 96 beats per minute, a commander could march his troops three miles in fifty minutes, allowing ten minutes each hour for a breather and a drink. [5]Another important instrument was a small flute called a fife. [6]The fife's role in an army was to entertain soldiers and communicate orders. [7]For example, the song "Pioneer's March" was the signal for road-clearing crews to get started ahead of the infantry. [8]Fifes were also used to give orders to soldiers during battle since they could be heard above the roar of firearms. [9]A third instrument used in warfare was the trumpet. [10]Requiring just one hand to play, it was used by soldiers on horseback to send messages to soldiers in battle and on the march.

_____B_____ 9. The main pattern of organization of the selection is
A. time order.   B. list of items.   C. comparison and/or contrast.

10. One transition that signals the pattern of organization of this paragraph
is _____*Any of the following:* One, Another, third_____.

The words *Three musical instruments* suggest a list will follow. Each of the three items in the list is introduced by an addition word.

RELATIONSHIPS I & II: Mastery Test 3

Each of the following selections uses **two** patterns of organization. Read each selection and then, in the spaces provided, write the letter of the two patterns of organization.

A. ¹A boycott is an expression of protest consisting of an organized refusal by a group of people to deal with another person or group. ²An <u>illustration</u> is the famous boycott that began in 1955 when Mrs. Rosa Parks of Montgomery, Alabama, refused to obey a local ordinance requiring black people to sit at the back of city buses. ³Mrs. Parks was arrested, which <u>resulted</u> in a boycott of the Montgomery bus system by blacks. ⁴The boycott was organized and led by Dr. Martin Luther King, Jr. ⁵Rather than continue to lose revenue needed to run the bus system, the city repealed the ordinance.

_____C_____ 1. The main patterns of organization of the selection are
    A. definition-example and list of items.
    B. cause-effect and contrast.
    C. definition-example and cause-effect.

The paragraph defines the term boycott *(sentence 1) and gives an example (sentences 2–4). Illustration word:* illustration. *Cause:* the arrest of Mrs. Parks. *Effect:* a boycott of the bus system by blacks. Cause and effect word: *resulted.*

B. ¹On May 18, 1980, Mt. St. Helens in the state of Washington erupted violently, killing nearly one hundred people and leveling thousands of acres of timber. ²<u>By contrast</u>, many volcanoes in Hawaii never explode, but simply have lava flowing out of them. ³The <u>difference</u> between volcanic eruptions and simple lava flows is the <u>result</u> of the <u>differing</u> composition of the molten rock that comes to the surface as lava. ⁴The lava from Mt. St. Helens is a type that cools more quickly, which causes it to build a lava dome that plugs up the flow. ⁵Eventually the pressure becomes so intense that a tremendous explosion blows the lava dome off and sends a massive cloud of ash into the air. ⁶<u>By contrast</u>, the lava from Hawaiian volcanoes contains enough iron to keep it from hardening to rock when it reaches the air; it flows down the side of the cone until it hits an obstacle or eventually cools and becomes solid. ⁷It never plugs the volcano; <u>therefore</u>, there is no explosion.

The paragraph contrasts Mt. St. Helens with the volcanoes in Hawaii. Contrast words: *By contrast, difference,* and *differing. Cause 1:* the amount of iron in the lava. *Effect 1:* the lava does or does not plug the volcano. *Cause 2:* lava does not plug volcano. *Effect 2:* no explosion. Cause and effect words: *result, causes,* and *therefore.*

_____B_____ 2. The main patterns of organization of the selection are
    A. definition-example and time order.
    B. contrast and cause-effect.
    C. list of items and comparison.

C. ¹The United States ranks near the bottom among the world's democracies in the percentage of eligible citizens who participate in national elections. ²One <u>reason</u> for the low voter turnout is that individual Americans are responsible for registering to vote, <u>whereas</u> in most other democracies, voters are automatically registered by government officials. ³In addition, <u>unlike</u> some other democracies, the United States does not

(Continues on next page)

encourage voting by holding elections on the weekend or by imposing penalties, such as fines, on those who do not participate.

_A_ 3. The main patterns of organization of the selection are
- A. cause-effect and contrast.
- B. time order and comparison.
- C. definition-example and time order.

Causes: registration methods and failure to encourage voting. *Effect:* low voter turnout. Cause and effect word: *reason.* The paragraph contrasts American methods of voter encouragement to those of other democracies. Contrast words: *whereas* and *unlike.*

D. ¹What caused our distant ancestors to move from walking on all fours to standing upright? ²First, and probably most important, standing upright freed the forelimbs to carry things. ³With dangerous animals around more than willing to make a meal out of a small primate, the ability to search for food while possibly carrying one's offspring and to carry the food back to a safe location would certainly be a benefit. ⁴Second, by elevating the head, walking upright provided better views of food and danger. ⁵In addition, the vertical orientation helped cool the body by presenting a smaller target to the intense equatorial rays of the sun and by placing more of the body above the ground to catch cooling air currents. ⁶Finally, standing upright, while using a great deal of energy for running, was very efficient for walking. ⁷Long periods of steady walking in search of food required less energy if done in an upright position.

_A_ 4. The main patterns of organization of the selection are
- A. cause-effect and list of items.
- B. definition-example and time order.
- C. list of items and time order.

Causes: standing upright freed the forelimbs, provided better views, helped cool the body, made walking easier. *Effect:* our ancestors started standing upright. Cause and effect word: *caused.* The four causes are given as a list. Addition words: *First, Second, In addition,* and *Finally.*

E. ¹When a honeybee finds a new source of food—flower pollen and nectar—she flies back to the hive. ²Within minutes, more bees emerge and, amazingly, fly straight to the food. ³Their ability to do this is a result of what goes on in the hive after that first bee flies in. ⁴Inside the hive, that bee does a dance, called a waggling dance, to communicate to the other bees the direction, distance, and identity of the food. ⁵First, because it's usually dark in the hive, she emits sound signals that help the other bees determine where she is and how she's moving. ⁶She then dances in a figure-eight pattern, waggling only when she is facing the direction of the food source in relation to the sun. ⁷The pace of her dancing tells how far away the food is; the faster she dances, the closer the food. ⁸At some point, the bees observing the dance emit sounds that vibrate the honeycomb. ⁹This causes the dancer to stop, and she gives the watchers small samples of the food so they know its taste, smell, and quality. ¹⁰After receiving the necessary information, the other bees then fly out to find the food.

_B_ 5. The main patterns of organization of the selection are
- A. definition-example and list of items.
- B. cause-effect and time order.
- C. comparison and time order.

Cause: the events that take place in the hive. *Effect:* the other bees are able to find the new source of food. Cause and effect words: *result, because, causes,* and *so.* The events in the hive are described in the time order in which they happen. Time words: *When, Within minutes, after, First, then,* and *At some point.*

7 Inferences

You have probably heard the expression "to read between the lines." When you "read between the lines," you pick up ideas that are not directly stated in what you are reading. These implied ideas are often important for a full understanding of what an author means. Discovering the ideas that are not stated directly in writing is called **making inferences**, or **drawing conclusions**.

Look at the cartoon below. What inferences can you make about it? Check (✓) the **two** inferences that are most logically based on the information suggested by the cartoon.

    ✓ A. The couple is not likely to have a good dining experience at the restaurant.

    ____ B. The couple will never eat at the restaurant.

    ____ C. The restaurant was recently closed for health violations.

    ✓ D. Whoever is running the restaurant is not doing a good job.

273

Explanation

A. *The couple is not likely to have a good dining experience at the restaurant.*

The "help wanted" sign indicates that the restaurant is seriously understaffed. It would be logical, then, to infer that the restaurant cannot provide patrons with a good dining experience. You should have checked this item.

B. *The couple will never eat at the restaurant.*

The man's comment that "this isn't the best time" suggests that he may be willing to try the restaurant once it has solved its staffing problems. Also, experience suggests that it is common for restaurants to change ownership and/or management. You should not have checked this item.

C. *The restaurant was recently closed for health violations.*

Nothing in the cartoon suggests that the restaurant was recently closed for health violations. Perhaps if it continues to operate without sufficient staff, it *may* be closed, but we have no way of knowing that. You should not have checked this item.

D. *Whoever is running the restaurant is not doing a good job.*

Experience tells us that good managers are able to hire and retain qualified employees. The "help wanted" sign suggests quite the opposite—that a number of employees have recently quit or been fired. The lack of staff, in turn, has caused the couple to decide against dining there. Clearly, this is no way to run a business!

Inferences in Reading

In reading, we make logical leaps from information stated directly to ideas that are not stated directly. As one scholar has said, inferences are "statements about the unknown made on the basis of the known." To draw inferences, we use all the clues provided by the writer, our own experience, and logic.

You have already practiced making inferences in this book. Do you remember the following sentence from "Vocabulary in Context" on page 21?

Many of us have *ambivalent* feelings about our politicians, admiring but also distrusting them.

That sentence does not tell us the meaning of *ambivalent*, but it does suggest that *ambivalent* involves both positive and negative feelings. Thus you can infer from this sentence that *ambivalent feelings* probably means "mixed feelings," and you'd be correct.

✓ *Check Your Understanding 1*

Read the following passage and check (✓) the **two** inferences that are most firmly based on the information given. Then read the explanation that follows.

[1]A sociology professor wrote on the board, "A woman without her man is nothing" and, with a smile, asked students to punctuate the sentence correctly. [2]The men all wrote, "A woman, without her man, is nothing." [3]However, the women wrote, "A woman: Without her, man is nothing."

_____ A. The professor was definitely a man.

_____ B. The professor did not believe students could punctuate the words correctly.

✓ C. The professor knew there was more than one way to punctuate the words correctly.

_____ D. The professor is not a good teacher.

✓ E. Gender differences caused students to read and punctuate the professor's words differently.

Explanation

A. There is no indication of the professor's gender in the passage. You should not have checked this item.

B. Nothing in the passage implies that the professor doubted students' ability to punctuate the words correctly. You should not have checked this item.

C. Since the professor chose the particular sentence and smiled while writing the words, we can conclude that the professor was aware of more than one punctuation possibility. Therefore, you should have checked this item.

D. There is no suggestion in the passage that the professor is a poor teacher. In fact, the professor has chosen a dramatic way to suggest that each sex sees the world from its own point of view. You should not have checked this item.

E. Male and female students had very different responses to the sentence. Gender was the only apparent difference among the students, so we can conclude that it caused the different responses. You should have checked this item.

✓ Check Your Understanding 2

Read the following passage and check (✓) the **three** inferences that can most logically be drawn from it. Then read the explanation that follows.

[1]A famous psychology experiment conducted by Dr. John B. Watson demonstrates that people, like animals, can be conditioned—trained to respond in a particular way to certain stimulations. [2]Watson gave an eleven-month-old baby named Albert a soft, furry white rat. [3]Each time Albert tried to stroke the rat, Dr. Watson hit a metal bar with a hammer. [4]Before long, Albert was afraid not only of white rats but also of white rabbits, white dogs, and white fur coats. [5]He even screamed at the sight of a Santa Claus mask.

_____ A. Dr. Watson did not like small children.

✓ B. Before the experiment, Albert was not afraid of white rats.

_____ C. Albert had been familiar with rats before the experiment.

_____ D. If he had seen a black fur coat, Albert would have screamed.

✓ E. Albert connected the loud noise of the hammer striking the metal bar with the white rat.

✓ F. Albert was afraid of unexpected loud noises.

Explanation

A. This is not a logical inference. We might certainly question the way the baby was used, but the passage doesn't give enough information for us to infer logically that Watson did not like small children.

B. This is a logical inference. Because Albert tried to pet the rat, it is fair to assume that he wasn't frightened of the animal.

C. This is not a logical inference. The passage gives no clues about Albert's having previous experience with rats.

D. This is not a logical inference. The passage makes no mention of Albert's response to any color but white.

E. This is a logical inference. Because the noise appears to have changed Albert's attitude toward the rat, we can assume he associated the noise with the rat.

F. This is a logical inference. Since the noise is what made Albert afraid of the rat, we have to infer that he was afraid of the noise. In addition, experience tells us that babies are likely to be frightened of unexpected loud noises.

Guidelines for Making Inferences in Reading

The exercises in this chapter provide practice in making careful inferences when you read. Here are three guidelines for that process:

1 **Never lose sight of the available information.** As much as possible, base your inferences on the facts. For instance, in the paragraph about Watson's experiment, we are told, "Albert tried to stroke the rat." On the basis of that fact, we can readily conclude that the baby had no fear of rats.

It's also important to note when a conclusion lacks support. For instance, the idea that Albert would have screamed at the sight of a black fur coat has no support in the paragraph. We are told only that Albert was frightened by white furry things.

2 **Use your background information and experience to help you in making inferences.** Our understanding and experience with babies, for example, help us realize that Albert was frightened of unexpected loud noises.

The more you know about a subject, the better your inferences are likely to be. So keep in mind that if your background in an area is weak, your inferences may be shaky. For example, if you develop a rash and fever that will not go away, a doctor's inferences about the cause are likely to be more helpful than your inferences.

3 **Consider the alternatives.** Don't simply accept the first inference that comes to mind. Instead, consider all the facts of a case and all the possible explanations. For example, the doctor analyzing your rash and fever may first think of and then eliminate several possibilities before coming to the right conclusion.

PRACTICE 1

Read the following passages. Then, in the space provided, write the letter of the most logical answer to each question, based on the information given in the passage.

A. ¹A corporate president recently made a visit to a nearby Native American reservation as part of his firm's public relations program. ²"We realize that we have not hired any Indians in the five years our company has been located in this area," he told the assembled tribespeople, "but we are looking into the matter very carefully." ³"Hora, hora," said some of the audience. ⁴"We would like to eventually hire 5 percent of our total work force from this reservation," he said. ⁵"Hora, hora," shouted more of the audience. ⁶Encouraged by their enthusiasm, the president closed his short address by telling them that he hoped his firm would be able to take some hiring action within the next couple of years. ⁷"Hora, hora, hora," cried the total group. ⁸With a feeling of satisfaction, the president left the hall and was taken on a tour of the reservation. ⁹Stopping in a field to admire some of the horses grazing there, the president asked if he could walk up closer to the animals. ¹⁰"Certainly," said his guide, "but be careful not to step in the *hora*."

The reader **C** 1. To get the main point of this passage, the reader must infer
must realize
what the audience   A. the location of the reservation.
was shouting
in order to   B. what kind of company the president headed.
understand
the point **B**   C. the meaning of the word *hora*.
of the passage.
2. From the passage, we can infer that the audience
     A. believed the president's speech.   The more he promised,
     B. did not believe the president's speech.   the more they shouted.
     C. was confused by the president's speech.

C 3. From the passage, we can infer that the president
See sentences 6 and 8.   A. thought the Native Americans deserved to be hired.
     B. thought his company should not hire the Native Americans.
     C. misinterpreted the Native Americans' reaction to his speech.

B 4. From the passage, we can infer that the main reason the president spoke
The speech is part   to the Native Americans about jobs was that
of a public relations
program, and the   A. they needed the jobs.
president makes
only vague hints   B. he thought promising jobs to Native Americans would make his
that he might ever   company look good.
consider hiring
Native Americans.   C. he thought hiring Native Americans would be good for his
     company.

B.   ¹Parents bewildered by their teen alien can take comfort from one sign that Junior may be from the same species as they are: High-school status ladders look just as they did when Corvettes were the hot cars of choice.
     ²A new study of social systems at eighteen high schools in various states reveals some familiar patterns, reports sociologist Murray Milner, Jr. ³Still tops in popularity: male athletes and attractive girls. ⁴Just beneath them stand well-dressed "preppies" who try to act indifferent to school and snag the "right" party invitations.
     ⁵"Nerds" cluster near the bottom. ⁶Their sin? ⁷Open preoccupation with academic success. ⁸But they're not lowest. ⁹The "dorks," Milner says, "were hopelessly inept" about clothes and social events. ¹⁰They often had low grades and poor athletic ability, too.
     ¹¹Kids typically date only within their status level, which is set in stone by the first year and seldom can be upgraded. ¹²Downgrading is a danger, though. ¹³A girl dating a star athlete who later got injured and couldn't play found his status—and hers—suddenly declining. ¹⁴And being seen talking to classmates "beneath" one's status can pull students down very fast.
     ¹⁵"High school is a very scary place," Milner says.
     ¹⁶It often is, agrees San Diego psychiatrist Martin Greenberg. ¹⁷To take the

pressure off at home, consider cutting teens some slack on minor disputes, he advises. [18]"Try to be flexible because a lot of them are having a hard time. [19]No matter how it looks," he says, "they're desperate for love."

_C_ 5. From the beginning of the passage, we can conclude that a generation ago

Sentences 1 and 3 support answer C as a logical inference.

  A. teens became popular for very different reasons than they do today.
  B. social status was not very important in high schools.
  C. good-looking girls and athletic boys were the most popular kids.
  D. only "dorks" drove Corvettes.

_B_ 6. We can infer from the passage that

Answer B is logical because high school is "very scary" (sentence 15) and many students have "a hard time" (sentence 18).

  A. teenagers generally don't care about their social status.
  B. the high-school years are stressful ones for many teens.
  C. most teens admire students who openly care about school.
  D. teens typically behave lovingly when they are home.

_A_ 7. The passage suggests that in high school,

Sentence 3 supports answer A as a logical inference.

  A. boys are most valued for their athletic ability and girls for their appearance.
  B. female athletes are generally as popular as male athletes.
  C. a nonathletic boy can be very popular as long as he is a good student.
  D. athletes don't care about getting invited to parties.

_C_ 8. The passage suggests that

Sentences 3 and 4 support answer C as a logical inference.

  A. teenagers are independent thinkers who aren't bothered by other people's opinions.
  B. popular teens often make friends with less popular kids.
  C. outward appearance is an important factor in determining high schoolers' status.
  D. a teenager's social status often changes from year to year.

C. [1]During World War II, the troop ship *SS Dorchester* steamed out of New York harbor with 904 men headed for Greenland. [2]Among those leaving anxious families behind were four chaplains: Methodist preacher George Fox, Rabbi Alexander Goode, Catholic priest John Washington, and Reformed Church minister Clark Poling. [3]Some 150 miles from their destination, a Nazi submarine sighted the *Dorchester* in its cross hairs. [4]Within moments of a torpedo's impact, reports a survivor, stunned men were pouring out from their bunks as the ship began tilting. [5]With power cut off, the escort vessels, unaware of the unfolding tragedy, pushed on in the darkness. [6]Onboard, chaos ruled as panicky men came up from the hold without life jackets and leaped into overcrowded lifeboats.

[7]When the four chaplains made it up to the steeply sloping deck, they began guiding the men to their boat stations. [8]They opened a storage locker, distributed life jackets, and coaxed the men over the side. [9]In the icy, oil-smeared water, Private William Bednar heard the chaplains preaching courage and found the strength to

swim until he reached a life raft. ¹⁰Still onboard, Grady Clark watched in awe as the chaplains handed out the last life jackets, and then, with ultimate selflessness, gave away their own. ¹¹As Clark slipped into the water, he saw the chaplains standing— their arms linked—praying, in Latin, Hebrew, and English. ¹²Other men, now calm, joined them in a huddle as the *Dorchester* slid beneath the sea.

_____ B _____   9. We can infer from this passage that

The families are "anxious" (sentence 2). Answers A and C are not suggested.

    A. the Nazis had been hunting for the *Dorchester* for a long time.
    B. the *Dorchester*'s passengers and their families knew that because the ship carried soldiers, it might be attacked.
    C. the Nazi submarine was eventually found and destroyed.

_____ A _____   10. We can infer that the chaplains and others remaining on the boat didn't jump off because

See sentence 9 ("icy . . . water") and sentence 10 ("handed out the last life jacket").

    A. there was no more room in the lifeboats, and they knew they could not survive in the icy sea without a life jacket.
    B. they couldn't swim.
    C. they assumed a friendly ship would soon pass by and save them.

_____ B _____   11. We can infer from the passage that Grady Clark

Sentence 11 supports answer B as a logical inference.

    A. was one of the men who died in the *Dorchester* tragedy.
    B. survived the attack and reported what the chaplains had done.
    C. was the sole survivor of the attack on the *Dorchester*.

_____ B _____   12. The passage suggests that

Sentences 9 and 11–12 support answer B as a logical inference.

    A. the chaplains had known each other for many years.
    B. religious faith may strengthen courage.
    C. the chaplains had no fear of death.

PRACTICE 2

Read the following textbook passages. Then put a check (✓) by the **three** inferences that are most logically based on the given facts in each passage.

A. ¹George Washington's honesty is a trait that has been well publicized. ²The famous story of how little George chopped down his father's favorite cherry tree, then bravely admitted to the deed, has an honored place in American presidential history. ³The cherry tree story was first recorded in 1806 by Parson Mason Weems, a Maryland preacher and storyteller. ⁴Unfortunately, Parson Weems was none too honest himself, and it appears that he invented the story of George and the cherry tree. ⁵There is no record of the cherry tree incident anywhere until it appears in Weems's book. ⁶The parson, it seems, thought it acceptable to teach the virtue of honesty through a made-up story. ⁷We can judge Weems's own truthfulness by the fact that he describes himself in the book as "formerly rector of Mount Vernon Parish." ⁸Such a parish never existed.

_____ 1. The passage suggests that George Washington was not so honest after all.

_____ 2. We can conclude that Parson Weems knew George Washington well.

✓ 3. Widely accepted stories about history are not necessarily true.

✓ 4. Parson Weems wrote about a virtue he didn't have himself.

_____ 5. The author of this passage doubts that George Washington was a great leader and president.

✓ 6. In his stories and sermons, Weems may well have told other false stories.   **Item 3:** Supported by sentences 4–5. **Item 4:** Supported by sentences 4 and 7–8. **Item 6:** Supported by sentences 6–8.

B. [1]The *Chicago Tribune* once wrote that Henry Ford, the founder of the Ford Motor Company, was an ignorant man. [2]Ford sued, challenging the paper to "prove it." [3]During the trial, Ford was asked dozens of simple, general information questions: "When was the Civil War?" "Name the presidents of the United States," and so on. [4]Ford, who had little formal education, could answer very few. [5]Finally, exasperated, he said, "I don't know the answers to those questions, but I could find a man in five minutes who does. [6]I use my brain to think, not store up a lot of useless facts."

Item 1:
Supported by sentence 2. (Ford must have been angry if he sued.)

Item 4:
Supported by sentence 5.

Item 6:
Supported by sentence 6.

✓ 1. Henry Ford was probably angered by the article in the *Chicago Tribune*.

_____ 2. Ford frequently sued people.

_____ 3. The *Tribune* won the case in court.

✓ 4. Ford believed that knowing where to find a fact is good enough.

_____ 5. Ford would have been even more successful in his career had he had a formal education.

✓ 6. Ford believed that knowing how to think is more important than knowing facts.

C. [1]Most people would like to think that they choose their friends solely on the basis of personal characteristics. [2]A classic study of a housing complex for married students at the Massachusetts Institute of Technology (MIT) suggests that proximity—nearness and availability—can be an important factor. [3]Researchers asked couples to list their friends in the complex. [4]They found that residents were far more likely to list the couple in the next apartment than one that lived two doors away, and more likely to visit with a couple two doors away than with one three or four doors away. [5]A distance of thirty feet or a short elevator ride made the difference between friends and strangers! [6]More recent studies have confirmed the importance of proximity. [7]One possible explanation is that whenever people encounter strangers, they feel tense. [8]The more they see a person, the more they come to think of that person as predictable and safe, and hence the more likely they are to strike up a conversation that leads to friendship. [9]This would explain why the most popular couples in the MIT housing complex were those who lived at the bottom of the stairs near the garbage cans that everyone used.

✓ 1. Most people probably think their personal preferences determine whom they choose for friends.

___ 2. In fact, our personal preferences have no effect on who our friends are.

___ 3. A person who lives in a big country is more likely to have more friends than someone who lives in a small country.

✓ 4. Someone living in an apartment house is likely to have more friends than someone who lives on a farm.

___ 5. A garbage collector is likely to have more friends than a letter carrier.

✓ 6. Someone who works in a busy office is likely to have more friends than someone who works at home.

> **Item 1:** Supported by sentence 1. **Items 4 and 6:** Supported by sentence 2. Both items describe situations of "nearness and availability."

Inferences in Literature

Inference is very important in reading literature. While writers of factual material usually state directly much of what they mean, creative writers often provide verbal pictures that *show* us what they mean. It is up to the reader to infer the point of what the creative writer has said. For instance, a nonfiction author might write the following:

> A man got angry at the person using a cell phone in the theater.

But a novelist might write this:

> Thomas turned to face the laughing red-haired girl sitting behind him in the theater. A vein on his forehead was throbbing. "Would you mind very much turning off that cell phone?" he hissed. "A few of us are here to actually see the movie."

Rather than merely stating that Thomas was angry, the author shows the anger with vivid details. To get the most out of literature, you must often infer meanings—just as you do in everyday life. Your may have inferred, for example, that the laughing girl is insensitive to the rights of others in the theater. You could also have concluded that Thomas has probably been waiting a while for her to quiet down, but she has not, and his temper is now boiling.

Now look at the following statement that a nonfiction writer might produce:

> A farmer is about to kill a small pig, but his daughter objects, so the farmer decides to let his daughter learn for herself that a small pig can be a problem.

Compare the above line with the following scene from *Charlotte's Web*, a literary classic that is beloved by young and old alike:

[1]"Fern," said Mr. Arable, "I know more about raising a litter of pigs than you do. [2]A weakling makes trouble. [3]Now run along!"

[4]"But it's unfair," cried Fern. [5]"The pig couldn't help being born small, could it? [6]If I had been very small at birth, would you have killed me?"

[7]Mr. Arable smiled. [8]"Certainly not," he said, looking down at his daughter with love. [9]"But this is different. [10]A little girl is one thing, a little runty pig is another."

[11]"I see no difference," replied Fern, still hanging on to the ax. [12]"This is the most terrible case of injustice I ever heard of."

[13]A queer look came over John Arable's face. [14]He seemed almost ready to cry himself.

[15]"All right," he said. [16]"You go back to the house and I will bring the runt when I come in. [17]I'll let you start it on a bottle, like a baby. [18]Then you'll see what trouble a pig can be."

✔ *Check Your Understanding*

See if you can answer the following inference questions about the excerpt.

_C_ 1. Fern and Mr. Arable probably live
   A. in a city.
   B. in a small town.
   C. on a farm.

_A_ 2. We can infer from the excerpt that Mr. Arable
   A. has probably raised many pigs in his lifetime.
   B. has had little experience raising pigs.
   C. does not like pigs.

_C_ 3. Mr. Arable appears almost ready to cry because he
   A. gets worried about how difficult it would be to raise the pig.
   B. does not like to lose an argument with his daughter.
   C. is touched by his daughter's willingness to stand up for the small pig.

_B_ 4. We can conclude that Mr. Arable agrees to spare the pig because
   A. Fern has convinced him that it is unfair to kill pigs, no matter what their size.
   B. he believes that raising a pig will teach Fern some lessons.
   C. he realizes that taking care of a runt pig is not that difficult.

_B_ 5. By the end of this passage, we can infer that Mr. Arable is
   A. a cruel man.
   B. a reasonable man.
   C. not a very patient man.

Explanation

1. Fern and Mr. Arable live in a place where pigs are born and raised. That strongly suggests that they live on a farm. The correct answer, then, is C.

2. Mr. Arable mentions that he knows about "raising a litter of pigs." He also tells Fern how to begin feeding the pig. These details suggest that he has raised pigs before. Therefore, the answer is A.

3. Mr. Arable seems near crying after Fern insists there's no difference between killing a runt pig and killing a small daughter. And the passage has already described Mr. Arable looking at his daughter with love. So we can conclude the plea for justice from the young daughter he adores is what touched him so. Thus the answer is C.

4. When Mr. Arable agrees to let his daughter raise the pig, he says "you'll see what trouble a pig can be." His words suggest that he expects Fern to learn a lesson. Therefore B is the answer.

5. Mr. Arable talks to Fern, listens to her opinions, and agrees to allow her to do something he does not fully support. These actions suggest he is a fair and reasonable man. So answer B is correct.

The excerpt from *Charlotte's Web* is a small example of how inference skills can increase your appreciation of literary forms—fiction, poetry, autobiographies, and other imaginative literature.

Poetry, especially, by its nature, implies much of its meaning. Poets often imply their meanings through comparisons. For example, Emily Dickinson begins one of her poems with the following lines:

> Hope is the thing with feathers
> That perches in the soul,
> And sings the tune without the words,
> And never stops at all . . . .

Here, Dickinson uses a figure of speech known as a metaphor, comparing hope to a singing bird. The comparison implies, among other things, that hope is a sweet and welcome thing. (More information about metaphors appears on the next page.)

A Note on Figures of Speech

Creative writers often use **figures of speech** to give us a fresh way of looking at something. The two most common figures of speech are similes and metaphors.

Simile—a stated comparison, introduced with the word *like* or *as*.

PEANUTS reproduced by permission of United Feature Syndicate, Inc.

In the cartoon, the boy, Linus, says that getting back his lost security blanket is "like seeing the flood waters recede . . . like a reunion with old friends . . . like a drop of water to a man lost in the desert . . . like coming out of a dark cave into the wonderful sunlight." (The joke, of course, is that he overdoes the similes, which is why Lucy ties the blanket around his mouth.)

Here is another example. Instead of saying, "The window shade snapped up," you could express it more vividly by saying, "The window shade snapped up like a gunshot." The simile shows that the noise of the window shade was loud and startling.

Here are some other similes:

- That Halloween night was *as dark as the inside of a witch's hat.*
- After you've broken up with a boyfriend or girlfriend, every day feels *like a cloudy, cold Monday morning.*
- If he senses you don't know the material, our math teacher attacks *like a shark.*
- That runner moves *as gracefully as a gazelle.*

Metaphor—an implied comparison, with *like* or *as* omitted.

The thought "No person can be self-sufficient" was expressed vividly in a metaphor by the poet John Donne, who wrote: "No man is an island." His comparison says no one can be completely disconnected from the mainland—the rest of humanity.

Here are some other metaphors:

- The grade on the paper was *a dash of ice water in my face.*
- When Nate got up to speak, he was *a mass of quivering Jell-O.*
- *The warm honey* of her voice melted my anger.
- Watching TV for hours, the children were *glassy-eyed statues.*
- The dancer's head was *a rose* on *the slender stem* of her neck.

PRACTICE 3

Use a check (✓) to identify each figure of speech as a simile or a metaphor. Then, in the space provided, answer each inference question that follows.

_B_ 1. His friendship is as genuine <u>as</u> a plastic Christmas tree.

✓ simile   ___ metaphor

You can infer that the friendship is

A. easy to maintain.

B. fake and cheap.

C. seasonal and glittery.

> The word indicating the simile is underlined.
> A plastic Christmas tree is a fake and cheap substitute for a real tree.

_C_ 2. A gang of teenaged boys moved through the mall <u>like</u> a pack of wild dogs.

✓ simile   ___ metaphor

You can infer that the boys were

A. polite and friendly.

B. sneaky and quiet.

C. loud and disruptive.

> The word indicating the simile is underlined.
> Wild dogs would be wild and disruptive.

_B_ 3. The executives did not admit that the company was a sinking ship until after they had taken millions of dollars for themselves.

___ simile   ✓ metaphor

You can infer that the company

A. was well-managed.

B. was failing.

C. was going in more than one direction.

> The metaphor of a sinking ship suggests the company will not last much longer.

_C_ 4. Everyone at work thinks that Jasmine is a real gem.

___ simile   ✓ metaphor

You can infer that Jasmine is

A. disliked and unfriendly.

B. shy and quiet.

C. admired and valued.

> A gem is something that is admired and valued.

_C_   5. I'm writing a family history so that my grandparents' stories do not go
     up in smoke and ashes.

   ___ simile   ✓ metaphor

   You can infer that the grandparents' stories are
   A. full of fire and passion.
   B. uneventful and unimportant.   Something that goes up in smoke and
   C. in danger of being lost forever.   ashes would be lost forever.

PRACTICE 4

George Orwell is famous for his novels *Animal Farm* and *1984* as well as his classic
literary essays. Following is an excerpt from "A Hanging," an essay Orwell wrote
about an execution he witnessed while he was an English police officer stationed in
Burma. Read the excerpt and then answer the inference questions that follow.

Note that the meanings of a few words in the excerpt are given below.

reiterated: repeated
Ram: Hindu god
abominable: hateful
timorously: timidly
oscillated: swung back and forth

¹We stood waiting, five yards away. ²The warders had formed in a rough
circle round the gallows. ³And then, when the noose was fixed, the prisoner began
crying out to his god. ⁴It was a high, reiterated° cry of "Ram°! Ram! Ram! Ram!" not
urgent and fearful like a prayer or a cry for help, but steady, rhythmical almost like
the tolling of a bell. ⁵The dog answered the sound with a whine. ⁶The hangman, still
standing on the gallows, produced a small cotton bag like a flour bag and drew it
down over the prisoner's face. ⁷But the sound, muffled by the cloth, still persisted,
over and over again: "Ram! Ram! Ram! Ram!"

⁸The hangman climbed down and stood ready, holding the lever. ⁹Minutes
seemed to pass. ¹⁰The steady, muffled crying from the prisoner went on and on,
"Ram! Ram! Ram!" never faltering for an instant. ¹¹The superintendent, his head on
his chest, was slowly poking the ground with his stick; perhaps he was counting
the cries, allowing the prisoner a fixed number—fifty, perhaps, or a hundred.
¹²Everyone had changed color. ¹³The Indians had gone grey like bad coffee, and
one or two of the bayonets were wavering. ¹⁴We looked at the lashed, hooded man
on the drop, and listened to his cries—each cry another second of life; the same
thought was in all our minds: oh, kill him quickly, get it over, stop that abominable°
noise!

¹⁵Suddenly the superintendent made up his mind. ¹⁶Throwing up his head he
made a swift motion with his stick. ¹⁷"Chalo!" he shouted almost fiercely.

¹⁸There was a clanking noise, and then dead silence. ¹⁹The prisoner had vanished, and the rope was twisting on itself. ²⁰I let go of the dog, and it galloped immediately to the back of the gallows; but when it got there it stopped short, barked, and then retreated into a corner of the yard, where it stood among the weeds, looking timorously° out at us. ²¹We went round the gallows to inspect the prisoner's body. ²²He was dangling with his toes pointed straight downward, very slowly revolving, as dead as a stone.

²³The superintendent reached out with his stick and poked the bare body; it oscillated°, slightly. ²⁴"*He's* all right," said the superintendent. ²⁵He backed out from under the gallows, and blew out a deep breath. ²⁶The moody look had gone out of his face quite suddenly. ²⁷He glanced at his wristwatch. ²⁸"Eight minutes past eight. ²⁹Well, that's all for this morning, thank God."

_B_ 1. We can infer from the simile below that the prisoner's cry was like
   A. wedding bells.
   B. a funeral bell.   Often, a rhythmically tolling bell
   C. a doorbell.   is part of a funeral service.

   "It was a high . . . cry . . . steady, rhythmical . . . like the tolling of a bell."

_B_ 2. The reaction of the Indian spectators, described in the simile below, suggests they are
   A. sympathetic to the superintendent's duty.   Bad coffee suggests being
   B. disturbed by the prisoner's hanging.   disturbed, rather than
   C. relieved that the prisoner was about to die.   sympathetic or relieved.

   "Everyone had changed color. The Indians had gone grey like bad coffee . . ."

_C_ 3. In the second paragraph, we can conclude that the superintendent waited for the prisoner to say his prayers because he
By allowing the   A. had the same religious beliefs as the prisoner.
prisoner a certain
number of chants,   B. was distracted by something on the ground.
the superintendent is
showing him respect. C. understood the prisoner's fear and showed him respect.

_C_ 4. We can infer from the passage that the word *chalo* was a
   A. word of protest against the hanging.   Immediately after the
   B. cheer in support of the hanging.   superintendent says the word,
   C. command used to begin the hanging.   the hangman proceeds.
                                              (See sentences 17 and 18.)

_A_ 5. Orwell's description of the prisoner being as "dead as a stone" is a simile that suggests the prisoner was
   A. still and lifeless.
   B. dirty and round.   A stone is still and lifeless.
   C. solid and strong.

_B_ 6. The author implies that the dog

See sentence 20.
The dog's actions suggest it senses something terrible.

A. belonged to the superintendent.
B. sensed that something terrible had happened.
C. had no understanding of what was going on around him.

_A_ 7. When the superintendent says, "Well, that's all for this morning," he implies that

Since it is only a little past 8 a.m., there will probably be other work to do in the morning, but no more executions.

A. there may be more executions in the afternoon.
B. there has been only one execution that morning.
C. there will be no other work to do in the morning.

_A_ 8. When the superintendent says, "*He's* all right," he means that

By emphasizing *he*, the superintendent is suggesting the rest of them may not be all right.

A. while the prisoner is at peace, everyone else is still shaken.
B. the prisoner got the punishment that he deserved.
C. the prisoner had wanted to die and got his wish.

_C_ 9. We can infer from the superintendent's behavior that he

The superintendent's reaction after the hanging (sentences 24–29) suggests inference C.

A. was a cruel man who enjoyed seeing others executed.
B. refused to attend any more executions after this one.
C. considered executions an unpleasant part of his duty.

_B_ 10. We can infer from the details in this passage and another excerpt from the essay, shown below, that the author probably was

A. in favor of capital punishment.
B. troubled by capital punishment.
C. not interested in the issue of capital punishment.

"He [the prisoner] and we were a party of men, walking together, seeing, hearing, feeling, understanding the same world; and in two minutes, with a sudden snap, one of us would be gone—one mind less, one world less."

The excerpt and the author's mention of "another second of life" (sentence 14) both suggest that he is not comfortable with the idea of killing a person as a punishment.

Inferences in Graphs and Tables

You have already tried your hand at making inferences from a picture, the cartoon about the couple deciding not to eat at the restaurant. Many of the cartoons in newspapers and magazines depend on your inference skills. Other "pictures" that require inferences are graphs and tables, which combine words with visual representations. Authors of textbooks, professional and newspaper articles, and other materials often organize large amounts of material into graphs and tables. Very often, the graphs and tables are used to show comparisons and changes that take place over time.

As with other reading material, to infer the ideas presented in graphs and tables, you must consider all the information presented.

Steps in Reading a Graph or Table

To find and make sense of the information in a graph or table, follow a few steps.

1 Read the title. It will tell you what the table or graph is about in general.

- What is the title of the graph on the next page? _____
  Changes in U.S. Workforce, 1900-2010

2 Check the source. At the bottom of a table or graph, you will usually find the source of the information, an indication of the reliability of its material.

- What is the source of the graph on the next page? _____
  Statistical Abstract 2005; James M. Henslin, 2007

3 Read any labels or captions at the top, the side, or underneath that tell exactly what each column, line, bar, number, or other item represents. This information includes such things as quantities, percentages, and years.

- What is the span of years covered in the graph? _____1900-2010_____
- Which types of work does the graph cover? _____
  White-collar, blue-collar, and farming

4 Once you have taken the above steps, you are ready to infer from the graph or table whatever information you seek from it.

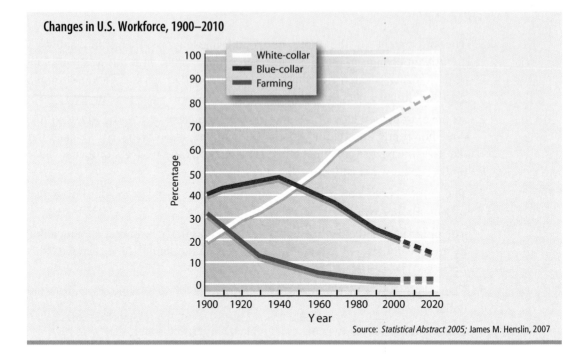

Changes in U.S. Workforce, 1900–2010

Source: *Statistical Abstract 2005;* James M. Henslin, 2007

✓ *Check Your Understanding*

See if you can put a check (✓) by the **three** inferences that are most logically based on the above graph.

✓ 1. The work force of 1900 was very different from the work force of today.

___ 2. Before 1900, farmers made up the smallest percentage of workers.

___ 3. In 1940, the percentages of farm workers and white-collar workers were about equal.

✓ 4. In general, as the number of farming and blue-collar workers has decreased, the number of white-collar workers has increased.

___ 5. In 1940, blue-collar workers made up about 25 percent of the U.S. work force.

✓ 6. In the future, most U.S. workers are likely to be white-collar workers.

Explanation

1. The movement of the three horizontal lines across the graph shows a significant change in the U.S. work force since 1900, with farmers and blue-collar workers decreasing sharply and white-collar workers rising strongly. You should have checked this item.

2. At the extreme left side of the graph, which represents 1900, the lowest of the three horizontal lines is for white-collar workers, not farmers. So we can infer that for at least a short time before 1900, white-collar workers probably made up the smallest percentage of the work force.

3. The graph shows that in 1940 the number of farm workers was far below that of white-collar workers.

4. The graph shows the decline of farmers and blue-collar workers accompanied by the steady rise of white-collar workers. You should have checked this item.

5. The graph shows that in 1940 over 50 percent of U.S. workers were blue-collar.

6. Given the trends shown on the graph, estimated through 2010, it seems a reasonable assumption that most U.S. workers will be white-collar workers. You should have checked this item.

PRACTICE 5

Read the table on the next page, following the steps for reading graphs and tables on page 290. Then put a check (✓) by the **three** inferences that are most logically based on the table.

      ___ 1. Most jobs which require short-term training pay about the same as those which require associate's degrees.

      ✓ 2. In general, as the education requirement of a job rises, so does the pay.

      ___ 3. There will be almost no need in the years ahead for new teachers and teaching assistants in United States classrooms.

      ___ 4. Retail salespeople require more training than carpenters.

      ✓ 5. Registered nursing pays well yet requires less education than other high-paying jobs.

      ✓ 6. There will be many opportunities in the years ahead in the health, education, and sales areas.

Occupations with the largest job growth, 2004–2014

OCCUPATION	SALARY RANKING	EDUCATION AND TRAINING CATEGORY
Retail salespersons	VL	Short-term on-the-job training
Registered nurses	VH	Associate's degree
Postsecondary teachers	VH	Doctoral degree
Customer service representatives	L	Moderate-term on-the-job training
Janitors and cleaners (no maids/housekeepers)	VL	Short-term on-the-job-training
Waiters and waitresses	VL	Short-term on-the-job-training
Food preparation/serving workers (including fast) food)	VL	Short-term on-the-job-training
Home Health aides	VL	Short-term on-the-job-training
Nursing aides, orderlies, and attendants	L	Postsecondary vocational award
General and operations managers	VH	Bachelor's or higher degree, plus work experience
Personal and home care aides	VL	Short-term on-the-job-training
Elementary school teachers, except special education	H	Bachelor's degree
Accountants and auditors	VH	Bachelor's degree
Office clerks, general	L	Short-term on-the-job-training
Laborers and freight, stock, and material movers, hand	VL	Short-term on-the-job-training
Receptionists and information clerks	L	Short-term on-the-job-training
Landscaping and groundskeeping workers	L	Short-term on-the-job-training
Truck drivers, heavy and tractor-trailer	H	Moderate-term on-the-job-training
Computer software engineers, applications	VH	Bachelor's degree
Maintenance and repair workers, general	H	Moderate-term on-the-job-training
Medical assistants	L	Moderate-term on-the-job-training
Executive secretaries and administrative assistants	H	Moderate-term on-the-job-training
Sales representatives (no technical/scientific products)	VH	Moderate-term on-the-job-training
Carpenters	H	Long-term on-the-job-training
Teacher assistants	VL	Short-term on-the-job-training
Child care workers	VL	Short-term on-the-job-training
Food preparation workers	VL	Short-term on-the-job-training
Maids and housekeeping cleaners	VL	Short-term on-the-job-training
Truck drivers, light or delivery services	L	Short-term on-the-job-training
Computers systems analysts	VH	Bachelor's degree

Salary rankings: VH = Very High ($43,605 and over), H = High ($28,590 to $43,604), L = Low ($20,185 to $28,589), VL = Very Low (up to $20,184)

Source: Bureau of Labor Statistics, December 12, 2005

Item 2: Most occupations with a salary ranking of H or VH require an associate's degree, a bachelor's degree, or more.

Item 5: Registered nurses need only an associate's degree.

Item 6: The heading indicates this is a list of "Occupations with the largest job growth." Many of the jobs listed are in health, education, and sales areas.

CHAPTER REVIEW

In this chapter, you learned the following:

- Many important ideas in reading are not stated directly but must be inferred. To make inferences about implied ideas, use the information provided as well as your own experience and logic.

- Inferences are also a key part of reading literature and such visual materials as cartoons, tables, and graphs.

The next chapter—Chapter 8—will help make you aware of an author's purpose and tone.

On the Web: If you are using this book in class, you can visit our website for additional practice in making inferences. Go to **www.townsendpress.com** and click on "Online Exercises."

REVIEW TEST 1

To review what you've learned in this chapter, answer each of the following questions about inferences.

1. An inference is an idea that is *(directly stated, suggested)* ___suggested___ by the author.

   See page 273.

2. When making inferences, it is *(a mistake, useful)* ___useful___ to use our own experience as well as the author's clues.

   See page 277.

3. When making inferences, it is *(a mistake, useful)* ___useful___ to use our sense of logic as well as the author's clues.

   See page 274.

4. ___T___ TRUE OR FALSE? A reader must make inferences when finding the meaning of words through context and when finding implied main ideas.

   See page 274.

5. Making inferences is a key skill in reading literature because writers of fiction do not so much *(tell, show)* ___tell___ us what they mean as *(tell, show)* ___show___ us with vivid specific details.

   See page 282.

REVIEW TEST 2

A. (1–4.) Put a check (✓) by the **four** inferences that are most logically based on the information given in the cartoon.

DILBERT reproduced by permission of UNIVERSAL PRESS SYNDICATE, Inc.

Item 1: Supported because man with the glasses says, "The dumpster seems a bit inappropriate."

Item 3: Supported with "no employee benefits."

Item 5: Supported with "I just love hiring . . ."

Item 7: Supported with "no union."

✓ 1. The man with glasses thinks the boss is unfair to temporary workers.

___ 2. The man with glasses agrees with the boss's behavior.

✓ 3. The boss values saving money more than he values caring for workers.

___ 4. The boss feels a bit guilty about his treatment of temporary workers.

✓ 5. The boss has probably hired and fired other temporary workers.

___ 6. The worker in the boss's arms is about to be promoted.

✓ 7. The cartoonist implies that temporary workers have no power in the workplace.

___ 8. The cartoonist implies that companies should not hire temporary workers.

B. (5–8.) Read the following textbook passage and then put a check (✓) by the **four** inferences that are most logically supported by the information given.

¹Your sister has a new boyfriend. ²The first time you meet him, he corners you and talks to you for an hour about football, a subject in which you have no interest at all. ³You come away with the impression that he is an inconsiderate bore. ⁴The next two times you see him, however, he says not a word about football; instead, he participates in the general conversation and makes some witty and intelligent remarks. ⁵What is your impression of him now? ⁶Do you find him likable and interesting on the basis of the last two encounters? ⁷Do you average out the early minus and the later plus and come out with a neutral zero? ⁸Neither is likely. ⁹What is likely is that you still think of him as an inconsiderate bore, for research suggests that first impressions, as our mothers and fathers told us, are quite lasting.

Item 2:
Supported by
sentence 9.

Item 4:
Supported by
sentences 2–3.

Item 6:
Supported by
sentence 7.

Item 7:
Being objective
would require us
to change first
opinions, but
we don't do that.

_____ 1. First impressions are usually negative.

✓ 2. It is useful to make good first impressions.

_____ 3. It's a bad idea to discuss football when you first meet someone.

✓ 4. To make a good impression, it helps to notice what interests the other person.

_____ 5. A "neutral zero" impression of someone would be negative.

✓ 6. A "neutral zero" impression of someone would be neither positive nor negative.

✓ 7. It's not so easy to be objective about others.

_____ 8. Second impressions can be even more powerful than first impressions.

C. (9–10.) After reading the following passage, put a check (✓) by the **two** inferences that are most firmly based on the given facts.

> ¹A man is talking to the Lord, trying to understand His eternal nature. ²"Lord," he asks, "what's a million years to you?" ³"A million years is but a second to me," the Lord explains. ⁴"And a million dollars?" ⁵"A penny," the Lord replies. ⁶The man feels bold and now proceeds to ask, "Lord, would you give me a million dollars?" ⁷"Sure," the Lord replies. ⁸"Just a second."

✓ 1. In comparison with eternity, a million years is a short time.

✓ 2. The man will not live long enough to collect his million dollars.

_____ 3. The Lord knows the man would just waste the money.

_____ 4. The man is poor.

Item 1: Supported by sentence 3.
Item 2: Supported by sentences 3 and 8.

REVIEW TEST 3

A. (1–4.) Read the graph below. Then put a check (✓) by the **four** statements that are most logically supported by the graph.

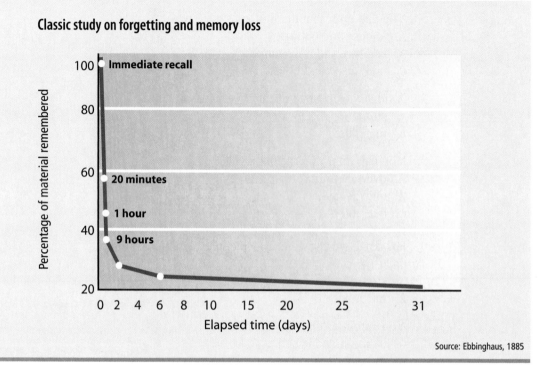

Classic study on forgetting and memory loss

Percentage of material remembered

100 ○ **Immediate recall**

80

60 ● **20 minutes**

● **1 hour**

40 ● **9 hours**

20

0 2 4 6 8 10   15   20   25   31

Elapsed time (days)

Source: Ebbinghaus, 1885

Item 1:
Over 40% loss in twenty minutes.

Item 3:
About 70%.

Item 5:
Over 70% in the first two days; less than 10% after day 2.

Item 6:
Common-sense ways to offset the speed of forgetting.

✓ 1. The most rapid memory loss takes place in the first twenty minutes after exposure to new material.

___ 2. After one month, most people remember only half of the new material they've learned.

✓ 3. In a single day, people are likely to forget over half of the new material they've learned.

___ 4. By the end of a month, people tend to forget 100 percent of new material learned.

✓ 5. After two days, the rate of forgetting slows down greatly.

✓ 6. Since people rapidly forget new material, taking notes in classes and reviewing them regularly are useful study techniques.

___ 7. A student who sits in class and listens carefully but does not take notes can often do just as well as a student who takes notes.

B. Identify each figure of speech as a simile or a metaphor. Then answer each inference question that follows.

_A_ 5. My mother's angry gaze bored into me <u>like</u> twin laser beams.
  A. simile   The word *like* signals the simile.
  B. metaphor

_A_ 6. You can infer that the mother's gaze was
  A. intense and cutting.
  B. exciting and adventurous.   Laser beams are intense and cutting.
  C. unfocused and bored.

_B_ 7. A tidal wave of bad events overtook the family.
  A. simile   Comparison that omits *like* or *as*.
  B. metaphor

_A_ 8. You can infer that the bad events were
  A. overwhelming.
  B. unexpected.   A tidal wave is overwhelming.
  C. bearable.

_A_ 9. His kind words were <u>as</u> welcome as a flash of sunlight on a cloudy day.
  A. simile   The word *as* signals the simile.
  B. metaphor

_C_ 10. You can infer that the words were
  A. depressing and sad.
  B. disorienting.   Sunlight on a cloudy day is
  C. warm and unexpected.   warm and unexpected.

REVIEW TEST 4

Here is a chance to apply your understanding of patterns of organization to a passage from a college textbook: *Essentials of Sociology: A Down-to-Earth Approach*, Seventh Edition, by James M. Henslin. To help you continue to strengthen your skills, the reading is followed by questions not only on what you've learned in this chapter but also on what you've learned in previous chapters.

Words to Watch

Below are some words in the reading that do not have strong context support. Each word is followed by the number of the paragraph in which it appears and its meaning there. These words are indicated in the article by a small circle (°).

perplexed (1): puzzled
blatant (5): obvious
resident (7): a doctor receiving specialized training
clinch (9): make sure of getting
industrialized (15): developed in the manufacturing and sales of goods

GENDER INEQUALITY IN HEALTH CARE AND IN THE WORKPLACE

James M. Henslin

GENDER INEQUALITY IN HEALTH CARE

1   Medical researchers were perplexed.° Reports were coming in from all over the country: Women were twice as likely as men to die after coronary bypass surgery. Researchers at Cedars-Sinai Medical Center in Los Angeles checked their own records. They found that of 2,300 coronary bypass patients, 4.6 percent of the women died as a result of the surgery, compared with 2.6 percent of the men.

2   These findings presented a sociological puzzle. To solve it, researchers first turned to biology. In coronary bypass surgery, a blood vessel is taken from one part of the body and stitched to an artery on the surface of the heart. Perhaps this operation was more difficult to perform on women because they have smaller arteries. To find out, researchers measured the amount of time that surgeons kept patients on the heart-lung machine while they operated. They were surprised to learn that women spent less time on the machine than men. This indicated that the operation was not more difficult to perform on women.

3   As the researchers probed, a surprising answer emerged: unintended sexual discrimination. Physicians had not taken the chest pains of their women patients as seriously as they took the complaints of their men patients. The physicians were ten times more likely to give men exercise stress tests and radioactive heart scans. They also sent men to surgery on the basis of abnormal stress tests, but waited until women

showed clear-cut symptoms of heart disease before sending them to surgery. Patients who have surgery after the disease is more advanced are less likely to survive.

4   As more women become physicians, perhaps this will change. We know that women doctors are more likely to order Pap smears and mammograms, so it is likely that they will be more responsive to the health complaints of women.

5   In the box below, we look at a more blatant° form of sexism in medicine.

Cold-Hearted Surgeons and Their Women Victims

6   Sociologist Sue Fisher, who did participant observation in a hospital, was surprised to hear surgeons recommend total hysterectomy (removal of both the uterus and the ovaries) when no cancer was present. When she asked why, the men doctors explained that the uterus and ovaries are "potentially disease-producing." They also said that they are unnecessary after the childbearing years, so why not remove them? Doctors who reviewed hysterectomies confirmed this bias: They found that three out of four of these surgeries were, in their term, inappropriate.

7   Surgical sexism has a powerful motive—greed. Surgeons make money by performing this surgery. But they have to "sell" the operation, for women, to understate the matter, are reluctant to part with these organs. Here is how one resident° explained the "hard sell" to sociologist Diana Scully:

8   "You have to look for your surgical procedures; you have to go after patients. Because no one is crazy enough to come and say, 'Hey, here I am. I want you to operate on me.' You have to sometimes convince the patient that she is really sick—if she is, of course [laughs], and that she is better off with a surgical procedure."

9   To "convince" a woman to have this surgery, the doctor tells her that, unfortunately, the examination has turned up fibroids in her uterus—and they might turn into cancer. This statement is often sufficient, for it frightens women, who picture themselves dying from cancer. To clinch° the sale, the surgeon withholds the rest of the truth—that the fibroids are common, that they most likely will not turn into cancer, and that the patient has several nonsurgical alternatives.

10   I wonder how men would feel if surgeons systematically suggested to them that they be castrated when they get older—since "that organ is no longer necessary, and it might cause disease."

GENDER INEQUALITY IN THE WORKPLACE

11   To examine the work setting is to make visible basic relations between men and women. Let's begin with one of the most remarkable areas of gender inequality at work, the pay gap.

The Gender Pay Gap

12   One of the chief characteristics of the U.S. work force is a steady growth in the numbers of women who work for wages outside the home. Figure 1 shows that in 1900 one of five people in the U.S. paid work force was a woman. By 1940, this ratio had grown to one of four, by 1960, to one of three, and today it is almost one of two.

13   After college, you might like to take a few years off, travel a bit, and sit under a palm tree and drink pina coladas. But chances are, you are going to work instead. Since you have to work, how would you like to earn an extra $635,000 on your job? If this sounds appealing, read on. I'm going to reveal how you can make an extra $1,300 a month between the ages of 25 and 65.

14   Is this hard to do? Actually, it is simple for some, but impossible for others. As Figure 2 shows, all you have to do is be born a male and graduate from college. If we compare full-time workers, based on current differences in earnings, this is how much more money the average male college graduate can expect to earn over the course of his career. Hardly any single factor

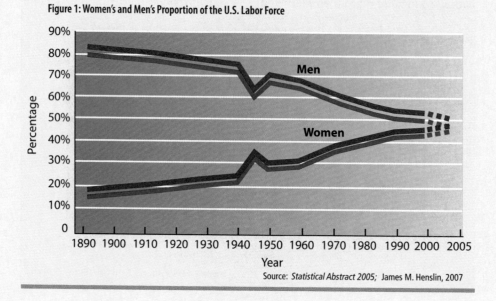

Figure 1: Women's and Men's Proportion of the U.S. Labor Force

Source: *Statistical Abstract 2005;* James M. Henslin, 2007

pinpoints gender discrimination better than this total. You can also see that the pay gap shows up at all levels of education.

15   The pay gap is so great that women who work full time average only 70 percent of what men are paid. As Figure 3 shows, the pay gap used to be even worse. You can also see that the gap closed a bit during the 1990s. Since then, it has held fairly constant, hovering between 65 percent and 70 percent. The gender gap in pay occurs not only in the United States but also in all industrialized° nations.

16   If $635,000 additional earnings aren't enough, how would you like to make another $166,000 extra at work? If so, just make sure that you are not only a man but also a tall man. Over their lifetimes, men who are over 6 feet tall average $166,000 more than men who

are 5 feet 5 inches or less. Taller women also make more than shorter women. But even when it comes to height, the gender pay gap persists, and tall men make more than tall women.

What logic can underlie the gender   17 pay gap? Earlier we saw that college degrees are gender-linked, so perhaps this gap is due to career choices. Maybe women are more likely to choose lower-paying jobs, such as teaching grade school, while men are more likely to go into better-paying fields, such as business and engineering. Actually, this is true, and researchers have found that about *half* the pay gap is due to such factors. And the balance? It consists of a combination of gender discrimination and what is called the "child penalty"—women missing out on work experience and opportunities while they care for children.

For college students, the gender   18

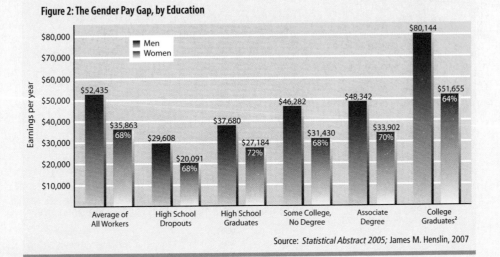

Figure 2: The Gender Pay Gap, by Education

Source: *Statistical Abstract 2005*; James M. Henslin, 2007

gap in pay begins with the first job after graduation. You might know of a particular woman who was offered a higher salary than most men in her class, but she would be an exception.

On average, men enjoy a "testosterone bonus," and employers start them out at higher salaries than women. Depending on your sex, then, you will either benefit from the pay gap or be victimized by it.

The Gender Gap Over Time:
What Percentage of Men's Income Do Women Earn?

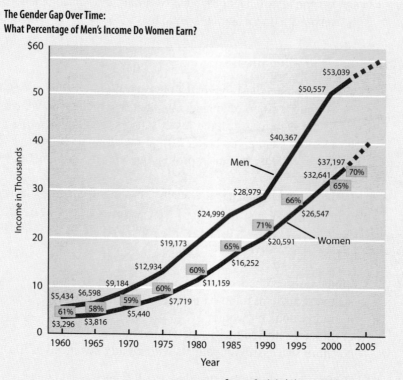

Source: *Statistical Abstract 2005;* James M. Henslin, 2007

Reading Comprehension Questions

Vocabulary in Context

___B___   1. In the sentence below, the word *probed* (prōbd) means
        A. decided.
        B. investigated.
        C. knew all along.
        D. gave up.

> If the answer unfolded, the researchers must have investigated to find it.

"As the researchers probed, a surprising answer unfolded—unintended sexual discrimination." (Paragraph 3)

Central Point and Main Ideas

___D___   2. Which sentence best expresses the central point of the selection?
        A. Among a group of business graduates, women who were as qualified as the men were offered lower salaries than the men.
        B. Doctors have given better care to men than to women.
        C. An excellent way to improve your lifetime earnings is to graduate from college.
        D. Discrimination against women exists in the country's health care and workplace.

> Answer A covers only Figure 2. Answer B ignores paragraphs 11–18. C ignores the issue of gender inequality.

Supporting Details

___C___   3. Medical researchers discovered that coronary bypass surgery is
        A. more difficult to do on people with smaller coronary arteries.
        B. rarely done on women.
        C. no more difficult to do on women than on men.
        D. more successful on patients with greatly advanced heart disease.

> See paragraph 2.

___C___   4. Half of the pay gap between men and women is due to
        A. the fact that men tend to be taller than women.
        B. the "child penalty."
        C. the fact that women are more likely than men to choose lower-paying jobs.
        D. the fact that fewer women than men graduate from college.

> See paragraph 17.

Transitions

___C___ 5. The sentence below expresses a relationship of
      A. addition.
      B. comparison.   The word *but* signals the contrast.
      C. contrast.
      D. time.

> "They . . . sent men to surgery on the basis of abnormal stress tests, but waited until women showed clear-cut symptoms of coronary heart disease . . ." (Paragraph 3)

Patterns of Organization

___A___ 6. Paragraph 17
      A. looks at the possible causes of the gender pay gap.
      B. lists instances of the pay gap according to profession.
      C. defines and illustrates the pay gap in the US work force.
      D. compares how similar men and women are in their salary
          expectations.   The paragraph names three possible causes: job choice, gender discrimination, and the "child penalty."

Inferences

___B___ 7. The author put the words *sell* and *hard sell* (paragraph 7) and *convince*
The terms are usually connected with effective salesmanship.   (paragraph 9) in quotation marks to imply that some surgeons
      A. must convince themselves of the need to remove a woman's uterus and ovaries.
      B. consider the total hysterectomy to be a money-making procedure for which good salesmanship is required.
      C. do not realize that fibroids will probably not turn into cancer and thus may not require any surgery.
      D. are not qualified or sufficiently experienced to do a total hysterectomy safely.

___D___ 8. Figure 1 suggests
      A. that in a few years, women are likely to make up half of the U.S. work force.
      B. that the proportion of women in the work force has increased almost continuously since the early 1900s.
      C. that in the early part of the twentieth century, a working mother would have been considered unusual.
      D. all of the above.   Answer A is supported by the fact that the percentage of women has been steadily increasing and is nearly 50%. B is supported because the percentage has increased from below 20% to almost 50% with only a brief decline between 1945 and 1950. C is supported by the fact that fewer than 25% of women were in the labor force between 1890 and 1940.

_D_ 9. Figure 2 suggests that

In all categories, the
bar representing
women's pay is
lower than the bar
representing
men's pay.

A. women with a college degree make less than men with a high school degree.

B. women are better off not working for a college degree.

C. more education decreases the gap between men's and women's pay.

D. men and women are paid unequally at all educational levels.

_B_ 10. From Figure 3, we can infer

Women's salaries
dropped from 71%
of men's salaries in
1990 to 66% in 1995.

A. there has not been much change in men's salaries between 1960 and 2000.

B. the gender gap actually increased from about 1990 to 1995.

C. in the near future, women's salaries are likely to catch up with men's.

D. in the near future, men's salaries are likely to stay the same.

Discussion Questions

1. Medical researchers discovered that men and women receive different health care because of "unintended sexual discrimination." How might such clear-cut discrimination be "unintended"? Do you know of any cases of gender health discrimination? Tell what happened.

2. According to Henslin, women suffer and men benefit from gender discrimination in the U.S. work force. Have you ever experienced or witnessed gender discrimination at work? Tell what happened.

3. Did it surprise you to learn that in modern U.S. society women earn significantly less than men? Explain. In your opinion, what are the causes of the gender gap, and what do you think would have to happen for it to end?

Note: Writing assignments for this selection appear on pages 603–604.

Check Your Performance   **INFERENCES**

Activity	Number Right	Points	Score
Review Test 1 (5 items)	_____	× 2 =	_____
Review Test 2 (10 items)	_____	× 3 =	_____
Review Test 3 (10 items)	_____	× 3 =	_____
Review Test 4 (10 items)	_____	× 3 =	_____
		TOTAL SCORE =	_____%

Enter your total score into the **Reading Performance Chart: Review Tests** on the inside back cover.

INFERENCES: Mastery Test 1

A. (1–3.) Put a check (✓) by the **three** inferences that are most logically based on the information suggested by the cartoon.

PEANUTS

PEANUTS reproduced by permission of United Feature Syndicate, Inc.

Item 1:
By saying that Linus "can't take destructive criticism," Lucy implies that she has recently criticized him.

Item 4:
Lucy's complaint suggests that she does not realize Linus might respond better to constructive criticism.

Item 6: The cartoonist makes us laugh at Lucy. We see that her destructive criticism of Linus has not been helpful.

✓ 1. Lucy has just criticized the boy, Linus.

___ 2. Linus feels Lucy's criticism is valid.

___ 3. Lucy feels very guilty that Linus has taken her criticism badly.

✓ 4. Lucy doesn't seem to realize that people may accept constructive criticism but not destructive criticism.

___ 5. The cartoonist believes we should never criticize others.

✓ 6. The cartoonist believes it's best to criticize others in a constructive way.

B. (4–6.) Read the passage below. Then check (✓) the **three** inferences that are most logically supported by the information given.

Item 2: The man "waved the smoke away" (sentence 2).

Item 3: Experience tells us that buses often have no-smoking signs. And sentence 2 tells us the smoke is bothering the man.

Item 4: The driver's reaction of shaking his head and continuing to drive (sentence 4) suggests that he refused to get involved.

[1]Shortly after the young woman sat down in the bus, she lit a cigarette. [2]The man next to her waved some smoke away, nudged her, and pointed to the sign at the front of the bus.

[3]The woman did not turn to look at the man and continued smoking calmly. [4]The man got up and spoke to the bus driver, who continued driving and shook his head. [5]At the next stop, the man, looking disgusted, got off the bus.

___ 1. The man had never smoked.

✓ 2. The smoke was bothering the man.

✓ 3. The man pointed to a no-smoking sign.

✓ 4. The driver refused to get involved.

___ 5. The man got off the bus because it was his stop.

___ 6. The driver was related to the woman.

(Continues on next page)

C. (7–10.) Read each passage below. Then check (✓) the **two** inferences after each passage which are most logically supported by the information given.

1.

Item 2: The descriptions in sentences 2 and 3 support this inference.

Item 5: The reactions of the daughter, wife, and son (sentences 4–6) would not restore a person's faith.

¹My day has not ended. ²When I get home I suddenly realize that I have between thirty and forty pounds of fish to clean—rockfish yet, all full of spines and pricklers and razor-sharp teeth. ³When I'm finished, I have so many holes in me I look like a composite of George Custer, Saint Sebastian, and Bonnie and Clyde, but my family comes out to view the catch and restore my faith in the whole enterprise.

⁴"Yuk," says my daughter.

⁵"That's a lot of rockfish for people who aren't all that into rockfish," says my wife.

⁶"I wouldn't eat that on a bet," says my son.

____ 1. The family is on vacation.

✓ 2. Rockfish are difficult to clean.

____ 3. The author's family appreciates his hard work to feed them.

____ 4. The man enjoys the challenge of cleaning rockfish.

✓ 5. When he praises his family for restoring his faith, the author is being sarcastic.

2.   ¹I guess I did it because I hadn't studied very much. ²And it seemed so easy—everybody knows that Mr. Wagner keeps his office door unlocked. ³It's just too bad things didn't work out for me. ⁴Now my classmates are mad at me because they must re-study for the new test Mr. Wagner is making up. ⁵My parents have taken away my car keys. ⁶And even worse, I'll have to go to summer school for biology.

✓ 1. The speaker stole a test.

____ 2. The speaker had been failing the course.

____ 3. The speaker deeply regrets not studying more.

____ 4. The speaker will never cheat again.

✓ 5. The speaker does not seem to have a guilty conscience about what he did.

Item 1: Sentences 1–2 support this inference.

Item 5: Sentences 3–6 suggest that the speaker is sorry that he got caught and is not happy about the consequences. But nothing he says suggests he feels remorse for stealing the test.

INFERENCES: Mastery Test 2

A. (1–3.) Put a check (✓) by the **three** inferences that are most logically based on the information suggested by the cartoon.

© 1997 Randy Glasbergen. www.glasbergen.com

GLASBERGEN

"Let's try getting up every night at 2:00 AM to feed the cat. If we enjoy doing that, then we can talk about having a baby."

Item 1: The man's comment implies that the woman has been talking about having a baby.

Item 4: The man's suggestion for putting off talking about having a baby shows his lack of enthusiasm.

Item 5: The expression on the woman's face suggests her dismay.

✓ 1. The woman would like to have a baby.

___ 2. The couple often have serious disagreements.

___ 3. The couple will divorce because of the man's unwillingness to have a baby.

✓ 4. The man is not enthusiastic about becoming a father.

✓ 5. The woman is dismayed by the man's lack of enthusiasm for having a baby.

___ 6. The woman has been trying to get pregnant for a long time.

B. (4–6.) Read the following quotation. Then put a check (✓) by the **three** inferences that are most logically based on the information given.

[1]"Good character is more to be praised than outstanding talent. [2]Most talents are, to some extent, a gift. [3]Good character, by contrast, is not given to us. [4]We have to build it piece by piece—by thought, choice, courage and determination."

— John Luther

Item 1: If talent is a gift, you can't earn it. But if character is consciously built, you can earn a reputation.

Item 3: See sentence 1.

✓ 1. You can't earn talent, but you can earn a reputation for being good.

___ 2. People of good character tend to look down on talented people.

✓ 3. People who possess outstanding talent don't deserve praise.

___ 4. In some ways, people with talent have it easier than people without talent.

(Continues on next page)

Item 6: The fact that sentence 1 needs to be stated suggests this inference.

_____ 5. People with outstanding talent are often selfish and lazy.

✓ 6. Talented people often receive more attention than people of good character.

C. Read the following passage. Then, in the spaces provided, write the letter of the most logical answer to each question, based on the information given in the passage.

> [1]My friends have no friends. [2]They are men. [3]They think they have friends, and if you ask them whether they have friends they will say yes, but they don't really. [4]They think, for instance, that I'm their friend, but I'm not. [5]It's OK. [6]They're not my friends either.
>
> [7]The reason for that is that we are all men—and men, I have come to believe, cannot or will not have real friends. [8]They have something else—companions, buddies, pals, chums, someone to drink with and someone to lunch with, but no one when it comes to saying how they feel—especially how they hurt.
>
> [9]Women know this. [10]They talk about it among themselves. [11]To women, this inability of men to say what they feel is a source of amazement and then anguish and then, finally, betrayal. [12]Women will tell you all the time that they don't know the men they live with. [13]They talk of long silences and of drifting off and of keeping feelings hidden and never letting on about troubles or bothers or whatever.

_C_ 7. We can infer that the author of this passage
    A. has genuine friends himself.   See sentence 7.
    B. believes men have no need of genuine friends.
    C. feels something prevents men from having genuine friends.

_B_ 8. We can infer that the author
    A. is proud he is able to share his feelings better than other men.
    B. believes women want the men in their lives to share their feelings.
    C. believes men have more hurt feelings than women do.
    See sentence 11.

_A_ 9. We can infer that the author believes women
    A. have genuine friends.
    B. prefer "strong, silent" men.   See sentence 7.
    C. understand why men do not talk about their feelings.

_C_ 10. We can conclude that the author thinks
    A. men realize they don't have friends.
    B. women should try to be more like men when it comes to friendship.
    C. men's relationships aren't deep enough to be genuine friendships.
    See sentence 8.

INFERENCES: Mastery Test 3

A. (1–3.) Put a check (✓) by the **three** inferences that are most logically based on the information suggested by the cartoon.

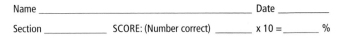

Item 3: The fact that the committee members are dressed as executioners suggests that the decision has already been made.

Item 4: Because the two young men are facing a roomful of executioners, it would be logical for them to expect something bad.

Item 6: The cartoon is called *Working Daze*, and the room in the drawing looks like a corporate meeting room.

_____ 1. The two young men have committed a serious crime.

_____ 2. The two young men will be invited to wear masks and carry axes, also.

✓ 3. The committee members have already made up their minds about the two young men.

✓ 4. The two young men in the doorway expect something bad is about to happen to them.

_____ 5. The two young men are powerful members of a corporation.

✓ 6. The two young men in the doorway work for a corporation.

B. (4–6.) Read the following textbook passage. Then put a check (✓) by the **three** inferences which are most logically supported by the information given.

> [1]The swim team at the University of California at Berkeley was having a practice. [2]After a race, the coach told each swimmer his time—but it wasn't his real time. [3]The coach falsified the time, making it slower than it really was. [4]During the next race, the coach watched what happened. [5]Some of his swimmers swam significantly faster than before, while others swam considerably slower than their usual pace.

(Continues on next page)

Item 4: Some of the swimmers "swam significantly faster than before" (sentence 5).

Item 5: Experience supports this inference. And the different reactions of the swimmers also support this inference.

___ 1. The swim coach at Berkeley expected his swimmers to react exactly the way they did.

___ 2. Some of the Berkeley swimmers probably knew about their coach's experiment before it took place.

___ 3. Giving disappointing news to athletes is the best way to increase their performance.

✓ 4. Disappointing news about performance can make some athletes try harder and perform better.

✓ 5. People's ability to perform certain tasks is often related to their thoughts and attitudes.

✓ 6. Disappointing news about performance can make some athletes grow discouraged and perform poorly.

Item 6: Some of the swimmers "swam considerably slower than their usual pace" (sentence 5).

C. Read the passage below, taken from the autobiographical book *Move On* by the television journalist Linda Ellerbee. Then, in the spaces provided, write the letter of the most logical answer to each question, based on the information given in the passage.

¹Television changed my family forever. ²We stopped eating dinner at the dining-room table after my mother found out about TV trays. ³We kept the TV trays behind the kitchen door and served ourselves from pots on the stove. ⁴Setting and clearing the dining-room table used to be my job; now, setting and clearing meant unfolding and wiping our TV trays, then, when we'd finished, wiping and folding our TV trays. ⁵Dinner was served in time for one program and finished in time for another. ⁶During dinner we used to talk to one another. ⁷Now television talked to us. ⁸If you had something you absolutely had to say, you waited until the commercial, which is, I suspect, where I learned to speak in thirty-second bursts. ⁹As a future writer, it was good practice in editing my thoughts. ¹⁰As a little girl, it was lonely as hell. ¹¹Once in a while, I'd pass our dining-room table and stop, thinking I heard our ghosts sitting around talking to one another, saying stuff.

_A_ 7. We can infer that as a child, Ellerbee
   A. preferred eating at the dining-room table to eating in front of TV.
   B. was glad that she no longer had to set and clear the dining-room table.
   C. wished that her parents watched TV programs that she enjoyed.

_B_ 8. Ellerbee suggests that   Sentences 10–11 support inference A.
   A. TV can help people feel less lonely.
   B. it's possible to feel lonely even when others are around.
   C. talking with others does not help to reduce loneliness.

_C_ 9. We can infer that in Ellerbee's home   Sentence 10 supports inference B.
   A. her mother was aware that Ellerbee was unhappy with TV.
   B. there were no other children for Ellerbee to talk to.
   C. watching TV became more important than talking and listening to family members.   Sentences 6–8 support inference C.

_A_ 10. We can infer that when Ellerbee imagined ghosts, she
   A. was remembering better times with her family.   Ellerbee is remembering
   B. was scared of passing by the dining room.   the times she describes
   C. realized her childhood home was haunted.   in sentence 6.

INFERENCES: Mastery Test 4

A. After reading the following textbook passage, write the letter of the best answer to each question.

[1]Suppose a man works six or seven days a week in a factory, trying to support his family, but never seems to be able to make ends meet. [2]If he analyzed his situation rationally, he would probably blame the well-to-do generally, and his employers specifically, for failing to pay him an adequate wage. [3]But these people have the power to cut off his income; to oppose them openly would be self-destructive. [4]He could also blame himself for his financial problems, but this too makes him uncomfortable. [5]Instead, he looks to the immigrants who have begun working in his factory. [6]He doesn't really know them, but he suspects they're willing to work for low wages and that many other immigrants are eager to take his job. [7]By a process of twisted logic, he blames these people for his poverty. [8]Soon he is exchanging rumors about "them" with his cronies and supporting efforts to close the border. [9]Hating immigrants makes the man and his friends feel a little better.

The author says the man works six or seven days a week but cannot support his family (sentence 1). This supports inference C. There is no support for inference A or inference B.

___C___ 1. We can infer that the author of the passage thinks
    A. factory workers are not good at managing money.
    B. all factory workers are underpaid.
    C. the man in the example is underpaid.

Sentences 2 and 7 support inference C.

___C___ 2. We can infer that the author
    A. agrees with what the man in the example thinks.
    B. feels that employers and other well-to-do's should hire only immigrants.
    C. is critical of both the man in the example and his well-to-do employers.

Sentence 6 supports inference C and contradicts inferences A and B.

___C___ 3. We can infer that the man in the example probably
    A. has many friends and neighbors who are immigrants.
    B. understands what immigrants think and is aware of their problems.
    C. has no understanding of or meaningful contact with immigrants.

If the man in the example hates immigrants, it is likely that he would oppose hiring them.

___B___ 4. We can infer from the passage that
    A. immigrants are eager to take other people's jobs.
    B. the man in the example would probably oppose hiring immigrants.
    C. most immigrants don't do their jobs as well as domestic workers.

Sentence 9 supports inference A. The passage does not offer an opinion on reducing immigration or on what is right or wrong for employers to do.

___A___ 5. The passage suggests that
    A. some people make themselves feel better by thinking less of others.
    B. immigration should be limited or reduced to protect workers' jobs.
    C. employers are wrong to hire immigrants when domestic workers are available.

(Continues on next page)

313

B. Read the following textbook passage. Then, in the space provided, write the letter of the best answer to each question.

> ¹People interrupt for various reasons. ²One is believing that what they have to say is more important than what the other person is saying. ³Another reason people interrupt is that they believe they know what the other person is going to say and want the person to know that they already know. ⁴People may also interrupt when they are not paying close attention. ⁵The interruption communicates a lack of sensitivity, a superior attitude, or both. ⁶People need to be able to verbalize their ideas and feelings fully; inappropriate interruptions are bound to damage their self-concepts or make them hostile—and possibly both. ⁷Simply stated, whatever you have to say is seldom so important that it requires you to interrupt a person. ⁸When you do interrupt, you should realize that you may be perceived as putting a person down. ⁹The more frequent the interruptions, the greater the potential harm.

_A_ 6. The author of the above passage suggests that people
   A. feel good if others listen carefully to their ideas.
   B. who interrupt don't mind being interrupted themselves.
   C. should learn not to feel insulted when they are interrupted.
                              Sentences 6 and 8 support inference A.

_A_ 7. The author suggests that people may interrupt because they
   A. don't realize that the speaker is in the middle of a point.
   B. are nervous and want the speaker to like and respect them.
   C. are angry at the speaker.   Sentence 4 suggests inference A.

_C_ 8. The author suggests that
   A. it is okay to interrupt others if you feel you are superior to them.
   B. you will never be interrupted if you don't interrupt others.
   C. interruptions can make people feel that their ideas are not worth listening to.   Sentences 6 and 8 support inference C.

_B_ 9. We can conclude from this paragraph that
   A. it is okay for a parent to interrupt a child.
   B. a boss will gain more cooperation by not interrupting workers.
   C. the author of the passage has never been interrupted in a conversation.
                              Sentences 6 and 8 support inference B.

_B_ 10. The passage suggests that people who interrupt
   A. usually are able to predict what others will think about their behavior.
   B. don't always realize how the other person will view the interruption.
   C. should not worry about trying to guess what others are thinking about them.   Sentences 2, 3, and 4 support inference B.

INFERENCES: Mastery Test 5

A. (1–6.) Read the passage below, taken from an essay titled "Darkness at Noon" by Harold Krents, an attorney who was born blind. Then check the **six** statements which are most logically supported by the information given.

Note that the meaning of one word in the passage is given below.

cum laude: with honor

¹There are those who assume that since I can't see, I obviously also cannot hear. ²Very often people will converse with me at the top of their lungs, enunciating each word very carefully. ³Conversely, people will also often whisper, assuming that since my eyes don't work, my ears don't either.

⁴For example, when I go to the airport and ask the ticket agent for assistance to the plane, he or she will invariably pick up the phone, call a ground hostess and whisper: "Hi, Jane, we've got a 76 here." ⁵I have concluded that the word "blind" is not used for one of two reasons: Either they fear that if the dread word is spoken, the ticket agent's retina will immediately detach, or they are reluctant to inform me of my condition, of which I may not have been previously aware.

⁶On the other hand, others know that of course I can hear but believe that I can't talk. ⁷Often, therefore, when my wife and I go out to dinner, a waiter or waitress will ask Kit if "he would like a drink," to which I respond that "indeed he would.". . .

⁸The toughest misconception of all is the view that because I can't see, I can't work. ⁹I was turned down by over forty law firms because of my blindness, even though my qualifications included a cum laude° degree from Harvard College and a good ranking in my Harvard Law School class.

____ 1. It would offend Krents if people were to use the word "blind" in reference to him.

Item 2:
See sentence 4.

✓ 2. The airline's code for a blind passenger was "76."

Item 4:
See sentences 2–3.

____ 3. It is better to whisper to blind people than to speak to them loudly.

Items 5 and 6:
See sentence 7.

✓ 4. Krents prefers that people speak to him in a normal tone of voice.

✓ 5. Sighted persons are sometimes uncomfortable directing conversation toward a blind person.

Item 8:
See sentence 9.

✓ 6. Krents's wife is not blind.

Item 10:
The entire passage supports this inference.

____ 7. Blindness seems to harm a person's intelligence.

✓ 8. Some employers are biased against blind workers.

____ 9. Harvard is apparently biased against blind students.

✓ 10. Krents speaks frankly about his blindness.

(Continues on next page)

B. (7–10.) Read the paragraph below. Then check the **four** statements which are most logically supported by the information given.

> [1]In 1995, the American Academy of Pediatrics declared that "advertising directed at children is inherently deceptive and exploits children under eight years of age." [2]The academy did not recommend a ban on such advertising because it seemed impractical and would infringe upon advertisers' freedom of speech. [3]Today the health risks faced by the nation's children far outweigh the needs of its mass marketers. [4]Congress should immediately ban all advertisements aimed at children that promote foods high in fat and sugar. [5]Thirty years ago Congress banned cigarette ads from radio and television as a public health measure—and those ads were directed at adults. [6]Smoking has declined ever since. [7]A ban on advertising unhealthy foods to children would discourage eating habits that are not only hard to break, but potentially life-threatening. [8]Moreover, such a ban would encourage the fast-food chains to alter the recipes for their children's meals. [9]Greatly reducing the fat content of McDonald's Happy Meals, for example, could have an immediate effect on the diet of the nation's kids. [10]Every month more than 90 percent of the children in the United States eat at McDonald's.

Item 1: Sentences 5–6 support this inference.

Item 3: Sentence 10 supports this inference.

Item 5: Sentence 4 supports this inference.

Item 8: Sentences 5–7 support this inference.

✓ 1. Cigarette advertisements were effective in encouraging people to continue smoking.

___ 2. The author values advertisers' freedom of speech, especially as it relates to commercials targeting children.

✓ 3. The author believes the number of children at risk of health problems due to poor diets has increased since 1995.

___ 4. Banning fast-food ads is unlikely to have any lasting effect on children's diets, according to the author.

✓ 5. The author feels that the advertisers' right to free speech is less important than the health of the nation's children.

___ 6. TV commercials and other ads probably have little effect on children's behaviors.

___ 7. The author believes fast-food chains can be convinced to voluntarily refrain from advertising unhealthy foods for young children.

✓ 8. The author suggests that children's poor eating habits are as serious a health problem as adults' smoking.

INFERENCES: Mastery Test 6

A. (1–5.) Read the table below. Then put a check by the **five** statements that are most logically based on the table.

Voter Turnout among the World's Democracies

Country	Approximate Voter Turnout	Automatic Registration	Election Day a Holiday or Weekend Day?
Belgium	90%	Yes	Yes
Italy	90%	Yes	Yes
Denmark	85%	Yes	No
Austria	80%	Yes	Yes
France	80%	No	Yes
Germany	80%	Yes	Yes
Great Britain	70%	Yes	No
Canada	65%	Yes	No
Japan	60%	Yes	Yes
United States	50%	No	No

Source: Thomas E. Patterson, *The American Democracy*, 2001.

Item 2: Five of the six countries with the highest voter turnout have Election Day holidays or Sunday elections.

Item 3: Countries that have both of these have higher voter turnout, so it is a logical inference.

Item 5: Japan's voter turnout is only 60%. This is 20% lower than other countries that have the same factors.

Item 6: All of the other countries follow one or both of the practices that make it easier for voters to participate.

Item 9: Their voter participation rate of 90% supports this inference.

_____ 1. About a third of voters in the United States do not vote.

✓ 2. Election Day holidays tend to increase voter turnout rates.

✓ 3. Voter turnout might increase if the United States had automatic voter registration and an Election Day holiday.

_____ 4. Low voter turnout in the United States probably has little to do with automatic voter registration or Election Day holidays.

✓ 5. Factors that have increased voter participation in other countries have not worked as well in Japan.

✓ 6. Compared to the United States, other countries make it easier for voters to participate in elections.

_____ 7. Voter turnout would be better if elections were held on weekend days rather than on holidays.

_____ 8. Voter turnout would be better if elections were held on holidays rather than on weekend days.

✓ 9. Voters in Belgium and Italy care more about political issues than U.S. voters do.

(Continues on next page)

B. Following is a passage from *A Hole in the World*, an autobiographical account by the Pulitzer Prize-winning author Richard Rhodes. Read the passage, and then choose the inferences which are most logically supported by the information given.

¹We played dodgeball at recess. ²Dodgeball was my sport. ³I was light and quick and often managed to escape being picked off until I was the last of my team inside the circle, the winner of the round. ⁴My friend was usually my competition. ⁵One day I kidded him too sharply when he lost and I won. ⁶He gathered a knot of classmates afterward, the girl I dreamed about among them. ⁷They strolled over and surrounded me. ⁸They were smiling and I thought they were friendly; it didn't occur to me to dodge. ⁹The boys grabbed me. ¹⁰My friend led them. ¹¹"You stink," he told me happily. ¹²"We think you're dirty. ¹³We want to see." ¹⁴They jerked down the straps on my bib overalls, held my arms high, peeled off my ragged shirt. ¹⁵They exposed my filth, my black armpits, my dirty neck for everyone to see. ¹⁶The faces of those children, the girl well forward among them, filled with horror perverted with glee. ¹⁷I went the only way I could go, down, dropping to the asphalt of the playground. ¹⁸They formed a circle around me, laughing and pointing. ¹⁹I couldn't get away. ²⁰I covered my head and drew up my knees. ²¹I knew how to make myself invisible. ²²I'd learned to make myself invisible when my stepmother attacked. ²³It worked because I couldn't see her even if she could still see me. ²⁴I made myself invisible. ²⁵They couldn't hear me crying.

_B_   6. We can infer from the passage that the author's friend
   A. felt sorry for him.
   B. meant to embarrass him.
   C. did not expect the other kids to laugh.

   The words and actions of the friend in sentences 10–15 support inference B.

_A_   7. We can infer from the passage that the girl in the crowd
   A. made the author's humiliation greater.
   B. had strong feelings for the author.
   C. was against teasing the author.

   Sentence 6 supports this inference.

_C_   8. The author implies that his stepmother
   A. was very fond of him.
   B. worried about him.
   C. abused him.

   Sentence 22 supports inference C and contradicts inferences A and B.

_A_   9. We can infer from the passage that the author
   A. probably wasn't very well cared for at home.
   B. was usually clean, but just happened to be dirty that day.
   C. expected kids to tease him about his dirtiness.

   Sentence 22 supports inference A.

_A_ 10. We can infer that when the author made himself "invisible,"
   A. he was really putting others out of sight.
   B. he was free from the hurt caused by the other kids.
   C. the other kids stopped teasing him.

   Sentence 23 supports inference A.

8 Purpose and Tone

There is an author—a person with thoughts, feelings, and opinions—behind everything you read. Whether this person is a cartoonist, a sportswriter, a newspaper columnist, a novelist, or a friend sending you a letter, he or she writes from a personal point of view. That point of view is reflected in (1) the *purpose* of a piece of writing—to inform, to persuade, or to entertain—as well as (2) its *tone:* the expression of attitude and feeling.

The *purpose* of the above cartoon, like all cartoons, is to entertain. Can you tell what the *tone* of each speaker is? Which one is sincere in what he says? Which is insincere? After you have decided on your answers, read the explanation that follows.

Explanation

The boss is insincere. If he decided to fire the worker, he most likely is not sorry. He doesn't know if the worker will "land on his feet" and find another job. The worker, on the other hand, is sincere in his anger at being fired and his wish that he could stomp on his ex-boss's chest.

Purpose

Authors write with a reason in mind, and you can better evaluate their ideas by determining what that reason is. The author's reason for writing is also called the **purpose** of a selection. Three common purposes are as follows:

● To **inform**—to give information about a subject. Authors with this purpose wish to provide facts that will explain or teach something to readers.

For example, the author of an informative paragraph about sandwiches might begin, "Eating food between two slices of bread—a sandwich—is a practice that has its origins in eighteenth-century England."

● To **persuade**—to convince the reader to agree with the author's point of view on a subject. Authors with this purpose may give facts, but their main goal is to argue or prove a point to readers.

The author of a persuasive paragraph about sandwiches might begin, "There are good reasons why every sandwich should be made with whole-grain bread."

● To **entertain**—to amuse and delight; to appeal to the reader's senses and imagination. Authors with this purpose entertain in various ways, through fiction and nonfiction.

The author of an entertaining paragraph about sandwiches might begin, "What I wanted was a midnight snack, but what I got was better—the biggest, most magical sandwich in the entire world."

While the cover and title of anything you read—books, articles, and so on—don't necessarily suggest the author's main purpose, often they do. On the next page are the covers of three books. See if you can guess the primary purpose of each of these books.

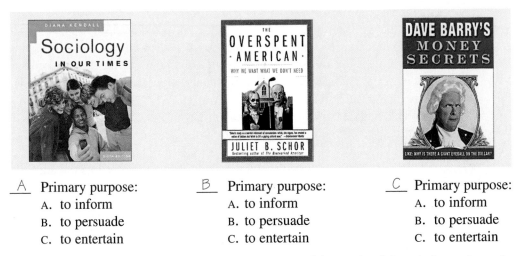

<u>A</u> Primary purpose:
   A. to inform
   B. to persuade
   C. to entertain

<u>B</u> Primary purpose:
   A. to inform
   B. to persuade
   C. to entertain

<u>C</u> Primary purpose:
   A. to inform
   B. to persuade
   C. to entertain

As you probably concluded, the main purpose of the textbook is to inform; the main purpose of *The Overspent American* is to persuade; and the main purpose of *Dave Barry's Money Secrets* is to entertain.

✔ *Check Your Understanding*

Read each of the three paragraphs below and decide whether the author's purpose is to inform, to persuade, or to entertain. Write in your answers, and then read the explanations that follow.

1. Each Saturday morning, TV commercials advertise fast foods and high-calorie cereals directly to children. These ads teach children unhealthy eating habits and have been linked to childhood obesity. Parents must realize how harmful such commercials are and should pressure companies to stop marketing unhealthy products to children.

    Purpose: _____ Persuade _____

2. About 113 billion people have lived and died in the history of our planet, according to scientific estimates. Of all these people, the names of about 7 billion, or approximately 6 percent, are recorded in some way—on monuments or in books, manuscripts, and public records. The other 106 billion people are gone without a trace.

    Purpose: _____ Inform _____

3. Because of the war between his medium-size shirts and pants and his extra-large-size body, my brother has made a commitment to only three meals a day. His definition of a meal, however, is as broad as his belly. If we spot a pretzel salesman or a hot-dog stand on our way to a restaurant, for example, he is not beyond suggesting that we stop. "It'll make a good appetizer," he says.

    Purpose: _____ Entertain _____

Explanation

In the first paragraph, the writer's purpose is to *persuade* the audience that parents should protest the marketing of unhealthy products to children. Words such as *must* in "must realize" and *should* in "should pressure" are meant to convince us rather than to inform us.

The purpose of the second paragraph is to *inform*. The author is simply providing readers with information about the people who have lived and died on Earth.

In paragraph 3, the playful and exaggerated details tell us the author's main goal is to *entertain* with humor.

A Note about Writing with More Than One Purpose

At times, writing may combine two or even all three purposes. A persuasive letter to an editor, for example, may contain factual information, or an informative article on losing weight may include comic touches and some implied persuasion.

● What would you say is the main purpose of this book?

   A. <u>To inform</u>   B. To persuade   C. To entertain

If you chose answer A, you're correct—my main purpose is to inform and provide practice. But I also have two other purposes at times. For example, on the first page (page 10) of an earlier section, "Reading for Pleasure and Power," what is my main purpose?

   A. To inform   B. <u>To persuade</u>   C. To entertain

My main purpose on page 10 was to persuade you about the importance of becoming a regular reader.

You'll notice, too, that I have included in this book high-interest readings such as the story of Lizzie Borden (page 515) or amusing passages such as the one about not stepping in the *hora* (page 277). What is my purpose in choosing such content?

   A. To inform   B. To persuade   C. <u>To entertain</u>

While my main purpose is to inform, I do at times have a second and even third purpose—to persuade and to entertain. And that is the case for other authors as well. What you need to remember when trying to determine purpose is to ask yourself, "What is the author's *main* purpose here?"

PRACTICE 1

Label each item according to its main purpose: to inform (**I**), to persuade (**P**), or to entertain (**E**).

_P_ 1. Professional athletes do not deserve their inflated salaries, nor does their behavior merit so much media attention.   *Persuasive clue: do not deserve.*

_I_ 2. The career of a professional athlete is usually quite short.

Direct statement of fact.

_P_ 3. Nurses assigned to intensive-care units should be given shorter shifts and higher pay because the work is unusually demanding and stressful.

Persuasive clue: should.

_I_ 4. On average, women dream more than men, and children dream more than adults.   *Objective information.*

_E_ 5. The best approach to take when you feel the urge to exercise is to lie down quickly in a darkened room until the feeling goes away.

Humorous advice for avoiding exercise.

_E_ 6. It's easy to quit smoking; I've done it hundreds of times.

Humorous twist on what it means to "quit smoking."

_P_ 7. More women should get involved in local politics and support the growing number of female candidates for public office.

Persuasive clue: should.

_I_ 8. An artificial odor is added to natural gas so that people can tell whether or not gas is leaking.   *Straightforward fact.*

_E_ 9. Once football season begins, Matt starts jogging every night—to the refrigerator during commercial breaks.   *The humor comes from Matt's jogging habits.*

_I_ 10. The first person to die of radiation poisoning was a co-discoverer of radium, Marie Curie.   *Straightforward information.*

PRACTICE 2

Following are three passages, one each from a textbook, a humor book, and a collection of essays. In the spaces provided, write the letter of the best description of the purpose of each passage.

_B_ 1. ¹We have all heard the story of how the young, impoverished Abraham Lincoln trekked miles to borrow books from a neighbor and then read them by firelight. ²We know that nineteenth-century readers would rush to the wharf to greet the ship carrying the latest chapters of a Dickens novel. ³Today, reading seems less urgent and less exciting to many of us. ⁴Worse, few people impart a passion for books to their children. ⁵Instead, they leave the children in front of the television and hope, weakly, that too much watching won't be bad for them. [6]But we cannot afford to stop reading. [7]Books shed a light that illuminates our problems and crises. [8]They are also mirrors that reflect the truest image of ourselves.

Impassioned phrases such as "we cannot afford to stop reading" are intended to persuade us that books are important.

The main purpose of this passage is to
A. explain something about Abraham Lincoln and Dickens to readers.
B. convince readers of the importance of books.
C. delight readers with entertaining material from books.

_C_ 2. [1]Most of what I know about carpentry, which is almost nothing, I learned in Shop. [2]You should know that I took Shop during the Eisenhower administration, when boys took Shop and girls took Home Economics—a code name for "cooking." [3]Schools are not allowed to separate boys and girls like that anymore. [4]They're also not allowed to put students' heads in vises and tighten them, which is what our Shop teacher, Mr. Schmidt, did to Ronnie Miller in the fifth grade when Ronnie used a chisel when he should have used a screwdriver. [5](Mr. Schmidt had strong feelings about how to use tools properly.) [6]I guess he shouldn't have put Ronnie's head in the vise, but it (Ronnie's head) was no great prize to begin with, and you can bet Ronnie never confused chisels and screwdrivers in later life—assuming he made it to later life.

The exaggerated details—for example, "put students' heads in vises"—are meant to entertain.

The main purpose of this passage is to
A. inform readers about the nature of shop classes.
B. argue that shop classes should be eliminated from public schools.
C. amuse readers with humorous details about shop classes.

_A_ 3. [1]Studies of job satisfaction indicate that the vast majority of workers are at least somewhat satisfied with their jobs and would continue to work even if they didn't have to. [2]The meaning of work varies from person to person. [3]To some, it is a source of self-respect and life purpose. [4]For others, work is a means of passing time. [5]To still others, it is primarily a source of financial independence. [6]Among women, available work is often less satisfying than home management. [7]Yet most women report increases in self-esteem when employed, especially if they experience support from their families.

The straightforward, factual language of this passage indicates that its purpose is to report information.

The main purpose of this passage is to
A. report on what has been learned through studies of job satisfaction.
B. convince readers of the importance of job satisfaction.
C. entertain readers with rich, sensual descriptions of job satisfaction.

Tone

A writer's **tone** reveals the attitude that he or she has toward a subject. Tone is expressed through the words and details the writer selects. Just as a speaker's voice can project a range of feelings, a writer's voice can project one or more tones, or feelings: anger, sympathy, hopefulness, sadness, respect, dislike, and so on. Understanding tone is, then, an important part of understanding what an author has written.

To appreciate the differences in tone that writers can employ, look at the following versions of a murder confession. Then read them aloud—in the tone of voice appropriate in each case.

"I just shot my husband five times in the chest with this .357 Magnum." (*Tone:* matter-of-fact, objective.)

"How could I ever have killed him? I just can't believe I did that!" (*Tone:* shocked, disbelieving.)

"Oh, my God. I've murdered my husband. How can I ever be forgiven for this dreadful deed?" (*Tone:* guilty, regretful.)

"That dirty rat. He's had it coming for years. I'm glad I finally had the nerve to do it." (*Tone:* revengeful, self-satisfied.)

PRACTICE 3

Following are five reactions to a fender-bender accident (in which one car hits and slightly damages the rear fender of another car). Label each statement with the tone of voice that you think is present. Choose each tone from the following box, and use each tone only once.

A. angry	B. apologetic	C. calm
D. concerned	E. defensive	

___D___ 1. "Are you hurt? Are you sure you're okay? Don't move too quickly. Take your time getting out of the car."   Both questions and both statements show the speaker's concern for the other person.

___B___ 2. "I am really sorry. I was daydreaming a bit, which is no excuse. I should have been more careful."   Statements of apology.

To the Instructor: In the practices and tests that follow, words that indicate tone are underlined in this *Instructor's Edition.*

_A_ 3. "You idiot! If you hadn't stopped short, I would never have hit you. You

Angry statements.   should be tossed in jail. You could have gotten us both killed."

_C_ 4. "It's no big deal. Neither of us was hurt, which is all that counts. The

Signs of calm.   damage is slight. Don't worry about it."

_E_ 5. "Hey, this wasn't my fault. Don't even think about blaming me. You're

Defensive   the one that stopped too quickly, not me. I did nothing wrong here."
statements.

Words That Describe Tone

Below and on the next page are two lists of words commonly used to describe tone. With the exception of the words *matter-of-fact* and *objective,* the words reflect a feeling or judgment. The words on this page are more familiar ones. Brief meanings are given in parentheses for the words on the next page. Refer to these meanings as needed to learn any words you don't know yet.

Some Words That Describe Tone

admiring	cruel	loving
affectionate	curious	playful
amused	defensive	praising
angry	doubtful	respectful
apologetic	encouraging	self-pitying
ashamed	excited	serious
calming	forgiving	sorrowful
caring	frightened	sympathetic
cheerful	grateful	threatening
conceited	humorous	tragic
concerned	insulting	warm
critical	joyous	worried

More Words That Describe Tone—with Their Meanings

ambivalent	*uncertain about a choice*
arrogant	*full of self-importance; conceited*
bewildered	*confused; puzzled*
bitter	*angry; full of hate*
compassionate	*deeply sympathetic*
depressed	*very sad or discouraged*
detached	*emotionally uninvolved*
disbelieving	*unbelieving*
distressed	*suffering sorrow, misery, or pain*
hypocritical	*false*
impassioned	*filled with strong feeling*
indignant	*angry about something unfair or mean*
instructive	*teaching*
ironic	*meaning the opposite of what is expressed*
lighthearted	*happy and carefree*
matter-of-fact	*sticking to facts; unemotional*
mocking	*making fun of and/or looking down upon something*
nostalgic	*longing for something or someone in the past*
objective	*not influenced by feelings or personal prejudices*
optimistic	*looking on the bright side of things*
pessimistic	*looking on the gloomy, unfavorable side of things*
pleading	*begging*
prideful	*full of pride or exaggerated self-esteem*
remorseful	*guilty over a wrong one has done*
revengeful	*wanting to hurt someone in return for an injury*
sarcastic	*sharp or wounding; ironic*
scheming	*tricky*
scornful	*looking down on someone or something*
self-mocking	*making fun of or looking down on oneself*
sentimental	*showing tender feelings; romantic; overly emotional*
solemn	*involved with serious concerns*
straightforward	*direct and honest*
superior	*looking down on others*
tolerant	*respectful of other views and behavior; patient about problems*
uncertain	*doubting*

✓ *Check Your Understanding*

Below are five statements expressing different attitudes about a shabby apartment. Five different tones are used:

bitter	humorous	optimistic
sentimental	tolerant	

Feel free to check the list on page 327 for the meanings of any unfamiliar tone words. Label each statement with the tone you think is present. Use each tone once. Then read the explanation that follows.

_____sentimental_____ 1. This place may be shabby, but since both of my children were born while we lived here, it has a special place in my heart.

_____tolerant_____ 2. This isn't the greatest apartment in the world, but it's not really that bad.

_____bitter_____ 3. If only there were some decent jobs out there, I wouldn't be reduced to living in this miserable dump.

_____optimistic_____ 4. This place does need some repairs, but I'm sure the landlord will be making improvements sometime soon.

_____humorous_____ 5. When we move away, we're planning to release three hundred cockroaches and two mice so we can leave the place exactly as we found it.

Explanation

The tone of item 1 is sentimental. "It has a special place in my heart" expresses tender emotions. In item 2, the words "it's not really that bad" show that the writer is tolerant, accepting the situation while recognizing that it could be better. We could describe the tone of item 3 as bitter. The writer resents a situation that forces him or her to live in a "miserable dump." Item 4 is optimistic since the writer is expecting the apartment to be improved soon. Finally, the tone of item 5 is humorous. Its writer claims to be planning a comic revenge on the landlord by returning the apartment to the terrible condition it was in when the tenants moved in.

A Note on Irony

One commonly used tone is irony. When writing has an **ironic** tone, it says one thing but means the opposite. Irony is found in everyday conversation as well as in writing. Following are a few examples; notice that the quotation in each says the opposite of what is meant.

- If at the beginning of a semester you discover that one of your instructors is particularly demanding, you might comment, "This class is sure going to be a piece of cake."

- After seeing a terrible performance in a movie, someone might say about the actor involved, "Now there's a person with a great chance for an Oscar."

- While standing in a long, slow line at a supermarket or bank, you might say to people in line with you, "My, this is exciting."

- If a friend arrives at your place two hours late, you might say, "Well, thanks for showing up on time."

- If you're suffering from the flu and someone asks how you feel, you might say: "I feel terrific today."

Irony also refers to situations in which what happens is the opposite of what we might expect. We would call it ironic, for example, if a young woman who failed English in high school went on to become a well-known writer, or if a young man who was cut from his Little League baseball team went on to star in the major leagues. Here are a few more examples of this type of irony:

- Security cameras installed to stop crime were stolen during a robbery.

- A new computer purchased to help a small business crashes, causing the business to lose many of its customers.

- An instructor at a health club smokes a cigarette during lunch break.

- Albert Einstein, one of the century's most brilliant scientists, did poorly in school.

- Beethoven's music teacher once said of him, "As a composer, he is hopeless."

- A newspaper editor fired Walt Disney because he "lacked imagination and had no good ideas."

As you can see, irony is a useful tone for humor and can be used to imply exactly the opposite of what is said or what is done.

✔ *Check Your Understanding*

Look now at the cartoon below. See if you can explain the irony.

GRAND AVENUE reproduced by permission of United Feature Syndicate, Inc.

The irony in the little girl's comment "People are so self-absorbed" is that *the little girl herself is self-absorbed.*

Explanation

The irony is that the little girl herself is completely self-absorbed. She shows no interest in the people around her and is concerned only about their paying attention to her new hair style.

PRACTICE 4

A. Below are five statements expressing different attitudes about a boss. Five different tones are used:

admiring	critical	ironic
objective	sympathetic	

For each statement, write the tone that you think is present. Use each tone once.

<u>admiring</u>   1. Tony is an <u>excellent</u> manager—the <u>best</u> one I've ever had.

_____sympathetic_____   2. I know Tony's daughter has been sick. Naturally it's <u>hard for him to concentrate</u> on work right now.

_____critical_____   3. Tony's <u>too ambitious for his own good. That ambition may destroy both him and the company.</u>

_____objective_____   4. Since Tony Roberts became manager, sales in the appliance division have increased 30 percent.

The lack of emotion demonstrates an objective tone.

_____ironic_____   5. Tony's wonderful, all right. <u>He's gotten as far as he has without the slightest idea of how to manage a division.</u>

These words suggest that Tony is actually *not* wonderful at all.

B. The following conversation between a mother and son involves five of the tones shown in the box below. For each statement, write the tone that you think is present. Five tones will be left over.

disbelieving	joyful	nostalgic	pessimistic
sarcastic	self-pitying	solemn	straightforward
sympathetic	threatening		

_____straightforward_____   6. "Please take the garbage out on your way to school this morning."   No emotion is expressed in this direct request.

_____sarcastic_____   7. "Sure, Mom. I've been looking forward to that chore all morning."   He has most assuredly *not* been looking forward all morning to taking the garbage out.

_____threatening_____   8. "Listen, young man, if you don't start fulfilling your responsibilities around this house, your father and I will start asking you to pay rent or find your own place."

The expression "if you don't…, your father and I will…." is a threat.

_____self-pitying_____   9. "Okay, I'll take the garbage out. But you know <u>it's not easy</u> going to school full-time and working twenty hours a week when <u>I'm just getting over a bad case of the flu</u>."   The underlined expressions suggest that the young man is feeling sorry for himself.

_____sympathetic_____   10. "I know, honey, this semester has been an especially difficult one for you."

Expressions like "I know, honey" and "especially difficult for you" suggest sympathy.

PRACTICE 5

Each passage illustrates one of the tones in the box below. In each space, put the letter of the tone that best applies. Don't use any letter more than once. Five tones will be left over.

Remember that the tone of a selection reflects the author's attitude. To find the tone of a paragraph, ask yourself what attitude is revealed by its words and phrases.

A. accepting	B. affectionate	C. alarmed	D. ambivalent
E. ashamed	F. bitter	G. forgiving	H. grateful
I. playful	J. revengeful		

_J_ 1. ¹In my fantasies I have ways of dealing with drivers who irritate the heck out of me. ²At times I have 50-caliber machine guns instead of headlights on the front of my car. ³That way, I can send several hundred rounds of burning lead into the slow-moving gas-guzzler car in front of me. ⁴I also have a fantasy to deal with another driver I really despise—the truck driver who tailgates just inches from my rear bumper. ⁵In his case, I have flame-throwers that rise up out of the trunk of my car and melt down his front tires; that gets him out of my life fast. ⁶I also have a way to deal at night with the guy behind me who has his high beams on. ⁷It feels like a spotlight is shining into my car. ⁸In this case, I'm driving a rented car, so I suddenly slam on my brakes, causing him to plow into me. ⁹That puts his lights out in a hurry. ¹⁰Then I drive on, leaving him to find his way home in the dark. ¹¹My motto is, "Don't just get mad, get even."

Signs of revenge.

_C_ 2. ¹The percentage of children who are classified as overweight has more than doubled in the last thirty years. ²A lack of exercise and increasingly unhealthy, junk-food-filled diets are making kids heavier and heavier. ³More than 22 percent—that's close to one in four—are classified as dangerously obese. ⁴One in four! ⁵This is an urgent public health crisis that people need to wake up to and recognize. ⁶Most overweight children become overweight adults, and overweight adults are at risk for developing heart disease, cancer, diabetes, and stroke. ⁷The costs of dealing with those health problems—from work-hours lost to medical expenses—are going to be immense. ⁸If we don't start dealing with this problem immediately, we're going to be in big trouble. ⁹Parents, schools, the government, and the media need to join forces to do something about it before it's too late.

Signs of alarm.

<u>A</u>   3.   ¹I'm at peace now with my husband's death. ²I had been out shopping when a sudden intuition prompted me to call him. ³My husband had been diagnosed six months before his death with a rare cancer of the body's soft tissues that had since spread to his lungs. ⁴"Are you all right?" I asked him. ⁵"No," he replied. ⁶"I'm having trouble breathing here." ⁷I rushed home and drove him to the ER. ⁸That's where the house of cards came tumbling down. ⁹During the week that followed, my husband developed serious complications. ¹⁰In his final hours, he told me he wanted everything done for him because he wanted to live so much. ¹¹But as I watched his condition deteriorate, I made the most difficult decision of my life. ¹²It had gotten to the point that life support wasn't the right thing to do. ¹³I went in and held him. ¹⁴And I said, "<u>I want you to let go and come into my heart because it's safe there.</u>" ¹⁵He stopped breathing. ¹⁶<u>And now he's in my heart.</u> ¹⁷I can feel his arms around me.

Signs of acceptance of the situation.

<u>D</u>   4.   ¹The proposal has been made that students in our schools be required to wear uniforms. ²<u>In some ways</u>, this sounds good. ³It is true that shopping for fashionable clothing and deciding what to wear in the morning take up a lot of money and time. ⁴<u>But</u> kids need to learn to deal with social pressure about things like clothing, and school might be as good a place as any for that lesson. ⁵<u>Also</u>, the way people dress is one way they express themselves, and <u>maybe</u> students should have that avenue of expression open to them too. ⁶<u>However</u>, it is a shame if they constantly worry about their appearance and waste valuable class time by wishing they could have the name-brand shirt across the room. ⁷So uniforms <u>might</u> be helpful in keeping students' minds on their education. ⁸Uniforms <u>could</u> save students and their parents money, too, which is certainly a good thing. ⁹<u>On the other hand</u>, those uniforms are not cheap, and most students will want to have several sets, so the savings might not be all that significant. ¹⁰<u>It's really hard to say whether uniforms are a good idea or not.</u>

Signs of ambivalence or uncertainty.

<u>F</u>   5.   ¹After twenty-two years of business in this community, Acme Supplies closed its doors for the final time today. ²Ninety-seven people lost their jobs. ³Many of them had worked for Acme since it opened. ⁴You might think the management of Acme would feel it owed those loyal workers something, but you would be wrong. ⁵Despite the factory's record of efficiency and high production, Acme executives leaped at the chance to make more money by moving the plant to Mexico, where wages are lower. ⁶In doing so, <u>they turned their backs on the men and women who have made their company so successful over the years.</u> ⁷Some of those employees were only months away from retirement. ⁸Instead of looking forward to some well-deserved rest, those employees are frantically trying to adjust to <u>having had the rug pulled out from under their feet by their greedy employers.</u> ⁹Although Acme always claimed to treat its workers "like family," the reality is that <u>those workers were never more than tools used to fatten the bank accounts of the company's unscrupulous managers.</u>

Signs of bitterness.

PRACTICE 6

Read the following letter to the late Ann Landers, along with her response. Then answer the questions about purpose and tone that follow.

[1]**Dear Ann Landers:** [2]When our daughter won a scholarship to a very fine university in the East last year, we were thrilled and proud of her.

[3]"Mary" does not drink or smoke and has high moral standards. [4]We were not the least bit uneasy about her moving so far from home to go to school, and we didn't worry about peer pressure. [5]She has always been a leader, not a follower.

[6]Mary's letters, however, are depressing. [7]She says so many people who live in her dorm (it's mixed, both men and women) get drunk at least four nights a week, and they make so much noise she can't study. [8]She also has spent several nights taking care of sick, hung-over friends. [9]Her roommate, she says, often stays out until 3 or 4 in the morning, comes in dead drunk, and throws up. [10]Mary resents having to clean up after her, but she has no choice.

[11]We did not anticipate this sort of thing when we sent our daughter away to college. [12]We asked Mary if she would consider changing schools next year (we would be willing to forgo the scholarship and pay her tuition). [13]She said, "No, an Ivy League school has always been my dream, and these problems exist all over."

[14]What on Earth is going on? [15]Can you tell us?

[16]**Dear Parents:** [17]You ask, "What's going on?" [18]You just described it, according to the information I receive regularly from the National Clearinghouse for Alcohol and Drug Information. [19]College students spend $5.5 billion a year on alcohol. [20]Harvard School of Public Health researchers have reported that excessive use of alcohol on college campuses may be hazardous not only to the health of drinkers but to nondrinkers as well. [21]Nondrinkers suffer from loss of sleep and study time, vandalism, physical assault, unwanted sexual advances, and rape.

[22]Dr. Henry Wechsler, director of college alcohol studies at the Harvard School of Public Health, was the lead author of a report that studied the drinking habits of 17,592 students from 140 colleges. [23]The study found that alcohol on college campuses poses a serious hazard to the physical health and emotional well-being of students. [24]One student said she was fed up with people urinating in the elevators, vomiting in the halls, wrecking the bathroom, and pounding holes in the walls.

[25]Wechsler's research revealed that nearly half the college students are binge drinkers who cause most of the trouble by depriving others of study time and sleep and by attacking classmates. [26]College security officers and administrators report that alcohol is involved in the majority of rapes and almost all violent incidents on campus.

[27]Wechsler urges students who do not drink to speak up and demand their rights. [28]*Time* magazine quoted Wechsler as saying, "If your roommate gets drunk every night, either insist on a new roommate or demand that you be moved." [29]He urges people who are bothered by excessive drinking to complain. [30]He said, "I want students to complain. [31]I want parents to complain. [32]That's the only way we will get change."

[33]Although Wechsler does not beat the drum for total abstinence (he says it is not "realistic"), I disagree. [34]If you don't drink at all, you will never have to worry about how much is too much.

_B_ 1. The first paragraph of the parents' letter has a
   A. tragic tone.
   B. prideful tone.
   C. pleading tone.

   The paragraph lists a positive achievement, and the parent says, "we were . . . proud of her."

_A_ 2. In its third paragraph, the parents' letter takes on a
   A. distressed tone.
   B. revengeful tone.
   C. doubtful tone.

   The details in the paragraph describe distressing situations such as frequently witnessing drunkenness and noise, constantly caring for hung-over friends, and repeatedly cleaning up when the roommate gets sick.

_B_ 3. The parents' letter ends in a(n)
   A. instructive tone.
   B. bewildered tone.
   C. sentimental tone.

   The question "What on Earth is going on?" shows bewilderment or confusion.

_A_ 4. The purpose of much of the parents' letter is to
   A. inform Ann Landers of their daughter's situation.
   B. persuade Ann Landers to convince their daughter to leave her school.
   C. amuse Ann Landers with the ridiculous behavior of today's college students.

   The parent presents the facts of the daughter's situation. None of the details support answer B or C.

_B_ 5. On the basis of the facts she has chosen to include and her last paragraph, we can conclude that Landers's main purpose is
   A. simply to inform people about various views of alcohol.
   B. to persuade readers that it is best to drink little or no alcohol.
   C. to entertain readers with colorful views about alcohol.

   Landers states that she disagrees with the idea that total abstinence is not realistic. And she states the advantage of not drinking at all. See the last paragraph of Landers's reply.

CHAPTER REVIEW

In this chapter, you learned that part of effective reading is to do the following:

- Be aware of an author's **purpose**: the reason why he or she writes. Three common purposes are to inform, to persuade, and to entertain.

- Be aware of **tone**: the expression of the author's attitude and feeling about a subject. A writer's tone might be objective—the case in most textbook writing—or it might be lighthearted, sympathetic, angry, affectionate, respectful, or any of many other tones shown on pages 326–327.

- One important tone to recognize is **irony**: saying one thing but meaning the opposite.

The next chapter—Chapter 9—will explain another part of effective reading: recognizing the point in an argument and evaluating the support for that point.

 On the Web: If you are using this book in class, you can visit our website for additional practice in identifying an author's purpose and tone. Go to **www.townsendpress.com** and click on "Online Exercises."

REVIEW TEST 1

To review what you've learned in this chapter, fill in the blank(s) or write, in the space provided, the letter of the correct answer for each question.

1. The author's reason for writing something is called the ___*purpose*___ of a selection.
   See page 320.

2–4. What is the purpose of each of the types of writing below? Label each according to its usual main purpose: to inform, to persuade, or to entertain.

   A news report: ___*inform*___

   A mystery novel: ___*entertain*___

   An editorial: ___*persuade*___

5. The tone of a selection reveals the author's ___*attitude*___ toward his or her subject.
   See page 325.

6. An ironic comment is one that means the ___*opposite*___ of what is said.
   See page 329.

___B___ 7. Imagine a bad morning when everything goes wrong—there is no hot water for the shower, milk for the cereal is sour, a pool of oil is under the car, and so on. Which of the following would be an ironic comment on the situation?
   A. "What a lousy start to the day."   To say it will be a "great day" when
   B. "What a great day this is going to be."   "everything goes wrong" is to say
   C. "Good grief. What did I do to deserve this?"   the opposite of what is meant.

___C___ 8. Which of the following tones reveals no personal feeling?
   A. Forgiving   *Matter-of-fact* means "unemotional."
   B. Critical   See page 327.
   C. Matter-of-fact

___C___ 9. An arrogant tone suggests that the speaker or writer
   A. is angry.   *Arrogant* means "conceited."
   B. looks on the unfavorable side of things.   See page 327.
   C. thinks a lot of himself or herself.

___B___ 10. An objective tone indicates that the speaker or writer is telling something   *Objective* means "not influenced
   A. dishonestly.   by personal prejudices."
   B. without personal prejudice.   See page 327.
   C. with a longing for something in the past.

REVIEW TEST 2: PURPOSE

In the space provided, indicate whether the primary purpose of each passage is to inform (**I**), to persuade (**P**), or to entertain (**E**).

___P___ 1. ¹Let's pretend for a moment. ²Suppose that in the hospital room where your mother lies dying with terminal cancer, there is a button. ³You have the power, by pushing that button, to quickly and painlessly end the life of this person you dearly love. ⁴You know your mother will be confined to that hospital room for her remaining days. ⁵Would you push the button for her? ⁶You watch as she is hooked up to a life-support machine, and you also watch and listen as her pain increases and she pleads for you to help. ⁷You watch her worsen day after day until she reaches a point where she can no longer talk or hear, and she is alive only because of that machine. ⁸Now would you push that button? ⁹If you can imagine the horror of what I have described, then you may agree our country should reconsider its laws against mercy killing. *Should* in sentence 9 indicates a persuasive purpose.

___I___ 2. ¹Traditionally, English grammar called for the use of the masculine pronoun *he* to stand for the entire class of humans regardless of sex. ²Thus in the past, the following sentence would have been considered proper English: "Everyone in class must hand in his paper tomorrow." ³Today, many language experts would consider that sentence sexist because it excludes females. ⁴They say that one way to avoid the problem is to recast a sentence using plurals: "All students in the class must hand in their papers tomorrow." ⁵Alternately, they advise using *both* male and female singular pronouns: "Everyone in class must hand in his or her paper tomorrow."

The passage offers facts in a straightforward way. It does not make judgments about the use of masculine and feminine pronouns.

___E___ 3. ¹An elderly woman in a Cadillac was preparing to back into a parking space. ²Suddenly a small red sports car appeared and pulled into the space. ³"That's what you can do when you're young and fast," the young man in the car yelled to the old woman. ⁴As he strolled away, laughing, he heard a terrible crunching sound. ⁵"What's that noise?" he asked. ⁶Turning around, he saw the old woman backing repeatedly into his small car and crushing it. ⁷"You can't do that, old lady!" he yelled.

⁸"What do you mean, I can't?" she yelled back, as metal grated against metal. ⁹"This is what you can do when you're old and rich."

This humorous description of the young man's comeuppance at the hands of the old woman is meant to amuse.

_____ I ___ 4.   ¹College students who contract mononucleosis ("mono") can be forced into a long period of bed rest during a semester when they can least afford it. ²Other common diseases can be managed with minimal disruption, but the overall weakness and fatigue seen in many people with mono sometimes requires a month or two of rest and recuperation. ³Mono is a viral infection in which the body produces an excess of one type of white blood cells. ⁴After an uncertain, perhaps long, incubation, the acute symptoms of mono can appear, including weakness, headache, low-grade fever, swollen lymph glands (especially in the neck), and sore throat. ⁵Mental fatigue and depression are sometimes reported as side effects of mono. ⁶After the acute symptoms disappear, the weakness and fatigue usually persist, sometimes for a few months.

> This passage offers facts about mono in a straightforward way.

_____ P ___ 5.   ¹Americans love parks and wildlife refuges, but the crowding they find there is a national disgrace. ²Parking lots are packed, and roadways through parks and refuges are often so jammed that they might as well be the parking lots. ³Playing fields and barbecue grills are claimed early in the day, and even on remote trails, voices can be heard from every direction. ⁴Americans badly need more land devoted to open space where nature walks, picnics, and camping can take place in uncrowded tranquillity. ⁵Communities across the nation should establish parks and trails that provide free access to open space for everyone.

> *Should* (sentence 5) indicates a persuasive purpose. The words *badly need* (sentence 4) also suggest the author's intent to persuade.

REVIEW TEST 3: TONE

The cartoon and the four passages that follow each illustrate one of the tones in the box below. In the space provided, put the letter of the tone that best applies in each case. Don't use any letter more than once. Three tones will be left over.

Remember that tone reflects an author's (or speaker's) attitude. In each case, ask yourself what attitude is revealed by the words used.

A. ashamed	B. forgiving	C. indignant	D. ironic
E. objective	F. pessimistic	G. sentimental	H. tolerant

_D_ 1. What is the tone of the man holding the cup of coffee in the cartoon below?

That much stomach acid would *not* be good for anyone. When the man says "Yep," he is saying the opposite of what he means, so his answer is ironic.

I HEAR THEY SAY COFFEE IS GOOD FOR YOU NOW.

YEP. JUST ONE SERVING OF THIS OFFICE COFFEE GIVES ME 4,000% OF THE MINIMUM DAILY REQUIREMENT OF STOMACH ACID.

_E_ 2. ¹Most animals have a "sweet tooth," and humans are no exception. ²That's why food manufacturers often add sugars and other sweeteners to their products. ³Indeed, many commercial breakfast cereals are 40% sugar by weight. ⁴Because added sugar provides calories but no essential nutrients, sugar is usually described as contributing "empty calories" to the diet. ⁵Excess calories from added sugar are converted to fat, which in some cases

The passage gives objective information. It does not make judgments about sugar in people's diets.

may contribute to overweight problems. [6]Populations that consume large amounts of sugar exhibit high rates of heart disease, obesity, diabetes, and tooth decay. [7]Sugar consumption in the United States averages about 133 pounds per person per year.

_____C_____ 3.

The impassioned language signals that the author is indignant.

[1]Relentless greed and horrifying dishonesty characterized the treatment of Indians in the 1860s and 1870s, when massacres of Native Americans were commonplace. [2]The massacre at Sand Creek in Colorado in 1864 was sadly typical. [3]The territorial governor had persuaded the Indians to gather there and had promised them protection. [4]Despite this pledge, Colonel J. M. Chivington's militia attacked the defenseless Indian camp. [5]They disregarded that sacred symbol, the American flag, and the white flag of truce that the Indians were flying at Sand Creek. [6]Four hundred fifty peaceful Indians—men, women, and children—were slaughtered in what has been called "the foulest and most unjustified crime in the annals of America." [7]This was only one of the heartless massacres of Native Americans recorded by history.

_____F_____ 4.

All of the details right down to "I'm done for" show pessimism.

[1]During my last physical, the doctor found a little lump in my throat. [2]I'm going into the hospital tomorrow so they can check out what it is. [3]The doctor said it was most likely a harmless cyst, but of course he would say that. [4]What's he going to say: "Sorry—looks like cancer to me"? [5]He also said that if it is cancer, it's probably of a kind that is easily treated. [6]Right, I thought. [7]He's trying to be nice, I know, but I also know how these things go. [8]First he'll say it's nothing; then he'll say it's cancer but no big deal; and finally he'll tell me the truth. [9]I'm done for.

_____A_____ 5.

Sentences 1–2 and 10–15 indicate that the writer feels ashamed of his behavior.

[1]I can't look my best friend in the eye. [2]He doesn't know what happened last weekend, and I hope he never will. [3]We were all at a party at a friend's house. [4]It was pretty loud and wild, and I was having a good time. [5]I found myself in the corner of a crowded room with the girl he's been dating all year. [6]We were joking around, and then we started dancing. [7]I don't even know how it began, but somehow we ended up alone in a bathroom. [8]I started kissing her and she kissed me back. [9]We stayed in there until somebody started pounding on the door. [10]That night it didn't seem like a big deal, but the next day I couldn't believe I had done it. [11]This is a girl he really cares for a lot, and she doesn't mean a thing to me. [12]Now everything is a mess. [13]I'm so uncomfortable around her I don't know what to do. [14]And I know he considers me one of his best friends. [15]I feel like such a jerk for betraying him.

REVIEW TEST 4

Here is a chance to apply your understanding of purpose and tone to a full-length selection. In "The Scholarship Jacket," Marta Salinas writes about a moment of disappointment in her childhood in southern Texas. By focusing on an award that school authorities decided she should not receive, Salinas shows us the pain of discrimination as well as the need for inner strength.

To help you continue to strengthen your skills, the reading is followed by questions not only on what you've learned in this chapter but also on what you've learned in previous chapters.

Words to Watch

Below are some words in the reading that do not have strong context support. Each word is followed by the number of the paragraph in which it appears and its meaning there. These words are indicated in the article by a small circle (°).

agile (2): able to move quickly
P.E. (3): the abbreviation for physical-education class
eavesdrop (4): secretly listen
filtered through (7): passed through
fidgeted (8): fussed
muster (12): call forth
mesquite (15): a sweet-smelling thorny tree
clod (15): lump of earth
gaunt (25): thin and bony
vile (29): very unpleasant
adrenaline (31): a hormone that responds to emotion, raising blood pressure and stimulating the heart

THE SCHOLARSHIP JACKET

Marta Salinas

1   The small Texas school that I attended carried out a tradition every year during the eighth grade graduation: a beautiful gold and green jacket, the school colors, was awarded to the class valedictorian, the student who had maintained the highest grades for eight years. The scholarship jacket had a big gold S on the left front side, and the winner's name was written in gold letters on the pocket.

2   My oldest sister, Rosie, had won the jacket a few years back, and I fully expected to win also. I was fourteen and in the eighth grade. I had been a straight-A student since the first grade, and the last year I had looked forward to owning that jacket. My father was a farm laborer who couldn't earn enough money to feed eight children, so when I

was six I was given to my grandparents to raise. We couldn't participate in sports at school because there were registration fees, uniform costs, and trips out of town; so even though we were quite agile° and athletic, there would never be a sports school jacket for us. This one, the scholarship jacket, was our only chance.

3   In May, close to graduation, spring fever struck, and no one paid any attention to class; instead we stared out the windows and at each other, wanting to speed up the last few weeks of school. I despaired every time I looked in the mirror. Pencil thin, not a curve anywhere, I was called "Beanpole" and "String Bean," and I knew that's what I looked like. A flat chest, no hips, and a brain, that's what I had. That really isn't much for a fourteen-year-old to work with, I thought, as I absentmindedly wandered from my history class to the gym. Another hour of sweating during basketball and displaying my toothpick legs was coming up. Then I remembered my P.E.° shorts were still in a bag under my desk where I'd forgotten them. I had to walk all the way back and get them. Coach Thompson was a real bear if anyone wasn't dressed for P.E. She had said I was a good forward and once she even tried to talk Grandma into letting me join the team. Grandma, of course, said no.

4   I was almost back at my classroom door when I heard angry voices and arguing. I stopped. I didn't mean to eavesdrop°; I just hesitated, not knowing what to do. I needed those shorts and I was going to be late, but I didn't want to interrupt an argument between my teachers. I recognized the voices: Mr. Schmidt, my history teacher, and Mr. Boone, my math teacher. They seemed to be arguing about me. I couldn't believe it. I still remember the shock that rooted me flat against the wall as if I were trying to blend in with the graffiti written there.

5   "I refuse to do it! I don't care who her father is, her grades don't even begin to compare to Martha's. I won't lie or falsify records. Martha has a straight-A-plus average and you know it." That was Mr. Schmidt, and he sounded very angry. Mr. Boone's voice sounded calm and quiet.

6   "Look, Joann's father is not only on the Board, he owns the only store in town; we could say it was a close tie and—"

7   The pounding in my ears drowned out the rest of the words, only a word here and there filtered through°. "Martha is Mexican . . . resign . . . won't do it . . . ." Mr. Schmidt came rushing out, and luckily for me went down the opposite way toward the auditorium, so he didn't see me. Shaking, I waited a few minutes and then went in and grabbed my bag and fled from the room. Mr. Boone looked up when I came in but didn't say anything. To this day I don't remember if I got in trouble in P.E. for being late or how I made it through the rest of the afternoon. I went home very sad and cried into my pillow that night so Grandmother wouldn't hear me. It seemed a cruel coincidence that I had overheard that conversation.

8   The next day when the principal called me into his office, I knew what it would be about. He looked uncomfortable and unhappy. I decided I wasn't going to make it any easier for him, so I looked him straight in the eye. He looked away and fidgeted° with the papers on his desk.

9   "Martha," he said, "there's been a change in policy this year regarding the scholarship jacket. As you know, it has always been free." He cleared his throat and continued. "This year the Board decided to charge fifteen dollars— which still won't cover the complete cost of the jacket."

10   I stared at him in shock, and a small sound of dismay escaped my throat. I hadn't expected this. He still avoided looking in my eyes.

11   "So if you are unable to pay the fifteen dollars for the jacket, it will be given to the next one in line."

12   Standing with all the dignity I could muster°, I said, "I'll speak to my grandfather about it, sir, and let you know tomorrow." I cried on the walk home from the bus stop. The dirt road was a quarter of a mile from the highway, so by the time I got home, my eyes were red and puffy.

13   "Where's Grandpa?" I asked Grandma, looking down at the floor so she wouldn't ask me why I'd been crying. She was sewing on a quilt and didn't look up.

14   "I think he's out back working in the bean field."

15   I went outside and looked out at the fields. There he was. I could see him walking between the rows, his body bent over the little plants, hoe in hand. I walked slowly out to him, trying to think how I could best ask him for the money. There was a cool breeze blowing and a sweet smell of mesquite° in the air, but I didn't appreciate it. I kicked at a dirt clod°. I wanted that jacket so much. It was more than just being a valedictorian and giving a little thank-you speech for the jacket on graduation night. It represented eight years of hard work and expectation. I knew I had to be honest with Grandpa; it was my only chance. He saw me and looked up.

16   He waited for me to speak. I cleared my throat nervously and clasped my hands behind my back so he wouldn't see them shaking. "Grandpa, I have a big favor to ask you," I said in Spanish, the only language he knew. He still waited silently. I tried again. "Grandpa, this year the principal said the scholarship jacket is not going to be free. It's going to cost fifteen dollars and I have to take the money in tomorrow, otherwise it'll be given to someone else." The last words came out in an eager rush. Grandpa straightened up tiredly and leaned his chin on the hoe handle. He looked out over the field that was filled with the tiny green bean plants. I waited, desperately hoping he'd say I could have the money.

17   He turned to me and asked quietly, "What does a scholarship jacket mean?"

18   I answered quickly; maybe there was a chance. "It means you've earned it by having the highest grades for eight years and that's why they're giving it to you." Too late I realized the significance of my words. Grandpa knew that I understood it was not a matter of money. It wasn't that. He went back to hoeing the weeds that sprang up between the delicate little bean plants. It was a time-consuming job; sometimes the small shoots were right next to each other. Finally he spoke again.

19   "Then if you pay for it, Marta, it's not a scholarship jacket, is it? Tell your principal I will not pay the fifteen dollars."

20   I walked back to the house and locked myself in the bathroom for a long time. I was angry with Grandfather even though I knew he was right, and I was angry with the Board, whoever they were. Why did they have to change the rules just when it was my turn to win the jacket?

21   It was a very sad and withdrawn girl who dragged into the principal's office the next day. This time he did look me in the eyes.

22   "What did your grandfather say?"

23   I sat very straight in my chair.

24   "He said to tell you he won't pay the fifteen dollars."

25   The principal muttered something I couldn't understand under his breath, and walked over to the window. He stood looking out at something outside. He looked bigger than usual when he stood up; he was a tall, gaunt° man with gray hair, and I watched the back of his head while I waited for him to speak.

26   "Why?" he finally asked. "Your grandfather has the money. Doesn't he own a small bean farm?"

27   I looked at him, forcing my eyes to stay dry. "He said if I had to pay for it, then it wouldn't be a scholarship jacket," I said and stood up to leave. "I guess you'll just have to give it to Joann." I hadn't meant to say that; it had just slipped out. I was almost to the door when he stopped me.

28   "Martha—wait."

29   I turned and looked at him, waiting. What did he want now? I could feel my heart pounding. Something bitter and vile° tasting was coming up in my mouth; I was afraid I was going to be sick. I didn't need any sympathy speeches. He sighed loudly and went back to his big desk. He looked at me, biting his lip, as if thinking.

30   "Okay, damn it. We'll make an exception in your case. I'll tell the Board, you'll get your jacket."

31   I could hardly believe it. I spoke in a trembling rush. "Oh, thank you, sir!" Suddenly I felt great. I didn't know about adrenaline° in those days, but I knew something was pumping through me, making me feel as tall as the sky. I wanted to yell, jump, run the mile, do something. I ran out so I could cry in the hall where there was no one to see me. At the end of the day, Mr. Schmidt winked at me and said, "I hear you're getting a scholarship jacket this year."

32   His face looked as happy and innocent as a baby's, but I knew better. Without answering I gave him a quick hug and ran to the bus. I cried on the walk home again, but this time because I was so happy. I couldn't wait to tell Grandpa and ran straight to the field. I joined him in the row where he was working and without saying anything I crouched down and started pulling up the weeds with my hands. Grandpa worked alongside me for a few minutes, but he didn't ask what had happened. After I had a little pile of weeds between the rows, I stood up and faced him.

33   "The principal said he's making an exception for me, Grandpa, and I'm getting the jacket after all. That's after I told him what you said."

34   Grandpa didn't say anything; he just gave me a pat on the shoulder and a smile. He pulled out the crumpled red handkerchief that he always carried in his back pocket and wiped the sweat off his forehead.

35   "Better go see if your grandmother needs any help with supper."

36   I gave him a big grin. He didn't fool me. I skipped and ran back to the house, whistling some silly tune.

Reading Comprehension Questions

Vocabulary in Context

_D_ 1. In the sentences below, the word *dismay* (dĭs-mā′) means

   A. joy.
   B. comfort.
   C. surprise and relief.
   D. sudden discouragement.

   > If Marta was "shocked" and received unexpected information, she would make a sound of sudden discouragement.

   > "I stared at him in shock, and a small sound of dismay escaped my throat. I hadn't expected this." (Paragraph 10)

Central Point and Main Ideas

_C_ 2. Which sentence best expresses the central point of this selection?

Answer A covers only paragraphs 4–7. Answer B covers only paragraph 1. Answer D covers only paragraph 2.

   A. When she went to pick up her gym clothes, Marta overheard a conversation between two teachers that shocked and saddened her.
   B. At Marta's school, it was a tradition to award a beautiful gold and green jacket to the eighth-grade valedictorian.
   C. Although fourteen-year-old Marta had earned a school jacket awarded for scholarship, she almost lost this award because of discrimination.
   D. Marta's sister had won the scholarship jacket, and Marta deeply wanted to win it as well.

_B_ 3. Which sentence best expresses the main idea of paragraph 7?

Expressions like "ears pounded," "shaking," "fled from the room," and "don't remember" show that Marta was shocked and saddened.

   A. Marta was unable to hear every word of Mr. Schmidt's and Mr. Boone's conversation.
   B. Marta was shocked and saddened when she overheard two teachers arguing about her.
   C. Mr. Schmidt didn't see Marta when he rushed out of the room.
   D. Marta didn't want her grandmother to know she was crying.

Supporting Details

_A_ 4. Which of the following statements is false?

See paragraph 2. Marta's parents were poor, not dead. Answer B is covered in paragraph 5 and the beginning of paragraph 7. Answer C is covered in paragraph 19. Answer D is covered in the third sentence of paragraph 3.

   A. Marta was being raised by her grandparents because her parents were dead.
   B. Mr. Schmidt was angry at the attempt to give the scholarship jacket to someone less deserving than Marta.
   C. Marta's grandfather refused to give her the money for the scholarship jacket.
   D. Marta was called by a different name at school.

Transitions

_D_ 5. The relationship between the two parts of the sentence below is one of

    A. time.

    B. contrast.

    C. comparison.

    D. cause and effect.

> *So* is a cause-effect word. The *cause* is the decision; the *effect* is looking him straight in the eye.

    "I decided I wasn't going to make it any easier for him, so I looked him straight in the eye." (Paragraph 8)

Patterns of Organization

_B_ 6. The overall pattern of organization of the selection is

    A. cause and effect.

    B. time order.

    C. comparison.

    D. contrast.

> The events are told in the order in which they occurred. Narrations such as this are usually in time order.

Inferences

_C_ 7. We can infer from paragraph 8 that the principal was "uncomfortable and unhappy" because

    A. the students had not been paying attention in class during the last few weeks before graduation.

    B. his office was very hot.

    C. he was ashamed to tell Marta that she had to pay fifteen dollars for a jacket that she had earned.

    D. Mr. Boone and Mr. Schmidt were fighting in the hallway.

> We suspect the principal is going to tell Marta that there is some sort of problem with the scholarship jacket that he knows she deserves, so it is logical to infer that this is why he looks "uncomfortable and unhappy."

_B_ 8. By saying, "If you pay for it, Marta, it's not a scholarship jacket, is it?" Marta's grandfather was implying that

    A. the jacket was not worth fifteen dollars.

    B. a real award should not have to be bought with money.

    C. Marta did not deserve to win the scholarship jacket.

    D. he did not understand the purpose of the scholarship jacket.

> Grandpa's question in paragraph 17 and Marta's statement that "Grandpa knew that I understood it was not a matter of money" (in paragraph 18) support this implication.

Purpose and Tone

___A___ 9. The author's purpose in this selection is to
   A. inform and engage readers with an interesting and meaningful anecdote.
   B. persuade schools not to charge students for academic awards.
   C. entertain with an amusing, light-hearted story about a young girl in school.

Answer B is incorrect because the selection says nothing about what schools should or should not do. Answer C is incorrect because there is nothing amusing or lighthearted about this story from Marta's youth.

___C___ 10. The tone of paragraph 31 can be described as
   A. contented.
   B. angry.
   C. joyous.
   D. conceited.

Expressions like "felt great," "adrenaline pumping," and "tall as the sky" describe an attitude of joy.

Discussion Questions

1. In her first meeting with the principal, Marta could have challenged him by telling what she had overheard the two teachers saying. Why do you think she stayed silent? What do you think the principal would have said or done if she'd told him she knew the real reason she wasn't being given the jacket?

2. Why do you think the principal gave in during his second meeting with Marta? What do you think that shows about Marta's grandfather's decision? What do you think might happen when the principal has to face the Board again? If you were the principal, what would you have said to the Board?

3. Marta implies that she was discriminated against because of her racial background (she was Mexican) and her family's economic condition (they were poor). Have you ever experienced discrimination, or do you know of a friend who has experienced it? Explain.

4. Marta stresses again and again how important the scholarship jacket was to her and how hard she worked to win it. Is there something you worked hard to achieve when you were younger? How long did you work toward that goal? How did you feel when you finally succeeded—or did not succeed? What lessons, if any, did you learn from the experience?

Note: Writing assignments for this selection appear on page 604.

Check Your Performance   PURPOSE AND TONE

Activity	Number Right	Points		Score
Review Test 1 (10 items)	_____	× 1	=	_____
Review Test 2 (5 items)	_____	× 6	=	_____
Review Test 3 (5 items)	_____	× 6	=	_____
Review Test 4 (10 items)	_____	× 3	=	_____
		TOTAL SCORE	=	_____%

Enter your total score into the **Reading Performance Chart: Review Tests** on the inside back cover.

PURPOSE AND TONE: Mastery Test 1

A. In the space provided, indicate whether the primary purpose of each item is to inform (**I**), to persuade (**P**), or to entertain (**E**).

_____I_____ 1. Every month more than 90 percent of the children in the United States eat at McDonald's.   Statistical information about where children eat.

_____P_____ 2. Fast-food chains must be encouraged to offer meals that are healthier for our children.   Persuasive clue: *must*.

_____E_____ 3. Fred's idea of healthy eating is to have a double cheeseburger without putting any salt on it.   Entertains by stating the silly idea that skipping the salt on a double cheeseburger will make it healthy.

_____P_____ 4. The federal government needs to hire more inspectors to insure the safety of the meals served to our schoolchildren.   Persuasive clue: *needs to*.

_____E_____ 5. Rachel says she eats a balanced diet by choosing items from the four major food groups: chips, soda, candy, and pastries.   Entertains by describing the four major food groups as "chips, soda, candy, and pastries."

B. Each of the following passages illustrates one of the five tones in the box below. In the space provided, write the letter of the tone that applies to each passage.

A. caring	B. critical	C. humorous
D. pessimistic	E. self-mocking	

_____C_____ 6. [1]Recently, my sister asked me to baby-sit her two sons for the evening. [2]I figured I would get them dinner, let them watch a little TV, and then put them to bed early. [3]The rest of the night I planned to watch TV and collect an easy twenty dollars. [4]Well, right before we sat down for a pizza dinner, Rickie let the parakeet out of its cage. [5]The dog started chasing the bird as it flew around the house, so I decided to catch it before the dog did. [6]The boys and I had the bird cornered by the fireplace when Rickie jumped for it and knocked over the hamster cage. [7]The hamsters took off under the sofa while the bird flew away. [8]Fortunately, the dog had disappeared at this point. [9]I took care of the hamsters while the boys caught the parakeet and put it back in its cage. [10]When we returned to the kitchen to eat cold pizza, I discovered why the dog had lost interest in the bird chase. [11]What was left of the pizza was lying on the floor, and tomato sauce was dripping like blood from the dog's chin. [12]Later, when my sister returned, I took the twenty dollars and told her to get someone else next time.   The author describes a series of amusing events that make the passage humorous.

(Continues on next page)

_B_   7.   ¹Whatever happened to the practice of saving up for what you want? ²It seems nobody has that kind of patience any more. ³Many Americans buy what they want when they want it and worry about paying for it later. ⁴The average American spends significantly more than he or she earns, much to the enjoyment of the credit-card companies. ⁵Apparently people need to reach a financial crisis before they realize that it's downright stupid to neglect balancing their budgets and saving for a rainy day.

Downright stupid signals that the author is being critical of the way many Americans handle their finances.

_E_   8.   ¹Machines are complete mysteries to me, and this has resulted in some embarrassing service calls at my home. ²For example, there was the time I called in a repairman because our refrigerator was too warm. ³Imagine my humiliation when he told me that the cause of the problem was a dirty filter, which I didn't know existed and therefore hadn't cleaned even once in the two years we owned the refrigerator. ⁴The best example of my brilliance with machines, however, has to be the time I called for someone to fix my washing machine. ⁵The repairman's solution was simply to put the plug back in the outlet, from which it had been jarred loose by the constant vibration of the washer.

The author makes fun of his or her own lack of understanding of machines. Talking about "my brilliance" in dealing with machines emphasizes the author's self-mockery.

_D_   9.   ¹Research on rats shows that when animals live in crowded conditions, they live disorderly, violent lives. ²Humans are no different. ³Crowded inner cities are models of lawlessness; the crowded highways of Los Angeles encourage aggression by drivers, and even shootings. ⁴As our urban areas continue to grow in population density, these types of problems will surely also grow. ⁵That means more family violence and more fighting over available resources. ⁶The American dream will become just that—only a dream.

The author presents only the negative side of life in America: disorderly and violent lives of lawlessness, freeway shootings, family violence. And these problems will only continue to get worse.

_A_   10.   ¹Those addicted to drugs and alcohol probably feel terrible about themselves—even if they don't show it—and harsh judgments only worsen their self-image. ²What these people need are programs to help rid themselves of their addictions. ³It is also important that we all open our hearts and minds to these troubled people. ⁴Their addiction does not make them any less "children of God"; nor does it mean that they deserve to be stripped of the dignity that is the birthright of every human being. ⁵We must strive to create an environment of hope and help for those who so desperately need it.

If the author feels we must "open our hearts and minds to these troubled people," he or she clearly cares about them. All of the rest of the details further support the idea that the author cares.

PURPOSE AND TONE: Mastery Test 2

A. In the space provided, indicate whether the primary purpose of each item is to inform (**I**), to persuade (**P**), or to entertain (**E**).

___I___ 1. The world's first ads were neither printed nor broadcast electronically; they were vocal, called out by street peddlers promoting their wares.
> Straightforward information about the world's first ads.

___P___ 2. Billboard advertising is a form of visual pollution and should be banned.
> Persuasive clue: *should*.

___E___ 3. Instead of nagging my father to lose weight, my mother bought him an extra-large T-shirt imprinted with the message "This space for rent."
> The amusing idea of renting space on the overweight father's extra-large T-shirt is intended to entertain us.

___I___ 4. For television, the top advertising spenders are manufacturers of cars and light trucks; automobile dealers spend the most on newspaper ads.
> Straightforward information about who spends the most money on television and newspaper ads.

___P___ 5. Advertisers should not be allowed to continue misleading consumers by lying or exaggerating.
> Persuasive clue: *should*.

___I___ 6. On average, each person in the United States and Canada uses more than 300 gigajoules (GJ) (equivalent to about 60 barrels) of oil per year. By contrast, in some of the poorest countries of the world, such as Ethiopia, Nepal, and Bhutan, each person generally consumes less than 1 GJ per year.
> Factual information about how much oil per person is used in various countries each year.

___P___ 7. The foundation of public education has always been reading, writing, and arithmetic—the "three R's." Yet the schools insist that students who have not mastered these fundamentals continue to take all the other subjects as well. What good does it do for young people to sit in a history or science class if they can't read or calculate well? Schools ought to require students who are very far behind in the fundamentals to devote all their time to the three R's until they are reading at or near grade level.
> Persuasive clue: *ought to*.

(Continues on next page)

B. Each of the following passages illustrates one of the tones identified in the box below. In each space provided, put the letter of the tone that applies to the passage. (Three tone choices will be left over.)

A. amused	B. arrogant	C. critical
D. depressed	E. objective	F. optimistic

_D_   8.

The author describes dreary details that are depressing. His or her inability to improve things (sentences 8 and 9) further suggests the depressed tone.

¹When I was younger, I thought that by this age, I would be pretty well set for life. ²I imagined that I would have a nice house, some money in the bank, and a decent job. ³But things haven't worked out that way at all. ⁴I'm living in a one-bedroom apartment with shabby furniture and a view of a parking lot. ⁵My office job is dull and unrewarding, and I bring home hardly enough to cover my rent and expenses, much less put anything away. ⁶My place is so unattractive that I don't want to invite anyone over, so I'm alone most of the time. ⁷Whatever dreams I had in my youth are pretty well gone now. ⁸Sometimes I think about going back to school and trying to prepare for a different career, but at my age there doesn't seem to be much point in doing that. ⁹I guess this is just what life had in store for me.

_C_   9.

The writer is criticizing parents who will not make time to read to their children. The words "Somehow they find time for those things . . . but can't find time to read to a child" emphasize the critical tone.

¹Parents who do not read to their children often excuse themselves by claiming a lack of time. ²But with few exceptions, their failure to read is a matter of priorities. ³Most parents find the time to put in a full workday, take several coffee breaks, eat lunch and dinner, read the newspaper, watch the nightly newscast or ball game, do the dishes, talk on the phone for thirty minutes (mostly about nothing), run to the store for a pack of cigarettes or a lottery ticket, drive to the mall, and never miss that favorite prime-time show. ⁴Somehow they find the time for those things—important or unimportant as they are—but can't find time to read to a child, which is much more important than all the other items on a leisure priority list.

_E_   10.

The author merely presents facts about the relationship between grilling meat and cancer.

¹Scientists say grilling meat creates cancer-causing substances that affect the meat in two ways. ²First, when fat drips onto the source of heat, the substances are formed and then carried up to the food by smoke. ³They are also formed when flames touch the meat. ⁴There are, however, a few ways that experts say will minimize the risk of grilling meat: (1) Use low-fat meats and nonfat sauces. ⁵(2) Partially cook meat before grilling. ⁶(3) Cover the grill with foil; punch holes in the foil to let fat drip down. ⁷(4) Avoid fire flare-ups, which cause harmful smoke. ⁸(5) Scrape off blackened material on the surface of meat before eating it. ⁹(6) Don't cook out every day.

PURPOSE AND TONE: Mastery Test 3

A. Seven quotations in the story below are preceded by a blank space. Identify the tone of each italicized quotation by writing in the letter of one of these tones. (Three tone choices will be left over.)

A. angry	B. curious	C. depressed	D. excited
E. frightened	F. pleading	G. scheming	H. straightforward
I. superior	J. sympathetic		

The television reporter knocked on the door of the small row home. A woman opened the door.

H 1. *"My name is Tod Hunter,"* the reporter said. *"I'm with* Action News, *and I'd like to talk to the woman who lost her daughter in the school fire last night."*

Item 1: The reporter is stating facts directly and honestly.

"Oh, I'm sorry, but she's not much in the mood for visitors."

"I understand," the reporter said. "Please tell her that we only want a moment of her time."

While the woman was gone, the reporter turned to his crew.

Item 2: The reporter is suggesting a sneaky way to try to get into the house.

G 2. *"You could shoot from this angle,"* he whispered, *"but let's try to get inside. If she's at all responsive to my questions, let's gradually move in* through the doorway."

Children in the neighborhood crowded around the TV crew.

Item 3: Shouting, laughing, and saying "Wow" suggest the children are excited.

D 3. *"Those are TV cameras!"* some shouted, laughing. *"Wow, real TV cameras!"*

B 4. Pausing to look at the crew standing outside the house, passersby asked, *"What do you suppose happened there?"*

Then the mother of the fire victim appeared at the door, looking drawn and exhausted. "What do you want?"

Item 4: Wondering about what is going on shows curiosity.

"I'm really very sorry for your great loss, Ma'am." Hunter continued, "I'm here for *Action News.* Do you know what caused the terrible fire?"

"Please, no interviews."

"Our viewers want to know about this awful fire."

Item 5: Shouting that it's none of the reporter's business shows anger.

A 5. *"I don't care about your viewers!"* she shouted. *"It's none of their business. It's none of your business, either, young man."*

Item 6: Running away shows the children are afraid.

E 6. *"Run! She's mad!"* shouted the children as they raced away.

F 7. *"All I want is two minutes,"* the reporter said. *"Please, just two minutes of your time."*

Item 7: The reporter is begging for the woman's time.

But the door had already slammed in his face.

"Let's get out of here," the frustrated reporter said to his crew. "I'm starved."

(Continues on next page)

B. In the space provided, indicate whether the primary purpose of each passage is to inform (**I**), to persuade (**P**), or to entertain (**E**).

_____I_____ 8. ¹Why do people swear and engage in coarse language? ²One researcher suggests that swearing is a way of asserting independence by breaking adult taboos. ³In a society that prizes adulthood and independence, the increasing use of vulgar and profane language at younger and younger ages is not surprising. ⁴When used infrequently, profanity and vulgar expressions communicate strong emotions for which there may be no other appropriate words. ⁵They are meant to shock and to communicate one's deep disgust or contempt.

The author provides straightforward
information about the use of profanity.

_____P_____ 9. ¹Advertising aimed at children is not just annoying—it is destructive and should be controlled. ²Especially around the holiday season, children are hammered with media messages intended to make them want the latest toy, game, computer, sneakers, doll, music, and clothing on the market. ³While manufacturers are busy sucking money from the pockets of children and their families, they are contributing to a growing sense of dissatisfaction and greed. ⁴That serves the manufacturers' purpose—after all, if children were ever satisfied, they would not ask their parents to buy more merchandise. ⁵But the effect is to produce a nation of selfish men and women whose lives are ruled by the need to have more, more, more. ⁶It is frightening to see a generation being trained from childhood to be greedy consumers. ⁷What chance do they have to ever become contented adults whose values extend beyond a price tag?

Should (sentence 1) is a word used to persuade. The emotional language— hammered with media messages (sentence 2), sucking money from the pockets (3), the need to have more, more, more (5), greedy consumers (6)— further supports the purpose of convincing us that the advertising is destructive.

_____E_____ 10. ¹While I was watching a cartoon with my daughter, she said, "Dad, why does Bugs Bunny wear gloves?" ²The question has bothered me ever since. ³Why do Mickey Mouse, Bugs and Woody Woodpecker all wear gloves? ⁴And who decides which characters get pants? ⁵Mickey always wears them, yet Donald Duck just wears that sailor shirt. ⁶Porky has a jacket and a bow tie, but no shirt or pants, and Daffy just has his feathers. ⁷And, come to think of it, how did Goofy, a dog, make the evolutionary leap to stand up on his hind legs, put on pants, a shirt, and a vest, and talk? ⁸Yet Pluto is content to hang out in the doghouse getting his butt kicked by the chipmunks Chip 'n Dale.

The passage raises amusing questions about the
clothing and habits of animal cartoon characters.

PURPOSE AND TONE: Mastery Test 4

A. Seven quotations in the story below are preceded by a blank space. Identify the tone of each italicized quotation by writing in the letter of one of these tones. (Three tone choices will be left over.)

A. amused	B. ashamed	C. cheerful	D. disgusted
E. joyous	F. outraged	G. sorrowful	H. straightforward
I. understanding	J. vengeful		

Item 1:
The word *chirped* emphasizes the cheerfulness of Annette's words.

Item 2:
Yuk emphasizes the man's disgust with the fish that makes him gag.

Item 3:
Smiling and *sighed* emphasize the speaker's joy.

Item 4:
The word *hissed* emphasizes the woman's outrage.

Item 5:
The word *instructing* emphasizes the manager's straightforward tone.

Item 6:
Annette's words show that she understands the manager's decision.

Item 7:
Ben's muttered words—he doesn't want anyone else to hear them—indicate that he wants revenge.

The scene is a busy restaurant on a Saturday evening.

_C_ 1. "Good evening!" a young waitress chirped to a table of diners. *"It's so nice to see you here tonight! My name is Annette, and I'll be your server this evening."*

_D_ 2. Meanwhile, across the room, a man stared at his food as he pushed it around with his fork. *"Yuk! They call this 'ocean-fresh fish,'"* he said, *"but it sure doesn't smell all that fresh. It's making me gag!"*

But at the next table, a young man said to his friend, "This great spaghetti really hits the spot. I was starved."

_E_ 3. Nearby, in a dimly lit corner of the restaurant, a young man and woman sat close together, smiling at the diamond ring on the woman's finger. "Oh, darling," sighed the woman. *"This is the happiest night of my life. This restaurant will always be my favorite because this is where you asked me to marry you."*

_F_ 4. A conversation of a different sort was taking place at another table: *"I cannot believe you would do this!"* a woman hissed at her husband. *"What kind of man takes his wife into a public place to tell her he's having an affair with her best friend? What am I supposed to do—order an appetizer?"*

_H_ 5. Back in the kitchen, the restaurant manager was instructing the staff. *"Annette, you cover tables one through four. Ben, you're responsible for five through eight. A party of sixteen people is coming in at eight o'clock; Lisa and Suzette will take care of them."*

"Well, we got passed over again, didn't we?" Ben remarked to Annette after the manager was gone. "Lisa and Suzette always get the big groups and the big tips. It makes me wonder why I try to do a good job here."

_I_ 6. "Oh, I don't mind," Annette said. *"Lisa and Suzette do work a lot more hours than you or I do. I can see why the manager thinks they deserve the best assignments."* Then Annette walked out of the kitchen.

_J_ 7. "Well, it's not okay with me," Ben muttered to himself. *"When I quit this lousy job, they're going to pay for the way they've treated me. I'll get back at them somehow."*

(Continues on next page)

B. (8.) In the space provided, indicate whether the primary purpose of the following passage is to inform (**I**), to persuade (**P**), or to entertain (**E**).

_____I_____

The passage provides us with direct factual information and statistics about eye contact.

[1]Eye contact, also referred to as gaze, is how and how much we look at people with whom we are communicating. [2]By maintaining our eye contact, we can tell when or whether people are paying attention to us, when people are involved in what we are saying, and whether what we are saying is eliciting feelings. [3]The amount of eye contact differs from person to person and from situation to situation. [4]Studies show that talkers hold eye contact about 40 percent of the time and listeners nearly 70 percent of the time. [5]We generally maintain better eye contact when we are discussing topics with which we are comfortable, when we are genuinely interested in a person's comments or reactions, or when we are trying to influence the other person. [6]On the other hand, we tend to avoid eye contact when we are discussing topics that make us uncomfortable, when we lack interest in the topic or person, or when we are embarrassed, ashamed, or trying to hide something.

C. Read the paragraph below. Then carefully consider the questions that follow, and write the letters of the best responses.

[1]There are certain types of people you <u>should</u> not trust. [2]One type is people who tell you that God told them to ask you to send them money. [3]You know the guys I mean. [4]They get on television and say: "God told me He wants you to send me some money, say $100, or even just $10, if that's all you can afford, but in all honesty I must point out that God is less likely to give you some horrible disease if your gift is in the $100 range." [5]The theory here seems to be that God talks only to the guys on television. [6]I always thought that if God needed money all that badly, He would get in touch with us directly.

_____C_____ 9. The purpose of this paragraph is
  A. to persuade readers that they should not send money to television evangelists.   The author persuades us by saying that we "*should* not
  B. to entertain readers by exaggerating points.   trust" these people. The
  C. both of the above.   author also entertains us by making fun of con men who try to get money from us.

_____B_____ 10. The tone of this paragraph can be described as
  A. straightforward and serious.
  B. humorous and mocking.   The author sets a tone of humor and mockery
  C. prayerful and respectful.   by presenting the claims these people make in
  D. sentimental and warm.   exaggerated form. (See sentence 4.)

PURPOSE AND TONE: Mastery Test 5

Read the paragraphs below. Then carefully consider the questions that follow, and, in the spaces provided, write the letters of the best responses.

A. ¹A successful doctor is scheduled to operate on a patient at 8 a.m., but it has snowed during the night, and driving is difficult. ²Do you think the doctor will stay home in bed? ³Not if he or she is professional. ⁴This attitude of professionalism is the key to being a successful college student, too. ⁵And it is <u>within your reach</u>, no matter how well or how poorly you have done in school up until now. ⁶You cannot undo the past, but <u>you can</u> adopt an attitude of professionalism from now on. ⁷All you have to do is intend to take school seriously, and the rest will follow. ⁸By attending classes, turning in assignments on time, and coming prepared for tests, <u>you will gradually build your skills.</u>

Words indicating the purpose and tone are underlined.

_B_ 1. The primary purpose of this paragraph is to
    A. present facts on student behavior.
    B. inspire students to be conscientious.
    C. entertain students with a dramatic story about professionalism.

_C_ 2. In general, the tone of this paragraph can be described as
    A. critical.
    B. pessimistic.
    C. encouraging.
    D. praising.

Item 1: The author is persuading students to be conscientious by comparing the successful student's attitude to the professional attitude of a successful doctor.
Item 2: Sentences 5–8 state in a positive way things a student can do to be successful.

B. ¹According to memory experts, there are ways you can improve your chances of remembering the names of people you meet. ²One way is to make associations between a person's name and looks. ³For example, if you meet a man named Baker, you might picture him wearing a baker's hat. ⁴If the name is a difficult one, ask for the spelling and visualize the letters mentally. ⁵It's also useful to repeat the person's name as you converse, keeping your mental images in mind. ⁶And when your conversation ends, repeat the person's name as you say goodbye.

_A_ 3. The primary purpose of this paragraph is to
    A. inform.
    B. persuade.
    C. entertain.

The paragraph gives specific information on how to remember the names of people you meet.

_D_ 4. The overall tone of this paragraph can be described as
    A. critical and angry.
    B. obviously humorous.
    C. doubtful.
    D. straightforward and instructive.

The passage presents a straightforward list of four tips for remembering names.

(Continues on next page)

359

C. ¹I was sitting on a beach one summer day, watching two children, a boy and a girl, playing in the sand. ²They were hard at work building an elaborate sandcastle by the water's edge, with gates and towers and moats and internal passages. ³Just when they had nearly finished their project, a big wave came along and knocked it down, reducing it to a heap of wet sand. ⁴I expected the children to burst into tears, devastated by what had happened to all their hard work. ⁵But they surprised me. ⁶Instead, they ran up the shore away from the water, laughing and holding hands, and sat down to build another castle. ⁷I realized that they had taught me an important lesson. ⁸All the things in our lives, all the complicated structures we spend so much time and energy creating, are built on sand. ⁹Only our relationships with other people endure. ¹⁰Sooner or later, a wave will come along and knock down what we have worked so hard to build up. ¹¹When that happens, only the person who has somebody's hand to hold will be able to laugh.

By relating this experience, the author hopes to persuade the reader that relationships are what is important in life.

_B_ 5. The primary purpose of this paragraph is to
   A. inform readers about how children behave.
   B. persuade readers of the importance of relationships.
   C. delight readers with a story of childhood playfulness.

_D_ 6. The tone of this paragraph can be described as
   A. forgiving.
   B. humorous.
   C. self-pitying.
   D. instructive.

Just as the author was instructed by the children's action, he or she hopes to instruct us by describing the event and the lesson.

D. ¹My best school report was in first grade from Mrs. Varulo. ²First, she told my parents about my amazing physical energy: "Lisa never tires of chasing and punching her classmates." ³Next, she praised my class participation and active, questioning mind: "After every instruction—even one as simple as 'Please take out your pencils'—Lisa asks 'Why?'" ⁴Mrs. Varulo was so impressed with my vocabulary that she commented, "I don't know where Lisa has picked up some of the words she uses—certainly not in my classroom." ⁵Somehow she even knew I would become a famous fiction writer. ⁶"More than any other student I have ever taught," she wrote, "Lisa is a born liar."

_C_ 7. The primary purpose of this paragraph is to
   A. inform.
   B. persuade.
   C. entertain.

The author describes each of the negative statements as a positive quality. This makes the paragraph entertaining.

_D_ 8. The tone of this paragraph can best be described as
   A. enthusiastic and cheerful.
   B. annoyed and bitter.
   C. cheerful and nostalgic.
   D. ironic and humorous.

The author uses irony by turning all of the teacher's negative comments into positive qualities. She pretends not to realize what the teacher actually meant.

PURPOSE AND TONE: Mastery Test 6

Read the paragraphs below. Then carefully consider the questions that follow, and, in the spaces provided, write the letters of the best responses.

A. ¹Throughout history, people have <u>suffered</u> from ailments that could have been easily avoided <u>if</u> they had <u>only</u> been understood. ²For instance, it used to be common for hat makers to be <u>tortured</u> by uncontrollable trembling, slurred speech, and mental confusion. ³The condition led to Lewis Carroll's creation of the Mad Hatter in his book *Alice's Adventures in Wonderland*. ⁴<u>Sadly</u>, the hatters did not know that the mercury they used in creating felt hats was poisoning them, leading to their strange symptoms. ⁵Similarly, many of the world's greatest artists <u>suffered</u> from terrible depression. ⁶Today we know that the lead in the paint they used probably affected their mental state. ⁷How <u>tragic that so many lives were destroyed</u> for want of a little knowledge.

__A__ 1. The primary purpose of the passage is
- A. to tell readers about formerly misunderstood ailments.
- B. to persuade readers to protect themselves against easily avoidable ailments.
- C. both of the above.

The author uses two straightforward factual examples to illustrate the point about formerly misunderstood ailments.

__A__ 2. The tone of the passage can be described as
- A. regretful.
- B. angry.
- C. alarmed.
- D. pessimistic.

Words suggesting the regretful tone are underlined.

B. ¹Al Smith, the Democratic candidate for President in 1928, was known for his ready wit and quick comebacks. ²Once he was heckled while making a campaign speech. ³"Tell 'em everything you know, Al," yelled the heckler. ⁴"It won't take very long."
⁵Al Smith answered with a grin, "I'll tell 'em everything we both know—it won't take any longer."

__A__ 3. The primary purpose of this passage is to
- A. inform students about a humorous aspect of a historical figure.
- B. persuade people to support the Democrats.
- C. argue that Al Smith should have won the 1928 presidential campaign.

Al Smith's comeback is entertaining. But the primary purpose is to inform us of this aspect of Smith.

__B__ 4. The tone of the passage can be described as
- A. forgiving.
- B. amused.
- C. bitter.
- D. disbelieving.

The author sets an amused tone by describing a humorous incident.

(Continues on next page)

C.   ¹Three people were killed because a man was angry that his girlfriend wanted to break up with him. ²He shot both her and two people who tried to stop him. ³Now the state is planning to kill him, and <u>that's as it should be</u>. ⁴Some may argue that taking a life is always wrong, that two wrongs don't make a right. ⁵But <u>there is nothing right</u> about making taxpayers give free room and board to a person who killed innocent people. ⁶And <u>there's nothing right</u> about putting such a dangerous person in prison, from which he will probably one day be released to again threaten society.   Words suggesting the purpose and tone are underlined.

_B_   5.   The primary purpose of this paragraph is to
   A.   report on facts about the death penalty.
   B.   persuade readers that the death penalty has merit.
   C.   entertain readers with a description of an interesting problem.

_A_   6.   The overall tone of this paragraph can be described as
   A.   forceful.
   B.   insulting.
   C.   compassionate.
   D.   excited.

D.   ¹When people are unemployed, two major sources of stress come into play. ²One is the loss of income, with all the financial hardships that this brings. ³Suddenly there are the difficulties of paying the monthly rent or mortgage, of making the car payment and paying credit-card bills, of dealing with utility costs, and the fundamental matter of putting enough food to eat on the table. ⁴The other source of stress is the effect of the loss of income on workers' feelings about themselves. ⁵Workers who derive their identity from their work, men who define manhood as supporting a family, and people who define their worth in terms of their work's dollar value lose more than their paychecks when they lose their jobs. ⁶They lose a piece of themselves; they lose their self-esteem.

_A_   7.   The primary purpose of this paragraph is
The author simply and   A.   to inform readers about the major sources of stress for the
clearly desribes the   unemployed.
two major sources of   B.   to persuade readers that unemployment should be eliminated.
stress that result from
the loss of a job.   C.   to amuse readers with observations about human nature.

_D_   8.   The tone of this paragraph can be described as
   A.   depressed and sorrowful.
   B.   angry and desperate.   The words *hardships* (sentence 2)
                                                and *difficulties* (sentence 3) suggest a
   C.   surprised but optimistic.   sympathetic tone. The serious tone comes
   D.   serious and sympathetic.   from the specifics the author includes.

9 Argument

"I shall now punch a huge hole in your argument."

Many of us enjoy a good argument. A good argument is not an emotional experience in which people's feelings get out of control, leaving them ready to start throwing things. Instead, it is a rational discussion in which each person advances and supports a point of view about some matter. We might argue with a friend, for example, about where to eat or what movie to go to. We might argue about whether a boss or a parent or an instructor is acting in a fair or an unfair manner. We might argue about whether certain performers or sports stars deserve to get paid as much as they do. In a good argument (such as the one that appears to be going on in the above cartoon), the other person listens carefully as we state our case, waiting to see if we really have solid evidence to support our point of view.

Argumentation is, then, a part of our everyday dealings with other people. It is also an important part of much of what we read. Authors often try to convince us of their opinions and interpretations. Very often there are three important things we must do as critical readers:

1 Recognize the **point** the author is making.

2 Decide if the author's support is **relevant**.

3 Decide if the author's support is **adequate**.

This chapter will give you practice in doing the above, first in everyday arguments and then in textbook material.

The Basics of Argument: Point and Support

A good **argument** is one in which you make a point and then provide persuasive and logical evidence to back it up. Here is a point:

Point: The Beef and Burger Shop is a poor fast-food restaurant.

This statement hardly discourages us from visiting the Beef and Burger Shop. "Why do you say that?" we might legitimately say. "Give your reasons." Support is needed so we can decide for ourselves whether a valid point has been made. Suppose the point is followed by these three reasons:

1. The burgers are full of gristle.

2. The roast beef sandwiches have a chemical taste.

3. The fries are lukewarm and soggy.

Clearly, the details provide solid support for the point. They give us a basis for understanding and agreeing with the point. In light of these details, our mouths are not watering for lunch at the Beef and Burger Shop.

We see here, then, a small example of what clear thinking in an argument is about: making a point and providing support that truly backs up that point. A **valid argument** may also be described as a conclusion supported by logical reasons, facts, examples, and other evidence.

Let's look at another example:

Point: There are certain creatures in particular that you would never want to bite you.

Of course, we would not want *any* creature to bite us. But in this statement we're told that certain creatures in particular can be nasty biters. We'd like to get supporting details so we can see and judge for ourselves. Here are details:

1. A bite from the venomous king cobra can cause muscle paralysis and lead to respiratory failure in a matter of minutes.

2. A lion's bite is powerful enough to rip off your arm or take large chunks out of your body.

3. A crocodile's jaws will snap closed like a steel trap, and if the crocodile then decides to roll, you can usually say goodbye to your arm, leg, or whatever is in its mouth.

With such solid support, you're likely to agree that the king cobra, lion, and crocodile are especially scary biters and that a logical point has been made.

The Point and Support of an Argument

In everyday life, of course, people don't simply say, "Here is my point" and "Here is my support." Nor do writers state their ideas so directly. Even so, the basic structure of point and support is still at work beneath the surface, and to evaluate an argument, you need to recognize its point and support.

The following activity will help you distinguish between a point and its support.

PRACTICE 1

In each group of statements, one statement is the point, and the other statement or statements are support for the point. Identify each point with a **P** and each statement of support with an **S**.

> *Hint:* If it sounds right to insert the word *because* in front of a sentence, you probably have a statement of support. For example, we could say, "Because the burgers are full of gristle, because the roast beef sandwiches have a chemical taste, and because the fries are lukewarm and soggy, I've come to the conclusion that the Beef and Burger Shop is a poor fast-food restaurant."

Answer A explains the reason you should see a doctor.

1. ___S___ A. You have constant headaches and blurred vision.
    ___P___ B. You should see a doctor.

Because a number of accidents have occurred, a traffic light is needed.

2. ___S___ A. A number of accidents have occurred at that intersection.
    ___P___ B. A traffic light is needed at the intersection.

Answers A and C give two reasons the student lounge is not a place for quiet study.

3. ___S___ A. A television is always blaring in one corner of the lounge.
    ___P___ B. The student lounge is not a place for quiet study.
    ___S___ C. There are always people there talking loudly to each other.

Answers B and C give two reasons high schools should teach personal finance skills.

4. __P__ A. High schools need to teach personal finance skills.

__S__ B. Many young people do not know how to budget their money.

__S__ C. More and more people are getting into serious credit-card debt.

Answers A and C give two examples of cats being sensible.

5. __S__ A. Cats refuse to learn silly tricks just to amuse people.

__P__ B. Cats are more sensible than dogs.

__S__ C. Dogs will accept cruel mistreatment, but if a cat is mistreated, it will run away.

Laws should be passed to reduce acid rain because it harms trees and bodies of water and because the damage is hard to undo.

6. __S__ A. Scientists have proved that acid rain harms trees and bodies of water.

__P__ B. Laws should be passed to reduce acid rain.

__S__ C. The damage done by acid rain is hard or impossible to undo.

Answers A and C give two reasons conditions in the workplace are tougher.

7. __S__ A. Fewer companies are offering health plans and retirement benefits.

__P__ B. Conditions in the workplace are tougher than they used to be.

__S__ C. In many industries, workers have had to take wage cuts.

Noise, roaches, and an unresponsive landlord are three reasons to look for another apartment.

8. __S__ A. The people upstairs make a lot of noise.

__P__ B. We'd better look for another apartment.

__S__ C. Roaches seem to be taking over this apartment.

__S__ D. The landlord does nothing but promise to fix the leaky faucets.

Answers A, B, and D give reasons why the shopping center is depressing.

9. __S__ A. Almost half of the stores in the shopping center are empty.

__S__ B. A deathly hush fills the building.

__P__ C. That shopping center is a depressing place.

__S__ D. Unhappy-looking store owners stare out at the few passing shoppers.

Answers A, B, and C describe three of the health benefits of drinking coffee.

10. __S__ A. The stimulant effects of a daily cup of coffee have been proved to reduce suicide rates.

__S__ B. Coffee flushes from the bloodstream the excess fat that clogs arteries.

__S__ C. Coffee supplies a large dose of antioxidants, chemicals which prevent the formation of tumors.

__P__ D. Even though coffee can make you jittery and interfere with sleep, there are real health benefits to drinking coffee.

Relevant Support

Once you identify the point and support of an argument, you need to decide if each piece of evidence is **relevant**—in other words, if it really applies to the point. The critical reader must ask, "Is this reason relevant support for the argument?" In their enthusiasm for making an argument, people often bring up irrelevant support. For example, in trying to persuade you to lend him some money this week, a friend might say, "You didn't lend me money last week when I needed it." But last week is beside the point; the question is whether or not you should lend him money *this* week.

An excellent way to develop your skill in recognizing relevant support is to work on simple point-support outlines of arguments. By isolating the reasons of an argument, such outlines help you think about whether each reason is truly relevant. Paying close attention to the relevance of support will help your writing as well as your reading.

✔ *Check Your Understanding*

Consider the following outline. The point is followed by six "facts," only three of which are relevant support for the point. See if you can check (✔) the **three** relevant statements of support.

Point: My dog Otis is not very bright.

✔ 1. He's five years old and doesn't respond to his name yet.

___ 2. He cries when I leave for work every day.

___ 3. He always gets excited when visitors arrive.

✔ 4. He often attacks the backyard hedge as if it's a hostile animal.

___ 5. He gets along very well with my neighbor's cat.

✔ 6. I often have to put food in front of him because he can't find it by himself.

Now read the following comments on the six items to see which ones you should have checked and why.

Explanation

1. Most dogs know their names, so Otis's unfamiliarity with his own name reveals a weak memory, and memory is one aspect of intelligence. You should have checked this item.

2. Even an intelligent dog might be sad when its companions leave the house.

3. Both bright and not-so-bright dogs are happy to see old and new human friends.

4. The inability to distinguish between a bush and an animal—friendly or hostile—suggests a lack of analytical skills. This is the second item you should have checked.

5. Dogs of all degrees of intelligence have been known to be friendly with cats.

6. Since most dogs recognize food much more often than their owners would like them to, Otis's inability to find food clearly indicates poor problem-solving skills. You should also have checked this item.

PRACTICE 2

Each point is followed by three statements that provide relevant support and three that do not. In the spaces, write the letters of the **three** relevant statements of support.

> *Hint:* To help you decide if a sentence is relevant or not, ask yourself, "Does this provide logical support for the point being argued?"

Answers A, C, and F are examples of wildlife found in the middle of the city. Answers B and D do not support the point. Answer E concerns domesticated animals, not wildlife.

1. **Point: Wildlife can be found even in the middle of the city.**

   A. Raccoons sometimes raid the garbage containers near urban apartments.
   B. Many animals have been pushed out of their homes by building development.
   C. Squirrels, chipmunks, and rabbits make their home in city parks.
   D. Heavy traffic makes it dangerous for animals in the city.
   E. Many city dwellers own a cat or a dog.
   F. Hawks build their nests on the window ledges of skyscrapers.

   Items that logically support the point: ___A___   ___C___   ___F___

Answers C, E, and F are three examples of the strict controls Singapore has on the behavior of its people. Answers A, B, and D do not address control issues.

2. **Point: Singapore is a society with strict controls on people's behavior.**

   A. There are four official languages spoken in Singapore.
   B. Singapore declared its independence from Malaysia in 1965.
   C. Chewing gum on the street is prohibited by law.
   D. Most Singaporeans are of Chinese, Malay, or Indian descent.
   E. Persons convicted of vandalism are whipped with a long rattan cane.
   F. There is a $95 fine for failing to flush a public toilet.

   Items that logically support the point: ___C___   ___E___   ___F___

3. **Point: Alcohol and tobacco are among the most dangerous drugs that Americans use today.**

Answers A, C, and F are examples of ways in which the drugs are dangerous today. Answer B refers to the past. Answers D and E do not concern the dangers of alcohol and tobacco.

A. Cancer from cigarette smoking kills numerous Americans every year.

B. During Prohibition (1920–1933), liquor bootleggers fought one another as drug dealers do today.

C. About half of all fatal traffic accidents are due to drunk driving.

D. Nothing is more annoying than trying to enjoy a restaurant meal when the people at nearby tables are smoking and drinking heavily.

E. We often don't think of alcohol and tobacco as "drugs" because they are legal.

F. Alcohol abuse causes many people to become more aggressive and violent.

Items that logically support the point: ___A___   ___C___   ___F___

4. **Point: Psychologically healthy people have some general characteristics in common.**

Answers B, D, and E explain the characteristics of psychologically healthy people. Answers A, C, and F do not address issues of good health.

A. Depression, stress, or fatigue can interfere with a person's normal functioning.

B. A person who is psychologically healthy is productive, doing tasks without making a big deal of them.

C. The culture we live in has a great deal to do with what we consider "normal" behavior.

D. People who are well-balanced psychologically get along well with most other people.

E. Psychologically healthy persons can focus their attention on people or things outside of themselves.

F. Consistently inappropriate behavior can be a symptom of mental illness.

Items that logically support the point: ___B___   ___D___   ___E___

Relevant Support in Paragraphs

The point, or main idea, of the argument in the paragraph on the next page is stated in the first sentence. One of the other sentences is **not** relevant support for that point.

✓ Check Your Understanding

Read the paragraph below and see if you can find the statement that does **not** support the point of the argument.

> ¹Every high-school student should be required to take a class in parenting skills. ²The absence of such classes shows how little our schools do for young people. ³Numerous young people today are bearing children without having the least idea of how to be a good parent. ⁴Many of them have grown up in families where poor parenting was the norm, and so they have no good parenting models. ⁵Well-planned parenting classes could give future parents at least an idea of what responsible parenting is all about. ⁶The classes might then reduce future problems, including child abuse.

The number of the irrelevant sentence: __2__

Explanation

The point of this argument is stated in the first sentence: "Every high-school student should be required to take a class in parenting skills." Any statement that doesn't help prove this point is irrelevant. Sentences 3–6 support that argument: Sentences 5–6 tell the benefits of parenting classes. Sentences 3–4 explain why students need those benefits. Sentence 2, however, is about something else altogether—it complains about the little that is being done for young people by schools. Whether that is true or not doesn't change the point and support of the argument. Even if the schools did much for young people, parenting classes could still be useful. Thus sentence 2 is irrelevant to the argument.

PRACTICE 3

The point of the argument in each paragraph that follows is stated in the first sentence. One sentence in the paragraph does not support that point. Read each paragraph, and decide which sentence is **not** relevant evidence. Then write its letter in the space provided.

> *Hint:* To decide if a sentence is relevant, ask yourself, "Does this really provide logical support for the point being argued?"

__B__ 1. ¹Nobody in this neighborhood will miss the Martins when they move. ²They keep their poor dog chained to a tree 24 hours a day, and it howls for most of that time. ³When the neighborhood kids play ball anywhere near their house, Mr. Martin yells at them, "Don't you dare hit that ball into my yard!"

Sentence 4 explains why Mr. Martin is short-tempered, not why nobody will miss the Martins.

⁴Of course he has had a lot of illness, so you can understand his being short-tempered. ⁵In addition, the Martins refuse to come to neighborhood block parties, and then they complain about the noise. ⁶And they mow their lawn at 6 a.m. on Saturday morning, when other people are trying to get a little extra sleep.

Which of the following statements does **not** support the author's argument that no one will miss the Martins when they move?

A. Sentence 3   C. Sentence 5
B. Sentence 4   D. Sentence 6

_B_ 2. ¹National health insurance is entirely possible, as many industrialized countries have proven. ²The National Health Service in Great Britain provides free health care to all citizens. ³The Health Service is almost completely tax-supported. ⁴That doesn't help the immigrants living in Britain, however. ⁵In Sweden, medical care is provided by publicly funded hospitals and clinics. ⁶A national health insurance system reimburses the providers. ⁷Canadians rely on private physicians and hospitals for day-to-day care, but health care is guaranteed as a right for all citizens. ⁸Income taxes are used to finance Canada's public medical insurance.

Sentence 4 states which people Great Britain's Health Service fails to help, instead of supporting the idea that national health insurance is possible.

Which of the following statements does **not** support the author's argument that providing national health insurance is entirely possible?

A. Sentence 3   C. Sentence 5
B. Sentence 4   D. Sentence 6

_B_ 3. ¹Short-term goals encourage self-discipline better than distant aims. ²For instance, dieters lose more weight by attempting to shed two pounds a week than by worrying about a total of twenty pounds or more. ³Low-fat diets are another help for dieters. ⁴Also, students who try to increase study time by a half hour each day do better than those who think only about compiling straight A averages. ⁵And alcoholics and drug addicts achieve more lasting recovery when they deal with their problems one day at a time.

Sentence 3 describes a diet, not how short-term goals encourage self-discipline.

Which sentence is **not** relevant support for the argument that short-term goals are better for will power than long-term goals?

A. Sentence 2   C. Sentence 4
B. Sentence 3   D. Sentence 5

_C_ 4. ¹The wish for acceptance by the dominant culture sometimes causes people to turn their backs on their own cultural tradition. ²In Australia, Aborigines who have become part of the dominant society may refuse to acknowledge their darker-skinned grandparents on the street. ³In India, the well-off Indians who dominate the culture copy the traditions and prejudices of the

Sentence 4 applies to India's winning its independence, not the point about people turning their backs on cultural tradition.

British, leaving many Hindus unhappy about their behavior. ⁴India won its independence from Britain after Mahatma Gandhi led a campaign of peaceful resistance. ⁵And in the United States, many descendants of immigrants have changed their ethnic-sounding family names to names like those of white Protestants. ⁶Also, children of U.S. immigrants are sometimes ashamed to let their school friends see that their parents speak another language.

Which sentence is **not** relevant support for the argument that people at times turn their backs on their own cultural tradition?

A. Sentence 2   C. Sentence 4
B. Sentence 3   D. Sentence 5

Adequate Support

A valid argument must include not only relevant support but also an **adequate** amount of support—enough to prove the point. For example, it would not be valid to argue "Abortion is wrong" if one's only support was "My sister had an abortion and has regretted it ever since." Such an important issue would require more support than the attitude and experience of a single relative. Arguing a point that doesn't have adequate support is called "jumping to a conclusion."

✔ Check Your Understanding

In the argument below, three supporting items are given, followed by four possible points. The evidence adequately supports only one of the points; it is insufficient to support the other three. Choose the **one** point you think is adequately supported, and put a check mark (✓) beside it.

Support

- The first time I went to that beach, I got a bad case of sunburn.
- The second time I went to that beach, I couldn't go in the water because of the pollution.
- The third time I went to that beach, I stepped on a starfish and had to go to the emergency room to have the spikes removed from my foot.

Which **point** is adequately supported by the evidence on the preceding page?

___ A. That beach is unsafe and should be closed.

✓ B. I've had a string of bad experiences at that beach.

___ C. Beaches are not safe places.

___ D. We're never going to get this planet cleaned up.

Explanation

The correct answer is B. Answer A is not adequately supported by three isolated instances; we'd need many more reports of dangerous conditions before considering having the beach closed. Answer C is even more poorly supported. We'd need many, many reports of dangerous conditions at beaches worldwide to come to the conclusion stated in C. Answer D is supported in part by the reference to pollution in the second statement of support, but the other two statements (about sunburn and the starfish) are not examples of pollution.

 **PRACTICE 4**

For each group, read the three items of support (the evidence). Then check (✓) the **one** point that is adequately supported by that evidence.

Group 1

Support

● Many credit cards do not carry an annual fee.

● Some cards give you cash back, frequent-flier miles, or other benefits.

● Some credit cards charge a lower rate of interest than others.

Which **point** is adequately supported by all the evidence above?

___ A. When used wisely, credit cards can be helpful.

___ B. Credit cards charge high interest rates on unpaid balances.

✓ C. You need to shop around for the right credit card.

___ D. Many people get into trouble by overusing credit cards.

Answer A is supported only by the second bulleted item.
Answers B and D are not supported by any of the items.

Group 2

Support

- Some people put off writing or calling a friend because they feel they do not have time to do it right, but a quick note or call is often better than nothing.

- Sometimes it makes sense to do a routine chore quickly rather than perfectly in order to save time for something more important.

- Even a desk and office need not be perfectly neat; sometimes cleaning them up is just an excuse for putting off more important work.

Which **point** is adequately supported by all the evidence above?

  ✓   A. Perfection is not always a worthwhile goal.

  ___   B. Striving for perfection always pays off in the end.

  ___   C. You can be better organized if you plan each day more carefully.

  ___   D. Getting things done haphazardly is always better than not getting them done at all.

Answer B is contradicted by the support. Answer C is not supported by any of the items. Answer D is incorrect because the support does not describe doing things haphazardly, and it does not say it is "always" better to do things less than perfectly.

Group 3

Support

- Some thieves who are sent to jail steal again as soon as they are released.

- A dog that has been hit for eating food off the table will often continue to gobble what it can find when the owner is not around.

- A teenage girl who is "grounded" because she sneaked out of the house may try to come up with a more creative plan to get out without being caught.

Which **point** is adequately supported by all the evidence above?

  ___   A. Many studies have found advantages and problems with punishment.

  ✓   B. Punishment does not always have the intended effects.

  ___   C. Punishment is rarely effective.

  ___   D. Punishment can be effective in some cases.

Answer A is incorrect because none of the evidence discusses research on or advantages of punishment. Answer C is incorrect because the support says nothing about how often punishment is ineffective. Answer D is incorrect because the evidence says nothing about when punishment is effective.

Group 4

Support

- Elderly nursing-home patients who have little control over their activities tend to decline faster and die sooner than do those given more control over their activities.

- If two rats receive simultaneous shocks, but only one of them can turn a wheel to stop the shocks, the helpless rat becomes more vulnerable to ulcers and has lower immunity to disease.

- When allowed to adjust office furnishings and control interruptions and distractions, workers experience less stress and illness.

Which **point** is adequately supported by all the evidence above?

_____ A. It is possible to gain full control over our lives.

_____ B. Many negative life events are uncontrollable.

_____ C. Loss of control is a major problem in our society.

✓ D. A loss of control is stressful and makes one more vulnerable to ill health.   Answers A, B, and C are incorrect because the evidence says nothing about gaining full control, uncontrollable negative life events, or how much of a problem loss of control is in our society.

Argument in Textbook Writing

In most textbook writing, argument takes the form of well-developed ideas or theories (in other words, points) that are supported with experiments, surveys, studies, expert testimony, reasons, examples, or other evidence. Textbook arguments generally have solid support, but recognizing the author's points and asking yourself whether the support is relevant and adequate will help you be an involved and critical reader.

A Final Note

This chapter has dealt with the basics of argument, including the need for relevant and adequate support. In the next chapter, "Critical Reading," you will learn about some common errors in reasoning—also known as **logical fallacies**—that people may make when advancing an argument.

CHAPTER REVIEW

In this chapter, you learned the following:

- A good argument is made up of a point, or a conclusion, and logical evidence to back it up.
- To critically read an argument, you must recognize the **point** the author is making.
- To think through an argument, you need to decide if each piece of evidence is **relevant**.
- To think through an argument, you also need to decide if the author's support is **adequate**.
- Textbook arguments generally have solid support, but recognizing the author's point and looking for for relevant and adequate support will help you become a more involved and critical reader.

The final chapter in Part One—Chapter 10—will explain other aspects of being a critical reader: separating fact from opinion, detecting propaganda, and recognizing errors in reasoning.

On the Web: If you are using this book in class, you can visit our website for additional practice in evaluating arguments. Go to **www.townsendpress.com** and click on "Online Exercises."

REVIEW TEST 1

To review what you've learned in this chapter, complete each sentence or write the letter of the correct answer in the space provided.

_C_   1. The point of an argument can also be called its
    A. relevance.   See page 364.
    B. evidence.
    C. conclusion.

_A_   2. The support for an argument can be referred to as the (A. evidence; B. conclusion) that backs up the point.   See page 364.

_C_   3. Relevant support for an argument is information that (A. enthusiastically; B. partially; C. logically) supports the point.   See page 368.

_B_   4. If there is too little information to support a point, we say the support is   See page 372.
    A. dull.
    B. inadequate.
    C. irrelevant.

_D_   5. Textbook authors may support their arguments with
    A. experiments.   C. studies.
    B. surveys.   D. all of the above and more.
    See page 375.

REVIEW TEST 2

A. In each group, one statement is the point, and the other statements are support for that point. Write the letter of the point in the space provided.

Hint: If it sounds right to insert the word *because* in front of a sentence, you probably have a statement of support.

You can insert the word *because* in front of answers A and C to explain why dark chocolate can be good for the human body.

_B_   1. A. Chemicals in dark chocolate help protect arteries from heart disease.
    B. Dark chocolate can be good for the human body.
    C. Dark chocolate contains ingredients that fight depression.

The word *should* in answer B is a clue to the point. Answers A, C, and D give three reasons for planting trees.

_B_   2. A. A healthy adult tree can produce 5 pounds of pure oxygen a day.
    B. People should plant more trees around their homes.
    C. Mature trees can increase property value by 10 percent.
    D. Trees planted properly around buildings provide shade that cuts air conditioning costs by 20 percent.

_D_   3. A. Teaching is a great way to learn because one needs to know the material well enough to explain it.

You can insert the word *because* in front of answers A, B, and C to explain why students should be required to teach.

B. By teaching a class, students will better appreciate their teachers' efforts.

C. Some students may pay more attention when another student teaches, out of curiosity if nothing else.

D. All students should be required to teach a class for a day.

_C_   4. A. In the 1700s, doctors in the American colonies were not required to attend college.

Answers A, B, and D explain how training for doctors has changed dramatically in the past two centuries.

B. In the mid-1800s, most doctors completed just two years of medical school.

C. The training for doctors has changed dramatically in the past two centuries.

D. Today, doctors receive about 10 years of education after high school.

B. Each point is followed by three statements that provide relevant support and three that do not. In the spaces, write the letters of the **three** relevant statements of support.

5–7. **Point: Drinking coffee can have unpleasant effects.**

Only answers B, D, and E support the point about unpleasant effects of drinking coffee. Answers A, C, and F are incorrect because they discuss people's dislike of decaffeinated coffee, the relative safety of coffee, and the cost of coffee.

A. Some people don't like the taste of decaffeinated coffee.

B. Coffee in the evening can interfere with sleep at night.

C. As addictions go, coffee is less dangerous than tobacco.

D. Too much coffee can cause the hands to shake.

E. Drinking too much coffee can lead to a faster heartbeat and light-headedness.

F. Most coffees cost under ten dollars a pound.

Items that logically support the point: _B_   _D_   _E_

8–10. **Point: Some people have very poor telephone manners.**

Only answers A, D, and F support the point about poor telephone manners. Answers B, C, and E are incorrect because they discuss cell phones, unlisted numbers, and people's dislike for talking on the phone.

A. They never identify themselves, but just begin the conversation.

B. They often make their calls on cell phones.

C. They have an unlisted telephone number.

D. They conduct conversations with people around them at the same time they're talking on the phone.

E. Some people don't like to talk on the phone.

F. They often call around 6 p.m., which is most people's dinner hour.

Items that logically support the point: _A_   _D_   _F_

REVIEW TEST 3

A. In the space provided, write the letter of the irrelevant sentence in each paragraph—the sentence that changes the subject.

_C_ 1. ¹Most people who have trouble with schoolwork don't lack intelligence—instead, they are tripped up by their own attitudes toward the work. ²For example, the "I can't do it" state of mind gets in many students' way. ³Instead of making an honest effort to do the work, the "I can't do it" type gives up before he or she begins. ⁴This type often also has trouble on the job. ⁵Then there's the "I'm too tired" attitude. ⁶Students with this problem give in to the temptation to nap whenever there is work to be done. ⁷Another view that leads to low achievement is "The instructor is boring." ⁸Students with that attitude expect every course to be highly entertaining and claim they can't be expected to learn anything otherwise.

Sentence 4 changes the subject from school problems to job problems.

Which sentence does **not** support the argument that people who have trouble with school work are tripped up by their own attitudes rather than a lack of intelligence?

A. Sentence 2   c. Sentence 4
B. Sentence 3   d. Sentence 7

_A_ 2. ¹Sigmund Freud was one of the most important scientists of the twentieth century. ²A loving father, he had three sons and three daughters. ³He was among the first to study mental disorders, such as hysteria and neurosis, in a systematic way. ⁴He developed the theory of the unconscious and showed how people's behavior is greatly affected by forgotten childhood events. ⁵His discoveries are the basis of psychoanalysis, a method of treating mental illness that is still important today.

Sentence 2 changes the subject from Freud's scientific contributions to his family.

Which sentence is **not** relevant support for the argument that Freud is one of the most important scientists of the twentieth century?

A. Sentence 2   c. Sentence 4
B. Sentence 3   d. Sentence 5

_D_ 3. ¹People's ability to remember what they see is less dependable than they think. ²In a famous experiment performed at Harvard, researchers showed people a videotape of a basketball game and asked them to count how many times players passed the ball. ³After about 45 seconds, a man dressed in a gorilla suit walked slowly across the scene, passing between the players. ⁴Although he was visible for five seconds, 40 percent of the viewers did not notice him at all. ⁵When the tape was played again, and they were asked simply to watch it, they saw him easily. ⁶Not surprisingly, some insisted that it could not be the same tape. ⁷They simply could not believe they had "tuned

Sentence 8 changes the subject from the experiment to what the participants got out of the experiment.

out" something as bizarre as a gorilla on the basketball floor. [8]At least they had a good story to tell when they got home.

Which of the following statements does **not** support the author's argument that people's ability to remember what they see is less dependable than they think?

A. Sentence 5   C. Sentence 7
B. Sentence 6   D. Sentence 8

B. For each group, read the three items of support (the evidence). Then, in the space provided, write the letter of the **one** point that is adequately supported by that evidence.

Remember that the point, or conclusion, should follow logically from the evidence. Do not jump to a conclusion that is not well supported.

Group 1

Support

- Many daycare facilities have health and safety standards that are barely satisfactory.
- Long waiting lists exist at most good daycare centers.
- Daycare centers can't get enough qualified help.

_D_ 4. Which **point** is adequately supported by all the evidence above?

A. Daycare is unreasonably expensive.
B. Mothers with young children should not work.
C. Our present birthrate must be drastically reduced.
D. Our present daycare system is inadequate.

The support names three reasons our daycare system is inadequate. Answers A, B, and C are not supported because the evidence says nothing about expense, whether or not mothers should work, or the birthrate.

Group 2

Support

All three items listed are shameful. Answers A and B are not supported. Answer D is contradicted by the second statement of support.

- Nearly all of those accused during the Salem, Massachusetts witch trials of 1692 had little political power or legal protection.

- On the basis of rumor and hearsay, innocent people in Salem were accused, tried, convicted and executed for the crime of witchcraft.

- The trial and execution of alleged witches in the Salem area ended suddenly when the wife of a "witch judge" found herself accused of practicing witchcraft.

_C_ 5. Which **point** is adequately supported by all the evidence above?

A. Many innocent people have been persecuted with charges of witchcraft over the centuries.

B. People in positions of power were less likely to be charged with witchcraft.
C. The Salem witch trials of 1692 were a shameful episode in American colonial history.
D. Some of the people executed during the Salem witch trials were guilty of serious crimes.

REVIEW TEST 4

Can failing a course be good for students? Here is a chance to apply your understanding of argument to an essay that addresses that question.

To help you continue to strengthen your skills, the reading is followed by questions not only on what you've learned in this chapter but also on what you've learned in previous chapters.

Words to Watch

Below are some words in the reading that do not have strong context support. Each word is followed by the number of the paragraph in which it appears and its meaning there. These words are indicated in the article by a small circle (°).

validity (1): soundness or worth
trump card (4): a tactic that gives one an advantage (like a trump suit in card games)
flustered (6): nervously confused
composure (6): calmness and self-control
radical (6): extreme
conspiracy (11): plot

IN PRAISE OF THE F WORD

Mary Sherry

1   Tens of thousands of eighteen-year-olds will graduate this year and be handed meaningless diplomas. These diplomas won't look any different from those awarded their luckier classmates. Their validity° will be questioned only when their employers discover that these graduates are semiliterate.

Eventually a fortunate few will 2 find their way into educational-repair shops—adult-literacy programs, such as the one where I teach basic grammar and writing. There, high-school graduates and high-school dropouts pursuing graduate-equivalency certificates will learn the skills they should have learned in school. They will also discover they have been cheated by our educational system.

3   As I teach, I learn a lot about our schools. Early in each session I ask my students to write about an unpleasant experience they had in school. No writers' block here! "I wish someone had made me stop doing drugs and made me study." "I liked to party and no one seemed to care." "I was a good kid and didn't cause any trouble, so they just passed me along even though I didn't read well and couldn't write." And so on.

4   I am your basic do-gooder, and prior to teaching this class I blamed the poor academic skills our kids have today on drugs, divorce, and other impediments to concentration necessary for doing well in school. But, as I rediscover each time I walk into the classroom, before a teacher can expect students to concentrate, he has to get their attention, no matter what distractions may be at hand. There are many ways to do this, and they have much to do with teaching style. However, if style alone won't do it, there is another way to show who holds the winning hand in the classroom. That is to reveal the trump card° of failure.

5   I will never forget a teacher who played that card to get the attention of one of my children. Our youngest, a world-class charmer, did little to develop his intellectual talents but always got by. Until Mrs. Stifter.

6   Our son was a high-school senior when he had her for English. "He sits in the back of the room talking to his friends," she told me. "Why don't you move him to the front row?" I urged, believing the embarrassment would get him to settle down. Mrs. Stifter looked at me steely-eyed over her glasses. "I don't move seniors," she said. "I flunk them." I was flustered°. Our son's academic life flashed before my eyes. No teacher had ever threatened him with that before. I regained my composure° and managed to say that I thought she was right. By the time I got home I was feeling pretty good about this. It was a radical° approach for these times, but, well, why not? "She's going to flunk you," I told my son. I did not discuss it any further. Suddenly English became a priority in his life. He finished out the semester with an A.

7   I know one example doesn't make a case, but at night I see a parade of students who are angry and resentful for having been passed along until they could no longer even pretend to keep up. Of average intelligence or better, they eventually quit school, concluding they were too dumb to finish. "I should have been held back," is a comment I hear frequently. Even sadder are those students who are high-school graduates who say to me after a few weeks of class, "I don't know how I ever got a high-school diploma."

8   Passing students who have not mastered the work cheats them and the employers who expect graduates to have basic skills. We excuse this dishonest behavior by saying kids can't learn if they come from terrible environments. No one seems to stop to think that—no matter what environments they come from—most kids don't put school first on their list unless they perceive something is at stake. They'd rather be sailing.

9   Many students I see at night could give expert testimony on unemployment, chemical dependency, abusive relationships. In spite of these difficulties, they have decided to make education a priority. They are motivated by the desire for a better job or the need to hang on to the one they've got. They have a healthy fear of failure.

10   People of all ages can rise above their problems, but they need to have a reason to do so. Young people generally don't have the maturity to value education in the same way my adult students value it. But fear of failure, whether economic or academic, can motivate both.

11   Flunking as a regular policy has just as much merit today as it did two generations ago. We must review the threat of flunking and see it as it really is—a positive teaching tool. It is an expression of confidence by both teachers and parents that the students have the ability to learn the material presented to them. However, making it work again would take a dedicated,

caring conspiracy° between teachers and parents. It would mean facing the tough reality that passing kids who haven't learned the material—while it might save them grief for the short term—dooms them to long-term illiteracy. It would mean that teachers would have to follow through on their threats, and parents would have to stand behind them, knowing their children's best interests are indeed at stake. This means no more doing Scott's assignments for him because he might fail. No more passing Jodi because she's such a nice kid.

12   This is a policy that worked in the past and can work today. A wise teacher, with my husband's and my support, gave our son the opportunity to succeed—or fail. It's time we return this choice to all students.

Reading Comprehension Questions

Vocabulary in Context

___C___ 1. In the excerpt below, the word *impediments* (ĭm-pĕd′ə-mənts) means
    A. questions.
    B. skills.
    C. obstacles.
    D. paths.

> " . . . I blamed the poor academic skills our kids have today on drugs, divorce, and other impediments to concentration. . . . " (Paragraph 4)

Drugs and divorce are obstacles to concentration.

Central Point and Main Ideas

___D___ 2. Which sentence best expresses the central point of the selection?

Answer A covers only paragraph 4. Answer B covers only paragraphs 1–2. Answer C covers only paragraphs 2–3.

    A. Before students will concentrate, the teacher must get their attention.
    B. Many adults cannot read or write well.
    C. English skills can be learned through adult literacy programs.
    D. The threat of failure should be returned to our classrooms.

___C___ 3. Which sentence best expresses the main idea of paragraph 6?

Answer A covers only the second sentence of the paragraph. Answer B covers only sentence 5. Answer D covers only sentence 7.

    A. According to his teacher, Sherry's son sat at the back of the room, talking to his friends.
    B. Mrs. Stifter said that she didn't move seniors; she flunked them.
    C. The fear of failure motivated Sherry's son to do well in English.
    D. Sherry was at first nervous and confused to learn that her son might fail English.

Supporting Details

___C___ 4. According to the author, many students who get "passed along"
    A. are lucky.   See paragraph 7.
    B. don't get into trouble.
    C. eventually feel angry and resentful.
    D. will never learn basic grammar and writing skills.

___A___ 5. According to the author, a fear of failure
    A. is healthy.   See paragraph 9.
    B. does not motivate people.
    C. hurts more than it helps.
    D. affects young students, but not her adult students.

Transitions

___D___ 6. Read the two sentences below and then answer the question that follows.

> "Many students I see at night could give expert testimony on unemployment, chemical dependency, abusive relationships. In spite of these difficulties, they have decided to make education a priority."
> (Paragraph 9)   The words *In spite of* signal the contrast.

What does the second sentence do?
A. It defines a problem and presents a solution.
B. It shows a time order relationship.
C. It compares the attitudes of day students with the attitudes of night students.
D. It contrasts the students' difficulties with their willingness to make education a priority.

Patterns of Organization

___A___ 7. The main pattern of organization of paragraph 6 is
A. time order.
B. list of items.   The paragraph tells a series of events in the order in which they happen.
C. definition and example.
D. comparison.

Inferences

___C___ 8. The author implies that our present educational system is
A. doing the best that it can.
B. the best in the world.   See paragraphs 8–12.
C. not demanding enough of students.
D. very short of teachers.

Purpose

___B___ 9. The author's primary purpose in this article is
A. to inform readers about the advantages and disadvantages of giving failing grades to students.
B. to persuade readers that failure (or the threat of failure) can be good for students.
C. to entertain readers with the true story of one teacher's experiences.

> The author doesn't simply explain the advantages and disadvantages of failing students—she supports the practice. (See the statement of the central point in item 2.)

Argument

10. Label the point of the following argument from the reading with a **P**; label the two statements of support for the point with an **S**. Label with an **X** the one statement that is neither the point nor the support of the argument.

    _S_ A. Fear of failure motivated the author's son to do well in English.

    _P_ B. Fear of failure is a good motivator.

    _X_ C. Some people learn skills after high school in adult literacy programs.

    _S_ D. Some kids won't put school first unless they know they might fail.

    Answers A and D give two pieces of evidence supporting the idea that failure is a good motivator—it motivated the author's son, and it helps some kids put school first. Answer C discusses learning in adult literacy programs instead of failure as a motivator.

Discussion Questions

1. Do you know anyone who has failed or almost failed a course? What effect did the experience have on that person?

2. Most people think of failing a course as a negative experience. Why, then, does Sherry consider the threat of failure to be a positive teaching tool? Do you agree?

3. People often look back on their education and realize that some of the teachers they learned the most from were their strictest teachers. Who do you think you learned more from, strict teachers or lenient ones? Give examples to support your point.

4. Besides the threat of failure, what are some other ways that teachers can motivate students? What have teachers done to make you want to work harder for a class?

Note: Writing assignments for this selection appear on page 605.

Check Your Performance   ARGUMENT

Activity	Number Right	Points		Score
Review Test 1 (5 items)	_____	× 2	=	_____
Review Test 2 (10 items)	_____	× 3	=	_____
Review Test 3 (5 items)	_____	× 6	=	_____
Review Test 4 (10 items)	_____	× 3	=	_____
		TOTAL SCORE	=	_____%

Enter your total score into the **Reading Performance Chart: Review Tests** on the inside back cover.

ARGUMENT: Mastery Test 1

A. In each group, one statement is the point of an argument, and the other statements are support for that point. Write the letter of the point of each group.

_B_ 1. Answers A, C, and D give three examples supporting the idea that certain animals are sensitive to the plight of others.

   A. Chimpanzees, who cannot swim, have drowned in zoo moats trying to save others.

   B. Some chimpanzees and monkeys are surprisingly sensitive to the plight of others.

   C. Given the chance to get food by pulling a chain that would also deliver an electric shock to a companion, rhesus monkeys will starve themselves for several days.

   D. Female chimps will sometimes head off a fight by taking stones out of the males' hands.

_D_ 2. Answers A, B, and C give three examples of punishments and executions that were public events.

   A. Colonial Boston had three well-used whipping posts in its public square.

   B. In some Italian cities, thieves and prostitutes were forced to run naked through the streets while being beaten with birch rods.

   C. In France, the hangman's scaffold was a permanent fixture in every city and town, and after the hanging, the corpse was allowed to remain until it crumbled.

   D. Far from being carried out "behind closed doors," hundreds of years ago punishments and executions were public events.

_C_ 3. Answers A, B, and D give three examples of slogans that don't translate well.

   A. Pepsi's slogan "Come Alive, You're in the Pepsi Generation" read to Chinese customers as "Pepsi Brings Your Ancestors Back from the Dead."

   B. Perdue Chicken's slogan "It Takes a Tough Man to Make a Tender Chicken" was interpreted in Spanish as "It Takes an Aroused Man to Make a Chicken Affectionate."

   C. Some American companies have found that their product slogans don't translate well into other languages.

   D. KFC's patented slogan "finger-lickin' good" was understood in Japanese as "Bite Your Fingers Off."

_B_ 4. Answers A, C, and D describe three assumptions about people—the pessimistic view, the optimistic view, and the middle-of-the-road theory. The words *several assumptions* in answer B are a clue to the point.

   A. The pessimistic view of human nature holds that people are basically lazy and have to be forced to work.

   B. Political and business leaders often base their policies on one of several assumptions about people.

   C. The optimistic view presumes people are interested in doing a job well and are capable of directing themselves.

   D. A middle-of-the-road theory is that while people do not dislike work, they do not work efficiently without appropriate direction.

(Continues on next page)

387

B. Each point is followed by three statements that provide relevant support and three that do not. In the spaces, write the letters of the **three** relevant statements of support.

5–7. **Point:** My boss is a very unpleasant man to work for.

Answers A, D, and E are all reasons the boss is unpleasant to work for. Answer B is about the boss's wife, not the boss. Answer C is about his office decorations. Answer F shows that he is not law-abiding, but this quality does not necessarily make him unpleasant to work for.

A. He barks orders and never asks for an employee's opinion.

B. His fashion-plate wife is said to be even nastier than he is.

C. His office is decorated in dull browns and grays.

D. Even when he invites employees out to lunch, he expects them to pick up their own checks.

E. He changes his mind so often that an employee who pleased him on Friday can be in the doghouse by Monday.

F. He once accumulated so many parking tickets that the police actually came to his home to arrest him.

Items that logically support the point: ___A___   ___D___   ___E___

8–10. **Point:** Stress has a negative effect on health.

Answers B, D, and E support the point that stress has a negative effect on health.
Answer A is a positive effect of stress.
Answer C is about the causes of stress.
Answer F is about ways to reduce stress.

A. Stress triggers a person's "flight or fight" response, which can save him or her from danger.

B. Stress can cause an irregular heartbeat, which can lead to a heart attack.

C. Stress can be caused by scary events or by pleasant ones, such as a romantic encounter.

D. Stress depresses the immune system, making people more vulnerable to illness.

E. Stress raises blood pressure, increasing the chance of stroke.

F. Yoga, meditation, and breathing exercises can all be used to reduce stress.

Items that logically support the point: ___B___   ___D___   ___E___

ARGUMENT: Mastery Test 2

A. In each group, one statement is the point of an argument, and the other statements are support for that point. In the space provided, write the letter of the point of each group.

_____A_____ 1.

Answers B, C, and D give three examples of animal species in Asia, Africa, and North America whose survival is threatened by poaching.

   A. Poaching (illegal hunting) is threatening the survival of animal species throughout the world.

   B. In Asia, poaching has driven Bengal tigers, snow leopards, and musk deer to the brink of extinction.

   C. In Africa, poaching has claimed thousands of leopards, cheetahs, rhinos, and elephants.

   D. In North America, illegal hunting has greatly reduced the number of bald eagles, grizzly bears, timber wolves, and giant otters.

_____B_____ 2.

Answers A, C, and D give evidence of food supplied in the 1800s that today would not be considered fit to eat.

   A. During the Spanish-American War, U.S. soldiers were supplied with tin cans containing decayed meat.

   B. Due to a lack of food safety standards, vendors in the 1800s often sold food that would not today be considered fit for people to eat.

   C. Store-bought butter was often stale and mixed with gelatin, fat or even mashed potatoes.

   D. To improve the color of milk from diseased cattle, dairymen sometimes added molasses, chalk, or plaster of Paris.

_____B_____ 3.

The word *should* in answer B is a clue to the point. Answers A, C, and D give three reasons why animal-rights activists should not attack others for using animals for fur and medical experiments.

   A. Most fur products are made from animals bred for that purpose, so few endangered species are threatened by the fur industry.

   B. Animal-rights activists should not attack others for using animals for fur and medical experiments.

   C. Many treatments that save human lives were developed through animal testing programs.

   D. Animals bred for fur coats are generally well cared for because breeders want a healthy coat.

(Continues on next page)

B. Each point is followed by three statements that provide relevant support and three that do not. In the spaces, write the letters of the **three** relevant statements of support.

4–6. **Point: Convenience stores live up to their name.**

Answers A, D, and E support the idea that convenience stores are convenient. Answer B urges people to support convenience stores. Answer C is about brand names. Answer F is about supermarkets, not convenience stores.

A. Convenience stores are close to home.

B. Small local businesses should be supported by the community.

C. Some convenience store chains sell products under their own brand name.

D. Convenience stores are open until late or all night.

E. Parking is right outside the convenience store's door.

F. The produce at most of our supermarkets is usually terrible.

Items that logically support the point: __A__   __D__   __E__

7–9. **Point: Eating yogurt is healthful.**

Answers A, C, and F support the point that yogurt is healthful. Answer B is about where you can get yogurt. Answer D is about how you can use yogurt. Answer E gives information about where yogurt is commonly eaten.

A. Yogurt contains natural antibiotics that can prevent certain kinds of infection.

B. Yogurt is available in nearly all food stores.

C. Yogurt kills the bacteria that can cause diarrhea.

D. You can substitute yogurt in many recipes calling for milk or sour cream.

E. Yogurt is a staple of the diet in many Middle Eastern countries.

F. Eating yogurt has been shown to lower cholesterol levels.

Items that logically support the point: __A__   __C__   __F__

C. Read the following paragraph and then answer the question that follows.

¹Sexual harassment in the workplace must be recognized for the serious problem it is. ²Too many people make light of the problem, believing sexual harassment to be nothing more than pleasant flirtation between coworkers. ³However, many women, and even some men, have been driven to quit their jobs because of unwanted sexual attention from their supervisors. ⁴An employer can more or less subtly pressure employees to grant sexual favors in order to keep their jobs. ⁵Even employers who do not demand sex can make their employees miserable through unwelcome remarks about their bodies or dress. ⁶Supervisors who sexually harass their employees must have a need to feel important or powerful. ⁷All degrees of sexual harassment have the effect of creating a hostile and degrading atmosphere in the workplace. ⁸To protect people from having to work in such an environment should be the aim of laws against sexual harassment.

The paragraph's main idea is that workers must be protected against sexual harassment. Sentence 6 suggests a possible reason for sexual harassment; this is a different topic and not relevant to the point of this argument.

__D__ 10. Which sentence is **not** relevant to the argument that laws should protect people from unwanted sexual attention?

A. Sentence 3   C. Sentence 5

B. Sentence 4   D. Sentence 6

ARGUMENT: Mastery Test 3

A. In the following groups, one statement is the point of an argument, and the other statements are support for that point. In the space provided, write the letter of the point of each group.

_____B_____ 1.

Answers A, C, and D give three examples of presidents who successfully used mass communication—Franklin Roosevelt, John F. Kennedy, and Ronald Reagan.

A. Franklin Roosevelt's masterful use of radio in his "fireside chats" gave many Americans the feeling that they knew him personally.

B. Some American presidents have been highly successful at using mass communication to get their message across.

C. John F. Kennedy's wit and self-assurance came across during his televised press conferences and contributed significantly to his popularity.

D. Ronald Reagan was known as "the great communicator" for his seemingly effortless ability to convey strength and sincerity to the American people.

_____D_____ 2.

Answers A, B, and C give three pieces of evidence that support the point that advertising has been used for thousands of years.

A. In the 6th century B.C., ships that came into port sent criers around town with signboards to announce their arrival.

B. The ancient Phoenicians painted advertisements on stones near the paths where people often walked.

C. The first printed advertisement was prepared by printer William Caxton in England in 1478 to sell one of his books.

D. Far from being a recent invention, advertising has been used to drum up business for thousands of years.

B. In the space provided, write the letter of the sentence that is **not** logical support for the argument in each paragraph.

_____C_____ 3.

Sentence 4 changes the subject from why proms should be discontinued to why rich people support proms.

¹Proms are one traditional part of the high-school experience that should be discontinued. ²For one thing, proms are just too expensive. ³Between the girl's dress, the guy's tuxedo, flowers, tickets, and probably dinner in a restaurant, it's way too much money for an average high-school couple to spend. ⁴Rich parents, however, are glad to show off their wealth by supporting such expensive occasions. ⁵Secondly, proms encourage destructive forms of social competition. ⁶Teenagers get caught up in worrying about who has the best-looking date, who spends most on a dress, or who arrives in a rented limousine. ⁷And finally, proms often turn into excuses for underage drinking-and-driving excursions.

Which sentence is **not** relevant to the argument that high-school proms should be discontinued?

A. Sentence 2   C. Sentence 4

B. Sentence 3   D. Sentence 5

(Continues on next page)

_D_ 4. ¹Statistics show that people travel more safely in airplanes than in cars. ²For that reason, it seems foolish to be afraid of flying and not be concerned about safety in a car. ³The figures are clear—planes, per passenger mile, are safer than cars. ⁴But statistics do not tell the whole story. ⁵Automobile accidents usually involve only a few people per occurrence and kill or injure only some of the victims. ⁶They involve situations which drivers believe they can avoid through skill or caution. ⁷On the other hand, airplane accidents usually involve large numbers of people and high death rates. ⁸One hundred percent is not uncommon. ⁹Surviving an airplane accident requires luck, not skill or caution, and passengers are totally dependent upon their crew. ¹⁰And to add insult to injury, passengers have paid unreasonably high amounts for tickets for this unsafe type of transportation. ¹¹There's no question about it: when driven by a safe and sober driver, a car is a safer bet than an airplane.

Sentence 10 changes the subject from safety to the cost of a ticket.

Which sentence is **not** relevant support for the argument that when a car is driven by a safe and sober driver, it is a safer bet than an airplane?

A. Sentence 5   C. Sentence 9
B. Sentence 8   D. Sentence 10

_B_ 5. ¹Non-human animals, even highly intelligent ones, are not capable of using language. ²In the 1930s, a husband and wife research team raised a young chimpanzee along with their human baby, treating the two youngsters exactly alike. ³The chimp didn't learn any language at all. ⁴It wasn't reported how the human baby was affected. ⁵In the 1950s, another team of married researchers gave a young chimp extensive language lessons. ⁶She finally learned to make sounds resembling "papa," "mama," and "cup," but nothing more. ⁷More recently, several chimps and gorillas have been taught to use some American Sign Language. ⁸But they use ASL only to request food or social rewards, not to communicate complex ideas or feelings.

Sentence 4 changes the subject from non-human animals to human ones.

Which sentence is **not** relevant support for the argument that that non-human animals cannot use language?

A. Sentence 3   C. Sentence 5
B. Sentence 4   D. Sentence 6

ARGUMENT: Mastery Test 4

A. Each point is followed by three statements that provide relevant support and three that do not. In the spaces, write the letters of the **three** relevant statements of support.

1–3. **Point: We should spend more of our tax dollars on mass transit systems such as subways, commuter rail lines, and buses.**

Answer A, C, and F support the point that we should spend tax dollars on mass transit systems. Answer B argues against mass transit systems. Answer D is about the history of subways in New York. Answer E just states how many cars there are in the U.S.

A. Our streets and roadways are becoming choked with traffic.

B. Hybrid cars, which get great gas mileage, are becoming increasingly popular.

C. Mass transit systems don't pollute nearly as much as automobiles.

D. The New York City Subway's first underground line opened in 1904.

E. There are currently over 200 million cars in the United States.

F. If more people took mass transit to work, we would reduce our dependence on foreign oil.

Items that logically support the point: ___A___ ___C___ ___F___

4–6. **Point: College students are particularly vulnerable to alcohol-related problems.**

Answers C, D, and F support the point that college students are vulnerable to alcohol-related problems. Answer A is about alcoholism running in families. Answer B is about the drinking age. Answer E is about attempts to reduce drinking.

A. People who have an alcoholic parent are at greater risk of becoming alcoholics themselves.

B. In America, most states limit the sale of alcohol to people who are 21 and older.

C. Many university customs and traditions encourage dangerous practices of alcohol use.

D. Alcohol use increases college students' already high risk for suicide, automobile crashes, and falls.

E. In recent years, some colleges and universities have attempted to crack down on campus drinking.

F. University campuses are heavily targeted by advertising and promotions from the alcohol beverage industry.

Items that logically support the point: ___C___ ___D___ ___F___

(Continues on next page)

7–9. **Point: Americans should cut down on their consumption of bottled water.**

Answers A, C, and
E give evidence
supporting cutting
down on the
consumption of
bottled water.
Answers B and F
are reasons to drink
bottled water.
Answer D is about
how many bottled
waters are available.

A. Studies indicate that the tap water in most communities is perfectly fit to drink.

B. Bottled water is very convenient when a person is participating in outdoor activities.

C. Discarded water bottles are contributing to our growing trash problem.

D. These days, there are many varieties of bottled water.

E. Bottled water must be transported by truck to stores and vending machines, thus contributing to air pollution.

F. Many people believe that drinking bottled water is healthier than drinking tap water.

Items that logically support the point: __A__   __C__   __E__

B. For the group below, read the three items of support (the evidence). Then, in the space provided, write the letter of the point that is adequately supported by that evidence.

Support

• Music is often quite effective in helping emotionally disturbed children communicate.

• Music can help relieve anxiety in patients about to undergo surgery.

• Music can help relieve persistent arthritis pain.

__D__ 10. Which point is adequately supported by all the evidence above?

A. Everyone should listen to music each day.

B. Music is one of our most effective medical tools.

C. More people should enter the field of music therapy.

D. Music is a useful treatment for physical and emotional ailments.

All three bulleted items tell why music is a useful treatment for physical and emotional ailments. Answers A and C are not mentioned in the items of support. Answer B is incorrect because music is not compared to other medical tools.

ARGUMENT: Mastery Test 5

A. Each point is followed by three statements that provide relevant support and three that do not. In the spaces, write the letters of the **three** relevant statements of support.

1–3. **Point: Professional boxing should be banned.**

Answers A, D, and F are reasons why boxing should be banned. Answer B changes the subject to broadcasting. Answer C is about women's boxing. Answer E states a positive effect of boxing.

A. Too many boxers have been critically injured and even killed in the ring.

B. Most important boxing matches are broadcast on a pay-per-view basis.

C. Women's boxing is becoming increasingly popular.

D. Boxing encourages people's cruelest, most savage instincts.

E. Boxing has given many young at-risk men a source of self-discipline and pride.

F. Boxers who survive their careers are often left with permanent brain damage.

Items that logically support the point: ___A___ ___D___ ___F___

4–6. **Point: Feeling guilty is not all bad.**

A. Some people feel guilty because they can't do everything others ask of them.

Answers B, C, and F state some positive results of guilt feelings. Answer A explains one reason for feeling guilty. Answers D and E state that some people feel guilty even when they themselves have done nothing wrong.

B. Feelings of guilt can encourage a person to think about his or her behavior and act differently the next time.

C. People who feel guilt are less likely to commit a crime than those who feel no guilt for their wrongdoings.

D. People often feel guilty even when they have done nothing wrong.

E. Parents often feel guilty when their children, even their adult children, do something wrong.

F. People who feel guilt have more understanding of and compassion for other people's imperfections.

Items that logically support the point: ___B___ ___C___ ___F___

B. Read the paragraph below, and then answer the questions that follow.

¹The death penalty is popular with voters, who are frightened of violent crime, but it is not very effective in reducing the murder rate. ²In the 1960s and 1970s, when murder rates were lower than today, the death penalty was hardly ever used. ³Even today, the states that use the death penalty most also often have the highest murder rates. ⁴In addition, every death sentence

(Continues on next page)

costs taxpayers hundreds of thousands of dollars in appeals and lawyers' fees. ⁵The number of executions that take place in a state doesn't seem to matter either. ⁶There have actually been some years in which states that had many executions experienced higher homicide rates than states with fewer executions.

All the details of the passage (except sentence 4) prove that the death penalty has not reduced the murder rate.

_B_ 7. Which statement is the point of the argument?

A. The death penalty is popular with voters, who are frightened of violent crime.

B. The death penalty is not very effective in reducing the murder rate.

C. The murder rate has gone up in this country since the 1960s and 1970s.

D. Executions cost more than they are worth.

Sentence 4 changes the subject from the reduction of the murder rate to the cost of a death sentence.

_B_ 8. Which sentence is **not** relevant support for the point of the argument?

A. Sentence 3   C. Sentence 5

B. Sentence 4   D. Sentence 6

C. Read the paragraph below, and then answer the questions that follow.

¹"I feel sorry for poor people, but it's not really my concern. ²I can't do anything about it. ³Right?" ⁴Wrong. ⁵Poverty is a problem that should concern every American of every economic class. ⁶When one American in eight—in *eight*—is living below the poverty line, that should worry every one of us. ⁷You and I may be comfortable today, but many of those millions of our fellow countrymen and women were once comfortable as well. ⁸The loss of jobs, the changing economy, and the slashing of social programs have meant that much of the American middle class is now hanging on by its fingertips, living from paycheck to paycheck, and feeling the ground give way beneath its feet. ⁹Other important social issues, such as the continued existence of racism, also demand attention in our country. ¹⁰In addition, we should care about poverty whether we ever personally experience it or not. ¹¹It is not merely an economic issue; it is a moral one. ¹²As a former vice president, Hubert Humphrey, once said, "A society is judged by how it treats its most vulnerable citizens."

All the details (except sentence 9) support the idea that poverty should be the economic and moral concern of every American.

_A_ 9. Which statement is the point of the argument?

A. Poverty should be the economic and moral concern of every American.

B. The middle class is hanging on by its fingertips.

C. Poverty is a moral issue.

D. Poverty has never been so widespread.

_C_ 10. Which sentence is **not** relevant support for the point of the argument?

A. Sentence 5   C. Sentence 9

B. Sentence 8   D. Sentence 12

Sentence 9 changes the subject from poverty to racism.

ARGUMENT: Mastery Test 6

A. Each point is followed by three statements that provide relevant support and three that do not. In the spaces, write the letters of the **three** relevant statements of support.

1–3. **Point: It makes sense to give alternative sentences, not jail, to some nonvolent offenders.**

Answers B, D, and F show that alternative sentences make sense. The other answers are about legal representation, the crime rate, and court backlogs, not about alternative sentences.

A. Everyone is entitled to legal representation.

B. Alternative sentences cost less than jail.

C. The crime rate goes up every year.

D. Prisons are overcrowded.

E. The courts always have a backlog of cases.

F. Evidence suggests that alternative sentences offer a better chance of rehabilitating the offender.

Items that logically support the point: __B__   __D__   __F__

4–6. **Point: Religion is a powerful force in modern American life.**

Answers B, C, and F explain how we know that religion is a powerful force in American life. The other answers change the subject to different aspects of religion in American life.

A. The main religion in America is Christianity.

B. Television evangelists can collect millions of dollars from contributors.

C. Religious leaders are often influential voices on public issues in America.

D. In America, there is no state religion.

E. The Pilgrims came to America seeking religious freedom.

F. Public opinion polls show that a majority of Americans consider religion personally important to them.

Items that logically support the point: __B__   __C__   __F__

B. In the following groups, one statement is the point of an argument, and the other statements are support for that point. In the space provided, write the letter of the point of each group.

__C__ 7.

Answers A, B, and D give reasons why legalizing narcotics would eliminate much of America's drug problem.

A. Harsh drug laws have not ended illegal drug use.

B. Legalizing drugs would put illegal street dealers out of business, thereby also putting an end to violent "turf battles" between dealers.

C. Much of America's drug problem could actually be eliminated by legalizing narcotics.

D. Profits from drug sales could be taxed to support drug treatment and education programs.

(Continues on next page)

_D_ 8. A. Death Valley, California, at 282 feet below sea level, is the lowest spot in America.

Answers A, B, and C state three facts that show Death Valley is a place of extremes— its distance below sea level, its extreme temperatures, and its lack of rainfall.

B. Temperatures in Death Valley can range from a high of 132° F to a low of 37° F.

C. The valley receives less than two inches of rain per year.

D. Death Valley is a place of extremes.

C. For each group below, read the three items of support (the evidence). Then, in the space provided, write the letter of the point that is adequately supported by that evidence.

Group 1

Support

- A growing number of Japanese women are choosing to stay single, viewing their traditional marriage role as a "raw deal."

- The cost of living and raising a child in Japan is very high.

- Long work days and lengthy commutes leave many Japanese working people too exhausted to deal with children.

_D_ 9. Which point is adequately supported by all the evidence above?

  A. Japanese women are demanding changes in their society.
  B. Japanese people work longer hours than workers in any other country.
  C. Japanese families have traditionally been large.
  D. There are a number of reasons why the birthrate in Japan is falling.

Group 2

Answer D covers all three of the items of support. Answers A and B each relate to only one of the items of support. Answer C is incorrect because none of the supporting items mentions the traditional size of the Japanese family.

Support

- Dolphins appear to be able to talk to one another through a language of squeals and grunts.

- There have been reports of dolphins helping people who were lost at sea.

- Dolphins in captivity have learned to perform sophisticated tasks, such as fetching objects in a particular order.

_B_ 10. Which point is adequately supported by the evidence above?

  A. There are no other animals as intelligent as dolphins.
  B. Dolphins appear to be highly intelligent animals.
  C. Dolphins are better off in captivity.
  D. Dolphins are good parents.

All three items of support show that dolphins are intelligent. Answer A is incorrect because none of the supporting items compare dolphins to other animals. Answers C and D are incorrect because neither is mentioned in the supporting items.

10 Critical Reading

Skilled readers are those who can *recognize* an author's point and the support for that point. **Critical readers** are those who can *evaluate* an author's support for a point and determine whether that support is solid or not. In this book, you have already had practice in evaluating support—deciding when inferences are valid and when they are not (pages 273–293) and determining whether supporting evidence is relevant (pages 367–372) and adequate (pages 372–375).

This chapter will extend your ability to read critically in three ways. It will explain and offer practice in each of the following:

● Separating fact from opinion

● Detecting propaganda

● Recognizing errors in reasoning

Separating Fact from Opinion

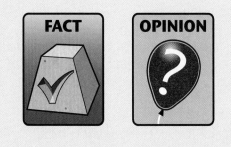

As the illustration suggests, facts are solidly grounded and can be checked for accuracy; opinions are afloat and open to question.

Look at the photograph below of my great-grandmother's gravestone and the information that it provides. In the spaces provided, do the following:

1. Write what you think are the **facts** on the gravestone.
2. Write what you think is the **opinion** it contains.

Facts: _____ Elizabeth L. Miller, wife of H.R. Miller, _____

_____ born December 4, 1823, died July 21, 1889 _____

Opinion: _____ Sweetly sleeping _____

Fact

A **fact** is information that can be proved true through objective evidence. This evidence may be physical proof or the spoken or written testimony of witnesses. The photograph above presents mostly facts: Elizabeth L. Miller was born on December 4, 1823, and died on July 21, 1889. She was the wife of H.R. Miller.

Following are some more facts—they can be checked for accuracy and thus proved true.

Fact: The Quad Tower is the tallest building in this city.

(A researcher could go out and, through inspection, confirm that the building is the tallest.)

Fact: Albert Einstein willed his violin to his grandson.

(This statement can be checked in historical publications or with Einstein's estate.)

Fact: On September 11, 2001, terrorists destroyed the New York World Trade Center, killing thousands.

(This event was witnessed in person or on television by millions, and it's in records worldwide.)

Opinion

An **opinion** is a belief, judgment, or conclusion that cannot be objectively proved true. As a result, it is open to question. For instance, on my great-grandmother's gravestone, we are told that she is "sweetly sleeping." Of course I certainly *hope* that she is sleeping sweetly, but I have no way of knowing for sure. The statement is an opinion.

Or consider this example: After watching a movie, someone might state that the film was too sentimental. The statement is an opinion because it cannot be objectively proved. Another person might see the same movie and find it realistic. Neither statement can be proved; both are opinions.

Here are some more opinions:

Opinion: The Quad Tower is the ugliest building in the city.

(There's no way to prove this statement because two people can look at the same building and come to different conclusions about its beauty. *Ugly* is a **value word**, a word we use to express a value judgment. Value or judgment words are signals that an opinion is being expressed. By their very nature, these words represent opinions, not facts.)

Opinion: Einstein should have willed his violin to a museum.

(Who says? Not his grandson. This is an opinion.)

Opinion: The attack on the World Trade Center was the worst act of terrorism in the history of humankind.

(Whether something is "worst" is always debatable. *Worst* is another value word.)

Writing Facts and Opinions

To get a better sense of fact and opinion, take a few minutes to write three facts about yourself and then to write three of your opinions. Here, for example, are three facts about me and three of my opinions.   *Answers will vary.*

Three facts about me:

- I am six feet tall.
- I do my writing on a Macintosh computer.
- I have two sisters and one wife.

Three of my opinions:

- Schools should encourage students to do a great deal of reading.
- Macintosh computers are much easier to use than PC's.
- People should not get special treatment just because they are rich.

Now write your facts and opinions in the space below.

Three facts about you:

- _____
  _____
- _____
  _____
- _____
  _____

Three of your opinions:

> *Hint:* To make sure that these are opinions, do not begin them with "I." For example, do not write "I think handguns should be banned." Simply write, "Handguns should be banned."

- _____
  _____
- _____
  _____
- _____
  _____

Points about Fact and Opinion

There are several points to keep in mind when considering fact and opinion.

1 Statements of fact may be found to be untrue.

Suppose you discovered that the Quad Tower is only the second-tallest building in the city. The statement would then be an error, not a fact. It is not unusual for evidence to show that a "fact" is not really true. It was once considered to be a fact that the world was flat, for example, but that "fact" turned out to be an error.

2 **Value words** (ones that contain a judgment) often represent opinions. Here are examples of these words:

Value Words

best	great	beautiful
worst	terrible	bad
better	lovely	good
worse	disgusting	wonderful

Value words often express judgments—they are generally subjective, not objective. While factual statements *report on* observed reality, subjective statements *interpret* reality. For example, the observation that it is raining outside is an objective one. The statement that the weather is bad, however, is subjective, an evaluation of reality. (Some people—for example, farmers whose crops need water—consider rain to be good weather.)

3 The words *should* and *ought to* often signal opinions. Those words introduce what people think should, or ought to, be done. Other people will disagree.

Couples should definitely not live together before marriage.

Couples ought to live together before getting married to be sure they are compatible.

4 Don't mistake widely held opinions for facts. Much information that sounds factual is really opinion. A real estate agent, for example, might say, "At the price listed, this rancher is a great buy." Buyers would be wise to wonder what the value word *great* means to the agent. Or an ad may claim that a particular automobile is "the most economical car on the road today," a statement that at first seems factual. But what is meant by *economical*? If the car offers the most miles per gallon but the worst record for expensive repairs, you might not agree that it's economical.

As we will see in later parts of this chapter, advertisers and politicans often try to manipulate us by presenting opinions as if they were facts. For instance, one politician may claim that another will be soft on terrorism or will waste our tax dollars. But accusations are often not facts. Clear-thinking citizens must aim to get below the surface of claims and charges and determine as much factual truth as possible.

5 Finally, remember that much of what we read and hear is a mixture of fact and opinion. Our job, then, is to draw upon existing fact and opinion and to arrive at an informed opinion. On our Supreme Court, for example, nine justices deliberate in order to deliver informed opinions about important issues of our time. But even these justices often disagree and deliver split decisions. The reality is that most of what matters in life is very complex and cannot be separated into simple fact and opinion. Our challenge always is to arrive at the best possible informed opinion, and even then there will be people who disagree with us.

Fact and Opinion in Reading

In general, textbook authors try to be as factual as possible. Most textbook material is based on scientific observation and study, and textbook authors do their best to present us with all the facts and objective informed opinion. On the other hand, many essays, editorials, political speeches, and advertisements may contain facts, but those facts are often carefully selected to back up the authors' opinions.

✔ *Check Your Understanding*

To sharpen your understanding of fact and opinion, read the following statements and decide whether each is fact or opinion. Put an **F** (for "fact") or an **O** (for "opinion") beside each statement. Put **F+O** beside the **two** statements that are a mixture of fact *and* opinion. Then read the explanation that follows.

> *Hint:* Remember that opinions are signaled by value words—words such as *great* or *hard* or *beautiful* or *terrible* that express a value judgment. Take care to note such words in your reading.

___F___ 1. Last night, a tree outside our house was struck by lightning.

___O___ 2. The waiters at that restaurant are rude, and the food costs twice as much as it's worth.

___F___ 3. Ostriches do not hide their heads in the sand.

___O___ 4. Brad Pitt and Halle Berry are the most gorgeous movie stars in Hollywood today.

F+O 5. Low-flow showerheads save water, so all homeowners should be required to buy and install them in their showers.

O 6. *Watchers*, by Dean R. Koontz, is a terrifying story that is bound to keep you awake at night.

F 7. The Grimm brothers collected their fairy tales from other storytellers.

O 8. There is nothing like a bottle of Coca-Cola to satisfy thirst.

F 9. In the late 1890s, when Coke was first sold, it included a small amount of cocaine, which was then legal.

F+O 10. One of the most delicious of soft drinks, Coca-Cola was first intended to cure various ills, including headaches.

Explanation

1. This is a statement of fact. You and your family might have seen or heard the lightning strike, or you could go outside later and see the type of damage done to the tree.

2. This is an opinion. Not every customer is likely to agree that all the waiters are rude and that the food is overpriced. The word *rude* is a value word.

3. This is a fact (contrary to popular belief) which can be checked through observation and scientific reports.

4. This is an opinion. Not everyone would regard Brad Pitt and Halle Berry in this way. Here the value word *gorgeous* shows us that a judgment is being expressed.

5. The first part of this statement is a fact; tests confirm that low-flow showerheads save water. The second part of the statement—that such showerheads should be *required*—is an opinion.

6. This is an opinion. The story may or may not be so scary that it would keep you awake at night.

7. This is a fact. It can be confirmed through the Grimms' writings and through research on the background of their stories.

8. This is an opinion. Many people might prefer cold water or some other drink as a thirst-quencher.

9. All the details here are facts that can be looked up and confirmed in historical records.

10. The first part of the statement is an opinion—not everyone would consider Coke to be one of the most delicious of soft drinks. (*Delicious* is another value word.) The second part of the statement is a fact that could be confirmed by researching historical records of the time.

PRACTICE 1

Some of the statements below are facts, and some are opinions; in addition, **two** include fact and opinion. Label facts with an **F**, opinions with an **O**, and statements of fact *and* opinion with an **F+O**.

_O_ 1. German shepherds are the scariest dogs alive.

> The word *scariest* is a value word.

_F_ 2. The dog that bites people the most often, according to one twenty-seven-year study, is the German shepherd.

> This fact can be checked by looking at the study.

The fact that German shepherds are used in police work and as guide dogs can be confirmed by research. Whether or not they make poor pets is an opinion.

_F+O_ 3. German shepherds, which always make poor pets, are used in police work and as guide dogs for the blind.

_F_ 4. Smoking has been found to be one cause of lung cancer.

_O_ 5. Executives of corporations that pollute the environment should be jailed.

_F_ 6. According to scientists, all the water on Earth has been recycled for millions of years, and we drink the same water as the dinosaurs did.

_F+O_ 7. Because many studies have concluded that smoking is a health hazard, cigarettes should be banned.

_F_ 8. Scientists predict that one-third of people who begin smoking under the age of 18 will die prematurely because of their habit.

_O_ 9. There's no illness harder to cope with than depression.

_F_ 10. Depression is most common among persons between the ages of 25 and 44.

Item 4: This fact can be confirmed by information from the American Cancer Society, medical literature, and the Surgeon General's office.

Item 5: The word *should* signals this opinion.

Item 6: This fact can be confirmed by looking up scientific information on water.

Item 7: The fact that smoking is a health hazard can be confirmed by looking at the studies. The word *should* signals the opinion part of the statement.

Item 8: The fact that scientists have made such a prediction can be confirmed by research in scientific journals.

Item 9: Some people might feel that other illnesses (for example, cancer) are harder to cope with.

Item 10: This fact can be confirmed by researching the age group among which depression is most common.

To the Instructor: In Practice 1, words indicating opinions are underlined in this *Instructor's Edition.*

Detecting Propaganda

Advertisers, salespeople, and politicians are constantly promoting their points: "Buy our product," "Believe what I say," and "Vote for me." Often they lack adequate factual support for their points, so they appeal to our emotions by using propaganda techniques.

Part of being a critical reader is having the ability to recognize these propaganda techniques for the emotional fluff that they are. The critical reader strips away the fluff to determine whether there is solid support for the point in question. None of us wants to accept someone else's point as a result of emotional manipulation.

This section will introduce you to six common propaganda techniques:

- Bandwagon
- Testimonial
- Transfer
- Plain Folks
- Name Calling
- Glittering Generalities

While there are other propaganda techniques, the ones described below are among the most common. They all use emotional appeals to distract from the fact they are not providing solid evidence to support their points.

1 Bandwagon

Old-fashioned parades usually began with a large wagon carrying a brass band. Therefore, to "jump on the bandwagon" means to join a parade, or to do what many others are doing. The **bandwagon** technique tells us to buy a product or support a certain issue because, in effect, "everybody else is doing it."

A TV commercial may claim that more and more people are watching the evening news with anchorperson Kerrie Berger. Or a cell phone ad may show people in many different kinds of occupations using a certain cell phone. Or a political ad may feature people from all walks of life speaking out in support of a certain candidate. The ads imply that if you don't jump on the bandwagon, the parade will pass you by.

Here are two examples of real TV ads that have used the bandwagon appeal:

> With appealing music in the background, flashing scenes show many people wearing the sponsor's jeans.

> On a beautiful day, almost everyone on the beach leaves in a hurry in order to attend the sponsor's sale.

● Check (✓) the ad below that uses the bandwagon appeal.

_____ 1. A famous actress explains that she loves to use a certain hair coloring.

_✓_ 2. A cable company claims that more and more people are switching to it to access the Internet.   The words *more and more people* suggest that you had better switch too, or you'll be left behind.

2 Testimonial

Famous athletes often appear on television as spokespersons for all sorts of products, from soft drinks to automobiles. Movie and TV stars make commercials endorsing products and political issues. The idea behind the **testimonial** approach is that the testimony of famous people influences the viewers that admire these people.

What consumers must remember is that famous people get paid to endorse products. In addition, these people are not necessarily experts about the products, or the political issues, they promote.

Here are two examples of real ads that have used the appeal of testimonials:

> An actor promotes a product intended to help a man's sexual performance.

> Popular country singers speak out on behalf of certain political candidates.

● Check (✓) the ad below that uses a testimonial.

_____ 1. An ad for a new movie shows people waiting to buy tickets in a line that extends halfway around the block.

_✓_ 2. A sports star praises the brand of sneakers he is putting on.   The fact that it is a sports star praising the sneakers signals the testimonial approach.

3 Transfer

The most common type of propaganda technique is **transfer**, in which products or candidates try to associate themselves with something that people admire or love. In the illustration on page 407, we see a political candidate holding a sign saying "Vote for Me" and standing next to a beauty queen wrapped in a U.S.A. banner.

There are countless variations on this ad, in which a beautiful and sexy woman (or an American flag or some other symbol of the U.S.A.) is used to promote a product or candidate or cause. The hope is that we will *transfer* the positive feelings we have toward a beautiful or sexy-looking person to the product being advertised, or that we will *transfer* the patriotism that we feel to a product or candidate. Over the years, advertisers have found that beauty and sex "sell" and that appeals to patriotism often succeed. In short, transfer usually works.

Here are two examples of real ads that have used the appeal of transfer:

> A beautiful woman in a slinky red dress is shown driving the sponsor's car.

> A hospital chain uses a portrait of Benjamin Franklin in its ads and claims that it, like Franklin, stands for new ideas.

● Check (✓) the ad below that uses transfer.

___✓___ 1. With the tune of "God Bless America" in the background, an announcer asks viewers to support the home baseball team by coming out to games.

_____ 2. A world-famous bike rider and cancer survivor appears in an ad for a company that sells anti-cancer medications.

> The use of "God Bless America" signals the transfer technique.

4 Plain Folks

Some people distrust political candidates who are rich or well-educated. They feel that these candidates, if elected, will not be able to understand the problems of the average working person. Therefore, candidates often use the **plain folks** technique, presenting themselves as ordinary, average citizens. They try to show they are just "plain folks" by referring in their speeches to hard times in their lives or by posing for photographs while wearing a hard hat or mingling with everyday people.

Similarly, the presidents of some companies appear in their own ads, trying to show that their giant corporations are just family businesses run by ordinary folks.

Here are two examples of real ads that have used the appeal of plain folks:

> Average-looking American kids are shown at home trying and enjoying a cereal.

> A president of an insurance company is shown with his family, talking about his concern for their safety and well-being if he should not be there some day.

● Check (✓) the ad below that uses plain-folks approach.

The grandmother and grandson suggest that this soup is made and eaten by regular people who cook at home.

_____ 1. A very attractive young woman wraps herself in a robe that has been washed in a particular brand of laundry detergent.

___✓___ 2. A grandmother, serving a canned vegetable soup to her grandson, says, "This has all the simple, healthy, and delicious ingredients I use in my own vegetable soup."

5   Name Calling

Name calling is the use of emotionally loaded language or negative comments to turn people against a rival product, candidate, or movement. An example of name calling would be a political candidate's labeling an opponent "soft," "radical," or "wimpy."

Here are two examples of name calling taken from real life:

> The fast-food industry labels critics of their industry as "food police," "cookie cops," and "the grease Gestapo."

> During a taste test, consumers describe the other leading brand of spaghetti sauce as "too salty" and "thin and tasteless."

● Check (✓) the ad below that uses name calling.

_____ 1. An ad for hard liquor shows a beautiful woman in a strapless gown having a drink and being admired by several handsome men.

__✓__ 2. "My opponent has lived in our state for only two years," says a candidate for state senator. "Let's not put an outsider into state office." Calling the opponent an outsider when he or she has lived in the state two years is name calling.

6   Glittering Generalities

A **glittering generality** is an important-sounding but unspecific claim about some product, candidate, or cause. It cannot be proved true or false because no evidence is offered to support the claim. Such claims use general words such as "great," "magical," or "ultimate." "Simply the best," an ad might say about a certain television set. But no specific evidence of any kind is offered to support such a generality. "The right candidate for our city," a campaign slogan might claim. But what does "right" really mean? It and similar phrases sound good but say nothing definite.

Here are two examples from real ads that use glittering generalities:

> A store ad claims, "Fashions that will bring out the rainbow in you."
> A canned-food ad boasts of "nutrition for today."

● Check (✓) the ad below that uses a glittering generality.

__✓__ 1. "Ed Dalton—a candidate that really cares," says the announcer.

_____ 2. A well-known athlete says he uses a certain kind of aspirin.

The words *really cares* tell us nothing specific about Ed Dalton.

PRACTICE 2

In each pair of sentences below, the first sentence does not illustrate a propaganda technique, but the second one does. On the line, write the letter of the propaganda technique used in the second sentence.

A. bandwagon	B. testimonial	C. transfer
D. plain folks	E. name calling	F. glittering generalities

Suggesting the competitors are money-grubbers is name calling.

_E_ 1. ● Kiddy Kare is the largest daycare center in town.
● Our competitor's daycare center is <u>more concerned about profits than about children</u>.

The testimony of the actress will influence people to buy the sunglasses.

_B_ 2. ● Sureguard sunglasses filter out harmful ultraviolet rays.
● "I'm proud to wear Sureguard sunglasses," says <u>actress Jennifer Barnes</u>. "You'll love them, too."

_A_ 3. ● In a recent election poll, Margo Levy was ahead of the other candidate.

The ad encourages people to do what it claims everybody else is doing.

● <u>Add your vote to the landslide victory</u> Margo Levy will win in next week's election.

The statement tells us nothing definite about Twin Oaks.

_F_ 4. ● Twin Oaks is a residential development near Des Moines, Iowa.
● There's <u>nothing else quite like</u> Twin Oaks, a great residential community <u>where you will be proud to live</u>.

If he lifted boxes and swept floors, he must be an ordinary, average citizen.

_D_ 5. ● As a young man, candidate Alan Wilson had a variety of jobs working in a department store and in his family's TV station.
● As a young man, candidate Alan Wilson learned what it means to work hard by <u>spending long hours lifting boxes and sweeping floors</u>.

Having a comedian deliver this serious message helps convince people.

_B_ 6. ● A college degree opens up job doors.
● <u>Comedian Jerry Klein</u> says, "A college degree opens up job doors."

Suggesting that the dogs know more than Smith is name calling.

_E_ 7. ● I'm voting for Jones because he has had ten years of experience on the Senate's Committee on International Affairs.
● I'll bet <u>my French poodle and German shepherd know more</u> about foreign affairs than Smith does. My vote goes to Jones.

The statement suggests we would be unpatriotic if we did not buy a used car from Markey's.

_C_ 8. ● Markey's Used Cars will be open on the Fourth of July.
● A <u>patriotic march</u> plays, and a <u>giant American flag</u> waves over a used-car lot. "Celebrate your freedom of choice on the <u>Fourth of July</u>!" says the announcer. "At Markey's, we'll <u>honor</u> the holiday by making some <u>star-spangled</u> deals."

To the Instructor:
In Practice 2, words indicating the propaganda technique are underlined in this *Instructor's Edition*.

_D_ 9. ● The presidential candidate supports our country's farmers.

● The presidential candidate has <u>her own small farm</u>, so she knows the farmers' concerns.

_F_ 10. ● At Triple-A Technical School, you can learn the skills needed to become a plumber, mechanic, or electrician.

● <u>Set the world on fire</u> with skills you learn at Triple-A Technical School!

Item 9: The presidential candidate wants to look like a regular person who understands the problems of average citizens.

Item 10: The words *Set the world on fire* tell us nothing specific about the school.

Recognizing Errors in Reasoning

So far in this chapter, you have gotten practice in separating fact from opinion and in spotting propaganda. In this section you will learn about some common errors in reasoning—also known as **fallacies**—that take the place of the real support needed in an argument. As shown in the illustration, a valid point is based on a rock-like foundation of solid support; a fallacious point is based on a house of cards that offers no real support at all. Regrettably, these fallacies appear all too often in political arguments, often as the result of deliberate manipulation, other times as the result of careless thinking.

You've already learned about two common fallacies in Chapter 9, "Argument." One of those fallacies is sometimes called **changing the subject**. Attention is diverted from the issue at hand by presenting irrelevant support—evidence that actually has nothing to do with the argument. The second fallacy covered in Chapter 9 is sometimes called **hasty generalization**—in which a point is based on inadequate support. To be valid, a point must be based on an adequate amount of evidence. To draw a conclusion on the basis of insufficient evidence is to make a hasty generalization.

Below are six other common fallacies that will be explained in this section.

Three Fallacies That Ignore the Issue

- Circular Reasoning
- Personal Attack
- Straw Man

Three Fallacies That Oversimplify the Issue

- False Cause
- False Comparison
- Either-Or

In all of these fallacies, a point is argued, but no true support is offered for that point.

Fallacies That Ignore the Issue

Circular Reasoning

Part of a point cannot reasonably be used as evidence to support it. The fallacy of including such illogical evidence is called **circular reasoning**; it is also known as **begging the question**.

Here is a simple and obvious example of such reasoning:

Mr. Green is a great teacher because he is so wonderful at teaching.

The supporting reason ("he is so wonderful at teaching") is really the same as the conclusion ("Mr. Green is a great teacher"). We still do not know *why* he is a great teacher. No real reasons have been given—the statement has merely been repeated.

Can you spot the circular reasoning in the following arguments?

1. Vitamins are healthful, for they improve your well-being.
2. Since people under 21 are too young to vote, the voting age shouldn't be lowered below age 21.
3. Abortion is an evil practice because it is so wrong.

Let's look more closely at these arguments:

1. The word *healthful*, which is used in the conclusion, conveys the same idea as *well-being*. We still don't know why vitamins are good for us.
2. The idea that people under 21 are too young to vote is both the conclusion and the reason of the argument. No real reason is given for why people under 21 are too young to vote.
3. The claim that abortion "is so wrong" simply restates the idea that it is an evil practice. No explanation is given for why abortion is evil or wrong.

In all these cases, the reasons merely repeat an important part of the conclusion. The careful reader wants to say, "Tell me something new. You are reasoning in circles. Give me supporting evidence, not a repetition."

● Check (✓) the item that contains an example of the circular reasoning fallacy.

    _✓_   1.   The government should lower our taxes because taxes are entirely too high.

    _____   2.   I'm not going to be paid what I'm worth until I get a boss who cares about being fair.   Saying that taxes are too high is merely a different way of saying that taxes should be lowered. (Item 2 is personal attack.)

Personal Attack

This fallacy often occurs in political debate. Here's an example:

> Senator Brill's opinions on public housing are worthless. He can't even manage to hold his own household together—he's been married and divorced three times already.

Senator Brill's family life may or may not reflect a weakness in his character, but it has nothing to do with the value of his opinions on public housing. **Personal attack** ignores the issue under discussion and concentrates instead on the character of the opponent.

Sometimes personal attacks take the form of accusing people of taking a stand only because it will benefit them personally. For instance, here's a personal attack on a congressman who is an outspoken member of the National Organization for Women (NOW): "He doesn't care about NOW. He supports it only in order to get more women to vote for him." This argument ignores the congressman's detailed defense of NOW as an organization that promotes equal rights for both men and women. The key to recognizing personal attack is that it always involves an opponent's personal life or character, rather than simply his or her public ideas.

● Check (✓) the item that contains an example of personal attack.

    _✓_   1.   Why support Ray O'Donnell's highway safety proposal? He's got the biggest collection of speeding tickets in the district.

    _____   2.   I feel my salary should be higher because it is so low.

       The statement attacks O'Donnell for his personal driving habits, not for his highway safety proposal. (Item 2 is circular reasoning.)

Straw Man

An opponent made of straw can be defeated very easily. Sometimes, if one's real opponent is putting up too good a fight, it can be tempting to build a scarecrow and battle it instead. For example, look at the following excerpt from a debate on the death penalty.

> Ms. Collins opposes capital punishment. But letting murderers out on the street to kill again is a crazy idea. If we did that, no one would be safe.

Ms. Collins, however, never advocated "letting murderers out on the street to kill again." In fact, she wants to keep them in jail for life rather than execute them. The **straw man** fallacy suggests that the opponent favors an obviously unpopular cause—when the opponent really doesn't support anything of the kind. Then that made-up position is opposed.

● Check (✓) the item that contains an example of straw man.

There may be valid reasons for favoring gun control. It is unlikely that those who do are unconcerned about criminals taking over the country. (Item 2 is personal attack.)

✓ 1. The people who are in favor of gun control are obviously not concerned about criminals taking control of this fine country.

_____ 2. Rose Curtis is a declared lesbian and should not be allowed to run for public office.

Fallacies That Oversimplify the Issue

False Cause

You have probably heard someone say as a joke, "I know it's going to rain today because I just washed the car." The idea that someone can make it rain by washing a car is funny because the two events obviously have nothing to do with each other. However, with more complicated issues, it is easy to make the mistake known as the fallacy of **false cause**. The mistake is to assume that because event B *follows* event A, event B *was caused by* event A.

Cause-and-effect situations can be difficult to analyze, and people are often tempted to oversimplify them by focusing on one "cause" and ignoring other possible causes. To identify an argument using a false cause, look for alternative causes.

Consider this argument:

The Macklin Company was more prosperous before Ms. Williams became president. Clearly, she is the cause of the decline.

(Event A: Ms. Williams became president.

Event B: The Macklin Company's earnings declined.)

However, Ms. Williams has been president for only a few months. What other possible causes could have been responsible for the decline? Perhaps the policies of the previous president are just now affecting the company. Perhaps the market for the company's product has changed. In any case, it's easy but dangerous to assume that just because A *came before* B, A *caused* B.

There are many ways the baby could have caught a cold besides being taken to the park. (Item 2 is false comparison.)

● Check (✓) the item that contains an example of false cause.

✓ 1. I knew I shouldn't have taken the baby to the park today. Now he's got a cold.

_____ 2. Of course the legalization of prostitution will work in America. It has worked in European countries, hasn't it?

False Comparison

When the poet Robert Burns wrote, "My love is like a red, red rose," he meant that both the woman he loved and a rose are beautiful. In other ways—such as having green leaves and thorns, for example—his love did not resemble a rose at all.

Comparisons are often a good way to clarify a point. But because two things are not alike in all respects, comparisons (sometimes called analogies) often make poor evidence for arguments. In the error in reasoning known as **false comparison**, the assumption is that two things are more alike than they really are. For example, read the following argument:

> It didn't hurt your grandfather to get to work without a car, and it won't hurt you either.

To judge whether or not this is a false comparison, consider how the two situations are alike and how they differ. They are similar in that both involve a young person's need to get to work. But the situations are different in that the grandfather didn't have to be at work an hour after his last class. In fact, he didn't go to school at all. In addition, his family didn't own a car he could use. The differences in this case are more important than the similarities, making it a false comparison.

- Check (✓) the item that contains an example of the false comparison.

  _____ 1. After visiting Hal today, I came home with a headache. I must be allergic to his dog.

  __✓__ 2. I don't know why you're so worried about my grades. Albert Einstein had lousy grades in high school, and he did all right.

  There are many differences between Albert Einstein and the person
making this statement. (Item 1 is false cause.)

Either-Or

It is often wrong to assume that there are only two sides to a question. Offering only two choices when more actually exist is an **either-or** fallacy. For example, the statement "You are either with us or against us" assumes that there is no middle ground. Or consider the following:

There may be other reasons for not studying three hours a night besides not being serious about college. For example, a student might have to work at night to pay for college. (Item 1 is false comparison.)

> People opposed to unrestricted free speech are really in favor of censorship.

This argument ignores the fact that a person could believe in free speech as well as in laws that prohibit slander or that punish someone for falsely yelling "Fire!" in a crowded theater. Some issues have only two sides (Will you pass the course, or won't you?), but most have several.

- Check (✓) the item that contains an example of the either-or fallacy.

  _____ 1. School prayer is a positive force in parochial schools, so why not try it in our public schools?

  __✓__ 2. If you don't study at least three hours a night, you're not really serious about being in college.

PRACTICE 3

A. In the space provided, write the letter of the fallacy contained in each argument. Choose from the three fallacies shown in the box below.

> A Circular reasoning (*a statement repeats itself rather than providing a real supporting reason to back up an argument*)
>
> B Personal attack (*ignores the issue under discussion and concentrates instead on the character of the opponent*)
>
> C Straw man (*an argument is made by claiming an opponent holds an extreme position and then opposing that extreme position*)

It is unlikely that supporters of lotteries think it is better to get something for nothing.

_C_ 1. Supporters of state lotteries apparently don't think people should work hard for what they get. They believe it's better to get something for nothing.

_B_ 2. Earl will make a lousy class treasurer because he's just a conceited jerk.   Earl's ability as class treasurer has nothing to do with whether or not he is a conceited jerk.

By definition, polluting is dirtying the environment.

_A_ 3. Pollution is wrong because it dirties the environment.

_C_ 4. Mr. Vincent supports sex education in junior high school. Maybe he thinks it's okay for 13-year-olds to be having babies, but I don't agree.   It is unlikely that Mr. Vincent takes the extreme position that it is all right for 13-year-olds to have babies.

_A_ 5. Watering new grass is important, since new lawns need a lot of water.   In effect, this statement says that new grass needs watering because new grass needs water.

B. In the space provided, write the letter of the fallacy contained in each argument. Choose from the three fallacies shown in the box below.

> A False cause (*the argument assumes that the order of events alone shows cause and effect*)
>
> B False comparison (*the argument assumes that two things being compared are more alike than they really are*)
>
> C Either-or (*the argument assumes that there are only two sides to a question*)

The rash could have been the result of any number of things besides Gary's dorm room.

_A_ 6. Stay away from Gary's filthy dorm room. After the last time I went there to study, I actually got a rash.

_C_ 7. Did you tell the boss off, or did you act like a wimp again?   Telling the boss off or being a wimp are not the only two possibilities. For example, one might discuss concerns with the boss rather than telling her off.

There are more differences between alcohol and pizza than there are similarities.

___B___ 8. There's a sign in the dorm lounge saying that excessive alcohol is dangerous. Well, so what? Too much pizza can be dangerous, too.

___C___ 9. Do you always tell the truth, or are you a liar?

___A___ 10. Last time there was an eclipse, the stock market went down. I'm going to sell all my stock before next week's eclipse takes place.

Item 9: If anyone who does not *always* tell the truth is called a liar, almost everyone must be a liar.

Item 10: It is highly unlikely that the eclipse had anything to do with the drop in the stock market.

CHAPTER REVIEW

In this chapter, you learned that critical readers evaluate an author's support for a point and determine whether that support is solid or not. Critical reading includes the following three abilities:

● **Separating fact from opinion.** A **fact** is information that can be proved true through objective evidence. An **opinion** is a belief, judgment, or conclusion that cannot be proved objectively true. Much of what we read is a mixture of fact and opinion, and our job as readers is to arrive at at the best possible informed opinion. Textbooks and other effective writing provide informed opinion—opinion based upon factual information.

● **Detecting propaganda.** Advertisers, salespeople, and politicians often try to promote their points by appealing to our emotions rather than our powers of reason. To do so, they practice six common propaganda techniques: bandwagon, testimonial, transfer, plain folks, name calling, and glittering generalities.

● **Recognizing errors in reasoning.** Politicians and others are at times guilty of errors in reasoning—fallacies—that take the place of the real support needed in an argument. Such fallacies include circular reasoning, personal attack, straw man, false cause, false comparison, and either-or.

On the Web: If you are using this book in class, you can visit our website for additional practice in critical reading. Go to **www.townsendpress.com** and click on "Online Exercises."

REVIEW TEST 1

To review what you've learned in this chapter, answer the following questions.

Fact and Opinion

1. *(A fact, An opinion)* _____A fact_____ can be proved true through objective evidence. See page 400.

A news report is supposed to present facts. An editorial presents the writer's opinion. A political speech presents opinions about why one candidate or proposal is better than another.

2. *(An editorial, A political speech, A news report)* ___A news report___ is likely to be totally factual.

3. Most of what we read is *(fact, opinion, a mixture of fact and opinion)* _____a mixture of fact and opinion_____. See page 404.

4. *(Facts, Opinions)* _____Opinions_____ often include words that express judgments. See page 401.

Propaganda Techniques

__B__ 5. Propaganda is intended to (A. inform; B. persuade). See page 407.

__A__ 6. An important difference between a testimonial and a plain-folks appeal is that testimonials feature (A. famous; B. ordinary) people. See page 408.

__A__ 7. The (A. transfer; B. plain-folks) technique associates a product with symbols and images that people respect. See page 408.

Fallacies

__T__ 8. TRUE OR FALSE? The fallacy of personal attack ignores the true issue. See pages 413–414.

__T__ 9. TRUE OR FALSE? The fallacy of straw man got its name because an opponent made of straw would be easily defeated. See page 414.

__B__ 10. In the either-or fallacy, the argument ignores the possibility of an additional See page 416.
    A. cause for something happening.
    B. side to a question.
    C. comparison.

REVIEW TEST 2

Read the following statements and decide whether each is fact or opinion. Put an **F** (for "fact") or an **O** (for "opinion") beside each statement. Put **F+O** beside the **one** statement that is a mixture of fact and opinion. Then read the explanation that follows.

Words indicating opinions are underlined.

___O___ 1. The <u>best</u> exercise for a healthy heart is walking.

Best is a value word.

___F___ 2. The heart pumps slightly more than a gallon of blood per minute through approximately 60,000 miles of blood vessels in the body.

This fact can be confirmed by looking

This information can be confirmed in scientific and medical literature.

___F___ 3. More Bibles have been printed than any other book in history.

at information on numbers of copies printed of various books.

___O___ 4. The Roman Catholic concept of God is <u>more correct</u> than the Protestant or the Jewish view.

The words *more correct* contain a judgment. Not everyone would agree with this opinion.

___O___ 5. Butterflies are the <u>most beautiful</u> of all insects.

___F+O___ 6. The <u>most amazing</u> thing about butterflies is that their taste sensors are located in their feet, so that by standing on food, they can taste it.

___F___ 7. Falling coconuts kill about 150 people worldwide each year, and sharks kill about 10 people.

___O___ 8. The <u>greatest</u> danger in swimming in the ocean is of being attacked by a shark.

___F___ 9. At the beginning of the twentieth century, only one of ten married women held a paying job.

___O___10. For self-fulfillment, mothers in today's world <u>should hold down an outside job</u> as well as care for their children.

Item 5: Some people find other insects (for example, dragonflies) more beautiful.

Item 6: That the taste sensors of butterflies are in their feet can be confirmed by researching information on butterflies. Whether or not this is the most amazing thing about them is a matter of opinion.

Item 7: These facts can be confirmed by checking statistics on deaths per year from falling coconuts and deaths per year from shark attacks.

Item 8: Some may feel that other dangers—such as drowning—are greater than the danger of being attacked by a shark.

Item 9: This fact can be confirmed by researching statistics on working women at the beginning of the twentieth century.

Item 10: The word *should* signals this opinion. Some people may feel there are other ways for mothers to find self-fulfillment.

REVIEW TEST 3

A. Each of the passages below illustrates a particular propaganda technique. On the line next to the passage, write the letter of the technique being used.

_____B_____ 1. Leslie Kendall, the television actress whose lovely hair is her

The television actress is giving a testimonial for Flirt.

trademark, reveals that her secret is Flirt shampoo. "Flirt softens my hair and gives it great body," Leslie says. "Thanks to Flirt, my hair has never looked better."

    A. Plain folks   C. Name calling
    B. Testimonial   D. Bandwagon

_____C_____ 2. Monroe Archer is a millionaire and the president of a large

Archer, in spite of his money and powerful position, seems as if he is just an average small-town boy.

corporation, yet he has never lost touch with his small-town roots. Despite his power and fame, he still likes returning to his hometown to enjoy a summer band concert and a simple supper at Charley's Diner.

    A. Name calling   C. Plain folks
    B. Bandwagon   D. Testimonial

_____C_____ 3. "I wear Form Fit jeans—if I wear anything at all," whispers a

If you wear Form-Fit jeans, you will look like the shapely model.

shapely model in tight jeans and low-cut T-shirt.

    A. Bandwagon   C. Transfer
    B. Name calling   D. Glittering generalities

_____B_____ 4. Come one! Come all! Everybody's going to Linwood Furniture for

If everybody else is going, you should jump on the bandwagon so you won't be left behind.

the big eighth annual sale, a sale so big we rented a tent to hold the crowds.

    A. Name calling   C. Transfer
    B. Bandwagon   D. Testimonial

_____A_____ 5. Cast your vote next Tuesday for Greg Lewis. This fine man has

These high-sounding words say nothing specific about Greg Lewis.

much to offer his community and his nation. As your representative, he pledges to do his best to improve conditions and to bring you closer to the fulfillment of your highest dreams.

    A. Glittering generalities   C. Bandwagon
    B. Transfer   D. Name calling

**To the Instructor:** Words indicating the propaganda technique are underlined.

B. In the space provided, write the letter of the fallacy contained in each argument. Choose from the three fallacies shown in the box below.

> A   Circular reasoning *(a statement repeats itself rather than providing a real supporting reason to back up an argument)*
> B   Personal attack *(ignores the issue under discussion and concentrates instead on the character of the opponent)*
> C   Straw man *(an argument is made by claiming an opponent holds an extreme position and then opposing that extreme position)*

___B___   6. Congressman Nagel's policy on welfare is nonsense. What do you expect from a man known to have cheated on his wife?

___A___   7. You can always trust an animal lover because people who like animals are more trustworthy than other people.

___C___   8. The mayor wants to allow liquor stores in town. He may not mind having all those drug pushers around, but I certainly do.

Now choose from the two fallacies shown in the box below.

> A   False cause *(the argument assumes that the order of events alone shows cause and effect)*
> B   Either-or *(the argument assumes that there are only two sides to a question)*

___A___   9. I ate in the company cafeteria yesterday, and today I have the flu. That's the last time I'll eat there.

___B___   10. There are only two types of citizens in this town: those who support building a new stadium and those who don't care about our town's future.

Item 6: Nagel's cheating on his wife has nothing to do with the quality of his welfare policy.

Item 7: In effect, this statement says that you can trust an animal lover because you can trust an animal lover.

Item 8: The statement illogically assumes that the mayor has no problem with having a lot of drug pushers in town.

Item 9: The person is just as likely to have gotten the flu somewhere else—in a meeting or on the bus, for example.

Item 10: There are other ways to demonstrate caring about the future of the town besides supporting building a new stadium.

REVIEW TEST 4

"To play at a game of chance." That's the definition of *gamble*. Put that way, gambling sounds like a lighthearted pastime. But for the increasing number of people who are addicted to gambling, it is anything but harmless fun.

The essay below about gambling is followed by questions on critical reading skills as well as on the skills that you learned in previous chapters.

Words to Watch

Below are some words in the reading that do not have strong context support. Each word is followed by the number of the paragraph in which it appears and its meaning there. These words are indicated in the article by a small circle (°).

groggy (3): sleepy
vastly (9): greatly
ventured (14): attempted
motto (14): saying or slogan
ironic (18): the opposite of what might be expected
surges (20): strong increases

GAMBLING—A DANGEROUS GAME

Jon Volkmer

1   When I was in college a few years back, every once in a while I would get a call from a classmate of mine, Tom. This one came in the middle of the night.

2   "Jon," a shaky voice said.

3   "Who's this?" I answered, still groggy°. And then reality hit. "Oh no, Tom. Not again."

4   "Jon, listen to me!" His voice was frantic. I could tell he had practiced his speech. "Jon, first I want you to promise me: if I ever call you again like this, I want you to promise me you'll say no, that you'll turn me down flat. Promise me that!"

5   "Okay, Tom," I said tiredly, "I promise."

6   "Just this one time, this last time, please, I need you to do me a big favor. I need you to call the airline and buy me a ticket home from Las Vegas. Whatever you do, do not send me any money! Just pay for the plane ticket, please! I'll pay you back soon, I swear."

7   I was angry. He'd promised never to do that again. I yelled at him. Next time, I said, I really would stick to the promise he'd just insisted I make. But this time I agreed to buy the ticket.

8   "Thanks, buddy," he said, "you're a lifesaver."

9   That was the last time Tom made me his last-resort call. After college we lost touch, but I will always remember that desperate voice. I have often wondered what became of him and his gambling problem. In the thirty years since, legal gambling in America has vastly° increased. In today's world, a one-way ticket out of Sin City is no "lifesaver" for anyone trying to avoid gambling.

10   In 1976, Atlantic City, New Jersey, set out to be the Vegas of the East. Over the next thirty years, 12.4 billion dollars was spent building casinos there. In 1988, American Indian tribes won rights to build casinos on reservation lands. At last count there were 354 casinos in 28 states, with combined revenues of over 14 billion dollars. This growth did not come at the expense of Las Vegas. On the contrary, Las Vegas has been the fastest-growing major city in America for the last decade, with newer, bigger casinos going up every year.

11   Betting on sporting events has also seen stunning growth. A recent federal study estimated that Americans spend up to 380 billion dollars a year betting on sports. And only 1 percent of that is legal! Eight billion dollars is bet on Super Bowl Sunday alone. For millions of Americans, "March Madness" means joining a pool to pick winners of the men's NCAA Division I basketball tournament.

12   In terms of dollars, gambling tops all other entertainments in America combined. It makes you wonder. What is it about gambling that is so attractive for so many, and so addictive for some? Maybe it's that gambling is part of human nature. Humans have always lived at the mercy of chance. Farmers gamble that their crops will grow. Hunters gamble on finding game. Traders gamble that their stocks will rise or fall.

13   America, in particular, could be called a nation built by gamblers. Columbus took a big chance in coming to the New World. The colonial army was a long shot against the British. The immigrants who populated this country bet all they owned that they could build a better life here.

14   Americans have always been in love with the rags-to-riches story.

The California Gold Rush is part of the national legend. The railroad barons of the 1800s, the oil tycoons of the 1900s, the Internet whiz kids of the 2000s—they are all celebrated as national heroes. People who make a lot of money on the stock market are considered geniuses. "Nothing ventured°, nothing gained" is practically the national motto°.

15 On the other hand, one could argue that those success stories all depended on skill, determination, and hard work. It wasn't just luck. One could say that the recent craze for gambling reflects national laziness. More and more people seem to want to get something for nothing. More and more act as if they are entitled to more money than they have. More and more think gambling is the way to make it happen.

16 Politicians, too, might be guilty of wanting the easy road to revenue. For much of our nation's history, lotteries were illegal. They were considered morally wrong and a threat to the common person. In 1964, New Hampshire became the first state in the modern era to start a lottery as a way to raise money. Thirty-seven states and the District of Columbia now have lotteries, and many also participate in multi-state lotteries such as "Powerball" and "Mega-Millions."

17 For state governments, lotteries are considered "painless" sources of revenue. Players voluntarily spend their money, as opposed to everyone being taxed. Lotteries are especially popular with voters when the money is for some specific cause, such as education. Enormous sums have been raised. In Georgia the state lottery provides a million dollars a day for education. Missouri's lottery provided 955 million dollars for public education in the year 2000.

18 It's ironic° that for all their popularity, lotteries have the worst odds of any form of legal gambling. In Minnesota, a typical example, the odds of winning a $5000 jackpot are 1 in 240,000. You are more likely to be struck by lightning. Your chance of winning California's Lotto Jackpot is 1 in 18,000,000. You are much more likely to die in a car crash on your way to buy the ticket. These odds are far worse than for slot machines or other kinds of casino games.

19 Lottery supporters say that the cost is so low that people do not mind long odds for a chance at winning a huge jackpot. It is a cheap, popular form of entertainment. Twenty-five percent of all Americans buy a lottery ticket at least once a week. Nobody forces these people to try their luck.

20 Some people are "forced," however, by addiction. The addictive qualities of gambling are well known. Like alcohol and drugs, gambling can actually change a person's brain chemistry. That person will crave the "gambler's high" and will do anything to get it, often with terribly destructive results. Opponents of gambling point to increased social problems in places it has been legalized. These include surges° in child abuse, domestic violence, and overall crime rates. An economist has estimated that casino gambling results in six dollars in social cost for every dollar of tax revenue.

21   Video lottery terminals, called VLT's, have been found to be particularly addictive. They are furnished with comfortable chairs and have high stimulation—plenty of sound and flashing lights. They set the stage for a person to make a lot of bets very quickly. VLT's are one of the fastest growing segments of the gambling market, and this worries many gambling experts. Some have called VLT's "the crack cocaine of gambling."

22   After learning more about gambling, I became more and more curious about my old friend Tom. It wasn't too hard to track him down through college contacts. I gave him a call. Although we hadn't spoken in decades, he was happy to hear from me.

23   Tom didn't mind talking about his own gambling history. He was eighteen years old the first time he went to a dog track. He asked a fellow how the betting was done, and the man said he was betting the two-four combination, called the "Daily Double." Tom bet the two-four and won three hundred dollars. "From that moment," he said, "I was hooked."

24   Tom remembered those phone calls to me in college and added some other chilling stories. Amazingly, twice he managed to sneak onto airplanes leaving Las Vegas. Once he ended up hitchhiking. "I was dead broke. I hadn't eaten or slept for days. I was wearing shorts and flip-flops, and it was snowing the whole way."

25   "It was terrible," he went on. "I stole money, I let people down, I thought a lot about suicide."

26   With the help of Gamblers Anonymous, a twelve-step program based on Alcoholics Anonymous, Tom eventually was able to stop gambling for years. He built a successful business and put three kids through college. I asked him if he thought that having so many more places to gamble these days created more gambling addicts. He said he was sure it did, and added that he had tried every one. He had spent a lot of time and money at Indian casinos before he quit.

27   I asked if he thought the government should restrict gambling. "I don't know if you can put that toothpaste back in the tube," he said. "State governments and tribal governments, they're all addicted too. They're addicted to the money they get from gambling." Tom did feel that governments and the companies that make profits from gambling should be required to spend a lot more in outreach, education and treatment for those addicted to gambling.

28   The most recent explosion in gambling has been on the Internet. Online gaming sites pose problems for authorities because they are hard to regulate and even harder to tax. Many of the companies are located outside of the country. A study cited by a U.S. senator estimates that online gambling grew from 2.2 billion dollars in 2000 to 12.6 billion dollars in 2006,

making it the fastest-growing segment of the gambling market. A gambling opposition group has called Internet gambling "the perfect storm" because it combines the quick addiction properties of VLT's with the instant access of the Internet. Without leaving their home or office, gamblers can go deeply into debt, since the standard form of payment for online gambling is the credit card.

29   For my last question, I asked my old friend Tom what he thought about Internet gambling sites. He told me this story. About two years ago he found his son playing online poker with play money. It was just a game. He watched his son for a few minutes, and within two days he himself was playing online poker, only with real money. Since then, he has not been able to control his addiction. He said he has been stealing money from his business, a lot of money. His gambling problem is as bad as it ever was, and no one knows. Even his wife doesn't know.

30   I was shocked that he confided in me. It seemed that he needed to tell someone, and I happened to call at the right moment. I didn't know what to say. I urged him to get help, and I wished him strength and courage. He said I could tell his story, adding, "Maybe it will help someone to not be like me." I said I would not use his real name or home town.

31   As we said our goodbyes, Tom added this. "You know what the worst thing is?" His voice cracked. "It's the time it steals. Gambling takes so much time. First you have to get the money, and then you take as much time as you can gambling with the money, trying to win. That's time I will never get back. Time I could have spent watching my kid play baseball, or snuggling with my wife, or doing something to make the world better. It's such a waste. It's all such a waste."

Reading Comprehension Questions

Vocabulary in Context

_____A_____ 1. In the excerpt below, the word *frantic* (frăn′tĭk) means

Tom's insistence and   A. upset.   C. angry.
the fact that he had to   B. depressed.   D. grateful.
practice the speech
show that he was upset.

> "Jon, listen to me!" His voice was frantic. I could tell he had practiced his speech. "Jon, first I want you to promise me: if I ever call you again like this, I want you to promise me you'll say no, that you'll turn me down flat. Promise me that!" (Paragraph 4)

Item 2: ### Central Point and Main Ideas
Answer A
is incorrect;   _____D_____ 2. Which sentence best expresses the central point of the selection?
paragraph
17 describes one way   A. Legalized gambling has both helped and harmed American society.
gambling helps, but   B. America was built by gamblers, and today gambling continues to be
this is far outweighed   highly popular.
by the many ways it
has harmed American   C. Although no one forces people to try their luck, the addictive qualities
society. Answer B covers   of gambling are well known.
only paragraphs 12–14. D. Gambling hurts Americans more than it helps them.
Answer C covers only paragraphs 19–20.

_____A_____ 3. The implied main idea of paragraph 20 is that
  A. gambling can be addictive and highly destructive.
  B. gambling can actually change a person's brain chemistry.
  C. legalized gambling has been connected with surges in child abuse
     and domestic violence.   The first half of the paragraph describes the
  D. casino gambling has high social costs.   addiction; the second half
                                describes the destructive outcomes.
                                Answer B covers only the third sentence.
                                Answer C covers only the sixth sentence.
Supporting Details   Answer D covers only the last sentence.

_____T_____ 4. TRUE OR FALSE? The odds of winning a state lottery are far worse than for slot machines or other kinds of casino games.
                                See paragraph 18.

Transitions

_____D_____ 5. Read the two sentences below and then answer the question that follows.

> "This growth did not come at the expense of Las Vegas. On the contrary, Las Vegas has been the fastest-growing major city in America for the last decade . . . ." (Paragraph 10)

The words *On the contrary* signal the contrast between the expected slowdown in the growth of Las Vegas and its rapid growth over the past ten years.

What does the second sentence do?

A. It establishes a cause and effect relationship with the first sentence.

B. It compares the growth of Las Vegas with the growth of other major American cities.

C. It shows a time order relationship.

D. It makes a contrast with the first sentence.

Patterns of Organization

___A___ 6. Paragraph 28 mainly

A. presents a series of cause and effect relationships.

B. defines a problem and presents a solution.

C. narrates a series of events in time order.

D. contrasts several attitudes toward gambling.

The cause-and-effect word *because* is used twice, and the word *since* is used once.

Inferences

___B___ 7. We can infer that the author of this selection

A. agrees that lotteries are "painless" sources of revenue.

B. feels that gambling has high social costs.

C. is disgusted that his friend Tom has once again started gambling.

D. believes that the government may once again restrict gambling.

See paragraphs 20–21 and 24–31.

Purpose and Tone

___B___ 8. On the whole, the author's tone is

A. angry.   C. disbelieving.

B. concerned.   D. detached.

The author's serious presentation of facts and of Tom's story shows his concern.

Critical Reading

___B___ 9. An ad featuring ten slot machine players who have recently "hit the jackpot" at a casino is an example of the propaganda technique of

If these people won, so can you.

A. glittering generalities.   C. plain folks.

B. bandwagon.   D. transfer.

___A___ 10. The statement "Tom is a gambling addict because he's hooked on gambling" is an example of the logical fallacy of

A. circular reasoning.   C. personal attack.

B. straw man.   D. either-or.

In effect, the statement says that because Tom is hooked on gambling, he is hooked on gambling.

Discussion Questions

1. Do you think Jon Volkmer did the right thing by helping Tom get home from Las Vegas? Why or why not?

2. Volkmer proposes several possible reasons why people find gambling attractive. Do you know anyone with a gambling problem? Why do you think this person (or people in general) cannot resist gambling?

3. If it were up to you, would you put more legal restrictions on gambling, or would you relax the legal restrictions on gambling? Explain.

4. Tom says he thinks those who profit from gambling, such as the government and casinos, should "spend a lot more in outreach, education and treatment for those addicted to gambling." Do you agree? Should the government and casinos share responsibility for the gamblers' addiction?

Note: Writing assignments for this selection appear on pages 605–606.

Check Your Performance   **CRITICAL READING**

Activity	Number Right	Points		Score
Review Test 1 (10 items)	_____	× 1	=	_____
Review Test 2 (10 items)	_____	× 3	=	_____
Review Test 3 (10 items)	_____	× 3	=	_____
Review Test 4 (10 items)	_____	× 3	=	_____
		TOTAL SCORE	=	_____%

Enter your total score into the **Reading Performance Chart: Review Tests** on the inside back cover.

CRITICAL READING: Mastery Test 1 (Fact and Opinion)

A. Identify facts with an **F**, opinions with an **O**, and the **one** combination of fact *and* opinion with an **F+O**.

_O_ 1. Local TV news shows devote too much coverage to violent crimes, accidents, and fires.

> Some may feel that there is not enough coverage of these stories.

_F_ 2. The percentage of people who get their news from the Internet is rising, while the percentage of broadcast-news viewers is declining.

> This fact can be confirmed by looking at statistics on where people get their news.

_O_ 3. High-school students should be required to study a foreign language.

> The word *should* signals that this is an opinion.

Item 4:
This fact can be verified through research on the use of Latin from the Roman Empire to the present.

_F_ 4. Although it is now considered a "dead" language, Latin was the language of the Roman Empire and later, the Roman Catholic Church.

Item 5:
By verifying the facts about Cleveland and Taft through biographical information, one would confirm the fact that some American presidents were large men.

_F_ 5. Some American presidents were large men: Grover Cleveland's nieces and nephews called him "Uncle Jumbo," and William Howard Taft tipped the scales at 330 pounds.

_O_ 6. Both Grover Cleveland and William Howard Taft rank as above-average presidents.

> Some people may feel that these two men rank as average or below-average presidents.

_F_ 7. The core of a pencil is made out of graphite and clay, not lead.

> This fact can be confirmed by analyzing the core of a pencil.

_O_ 8. It is always better to use a ball-point pen rather than a pencil when taking notes in class.

> Some people may prefer a pencil for taking notes.

_F_ 9. In the late 1800s, it was common for American children under fifteen to work in mines, factories, and in the homes of the wealthy.

> This fact can be confirmed through research on child labor in the late 1800s.

_F+O_ 10. In the 20th century, child labor laws put a stop to such outrageous practices as having five-year-olds working sixteen-hour days.

> Research on child labor laws would confirm that the laws stopped the practice of sixteen-hour days. *Outrageous* is a value word indicating an opinion.

To the Instructor: In Tests 1 and 2, words indicating opinions are underlined in this *Instructor's Edition.*

(Continues on next page)

B. Identify facts with an **F**, opinions with an **O**, and the **one** combination of fact *and* opinion with an **F+O**.

_O_ 11. Cats are much easier to care for than dogs.

> Some people may feel that dogs are easier to care for.

_F_ 12. A cat once fell from a building's twentieth floor and suffered only a pelvic fracture.

> This fact can be confirmed by researching the story.

_O_ 13. The Model T Ford was the most significant invention of the twentieth century.

> Some people would say that other inventions—such as the computer—were more significant.

_F_ 14. In 1924, the Model T Ford could be purchased for $290.

> This can be confirmed by researching the price of cars in 1924.

_F_ 15. Bessie Smith, known as the "empress of the blues," was killed in a car accident in 1937.

> These two facts could be checked in biographical information on Bessie Smith.

_O_ 16. No singer alive today can sing the blues better than Bessie Smith did.

> Some people would feel that there are singers alive today who can sing the blues better than Bessie Smith.

_F_ 17. The first bathing suits for women were created in the mid-1800s.

> This fact can be checked by researching the history of women's bathing suits.

_F+O_ 18. Invented by a man, they were ridiculous-looking, high-necked costumes that included knee-length skirts, elbow-length sleeves, black stockings, and shoes.

> The facts about who invented these bathing suits and what they looked like can be verified by historical research. Whether or not the suits were ridiculous-looking is a matter of opinion.

_F_ 19. Once such suits became wet, they could weigh as much as the bather, and there is evidence they may have caused drowning on more than one occasion.

> These facts can be verified by historical research.

_O_ 20. Only a man could have invented something quite so impractical for women.

> Some people might think that it would be possible for a woman to invent something so impractical.

CRITICAL READING: Mastery Test 2 (Fact and Opinion)

A. Identify facts with an **F**, opinions with an **O**, and the **one** combination of fact *and* opinion with an **F+O**.

_F_ 1. The globefish keeps from being eaten by gulping so much water that it becomes too large to be swallowed by its enemies.

> This fact can be verified in scientific material.

_O_ 2. The globefish is nature's <u>strangest</u> creature.

> Some people may feel that other creatures are stranger.

Item 3:
Some people would argue that many comic strips are quite suitable reading for young children.

_O_ 3. Comic strips are <u>never suitable</u> reading for young children.

_F_ 4. In 1907, the San Francisco Chronicle began publishing the first daily comic strip—"Mr. Mutt," later named "Mutt and Jeff."

> This is a fact that can be checked in historical information on comic strips.

_F_ 5. Sushi, a Japanese dish, usually consists of rice and uncooked fish.

> This fact can be confirmed by researching recipes for sushi.

Item 6:
People who do not like the taste of sushi would disagree with this opinion.

_O_ 6. People who refuse to eat sushi are missing a <u>delicious</u> taste experience.

_O_ 7. Americans have become <u>much too concerned</u> about material success and owning things.

> Some people may feel that Americans' concern about material success and owning things is what makes America strong and powerful.

_F_ 8. Studies show that Americans use as much as 50 percent of their paychecks to pay back consumer loans.

> This statistic can be confirmed by reading the studies mentioned.

_F+O_ 9. For their clothing alone, consumers each year pay out millions of dollars, dollars that <u>should</u> go instead to such <u>worthy</u> projects as health care research and housing for the homeless.

_O_ 10. It is time for Americans to become <u>less selfish</u> and <u>contribute more</u> to the community.

> **Item 9:** Not everyone would agree that projects like these are where the money should go. The fact that consumers spend millions of dollars each year for clothing can be checked by looking up information on consumer spending.
>
> **Item 10:** Some people would disagree. They might argue that doing so would harm the economy.

(Continues on next page)

B. Identify facts with an **F**, opinions with an **O**, and the **one** combination of fact *and* opinion with an **F+O**.

_O_ 11. Organ transplantation is the <u>most important</u> medical achievement of the twentieth century.   Some people would argue that other medical achievements—such as the eradication of smallpox— are more important.

_F_ 12. Through transplants, more than two thousand people each year receive a heart that once belonged to someone else.

This fact can be confirmed in medical literature.

_F_ 13. In the Middle Ages it was commonly believed that the seat of human intelligence was the heart.   This fact can be confirmed in history books.

Item 14:
Whether or not the Middle Ages was the worst time to be alive is an opinion.
The fact   _F+O_ 14. The Middle Ages was the <u>worst</u> time to be alive; for example, in the
that
bubonic plague killed   mid-fourteenth century, bubonic plague killed millions of people.
millions of people in the mid-fourteenth century can be checked in history books or on the Internet.

_F_ 15. During the Middle Ages it was mainly the clergy that could read and write; most other people—including royalty—did not have these skills.

This factual information can be confirmed by researching the Middle Ages.

Item 16:   _F_ 16. Because of its location on the San Andreas Fault, San Francisco has
These facts
can be confirmed   experienced several major earthquakes in the 1800s.
by researching the history of San Francisco as well as geological information.

_O_ 17. Due to its <u>stunning</u> location and <u>magnificent</u> architecture, San Francisco is the <u>most beautiful</u> city in America.

The value words express opinions that some people might disagree with.

_F_ 18. Bram Stoker's *Dracula* begins with the story of Jonathan Harker, a young English lawyer hired by Count Dracula.

_F_ 19. After he arrives at Dracula's castle in Transylvania, Jonathan finds himself the prisoner of the Count, who he slowly realizes is a bloodthirsty vampire.

_O_ 20. From that point on, the reader will <u>find it impossible to stop reading</u> what is clearly the <u>most enjoyably scary horror story of all time</u>.

Items 18–19: The information about what happens in the book is factual. It can be confirmed by reading the book. (In this case, *bloodthirsty* is a factual description of the vampire.)

Item 20: Some people might find it easy to put the book down and might not find the book enjoyable. Others might think a novel by a different author—for example, Stephen King or Dean Koontz— deserves being called "the most enjoyably scary horror story of all time."

CRITICAL READING: Mastery Test 3 (Propaganda Techniques)

A. Each pair of items below illustrates a particular propaganda technique. On the line next to each pair, write the letter of the main technique being used.

The inventor and the champion racer are famous people selling a product.

__A__ 1. ● <u>The inventor of an artificial heart</u> encourages people at risk of heart disease to try a drug which lowers cholesterol.

● "I get each day off to a roaring start with Zip breakfast cereal," says <u>champion stock car racer Miles Leonard.</u>

    A. Testimonial   C. Bandwagon

    B. Plain folks   D. Name calling

__D__ 2. ● A <u>man in painter's overalls</u> is dipping his brush into a can of Olsen Paint. "Most of the week I'm president of Olsen Paint," he says. "On Saturdays, <u>I'm a housepainter myself.</u> So I know what people look for in a quality house paint."

The first item shows that the president of Olsen Paint is just an average guy. The second shows that Wilson's appeals to regular people like bank clerks and homemakers.

● "I shop for my family's wardrobe at Wilson's Department Store. I want good values, not necessarily designer labels," says Anna Hendricks, <u>bank clerk and homemaker.</u>

    A. Transfer   C. Bandwagon

    B. Name calling   D. Plain folks

__B__ 3. ● After six terms, the incumbent, Representative Lou Snark, is part of the <u>pampered Washington crowd, out of touch</u> with the people who elected him. Vote for Loretta Reese!

Reese calls Snark "pampered" and "out of touch." And who would want their dog to have artificial "fillers" when they can have wholesome, all-natural ingredients?

● Unlike some other brands of dog food which contain <u>artificial "fillers,"</u> Hearty Dog contains wholesome, all-natural ingredients.

    A. Transfer   C. Bandwagon

    B. Name calling   D. Plain folks

__D__ 4. ● The U.S. Heritage Committee has selected Bubble-O as the official soft <u>drink of the Heritage Celebration</u> to be held in the nation's capital this summer. Bubble-O: an important <u>part of your heritage.</u>

The first item encourages us to transfer our warm and patriotic feelings for our heritage to Bubble-O. The second item suggests that we, too, can be as beautiful and elegant as the model.

● A beautiful, <u>nearly nude model</u> lies on <u>blue satin sheets</u> in an ad for a skin care product containing cocoa butter.

    A. Plain folks   C. Bandwagon

    B. Glittering generalities   D. Transfer

To the Instructor: In Tests 3 and 4, words indicating a particular propaganda technique are underlined in this *Instructor's Edition.*

(Continues on next page)

_B_   5. ● A Pacekeeper pickup truck is climbing a dirt road in the desert. "Pacekeeper," says the announcer. "The perfect vehicle to drive you into a new century."

These statements tell us nothing about the products.

● Buy your next suit at West's Tall Men's Store, and you'll be walking tall.

A. Plain folks   C. Bandwagon
B. Glittering generalities D. Transfer

_C_   6. ● Don't miss out on the vacation cruise enjoyed by thousands of travelers. Ask your agent for details about Sea Fair's very popular tour of the Caribbean.

Both items suggest that you will be left behind if you don't do what they are urging.

● You can be part of the growing number of people who are saying "No" to drugs and "Yes" to achievement. Be part of the crowd that makes a difference.

A. Testimonial   C. Bandwagon
B. Plain folks   D. Glittering generalities

B. Below are descriptions of four actual ads. On each line, write the letter of the main propaganda technique that applies to the ad.

A	Bandwagon	D	Plain folks
B	Testimonial	E	Name calling
C	Transfer	F	Glittering generalities

_C_   7. An ad for Tide laundry detergent features a cute little girl wearing a star-spangled red, white, and blue dress. "Stay true to her reds, whites, blues, and everything in between," reads the ad.

_F_   8. An ad for Bermuda tourism proclaims: "Bermuda: Feel the love."

_A_   9. A TV commercial for the Showboat casino shows crowds of people enjoying themselves around various gaming tables and asks the question, "Showboat . . . who *doesn't* want to play?"

_B_   10. Actress Sally Field urges post-menopausal women to take Boniva to build strong, healthy bones.

Item 7: The company hopes we feel the same allegiance to Tide that we feel to the American flag.

Item 8: The statement tells us nothing about Bermuda as a vacation destination.

Item 9: There must be something wrong with you if you don't want to gamble at the Showboat.

Item 10: Our admiration for Sally Field should extend to Boniva.

CRITICAL READING: Mastery Test 4 (Propaganda Techniques)

A. Each pair of items below illustrates a particular propaganda technique. On the line next to each pair, write the letter of the main technique being used.

_B_ 1. ● An ad for NyQuil Cough Syrup says, "Unlike those cough medicines you take every four hours, NyQuil Cough is made to last through the night."

Both ads refer to their competitors' products in negative terms.

● Sal's Pizza is like the thick cardboard we use to wrap take-home orders of Cheesy Pizza. Eat Cheesy Pizza if you're a pizza lover; eat Sal's if you love cardboard.

  A. Glittering generalities   C. Testimonial
  B. Name calling   D. Plain folks

_D_ 2. ● A cable company advertises that more and more people are making the switch to its cable service.

In both cases, you will be left out if you don't do what everyone else is doing.

● A small group comes onto a crowded beach carrying buckets of Deep Southern brand friend chicken. Other people nearby notice the group, leave, and come back with buckets of Deep Southern fried chicken. Soon everyone on the beach is either eating Deep Southern or going to get some.

  A. Glittering generalities   C. Transfer
  B. Name calling   D. Bandwagon

_A_ 3. ● Try Choco-Chip Cookies—the cookies with goodness that doesn't quit.

The claims made about the cookie and the camera sound appealing, but offer no specific information.

● An Arnold Autofocus camera is the camera of your dreams. This delightful camera will make all your photography a pleasure. You'll love your new Arnold Autofocus.

  A. Glittering generalities   C. Transfer
  B. Name calling   D. Bandwagon

_C_ 4. ● We cannot tell a lie—we honor America's presidents with beauty and savings. Come to Cherry Tree Carpets to see the amazing quality and discounts at our Presidents' Day Sale.

The carpet company associates itself with patriotism and with George Washington's legendary honesty. The cigarettes associate themselves with being hip and graceful.

● An ad for a brand of cigarettes shows a hip young couple performing a graceful dance move.

  A. Glittering generalities   C. Transfer
  B. Name calling   D. Bandwagon

(Continues on next page)

_____D_____ 5. ● "Out here in <u>farm country</u>, I work <u>hard and live simply</u>," says a farmer. "I don't <u>look for fancy</u>, but I do require quality. That's why, for <u>everyday down-home</u> toughness, I drive a Wellbilt truck."

The trucks appeal to everyday country people. And the mayoral candidate drops his daughter off at public school just like everybody else.

● A big-city mayoral candidate is shown <u>dropping off his daughter at the public school</u> she attends in that city.

    A. Glittering generalities   C. Testimonial
    B. Name calling   D. Plain folks

_____C_____ 6. ● <u>Movie star Brad Clooney</u> says, "I think this is the most entertaining movie I've ever been part of."

The movie star and the television actress use their fame to influence people to listen to their messages.

● <u>Television actress Tamara Archer</u> encourages overweight women to try the diet system that helped her shed seventy-five pounds.

    A. Glittering generalities   C. Testimonial
    B. Name calling   D. Plain folks

B. Below are descriptions of four actual ads. On each line, write the letter of the main propaganda technique that applies to the ad.

A	Bandwagon	D	Plain folks
B	Testimonial	E	Name calling
C	Transfer	F	Glittering generalities

_____F_____ 7. What is it about owning a Weber grill that can make you <u>wear your heart on your sleeve</u>? <u>Everything</u>. From the thoughtful design to the careful construction to <u>the way it treats your $40 filets</u>, it all adds up to <u>an ownership experience as beautiful as the grill itself</u>. That's why <u>millions of people around the world love their Weber grills</u>.

None of these impressive-sounding words tells us anything specific about the grill.

_____F_____ 8. A picture of a new-model Jeep simply states, "Jeep: <u>There's only one</u>."

_____C_____ 9. In an ad for Samsung televisions, a <u>beautiful young woman in a slinky black dress</u> looks at a television which features Samsung's new black-screen technology.

_____B_____ 10. Actor James Brolin is shown with a bottle of Flex-a-min dietary supplement. He says, "I have a pretty active lifestyle, and I can't let sore, stiff joints slow me down. So I take Flex-a-min every day. It works for me."

Item 8:   Unless the ad means that they have built only one of these vehicles, it tells us nothing about the Jeep.

Item 9:   Owning one of these TV sets will make you beautiful and slinky—or, if you're male, will attract a beautiful and slinky woman to you.

Item 10: If Flex-a-min is good enough for the famous James Brolin, it must be good enough for everybody else.

CRITICAL READING: Mastery Test 5 (Errors in Reasoning)

A. Each pair of items below illustrates a particular error in reasoning. On the line next to each pair, write the letter of the logical fallacy contained in both items. Choose from the three fallacies shown in the box below.

> A **Circular reasoning** *(a statement repeats itself rather than providing a real supporting reason to back up an argument)*
>
> B **Personal attack** *(ignores the issue under discussion and concentrates instead on the character of the opponent)*
>
> C **Straw man** *(an argument is made by claiming an opponent holds an extreme position and then opposing that extreme position)*

Item 1: The son's dropping out of college does not make the father's views on higher education worthless. And being an atheist has nothing to do with how good a math teacher Jones is.

_B_ 1. ● Governor Donovan's views on higher education are worthless. His own son dropped out of college.

● Ms. Jones is an atheist and should not be hired as a math teacher.

Item 2: Both items claim extreme positions. It is unlikely that Fred doesn't care if terrorists attack us. And it is unlikely that establishing the halfway house will result in dangerous psychopaths roaming the streets.

_C_ 2. ● My neighbor Fred didn't support our invasion of Iraq. He obviously doesn't care if the terrorists attack us again.

● A local association wants to establish a halfway house for former mental patients in our neighborhood. But the neighbors oppose the idea; they say they don't want dangerous psychopaths roaming our streets.

_A_ 3. ● Ronald Reagan was a great president because he was so effective in office.

● The government should raise the minimum wage because the minimum wage today is entirely too low.

_B_ 4. ● Our congressman supports gay rights. How can he dare consider himself a Christian?

● I would never vote for Sarah Ratcliffe for mayor. Her own daughter was convicted of drinking and driving.

_A_ 5. ● People should not wear fur coats because it's the wrong thing to do.

● Football is fun to watch because it's such an enjoyable game.

Item 3: All great presidents are effective in office; we still don't know *why* Reagan was a great president. And, in effect, saying the minimum wage is too low and saying it should be raised are the same thing.

Item 4: Some Christians support gay rights. The daughter's conviction has nothing to do with Ratcliff's qualifications to be mayor.

Item 5: By definition, if something is wrong, people should not do it. Saying that football is fun is the same as saying that it is enjoyable.

(Continues on next page)

B. In the space provided, write the letter of the fallacy contained in each pair of arguments. Choose from the three fallacies shown in the box below.

> A   False cause *(the argument assumes that the order of events alone shows cause and effect)*
>
> B   False comparison *(the argument assumes that two things being compared are more alike than they really are)*
>
> C   Either-or *(the argument assumes that there are only two sides to a question)*

Item 6: Some doctors who get their degrees overseas are good— and some who get their degrees in the U.S. are bad. Some careers allow one to earn a decent living *and* help fellow human beings.

_C_   6. ● Is he a good doctor, or did he get his medical degree overseas?

● Young people must choose between a career that will help their fellow human beings and one that will earn them a decent living.

_B_   7. ● Back in my day, private-school teachers were allowed to give pupils who misbehaved a good whack with a ruler, so I don't see why teachers today can't do the same.

● Children are like flowers—you only have to feed them and let them have plenty of sunshine, and they'll grow up hardy and beautiful.

_A_   8. ● My son is failing algebra. Evidently his teacher, Mr. Williamson, isn't doing a good job.

● A month after the president took office, the stock market went into a tailspin. I don't think he knows the first thing about managing the economy.

_C_   9. ● Are you going bar-hopping with us, or are you going to chicken out?

● You'll either have to get a good job soon or face the fact that you'll never be successful.

_A_ 10. ● Ever since the new mayor took office, our town has had a string of burglaries. He must be soft on crime.

● The day Rosa wore her pink crystal bracelet, she finished first in the 100-meter run. Now she plans to wear that bracelet every time she races.

Item 7: There are many differences between what was considered all right "back in my day" and what is considered all right today. There are many differences between children and flowers that make the comparison false.

Item 8: There could be many reasons the student is failing algebra—such as not studying for tests. There are many factors that influence the economy much more than the president can.

Item 9: There can be reasons for not going bar-hopping besides chickening out. It is possible to be successful without getting a good job right now.

Item 10: The new mayor's stand on crime may have little relation to the string of burglaries. It is unlikely that the pink bracelet caused Rosa to win the race.

CRITICAL READING: Mastery Test 6 (Errors in Reasoning)

A. Each pair of items below illustrates a particular error in reasoning. On the line next to each pair, write the letter of the logical fallacy contained in both items. Choose from the three fallacies shown in the box below.

> A **Circular reasoning** (*a statement repeats itself rather than providing a real supporting reason to back up an argument*)
>
> B **Personal attack** (*ignores the issue under discussion and concentrates instead on the character of the opponent*)
>
> C **Straw man** (*an argument is made by claiming an opponent holds an extreme position and then opposing that extreme position*)

Item 1: It is likely that there are women and minorities who are extremely qualified. It is unlikely that Anthony does not care if gangs trash his neighborhood.

_C_ 1.
- George wants the firm to hire more women and minorities. He doesn't seem to care how qualified our workers are.
- Anthony is in favor of building the new sports arena just a few blocks from here. He must not care if gangs of roughnecks trash our neighborhood.

Item 2: Having once been treated for depression or being a homosexual does not weaken one's ability to serve in an elected office.

_B_ 2.
- I would never vote for Gary Blakely for Congress. At one time, he was being treated for depression.
- Councilman Hawkins is wholly unqualified to be elected mayor. He is a well-known homosexual.

Item 3: Saying that Aaron had great athletic ability and saying he was a great baseball player are essentially the same. By definition, being cheap is refusing to spend money on anything.

_A_ 3.
- Hank Aaron was one of the greatest baseball players of all time because he had great athletic ability.
- Todd is so cheap because he absolutely refuses to spend money on anything.

Item 4: The wife's nervous breakdown ignores Meyer's position on health care. The age of Green's clothing and car has nothing to do with his argument for raising the sales tax.

_B_ 4.
- Senator Meyer's position on health care is nonsense. I understand his own wife suffered a nervous breakdown.
- Who can take Jake Green's argument for raising the sales tax seriously? Judging by the age of his wardrobe and car, the man hasn't paid a sales tax himself in decades.

Item 5: It is unlikely that Rudolph wants to bankrupt the whole American auto industry. It is unlikely that the brother-in-law wants to make it harder for young people to get jobs.

_C_ 5.
- Governor Rudolph favors tightening fuel efficiency standards on new vehicles. What does he want to do, bankrupt the whole American auto industry?
- My brother-in-law is opposed to the building of a new Wal-Mart outside of town. Evidently he wants to make it even harder for our young people to get jobs.

(Continues on next page)

B. In the space provided, write the letter of the fallacy contained in each pair of arguments. Choose from the three fallacies shown in the box below.

> A **False cause** (*the argument assumes that the order of events alone shows cause and effect*)
>
> B **False comparison** (*the argument assumes that two things being compared are more alike than they really are*)
>
> C **Either-or** (*the argument assumes that there are only two sides to a question*)

Item 6: Eating Oreos is probably not the cause of the speaker's doing well on the finals. There could be many causes (besides Jeremy's pool) for the rash.

___A___ 6. ● I did well on the finals last semester after having Oreos for breakfast. I must remember to buy a bag of Oreos before this semester's finals begin.

● I got a rash a couple of days after swimming in Jeremy's pool. That's the last time I swim there.

Item 7: One can support good causes in ways other than buying Girl Scout cookies. There are other possibilities besides supporting stricter gun control laws and favoring shooting rampages.

___C___ 7. ● Mrs. Newhart didn't buy any Girl Scout cookies from my daughter. She must not believe in supporting a good cause.

● Do you support stricter gun control laws, or are you in favor of more tragedies such as Columbine and Virginia Tech?

Item 8: There are many differences between the past and the present that make these comparisons invalid.

___B___ 8. ● When I was a kid, we never took our dogs and cats to the vet, so I don't see why my children shell out a lot of money to take their pets there.

● Back in my day, our teachers never went out on strike, so I don't know why teachers today feel they need to do so.

Item 9: The plant may have died for many reasons—such as not being watered properly. And James's reading probably is not the cause of his needing glasses.

___A___ 9. ● The houseplant I bought at Eden's Garden Center died a month after I bought it. They must be selling sickly plants.

● James is always reading, and now he needs glasses. That's what too much reading will do to you.

___C___ 10. ● Unless you work out daily and carefully monitor your intake of fats, you're not really serious about staying in shape.

● Are you going to tell your girlfriend who's boss, or are you going to let her keep walking all over you?

> **Item 10:** There are other ways (besides daily workouts and monitoring fat intake) to be serious about staying in shape. And there are other ways of having a relationship besides somebody being the boss. For example, one could have a relationship based on mutual respect.

Part Two

Ten Reading Selections

1 The Yellow Ribbon
Pete Hamill

Preview

When is a yellow handkerchief like a pair of open arms? For the answer, read this selection, which first appeared in a *New York Post* newspaper column by Pete Hamill. The story became the inspiration for the popular song "Tie a Yellow Ribbon 'Round the Old Oak Tree." This moving article probably also suggests the origin of using yellow ribbons as a symbol of America's wish to see her troops return home safely.

Words to Watch

cocoon (2): protective covering
bluntness (13): abruptness
exaltation (22): joy

They were going to Fort Lauderdale, 1 the girl remembered later. There were six of them, three boys and three girls, and they picked up the bus at the old terminal on 34th Street, carrying sandwiches and wine in paper bags, dreaming of golden beaches and the tides of the sea as the gray cold spring of New York vanished behind them. Vingo was on board from the beginning.

As the bus passed through Jersey 2 and into Philly, they began to notice that Vingo never moved. He sat in front of the young people, his dusty face masking his age, dressed in a plain brown ill-fitting suit. His fingers were stained from cigarettes and he chewed

the inside of his lip a lot, frozen into some personal cocoon° of silence.

3   Somewhere outside of Washington, deep into the night, the bus pulled into a Howard Johnson's, and everybody got off except Vingo. He sat rooted in his seat, and the young people began to wonder about him, trying to imagine his life: Perhaps he was a sea captain, maybe he had run away from his wife, he could be an old soldier going home. When they went back to the bus, the girl sat beside him and introduced herself.

4   "We're going to Florida," the girl said brightly. "You going that far?"

5   "I don't know." Vingo said.

6   "I've never been there," she said. "I hear it's beautiful."

7   "It is," he said quietly, as if remembering something he had tried to forget.

8   "You live there?"

9   "I did some time there in the Navy. Jacksonville."

10   "Want some wine?" she said. He smiled and took the bottle of Chianti and took a swig. He thanked her and retreated again into his silence. After a while, she went back to the others, as Vingo nodded in sleep.

11   In the morning they awoke outside another Howard Johnson's, and this time Vingo went in. The girl insisted that he join them. He seemed very shy and ordered black coffee and smoked nervously, as the young people chattered about sleeping on the beaches. When they went back on the bus, the girl sat with Vingo again, and after a while, slowly and painfully and with great hesitation, he began to tell his story. He had been in jail in New York for the last four years, and now he was going home.

12   "Four years!" the girl said. "What did you do?"

13   "It doesn't matter," he said with quiet bluntness°. "I did it and I went to jail. If you can't do the time, don't do the crime. That's what they say and they're right."

14   "Are you married?"

15   "I don't know."

16   "You don't know?" she said.

17   "Well, when I was in the can I wrote to my wife," he said. "I told her, I said, Martha, I understand if you can't stay married to me. I told her that. I said I was gonna be away a long time, and that if she couldn't stand it, if the kids kept askin' questions, if it hurt her too much, well, she could just forget me. Get a new guy—she's a wonderful woman, really something—and forget about me. I told her she didn't have to write me or nothing. And she didn't. Not for three and a half years."

18   "And you're going home now, not knowing?"

19   "Yeah," he said shyly. "Well, last week, when I was sure the parole was coming through I wrote her. I told her that if she had a new guy, I understood. But if she didn't, if she would take me back, she should let me know. We used to live in this town, Brunswick, just before

Jacksonville, and there's a great big oak tree just as you come into town, a very famous tree, huge. I told her if she would take me back, she should put a yellow handkerchief on the tree, and I would get off and come home. If she didn't want me, forget it, no handkerchief, and I'd keep going on through."

20   "Wow," the girl said. "Wow."

21   She told the others, and soon all of them were in it, caught up in the approach of Brunswick, looking at the pictures Vingo showed them of his wife and three children, the woman handsome in a plain way, the children still unformed in a cracked, much-handled snapshot. Now they were twenty miles from Brunswick and the young people took over window seats on the right side, waiting for the approach of the great oak tree. Vingo stopped looking, tightening his face into the ex-con's mask, as if fortifying himself against still another disappointment. Then it was ten miles, and then five, and the bus acquired a dark hushed mood, full of silence, of absence, of lost years, of the woman's plain face, of the sudden letter on the breakfast table, of the wonder of children, of the iron bars of solitude.

22   Then suddenly all of the young people were up out of their seats, screaming and shouting and crying, doing small dances, shaking clenched fists in triumph and exaltation°. All except Vingo.

23   Vingo sat there stunned, looking at the oak tree. It was covered with yellow handkerchiefs, twenty of them, thirty of them, maybe hundreds, a tree that stood like a banner of welcome blowing and billowing in the wind, turned into a gorgeous yellow blur by the passing bus. As the young people shouted, the old con slowly rose from his seat, holding himself tightly, and made his way to the front of the bus to go home.

Basic Skill Questions

Vocabulary in Context

___A___ 1. In the sentence below, the word *fortifying* (fôr′tə-fī′ĭng) means

A. strengthening.
B. watching.
C. hurrying.
D. losing.

If he is expecting a disappointment, he would strengthen himself to prepare for it.

"Vingo stopped looking, tightening his face into the ex-con's mask, as if fortifying himself against still another disappointment." (Paragraph 21)

_B_ 2. In the excerpt below, the word *acquired* (ə-kwīrd′) means

A. needed.

B. took on.

C. stopped.

D. lost.

As the people anticipated reaching the tree, the bus would take on a hushed mood.

"Then it was ten miles, and then five, and the bus acquired a dark hushed mood...." (Paragraph 21)

Central Point and Main Ideas

Answer A is not supported. Answer B covers only paragraph 13. Answer C covers only paragraphs 14–21; it overlooks the outcome.

_D_ 3. Which sentence best expresses the main idea of this selection?

A. Prison sentences can ruin marriages.

B. If you commit a crime, you must pay for it.

C. Vingo did not know what to expect.

D. Vingo returned from prison to find that his wife still loved him.

Answers A and D cover only sentence 1. Answer C covers only sentence 2.

_B_ 4. Which sentence best expresses the main idea of paragraph 3?

A. The bus stopped at a Howard Johnson's.

B. The young people began to be curious about Vingo.

C. Vingo might have been a sea captain.

D. Everyone got off the bus except Vingo.

Supporting Details

_F_ 5. TRUE OR FALSE? Vingo felt he should not have been put in prison.

See paragraph 13.

Transitions

_B_ 6. The relationship between the two sentences below is one of

A. time.

B. contrast.

C. comparison.

D. illustration.

Vingo is contrasting the two possible reactions by his wife.

"... I told her that if she had a new guy, I understood. But if she didn't, if she would take me back, she should let me know." (Paragraph 19)

_D_ 7. The transition words *as, when, after, now,* and *then,* which Hamill uses throughout this selection, all signal

A. cause and effect.

B. examples.

C. contrast.

D. time.

Because narratives tell about events in the order in which they happen, they use many time signals.

___B___ 8. The relationship expressed in the phrase "a tree that stood <u>like</u> a banner of welcome" (paragraph 23) is one of

    A. contrast.

    B. comparison.

    C. cause and effect.

    D. time.

> The tree with handkerchiefs is being compared to a banner. *Like* is a comparison word.

Patterns of Organization

___C___ 9. The main pattern of organization of paragraph 2 is

    A. cause and effect.

    B. comparison and/or contrast.

    C. list of items.

    D. time order.

> The items listed are details that describe Vingo.

___D___ 10. The main pattern of organization of the entire selection is

    A. cause and effect.

    B. comparison and/or contrast.

    C. list of items.

    D. time order.

> Narratives tell about events in the order in which they happened.

Advanced Skill Questions

Inferences

___C___ 11. We can infer that the young people were going to Florida

    A. on business.

    B. to visit relatives.

    C. on vacation.

    D. to get married.

> Hamill states that the young people were "dreaming of golden beaches and the tides of the sea" (paragraph 1).

___B___ 12. The author implies that Vingo thought

    A. he would someday be in prison again.

    B. there might be no yellow handkerchief on the tree.

    C. his wife was wrong for not writing to him in prison.

    D. his wife was sure to want him back.

> Vingo's nervousness and the fact that his wife hadn't written imply the possibility that she might not want him back.

___T___ 13. TRUE OR FALSE? The statement that Vingo "rose from his seat, holding himself tightly" (paragraph 23) implies that Vingo was trying to contain his emotions.

> We can make this inference based on the "message" Vingo has just received.

_C_ 14. By telling us that the picture of Vingo's family was a "cracked, much-handled snapshot," the author implies that
   A. Vingo didn't know how to take good care of photos.
   B. the pictures were not really of Vingo's family.
   C. Vingo had looked at the snapshot a great deal while in jail.
   D. the photo was relatively new.

For the four years that Vingo was in jail, the photo may have been his only concrete connection with his family.

Purpose and Tone

_C_ 15. The main purpose of "The Yellow Ribbon" is to

Answers A and B are not supported.

   A. inform readers that a convict's life can be rebuilt after prison.
   B. persuade readers to avoid a life of crime.
   C. entertain readers with a heartwarming story.

_C_ 16. In paragraphs 17 through 21, the author's tone becomes increasingly
   A. bitter.
   B. amused.
   C. suspenseful.
   D. disbelieving.

The author chooses details that increase suspense about whether there will be a yellow handkerchief on the oak tree.

Argument

_A_ 17. Which of the following points is well supported by the evidence below?

Nothing in the sentence suggests the points in answers B, C, and D.

   A. Vingo was nervous about something.
   B. Vingo was on the verge of a nervous breakdown.
   C. Vingo had a hostile personality.
   D. Vingo disliked young people.

"[Vingo's] fingers were stained from cigarettes and he chewed the inside of his lip a lot, frozen into some personal cocoon of silence." (Paragraph 2)

_C_ 18. Which statement does **not** support the following point?

The point in answer C would be a reason for Vingo's family to reject him.

Point: Vingo deserved the yellow handkerchiefs.

   A. He admitted his mistake.
   B. He paid for his crime by serving four years in jail.
   C. He probably caused his wife and children a lot of pain and embarrassment.
   D. He seemed to regret causing his wife pain.

Critical Reading

_D_ 19. In telling this narrative, Hamill
  A. stresses his own opinions.
  B. leaves out any of Vingo's opinions.
  C. reveals the bus driver's opinions.
  D. reveals through the young people's actions how they feel about Vingo.

This is reflected in paragraphs 3–22. It is particularly emphasized in paragraphs 20–22.

_C_ 20. Judging by the first sentence of the selection, Hamill got some facts for this nonfiction narrative by
  A. observing everything as a passenger on the bus ride.
  B. only imagining what might have happened on such a ride.
  C. interviewing at least one passenger.
  D. using a tape recording of the bus ride.

The words the girl remembered later suggest that Hamill talked with her sometime after the events of the narrative occurred.

Summarizing

Following is an incomplete summary of "The Yellow Ribbon." In the space provided, write the letter (A, B, or C) of the item below that best completes the summary.

_B_

Answer A does not include paragraphs 22–23. Answer C does not include paragraphs 20–23.

A man named Vingo had just been released from prison and was on a bus headed home. Some young people were also on the bus, and they got Vingo to tell his story. He said he had written to his wife when he went to prison to explain he would understand if she found another man. He hadn't heard from her since but still loved her very much. So he recently wrote to her, telling her to put a yellow handkerchief on a well-known oak tree in town if she wanted him to come home. If the handkerchief wasn't on the tree, he wouldn't get off the bus there. . . .

  A. Vingo showed pictures of his wife and children to the young people, who got caught up in waiting to see the oak tree. As the bus got closer to Vingo's hometown, the bus became quiet and filled with suspense.
  B. The young people got caught up in Vingo's situation. After a tense ride to his hometown, he and his fellow travelers finally got his wife's answer: not one, but scores of handkerchiefs fluttering on the tree.
  C. Vingo would just continue on the bus to Florida, which is where the young people were going. He understood that while he was in prison, his wife might have started a new life for herself and their children.

Discussion Questions

1. According to the information in the selection, what is Vingo's attitude toward his wife?

2. Has Vingo assumed responsibility for his crime, in your opinion?

3. While there is much we don't learn about Vingo in this very short narrative, Hamill does provide us with clues to some important aspects of his personality. What evidence is there that he is a decent man, a person who we could feel deserves a second chance?

4. Many people are thrilled, some even to tears, by this story. Why do you think "The Yellow Ribbon" has such a powerful effect on readers?

Note: Writing assignments for this selection appear on page 607.

Check Your Performance   THE YELLOW RIBBON

Activity	Number Right	Points	Score
Basic Skill Questions			
Vocabulary in Context (2 items)	_____	× 4 =	_____
Central Point and Main Ideas (2 items)	_____	× 4 =	_____
Supporting Details (1 item)	_____	× 4 =	_____
Transitions (3 items)	_____	× 4 =	_____
Patterns of Organization (2 items)	_____	× 4 =	_____
Advanced Skill Questions			
Inferences (4 items)	_____	× 4 =	_____
Purpose and Tone (2 items)	_____	× 4 =	_____
Argument (2 items)	_____	× 4 =	_____
Critical Reading (2 items)	_____	× 4 =	_____
Summarizing (1 item)	_____	× 20 =	_____
		TOTAL SCORE =	_____ %

Enter your total score into the **Reading Performance Chart: Ten Reading Selections** on the inside back cover.

2 The Certainty of Fear
Audra Kendall

Preview

What are you afraid of? Were your fears different five years ago? According to this essay, every stage of life brings its particular fears. Do you fit the pattern?

Words to Watch

provocation (6): irritation
conspicuous (14): noticeable
intoxicated (16): drunk
obsessed (17): constantly preoccupied
turmoil (19): confusion
priorities (21): what a person considers most important
frailty (23): physical weakness

1 I had all the usual childhood fears. I couldn't go to sleep unless the light in my bedroom closet was on. I dreaded that someday when my mother was distracted, Crazy Betty (our local small-town oddball) would grab me in the grocery store. On the hottest summer nights, my feet had to be wrapped tightly in my bedsheets; if one of them hung bare over the side of the bed, who knew what might grab it in its cold, slimy claw?

2 But all other frights paled before the Great Fear, the *Titanic* of my childhood terrors. That fear—and I admit, I feel a tightening in my stomach typing the words even today—was that something would happen to Monk-Monk.

3   Looking at Monk-Monk today, you wouldn't see what I see. You'd see a torn, discolored sock monkey, very much past his prime, stuffing leaking from his stumpy tail, holes on his sock-body inexpertly stitched up with thread that doesn't match. I see my dearest childhood friend, my companion of a thousand nights. When I was only two and very ill, an aunt made him for me and delivered him to the hospital. I bonded with him fiercely and rarely let him out of my sight. When no one else was around, Monk-Monk played endless games with me, soaked up my tears, and listened to my secrets.

4   And then Uncle Ken came to visit. I didn't know Uncle Ken well, and I didn't like him very much. I had the feeling he didn't really like me, either. He clearly thought it was pretty silly that a big first-grader was dragging a sock monkey around, and he teased me by saying he thought he'd take Monk-Monk home to Ohio with him. I clutched Monk-Monk more tightly.

5   I was at school a few days later when Uncle Ken left. When I came home, I couldn't find Monk-Monk anywhere. I can hardly describe the depths of my panic. I don't think I cried; my terror was beyond that. I could barely breathe. My thoughts raced like a wild animal in a tiny cage. Where was Monk-Monk? What had Uncle Ken done to him? Was he safe somewhere, or had Uncle Ken (and this thought made my heart nearly stop) thrown him out the car window? Was Monk-Monk lying in a weedy strip along the interstate, lonely and cold, never to be loved again?

6   When we found Monk-Monk wedged behind the sofa (could Uncle Ken really have been mean enough to do that? I never found out), I was limp with relief. For days afterwards I was shaken, crying at the least provocation°.

7   As far as I can remember, that near-loss of Monk-Monk was my first encounter with real, deep-down fear. I felt the threatened loss of something precious to me. And that, I think, is the essence of fear—the threat of loss.

8   Small children fear the loss of a favorite toy. The fears of adolescents are different. Above almost anything, adolescents fear losing their cool—looking "stupid." They will risk almost anything in order to maintain the illusion that they are cool, composed and in control.

9   Let me give you an example. A friend of mine had the opportunity to work in Florence, Italy, for a few months. While he was gone, he arranged for his two teenage sons to visit him for a week. The excited boys arrived at the airport and checked in. After sitting down to wait for their flight, one nudged the other. "Look at the tickets," he told his brother. "They don't say 'Florence.'" Indeed, the tickets did not list Florence as the destination. They said "Firenze."

10   Now, it so happens that Firenze is the Italian name for Florence, so everything was fine. But the boys didn't know that. They thought that through some error, they were being put on the wrong plane for the wrong destination.

11   So what did they do?

12   Nothing.

13   At the appointed time, they unhappily boarded the plane for Firenze, sat down, and worried silently for six hours that they were going to end up in, oh, maybe South America. Possibly Asia. They had no idea. But the thought of admitting to a ticket agent that they didn't know what "Firenze" meant was more terrifying than the prospect of being dumped, alone, in a strange city on an unknown continent.

14   The fear of being conspicuous° does not usually land teenagers on jet airplanes bound for unknown destinations. But for many adolescents, it rules their daily lives. Such fear is rooted in the enormous self-consciousness that afflicts many adolescents. Psychologist David Elkind has come up with what he calls the "Imaginary Audience Theory" to help explain this period of life.

15   During adolescence, Elkind says, kids are changing so much so fast (physically, mentally, and emotionally) that they become intensely self-centered. It is literally difficult for them to remember that other individuals have their own lives, thoughts, and feelings, and that they are not focusing their attention on the adolescents. According to Elkind, the adolescent feels as though he or she is on an enormous stage before a watchful audience that is noticing every aspect of his or her behavior. As a result, the adolescent is terrified of doing or saying something that will attract scorn or criticism. As a result, we end up with the teenager whose life is "ruined" by an outbreak of acne; an adolescent who won't leave the house on a bad hair day, or the teen who refuses to return to school after making an embarrassing slip during a speech.

16   In general, typical adolescent fears don't do great harm. Kids mature and eventually realize a moment's embarrassment isn't that big a deal, and that, in fact, most people aren't paying much attention to them at all. But the fear of being conspicuous can have serious, even tragic results. Adolescents can be so fearful of being criticized that they sometimes go along with the crowd when it is in their best interests not to. Teens get into cars with obviously intoxicated° drivers; they go along with the crowd on a shoplifting expedition; they engage in risky sexual behavior, etc., in large part because they are afraid to speak up and risk the scorn of the "audience."

17   In midlife, we generally become more confident and less obsessed° with what others are thinking of us. But underneath that veneer of confidence, a new kind of fear grips many middle-aged people. That fear has been expressed in timeless fashion by the Italian poet Dante in his famous poem *The Inferno:* "In the middle of the road, I found myself in a dark wood, with no clear path through."

18   The key word here is "middle." As people enter middle age, they face the unsettling fact that their lives are halfway over. They are no longer youngsters, looking ahead at decades filled with unlimited potential. In looking back at what they have accomplished, many people feel unsatisfied. They may not

have achieved the career success they had hoped for. They fear they do not have time to reach goals that they had once dreamed of. They become critical of their own aging bodies. As their parents die and their children grow up and leave home, they feel adrift, no longer certain of their roles in life. Frightening thoughts press in: "My life is heading downhill. I'm running out of time."

19 The result of all this inner turmoil° is what is often termed a midlife crisis. Movies and sitcoms often present such a crisis in tragicomic style: the middle-aged guy dumps his wife, dyes his hair, buys a sports car, and begins romancing a woman young enough to be his daughter. The middle-aged woman gets liposuction and a facelift and has an affair with a young personal trainer.

20 There is plenty of evidence that such behavior does occur. Many long-term marriages break up as a result of one or both partners' midlife crisis. The panicky feelings that can result from thinking "Is this all there is?" can make even a formerly happy marriage seem suffocating.

21 However, most midlife crises do not have such dramatic results. More typically, the midlife crisis is a time of inner exploration, of reconsidering one's priorities°. It may involve a period of depression, but, fortunately, most people emerge from a midlife crisis feeling relatively satisfied. They come to terms with the idea that youth and its promise are behind them, and learn to appreciate the perhaps quieter joys of mature life.

22 Those joys and a sense of certainty about life's priorities often carry over into the elderly years. Senior citizens' self-knowledge often allows them to state their opinions and explore new interests in a way they did not feel free to in their younger years.

23 But along with the relief from self-consciousness comes another set of fears for the elderly. Those fears center around the increasing frailty° of the body and the accompanying loss of independence.

24 Some years ago, a television ad featured an elderly woman saying, "Help! I've fallen and I can't get up." The ad became the punch line of many jokes, but the message was serious. Many elderly people report falling as their greatest fear. They are not simply concerned with the injury they might suffer. They worry that a fall might lead to being institutionalized, a step that many elderly people fear deeply. After a lifetime of independence and, often, of taking care of others, they dread the idea of being helpless, even a burden to their families.

25 As a result, many elderly people—especially after having suffered a fall or another injury—become increasingly reluctant to go out into the world to try new things and keep up with friends. Afraid of being hurt, they become hermit-like, staying within the confines of their homes. Ironically, this isolation and lack of exercise can actually hasten the dreaded loss of independence. Mental and physical activity are both

key elements in keeping elderly people in good health.

26   Benjamin Franklin once wrote, "In this world nothing is certain but death and taxes." Franklin might have added, "and fears." Every stage of life brings them; while we may say goodbye to childish fears, there are always others in the wings, waiting to take their place. By being aware of them, we can keep their dark shadows from adversely affecting our lives.

Basic Skill Questions

Vocabulary in Context

_B_ 1. In the excerpt below, the word *veneer* (və-nîr′) means
    A. center.
    B. thin layer.
    C. rusty surface.
    D. logic.

> If we seem confident but in fact feel fear, our confidence is just a thin layer on the surface.

"In midlife, we generally become more confident and less obsessed with what others are thinking of us. But underneath that veneer of confidence, a new kind of fear grips many middle-aged people." (Paragraph 17)

_B_ 2. In the excerpt below, the word *adversely* (ăd-vûrs′lē) means
    A. positively.
    B. negatively.
    C. happily.
    D. mildly.

> The dark shadows of fears can have a negative effect on a person's life.

". . . while we may say goodbye to childish fears, there are always others in the wings, waiting to take their place. By being aware of them, we can keep their dark shadows from adversely affecting our lives." (Paragraph 26)

Central Point and Main Ideas

_C_ 3. Which sentence best expresses the central point of the selection?
    A. It is impossible to be totally fearless.
    B. Many people allow their fears to negatively affect their behavior.
    C. People fear different things at different stages in their lives.
    D. Some people handle fear better than others.

> Answer A is not supported. Answer B covers only paragraphs 16, 20, and 25. Answer D covers only paragraphs 16 and 21.

_D_ 4. Which sentence best expresses the main idea of paragraph 16?

Answer A covers only sentence 1. Answer B covers only sentence 2. Answer C covers only the last sentence.

A. In general, typical adolescent fears don't do great harm.

B. Teenagers eventually realize that most people aren't paying much attention to them at all.

C. Some teens engaged in risky behavior such as getting into cars with drunken drivers, going on shoplifting expeditions, and engaging in risky sexual behavior.

D. Adolescent fear of criticism can have serious, even tragic results.

_B_ 5. Which sentence best expresses the main idea of paragraphs 17–21?

Answer A covers only the first sentence of paragraph 17. Answer C covers only part of paragraph 18. Answer D covers only part of paragraph 21.

A. In midlife, people generally become more confident and less obsessed with what others think of them.

B. The midlife period may involve fear, turmoil, crisis, and depression, but most people are able to emerge from it relatively satisfied.

C. Middle-aged people often fear that they're running out of time and experience a midlife crisis.

D. Some middle-aged people learn to appreciate the quiet joys of mature life.

Supporting Details

_A_ 6. According to the selection, the thing that adolescents fear most of all is

A. looking "stupid."   See paragraph 8.

B. flying to overseas destinations.

C. appearing to be self-conscious.

D. engaging in risky behavior.

_B_ 7. According to the selection, elderly people

A. are better off leading a quiet existence.   See paragraph 25.

B. need both mental and physical activity to stay healthy.

C. sometimes feel relief when they are institutionalized.

D. have less to fear than adolescents and middle-aged people.

Transitions

_D_ 8. The sentences below expresses a relationship of

A. contrast.   C. addition.

B. cause and effect.   D. time.

"I was at school a few days later _when_ Uncle Ken left. _When_ I came home, I couldn't find Monk-Monk anywhere." (Paragraph 5)

When is a time transition. At the time Uncle Ken left, the author was at school. Then, at the time the author came home from school, she couldn't find her sock monkey.

_____ A ____ 9. The relationship of the second sentence below to the first is one of

The two sentences
contrast the greater
confidence we feel
during midlife with
the new kind of fear
it brings.

A. contrast.   C. addition.
B. cause and effect.   D. time.

> "In midlife, we generally become more confident and less obsessed with
> what others are thinking of us. But underneath that veneer of confidence,
> a new kind of fear grips many middle-aged people." (Paragraph 17)

Patterns of Organization

_____ B ____ 10. Paragraphs 9–14

Before the term is
introduced, the author
presents an example
of how it affects
adolescents.

A. define the term "Imaginary Audience Theory."
B. illustrate the term "Imaginary Audience Theory."
C. contrast American teenagers with teenagers in other parts of the
   world.
D. list reasons why two teenage boys were reluctant to admit to a ticket
   agent that they didn't know what "Firenze" meant.

_____ C ____ 11. The main pattern of organization in paragraph 15 is

A. list of items.
B. contrast.
C. cause and effect.
D. time order.

The cause and effect words *as a result* are
used twice. *Cause 1:* adolescent feels on stage.
Effect 1: adolescent terrified of attracting criticism.
Cause 2: adolescent terrified of attracting criticism.
Effect 2: adolescent's life "ruined" by small events.

Advanced Skill Questions

Inferences

Uncle Ken's
teasing and the
possibility that he may
have hidden Monk-Monk
suggest these qualities.
Answers B, C, and D
are not supported.

_____ A ____ 12. On the basis of paragraphs 4–6, we can infer that Uncle Ken was

A. an insensitive, mean-spirited man.
B. kind-hearted, but silly.
C. wise to conclude that a first-grader should not be dragging around a
   sock monkey.
D. probably a child molester.

_____ D ____ 13. On the basis of paragraphs 20–21, we can infer that the author

See the final sentence of
paragraph 21. Answers
A, B, and C are not
supported.

A. strongly disapproves of middle-aged people who have affairs with
   younger partners.
B. respects middle-aged people who do new things, like taking up with
   younger partners, buying sports cars, and having plastic surgery.
C. is not yet middle-aged.
D. believes it is important for middle-aged people to learn to appreciate
   the quieter joys of mature life.

_A_ 14. Paragraph 26 suggests that

See the final sentence of paragraph 26. Answers B, C, and D are not supported.

A. recognizing our fears helps us to keep them from becoming crippling.

B. Ben Franklin was himself fearless.

C. all fears are childish.

D. it is possible, with effort, to become completely fearless.

Purpose and Tone

_A_ 15. The main purpose of this article is to

A. inform.

B. persuade.

C. entertain.

The article informs us about the fears experienced at different stages of life. As the final sentence indicates, making us aware of fears will help keep us from being adversely affected by them.

_D_ 16. The tone of the last paragraph of this article can be described as

A. pessimistic.

B. detached.

C. solemn.

D. encouraging.

By suggesting that these fears are manageable, the author sets an encouraging tone.

Argument

_C_ 17. Write the letter of the statement that is the point of the following argument. The other statements are support for that point.

Answers A, B, and D give examples of times when teenagers go along even though it is not in their best interests.

A. Teens sometimes get into cars with obviously intoxicated drivers.

B. Teens sometimes go along with the crowd on shoplifting expeditions.

C. Teens sometimes go along with the crowd when it is in their best interests not to.

D. Teens sometimes engage in risky sexual behavior, in large part because they are afraid to speak up and risk the scorn of the "audience."

_B_ 18. Write the letter of the statement that is the point of the following argument. The other statements are support for that point.

A. Small children fear the loss of a favorite toy.

B. Every stage of life has its own fears.

C. Adolescents fear losing their cool.

D. Elderly people fear the idea of being helpless.

Answers A, C, and D give examples of fears at three stages of life.

Critical Reading

_C_ 19. The following sentence is a statement of

A. fact.

B. opinion.

C. both fact and opinion.

The facts that the midlife crisis "may involve a period of depression" but that afterward, people feel "relatively satisfied" with their lives can be verified by reading the results of research on the midlife crisis. The word *fortunately* expresses the author's opinion of the second fact.

"[The midlife crisis] may involve a period of depression, but, fortunately, most people emerge from a midlife crisis feeling relatively satisfied." (Paragraph 21)

_C_ 20. An adolescent who taunts another by telling him that he is a "chicken" unless he joins a shoplifting expedition is illustrating the fallacy of

A. straw man.

B. circular reasoning.

C. either-or.

D. false cause.

There may be other reasons for not joining the shoplifting expedition besides lacking courage—for example, the idea that shoplifting is morally wrong.

Mapping

Complete the map of the selection by filling in the four missing major details.

Wording of answers may vary.

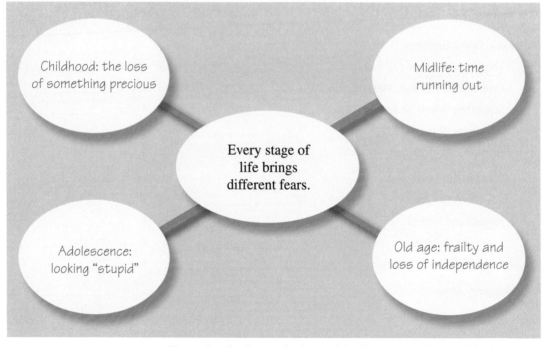

The major details are the fears of the four stages discussed in the article. Childhood—see paragraph 7. Adolescence—see paragraph 8. Midlife—see paragraph 18. Old age—see paragraph 23.

Discussion Questions

1. Did you, like the author, have a beloved toy or doll when you were a small child? Why was it so special to you? How would you have responded if you had lost it?

2. What do you think of psychologist David Elkind's "Imaginary Audience Theory" of adolescence? Did you feel the kind of self-consciousness he describes when you were an adolescent? Do you observe that kind of behavior in other teens?

3. Have you observed someone going through what seemed to be a midlife crisis? What behaviors did you notice?

4. The author writes, "And that, I think, is the essence of fear—the threat of loss." Do you agree with her? What are some examples you can think of in which fears are caused by the threat of loss?

Note: Writing assignments for this selection appear on page 608.

Check Your Performance   THE CERTAINTY OF FEAR

Activity	Number Right	Points	Score
Basic Skill Questions			
Vocabulary in Context (2 items)	_____	× 4 =	_____
Central Point and Main Ideas (3 items)	_____	× 4 =	_____
Supporting Details (2 items)	_____	× 4 =	_____
Transitions (2 items)	_____	× 4 =	_____
Patterns of Organization (2 items)	_____	× 4 =	_____
Advanced Skill Questions			
Inferences (3 items)	_____	× 4 =	_____
Purpose and Tone (2 items)	_____	× 4 =	_____
Argument (2 items)	_____	× 4 =	_____
Critical Reading (2 items)	_____	× 4 =	_____
Mapping (4 items)	_____	× 5 =	_____
	TOTAL SCORE	=	_____%

Enter your total score into the **Reading Performance Chart: Ten Reading Selections** on the inside back cover.

3 Shame

Dick Gregory

Preview

When we receive help, most of us feel grateful. But what if the help is given in an inconsiderate way? In this autobiographical piece, the comedian and social activist Dick Gregory shows that the good intentions of a giver are not enough if they don't take the recipient's pride into account.

Words to Watch

light-complected (1): light-skinned
stoop (2): an outside stairway, porch, or platform at the entrance to a house
mackinaw (28): a short plaid coat or jacket
googobs (29): Gregory's slang for *gobs*, a large amount

1   I never learned hate at home, or shame. I had to go to school for that. I was about seven years old when I got my first big lesson. I was in love with a little girl named Helene Tucker, a light-complected° little girl with pigtails and nice manners. She was always clean and she was smart in school. I think I went to school then mostly to look at her. I brushed my hair and even got me a little old handkerchief. It was a lady's handkerchief, but I didn't want Helene to see me wipe my nose on my hand. The pipes were frozen again, there was no water in the house, but I washed my socks and shirt every night. I'd get a pot, and go over to Mister Ben's grocery store, and stick my pot down into his soda machine. Scoop out some chopped ice. By evening the ice melted to water for washing. I got sick a lot that winter because the fire would go out at night before the clothes were dry. In the morning I'd put them on, wet or dry, because they were the only clothes I had.

2   Everybody's got a Helene Tucker, a symbol of everything you want. I loved

her for her goodness, her cleanness, her popularity. She'd walk down my street and my brothers and sisters would yell, "Here comes Helene," and I'd rub my tennis sneakers* on the back of my pants and wish my hair wasn't so nappy and the white folks' shirt fit me better. I'd run out on the street. If I knew my place and didn't come too close, she'd wink at me and say hello. That was a good feeling. Sometimes I'd follow her all the way home, and shovel the snow off her walk and try to make friends with her Momma and her aunts. I'd drop money on her stoop° late at night on my way back from shining shoes in the taverns. And she had a Daddy, and he had a good job. He was a paper hanger.

3   I guess I would have gotten over Helene by summertime, but something happened in that classroom that made her face hang in front of me for the next twenty-two years. When I played the drums in high school it was for Helene and when I broke track records in college it was for Helene and when I started standing behind microphones and heard applause I wished Helene could hear it, too. It wasn't until I was twenty-nine years old and married and making money that I finally got her out of my system. Helene was sitting in that classroom when I learned to be ashamed of myself.

4   It was on a Thursday. I was sitting in the back of the room, in a seat with a chalk circle drawn around it. The idiot's seat, the troublemaker's seat.

5   The teacher thought I was stupid. Couldn't spell, couldn't read, couldn't do arithmetic. Just stupid. Teachers were never interested in finding out that you couldn't concentrate because you were so hungry, because you hadn't had any breakfast. All you could think about was noontime, would it ever come? Maybe you could sneak into the cloakroom and steal a bite of some kid's lunch out of a coat pocket. A bite of something. Paste. You can't really make a meal of paste, or put it on bread for a sandwich, but sometimes I'd scoop a few spoonfuls out of the big paste jar in the back of the room. Pregnant people get strange tastes. I was pregnant with poverty. Pregnant with dirt and pregnant with smells that made people turn away, pregnant with cold and pregnant with shoes that were never bought for me, pregnant with five other people in my bed and no Daddy in the next room, and pregnant with hunger. Paste doesn't taste too bad when you're hungry.

6   The teacher thought I was a troublemaker. All she saw from the front of the room was a little black boy who squirmed in his idiot's seat and made noises and poked the kids around him. I guess she couldn't see a kid who made noises because he wanted someone to know he was there.

7   It was on a Thursday, the day before the Negro payday. The eagle always flew on Friday.* The teacher was asking each

---

* All sneakers used to be called "tennis sneakers."

* In Gregory's day, ten-dollar bills were known as "eagles." On payday, people would have some ten-dollar bills to spend.

student how much his father would give to the Community Chest*. On Friday night, each kid would get the money from his father, and on Monday he would bring it to the school. I decided I was going to buy a Daddy right then. I had money in my pocket from shining shoes and selling papers, and whatever Helene Tucker pledged for her Daddy, I was going to top it. And I'd hand the money right in. I wasn't going to wait until Monday to buy me a Daddy.

8   I was shaking, scared to death. The teacher opened her book and started calling out names alphabetically.

9   "Helene Tucker?"

10   "My Daddy said he'd give two dollars and fifty cents."

11   "That's very nice, Helene. Very, very nice indeed."

12   That made me feel pretty good. It wouldn't take too much to top that. I had almost three dollars in dimes and quarters in my pocket. I stuck my hand in my pocket and held onto the money, waiting for her to call my name. But the teacher closed her book after she called on everybody else in the class.

13   I stood up and raised my hand.

14   "What is it now?"

15   "You forgot me."

16   She turned toward the blackboard. "I don't have time to be playing with you, Richard."

17   "My Daddy said he'd . . . ."

18   "Sit down, Richard, you're disturbing the class."

19   "My Daddy said he'd give . . . fifteen dollars."

20   She turned around and looked mad. "We are collecting this money for you and your kind, Richard Gregory. If your Daddy can give fifteen dollars you have no business being on relief*."

21   "I got it right now, I got it right now, my Daddy gave it to me to turn in today, my Daddy said . . . ."

22   "And furthermore," she said, looking right at me, her nostrils getting big and her lips getting thin and her eyes opening wide, "we know you don't have a Daddy."

23   Helene Tucker turned around, her eyes full of tears. She felt sorry for me. Then I couldn't see her too well because I was crying, too.

24   "Sit down, Richard."

25   And I always thought the teacher kind of liked me. She always picked me to wash the blackboard on Friday, after school. That was a big thrill, it made me feel important. If I didn't wash it, come Monday the school might not function right.

26   "Where are you going, Richard?"

27   I walked out of school that day, and for a long time I didn't go back very often. There was shame there.

28   Now there was shame everywhere. It seemed like the whole world had been inside that classroom, everyone had heard what the teacher had said, everyone had turned around and felt sorry for me. There was shame in going to the Worthy Boys Annual Christmas

---

* In Gregory's day, the charitable organization we call the United Way was known as the Community Chest.

* welfare

Dinner for you and your kind, because everybody knew what a worthy boy was. Why couldn't they just call it the Boys Annual Dinner, why'd they have to give it a name? There was shame in wearing the brown and orange and white plaid mackinaw° the welfare gave to three thousand boys. Why'd it have to be the same for everybody so when you walked down the street the people could see you were on relief? It was a nice warm mackinaw and it had a hood, and my Momma beat me and called me a little rat when she found out I stuffed it in the bottom of a pail full of garbage way over on Cottage Street. There was shame in running over to Mister Ben's at the end of the day and asking for his rotten peaches, there was shame in asking Mrs. Simmons for a spoonful of sugar, there was shame in running out to meet the relief truck. I hated that truck, full of food for you and your kind. I ran into the house and hid when it came. And then I started to sneak through alleys, to take the long way home so the people going into White's Eat Shop wouldn't see me. Yeah, the whole world heard the teacher that day, we all know you don't have a Daddy.

29   It lasted for a while, this kind of numbness. I spent a lot of time feeling sorry for myself. And then one day I met this wino in a restaurant. I'd been out hustling all day, shining shoes, selling newspapers, and I had googobs° of money in my pocket. Bought me a bowl of chili for fifteen cents, and a cheeseburger for fifteen cents, and a Pepsi for five cents, and a piece of chocolate cake for ten cents. That was a good meal. I was eating when this old wino came in. I love winos because they never hurt anyone but themselves.

30   The old wino sat down at the counter and ordered twenty-six cents' worth of food. He ate it like he really enjoyed it. When the owner, Mister Williams, asked him to pay the check, the old wino didn't lie or go through his pocket like he suddenly found a hole.

31   He just said: "Don't have no money."

32   The owner yelled: "Why in hell you come in here and eat my food if you don't have no money? That food cost me money."

33   Mister Williams jumped over the counter and knocked the wino off his stool and beat him over the head with a pop bottle. Then he stepped back and watched the wino bleed. Then he kicked him. And he kicked him again.

34   I looked at the wino with blood all over his face and I went over. "Leave him alone, Mister Williams. I'll pay the twenty-six cents."

35   The wino got up, slowly, pulling himself up to the stool, then up to the counter, holding on for a minute until his legs stopped shaking so bad. He looked at me with pure hate. "Keep your twenty-six cents. You don't have to pay, not now. I just finished paying for it."

36   He started to walk out, and as he passed me, he reached down and touched my shoulder. "Thanks, sonny, but it's too late now. Why didn't you pay it before?"

37   I was pretty sick about that. I waited too long to help another man.

Basic Skill Questions

Vocabulary in Context

_C_ 1. In the excerpt below, the word *pledged* (plĕjd) means

Each child has been asked how much his or her father would give, so Dick Gregory plans to top whatever amount Helene promises her father will give.

A. repeated.
B. studied.
C. promised to give.
D. brought home.

> "I had money in my pocket . . . and whatever Helene Tucker pledged for her Daddy, I was going to top it." (Paragraph 7)

_D_ 2. In the sentence below, the word *hustling* (hŭs′lĭng) means

Shining shoes and selling newspapers all day are examples of working energetically.

A. complaining.
B. relaxing.
C. studying hard.
D. working energetically.

> "I'd been out hustling all day, shining shoes, selling newspapers, and I had googobs of money in my pocket." (Paragraph 29)

Central Point and Main Ideas

_C_ 3. Which sentence best expresses the central point of this selection?

Answer A covers only paragraphs 1–3. Answer B covers only paragraph 28. Answer D covers only paragraphs 1–2 .

A. Dick Gregory had a long-standing crush on a girl named Helene Tucker.
B. The charity Gregory received was given in a way that labeled him as poor, which made him ashamed.
C. As both a receiver and a giver, young Gregory learned that how something is given is as important as what is given.
D. Gregory grew up in a poor and fatherless family.

_A_ 4. Which sentence best expresses the main idea of paragraph 2?

Answer B covers only the first sentence. Answer C covers only sentence 3. Answer D covers only the last sentence.

A. The author adored Helene Tucker, a symbol of everything he wanted.
B. Everybody has a symbol of everything he or she wants.
C. Helene Tucker made the author feel ashamed of his looks.
D. Unlike the author, Helene Tucker had a father.

_D_ 5. Which sentence best expresses the main idea of paragraph 5?

Answer A is incorrect because he does not say he liked to eat it, only that it doesn't taste bad if you are hungry. Answer B covers only sentences 1–3. Answer C covers only sentence 4.

A. Gregory liked to eat paste.
B. The teacher assumed that Gregory was stupid.
C. The teacher never realized that Gregory was hungry all the time.
D. The teacher assumed that Gregory was stupid and never realized that his poor work was the result of hunger.

Supporting Details

_B_ 6. After the teacher told him he was the type of person the Community

See the first two sentences of paragraph 29.

Chest helped and that he was fatherless, Gregory
A. never went back to school.
B. felt sorry for himself for a while.
C. stopped working.
D. felt that Helene Tucker did not feel sorry for him.

_C_ 7. As support for his central point, the author uses several

Gregory describes his early experiences in feeling shame.

A. statistics.
B. expert opinions.
C. personal experiences.
D. famous quotations.

Transitions

_D_ 8. The sentence below contains a(n)

Cause: The fire went out before the clothes dried. *Effect:* Gregory got sick a lot.

A. contrast signal.
B. comparison signal.
C. illustration signal.
D. cause-effect signal.

"I got sick a lot that winter <u>because</u> the fire would go out at night before the clothes were dry." (Paragraph 1)

_C_ 9. The relationship of the second sentence below to the first is one of

The teacher's action is contrasted with Gregory's expectation.

A. addition.
B. comparison.
C. contrast.
D. illustration.

"I stuck my hand in my pocket and held onto the money, waiting for her to call my name. <u>But</u> the teacher closed her book after she called on everybody else in the class." (Paragraph 12)

Patterns of Organization

_B_ 10. The main pattern of organization of paragraph 28 is

Gregory lists some of the situations in which he felt shame.

A. time order.
B. list of items.
C. definition and example.
D. contrast.

_B_ 11. The pattern of organization used in paragraphs 30–36 is
A. list of items.
B. time order.
C. cause and effect.
D. comparison.

In these paragraphs, the author narrates a series of events in the order in which they happened.

Advanced Skill Questions

Inferences

_T_ 12. TRUE OR FALSE? The author implies that the wino taught him a valuable
lesson.
Gregory implies this by including the wino story in his essay on shame and by stating, in the last sentence, the lesson he learned.

_C_ 13. In paragraph 5, the author implies that

Gregory writes that
teachers "weren't
interested in finding
out that you couldn't
concentrate because
you were so hungry."

    A. he is stupid.
    B. teachers understood him well.
    C. it was difficult for him to concentrate in school.
    D. the only way he ever got food was to steal it.

Purpose and Tone

_T_ 14. TRUE OR FALSE? One of the author's purposes is to inform readers of how
he learned the meaning of shame.   Gregory suggests this purpose in the
first two sentences of the selection.

_D_ 15. The word that best describes the tone of the last paragraph of the

Saying that he was
"pretty sick about"
waiting too long to help
the wino shows that he
feels ashamed.

selection is
    A. angry.   C. sentimental.
    B. objective.   D. ashamed.

Argument

_T_ 16. TRUE OR FALSE? The teacher's conclusion that Gregory was stupid did

See paragraph 5.

not take into account all the relevant evidence.

_A_ 17. Which evidence from the selection supports Gregory's statement that,

See paragraph 28.

after the school incident, he felt shame everywhere?
    A. Gregory stuffed the plaid mackinaw into a garbage can.
    B. Gregory was always chosen to wash the blackboards on Fridays.
    C. Helene Tucker's eyes were full of tears.
    D. Gregory wanted to pay for the wino's dinner.

Critical Reading

_B_ 18. Which of the following is a statement of opinion?

How something tastes
is a matter of opinion.

    A. "I was sitting in the back of the room, in a seat with a chalk circle
       drawn around it."
    B. "Paste doesn't taste too bad when you're hungry."
    C. "She turned toward the blackboard."
    D. "Helene Tucker turned around, her eyes full of tears."

_C_ 19. In a TV commercial for a public university, a <u>famous comedian</u> states
that he benefited from attending that university and so can others. The
commercial is employing the propaganda technique of
    A. glittering generalities.   C. testimonial.
    B. plain folks.   D. bandwagon.

The university is using the testimony of the famous comedian to
convince people they can benefit from attending that school.

_C_ 20. The following statement illustrates the logical fallacy of

    A. either-or.

    B. false cause.

    C. false comparison.

    D. personal attack.

> There are many differences between students today and students in the past.

> "Students today have it far easier than we had it. They get free lunches in school."

Outlining

The following outline of "Shame" is missing two major supporting details and three minor supporting details. Complete the outline by filling in the missing details, which are listed after the outline.

Central point: **Young Gregory learned both the shame of being let down by those who were supposed to help him and the shame of letting down another person.**

  A. _Becomes ashamed of his poverty_

    1. Intends to impress Helene Tucker by pledging to Community Chest

    2. _Is humiliated by teacher_

    3. _Leaves school and avoids it in the future_

  B. _Becomes ashamed of his own failure to help another_

    1. Earns a lot of money one day and goes to a restaurant for a good meal

    2. Sees wino being beaten for not being able to pay for his meal

    3. _Offers to pay for meal, but too late_

Items Missing from the Outline

- Offers to pay for meal, but too late
- Becomes ashamed of his own failure to help another
- Is humiliated by teacher
- Becomes ashamed of his poverty
- Leaves school and avoids it in the future

Discussion Questions

1. Why did Gregory include both the classroom and the restaurant anecdotes in one selection? What is the difference between the shame he felt in the first incident and the shame he felt in the second? What are the similarities between the two incidents?

2. The Community Chest incident could have had very different results if Gregory's teacher had handled the situation in another way. What do you think she should have done when Gregory said, "You forgot me"?

3. One type of irony is an event or an effect that is the opposite of what might be expected. In what ways are the following parts of "Shame" ironic?

   ● I never learned hate at home, or shame. I had to go to school for that.

   ● If I knew my place and didn't come too close, she'd wink at me and say hello. That was a good feeling.

   ● I looked at the wino with blood all over his face and I went over. "Leave him alone, Mister Williams. I'll pay the twenty-six cents." The wino got up. . . . He looked at me with pure hate.

4. Has anyone ever tried to help you in a way that didn't take all your needs into account? If so, how did you feel toward that person? In what ways might activities that are meant to help people also hurt them?

Note: Writing assignments for this selection appear on pages 608–609.

Check Your Performance   SHAME

Activity	Number Right	Points	Score
Basic Skill Questions			
Vocabulary in Context (2 items)	_____	× 4 =	_____
Central Point and Main Ideas (3 items)	_____	× 4 =	_____
Supporting Details (2 items)	_____	× 4 =	_____
Transitions (2 items)	_____	× 4 =	_____
Patterns of Organization (2 items)	_____	× 4 =	_____
Advanced Skill Questions			
Inferences (2 items)	_____	× 4 =	_____
Purpose and Tone (2 items)	_____	× 4 =	_____
Argument (2 items)	_____	× 4 =	_____
Critical Reading (3 items)	_____	× 4 =	_____
Outlining (5 items)	_____	× 4 =	_____
	TOTAL SCORE	=	_____%

Enter your total score into the **Reading Performance Chart: Ten Reading Selections** on the inside back cover.

4 The Bystander Effect
Dorothy Barkin

Preview

On a chilly March night, thirty-eight people witnessed a brutal attack—and hardly raised a finger to stop it. That kind of unwillingness to get involved is the topic of this article by Dorothy Barkin, who analyzes the confusion and lack of responsibility bystanders often feel when witnessing a crime or medical emergency. She begins by describing four crisis situations—and placing you right there at the scene. How would you react?

Words to Watch

intervene (2): interfere
phenomena (4): facts
apathy (23): indifference
diffusion (32): spreading thin
paralysis (32): inability to act

1   It is a pleasant fall afternoon. The sun is shining. You are heading toward the parking lot after your last class of the day. All of a sudden, you come across the following situations. What do you think you'd do in each case?

Situation One: A man in his early twenties dressed in jeans and a T-shirt is using a coat hanger to pry open a door of a late-model Ford sedan. An overcoat and a camera are visible on the back seat of the car. You're the only one who sees this.

Situation Two: A man and woman are wrestling with each other. The woman is in tears. Attempting to fight the man off, she screams, "Who are you? Get away from me!" You're the only one who witnesses this.

Situation Three: Imagine the same scenario as in Situation Two except

that this time the woman screams, "Get away from me! I don't know why I ever married you!"

Situation Four: Again imagine Situation Three. This time, however, there are a few other people (strangers to you and each other) who also observe the incident.

2 Many people would choose not to get involved in situations like these. Bystanders are often reluctant to intervene° in criminal or medical emergencies for reasons they are well aware of. They fear possible danger to themselves or getting caught up in a situation that could lead to complicated and time-consuming legal proceedings.

3 There are, however, other, less obvious factors which influence the decision to get involved in emergency situations. Complex psychological factors, which many people are unaware of, play an important part in the behavior of bystanders; knowing about these factors can help people to act more responsibly when faced with emergencies.

4 To understand these psychological phenomena°, it is helpful to look at what researchers have learned about behavior in the situations mentioned at the beginning of this article.

Situation One: Research reveals a remarkably low rate of bystander intervention to protect property. In one study, more than 3,000 people walked past 214 staged car break-ins like the one described in this situation. The vast majority of passers-by completely ignored what appeared to be a crime in progress. Not one of the 3,000 bothered to report the incident to the police.

Situation Two: Another experiment involved staging scenarios like this and the next situation. In Situation Two, bystanders offered some sort of assistance to the young woman 65 percent of the time.

Situation Three: Here the rate of bystander assistance dropped down to 19 percent. This demonstrates that bystanders are more reluctant to help a woman when they believe she's fighting with her husband. Not only do they consider a wife in less need of help; they think interfering with a married couple may be more dangerous. The husband, unlike a stranger, will not flee the situation.

Situation Four: The important idea in this situation is being a member of a group of bystanders. In more than fifty studies involving many different conditions, one outcome has been consistent: bystanders are much less likely to get involved when other witnesses are present than when they are alone.

5 Thus, membership in a group of bystanders lowers the likelihood that each member of the group will become involved. This finding may seem surprising. You might think there would

be safety in numbers and that being a member of a group would increase the likelihood of intervention. How can we explain this aspect of group behavior?

6   A flood of research has tried to answer this and other questions about bystanders in emergencies ever since the infamous case of the murder of Kitty Genovese.

7   In 1964 in the borough of Queens in New York City, Catherine "Kitty" Genovese, twenty-eight, was brutally murdered in a shocking crime that outraged the nation.

8   The crime began at 3 a.m. Kitty Genovese was coming home from her job as manager of a bar. After parking her car in a parking lot, she began the hundred-foot walk to the entrance of her apartment. But she soon noticed a man in the lot and decided instead to walk toward a police call box. As she walked by a bookstore on her way there, the man grabbed her. She screamed.

9   Lights went on and windows opened in the ten-story apartment building.

10   Next, the attacker stabbed Genovese. She shrieked, "Oh, my God, he stabbed me! Please help me! Please help me!"

11   From an upper window in the apartment house, a man shouted, "Let that girl alone!"

12   The assailant, alarmed by the man's shout, started toward his car, which was parked nearby. However, the lights in the building soon went out, and the man returned. He found Genovese struggling to reach her apartment—and stabbed her again.

13   She screamed, "I'm dying! I'm dying!"

14   Once more lights went on and windows opened in the apartment building. The attacker then went to his car and drove off. Struggling, Genovese made her way inside the building.

15   But the assailant returned to attack Genovese yet a third time. He found her slumped on the floor at the foot of the stairs and stabbed her again, this time fatally.

16   The murder took over a half hour, and Kitty Genovese's desperate cries for help were heard by at least thirty-eight people. Not a single one of the thirty-eight who later admitted to having witnessed the murder bothered to pick up the phone during the attack and call the police. One man called after Genovese was dead.

17   Comments made by bystanders after this murder provide important insight into what group members think when they consider intervening in an emergency.

18   These are some of the comments:

19   "I didn't want my husband to get involved."

20   "Frankly, we were afraid."

21   "We thought it was a lovers' quarrel."

22   "I was tired."

23   The Genovese murder sparked a national debate on the questions of public apathy° and fear and became the basis for thousands of sermons,

editorials, classroom discussions, and even a made-for-television movie. The same question was on everybody's mind—how could thirty-eight people have done so little?

24   Nine years later, another well-publicized incident provided additional information about the psychology of a group witnessing a crime.

25   On a summer afternoon in Trenton, New Jersey, a twenty-year-old woman was brutally raped in a parking lot in full view of twenty-five employees of a nearby roofing company. Though the workers witnessed the entire incident and the woman repeatedly screamed for help, no one came to her assistance.

26   Comments made by witnesses to the rape were remarkably similar to those made by the bystanders to the Genovese murder. For example, one witness said, "We thought, well, it might turn out to be her boyfriend or something like that."

27   It's not surprising to find similar excuses for not helping in cases involving a group of bystanders. The same psychological principles apply to each. Research conducted since the Genovese murder indicates that the failure of bystanders to get involved can't be simply dismissed as a symptom of an uncaring society. Rather, the *bystander effect,* as it is called by social scientists, is the product of a complex set of psychological factors.

28   Two factors appear to be most important in understanding the reactions of bystanders to emergencies.

29   First is the level of ambiguity involved in the situation. Bystanders are afraid to endanger themselves or look foolish if they take the wrong action in a situation they're not sure how to interpret. A person lying face down on the floor of a subway train may have just suffered a heart attack and be in need of immediate medical assistance—or he may be a dangerous drunk.

30   Determining what is happening is especially difficult when a man is attacking a woman. Many times lovers do quarrel, sometimes violently. But they may strongly resent an outsider, no matter how well-meaning, intruding into their affairs.

31   When a group of bystanders is around, interpreting an event can be even more difficult than when one is alone. Bystanders look to others for cues as to what is happening. Frequently other witnesses, just as confused, try to look calm. Thus bystanders can mislead each other about the seriousness of an incident.

32   The second factor in determining the reactions of bystanders to emergencies is what psychologists call the principle of moral diffusion°. Moral diffusion is the lessening of a sense of individual responsibility when someone is a member of a group. Responsibility to act diffuses throughout the crowd. When a member of the group is able to escape the collective paralysis° and take action, others in the group tend to act as well. But the larger the crowd, the greater the diffusion of responsibility, and the less

likely someone is to intervene.

33 The more social scientists are able to teach us about how bystanders react to an emergency, the better the chances that we will take appropriate action when faced with one. Knowing about moral diffusion, for example, makes it easier for us to escape it. If you find yourself witnessing an emergency with a group, remember that everybody is waiting for someone else to do something first. If you take action, others may also help.

34 Also realize that any one of us could at some time be in desperate need of help. Imagine what it feels like to need help and have a crowd watching you suffer—and doing nothing. Remember Kitty Genovese.

Basic Skill Questions

Vocabulary in Context

__C__ 1. In the sentence below, the word *scenario* (sĭ-nâr′ē-ō′) means
   A. fight.
   B. relationship.
   C. suggested scene.
   D. quotation.

   Situation Two has described a suggested scene.

   "Imagine the same scenario as in Situation Two except that this time the woman screams, 'Get away from me! I don't know why I ever married you!'" (Paragraph 1)

__D__ 2. In the excerpt below, the word *assailant* (ə-sā′lənt) means
   A. observer.
   B. bystander.
   C. victim.
   D. attacker.

   If someone shouted while the attack was in progress, who would be scared away? The word *attacker* in the first sentence is a synonym clue.

   "Next, the attacker stabbed Genovese. . . . From an upper window in the apartment house, a man shouted, 'Let that girl alone!'

   "The assailant, alarmed by the man's shout, started toward his car. . . ." (Paragraphs 10–12)

_B_ 3. In the excerpt below, the word *ambiguity* (ăm′bĭ-gyoo′ĭ-tē) means

A. argument.

B. uncertainty.

C. lack of interest.

D. crowding.

> If the bystanders are in a situation they are not sure how to interpret, there is a level of uncertainty involved.

"First is the level of ambiguity involved. . . . Bystanders are afraid to endanger themselves or look foolish . . . in a situation they're not sure how to interpret." (Paragraph 29)

Central Point and Main Ideas

Answer A ignores the issue of why people don't want to be involved. Answer B covers only paragraphs 7–16. Answer C is contradicted by paragraph 27.

_D_ 4. Which sentence best expresses the central point of this selection?

A. People don't want to get involved in emergencies.

B. Kitty Genovese was murdered because no one helped enough.

C. People don't care what happens to others.

D. Understanding why bystanders react as they do in a crisis can help people act more responsibly.

_D_ 5. Which sentence best expresses the main idea of paragraph 27?

Answer A covers only sentence 1. Answer B covers only sentence 3. Answer C is contradicted by sentence 3.

A. Bystanders always have the same excuses for not helping.

B. There has been research on bystanders since the Genovese murder.

C. The "bystander effect" is a symptom of an uncaring society.

D. Research shows that a number of psychological factors, not a simple lack of caring, keeps bystanders from getting involved.

_D_ 6. The sentence that makes up paragraph 28 states the main idea of

A. paragraph 29.

B. paragraphs 29–30.

C. paragraphs 29–31.

D. paragraphs 29–32.

> Paragraph 28 says there are two factors. Paragraphs 29–31 describe the first factor (introduced by the word *First*). Paragraph 32 describes the second factor (introduced by the word *second*).

Supporting Details

_C_ 7. Bystanders are most likely to help   See paragraph 4.

A. a woman being attacked by her husband.

B. in any emergency when others are around.

C. a woman being attacked by a stranger.

D. when property is being stolen.

_D_ 8. According to the author, when there is a group of bystanders,

See paragraph 32.
   A. everyone is more likely to help.
   B. it is easier to understand what is happening.
   C. they are not influenced at all by each other.
   D. each is more likely to act after someone else takes action.

_C_ 9. The author supports her statement that "bystanders are much less likely to get involved when other witnesses are present" with

   A. opinions.
   B. quotations from experts.
   C. research and examples.
   D. no evidence.

The examples are the Genovese murder and the Trenton rape. The research-based information precedes and follows the examples.

Transitions

_D_ 10. In the excerpt below, what does the second sentence do?

The word *Thus* signals a cause and effect relationship. *Cause:* confused witnesses try to look calm. *Effect:* bystanders mislead one another about how serious the incident is.

   A. It compares the behavior of some bystanders with the behavior of others.
   B. It contrasts the behavior of confused bystanders with that of calm bystanders.
   C. It adds more detail to the first sentence.
   D. It establishes a cause and effect relationship.

   "Frequently other witnesses, just as confused, try to look calm. Thus bystanders can mislead each other about the seriousness of an incident." (Paragraph 31)

_B_ 11. In the excerpt below, what does the second sentence do?

The words *For example* are illustration words. The second sentence gives an example of a comment made by a witness to the rape.

   A. It contrasts the comments made by witnesses to the rape with comments made by witnesses to the Genovese murder.
   B. It illustrates a point made in the first sentence.
   C. It compares two serious crimes.
   D. It establishes a cause and effect relationship.

   "Comments made by witnesses to the rape were remarkably similar to those made by the bystanders to the Genovese murder. For example, one witness said, "We thought, well, it might turn out to be her boyfriend or something like that." (Paragraph 26)

Patterns of Organization

_D_ 12. The pattern of organization of paragraphs 7–16 is
    A. comparison and/or contrast.   The paragraphs narrate a series of events
    B. list of items.   in the order in which they happened.
    C. definition and example.
    D. time order.

Advanced Skill Questions

Inferences

_C_ 13. The reading suggests that people tend to believe

See "Situation One"
and "Situation Two"
in paragraph 4.

    A. theft is okay.
    B. loss of property is worse than bodily harm.
    C. bodily harm is worse than loss of property.
    D. rape is worse than murder.

_D_ 14. From the article, we can conclude that Kitty Genovese's killer

See paragraphs 12–15.

    A. knew his victim.
    B. was unaware of the witnesses.
    C. stabbed her too quickly for her to get help.
    D. kept attacking when he realized no one was coming to help her.

_B_ 15. From the article, we can conclude that of the following situations, the bystander is most likely to get involved when

See paragraphs 4–5.
They suggest that
bystanders tend not to
help in cases of loss of
property or family feuds,
and when others are
around.

    A. a man passes a clothing store from which people are carrying away clothes.
    B. a college student sees a man collapsing on a street where no one else is present.
    C. a neighbor sees a father and son fighting in their yard.
    D. a softball team sees the coach angrily chasing his wife.

Purpose and Tone

_C_ 16. The main purpose of this article is to

The article explains the
bystander effect.
In paragraphs 33–34, the
author appeals directly
to readers in an effort to
persuade people to help
in emergency situations.

    A. inform readers about the bystander effect and the factors that contribute to it.
    B. persuade people to be more helpful in emergency situations.
    C. both of the above.

_C_ 17. The tone of the last paragraph of this article can be described as

A. surprised.

B. confused.

C. pleading.

D. lighthearted.

By urging us to imagine ourselves in a situation
of needing help and asking us to remember
Genovese, the author sets a pleading tone.

Argument

_B_ 18. Write the letter of the statement that is the point of the following argument. The other statements are support for that point.

A. "When a member of the group is able to escape the collective paralysis and take action, others in the group tend to act as well."

B. "If you take action [in an emergency], others may also help."

C. "Bystanders are afraid to endanger themselves or look foolish if they take the wrong action in a situation they're not sure how to interpret."

Statements A and C explain statement B.

Critical Reading

_A_ 19. The following sentence is a statement of

A. fact.

B. opinion.

C. fact and opinion.

This fact can be confirmed by reading the studies.

"In more than fifty studies involving many different conditions, one outcome has been consistent: bystanders are much less likely to get involved when other witnesses are present than when they are alone." (Paragraph 4)

_A_ 20. A man who explains that a woman was raped because she wore sexy clothing is illustrating the logical fallacy of

A. false cause.

B. straw man.

C. personal attack.

D. circular reasoning.

There could be many reasons that the
woman was raped besides the clothing she
was wearing, including causes that have to
do with the rapist rather than the woman.

Summarizing

Wording of answers may vary.

Add the ideas needed to complete the following summary of "The Bystander Effect."

Witnesses to crisis situations are less likely to help when only property is at risk and when a woman is being attacked by a man who may be her husband. Numerous studies have shown that witnesses' resistance to helping is also increased when there are other _____ *witnesses*

See "Situation Four" in paragraph 4.

_____ *present* _____. A famous example is the case of Kitty Genovese, who was stabbed to death at 3 a.m. while returning to her apartment. The attack went on for over half an hour. Thirty-eight people

See paragraph 16.

listened to her cries for help, but _____ *no one called the police* _____ *during the attack* _____. In another example, employees of a roofing company ignored a rape taking place on a nearby

See paragraph 28.

parking lot. Two psychological factors seem to explain _____ *the reactions* _____ *of bystanders to emergencies* _____. One is the level of uncertainty in the situation. If the bystanders don't know how to _____

See paragraphs 29–31.

_____ *interpret* _____ a situation, they don't want to take action. The other factor is the principle of moral diffusion. The larger the crowd that

See paragraph 32.

is watching, the less responsibility _____ *is felt by* _____ *each member of the crowd* _____. Understanding these factors can help people be more useful in emergency situations.

Discussion Questions

1. Have you ever been in a situation in which the bystander effect played a part? Would your behavior be any different in light of what you have learned from this article?

2. The author states in paragraph 31, "Bystanders look to others for cues as to what is happening. Frequently other witnesses, just as confused, try to look calm." Why do you think witnesses would try to look calm during an emergency?

3. In paragraph 33, the author suggests that if you understand what causes "the bystander effect," you can act appropriately in an emergency: "If you take action, others may also help." If, say, you were in a group of onlookers while a fight was in progress, what could you do that would encourage others to intervene?

4. How does the conclusion of this article clarify the author's purpose for the reader? How does the article's beginning fit in with that purpose?

Note: Writing assignments for this selection appear on pages 609–610.

Check Your Performance   THE BYSTANDER EFFECT

Activity	Number Right	Points		Score
Basic Skill Questions				
Vocabulary in Context (3 items)	_____	× 4	=	_____
Central Point and Main Ideas (3 items)	_____	× 4	=	_____
Supporting Details (3 items)	_____	× 4	=	_____
Transitions (2 items)	_____	× 4	=	_____
Patterns of Organization (1 item)	_____	× 4	=	_____
Advanced Skill Questions				
Inferences (3 items)	_____	× 4	=	_____
Purpose and Tone (2 items)	_____	× 4	=	_____
Argument (1 item)	_____	× 4	=	_____
Critical Reading (2 items)	_____	× 4	=	_____
Summarizing (5 items)	_____	× 4	=	_____
		TOTAL SCORE	=	_____ %

Enter your total score into the **Reading Performance Chart: Ten Reading Selections** on the inside back cover.

5 "Let's Roll."
Karen Breslau, Eleanor Clift, and Evan Thomas

Preview

The terrorists had years to plan their hijacking. The passengers had just minutes to respond. But a band of patriots came together to defy death and save a symbol of freedom. Here's their story, taken from *Newsweek* magazine.

Words to Watch

chronically (5): continuously
sparsely (6): thinly
muffled (9): unable to be heard clearly
speculate (11): think
derision (17): ridicule
submission (19): nonresistance
subdue (21): control
lurching (21): moving suddenly up, down, or to the side
valiantly (32): courageously

In the first few days after September 11, 2001, Lisa Beamer could not sleep for more than an hour. Then she would wake up and cry. She worried about the boys, David, 3, and Drew, 19 months, and the new baby due in January. David wanted to know why, if their father loved them so much, he had gone to be with Jesus. And there was that one nagging question. Why had her husband not called her from the plane? Other passengers had called home from Flight 93 to say goodbye and talk to their loved ones. Why not Todd?

Then on Friday night, September 14, she got a call from her crisis counselor at United Airlines. Todd Beamer, it turned

out, had made a call; it had been routed to an Airfone operator in Chicago. The counselor said she had a message for Lisa, but she was worried it might be too much to handle. "Read it to me right now," said Lisa. The letter recounted a conversation between Todd and an Airfone supervisor, Lisa Jefferson, and some last words that will never be forgotten. The next morning the two Lisas had a tearful conversation. Jefferson told Beamer that her husband had been calm and matter-of-fact. Lisa Beamer was relieved; she had not wanted her husband to die in terror.

3   Actually, Todd had been afraid. They all had been deathly afraid. But Beamer, like so many others aboard Flight 93, did not wait to die. The passengers and crew of Flight 93 went out bravely and heroically, and by doing so they may have saved countless others and spared a symbol of democracy and freedom in our nation's capitol from destruction.

4   The terrorist Osama bin Laden is said to have thought that the United States has become soft and weak. He might have been wise to have learned more about the historical willingness of Americans to die for liberty. The first American flag flown by the patriots of the early Revolutionary War was not the Stars and Stripes but a banner showing a coiled snake, with the inscription "Don't Tread on Me." America's latest war for freedom did not begin with a cruise-missile attack on a terrorist-training camp in Afghanistan. It began with a group of citizen soldiers on Flight 93 who rose up, like their forefathers, to defy tyranny. And when they came storming down the aisle, it wasn't the Americans who were afraid. It was the terrorists.

5   The four hijackers who took over Flight 93 were not supermen by any means. From the outset their timing was off. Flight 93 was delayed at chronically° clogged Newark International Airport for nearly 45 minutes. It did not take off until 8:42. Aboard the other planes, the hijackers moved quickly to seize control. But on Flight 93 the four terrorists waited for breakfast to be served.

6   At about 9:25 a.m., in the sparsely° filled main cabin, passengers were settling back for a snooze or popping open their laptops or picking up a novel for the long coast-to-coast flight. But passengers up front in first class may have observed something unsettling: four Middle Eastern-looking passengers tying red bandannas around their heads.

7   In the cockpit, the captain and his first officer had already been warned to be on the alert for trouble. A message had flashed on the cockpit computer screen, sent out to all United Airlines pilots by the home office. American Flight 11 had already crashed into the first World Trade Center tower, and United 175 had just plowed into the second tower. American Flight 77 had been hijacked and was headed for Washington, D.C. Flight 93's pilots, Captain Jason Dahl and First Officer LeRoy Homer, were not told these details, just given a general warning: "Beware, cockpit intrusion." One of the two pilots simply typed, "Confirmed."

8   At about 9:25 the pilots checked in with Cleveland air-traffic control.

Suddenly the air-traffic controller could hear the sound of screaming and scuffling over the open mike. "Did somebody call Cleveland?" the controller asked.

9   No answer. Just the muffled° sounds of struggle. Then silence.

10   It's not clear what was happening in the passenger cabin. After 40 seconds of silence, one of the pilots turned on the microphone again, allowing Cleveland air control to hear more muffled clamor and someone frantically shouting, "Get out of here! Get out of here!" The mike went dead again.

11   The tape of the automatic cockpit voice recorder of Flight 93 begins shortly after 9:30 a.m. The sounds it picked up were grim. Someone is crying and moaning, pleading not to be hurt, not to be killed. Some investigators speculate° that the hijackers may have slashed the throats of the pilots as the two men were still strapped into their seats.

12   In San Ramon, California, a prosperous suburb in the hills of the East Bay across from San Francisco, Deena Burnett was preparing breakfast for her three girls. The phone rang. It was her husband, Tom. "Are you OK?" she asked. "No," he said. "I'm on a plane, and we've been hijacked. They've knifed a guy, and there's a bomb onboard. Call the authorities, Deena." Then he hung up.

13   At Cleveland Center, the air-traffic controllers furiously tried to contact Flight 93. A thickly accented voice came back on the air: "Hi, this is the captain. We'd like you all to remain seated. There is a bomb onboard. We are going to turn back to the airport. And they have our demands, so please be quiet."

Investigators think the hijacker had flipped the wrong switch, thinking he was addressing the passengers over the PA system when he was calling Cleveland control instead.

14   In upstate Windham, New York, where Lyz Glick had taken her 12-week-old baby to visit her parents, the phone rang. Her husband, Jeremy, was calling from Flight 93, pouring out an incredible story. He described "three Iranian-looking men" wearing red headbands and saying they had a bomb.

15   Jeremy Glick was a 6-foot-1, 220-pound former NCAA judo champion. He told his wife that there were some other big men on the plane. Herded into the back by the hijackers, the passengers were beginning to whisper among themselves. They were talking about "rushing the hijackers."

16   United flight attendant Sandy Bradshaw called her husband, Phil, in Greensboro, North Carolina. "Have you heard what happened?" she began. "We've been hijacked." There was talk of doing something, she said. She and several of the other flight attendants were filling coffeepots with boiling water—to throw at the hijackers.

17   Back in rows 30 to 34, where most of the passengers had been confined, a rebellion was in the works. No one seems to have paid too much heed to the guard who had a red box strapped around his waist. He said it was a bomb, but he seems to have inspired more derision° than fear. If the hijackers had hoped for a timorous group of passengers, they picked the wrong plane. In addition to judo expert Glick and Tom Burnett,

a take-charge type who had been a quarterback in college, there was Todd Beamer, who had never been the biggest or fastest guy on the court but who was known as a "gamer," the team member who makes the winning play. Mark Bingham, 6 feet 5, had played rugby at Cal on a national-championship team. A risk taker, he had once been arrested for tackling the Stanford mascot at a football game. Lou Nacke, at 5 feet 3 and 200 pounds, was a weight lifter with a Superman tattoo on his shoulder. Rich Guadagno, an enforcement officer with California Fish and Wildlife, had been trained in hand-to-hand combat. Flight attendant CeeCee Lyles had been a police detective. William Cashman was a former paratrooper. Linda Gronlund, a lawyer, had a brown belt in karate. Lauren Grandcolas had organized a sky-diving expedition. Alan Beaven was a rock climber and former Scotland Yard prosecutor. The hijackers had been training for two years; the passengers came together in a few minutes. But the odds were not hopeless. There was even a pilot among them: Don Greene, the vice president of a company that made safety devices for airlines, had flown single-engine aircraft.

18   At about 9:45 a.m., Tom Burnett called Deena again. He told her that the hijackers claimed to have a bomb, but he was skeptical. "I think they're bluffing," he said. "We're going to do something," he went on. "I've got to go."

19   Todd Beamer may have been having trouble with his credit card, or he may just have punched 0 into the Airfone. In any case, his call at 9:45 was routed to the GTE Customer Center in Oakbrook, Illinois. An operator told supervisor Lisa Jefferson that she had a call from a man who said his plane was being hijacked. "This is Mrs. Jefferson," said the GTE supervisor, in her calmest, most professional voice. "What is your situation?" In an equally calm and businesslike way, Beamer told her. In the cabin, the hijackers must have realized that the passengers were stirring against them. One of the hijackers begins praying. Another suggests using an ax—there is one hanging in the back of the cockpit, to break out in case of fire—to scare the passengers into submission°.

20   In the back of the plane, knots of passengers were talking to each other, debating how to strike. At one point Jeremy Glick told Lyz that the passengers were taking a vote. "What do you think we should do?" he asked. "Go for it," answered Lyz. She was no longer panicked. "Do what you have to do." Jeremy took heart. There was some discussion, he said, among the passengers about what they could use for weapons. "I've got my butter knife from breakfast," he joked.

21   In the cockpit, the hijackers apparently decided to try to subdue° the restless passengers by knocking them off their feet. Switching off the autopilot, the hijacker pilot sent the plane lurching° and bobbing.

22   For a moment Todd Beamer's composure cracked. "Jesus, we're going down," he said, his voice rising. Then he steadied. "We're coming back up," he told Lisa Jefferson. "No, I think we're just

turning around. We're heading north. I don't know where we're heading."

23 Up to this moment, Beamer had been all business. "Lisa," he said suddenly. "Yes?" responded Jefferson. "That's my wife," said Beamer. "Well, that's my name, too, Todd," said Jefferson. "Oh, my God," said Beamer. "I don't think we're going to get out of this thing. I'm going to have to go out on faith." Beamer asked her to promise to call his wife if he didn't make it home. He told her about his little boys and the new baby on the way. Then he said that the passengers were going to try to jump the hijackers. He asked her to pray with him. He began to recite the ancient litany, and she joined him:

Our Father which art in heaven,
Hallowed be thy name.
Thy kingdom come. Thy will be done in earth, as it is in heaven.
Give us this day our daily bread.
And forgive us our trespasses, as we forgive those who trespass against us.
And lead us not into temptation, but deliver us from evil: For thine is the kingdom, and the power, and the glory, for ever. Amen.

24 "Jesus help me," Beamer said. He recited the 23rd Psalm. Then Jefferson heard him say:

25 "Are you guys ready? Let's roll."

26 In the minutes before they fought to save their dignity and honor, if not their lives, the passengers of Flight 93 showed small acts of kindness and grace. They said goodbye to their families and to each other. Lauren Grandcolas left a message for her husband, Jack, on the answering machine, telling him how much she loved him and her family. Elizabeth Wainio, 28, reached her stepmother, Esther, in Catonsville, Maryland. She said she had been frightened, but that a nice woman next to her had comforted her and told her to call home.

27 In Greensboro, North Carolina, as he talked to his wife, flight attendant Sandy, Phil Bradshaw could hear a group of men reciting the 23rd Psalm: "Yea, though I walk through the valley of the shadow of death, I will fear no evil . . ."

28 Sandy told him it was time to go. "We're running to first class now," she said. CeeCee Lyles called her husband, Lorne. "Babe," she said, "my plane's been hijacked." They talked about their love and their four boys. Suddenly Lorne heard screaming, and CeeCee yelled, "They're doing it! They're doing it!" Elizabeth Wainio ended her phone call with her stepmother, saying, "I've got to go, they're breaking into the cockpit. I love you. Goodbye."

29 The distance on a Boeing 757 from the rear galley to the cockpit door is 110 feet. It's not known who led the charge, or how many followed. When Newsweek interviewed the families and friends of the passengers of Flight 93, they all imagined their loved one in the hero's role—whether it was a grandmother whacking away at a hijacker with her purse or a disabled sister tripping a hijacker with her cane. In a sense they were all right; resistance—fierce, unyielding resistance—was the spirit of Flight 93.

30 Beginning at 9:57, the cockpit voice

recorder began to pick up the sounds of a death struggle. There is the crash of galley dishes and trays being hurled, a man's voice screaming loudly. One of the passengers cries out, "Let's get them!" The end is near. The hijackers can be heard talking about finishing off the plane, which has begun to dive. The cockpit voice recorder picks up shouting by one of the male passengers. It is unclear whether the passengers have broken into the cockpit or are just outside the door. The hijackers apparently begin to fight among themselves for the controls, demanding, "Give it to me."

31   In the hilly country of Somerset County, Pennsylvania, eyewitnesses saw a plane rocking from side to side, like a seesaw, as it plunged toward the earth. The crater in the field was 50 feet deep after it hit, but nothing compared with what the Capitol or the White House might have looked like if Flight 93 had kept on its course.

32   Amid her sorrow, Lisa Beamer can laugh a little now about her strange celebrity as the Hero Widow, about the time she asked the CNN limo to stop at Macy's so she could get a new maternity dress on the way to *Larry King Live*. She still goes from time to time to Todd's den. It was on his desk that she found, on a folded piece of paper at the bottom of his in-box, a passage quoting Teddy Roosevelt:

The credit belongs to the man who is actually in the arena . . . who strives valiantly°, who knows the great enthusiasms, the great devotions, and spends himself in worthy causes. Who, at best, knows the triumph of high achievement and who, at worst, if he fails, fails while daring greatly so that his place shall never be with those cold and timid souls who know neither victory nor defeat.

33   In daring and dying, the passengers and crew of Flight 93 found victory for us all.

Basic Skill Questions

Vocabulary in Context

In contrast with the 40 seconds of silence, there would be muffled noise along with the frantic shouting.

_D_ 1. In the sentence below, the word *clamor* (klăm′ər) means
    A. celebration.   C. music.
    B. silence.   D. noise.

"After 40 seconds of silence, one of the pilots turned on the microphone again, allowing Cleveland air control to hear more muffled clamor and someone frantically shouting, 'Get out of here! Get out of here!'" (Paragraph 10)

The words "they picked the wrong plane" are an antonym clue. "Timid" is the opposite of how the passengers are described and what the hijackers had hoped for.

_B_ 2. In the excerpt on the next page, the word *timorous* (tĭm′ər-əs) means
    A. bold.   C. knowledgeable.
    B. timid.   D. young.

"If the hijackers had hoped for a timorous group of passengers, they picked the wrong plane. In addition to judo expert Glick and Tom Burnett, a take-charge type who had been a quarterback in college, there was Todd Beamer, . . . who was known as . . . the team member who makes the winning play." (Paragraph 17)

Central Point and Main Ideas

__B__ 3. The central point of the article is best expressed in the
A. first sentence of the selection.
B. last sentence of paragraph 3.
C. first sentence of paragraph 28.
D. last sentence of paragraph 31.

> Answers A, C, and D are details about the people and events.

__A__ 4. The main idea of paragraph 26 is best expressed in its
A. first sentence.   C. third sentence.
B. second sentence.   D. fourth sentence.

> The first sentence states the passengers showed "small acts of kindness and grace." The rest of the paragraph describes such acts.

Supporting Details

__F__ 5. TRUE OR FALSE? When Jeremy Glick asked his wife Lyz whether she thought the passengers should challenge the hijackers, she begged him to quietly remain in his seat.

> See paragraph 20.

Transitions

__C__ 6. The relationship of the second sentence to the first one is one of

> The behavior of the other hijackers is contrasted with that of the four terrorists on Flight 93.

A. time.   C. contrast.
B. addition.   D. illustration.

"Aboard the other planes, the hijackers moved quickly to seize control. But on Flight 93, the four terrorists waited for breakfast to be served." (Paragraph 5)

__A__ 7. The relationship of the second sentence below to the first is one of

> The sentences report what Beamer said in the order in which he said it. First he told her about his family. Then he told her about the passengers' plan.

A. time.   C. contrast.
B. addition.   D. illustration.

"He told her about his little boys and the new baby on the way. Then he said that the passengers were going to try to jump the hijackers." (Paragraph 23)

Patterns of Organization

_A_ 8. Paragraph 4 (A. compares; B. contrasts; C. defines; D. illustrates) the passengers on Flight 93 and the heroes of the American Revolution.

> Both groups were willing "to die for liberty." The comparison word _like_ (in the fifth sentence) is a clue.

_D_ 9. The main pattern of organization of paragraph 17 is

> Most of the details in paragraph 17 list the passengers and describe the attributes of each.

A. definition and example.

B. cause and effect.

C. comparison.

D. list of items.

_C_ 10. The main overall pattern of organization of the selection is

A. definition.

B. contrast.

C. time order.

D. comparison.

> For the most part, the selection describes what happened during the last flight of Flight 93 on the morning of September 11, 2001.

Advanced Skill Questions

Inferences

> **Item 11:** Expressions such as "not supermen," "their timing was off," "Aboard the other planes, the hijackers moved quickly. . . . But on Flight 93 the four terrorists waited for breakfast. . . ." show that the hijackers on Flight 93 were not as organized and single-minded as those on the other planes.

_B_ 11. In paragraph 5, the authors imply that

A. various political conditions justified the actions of the Flight 93 hijackers.

B. the hijackers of Flight 93 were less competent than the other September 11th hijackers.

C. if Flight 93 had departed on time, it would never have been hijacked.

D. officials at Newark International Airport could have prevented the hijacking of Flight 93.

_D_ 12. We can infer from paragraph 29 that

> The words "they all imagined their loved one in the hero's role" show that families and friends believe in the heroism of those lost in the crash of Flight 93.

A. the families and friends of the Flight 93 victims all have unhealthy imaginations.

B. there is evidence that a grandmother and a disabled woman led the attack against the hijackers.

C. the hijackers admired the bravery and resolve of the passengers.

D. the surviving families and friends find comfort in the idea of the passengers' heroism.

_D_ 13. The authors imply that the note Lisa Beamer found on her late husband's desk illustrates

> See paragraph 32.

A. that Todd was an expert on Teddy Roosevelt.

B. Todd's belief that people should avoid violence at all costs.

C. that Todd liked to keep secrets from his wife.

D. Todd's belief that heroism comes through decisive action.

_D_ 14. We can infer that the authors got information for their article from
A. interviews with friends and family of the passengers and Phil Bradshaw.
B. the cockpit voice recorder.
C. eyewitnesses of the crash.
D. all of the above.

Answer A has supporting details in many paragraphs. Answer B has supporting details in paragraphs 11 and 30. Answer C has supporting details in paragraph 31.

Purpose and Tone

_A_ 15. The main purpose of this selection is to
A. inform and inspire.
B. persuade readers to act.
C. entertain.

The article makes no attempt to persuade the reader to think or act differently, not it is meant merely to entertain. It simply informs us of the events on the morning of September 11 and shows the heroism of which ordinary Americans are capable.

The descriptions of the character and actions of the passengers show the author's respect for them. Details are presented in a serious manner.

_C_ 16. In general, the authors' tone in the selection is
A. lighthearted and optimistic.
B. objective and scientific.
C. serious and respectful.
D. angry and scornful.

_B_ 17. The tone of paragraph 4 can be described as being
A. sorrowful.
B. prideful.
C. bitter.
D. forgiving.

The descriptions show pride in both the forefathers and the passengers.

Argument

_D_ 18. Write the letter of the statement that is the point of the following argument. The other statements are support for that point.
A. Several of the Flight 93 passengers were athletes or had been trained in combat.
B. Todd Beamer told Lisa Jefferson that the passengers would try to "jump" the hijackers.
C. Beginning at 9:57, the cockpit voice recorder picked up the sounds of a struggle between the passengers and the hijackers.
D. Osama bin Laden was wrong to think Americans were soft and weak.

Answers A, B, and C give evidence that these Americans were strong, not soft and weak.

Critical Reading

___B___ 19. The sentence below is
   A. a fact.
   B. an opinion.

   These details about Jeremy Glick can be verified by research.

   "Jeremy Glick was a 6 foot 1, 220-pound former NCAA judo champion." (Paragraph 15)

___B___ 20. A politician who appears in a TV commercial and accuses his opponents of being a tool of terrorists such as Osama bin Laden is using the propaganda technique of
   A. transfer.
   B. name calling.
   C. bandwagon.
   D. testimonial.

   Calling one's opponent "a tool of terrorists such as Osama bin Laden" is using emotionally loaded language to turn people against the opponent.

Outlining

Complete the following general outline of "Let's Roll" by filling in the missing topics.

   A. Introduction—paragraphs 1 to 4
      1. Lisa Beamer's conversations with counselor and Airfone supervisor
      2. Fighting of Flight 93 passengers despite fear
      3. Americans' willingness to die for liberty
   B. Narrative of the events of Flight 93 —paragraphs 5 to 31
   C. Conclusion—paragraphs 32 to 33
      1. Lisa Beamer as hero's widow
      2. Teddy Roosevelt's words
      3. Final statement of admiration and gratitude

Items Missing from the Outline
   ● Narrative of the events of Flight 93
   ● Teddy Roosevelt's words
   ● Lisa Beamer as hero's widow
   ● Lisa Beamer's conversations with counselor and Airfone supervisor

Discussion Questions

1. Where were you on the terrible day of September 11th, 2001, and what were your reactions to the events of that day?

2. How did reading this selection affect you? For example, as you were reading, did you feel pity, anger, horror, surprise, admiration, pride, or a combination of the above? Explain.

3. While the selection focuses mainly on the struggle between a group of passengers and the hijackers, we are also given specific details about individual passengers. Which details would you say are particularly effective in making you see these people as individuals? If you could interview any of the passengers, whom would you choose, and what questions would you want to ask?

Note: Writing assignments for this selection appear on page 610.

Check Your Performance   "LET'S ROLL."

Activity	Number Right	Points	Score
Basic Skill Questions			
Vocabulary in Context (2 items)	_____	× 4 =	_____
Central Point and Main Ideas (2 items)	_____	× 4 =	_____
Supporting Details (1 item)	_____	× 4 =	_____
Transitions (2 items)	_____	× 4 =	_____
Patterns of Organization (3 items)	_____	× 4 =	_____
Advanced Skill Questions			
Inferences (4 items)	_____	× 4 =	_____
Purpose and Tone (3 items)	_____	× 4 =	_____
Argument (1 item)	_____	× 4 =	_____
Critical Reading (2 items)	_____	× 4 =	_____
Outlining (4 items)	_____	× 5 =	_____
		TOTAL SCORE =	_____%

Enter your total score into the **Reading Performance Chart: Ten Reading Selections** on the inside back cover.

6 Coping with Nervousness

Rudolph F. Verderber

Preview

Do you have trouble relaxing when you speak in front of a group? Do your legs tremble, does your heart pound, is your mouth dry? For many people, public speaking can be a nerve-racking experience. However, there are ways to deal with the nervousness. In this selection from his widely used college textbook *Communicate!* Seventh Edition, Rudolph F. Verderber provides information that may make your future speaking assignments less painful.

Words to Watch

virtually (2): almost
channel (3): direct
adrenaline (4): a hormone that stimulates and strengthens parts of the body
flabbergasted (5): amazed
eliciting (5): drawing out
psyching . . . up (9): preparing (oneself) psychologically
initial (10): first

1   Most people confess to extreme nervousness at even the thought of giving a speech. Yet you must learn to cope with nervousness because speaking is important. Through speaking, we gain the power to share what we are thinking with others. Each of us has vital information to share: we may have the data needed to solve a problem; we may have an idea for a procedure that will save money for our company or group; we may have insights that will influence the way people see an issue. We can only imagine the tremendous loss to business, governmental, educational, professional, and fraternal groups because anxiety prevents people from speaking up.

2   Let's start with the assumption that you are indeed nervous—you may in fact be scared to death. Now what? Experience has proved that virtually° anyone can learn to cope with the fear of public speaking. Consider the following points:

3   **1. You are in good company.** Not only do most beginning speakers suffer anxiety at the thought of speaking in public, but many experienced speakers confess to nervousness when they speak as well. Now, you may think, "Don't

give me that line—you can't tell me that [fill in the name of a good speaker you know] is nervous when speaking in public!" Ask the person. He or she will tell you. Even powerful speakers like Abraham Lincoln and Franklin D. Roosevelt were nervous before speaking. The difference in nervousness among people is a matter of degree. Some people tremble, perspire, and experience shortness of breath and increased heartbeat. As they go through their speech, they may be so preoccupied with themselves that they lose contact with the audience, jump back and forth from point to point, and on occasion forget what they had planned to say. Others, however, may get butterflies in their stomachs and feel weak in the knees—and still go on to deliver a strong speech. The secret is not to

get rid of all of your feelings but to learn to channel° and control your nervousness.

2. **Despite nervousness, you can make it through a speech.** Very few people are so bothered by anxiety that they are unable to proceed with the speech. You may not enjoy the experience— especially the first time—but you can do it. In fact, it would be detrimental if you were not nervous. Why? Because you must be a little more aroused than usual to do your best. A bit of nervousness gets the adrenaline° flowing—and that brings you to speaking readiness.

3. **Your listeners aren't nearly as likely to recognize your fear as you might think.** "The only thing we have to fear," Franklin Roosevelt said, "is fear itself." Many speakers worry that others will notice how nervous they are—and that makes them even more self-conscious and nervous. The fact is that people, even speech instructors, will greatly underrate the amount of stage fright they believe a person has. Recently, a young woman reported that she broke out in hives before each speech. She was flabbergasted° when other students said to her, "You seem so calm when you speak." Try eliciting° feedback from your listeners after a speech. Once you realize that your audience does not perceive your nervousness

4

5

to the degree that you imagine, you will remove one unnecessary source of anxiety.

6   **4. The more experience you get in speaking, the better you become at coping with nervousness.** As you gain experience, you learn to think more about the audience and the message and less about yourself. Moreover, you come to realize that audiences, your classmates especially, are very supportive, especially in informative speech situations. After all, most people are in the audience because they want to hear you. As time goes on, you will come to find that having a group of people listening to you alone is a very satisfying experience.

7   Now let's consider what you can do about your nervousness. Coping with nervousness begins during the preparation process and extends to the time you actually begin the speech.

8   The best way to control nervousness is to pick a topic you know something about and are interested in. Public speakers cannot allow themselves to be saddled with a topic they don't care about. An unsatisfactory topic lays the groundwork for a psychological mindset that almost guarantees nervousness at the time of the speech. By the same token, selecting a topic you are truly interested in will help you focus on what you want to communicate and so lay the groundwork for a satisfying speech experience.

9   A second key to controlling nervousness is to prepare adequately for your speech. If you feel in command of your material and delivery, you'll be far more confident. During the preparation period, you can also be "psyching yourself up°" for the speech. Even in your classroom speeches, if you have a suitable topic, and if you are well prepared, your audience will feel they profited from listening to you. Before you say, "Come on, who are you trying to kid!" think of lectures, talks, and speeches you have heard. When the speaker seemed knowledgeable and conveyed enthusiasm, weren't you impressed? The fact is that some of the speeches you hear in class are likely to be among the best and most informative or moving speeches you are ever going to hear. Public speaking students learn to put time and effort into their speeches, and many classroom speeches turn out to be surprisingly interesting and valuable. If you work at your speech, you will probably sense that your class looks forward to listening to you.

10   Perhaps the most important time for coping with nervousness is shortly before you give your speech. Research indicates that it is during the period right before you walk up to give your speech and the time when you have your initial° contact with the audience that your fear is most likely to be at its greatest.

11   When speeches are being scheduled, you may be able to control when you speak. Are you better off "getting it over with," that is, being the first person

to speak that day? If so, you may be able to volunteer to go first. But regardless of when you are scheduled to speak, try not to spend your time thinking about yourself or your speech. At the moment the class begins, you have done all you can to be prepared. This is the time to focus your mind on something else. Try to listen to each of the speeches that come before yours. Get involved with what each speaker is saying. When your turn comes, you will be far more relaxed than if you had spent the time worrying about your own speech.

12   As you walk to the speaker's stand, remind yourself that you have ideas you want to convey, that you are well prepared, and that your audience is going to want to hear what you have to say. Even if you make mistakes, the audience will be focusing on your ideas and will profit from your speech.

When you reach the stand, pause   13 a few seconds before you start and establish eye contact with the audience. Take a deep breath to help get your breathing in order. Try to move about a little during the first few sentences— sometimes, a few gestures or a step one way or another is enough to break some of the tension. Above all, concentrate on communicating with your audience— your goal is to share your ideas, not to give a performance.

Basic Skill Questions

Vocabulary in Context

_C_   1. In the excerpt below, the word *detrimental* (dĕt′rə-mĕn′tl) means
   A. helpful.
   B. expensive.
   C. harmful.
   D. funny.

   If being a little nervous helps you do your best, not being nervous would be harmful.

   "Despite nervousness, you can make it through a speech. . . . In fact, it would be detrimental if you were not nervous. Why? Because you must be a little more aroused than usual to do your best." (Paragraph 4)

_B_   2. In the sentence below, the word *conveyed* (kən-vād′) means
   A. prevented.
   B. communicated.
   C. forgot.
   D. delayed.

   You would be impressed if the speaker seemed knowledgeable and communicated enthusiasm.

   "When the speaker seemed knowledgeable and conveyed enthusiasm, weren't you impressed?" (Paragraph 9)

Central Point and Main Ideas

Answer A covers only the first sentence of the selection and paragraph 3. Answer C covers only paragraph 8. Answer D covers only the first half of paragraph 3.

_B_ 3. Which sentence best expresses the central point of the selection?

A. Nearly everyone feels nervous about speaking in public.
B. It is possible to control the fear of public speaking.
C. You can control your nervousness about speaking by picking a topic that interests you.
D. Even famous speakers report feeling nervous before giving speeches.

Answers B, C, and D each cover only one or two sentences of the paragraph.

_A_ 4. Which sentence best expresses the main idea of paragraph 3?

A. Nearly everyone gets nervous before giving a speech, but good speakers are able to channel and control their nervousness.
B. Franklin D. Roosevelt and Abraham Lincoln were nervous before speaking.
C. Giving a speech can be a stressful experience.
D. Speakers who tremble, perspire, and experience shortness of breath and increased heartbeat may lose contact with the audience.

Answer A covers only paragraph 8. Answer B covers only paragraph 9. Answer D covers only paragraph 10.

_C_ 5. Which sentence best expresses the main idea of paragraphs 7–13?

A. When preparing a speech, choose a topic you know something about and are interested in.
B. You will feel far more confident about a speech if you prepare adequately for it.
C. There are various things you can do to cope with nervousness during the preparation for and beginning of a speech.
D. According to research, it is just before you walk up to give your speech and the time of your first contact with the audience that your fear is likely to be at its greatest.

Supporting Details

See paragraph 2.

_C_ 6. The supporting details in paragraphs 3–6 are

A. reasons public speaking is important.
B. suggestions for avoiding the fear of public speaking.
C. evidence that people learn to deal with the fear of public speaking.
D. steps in the process of public speaking.

See paragraph 4.

_B_ 7. Nervousness

A. is rarely experienced by people who give speeches on a regular basis.
B. can actually help a speaker to do his or her best.
C. cannot be effectively controlled.
D. always interferes with the effectiveness of a speech.

_B_ 8. One way to control being nervous about a speech is to
- A. speak loudly.   See paragraph 9.
- B. prepare adequately.
- C. avoid eye contact.
- D. all of the above.

Transitions

_D_ 9. The sentence below expresses a relationship of
- A. addition.   How you feel is contrasted with what you can achieve.
- B. time.
- C. cause and effect.
- D. contrast.

"Despite nervousness, you can make it through a speech." (Paragraph 4)

_A_ 10. The relationship of the second sentence below to the first is one of
- A. addition.   A second thing learned from the
- B. illustration.   experience is being added to the first one.
- C. contrast.
- D. cause and effect.

"As you gain experience, you learn to think more about the audience and the message and less about yourself. Moreover, you come to realize that audiences, your classmates especially, are very supportive, especially in informative speech situations." (Paragraph 6)

Patterns of Organization

_A_ 11. The main pattern of organization of paragraphs 3–6 is
- A. list of items.   The paragraphs list points that prove "anyone can learn
- B. time order.   to cope with the fear of public speaking."
- C. contrast.
- D. definition and example.

_A_ 12. The main pattern of organization of paragraphs 7–13 is
- A. time order.   These paragraphs present steps that take place "during
- B. contrast.   the preparation process" and continue through "the
- C. comparison.   time you actually begin the speech."
- D. definition and example.

Advanced Skill Questions

Inferences

_A_ 13. The author suggests that

See paragraph 11.

    A. thinking about your speech shortly before giving it is likely to make you more nervous.

    B. you should revise your speech up until the last possible moment.

    C. it is always best to try to be the first speaker of the day.

    D. with proper preparation, you will certainly not be nervous once your speech begins.

_D_ 14. The author suggests that with practice, you

See, for example, the end of paragraph 5 and the end of paragraph 11.

    A. can completely get over all fear of speaking in public.

    B. will find it is no longer so necessary to be in command of your speech material.

    C. will choose better and better topics for your speeches.

    D. will experience less fear when speaking.

_D_ 15. The author implies that

For answer A, see paragraph 11. For answer B, see paragraph 1. For answer C, see paragraph 12.

    A. it is possible to think about your speech too much.

    B. everyone has worthwhile ideas to share in a speech.

    C. making mistakes in a speech doesn't ruin it.

    D. all of the above.

Purpose and Tone

_C_ 16. The purpose of this reading is

    A. to inform.

    B. to persuade.

    C. both of the above.

The author wishes to persuade us "to cope with nervousness because speaking is important" and to inform us about how to do so.

_A_ 17. The tone of this reading is

    A. optimistic and helpful.

    B. outspoken and critical.

    C. sympathetic and forgiving.

    D. excited and joyous.

The author stresses the positive aspects of speaking and the likelihood of success. He also provides encouraging advice.

Argument

_A_ 18. One of the following statements is the point of the author's argument in paragraph 1. The other statements are support for that point. Write the letter of the point of the argument.

Answers B, C, and D are reasons why speaking is important.

A. Speaking is important.
B. Speaking gives us the power to share our thoughts with others.
C. Through speaking, we can provide the data needed to solve a problem.
D. We may be able to share a money-saving idea for our company.

Critical Reading

_A_ 19. The sentence below is
A. a fact.
B. an opinion.
C. both fact and opinion.

While fear is subjective, it is real and can be studied factually. One can look at the results of the research to confirm this fact.

"Research indicates that it is during the period right before you walk up to give your speech and the time when you have your initial contact with the audience that your fear is most likely to be at its greatest." (Paragraph 10)

_D_ 20. The following statement illustrates the logical fallacy of
A. circular reasoning.
B. false cause.
C. false comparison.
D. either-or.

"Either you get rid of your nervousness or you'll never become an effective public speaker."

It is possible to be nervous and to be an effective speaker, if one learns to manage the nervousness.

Outlining

Complete the outline by filling in the missing major and minor details. The missing items are listed in random order below the outline.

Central point: You can cope with the nervousness of public speaking.

A. Introduction: Since speaking is important, it's important to learn to cope with nervousness.

See paragraph 2.

B. _People can learn to cope with the fear of public speaking._

_____

1. Even good speakers get nervous; they just learn to channel and control their nervousness.
2. Nervousness won't stop you from completing a speech, and it will even help you.

3. Your nervousness during a speech won't show nearly as much as you might think it will.
4. The more experience you get in speaking, the better you become at coping with nervousness.

C. <u>There are various ways to cope with your nervousness</u>

See paragraph 7.   <u>about public speaking.</u>

1. Pick a topic you know something about and are interested in.

See paragraph 9.   2. <u>Prepare adequately for your speech.</u>

_____

3. Try to control your nervousness just before you walk up to give your speech.

   a. Try to schedule your speech at a comfortable time.
   b. Focus your mind on something other than your speech.

See paragraph 12.   4. <u>Use certain techniques as you walk to the speaker's stand and just</u>

<u>after.</u>

   a. As you walk to the speaker's stand, focus on your ideas and the fact that you're well prepared.
   b. When you reach the stand, do a few things to break some of the tension.
     1) Pause a few seconds and establish eye contact with the audience.
     2) Take a deep breath.
     3) Move about a little during your first few sentences.
     4) Concentrate on communicating with your audience.

Items Missing from the Outline

- There are various ways to cope with your nervousness about public speaking.
- Prepare adequately for your speech.
- Use certain techniques as you walk to the speaker's stand and just after.
- People can learn to cope with the fear of public speaking.

Discussion Questions

1. What have your public speaking experiences been like? Have some speeches gone better than others? If so, what were the differences, and what do you think were the reasons for those differences? What did you find helpful in preparing and giving speeches?

2. Why might it be a good idea to speak on a topic you know a great deal about and are interested in? Can you think of any examples from the speeches you've given or heard?

3. You may need to give speeches in your classes, but do you think you will have to speak in public after you graduate from school? In what situations might you have to give a speech or even a presentation to a small group?

4. Obviously, Verderber feels that nervousness is no reason to avoid speaking in public. What other activities have you willingly done despite the fact that they made you nervous in some way? Was being nervous in these situations helpful in some ways? If so, how?

Note: Writing assignments for this selection appear on page 611.

Check Your Performance   COPING WITH NERVOUSNESS

Activity	Number Right	Points	Score
Basic Skill Questions			
Vocabulary in Context (2 items)	_____	× 4 =	_____
Central Point and Main Ideas (3 items)	_____	× 4 =	_____
Supporting Details (3 items)	_____	× 4 =	_____
Transitions (2 items)	_____	× 4 =	_____
Patterns of Organization (2 items)	_____	× 4 =	_____
Advanced Skill Questions			
Inferences (3 items)	_____	× 4 =	_____
Purpose and Tone (2 items)	_____	× 4 =	_____
Argument (1 item)	_____	× 4 =	_____
Critical Reading (2 items)	_____	× 4 =	_____
Outlining (4 items)	_____	× 5 =	_____
		TOTAL SCORE =	_____%

Enter your total score into the **Reading Performance Chart: Ten Reading Selections** on the inside back cover.

7 Compliance Techniques: Getting People to Say Yes

Shelley E. Taylor, Letitia Anne Peplau, and David O. Sears

Preview

People who make a living selling products or ideas do not rely on mere chance as they make their pitch. They use time-proven techniques to convince buyers that they are getting a good deal. This selection from *Social Psychology*, Eighth Edition, reveals some widely used compliance techniques. See if you recognize any of them.

Words to Watch

compliance (1): going along with someone else's wishes
induce (2): persuade
explicitly (2): in a clear way
implicitly (2): in a way that is not obvious
replicated (4): duplicated
self-perception (5): how one views oneself
proposition (10): suggested plan
unscrupulous (10): without moral standards

1   Research has investigated the specific techniques that people use to gain compliance°. Robert Cialdini has studied car salesmen, con artists, and other professionals who earn a living by getting people to buy their products or go along with their schemes. He and other social psychology researchers have identified several important compliance techniques.

The Foot-in-the-Door Technique

2   One way of increasing compliance is to induce° a person to agree first to a small request. Once someone has agreed to the small action, he or she is more likely to agree to a larger request. This is the so-called foot-in-the-door technique. It is used explicitly° or implicitly° in many advertising campaigns. Advertisers often concentrate on getting consumers to do something connected with the product—even sending back a card saying that they do not want it. The advertisers apparently think that any act connected with the product increases the likelihood that the consumer will buy it in the future.

3   A classic study by Freedman and Fraser demonstrated this effect. Experimenters went from door to door and told homemakers they were working for the Committee for Safe Driving. They said they wanted the women's support for this campaign and asked them to sign a petition that was to be sent to the state's senators. The petition requested the senators to work for legislation to encourage safe driving. Almost all the women agreed to sign. Several weeks later, different experimenters contacted the same women and also other women who had not been approached before. At this time, all the women were asked to put in their front yards a large, unattractive sign that read "Drive Carefully."

4   The results were striking. Over 55 percent of the women who had previously endorsed the petition (a small request) also agreed to post the sign (a relatively large request). In contrast, less than 17 percent of the other women agreed to post the sign. Getting the women to agree to the initial small request tripled the amount of compliance to the large request. This effect has been replicated° in several studies.

5   Why this technique works is not entirely clear. One explanation is that people who agree to a small request get involved and committed to the issue itself, to the behavior they perform, or perhaps simply to the idea of taking some kind of action. Another explanation is based on self-perception° theory. The idea here is that in some ways the individual's self-image changes as a result of the initial act of compliance. In the safe-driving experiment, for example, a woman may have thought of herself as the kind of person who does not take social action, who does not sign petitions, who does not post signs, or, perhaps, who does not agree to things that are asked of her by someone at the door. Once she has agreed to the small request, which was actually difficult to refuse, she may have changed her perception of herself slightly. Once she has agreed to sign a petition, she may come to think of herself as the kind of person who does this sort of thing. Then, when the second request was made, she was more likely to comply than she would have been otherwise.

The Door-in-the-Face Technique

6   Sometimes a technique opposite to the foot-in-the-door also works. First asking for a very large request and then making a smaller request can increase

compliance to the small request. This is sometimes called the door-in-the-face technique, since the first request is typically so outrageously large that people might be tempted to slam the door in the requester's face. In one study, subjects were asked to volunteer time for a good cause. Some were asked first to give a huge amount of time. When they refused, as almost all did, the experimenter immediately said then perhaps they might agree to a much smaller commitment of time. Other subjects were asked only the smaller request, while a third group was given a choice between the two. The results were striking. In the small-request-only condition, 17 percent of subjects agreed. In the choice condition, 25 percent of subjects complied with the smaller request. But in the condition where subjects had first turned down a big request, 50 percent agreed to the smaller request.

7   This effect is familiar to anyone who has ever bargained about the price of a used car or been involved in negotiations between a labor union and management. The tactic is to ask for the moon and then settle for less. The more you ask for at first, the more you expect to end up with eventually. The idea is that when you reduce your demands, the other person thinks you are compromising and the amount seems smaller. In a compliance situation, such as asking for money for charity, the same might apply. Five dollars doesn't seem like so much when the organization initially asked for a hundred dollars.

Clearly, both the foot-in-the-door 8 and the reverse tactic work at times, but we do not yet know when each will be more effective. Both seem to work best when the behavior involved is prosocial, that is, when the request is to give money or help a worthwhile cause. One difference seems to be that the door-in-the-face technique works when the smaller request follows the larger request immediately and is obviously connected. The foot-in-the-door technique works even when the two requests are seemingly unconnected.

The Low-Ball Technique

Consider how likely you would be 9 to agree to the following requests. In one case, a researcher calls you on the phone and asks you to participate in an experiment scheduled for 7:00 in the morning. In a second case, a researcher calls and asks you to participate in a study. Only after you initially agree to participate does the researcher inform you that the study will be scheduled at 7:00 a.m. When Robert Cialdini and his associates compared these two procedures, they found that the second approach was much more effective. When students were told from the outset that an experiment would be conducted early in the morning, only 25 percent agreed to participate and showed up on time. In contrast, using the second approach of initially concealing the time of the study, 55 percent of students agreed to the request and almost all of them actually showed up for the early morning appointment. Once having agreed to participate, few people backed out of their agreement when they were informed about the time of day.

10   This tactic, in which a person is asked to agree to something on the basis of incomplete information and is later told the full story, is called the low-ball technique. Essentially, the person is tricked into agreeing to a relatively attractive proposition°, only to discover later that the terms are actually different from those expected. This technique appears to work because once an individual has made an initial commitment to a course of action, he or she is reluctant to withdraw, even when the ground rules are changed. Although this technique can be effective (Burger & Petty, 1981), it is clearly deceptive. To protect consumers from unscrupulous° salespersons, laws have been enacted to make low-balling illegal for several industries, such as automobile dealerships.

11   Our discussion of the foot-in-the-door, door-in-the-face, and low-ball techniques by no means exhausts the possible tactics people use to gain compliance. Research by Jerry Burger has begun to explore another strategy that he calls the **that's-not-all technique**. Consider this situation: A salesperson describes a new microwave oven to a potential customer and quotes a price. Then, while the customer is mulling over the decision, the salesperson adds, "But that's not all.

Today only, we're having a special deal. If you buy the microwave now, we'll give you a five-piece set of microwave dishes at no additional cost." In actuality, the dishes always come with the oven, but by presenting the dishes as a "special deal" or something "just for you," the salesperson hopes to make the purchase even more attractive. The essence of this technique is to present a product at a high price, allow the customer to think about the price, and then improve the deal either by adding an additional product or by lowering the price.

12   In a series of seven experiments, Burger has demonstrated the potential effectiveness of the "that's-not-all" approach. In one illustrative study, experimenters held a psychology club bake sale on campus. At random, half the people who stopped at the table and asked about the cupcakes were told that they could buy a prepackaged set including one cupcake and two cookies for 75 cents. In this control condition, 40 percent of those who inquired actually purchased a cupcake. In the "that's-not-all condition," people who inquired were first told that the cupcakes were 75 cents each. A moment later, they were told that actually, they would get not only the cupcake but also 2 cookies for the 75-cent price. In this "that's-not-all" condition, 73 percent of people bought a cupcake, a substantially higher proportion than in the control condition.

Basic Skill Questions

Vocabulary in Context

_C_ 1. In the sentence below, the word *endorsed* (ĕn-dôrst′ *or* ĭn-dôrst′)
   means

   A. rejected.
   B. asked for.
   C. supported.
   D. ignored.

   If the women "also agreed" to the large request, they must have previously supported the small request.

   "Over 55 percent of the women who had previously endorsed the petition (a small request) also agreed to post the sign (a relatively large request)." (Paragraph 4)

_D_ 2. In the excerpt below, the words *mulling over* (mŭl′ĭng ō′vər) mean

   A. regretting.
   B. paying for.
   C. agreeing to.
   D. thinking about.

   After the salesman has quoted a price, the customer would think over whether or not to buy the microwave.

   "A salesperson describes a new microwave oven to a potential customer and quotes a price. Then, while the customer is mulling over the decision, the salesperson adds, 'But that's not all. Today only, we're having a special deal.'" (Paragraph 11)

Central Point and Main Ideas

_A_ 3. Which sentence best expresses the central point of the selection?

   A. Certain techniques are widely used to persuade consumers to buy a product or go along with a plan.
   B. The foot-in-the-door technique relies on people's tendency to agree to a larger request after they have agreed to a small one.
   C. Anyone who has bargained to buy a car will recognize the door-in-the-face technique.
   D. Social psychologists study why people are influenced by certain kinds of sales techniques.

Answer B covers only paragraph 2. Answer C covers only paragraph 7, sentence 1. Answer D covers only paragraph 1.

_A_ 4. Which sentence best expresses the main idea of paragraph 5?

   A. While it is not certain why the foot-in-the-door technique works, there are some likely explanations.
   B. People adjust their actions based on changes in their self-perception.
   C. It is difficult to refuse a small, reasonable request.
   D. A woman may not have considered herself to be the sort of person who takes social action.

Answer B ignores the first two sentences of paragraph 5. Answer C covers only sentence 6. Answer D covers only sentence 5.

_B_ 5. Which sentence best expresses the main idea of paragraph 7?

Answer A covers only sentence 1.
Answer C covers only the last sentence.
Answer D covers only sentences 2–3.

A. The door-in-the-face technique is commonly used when one bargains for a used car.

B. When someone starts out making a large request and then replaces it with a smaller one, the second request seems reasonable by contrast.

C. Compared with one hundred dollars, five dollars does not seem like much.

D. People often begin negotiations by asking for more than they expect.

Supporting Details

_C_ 6. The major supporting details of the reading are a series of

A. questions.   See paragraph 1.
B. events.
C. techniques.
D. steps.

_D_ 7. One explanation given for why the foot-in-the-door technique works is that agreeing to a small task   See paragraph 5.

A. makes the person feel he or she has done enough.
B. angers the person.
C. improves a person's opinion of the requester.
D. changes the person's self-image.

Transitions

_D_ 8. The relationship of the second sentence below to the first one is one of

A. cause and effect.
B. comparison.
C. illustration.
D. time.

The two events happened in sequence. First, almost all the women agreed to sign. Then, different experimenters contacted them and also contacted other women.

"Almost all the women agreed to sign. Several weeks later, different experimenters contacted the same women and also other women who had not been approached before." (Paragraph 3)

_C_ 9. In the excerpt below, what does the second sentence do?

The degree of
compliance in the
first condition
contrasts with
that in the
second condition.

A. It establishes a cause and effect relationship.
B. It presents a solution to a problem.
C. It contrasts the responses of two groups of people to a smaller request.
D. It adds more detail to the first sentence.

"In the choice condition, 25 percent of subjects complied with the smaller request. But in the condition where subjects had first turned down a big request, 50 percent agreed to the smaller request." (Paragraph 6)

Patterns of Organization

_C_ 10. The main pattern of organization of paragraph 6 is
A. list of items.
B. time order.
C. definition and example.
D. comparison.

The door-in-the-face technique is defined and then illustrated in the context of a study.

_D_ 11. The main pattern of organization of paragraph 8 is
A. list of items.
B. time order.
C. definition and example.
D. comparison and/or contrast.

The foot-in-the-door and the door-in-the-face techniques are compared in the second sentence and contrasted in the next two sentences.

Advanced Skill Questions

Inferences

Item 12: Since the report characterizes the sign as unattractive, that feature must have been part of the study. This makes it fit in with the requirement that the second request should be something people would think twice about doing.

_C_ 12. We can infer from paragraph 3 that
A. women are more likely to be concerned about safe driving than men.
B. the experimenters were aggressive and pushy in their dealings with the homemakers.
C. the "Safe Driving" signs were deliberately made unattractive.
D. the researchers were truly employees of the Committee for Safe Driving.

_B_ 13. We can conclude from paragraph 5 that

See the first sentence
of paragraph 5.

A. experiments often reveal very little.
B. even though an experiment proves something, that doesn't mean it is fully understood.
C. human behavior is generally easy to explain.
D. we will never know why the foot-in-the-door technique works.

_D_ 14. We can conclude that the "that's-not-all" technique works because

See the end of
paragraph 11.

   A. people like to buy things.
   B. microwave ovens are especially popular these days.
   C. people buy what they need or want.
   D. people like to feel that they are getting more for their money.

Purpose and Tone

_B_ 15. The tone of the reading can be identified as

In general, the authors
simply report on the
relevant facts.

   A. upbeat and positive.
   B. scholarly and matter-of-fact.
   C. concerned and angry.
   D. forgiving and understanding.

Argument

_C_ 16. Which of the statements does **not** support the point of the argument?

Whether or not it is right
to try to influence people
has nothing to do with
the point that there are
effective ways to
influence people.

   Point: There are ways to make it more likely that people will do what you want them to do.

   A. Experiments have shown that some compliance techniques work.
   B. Salespeople find that certain techniques work better than others.
   C. There is nothing wrong with trying to influence people.
   D. People are more likely to buy something if they are made to feel it's a great bargain.

Critical Reading

_A_ 17. The sentence below is

   A. all factual.
   B. all opinion.
   C. a mix of fact and opinion.

While people might argue about what "unscrupulous salespersons" are, it is a fact that the laws have been passed for the reasons stated.

   "To protect consumers from unscrupulous salespersons, laws have been enacted to make low-balling illegal for several industries, such as automobile dealerships." (Paragraph 10)

_B_ 18. A fund-raising group which displays a large sign illustrating <u>how many people have already donated</u> to their cause is using the propaganda technique of

   A. plain folks.
   B. bandwagon.
   C. testimonial.
   D. glittering generalities.

The sign encourages people to join this group of "many people" that have already donated.

_D_ 19. A TV commercial which encourages us to purchase "The <u>amazing</u> Miracle Knives—guaranteed to make meal preparation a <u>breeze</u>" is using the propaganda technique of
A. plain folks.   The commercial tells us nothing specific about the knives.
B. bandwagon.
C. testimonial.
D. glittering generalities.

_D_ 20. The following statement illustrates the logical fallacy of
A. false comparison.
B. either-or.   A great buy and a real bargain are the same thing.
C. false cause.
D. circular reasoning.

"This product is a great buy because it's a real bargain."

Summarizing

Study notes on this reading might be made up of a summary of each compliance technique, including 1) a definition, 2) an example, and 3) an explanation of why the technique works. Complete the summary below by filling in the incomplete or missing items.

Wording of answers may vary.

Compliance Techniques

1. Foot-in-the-door technique—getting a person to agree first to a small request so that he or she is more likely to agree to a larger one. This technique may work either because people become more committed or because they change their self-image. It works even when the requests appear unconnected.

   Example: Women were more likely to agree to put a large, unattractive "Drive Carefully" sign in their front yards if they had first signed a petition asking senators to work for legislation encouraging safe driving.

2. Door-in-the-face technique—first asking for a very large request and then

   making a smaller request. The first request is so outrageously large that

   See paragraph 6, sentences 3–4.

   people might be tempted to slam the door in the requester's face.

   This works when the smaller request follows the larger one immediately and is obviously connected to it.

   See paragraph 6 from sentence 5 to the end.

   Example: Study subjects were more likely to volunteer a small amount of time for a good cause if they were first asked _____

   to give a great deal of time.

See paragraph 10, the first sentence.

3. Low-ball technique— _asking a person to agree to something on the basis_ _of incomplete information and then later telling the full story._

This may work because people are reluctant to withdraw after making a commitment.

> Example: Students were more likely to take part in an experiment at 7 a.m. if they weren't told about the time until after agreeing to participate.

4. That's-not-all technique—presenting a product at a high price, allowing the customer to think about the price, and then improving the deal either by adding an additional product or by lowering the price.

See paragraph 12.

> Example: _At a bake sale, customers were more likely to buy cupcakes_ _for 75 cents if they were told they would also get two free cookies._

Discussion Questions

1. While reading this selection, did you recognize techniques that have been used to influence you to make a purchase or support someone's plan? How were the techniques used?

2. Which of the compliance techniques do you feel is most clearly deceptive? Why?

3. The authors state that no one is really sure why the foot-in-the-door technique is effective, but they offer two possible explanations. Does either of these theories seem to you to adequately explain why the technique works? Can you think of an alternative explanation?

4. Imagine that you are in the business of selling home computers. Describe how you would use the foot-in-the-door technique, the door-in-the-face technique, and the low-ball technique to try to make a sale.

Note: Writing assignments for this selection appear on pages 611–612.

Check Your Performance

COMPLIANCE TECHNIQUES

Activity	Number Right		Points		Score
Basic Skill Questions					
Vocabulary in Context (2 items)	_____	×	4	=	_____
Central Point and Main Ideas (3 items)	_____	×	4	=	_____
Supporting Details (2 items)	_____	×	4	=	_____
Transitions (2 items)	_____	×	4	=	_____
Patterns of Organization (2 items)	_____	×	4	=	_____
Advanced Skill Questions					
Inferences (3 items)	_____	×	4	=	_____
Purpose and Tone (1 item)	_____	×	4	=	_____
Argument (1 item)	_____	×	4	=	_____
Critical Reading (4 items)	_____	×	4	=	_____
Summarizing (4 items)	_____	×	5	=	_____

TOTAL SCORE = _____ %

Enter your total score into the **Reading Performance Chart: Ten Reading Selections** on the inside back cover.

8 Lizzie Borden
James Kirby Martin and others

Preview

A prosperous businessman and his wife lay dead, murdered with an ax. Their unhappy daughter had the motive and opportunity to kill. Modern experts strongly believe that Lizzie Borden was guilty of her parents' murder. Yet she was swiftly found innocent. In this selection taken from the history textbook *America and Its People*, Second Edition, Lizzie's acquittal is examined in light of the social views of the late nineteenth century.

Words to Watch

maintained (1): claimed
alienated (3): set apart from
grisly (5): causing horror
preponderance (7): great amount
unanimous (7): agreed upon by everyone
affirmed (7): stated
preconceived (9): decided before knowing all the facts
docile (9): obedient
frivolous (9): silly

1   Andrew Borden had, as the old Scottish saying goes, short arms and long pockets. He was cheap, not because he had to be frugal but because he hated to spend money. He had dedicated his entire life to making and saving money, and tales of his unethical and parsimonious business behavior were legendary in his hometown of Fall River, Massachusetts. Local gossips maintained° that as an undertaker, he cut off the feet of corpses so that he could fit them into undersized coffins that he had purchased at a very good price. Andrew, however, was not interested in rumors or the opinions of other people; he was concerned with his own rising fortunes. By 1892 he had amassed over half a million dollars, and he controlled the Fall River Union Savings Bank as well as serving as the director of the Globe Yard Mill Company, the First National Bank, the Troy Cotton and Manufacturing Company, and the Merchants Manufacturing Company.

2   Andrew was rich, but he did not live like a wealthy man. Instead of living alongside the other prosperous Fall River citizens in the elite neighborhood known as "the Hill," Andrew resided

in an area near the business district called "the Flats." He liked to save time as well as money, and from the Flats he could conveniently walk to work. For his daughters Lizzie and Emma, whose eyes and dreams focused on the Hill, life in the Flats was an intolerable embarrassment. Their house was a grim, boxlike structure that lacked comfort and privacy. Since Andrew believed that running water on each floor was a wasteful luxury, the only washing facilities were a cold-water faucet in the kitchen and a laundry-room water tap in the cellar. Also in the cellar was the only toilet in the house. To make matters worse, the house was not connected to the Fall River gas main. Andrew preferred to use kerosene to light his house. Although it did not provide as good light or burn as cleanly as gas, it was less expensive. To save even more money, he and his family frequently sat in the dark.

3   The Borden home was far from happy. Lizzie and Emma, ages 32 and 42 in 1892, strongly disliked their stepmother, Abby, and resented Andrew's penny-pinching ways. Lizzie especially felt alienated° from the world around her. Although Fall River was the largest cotton-manufacturing town in America, it offered few opportunities for the unmarried daughter of a prosperous man. Society expected a woman of social position to marry, and while she waited for a proper suitor, her only respectable social outlets were church and community service. So Lizzie taught a Sunday school class and was active in the Women's Christian Temperance Union, the Ladies' Fruit and Flower Mission, and other organizations. She kept herself busy, but she was not happy.

4   In August, 1892, strange things started to happen in the Borden home. They began after Lizzie and Emma learned that Andrew had secretly changed his will. Abby became violently ill. In time so did the Bordens' maid Bridget Sullivan and Andrew himself. Abby told a neighborhood doctor that she had been poisoned, but Andrew refused to listen to her wild ideas.

Shortly thereafter, Lizzie went shopping for prussic acid, a deadly poison she said she needed to clean her sealskin cape. When a Fall River druggist refused her request, she left the store in an agitated state. Later in the day, she told a friend that she feared an unknown enemy of her father's was after him. "I'm afraid somebody will do something," she said.

5   On August 4, 1892, Bridget awoke early and ill, but she still managed to prepare a large breakfast of johnnycakes, fresh-baked bread, ginger and oatmeal cookies and raisins, and some three-day-old mutton and hot mutton soup. After eating a hearty meal, Andrew left for work. Bridget also left to do some work outside. This left Abby and Lizzie in the house alone. Then somebody did something very specific and very grisly°. As Abby was bent over making the bed in the guest room, someone moved into the room unobserved and killed her with an ax.

6   Andrew came home for lunch earlier than usual. He asked Lizzie where Abby was, and she said she did not know. Unconcerned, Andrew, who was not feeling well, lay down on the parlor sofa for a nap. He never awoke. Like Abby, he was slaughtered by someone with an ax. Lizzie "discovered" his body still lying on the sofa. She called Bridget, who had taken the back stairs to her attic room. "Come down quick; Father's dead; somebody came in and killed him."

7   Experts have examined and reexamined the crime, and most have reached the same conclusion: Lizzie killed her father and stepmother. In fact, Lizzie was tried for the gruesome murders. Despite a preponderance° of evidence, however, an all-male jury found her not guilty. Their verdict was unanimous° and was arrived at without debate or disagreement. A woman of Lizzie's social position, they affirmed°, simply could not have committed such a terrible crime.

8   Even before the trial began, newspaper and magazine writers had judged Lizzie innocent for the same reasons. As historian Kathryn Allamong Jacob, an expert on the case, noted, "Americans were certain that well-brought up daughters could not commit murder with a hatchet on sunny summer mornings." Criminal women, they believed, originated in the lower classes and even looked evil. They did not look like round-faced Lizzie, and did not belong to the Ladies' Fruit and Flower Mission.

9   Jurors and editorialists alike judged Lizzie according to their preconceived° notions of Victorian womanhood. They believed that such a woman was gentle, docile°, and physically frail, short on analytical ability but long on nurturing instincts. "Women," wrote an editorialist for *Scribner's*, "are merely large babies. They are shortsighted, frivolous°, and occupy an intermediate stage between children and men." Too uncoordinated and weak to accurately swing an ax and too gentle and unintelligent to coldly plan a double murder, women of Lizzie's background simply had to be innocent because of their basic innocence.

Basic Skill Questions

Vocabulary in Context

___C___ 1. In the excerpt below, the word *parsimonious* (pär′sə-mō′nē-əs) means

    A. generous.

    B. lazy.

    c. stingy.

    D. deadly.

> If he cuts the feet off corpses to make the bodies fit into cheap coffins, he must be stingy.

". . . tales of his unethical and parsimonious business behavior were legendary in his hometown . . . Local gossips maintained that as an undertaker, he cut off the feet of corpses so that he could fit them into undersized coffins that he had purchased at a very good price." (Paragraph 1)

___C___ 2. In the excerpt below, the word *amassed* (ə-măst′) means

    A. spent.

    B. found.

    c. accumulated.

    D. donated.

> The rest of the paragraph tells us he was stingy and he ran several businesses, so he must have accumulated this large amount of money.

"By 1892 [Andrew Borden] had amassed over half a million dollars . . . " (Paragraph 1)

Central Point and Main Ideas

___C___ 3. Which sentence best expresses the central point of the selection?

Answer A is incorrect; Borden had these qualities, but there is no indication that they directly caused his murder.
Answer B is not addressed by the authors.
Answer D covers only paragraph 9.

    A. Andrew Borden's unpleasant personality and cheap ways probably led to his murder.

    B. The case of Lizzie Borden should be reopened and reexamined to determine if she was truly guilty.

    c. Despite much evidence of her guilt, Lizzie Borden was found innocent of murder because of society's beliefs about women of her social class.

    D. In the late 1800s, Americans assumed that middle-class women who were well brought up were weak and gentle people who could not possibly commit a murder.

___A___ 4. The main idea of paragraph 2 is expressed in its

    A. first sentence.

    B. second sentence.

    c. third sentence.

    D. last sentence.

> The rest of the paragraph illustrates the fact that Andrew "did not live like a wealthy man."

_B_ 5. Which sentence best expresses the main idea of paragraph 8?

Answer A covers
only the last sentence.
Answer C is not stated.
Answer D covers
only sentence 3.

    A. Lizzie had a round face and belonged to the Ladies' Fruit and Flower Mission.

    B. Americans couldn't believe a pleasant-looking, respectable woman like Lizzie could be a killer.

    C. Trials in the late 1800s were widely covered in newspapers and magazines.

    D. Americans of Lizzie's day believed that killers looked evil.

Supporting Details

_A_ 6. The supporting details of paragraph 2 are mainly about

The ways Borden
saved money are the
supporting details
for the main idea.
(See question 4.)

    A. the ways in which Andrew Borden saved money.

    B. Lizzie's and Emma's embarrassment with their home.

    C. the reason the Bordens often sat in the dark.

    D. the fact that the Bordens used kerosene rather than gas for light.

_C_ 7. The odd occurrences in the Borden home began after

See paragraph 4.

    A. Bridget Sullivan was hired to be the maid.

    B. Andrew Borden brought Abby home to be Lizzie and Emma's stepmother.

    C. Andrew Borden changed his will.

    D. Lizzie joined the church's Fruit and Flower Mission.

Transitions

_B_ 8. The relationship between the two parts of the sentence below is one of

    A. cause and effect.

    B. contrast.

    C. time order.

    D. addition.

The sentence contrasts the two neighborhoods.

"Instead of living alongside the other prosperous Fall River citizens in the elite neighborhood known as 'the Hill,' Andrew resided in an area near the business district called 'the Flats.'" (Paragraph 2)

_A_ 9. In the following excerpt, what does the second sentence do?

Cause: Lizzie's only
respectable social
outlets were church
and community
service (first sentence).
Effect: Lizzie taught
Sunday school and was
active in community
organizations
(second sentence).

    A. It establishes a cause and effect relationship.

    B. It contrasts Lizzie Borden's behavior with that of other women.

    C. It defines a term in the first sentence.

    D. It compares Lizzie Borden to other women of social position.

"Society expected a woman of social position to marry, and while she waited for a proper suitor, her only respectable social outlets were church and community service. So Lizzie taught a Sunday school class and was active in the the Women's Christian Temperance Union, the Ladies' Fruit and Flower Mission, and other organizations." (Paragraph 3)

Patterns of Organization

_B_ 10. Paragraph 2 is organized as a

The ways the
Bordens saved
money are listed.

A. series of events in the Borden household.
B. list of ways in which the Bordens lived very thriftily.
C. comparison and contrast between the members of the Borden household.
D. definition of *wealthy* followed by examples.

_A_ 11. The pattern of organization of paragraphs 4–6 is

The author narrates
the events at the
time of the murder
in the order in which
they occurred.

A. time order.
B. list of items.
C. comparison and contrast.
D. definition and example.

Advanced Skill Questions

Inferences

_C_ 12. We can infer from the mention of Andrew Borden's changing his will that

Lizzie apparently
took action because
the will was changed
(paragraph 4).

A. he had decided to leave all of his money to his daughters.
B. he was a lawyer.
C. his new will was unfavorable to Lizzie.
D. his new wife was not going to inherit any of his money.

_C_ 13. The authors imply that Bridget, Andrew, and Abby all became ill at about the same time because

See paragraph 4.

A. they became sick from living in the cold, dark house.
B. they suffered from food poisoning as a result of eating three-day-old mutton.
C. Lizzie poisoned them.
D. Bridget poisoned them, but pretended to be ill herself to hide her actions.

_C_ 14. Which of the following statements is a valid conclusion based on the information in paragraph 9?

Women are
described as
occupying "an
intermediate stage
between children
and men"
(paragraph 9).

A. The editorialist for *Scribner's* expressed opinions that were unusual for the day.
B. Lizzie Borden was an exceptionally unintelligent, gentle person.
C. Men were thought to be more competent, mature, and intelligent than women.
D. The ax used in the Borden murders was very heavy.

Purpose and Tone

_A_ 15. The main purpose of this selection is to

The authors show
why they feel the
jury was wrong
(paragraphs 7–9).

    A. persuade the reader that society's views about women led to Lizzie
       Borden's being found innocent of two murders that she probably
       committed.

    B. inform the reader about the everyday life of a well-known nineteenth-
       century family and about a famous trial of the time.

    C. entertain the reader with a crime story.

_B_ 16. In general, the authors' tone is

The authors present
facts and then
analyze them.

    A. sad and hopeless.
    B. objective and analytical.
    C. light and amusing.
    D. bitterly critical.

Argument

_D_ 17. Which statement does **not** support the following point?

Answer D has nothing
to do with her guilt or
innocence.

Point: Lizzie Borden was probably guilty.

    A. She had attempted to buy poison shortly before the killings.
    B. She was miserable living with her stingy father and disliked her
       stepmother.
    C. She was alone in the house with her parents when the killings
       occurred.
    D. She was active in church and community organizations.

_B_ 18. One of the following statements is the point of an argument. The other
    statements support that point. Write the letter of the point.

Statements A, C, and
D are reasons for the
conclusion in B.

    A. The common belief that upper-class women were unable to swing an
       ax well was false.
    B. The jurors' reasoning in finding Lizzie Borden innocent was faulty.
    C. The jurors' idea that criminals looked a certain way was mistaken.
    D. The jurors' belief that women were too gentle and unintelligent to
       plan a murder was false.

Critical Reading

___A___ 19. The sentence below contains

Everything in the sentence can be verified in historical records.

A. only facts.
B. only opinions.
C. a mixture of both fact and opinion.

> "By 1892 he had amassed over half a million dollars, and he controlled the Fall River Union Savings Bank as well as serving as the director of the Globe Yard Mill Company, the First National Bank, the Troy Cotton and Manufacturing Company, and the Merchants Manufacturing Company." (Paragraph 1)

___D___ 20. The following excerpt is an example of which logical fallacy?

The statement says that women like Lizzie were innocent because they were innocent.

A. False comparison
B. Either-or
C. False cause
D. Circular reasoning

> "Too uncoordinated and weak to accurately swing an ax and too gentle and unintelligent to coldly plan a double murder, women of Lizzie's background simply had to be innocent because of their basic innocence." (Paragraph 9)

Summarizing

In the space provided, write the letter of the paragraph (A, B, or C) that best summarizes the reading "Lizzie Borden."

As you read the three choices, keep in mind that a good summary will include general statements that sum up the selection. It will cover the key elements of the reading. Some specific details may be included as well.

___B___ is the best summary of the reading.

Answer A omits paragraphs 1–2 and 8–9.
Answer C omits much of paragraphs 4–6 and all of paragraphs 7–9.

A. Lizzie Borden lived the respectable life expected of a woman of social position. One day she and her sister discovered that their father, Andrew, had secretly changed his will. Strange things then began to happen in the Borden household. First of all, their stepmother, Abby, became violently ill. After that, the Bordens' maid, Bridget Sullivan, and Andrew himself became ill too. Then Lizzie went shopping for a deadly poison, prussic acid. She said she needed it to clean her sealskin cape. However, the local druggist refused to sell the poison to her. Lizzie later told a friend that she feared an enemy would do something to her father. On August 4,

Lizzie was alone in the house with her stepmother. As Abby was making a bed in the guest room, someone came into the room unobserved and killed her with an ax. Later that day, Andrew came home for lunch and, feeling unwell, lay down on the parlor sofa and napped. He never woke up. Like Abby, he was axed to death. Although there is strong evidence that Lizzie was the murderer, she was found innocent in a trial.

B. Lizzie Borden lived the respectable life expected of unmarried women of her social class, but she wasn't happy. Although her father, Andrew, was rich, he was miserly, and the Borden home was grim. In addition, Lizzie disliked her stepmother, Abby. In 1892, she and her sister learned their father had changed his will. Soon after, Abby and then the maid and Andrew became very ill. After that, Lizzie tried unsuccessfully to buy a deadly poison. Then, on August 4, both Abby and Andrew were found axed to death. Lizzie was tried for the crimes. Although experts today conclude she was guilty, the jury found her innocent. Like others of their day, they believed that upper-class women were too gentle, weak, and stupid to plan and carry out a murder. Also, they believed that criminal women came from the lower classes and looked evil.

C. Andrew Borden was rich but miserly. The Borden home, therefore, lacked comforts. It had no running water on each floor, and the only toilet in the house was in the cellar. To save money, since kerosene was cheaper than gas, the house was not connected to the town gas main. And to save yet more money, the Bordens often sat in the dark. Furthermore, the house was in a neighborhood near the business district, not the elite neighborhood that his daughters, Lizzie and Emma, felt was equal to their social class. The sisters also disliked their stepmother, Abby. Women of the time were expected to marry and, while waiting for the proper man, to do volunteer work for the church and community. So Lizzie taught a Sunday school class and was active in such organizations as the Women's Christian Temperance Union and the Ladies' Fruit and Flower Mission. One day she discovered her father had changed his will; not long after that, he and Abby were found axed to death.

Discussion Questions

1. On the basis of the information in the reading, do you agree or disagree with the experts who say Lizzie was guilty? Explain your answer.

2. As you read this selection, what impression did you form of life in the Borden household? What particular details helped you form that opinion?

3. The authors imply that the story about Andrew Borden's cutting off the feet of corpses to make them fit undersized coffins was a rumor, not a proved fact. Why, then, do you think they include the story in this piece?

4. Do you believe that any of the notions about women that existed in Lizzie Borden's day are still at work in some ways today? Explain your answer.

Note: Writing assignments for this selection appear on page 612.

Check Your Performance   LIZZIE BORDEN

Activity	Number Right	Points	Score
Basic Skill Questions			
Vocabulary in Context (2 items)	_____	× 4 =	_____
Central Point and Main Ideas (3 items)	_____	× 4 =	_____
Supporting Details (2 items)	_____	× 4 =	_____
Transitions (2 items)	_____	× 4 =	_____
Patterns of Organization (2 items)	_____	× 4 =	_____
Advanced Skill Questions			
Inferences (3 items)	_____	× 4 =	_____
Purpose and Tone (2 items)	_____	× 4 =	_____
Argument (2 items)	_____	× 4 =	_____
Critical Reading (2 items)	_____	× 4 =	_____
Summarizing (1 item)	_____	× 20 =	_____
		TOTAL SCORE =	_____%

Enter your total score into the **Reading Performance Chart: Ten Reading Selections** on the inside back cover.

9 Nonverbal Communication
Anthony F. Grasha

Preview

When we think of communication, we usually think of language. But a great deal of human communication takes place without speaking. When we are angry, we may make a fist. When we are happy, our faces give us away. The extent to which we reveal our feelings without words, however, goes much further than we are often aware of. In this excerpt from a college textbook titled *Practical Applications of Psychology,* Third Edition, Anthony F. Grasha provides an overview of just how much we really say without words.

Words to Watch

norms (2): normal standards
culprit (6): guilty one
manipulate (7): use
utterances (7): expressions
quivering (8): trembling

1   The way we dress, our mannerisms, how close we stand to people, eye contact, touching, and the ways we mark our personal spaces convey certain messages. *Such nonverbal behaviors communicate certain messages by themselves and also enhance the meaning of our verbal communications.* Pounding your fist on a table, for example, suggests anger without anything being spoken. Holding someone close to you conveys the message that you care. To say "I don't like you" with a loud voice or waving fists increases the intensity of the verbal message. Let us examine the concepts of *personal space* and *body language* to gain additional insights into the nonverbal side of interpersonal communication.

NONVERBAL MESSAGES: The Use of Personal Space

2   Edward Hall notes that we have personal spatial territories or zones that allow certain types of behaviors and communications. We allow only certain people to enter or events to occur within a zone. Let us look at how some nonverbal messages can be triggered by behaviors that violate the norms° of each zone. The four personal zones identified by Hall are as follows:

3   **1. Intimate distance.** This personal zone covers a range of distance from

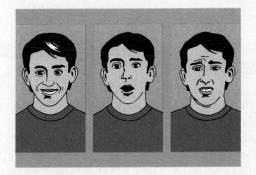

ever happened to you?

body contact to one foot. Relationships between a parent and child, lovers, and close friends occur within this zone. As a general rule, we allow only people we know and have some affection for to enter this zone. When people try to enter without our permission, they are strongly repelled by our telling them to stay away from us or by our pushing them away. Why do you think we allow a doctor to easily violate our intimate distance zone?

4   **2. Personal distance.** The spatial range covered by this zone extends from one to four feet. Activities like eating in a restaurant with two or three other people, sitting on chairs or on the floor in small groups at parties, or playing cards occur within this zone. Violations of the zone make people feel uneasy and act nervously. When you are eating at a restaurant, the amount of table space that is considered yours is usually divided equally by the number of people present. I can remember becoming angry and generally irritated when a friend of mine placed a plate and glass in my space. As we talked I was visibly irritated, but my anger had nothing to do with the topic we discussed. Has this

3. Social distance. Four to twelve 5 feet is the social distance zone. Business meetings, large formal dinners, and small classroom seminars occur within the boundaries of the social distance zone. Discussions concerning everyday topics like the weather, politics, or a best seller are considered acceptable. For a husband and wife to launch into a heated argument during a party in front of ten other people would violate the accepted norms for behavior in the social zone. This once happened at a formal party I attended. The nonverbal behaviors that resulted consisted of several people leaving the room, others looking angry or uncomfortable, and a few standing and watching quietly with an occasional upward glance and a rolling of their eyeballs. What would violate the social distance norms in a classroom?

4. Public distance. This zone in- 6 cludes the area beyond twelve feet. Addressing a crowd, watching a sports event, and sitting in a large lecture section are behaviors we engage in within this zone. As is true for the other zones, behaviors unacceptable for this zone can trigger nonverbal messages. At a recent World Series game a young male took his clothes off and ran around the outfield. Some watched with amusement on their faces, others looked away, and a few waved their fists at the culprit°. The respective messages were "That's funny," "I'm afraid or ashamed to look," and "How dare you interrupt the game." What would your reaction be in this situation?

NONVERBAL MESSAGES:
The Use of Body Language

7   *Body language* refers to the various arm and hand gestures, facial expressions, tones of voice, postures, and body movements we use to convey certain messages. According to Erving Goffman, they are the things we "give off" when talking to other people. Goffman notes that our body language is generally difficult to manipulate° at will. Unlike our verbal utterances°, we have less conscious control over the specific body gestures or expressions we might make while talking. Unless we are acting on a stage or purposely trying to create a certain effect, they occur automatically without much thought on our part.

8   Michael Argyle notes that body language serves several functions for us. *It helps us to communicate certain emotions, attitudes, and preferences.* A hug by someone close to us lets us know we are appreciated. A friendly wave and smile as someone we know passes us lets us know we are recognized. A quivering° lip tells us that someone is upset. Each of us has become quite sensitive to the meaning of various body gestures and expressions. Robert Rosenthal has demonstrated that this sensitivity is rather remarkable. When shown films of people expressing various emotions, individuals were able to identify the emotion correctly 66 percent of the time even when each frame was exposed for one twenty-fourth of a second. *Body language also supports our verbal communications.* Vocal signals of timing, pitch, voice stress, and various gestures add meaning to our verbal utterances. Argyle suggests that we may speak with our vocal organs, but we converse with our whole body. *Body language helps to control our conversations.* It helps us to decide when it is time to stop talking, to interrupt the other person, and to know when to shift topics or elaborate on something because our listeners are bored, do not understand us, or are not paying attention.

Basic Skill Questions

Vocabulary in Context

_____B_____ 1. In the excerpt below, the word *enhance* (ĕn-hăns′) means

If nonverbal behaviors can communicate messages by themselves, they would also reinforce the meaning of verbal communications.

A. replace.   C. contradict.
B. reinforce.   D. delay.

"The way we dress, our mannerisms . . . convey certain messages. Such nonverbal behaviors communicate certain messages by themselves and also enhance the meaning of our verbal communications." (Paragraph 1)

_B_ 2. In the excerpt below, the word *repelled* (rĭ-pĕld´) means

Telling people to stay away would make them turn away from us.

A. greeted.   C. encouraged.
B. turned away.   D. ignored.

"When people try to enter without our permission, they are strongly repelled by our telling them to stay away from us. . . ." (Paragraph 3)

Central Point and Main Ideas

Answer A covers only the third sentence of paragraph 1. Answer B is too broad because the selection deals with only two types of nonverbal messages. Answer D covers only paragraph 8.

_C_ 3. Which sentence best expresses the central point of the selection?

A. It is possible to express anger without words.
B. People communicate with each other in various ways.
C. We can convey nonverbal messages and emphasize verbal messages through the use of personal space and body language.
D. According to Michael Argyle, body language has several functions.

Answer A is contradicted in the paragraph. Answer B ignores sentences 1–2. Answer C covers only the last sentence.

_D_ 4. Which sentence best expresses the main idea of paragraph 7?

A. We must plan our body language.
B. It is hard to control body language.
C. Actors use body language to create an effect.
D. *Body language* refers to the nonverbal ways we communicate, usually without conscious control.

_A_ 5. The main idea of paragraph 8 is expressed in its

A. first sentence.
B. second sentence.
C. next-to-last sentence.
D. last sentence.

The first sentence states that body language serves several functions, according to Argyle. The paragraph goes on to name and discuss three functions, highlighted in italics.

Supporting Details

_A_ 6. According to Rosenthal's work, we

A. frequently understand body language.
B. rarely understand body language.
C. always understand body language.
D. never understand body language.

See paragraph 8, sentences 7–8.

Item 7: For answer A: see paragraphs 3–6. For answer B: see paragraph 8, for example. For answer C: the four categories of personal space, for instance, represent Hall's opinions on how to categorize personal space.

_D_ 7. To support his central point, the author uses

A. examples.   C. opinions of other experts.
B. research.   D. all of the above.

_D_ 8. The major supporting details of the reading are

A. nonverbal messages and verbal messages.
B. communicating well and communicating poorly.
C. intimate distance and body language.
D. communicating through personal space and through body language.

Item 8: See the headings in the reading.

Transitions

_A_ 9. In the following excerpt, what does the second sentence do?

The second sentence gives a specific example (pounding your fist) to illustrate a behavior that communicates a message by itself.

A. It illustrates and adds detail to the first sentence.
B. It establishes a cause and effect relationship.
C. It shows a time order relationship.
D. It contrasts verbal and nonverbal forms of communication.

> *"Such nonverbal behaviors communicate certain messages by themselves and also enhance the meaning of our verbal communications. Pounding your fist on a table, for example, suggests anger without anything being spoken."* (Paragraph 1)

Patterns of Organization

_C_ 10. The pattern of organization of paragraph 3 (as well as 4, 5, and 6) is

A. time order.   Each of these paragraphs begins with a boldfaced
B. cause and effect.   term which is then defined and illustrated.
C. definition and example.
D. list of items.

Item 11:
The words *several functions* in the first sentence suggest that a list will follow. The rest of the paragraph goes on to name and discuss three functions.

_B_ 11. On the whole, paragraph 8

A. compares and contrasts body language and verbal expression.
B. lists the functions of body language.
C. defines body language and gives examples of it.
D. uses time order to narrate an incident about body language.

Advanced Skill Questions

Inferences

Item 12: In paragraphs 4, 5, and 6, the author gives examples of people's automatic reactions to others who invade their personal space.

_T_ 12. TRUE OR FALSE? Just as body language generally occurs automatically, so do our reactions to the use or misuse of our personal space.

Item 13: If our body language occurs "automatically without much thought on our part," we can conclude that we sometimes unknowingly move in ways that reveal our true feelings.

_B_ 13. Goffman's ideas on body language (paragraph 7) imply that

A. we usually are aware of our own body language.
B. our body language might reveal emotions we wish to hide.
C. we can never manipulate our body language.
D. we should learn to manipulate our body language.

_A_ 14. We can conclude from the reading and our own experience that body language

A. communicates positive and negative messages of all sorts.
B. is best at communicating friendly messages.
C. communicates poorly.   Paragraph 8 supports this conclusion.
D. communicates rarely.

_B_ 15. Two students reviewing together for a test would be working within
   A. an intimate distance.
   B. a personal distance.   See paragraph 4.
   C. a social distance.
   D. a public distance.

Purpose and Tone

_A_ 16. The author's primary purpose in this selection is to
   A. inform us about nonverbal communication and how it works.
   B. persuade us that nonverbal communication is as important as conversation.
   C. entertain us with anecdotes involving funny or embarassing public behavior.

The author is simply presenting information.

_B_ 17. On the whole, the author's tone is
   A. humorous.
   B. objective.   The author presents the information in a straightforward, factual manner.
   C. scornful.
   D. enthusiastic.

Argument

_D_ 18. Write the letter of the statement that is the point of the following argument. Note that two other statements support the point, and that one statement expresses another point.
   A. I became angry and generally irritated when a friend of mine placed a plate and glass in my space.
   B. As we talked I was visibly irritated, but my anger had nothing to do with the topic we discussed.
   C. Business meetings take place within the boundaries of the social distance zone.
   D. Violations of the personal zone make people feel uneasy and act nervously.

Statements A and B give examples of uneasy and nervous reactions to a violation of the personal zone. Statement C is about the social distance zone, not the personal zone.

Critical Reading

_A_ 19. The sentence below is
   A. totally factual.
   B. only opinion.
   C. both fact and opinion.

The information can be verified in records of Rosenthal's study.

"When shown films of people expressing various emotions, individuals were able to identify the emotion correctly 66 percent of the time even when each frame was exposed for one twenty-fourth of a second." (Paragraph 8)

_B_ 20. An ad featuring a beautiful young woman draped over a luxury convertible is using the propaganda technique of

Owning this car will make you seem attractive and young.

- A. bandwagon.
- B. transfer.
- C. testimonial.
- D. plain folks.

Outlining

Complete the following outline of "Nonverbal Communication" by using the information in the boldfaced headings, italics, and numbers in the selection. (Five items need to be added to the outline.)   *Wording of answers may vary.*

Central point: **Our use of personal space and body language communicates meaning and emphasizes verbal communication.**

See heading before paragraph 2.

A. Nonverbal message: the use of personal space

1. Intimate distance

2. Personal distance

3. Social distance   See boldfaced term in paragraph 5.

4. Public distance   See boldfaced term in paragraph 6.

B. Nonverbal messages: the use of body language

1. Definition and explanation of body language

2. Functions of body language

See paragraph 8, first italicized sentence.

a. Helps communicate certain emotions, attitudes, and preferences

See paragraph 8, second italicized sentence.

b. Supports our verbal communications

c. Helps control our conversations

Discussion Questions

1. What are your answers to the following questions from the selection? Why do you think the author included these questions?

- Why do you think we allow a doctor to easily violate our intimate distance zone?

- I can remember becoming angry and generally irritated when a friend of mine placed a plate and glass in my space. . . . Has this ever happened to you?

- What would violate the social distance norms in a classroom?

2. This selection includes headings, italics, labels, and numbered items. How are these related to the author's purpose?

3. What are some examples of a dating or business situation in which someone's body language might contradict his or her verbal communication?

4. Give examples from your own experience of all four types of personal space.

Note: Writing assignments for this selection appear on page 613.

Check Your Performance   NONVERBAL COMMUNICATION

Activity	Number Right	Points	Score
Basic Skill Questions			
Vocabulary in Context (2 items)	_____	× 4 =	_____
Central Point and Main Ideas (3 items)	_____	× 4 =	_____
Supporting Details (3 items)	_____	× 4 =	_____
Transitions (1 item)	_____	× 4 =	_____
Patterns of Organization (2 items)	_____	× 4 =	_____
Advanced Skill Questions			
Inferences (4 items)	_____	× 4 =	_____
Purpose and Tone (2 items)	_____	× 4 =	_____
Argument (1 item)	_____	× 4 =	_____
Critical Reading (2 items)	_____	× 4 =	_____
Outlining (5 items)	_____	× 4 =	_____
	TOTAL SCORE	=	_____%

Enter your total score into the **Reading Performance Chart: Ten Reading Selections** on the inside back cover.

10 The Power Within
John Langan

Preview

Year after year, teachers watch the latest group of college students arrive in their classrooms. After a while, an observant teacher can begin to predict, with pretty good accuracy, which students will succeed and which will not. Here a veteran teacher explains that the most important factor is not a student's IQ. Read on to discover the real secrets behind college (and life!) success.

Words to Watch

slouching (10): hunched over
resignation (11): acceptance of defeat
peers (17): buddies
succumb (19): surrender
passive (29); inactive
clique (42): gang

1   In the first college writing class that I taught, I had a student who was drowning.

2   Gerald was a quiet young man who wore sunglasses, did not speak in class, and sat in the back of the room. I didn't know he was drowning until I collected a mid-semester assignment which asked students to write about what they had done—or not done—to take charge of their lives.

3   I still remember reading Gerald's essay, listening to the voice of a young person flooded with pain and regret. It was so moving I asked him if I could copy and share it with other students. He agreed, and then, several weeks later, he stopped coming to class and I never saw him again. All that remains are his words:

MY LIFE

4   Somewhere, a little piece of me is lost and crying. Someplace, deep in the shadows of my subconscious, a piece of my soul has sat down and anchored itself in defeat and is trying to pull me down into the darkness with it. This might sound strange to someone who is not familiar with the inner conflicts that can tear and pull at a person's soul until he begins to stop and sink in his own deep-hollow depths. But sinking doesn't take much. It takes only one

little flaw which left unattended will grow and grow . . . until, like cancer, it consumes the soul.

5   I know now, and I have always known, that help comes first from within. I know that if one doesn't come to one's own rescue, then all is lost. I know it is time for me to look at myself, which I would rather avoid. But in order to break free of my own chains, I must look at myself.

6   I could relate the incidents of youth. I could tell of many past failures and what I think caused them. But I won't, for one example will show where I'm at. At the beginning of this summer I set my goals. These goals consisted of the college courses I wanted to complete and where I wanted to be physically and mentally when the summer was over. Listed among the goals to be accomplished were courses I needed in writing and accounting. But now I am so far behind in both courses it looks as if I will fail them both. I ask myself, "Why?" I know that if I work enough, I can handle the courses. So why am I so lazy? Why is it that the things I seem to want most, I either give up or in some way do not strive for? These are the questions I must try to answer.

7   I think I've spent too much of my life just waiting for good things to come. I've waited for a magic rainbow to appear in the sky and to drop a pot of gold in my lap. I've been hurt so much in life and I just wanted it handed to me.

8   But it's time for me to stop chasing rainbows. It's time to stop looking into the sky waiting for help to arrive. It's time for me to start bailing the rot out of my mind, to stop dreaming and not acting, before I have nothing left to hope for. I can see now that I've never given it the total effort, that I've always been afraid I would fail or not measure up. So I've quit early. Instead of acting on my dreams, I've laid back and just drifted along. I've lived too much time in this world unfulfilled. I've got to make my dreams work. I must do this now, and what it takes is the doing. Somehow I must learn to succeed at success rather than at failure, and the time to start is now.

9   I have known other students over the years who, like Gerald, were involved in an inner battle. It's often clear they regard themselves as unlikely to succeed in school. They walk into the classroom carrying defeat on their shoulders the way other students carry textbooks under their arms.

10   I'd look at them slouching° in their seats and staring into space and think, "What terrible things have gone on in their lives that they've quit already? They have so little faith in their ability to learn that they're not even trying." Such students often suddenly disappear one day, just as Gerald did, and no one pays much notice because they had already disappeared in spirit long before.

11   When I have seen such students with resignation° in their eyes, I have wanted to shake them by the shoulders and say, "You are not dead. Be proud and pleased that you have brought yourself this far. Yes, life has probably been very hard, but you can still be someone. Get off the bench. Come onto the playing field. Give it a shot. You'll never learn to succeed if you don't try."

Running from the Power Within

12   For years I have watched what happens when a school year unfolds. As the crunch of work begins, students are put up against the wall. Like it or not, they must define their role in school. There are only two roads to take. One road is to do the work: to click off the stereo or television, reject the invitation to go out, shut off the cell phone, stop everything and anything else, and go do the essentially lonely work that studying is. The other road is to escape the work.

13   Below I describe escape routes I've seen students take. If you see yourself in any of these situations, you need to know it. Self-knowledge is power. Once you are aware of what you are doing, you can begin to deal with it.

"I Can't Do It."

14   Some people will let themselves be discouraged by bad grades. They'll think, "There's no use trying. I'm just not any good at this." But the only way people will really know that they cannot do something is by first trying—giving it their best shot. They must not let a defeatist attitude keep them from making a real effort. If you think you "can't do it," the reason may be that you have given up far too soon.

"I'm Too Busy."

15   Some people make themselves too busy, perhaps working more hours on a part-time job than they need to. Others get overly involved in social activities. Others allow personal or family problems to become so distracting that they cannot concentrate on their work. There are situations in which people are so busy or troubled that they cannot do their work. But there are also situations where people exaggerate conflicts or stress. They create an excuse for not doing what they know they should do.

"I'm Too Tired."

16   People with this excuse usually become tired as soon as it's time to write a paper or study a book or go to class. Their weariness clears up when the work period ends. The "sleepiness syndrome" also expresses itself in the imagined need for naps during the day and then ten hours or more of sleep at night. Such students are, often literally, closing their eyes to the hard work that school demands.

"I'll Do It Later."

17   Everyone tends at times to procrastinate—to put things off. Some students, however, constantly postpone assignments and study. Time and time again they put off what needs to be done so they can watch TV, talk to a friend, hang out with their peers,° or do any one of a hundred other things. They typically wind up cramming for tests and writing last-minute papers, and they often seem surprised and angry at their low grades.

"I'm Bored with the Subject."

18   Students sometimes explain that they are doing poorly in a course because the instructor or the subject matter is boring. These students want education to be entertainment—an unrealistic expectation. On the whole, courses and instructors balance out: Some are boring, some are exciting, many are in between. If a course is not interesting, students should be all the more motivated to do the work so that they can leave the course behind once and for all.

"I'm Here, and That's What Counts."

19   Some students spend their time at school lost in a dangerous kind of fantasy. They feel, "All will be well, for here I am in school. I have a student ID in my pocket, a sweatshirt with the school name on it, and textbooks on my desk. All this proves I am a student." Such students have given in to a fantasy we all at times succumb° to: the belief that we will get something for nothing. But we find out soon enough that such a hope is a false one. Life seldom gives us something for nothing—and school won't either.

20   We have probably all known students who escape. They make excuses. They never really determine to try their best. They know what they should do but don't do it. They fool themselves, time and time again. They try to have as much fun as they can, and they keep saying, "Tomorrow. Tomorrow I will get serious. Tomorrow I will start working hard." There is often a terrible hurt deep inside them. And for some reason a switch within never turns on, a spark of determination never ignites. They are individuals who are unable to take charge of their own lives and to work hard, as Gerald puts it, "to succeed at success."

Turning On
the Power Within

21   Wouldn't be great if we could go to a drugstore and buy motivational pills? These personal power pills would energize our attitude. We would turn on to success and take charge of our lives and pursue worthy goals. We would be determined and self-disciplined, and nothing would stop us. Of course, there are no such pills. What I am going to offer you instead are some thoughts. Read and think about them and see if you can get them into your soul.

Thought #1:
Having a Dream

22   Several years ago, my wife and I were vacationing in New Mexico. As we drove into one small town, we suddenly came upon a huge billboard. I was so struck by what it said that I stopped our car and wrote down the words.

> **If you never have a dream, you'll never have a dream come *true*.**

23   You need to have a dream within you—a belief and resolve in your heart that you will take charge of your life and make yourself proud.

24   Consider this basic truth about human nature: we all want to respect ourselves. We all want to live our lives in such a way that we think well of our behavior and others think well of us. We do not want to be disrespected or seen as bad people. An equally basic truth is that the only way we can get respect is to earn it. At a certain point in growing up, we realize that life doesn't give us something for nothing. What is important and meaningful is what we earn through trying hard and working hard.

25   Take a minute to think about the following question: Imagine two people. The first person has drifted unhappily through life, putting in a minimal effort at a series of jobs and maybe even at times living off others. One morning the telephone rings and someone says to this person, "Congratulations. You have just won a million dollars in the state lottery." The second person works hard and eventually earns a million dollars; that person is well-regarded by others and has a strong sense of accomplishment and self-worth. Which person would you rather be—the one who *won* a million dollars or the one who *earned* a million dollars?

26   Of course, we'd all like to wake up one morning and learn that we've just won a million dollars. But let's face it: this isn't very likely. In fact, it's close to impossible. So if you're realistic, chances are you would choose to be the person who worked hard, overcame obstacles, and achieved success. If you relate

to that person, your attitude may be something like this: "I want to respect myself and have others respect me. To get this respect, I'm going to work hard to succeed. At this stage in my life, that means doing well in school because education is clearly a key to success." And if you've made mistakes in the past (and many of us have), your attitude should be: "I can change my behavior. I'm going to learn to work hard so I can get somewhere and be someone."

Thought #2
Your Attitude about Learning

27   Think about your own attitude toward learning. Put a check by the item or items that apply to you. (If you agree with some sentences in an item but not others, cross out the ones you do not agree with.)

28   _____ School has never really turned me on. I feel I can start to study if I need to, but I don't want to. What's wrong with being a bit lazy? Life is supposed to be about enjoying yourself and having some fun. I want to take it easy and have as much good time as I can for now.

29   _____ I suppose I am passive° about studying, but it's not all my fault. I'm tired of being told what to do. I'm tired of being force-fed what other people think I need to learn. A lot of the stuff is not going to be of any value to me as far as I can see. I can't wait to get out of school and be on my own so I can start living my life.

30   _____ If I study too much, I'll miss out on the good times that school has to offer. I won't have time to go to games or parties. And I don't want to be alone. If I start studying, some of my friends are going to think twice about hanging out with me.

31   _____ I want to do more in school, but I'm afraid of really giving it a good effort. What if I try my best and I still get lousy grades? People will just laugh at me. I don't want to look foolish, so I'm probably just going to drift along and not call any attention to myself.

32   _____ I guess I've just been out of it for a long time. There are probably lots of reasons why. I never got any encouragement along the way. I pretty much just let things happen to me. I feel like a piece of driftwood that's been tossed about on a stormy sea. I do want to do something and to become someone. I've felt like this for a while, and at times I really want to get serious. But so far I just haven't done so.

33   _____ I'm not an active student who tries my best all the time. But I'm not a zombie either. I do some studying, just not as much as other people would like me to. I should probably do more, and I'm going to work on that and try to do a better job of taking charge of my studies.

34   _____ I feel something stirring within me. For a long time I was dead to learning, but I want to get somewhere. I'm ready

to be a serious student. It's true that some of the stuff I have to study is boring, and some teachers do not care. But I feel now that these are just hurdles that will not stop me. I'm going to start doing more to get where I want to go.

35 _____ I'm on the move, and I have taken charge of my life. There is something inside me that is strong and determined to succeed. I feel in my heart of hearts that nothing is going to stop me. It's my life, and I'm going to work hard and respect myself and gain success and happiness.

36 So where do you fit? The items above will help you think about what your attitude is and how you can improve it.

Thought #3
Doing the Work

37 The heart of the matter is not the speed at which a person learns; the heart of the matter is his or her determination—"I *will* learn." I have seen people who had this quality of determination or persistence do poorly in a course (often because of out-of-class problems or events), come back and repeat it, and finally succeed.

38 Through knowing such determined people, I've come to feel that the single most important factor for school survival and success is an inner commitment to doing the work. When the crunch comes—and the crunch is the plain hard work that school requires—the person with the commitment meets it head-on; the person without the commitment avoids it in a hundred different ways.

39 On the following scale of *Passive* to *Determined*, where would you rate yourself?

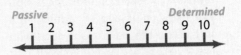

Passive   *Determined*

1 2 3 4 5 6 7 8 9 10

40 Why have you rated yourself at that point on the scale? What strengths can you build upon? What are the personal challenges you must overcome?

Thought # 4
An Unequal Playing Field

41 There is a popular idea in America that has always made me uneasy. It is the idea that success is within us—that we can all "pull ourselves up by our bootstraps" and triumph over tough odds.

42 Now there is truth to this idea, but it is not the whole truth. Life is like a race, and there are different lanes on the racetrack. Some of us are in lanes where there are no obstacles on the track. Some of us are in lanes where there are all kinds of obstacles—for example, personal health challenges, family neglect or abuse, poverty, racism, a neighborhood environment with violence and drugs, a school where one's peers are not into studies but into "respecting themselves" by being in the

right clique,° wearing the right kind of footwear, having the right hair style, or whatever.

43   If you're in a track that is full of obstacles, you can get worn down. You can start losing hope. And then it is harder to ignite the spark of determination within. In such circumstances, you must try your best to be a hero. You must battle the odds. You must keep alive a belief deep inside yourself that you can make your world a better one. And the first step in doing that is to know your life has been hard but that you will not give up. If you have read this essay so far, chances are that you can do it. You can be a fighter. You can be a hero.

Thought # 5
A Quotation to Live By

44   If I could pass along one quotation, it would be this line from the great religious and political leader Mahatma Gandhi: **"Be the change you want to see in the world."** These ten words are all simple ones, but put together they express an idea with unlimited power. The key to changing your world is to take personal responsibility for your actions and behavior. No one else can do this for you; it must be you alone.

45   To put Gandhi's idea another way, each one of us has his or her own ship to sail. Some people don't sail their own ships; they just kind of drift with the tides. That's not a very satisfying way to live one's life, just drifting along with

others who are also drifting, and yet a lot of people do it. If their friends and peers are into enjoying the moment and taking the easy way out and not into setting larger goals in life, that's what they do.

46   I urge you to actively sail your own ship. That ship of yours is unique and precious, and no one else should sail it for you. That ship is the journey of your life. You get to go on that journey only once, with a one-way ticket, so make the most of it. Dream dreams, set meaningful goals, make something happen. Don't just drift along with the tides. Become someone.

47   In the opening story, my student Gerald realized he was not sailing his own ship, and you could almost hear him crying out in disillusionment and regret. Do not let that happen to you. You do not want to wake up some day with a taste of dust and ashes in your mouth and a terrible pain in your soul.

Thought # 6
The Fear of Loneliness

48   Perhaps the biggest reason it is so hard to take responsibility for one's life and sail one's own ship is the fear of being alone.

49   To grow, we must sometimes set sail in new directions and leave acquaintances and friends behind. At such times, we must have the courage and strength to depend on ourselves. We must be ready to handle the loneliness that may be part of marching to the

beat of our own drummer. We must not cling to the crowd when it prevents our personal growth. When the adventurer Columbus set sail for America, it was a terrifying thing to do. But he discovered a new world, and if we have the courage to sail our own ship, so might we.

Thought #7
The Opportunity to Help Others

50 There are many self-help books on the market that present the following idea: If you take charge of your life, you can achieve financial success. That may (or may not) be true, but it is not the full story of what happiness is about. As you seek to grow, the larger goal to keep in mind is that by gaining power for yourself, you will gain the power to be of help to others.

51 Robert Kennedy said, "The purpose of life is to contribute in some way to making things better." Dr. Martin Luther King wrote, "Life's most persistent and urgent question is, 'What are you doing for others?'" If we take control of our lives and achieve a measure of success, we will have the opportunity to work on behalf of others. At that stage, many religious leaders believe, we become fully blessed.

Thought #8
The Power of Regular Reading

52 If you have read this essay so far, you may be saying, "OK, I'm ready to do what it takes. I'll stick to my studies because I know they're a means to an end. I'll have some fun and games but remember they're a side show and not the main event. I'm OK with being alone a bit along the way. But what else can I do to keep myself inspired? What practical strategy do you have for me?"

53 I do have one strategy: Read. No one expresses the power of reading better than Oprah Winfrey: "I can't imagine," she said, "how I could have become the person I am now without books. How would I know there was another world beyond my small, isolated, feeling-abandoned world? Books became synonymous with freedom. They showed that you can open doors and walk through."

54 Many people (and I am one of them) believe that regular reading is the very heart of education. Here is what the experts say:

55 **1. Reading provides language power.** Research has shown *beyond any question* that frequent reading improves vocabulary, spelling, and reading speed and comprehension, as well as grammar and writing style. If you become a regular reader, all of these language and thinking abilities develop almost automatically.

56 **2. Reading increases the chances for job success.** In today's world more than ever before, jobs involve the processing of information, with words being the tools of the trade. Studies have found

that the better your command of words, the more success you are likely to have. Nothing will give you a command of words like regular reading.

57   **3. Reading creates human power.** Reading enlarges the mind and the heart. It frees us from the narrow confines of our own experience. Knowing how other people view important matters helps us decide what we ourselves think and feel. Reading also helps us connect with others and realize our shared humanity. The novelist C.S. Lewis wrote, "We read in order to know that we are not alone." We become less isolated as we share the common experiences, emotions, and thoughts that make us human. We grow more sympathetic and understanding because we realize that others are like us.

58   Regular reading can, in short, change your life. It can open the door to a lifetime of pleasure, learning, and personal growth. But you must be the one to decide whether to walk through that door.

Finally . . .

59   There are no fireworks to set off here, just some final words.

60   Understand that your ship is yours alone to sail, and no one else can sail it for you. The power within you is enormous, but you must turn it on. Work on your studies. Reread this essay. Order some books. I wish you a strong and courageous heart as you set sail on the adventure of your life.

Basic Skill Questions

Vocabulary in Context

_C_   1. In the sentence below, the word *syndrome* (sĭn′drōm′) means
    A. complaint.
    B. reaction.
    C. pattern.
    D. idea.

> Frequent naps and ten hours of sleep a night are a pattern of sleepiness.

"The "sleepiness syndrome" also expresses itself in the imagined need for naps during the day and then ten hours or more of sleep at night." (Paragraph 16)

___B___ 2. In the excerpt below, the words *synonymous* (sĭ-nŏn'ə-məs) *with* mean
       A. related to.
       B. the same as.
       C. unlike.
       D. more important than.

> If books enabled Oprah to open doors and walk through, they became the same as freedom for her.

> "How would I know there was another world beyond my small, isolated, feeling-abandoned world? Books became synonymous with freedom. They showed that you can open doors and walk through." (Paragraph 53)

Central Point and Main Ideas

___D___ 3. Which sentence best expresses the central point of the selection?
       A. Some students fail to realize that they have the ability to become heroes.
       B. There are a number of escape routes that students take to avoid studying.
       C. To succeed in school, students must first honestly examine their attitude about learning.
       D. Students can succeed in school by turning on the power within themselves.

Answer A covers only paragraph 13. Answer B covers only paragraphs 13–19. Answer C covers only paragraphs 27–36.

___D___ 4. The main idea of paragraphs 37–38 is that
       A. some people must repeat courses before they succeed at them.
       B. Langan has known some very determined people.
       C. school is hard work.
       D. determination is the key to success in school.

Answers A and B cover only paragraph 37, sentence 2. Answer C covers only paragraph 38, sentence 2.

___C___ 5. The main idea of paragraphs 41–43 is that
       A. Langan is uncomfortable with the idea that we can all "pull ourselves up by our own bootstraps."
       B. if you're on a track that is full of obstacles, it's easy to get worn down.
       C. people who face more obstacles than others must try their best to be heroes.
       D. in some schools, being in the right clique is more important than studying.

Answer A covers only paragraph 41. Answer B covers only paragraph 43, sentences 1–2. Answer D covers only paragraph 42, sentence 4.

Supporting Details

___B___ 6. According to Langan, happiness is best achieved by
       A. achieving financial success.
       B. gaining the opportunity to work on behalf of others.
       C. gaining power for yourself.
       D. overcoming obstacles such as personal health challenges, family neglect or abuse, and bad neighborhoods.

See paragraphs 50–51.

_____A_____ 7. The major supporting details of paragraphs 14–19 are

  A. excuses students use to avoid studying.

  B. obstacles that make it impossible for some students to succeed.

  C. ways that students deal with failure.   In paragraph 13, Langan says he

  D. typical attitudes toward learning. will "describe escape routes" students
                                                take to avoid studying. In paragraphs 14–19,
Transitions   he presents six excuses students use.

_____D_____ 8. The sentence below expresses a relationship of

  A. addition.   *When* is a time transition. At the time the author has

  B. cause and effect.   seen these students, he has wanted to shake them.

  C. comparison.

  D. time.

  > "When I have seen such students with resignation in their eyes, I have wanted to shake them by the shoulders and say, "You are not dead."
  > (Paragraph 11)

_____B_____ 9. The relationship of the second sentence below to the first sentence is one of

  A. comparison.   *Cause:* obstacles in the track that wear you down. *Effect:*

  B. cause and effect.   you'll find it harder to be determined to succeed.

  C. illustration.

  D. contrast.

  > "If you're in a track that is full of obstacles, you can get worn down.... And then it is harder to ignite the spark of determination within." (Paragraph 43)

Patterns of Organization

The "person   _____C_____ 10. Paragraph 25
who has
drifted unhappily   A. narrates in time order a day in the life of a lottery winner.
through life"
(sentences 3–4) is   B. illustrates what it feels like to win a million dollars.
contrasted with the
person who is   C. contrasts a lottery winner with a person who worked hard and earned
respected and feels   a million dollars.
self-worth (sentence 5). D. gives reasons why it's better to earn a million dollars than to win a
                          million dollars.

_____C_____ 11. The main pattern of organization of this selection is

  A. time order.
                    The list of excuses for not working (paragraphs 14–19)
  B. contrast.   and the list of eight thoughts for turning on the
                          power within (paragraphs 22–57) make up
  C. list of items.   the major portion of the selection.

  D. definition and example.

Advanced Skill Questions

Inferences

Item 12: See paragraph 43 in particular. Answer B is not supported. Paragraph 43 suggests C is not a valid inference. Answer D is contradicted by paragraph 42, sentences 3–4.

_A_ 12. On the basis of paragraphs 41–43, we can infer that
  A. some students use real obstacles as an excuse for giving up.
  B. many students exaggerate the obstacles they face.
  C. it is nearly impossible to become a hero.
  D. most students face similar obstacles in life.

_D_ 13. On the basis of Gerald's essay, we can conclude that he
  A. lacked the intelligence to succeed in school.
  B. eventually became a success.
  C. was not a good writer.
  D. was his own worst enemy when it came to school.

Throughout the essay Gerald says things such as a piece of his soul "is trying to pull [him] down" (paragraph 4) and that he has "spent too much of [his] life just waiting for good things to come" (paragraph 7).

Purpose and Tone

_C_ 14. In general, the author's tone is
  A. tolerant.
  B. solemn.
  C. encouraging.
  D. matter-of-fact.

A few of the many examples of the encouraging tone can be found in the last sentences of paragraphs 13, 30, 43, and 49. In addition, paragraph 60 strongly reinforces this tone.

_B_ 15. The author's main purpose is to
  A. inform readers of strategies to succeed in school and in life.
  B. persuade readers that they can succeed in school and in life.
  C. entertain readers with the silly excuses some students use to get out of studying.

Statements such as "you must be the one to decide whether to walk through that door," coupled with the encouraging tone throughout, are intended to persuade the reader that he or she can turn on the power within.

Argument

16. Complete the following argument by adding a statement of support.

Point: Leaders agree that helping others is life's larger goal.

Support: Robert Kennedy said, "The purpose of life is to contribute in some way to making things better."

Support: Dr. Martin Luther King wrote, "Life's most persistent and urgent question is, 'What are you doing for others?'"

See paragraph 51.

_B_ 17. Write the letter of the statement that is the point of the following argument. The other statements are support for that point.

Statements A, C, and D describe specific ways that reading is the heart of education.

A. Research has shown beyond any question that frequent reading improves vocabulary, spelling, and reading speed and comprehension, as well as grammar and writing style.

B. Reading is the heart of education.

C. Reading increases the chance for job success.

D. Reading frees us from the narrow confines of our own experience.

Critical Reading

_A_ 18. The sentence below contains

A. facts.   This fact can be confirmed by looking at self-help books available in a bookstore or online. (The idea the authors of these books present may be opinion, but it is a fact that the books present this idea.)

B. opinions.

C. both facts and opinions.

There are many self-help books on the market that present the following idea: If you take charge of your life, you can achieve financial success.

_B_ 19. Students who like to do what their friends are doing would probably be strongly influenced by the propaganda technique of

A. name-calling.   If the students are following along with what their friends are doing, they probably do not want to be left behind.

B. bandwagon.

C. glittering generalities.

D. testimonial.

_C_ 20. Students who believe that if they study too much, they will miss out on the good times that school has to offer are committing the logical fallacy of

A. false cause (*the argument assumes that the order of events alone shows cause and effect*).

B. circular reasoning (*a statement repeats itself rather than providing a real supporting reason to back up an argument*).

C. either-or (*the argument assumes that there are only two sides to a question*).

D. false comparison (*the argument assumes that two things being compared are more alike than they really are*).

The belief assumes that they must choose one of two possibilities: studying hard or having a good time. There may be a middle ground.

Outlining

Complete the following outline of the selection. Some items and parts of items are already filled in for you.   *Wording of some answers may vary.*

Central point: Students can become successful if they take charge of their lives by activating the power within themselves.

A. Gerald—an example of a student with a self-defeating attitude

B. Running from the Power Within—escape routes students take to avoid studying

  1. "I can't do it."

  2. "I'm too busy."   See paragraph 15.

  3. "I'm too tired."

  4. "I'll do it later."

  5. "I'm bored with the subject."   See paragraph 18.

  6. "I'm here and that's what counts."

C. Turning On the Power Within—some motivational thoughts

  1. Have a dream.   See paragraphs 22–26.

  2. Know your attitude about learning.

  3. Have the determination and commitment to do the work.

  4. Battle the odds of an unequal playing field.   See paragraphs 37–40.

  5. Live by the quotation: "Be the change you want to see in the world."

  6. Be ready to handle loneliness.

  7. Seek to help others.

  8. Read a lot because reading:

    a. Provides language power.

    b. Increases the chances for job success.

    c. Creates human power.   See paragraph 56.

Discussion Questions

1. In the course of your education, have you met any students like Gerald—or have you ever had a bit of Gerald in yourself? What do you think people like Gerald have to do to take charge of their lives?

2. What escape routes are you most likely to use to avoid studying? What can you do to avoid them?

3. Describe someone you know (it could be you) who has a dream—and who is the better off for it. Also describe someone you know who does *not* have a dream. Do you agree or disagree that it's important to have a dream?

4. In "The Power Within," the author quotes such inspirational figures as Mahatma Gandhi, Robert Kennedy, Dr. Martin Luther King, and Oprah Winfrey. Who inspires you? Why?

Note: Writing assignments for this selection appear on page 614.

Check Your Performance   THE POWER WITHIN

Activity	Number Right	Points	Score
Basic Skill Questions			
Vocabulary in Context (2 items)	_____	× 4 =	_____
Central Point and Main Ideas (3 items)	_____	× 4 =	_____
Supporting Details (2 items)	_____	× 4 =	_____
Transitions (2 items)	_____	× 4 =	_____
Patterns of Organization (2 items)	_____	× 4 =	_____
Advanced Skill Questions			
Inferences (2 items)	_____	× 4 =	_____
Purpose and Tone (2 items)	_____	× 4 =	_____
Argument (2 items)	_____	× 4 =	_____
Critical Reading (3 items)	_____	× 4 =	_____
Outlining (5 items)	_____	× 4 =	_____
		TOTAL SCORE =	_____%

Enter your total score into the **Reading Performance Chart: Ten Reading Selections** on the inside back cover.

Part Three

Combined-Skills Tests

Following are twenty tests that cover many of the skills taught in Part One and reinforced in Part Two of this book. Each test consists of a short reading passage followed by questions on any of the following: vocabulary in context, central points and main ideas, supporting details, relationships, inferences, purpose and tone, argument, and critical reading.

Notes:

1. In the comments on test questions, the term "too narrow" describes an item that is only a detail within the selection. "Too broad" describes an item that covers a great deal more than is in the selection.

2. Because these combined-skills tests are on facing pages—**specifically so that students can see the full text and the questions on a single spread without having to flip back and forth**—you might not want to ask students to remove them from the book. One option instead would be to pass out copies of the model answer sheet that is on the next page. Or you could ask students to use a piece of notebook paper as their answer sheet.

Sample Answer Sheet

Use the form below as a model answer sheet for the twenty combined-skills tests on the following pages.

Name _____ Date _____

Section _____ SCORE: (Number correct) _____ x 12.5 = _____ %

COMBINED SKILLS: Mastery Test _____

1. _____

2. _____

3. _____

4. _____

5. _____

6. _____

7. _____

8. _____

COMBINED SKILLS: Mastery Test 1

Read the passage below. Then write the letter of the best answer to each question that follows.

[1]In his book *About Alice*, in which he remembers his late wife, the writer Calvin Trillin writes about Alice and her beliefs about parenting. [2]He describes a time that Alice volunteered at a camp for children with disabilities. [3]Alice was especially good friends with a little girl she called by her initial, L. [4]L. had genetic diseases that kept her from growing normally and from digesting food. [5]She had difficulty walking. [6]She had to be fed through a tube at night. [7]Still, the little girl was, in Alice's words, "the most optimistic, most enthusiastic, most hopeful human being I had ever encountered." [8]As Alice became closer to the little girl, she became more curious about L. [9]What had given her such strength, such joy and optimism? [10]What was her secret? [11]Then one day at camp, while the children were playing a game, L. asked Alice to hold her mail. [12]On top of the pile was a note from L.'s mother. [13]Alice glanced at it and saw the words that L.'s mother had written to her daughter. [14]"If God had given us all the children in the world to choose from, L., we would only have chosen you."

_C_   1. Alice learned the secret of L.'s optimism when she

See sentences 11–14.
    A. met the girl's charming mother.
    B. read a note that L. had written to her mother.
    C. glanced at a note that L.'s mother had written to her daughter.
    D. helped feed her through a tube at night.

_D_   2. The relationship between sentence 7 and sentences 4–6 is one of
    A. cause and effect.
    B. addition.

The sentences contrast L.'s optimism, enthusiasm, and hope with her physical disabilities. The contrast word still *signals the relationship.*

    C. comparison.
    D. contrast.

_B_   3. The author implies that

See sentences 13–14.
    A. some parents are willing to overlook their children's disabilities.
    B. the secret of L.'s optimism was that she knew her parents loved her dearly.
    C. Alice had never met a child who had as many disabilities as L.
    D. Alice envied L.'s joyful nature.

To the Instructor: In the combined-skills tests in Part Three, transitions and other words relevant to the answers are underlined in this *Instructor's Edition*.

___C___ 4. We can infer that Calvin Trillin

The way in which Trillin describes his wife's friendship with L. suggests his admiration for her work with children with disabilities.

- A. was shocked when he learned that his wife had secretly read the note that L.'s mother had written her.
- B. could not understand his wife's curiosity about L.
- C. admired his wife for volunteering at a camp for children with disabilities.
- D. was annoyed that his wife spent time volunteering at a summer camp rather than staying at home with him.

___B___ 5. We can infer that L.'s mother

The love reflected in the mother's letter shows that she was more than equal to the challenge.

- A. was frustrated that her disabled daughter required so much assistance.
- B. was more than equal to the challenge of being the parent of a disabled child.
- C. felt guilty about sending her disabled daughter off to summer camp.
- D. also suffered from serious disabilities.

___C___ 6. The author's main purpose is to

Trillin entertains us with this touching story about the impact that L.'s mother's love had on L.'s life.

- A. inform us about some of the needs of a particular disabled child.
- B. persuade us that disabled children deserve better treatment.
- C. entertain us with a heartwarming story of the power of love.

___A___ 7. The tone of the passage can be described as mainly

- A. admiring.
- B. concerned.
- C. humorous.
- D. detached.

Trillin admires his wife's volunteer work; Alice admires L.'s positive attitude; both of them (and all of us) admire L.'s mother's loving support of her child.

___D___ 8. Which is an appropriate title for this selection?

See sentence 14. The child's attitude, despite her disabilities, shows the power of love.

- A. Little Girl Lost
- B. Doing More for Disabled Children
- C. An Uncomplaining Child
- D. The Power of Love

COMBINED SKILLS: Mastery Test 2

Read the passage below. Then write the letter of the best answer to each question that follows.

¹I remember the day we were driving to a friend's house. ²We were trying to turn left into a residential neighborhood, but there was a car stopped, blocking the lane ahead. ³I could see a man in the car holding a woman around the neck with his right arm and slugging her in the face with his left fist. ⁴I jumped out of the car and pulled open her door. ⁵As I pulled her out of the car, he swung open his door and headed for us both. ⁶It occurred to me then that I had always inserted myself into these situations on the premise that a man wouldn't hit a woman, and that premise clearly didn't apply here. ⁷But as he stepped toward us, my husband was standing there. ⁸"Calm down, man," my husband said. ⁹He walked the man back along the road, talking to him, almost whispering to him, as I took the woman across the street, into someone's yard under a tree and went to the house to get help. ¹⁰Her face was covered in blood. ¹¹The police came, but the woman wouldn't press charges. ¹²The police would not arrest him based on what I saw without her complaint, and so we all got back in our cars and drove away.

¹³I saw them both about a year later at the grocery store, an old yellow bruise on her cheek. ¹⁴I suppose I had always thought that even strangers could intervene and make things right, if only they would, and this was a hard lesson that it wasn't that easy. ¹⁵You couldn't always fix everything.

_A_ 1. In sentence 6, the word *premise* means
- A. belief.
- B. misunderstanding.
- C. report.
- D. invitation.

> The writer would insert herself into dangerous situations because of her belief she was not in danger.

_B_ 2. In sentence 14, the word *intervene* means
- A. seek revenge.
- B. come between.
- C. explain.
- D. decide.

> The writer had come between the man and the woman to try to make the situation right.

_C_ 3. When the writer pulls the injured woman out of the car, her husband
- A. fights with the abusive man.
- B. shouts at the abusive man that he has called the police.
- C. walks the abusive man back along the road, talking to him.
- D. remains in the car in order to call the police on his cell phone.

See sentence 9.

_C_ 4. The passage

The events of the story are told in the order in which they occurred. The words *as* and *a year later* signal the time pattern.

A. contrasts abusive men with men who aren't abusive.
B. compares the writer's attitude toward abuse with that of her husband.
C. presents a sequence of events in time order.
D. lists reasons why some women accept being abused.

_D_ 5. On the basis of sentence 6, we can infer that the writer

By saying that the belief that a man would not hit a woman "didn't apply here," the writer implies she fears that the man will attack her as well.

A. knows that the man who slugged and choked the woman won't hit her.
B. regrets that she ever got involved with the couple.
C. wants to attack the man herself.
D. fears that the man will attack her.

_C_ 6. The author's tone is mainly

A. tolerant.
B. apologetic.
C. concerned.
D. frightened.

The writer's description of her efforts to help and her disappointment at her inability to "make things right" set the concerned tone.

_D_ 7. You could conclude from the passage that the writer

See sentences 11–15.

A. will be unwilling to intervene in another case of domestic abuse.
B. will try once more to get the woman to press charges against the abusive man.
C. regrets becoming involved in the couple's business.
D. now sees that there is little anyone can do if a woman who is being abused refuses to press charges against her abuser.

_A_ 8. Which of the following statements best expresses the main idea of the passage?

A. Sometimes there is no "quick fix" for abusive relationships.
B. Some women love their men so much that they are willing to endure being abused by them.
C. Violent behavior can be observed even in seemingly "nice" neighborhoods.
D. Domestic violence is the most serious social problem facing Americans today.

See sentence 15. Answer B is incorrect because we do not know why this woman endures the abuse. Answer C covers only sentence 2. Answer D is too broad because the focus is on one particular situation of abuse and what the writer learned from it.

COMBINED SKILLS: Mastery Test 3

Read the passage below. Then write the letter of the best answer to each question that follows.

¹Most people dislike bats, and surely the most feared of all the species is the dreaded vampire bat. ²Vampire bats live up to their horror-story reputation as greedy and efficient stealers of blood.

³Depending upon its type, the vampire bat may prefer to dine on the blood of mammals (including humans) or birds. ⁴The bat begins its meal by circling above its usually sleeping target for several minutes, probably to allow heat-sensitive patches on its face to determine where best to bite. ⁵It then inflicts a small wound with its teeth, which are so razor-sharp that they make the incision virtually painless. ⁶The wound bleeds freely as long as the bat continues feeding, thanks to a substance in the bat's saliva that prevents clotting. ⁷As many as a half dozen of the bat's fellows may join it to feed from one wound.

⁸Vampire bats have such great appetites for blood that they may drink more than their own weight at one feeding, thus making it briefly impossible for them to fly. ⁹A single vampire drinks about twenty-five gallons of blood in its lifetime. ¹⁰Although vampire bats are sometimes responsible for the death of humans or animals, those deaths are not due to loss of blood. ¹¹Rather, the deaths are the result of rabies or other diseases spread by the bats.

_B_   1. In sentence 5, *incision* means
        A. heat-sensitive patch.
        B. cut.
        C. blood.
        D. saliva.

"Wound with its teeth" (sentence 5) suggests that *incision* means "cut."

_D_   2. Sentences 10 and 11
        A. narrate events.
        B. define a term.
        C. compare two things.
        D. discuss a cause and effect relationship.

Sentences 10 and 11 tell why people sometimes die from vampire bat bites. *Cause:* the diseases the bats carry. *Effect:* humans and animals die from the disease transmitted by the bite. The words *due to* and *result* signal the relationship.

_C_   3. The main patterns of organization of the second paragraph are cause-effect and
        A. contrast.
        B. comparison.
        C. time order.
        D. definition and example.

The second paragraph describes the sequence of steps in a vampire bat's feeding process. The words *begins* and *then* signal a time relationship.

_B_   4.   We can conclude that vampire bats use their heat-sensitive patches

See sentence 4. The best place for the bat to bite would be where the blood is close to the skin.

- A. for personal temperature control.
- B. to find where blood is close to their victims' skin.
- C. to find sleeping victims.
- D. to find out which potential victims have the best blood.

_D_   5.   The passage suggests that

See sentence 4. If the target is "usually sleeping," it would be lying still.

- A. bats are usually solitary feeders.
- B. all vampire bats have rabies.
- C. vampire bats intend to kill their victims.
- D. vampire bats prefer victims that lie still.

_A_   6.   The author's main purpose is to

The author presents factual information without value judgments or evaluations.

- A. inform readers about how vampire bats are able to locate and drink blood.
- B. persuade readers that vampire bats deserve to be feared.
- C. entertain readers with scary details about vampire bats.
- D. predict that vampire bats will soon become extinct.

_B_   7.   On the whole, the tone of the passage is

- A. fearful.
- B. objective.
- C. disbelieving.
- D. playful.

The author presents mostly facts without value words or opinions.

_A_   8.   Which is the most appropriate title for this passage?

- A. Vampire Bats' Feeding Habits
- B. Bats and Disease
- C. Bats in Social Groups
- D. How Bats Live

Most of the details focus on the feeding habits of vampire bats. Answer B covers only sentence 11. Answer C covers only sentence 7. Answer D is too broad because the passage does not discuss how vampire bats live in general.

COMBINED SKILLS: Mastery Test 4

Read the passage below. Then write the letter of the best answer to each question that follows.

[1]Have you ever seen someone walk across a bed of hot coals and wondered how in the world he or she did it? [2]"Firewalkers" seem to trot right across the fire without a hint of a grimace and without any damage done to the soles of their feet. [3]And while firewalkers would like their performances to appear to be the result of some secret and mystical power, the "secrets" behind firewalking are really pretty simple. [4]To begin with, you may have noticed that firewalking always happens at night. [5]The reason for this is that if the walks happened during daylight, the fiery coals would appear to be no more than a pile of gray ashes. [6]In reality, the coals that you see the firewalkers move across have been burning for a very long time, so they are covered with a thick layer of ash. [7]However, in darkness, the red glow of the coals is visible. [8]And *after* the firewalker steps onto the coals, sparks and flames often shoot up, giving the impression of walking through fire. [9]But the fact is, if the walker moves quickly enough, his or her feet are protected by ash, which is a remarkably poor conductor of heat. [10]A walker would have to stand still on the coals for a few seconds in order for them to actually cause a burn. [11]Therefore, the real skill of a firewalker lies in his or her ability to move calmly and slowly enough to amaze an audience, yet quickly enough to avoid roasted feet.

___D___ 1. As used in sentence 2, the word *grimace* means
   A. bored expression.
   B. smile.
   C. doubt.
   D. pained expression.

   One would expect that walking on hot coals would result in a pained expression.

___C___ 2. In order for their feet to get burned, firewalkers would have to stand on hot coals for
   A. about 15 seconds.
   B. a fraction of a second.
   C. a few seconds.
   D. a minute or more.

   See sentence 10.

___A___ 3. Sentence 6 expresses a relationship of
   A. cause and effect.
   B. time.
   C. comparison.
   D. contrast.

   Cause: the coals have been burning for a very long time.
   Effect: the coals are covered with a thick layer of ash.
   The word *so* signals the relationship.

_B_ 4. The passage discusses

See sentence 3.

  A. stages in the training of a professional firewalker.
  B. reasons why firewalking isn't as risky as it seems.
  C. a definition and example of the term *firewalker.*
  D. differences between professional and amateur firewalkers.

_B_ 5. We can infer that if firewalkers performed during the day,

See sentence 5.

  A. many of them would get seriously burned.
  B. their audiences would not be as impressed with them.
  C. the coals they walk across would be hotter.
  D. both A and C.

_D_ 6. The author of this passage would probably agree with which of the following statements?

See sentence 11.
Answers A, B, and C
are not supported.

  A. Firewalkers are fakes who should be arrested for tricking people.
  B. Firewalking should be outlawed since it can lead to serious burns.
  C. It is easy to learn to be a firewalker.
  D. Firewalking involves skill rather than magic.

_A_ 7. The author's tone can be described as

  A. mocking.
  B. amazed.
  C. critical.
  D. straightforward.

The mildly mocking tone is indicated by words and phrases such as *trot right across,* "*secrets,*" and *avoid roasted feet.*

_B_ 8. Which statement best states the main idea of the passage?

  A. To many people, firewalking seems amazing.
  B. Firewalkers do not possess mystical powers, but instead they have an awareness of some simple secrets.
  C. Coals which have been burning for a long time produce lots of ash, which is a poor conductor of heat.
  D. Firewalkers must not walk too slow or too fast.

Answer A covers only sentence 1. Answer C covers only sentences 6 and 9. Answer D covers only sentence 11.

COMBINED SKILLS: Mastery Test 5

Read the passage below. Then write the letter of the best answer to each question that follows.

¹Little League baseball in its present form <u>should</u> be abolished. ²For one thing, the pressure that children are put under to succeed may harm them more than help them. ³One mother discovered her son taking Maalox tablets from the medicine chest whenever a game approached. ⁴He explained that they helped relieve the stomach burn he would feel during the game. ⁵Other children have been found taking tranquilizers. ⁶<u>Another</u> drawback to today's Little League baseball is that some parents take the game too seriously and set a bad example for their children. ⁷Recently, a disillusioned coach said, "At our field, we put the bleachers way back from the dugout where the players are. ⁸That way, parents can't be hissing down advice to their children all the time and getting them upset." ⁹A final reason Little League should be abolished is that it doesn't offer enough success to most players. ¹⁰Instead, the game revolves around the more developed kids who are able to hit and throw the ball harder than the smaller children. ¹¹In one recent game, most of the batters were clearly afraid of the speed of the hardball, which was pitched by a boy bigger than many of the other players.

¹²A workable alternative to Little League hardball would be slow-pitch softball. ¹³The ball is pitched slowly and underhand, which offers a high level of success to kids without a high level of ability. ¹⁴Slow-pitch softball would get more children involved in the game, and help people remember that it *is* a game—not an adult arena where one is branded with success or failure.

_B_ 1. In sentences 1 and 9, the word *abolished* means
   A. supported.   All of the arguments in the first paragraph show how
   B. done away with.   Little League baseball harms children, and if it harms
   C. expanded.   children, we would want to do away with it.
   D. imitated.

_D_ 2. According to the author, one advantage of slow-pitch softball is the
   A. weight of the ball.   See sentence 13.
   B. age of the players.
   C. size of the field.
   D. lesser degree of skill required.

_B_ 3. The relationship of sentence 6 to the sentences that come before it is one of
                                              The word *Another* signals that this is
   A. time.   one more in a list of drawbacks.
   B. addition.
   C. contrast.
   D. comparison.

_B_ 4. Sentence 1 is a statement of
    A. fact.
    B. opinion.
    C. fact and opinion.

The word *should* is a signal that this is an opinion.
Not everyone would agree with this opinion.

See sentence 14.

_A_ 5. From the passage, you can conclude the author would agree with the idea that
    A. it's not whether you win or lose; it's how you play the game.
    B. competition in baseball helps prepare people for competition in life.
    C. children's games should imitate adults' games.
    D. sports should help children learn that there are winners and losers in life.

_B_ 6. The author's main purpose is to
    A. inform readers how Little League baseball works.
    B. persuade readers that Little League baseball is harmful to children.
    C. entertain readers with true stories involving Little League games.
    D. predict that Little League baseball will soon be abolished.

_A_ 7. The main idea of paragraph 1 is best stated in
    A. sentence 1.
    B. sentence 2.
    C. sentence 9.
    D. sentence 11.

_C_ 8. What is the most appropriate title for this selection?
    A. The Pressures on Today's Children
    B. Slow-Pitch Softball
    C. Let's Reform Little League
    D. Sportsmanship in Baseball

Item 6: All of the major details in paragraph 1 describe ways in which Little League baseball harms children. Paragraph 2 describes an alternative that would not be so harmful. The word *should* in the main idea shows the author's intent to persuade.

Item 7: Answers B and C are major details. Answer D is a minor detail. All of the details in the paragraph support the idea, in sentence 1, that Little League baseball should be abolished.

Item 8: Answer A is too broad because the passage refers only to the pressures in Little League baseball. Answer B covers only sentences 12–14. Answer D is incorrect because the passage discusses only Little League baseball, not baseball in general.

COMBINED SKILLS: Mastery Test 6

Read the passage below. Then write the letter of the best answer to each question that follows.

¹The social psychologist Philip Zimbardo set out to test a theory that the anonymity of city life encourages crime. ²He arranged to have automobiles abandoned in two different locations: New York City and Palo Alto, California, a medium-sized suburban community. ³The cars' license plates were removed and their hoods were raised to signal that the autos were abandoned. ⁴Then each car was secretly watched for sixty-four hours.

⁵The person assigned to watch the New York car did not have long to wait. <u>⁶Within ten minutes</u> the car received its first auto strippers—a father, mother, and eight-year-old son. ⁷The mother appeared to be a lookout, <u>while</u> the son aided the father's search of the trunk, glove compartment, and motor. ⁸He <u>then</u> handed his father the tools necessary to remove the battery and radiator. ⁹Total time of destructive contact: seven minutes.

¹⁰This, however, was only the first "contact." ¹¹By the end of the sixty-four hours, the car had been vandalized twenty-four times, often by well-dressed, seemingly middle-class adults. ¹²What remained when the experiment was over was a useless hunk of metal. ¹³In contrast, the Palo Alto car was approached only once: when it started to rain, a passerby stopped to lower the hood.

¹⁴According to Zimbardo, the crucial factor in the different fates of the two cars was anonymity. ¹⁵In a large city, where the chances of being recognized outside one's own neighborhood are extremely slim, even "upstanding citizens" can afford a temporary turn at thievery. <u>¹⁶In a smaller community, on the other hand</u>, the higher probability of being recognized and caught keeps people honest.

_B_ 1. In sentence 14, the word *crucial* means
   A. least interesting.
   B. most important.
   C. most unlikely.
   D. most helpful.

   Sentences 15 and 16 indicate that the degree of fear of being caught is significant in determining people's actions. Therefore, anonymity would be a very important factor.

_B_ 2. According to the passage, Zimbardo's main purpose in doing the experiment was to
   A. illustrate a point.
   B. test a theory.
   C. catch thieves.
   D. teach honesty.

   See sentence 1: "Zimbardo set out to test a theory."

_A_ 3. The pattern of organization in sentences 5 through 9 is one of

    A. time order.   The events of the first destructive contact are described
    B. list of items.   in the order in which they occurred during a
    C. comparison.   seven-minute period. The words *Within ten minutes*
    D. contrast.   (sentence 6), *while* (sentence 7), and *then*
    (sentence 8) signal the time order.

_C_ 4. The relationship between sentences 15 and 16 is one of

    A. time.   The sentences contrast the chances of being recognized
    B. comparison.   in a large city with those in a smaller community. The
    C. contrast.   words *On the other hand* signal the contrast.
    D. cause and effect.

_A_ 5. Sentence 13 is a statement of

    A. fact.   Sentence 4 offers verification for sentence 13.
    B. opinion.   Sentence 13 can also be verified by reading
    C. fact and opinion.   Zimbardo's account of his experiment.

_C_ 6. The passage suggests that

See sentences 15 and 16.   A. people who vandalize cars always travel in groups.
    B. New Yorkers are more dishonest than people in most other big cities.
    C. social pressure promotes honesty.
    D. the car used in Palo Alto was probably in better condition than the car in New York City.

_A_ 7. The tone of the passage can be described as mainly

    A. objective.   The passage describes the experiment and
    B. doubtful.   the results in a straightforward manner
    C. alarmed.   and without making value judgments.
    D. scornful.

_D_ 8. Which statement best states the main idea of the passage?

    A. Philip Zimbardo is a creative social psychologist.
    B. People are now more dishonest than ever.
    C. In big cities, ordinary people's chances of being recognized outside of their neighborhood are quite slim.
    D. Zimbardo's experiment suggests that the impersonal nature of city life encourages crime.

    Answer A covers only sentences 1–2. Answer B is not addressed at all. Answer C covers only sentence 15.

COMBINED SKILLS: Mastery Test 7

Read the passage below. Then write the letter of the best answer to each question that follows.

> [1]Perception is strongly influenced by attention. [2]Unfortunately, if you daydream during a lecture, little or nothing will reach your brain. [3]Attending is not always easy, so so you take notes and make conscious efforts to remain alert. [4]Did you notice an error in the previous sentence? [5]You probably were concentrating on the content, and although your eyes saw the word *so* repeated, you ignored it. [6]Similarly, you were probably not focusing any attention on your thumb until you read this sentence. [7]You simply cannot attend to every stimulus around you, so only certain things are selected. [8]Have you ever driven down a highway with your gas needle nearing "empty"? [9]Chances are you become preoccupied with the location of gas stations. [10]Another day when your tank was full but your stomach was empty, the gas stations might have been overlooked, but every diner and restaurant would have caught your eye. [11]Attention is usually focused on needed things. [12]If you are hungry or thirsty right now, you might have a problem keeping your attention focused on the reading rather than on the refrigerator.

_B_ 1. As used in sentence 3, the word *attending* means
  A. showing up.
  B. paying attention.
  C. taking care.
  D. waiting.

  Taking notes and making conscious efforts to remain alert are ways of paying attention.

_A_ 2. In sentence 9, the words *preoccupied with* mean
  A. fully interested in.
  B. forgetful about.
  C. expert in.
  D. confident about.

  If your gas needle were near "empty," you'd be very interested in the location of gas stations.

_D_ 3. According to the author, we usually concentrate on
  A. what we are expected to pay attention to.
  B. random things.
  C. daydreaming.
  D. needed things.

  See sentence 11.

_C_ 4. The relationship between sentences 5 and 6 is one of
  A. time.
  B. contrast.
  C. comparison.
  D. illustration.

  The sentences compare the ignored words with the ignored thumb. The word Similarly signals the comparison.

_D_ 5. Sentence 12 discusses a
    A. series of events.
    B. contrast.
    C. comparison.
    D. cause and effect.

Cause: hunger or thirst. *Effect:* your attention is on the refrigerator instead of the reading. The word *If* and the implied *then* signal the pattern.

Sentences 10–12 suggest that going to class hungry would cause one to not pay attention.

_B_ 6. You might conclude from the paragraph that it would be a good idea to
    A. forget about taking notes in classes.
    B. avoid being hungry when you go to your classes.
    C. take a difficult class just before lunchtime.
    D. eat less.

See sentence 1. Answer A covers only sentence 2. Answer B ignores the subject of attention. Answer D covers only sentences 10–12.

_C_ 7. What is the best title for this selection?
    A. Daydreaming
    B. Perception
    C. The Relationship between Perception and Attention
    D. How Hunger Influences Attention

_D_ 8. Which statement best expresses the main idea of the paragraph?
    A. You are unlikely to notice an error in writing if you are concentrating on its content.
    B. If you are hungry, you will focus on eating.
    C. Unfortunately, when students daydream during lectures, nothing will reach their brains.
    D. Perception is strongly influenced by attention, which is usually focused on needed things.

Answer A covers only sentences 3–5. Answer B covers only sentences 10 and 12. Answer C covers only sentence 2.

COMBINED SKILLS: Mastery Test 8

Read the passage below. Then write the letter of the best answer to each question that follows.

¹We live in an era in which more women are entering formerly male-dominated professions, demanding equal pay for equal work, and generally rejecting the societal double standard which has held them back from reaching their full potential. ²Yet many women are still bound by old-fashioned and harmful ideas about sexuality. ³An epidemic of "date rapes" on college campuses is evidence that warped beliefs about sexuality are barriers that women—as well as men—need to break in order to achieve a full human partnership. ⁴As many as 25 percent of all college women may become victims of rape or attempted rape. ⁵Women at the beginning of their college careers are especially vulnerable to date rape. ⁶They may be living in coed dorms with men whom they assume they can trust. ⁷They are eager to appear cool and sophisticated, not paranoid or uptight. ⁸Most destructively of all, many women still subscribe, at least subconsciously, to the belief that they "owe" sexual favors to a man they date. ⁹After a sexual attack by a date, many women are racked with guilt rather than anger. ¹⁰Were they to blame, they ask themselves, because they drank too much? ¹¹Because they wore a short skirt? ¹²Similarly, men have grown up in a culture which suggests that once they have spent "good money" entertaining a date, they are owed sex in return.

_B_ 1. In sentence 8, the words *subscribe . . . to* mean
   A. describe.
   B. agree with.
   C. ignore.
   D. argue with.

   If women feel guilt rather than anger after being attacked by a date, they must at some level agree with the idea that they "owe" sexual favors.

_C_ 2. The relationship of sentence 2 to sentence 1 is one of
   A. addition.
   B. illustration.
   C. contrast.
   D. comparison.

   The current idea of equality between the sexes is being contrasted with the "old-fashioned and harmful ideas about sexuality" that many women still hold onto. The word *Yet* signals the contrast.

_C_ 3. The relationship of sentence 12 to sentences 9–11 is one of
   A. time.
   B. contrast.
   C. comparison.
   D. cause and effect.

   Women's beliefs are being compared to men's beliefs about sexual "owing." The word *Similarly* signals the comparison.

Answer A is
supported by
sentences 2–3.
The words *need to* are
a clue. Answer B is
supported by sentences
1–2. Answer C is
supported by sentences
9–11.

___D___ 4. You can conclude that the author believes
A. many men and women should change their attitudes about sexuality.
B. attitudes about rights in the workplace have changed more than attitudes about sexuality.
C. victims of date rape often feel responsible for having been attacked.
D. all of the above.

___B___ 5. The main purpose of this passage is to
A. inform readers about interesting sexual attitudes.
B. use facts to argue that sexual attitudes need improving.
C. entertain readers with dramatic sexual images.
D. predict the future of the American sex scene.

___D___ 6. The author's tone can be described as
A. sarcastic.
B. optimistic.
C. arrogant.
D. concerned.

___C___ 7. The point made in sentence 2 is best supported by
A. sentence 1.
B. sentence 4.
C. sentence 8.
D. sentence 12.

___B___ 8. The main idea of the passage is that
A. women are now close to reaching their full potential.
B. societal attitudes toward sexuality are old-fashioned and harmful.
C. colleges should provide better security in coed dorms.
D. men's sexual attitudes are strongly in need of change.

Item 5: Facts presented in sentences 4–12 support the idea of what women "need to" do, as stated in sentence 3. Answer A is incorrect because the author does more than just inform us. Answer C is incorrect because there is no attempt to entertain us in the discussion of this serious subject. Answer D is incorrect because, although the past and present are discussed, there is no prediction of what will happen.

Item 6: The concern is especially clear in sentences 2–4.

Item 7: The words *"Most destructively of all. . . still subscribe. . . to the belief"* (sentence 8) suggest that the belief is an old-fashioned and harmful one.

Item 8: See sentences 2–3. Answers A and C are not discussed. Answer D covers only sentences 3 and 12.

COMBINED SKILLS: Mastery Test 9

Read the passage below. Then write the letter of the best answer to each question that follows.

[1]Mary was watching a mystery on television. [2]The end of the movie was near, and she was totally engrossed. [3]Then her baby started crying. [4]She shouted at him to shut up. [5]His response was intensified crying. [6]Mary got angry and shook him. [7]The baby cried even louder. [8]Meanwhile, the mystery's conclusion took place, and Mary missed it. [9]Angrily, she slapped her son's face. [10]In this situation, someone was pursuing a goal— seeing the end of a suspenseful television show. [11]But something happened to block the achievement of that goal. [12]The person thus became frustrated, anger built up, and direct aggression occurred.

[13]Aggression is not always aimed at the original frustrater. [14]For example, consider a businessman who had a hard day at the office. [15]He was about to close a deal with a client when his boss clumsily interfered and lost the sale. [16]On the way home in his car, the frustrated businessman blew his horn angrily at a car ahead when it didn't immediately pull away from a stoplight. [17]As he entered his home, his dog jumped up on him, only to receive a quick kick. [18]He then shouted at his wife during supper. [19]All these aggressive behaviors are examples of displaced aggression. [20]Aggression against the person who caused the original frustration can often be harmful. [21]In this case, assaulting or swearing at the boss could cost the businessman his job. [22]When the original frustrater has status and power over the frustrated person, aggression may be displaced onto a less threatening target, who may have nothing at all to do with the original frustration.

_____A_____ 1. In sentence 2, the word *engrossed* means
      A. involved.   Mary's actions when she was interrupted suggest that
      B. disgusted.   she had been completely involved in the movie.
      C. disappointed.
      D. bored.

_____B_____ 2. The topic of the first paragraph is
      A. parent-child relationships.   See sentence 12.
      B. direct aggression.
      C. displaced aggression.
      D. suspense.

_____B_____ 3. Aggression is more likely to be displaced if the original frustrater
      A. is a family member.   See sentence 22.
      B. has power over the frustrated person.
      C. is angry at the frustrated person.
      D. is unfair to the frustrated person.

___D___ 4. The relationship between sentences 11 and 12 is one of
- A. definition and example.
- B. comparison.
- C. contrast.
- D. cause and effect.

> The word *thus* signals the cause and effect relationship. *Cause:* something happened to block the achievement of the goal. *Effect:* the person became frustrated, anger built, and direct aggression occurred.

___C___ 5. The organizational pattern of the second paragraph is
- A. a series of steps in a process.
- B. a contrast of events.
- C. illustration and explanation of a general concept.
- D. a comparison of two or more events.

___B___ 6. The writer's main purpose in writing this selection is to
- A. predict how aggression influences relationships.
- B. inform readers about two types of aggression.
- C. persuade readers to be careful not to take out their aggression on the wrong people.
- D. entertain readers with dramatic anecdotes about aggressive behavior.

___C___ 7. What is the best title for the selection?
- A. Family Relationships
- B. The Causes of Aggression
- C. Direct and Displaced Aggression
- D. Displaced Aggression

___B___ 8. Which sentence best states the main idea of the selection?
- A. A great deal of frustration is aimed against family members.
- B. When frustration and anger build up, direct or displaced aggression may occur.
- C. Sometimes a frustrater may have a great deal more power or status than the person who is frustrated.
- D. Direct aggression is more satisfying than indirect aggression.

Item 5: The general concept of displaced aggression is discussed in sentences 13 and 19–22. It is illustrated with the example of the businessman in sentences 14–18.

Item 6: The first paragraph explains and illustrates direct aggression. The second paragraph explains and illustrates displaced aggression.

Item 7: Answer A is too broad because family relationships are mentioned only as part of the illustration for each type of aggression. Answer B is too narrow because the passage discusses both the cause and the types of aggression. Answer D ignores direct aggression (paragraph 1).

Item 8: Answer A is true in the two examples given, but it ignores the types of aggression. Answer C is just one detail of the second paragraph. Answer D is incorrect because the passage does not discuss degrees of satisfaction in different types of aggression.

COMBINED SKILLS: Mastery Test 10

Read the passage below. Then write the letter of the best answer to each question that follows.

¹Thousands of years ago, ancient Greeks firmly believed that many illnesses, from colds to migraines, were caused by too much blood in the body. ²Because they didn't realize that blood constantly circulated through the body, they felt that blood could become stagnant and rot inside people. ³As a result, Greek physicians regularly prescribed "bloodletting," a procedure that involved cutting patients and draining blood from them—sometimes more than a quart! ⁴Often, patients who had been only slightly ill with a little head cold became deathly ill from blood loss. ⁵Meanwhile, as recently as 120 years ago, many doctors prescribed what was known as the "Rest Cure" for female patients who complained of sadness or lack of energy. ⁶This "cure" involved confining the patient to bed for months at a time and strictly forbidding any creative activity. ⁷Doctors believed that pastimes of painting or writing or playing music were much too intense for even a healthy woman. ⁸Therefore, tired or disturbed women should certainly avoid creative activities. ⁹Additionally, little to no social interaction was allowed since it was felt that the distraction of friends and loved ones would further exhaust a patient. ¹⁰The result of this "cure" was that moderately depressed women often became terribly depressed at best, and suicidal at worst. ¹¹From ancient Greek medicine to near-modern medicine, sometimes the treatment has been more dangerous than the illness!

_B_ 1. In sentence 2, the word *stagnant* means
   A. powerful.
   B. inactive.
   C. overheated.
   D. cold.

   If the ancient Greeks did not realize that the blood circulated constantly, they would think it could become inactive and rot.

_C_ 2. The ancient Greeks didn't realize

See sentence 2.
   A. that bodies sometimes contain too much blood.
   B. that colds and migraines differ from other illnesses.
   C. that blood circulates throughout the body.
   D. all of the above.

_C_ 3. As recently as 120 years ago, doctors believed that

See sentences 5 and 7.
   A. creative activity could benefit only healthy women.
   B. depression could be cured through intense activity.
   C. creative activities such as painting or writing were too intense for even healthy women.
   D. most women were emotionally disturbed.

_B_   4. The relationship of sentence 3 to sentence 2 is one of
        A. contrast.
        B. cause and effect.
        C. comparison.
        D. time.

> The words *As a result* signal the cause and effect relationship. *Cause:* the ancient Greeks felt the blood could become inactive and rot. *Effect:* their doctors drained blood from people.

For answers
A and C, see
sentence 10.
For answer B, see
sentences 7–9.

_D_   5. We can infer that doctors who prescribed the "Rest Cure" for women
        A. did not realize that their "cure" was driving some women to suicide.
        B. believed that, in general, women were "the weaker sex."
        C. had no knowledge of how to effectively treat depression.
        D. all of the above.

See sentence 4. If
patients often "became
deathly ill," many of
them must have died.

_A_   6. The passage suggests that bloodletting
        A. led to the deaths of a number of patients.
        B. often drove patients to suicide.
        C. was sometimes an effective method of treating blood disorders.
        D. all of the above.

_D_   7. The author's tone seems to be
        A. nostalgic.
        B. detached.
        C. ashamed.
        D. critical.

_D_   8. The main idea of the passage is expressed in
        A. sentence 1.
        B. sentence 2.
        C. sentence 5.
        D. sentence 11.

Item 7: Saying that the patients became "deathly ill" (sentence 4) and "terribly depressed . . . and suicidal" suggests criticism, as does saying that the treatment was "more dangerous than the illness" (sentence 11). The use of quotation marks around the word *cure* (sentences 6 and 10) and the exclamation points at the ends of sentences 3 and 11 also suggest criticism.

Item 8: Answers A and B are incorrect because these sentences explain only one of the two dangerous treatments described in the paragraph. Answer C is incorrect because sentence 5 introduces the second major detail, the "Rest Cure."

COMBINED SKILLS: Mastery Test 11

Read the passage below. Then write the letter of the best answer to each question that follows.

[1]It would be a mistake to assume that primitive societies are mentally backward—unable to benefit from their environment or understand how to cope effectively with it. [2]Given the general level of technology available, they do adapt to and manipulate their environment in a sophisticated and understanding manner. [3]Countless examples can be cited to illustrate this point. [4]Among some Eskimo groups, wolves are a menace—a dangerous environmental feature that must be dealt with. [5]They could perhaps be hunted down and killed, but this involves danger as well as considerable expenditure in time and energy. [6]So a simple yet clever device is employed. [7]A sharp sliver of bone is curled into a springlike shape, and seal blubber is molded around it and permitted to freeze. [8]This is then placed where it can be discovered by a hungry wolf, which, living up to its reputation, "wolfs it down." [9]Later, as this "time bomb" is digested and the blubber disappears, the bone uncurls and its sharp ends pierce the stomach of the wolf, causing internal bleeding and death. [10]This method, though harsh, is undeniably practical. [11]It is a simple yet fairly safe technique that involves an understanding of the environment as well as wolf psychology and habits.

_C_ 1. As used in sentence 6, the word *employed* means
    A. hired.
    B. recognized.
    C. used.
    D. known.

> Answer A is incorrect because people, not objects, are hired. Answers B and D are incorrect because the Eskimos did more than just recognize or know the device—they used it, as described in sentences 7–9.

_C_ 2. The relationship between the two parts of sentence 5 is one of
    A. time.
    B. comparison.
    C. contrast.
    D. addition.

> The sentence contrasts the advantages of killing the wolves (eliminate the threat) with the disadvantages (danger, time spent, and wasted energy). The word *but* signals the contrast.

_B_ 3. The author implies that among primitive societies, the Eskimos' cleverness is
    A. superior.
    B. typical.
    C. rare.
    D. inferior.

> Sentence 2 implies that the Eskimos are typically clever, and sentence 3 mentions that "countless examples" can illustrate this point.

_B_ 4. The author implies that certain societies are considered "primitive"
because of their   See sentences 1, 2, 10, and 11.
   A. attitude toward animals.
   B. level of technology.
   C. creative ability.
   D. understanding of their environment.

_C_ 5. The author's attitude toward the Eskimos who created the weapon
appears to be   The author never accuses, sounds disgusted, or seems
   A. accusing.   puzzled; therefore, the tone is generally objective.
   B. disgusted.   Reference to the method as "harsh" (sentence 10)
   C. objective.   does not imply disapproval of Eskimos.
   D. puzzled.

_C_ 6. Which is an appropriate title for this selection?
   A. Mentally Backward Societies
   B. Dangerous Environmental Features
   C. Intelligence in Primitive Societies
   D. Land of the Eskimos

_D_ 7. Which sentence best expresses the main idea of the passage?
   A. The greatest challenge to a society is controlling its environment.
   B. Eskimos are able to control wolves.
   C. With increased technology, primitive societies should be able to
      cope even more effectively with their environment.
   D. Primitive societies can deal shrewdly and effectively with the
      demands of their environment.

_D_ 8. The author supports the main idea with a
   A. list of several reasons.
   B. comparison of two things.
   C. contrast between two things.
   D. detailed example.

Item 6: Answer A contradicts the point the author makes and the example
   given. Answer B is too broad because the wolf is the only dangerous
   environmental feature mentioned. Answer D is too broad because the
   passage does not discuss the land of the Eskimos in general.

Item 7: Answers A and C are not discussed in the passage. Answer B covers
   only the example, ignoring sentences 1–3.

Item 8: Answers A, B, and C are not accurate. Sentences 4–11 give the
   detailed example of the Eskimo and the wolf. It is introduced by the
   word *examples* in sentence 3.

COMBINED SKILLS: Mastery Test 12

Read the passage below. Then write the letter of the best answer to each question that follows.

¹It's not easy to tell when someone's lying to you. ²But most liars feel a little bad about their deception, whether it's complimenting Grandma on her tasteless cake or covering up a major scandal. ³And often that twinge of guilt, anxiety, or fear is strong enough to give lies away. ⁴The tone of a person's voice, <u>for example</u>, is one of the best cues. ⁵Research indicates that people's voices often get noticeably higher in pitch when they lie. ⁶Also, they're more likely to stammer or stumble over words. ⁷Liars also often sound distant when they're making something up, using few descriptive phrases or hand motions. ⁸In one study, students pretending to like a person they in fact disliked said such things as, "Yeah, I really like her because she's a good person." ⁹In addition, liars tend to lace their speech with denials and hedging, such as, "I didn't really read the book very carefully, so I'm not sure," or "I don't remember for sure who I played against in that tournament." ¹⁰And they're prone to frequent blinking and fidgeting, such as head-scratching or nail-biting. ¹¹<u>On the other hand</u>, many behaviors we think are signs of deception are not. ¹²Shifty eyes, for example, are not a good sign that someone is lying. ¹³When people speak slowly, take a long time to answer questions, shift their gaze or their posture, or don't smile much, they're *perceived* to be deceptive. ¹⁴According to researchers, however, these behaviors are as likely to show up during lie-telling as truth-telling.

_D_ 1. As used in sentence 10, the words *prone to* mean
   A. responsive to.
   B. afraid to show.
   C. likely to hide.
   D. likely to show.

   The larger context is the clue. Sentences 4–10 all describe behaviors people are likely to show when lying.

_C_ 2. According to the selection, one behavior that does **not** indicate that someone is lying is
   A. a higher-sounding voice.
   B. stammering and stumbling over words.
   C. shifty eyes.
   D. head-scratching and nail-biting.

   See sentence 12.

_A_ 3. Sentences 4–10
   A. provide examples of types of behavior which indicate that a person is lying.
   B. list reasons why some people feel the need to lie.
   C. compare liars with honest people.
   D. define the term *deceptive behavior*.

Sentences 4–10 give five examples of behavior that may indicate a person is lying. The words *for example* signal the pattern. (Notice that the examples are given as a list.)

_B_ 4. The relationship of sentence 11 to sentence 10 is one of
   A. cause and effect.
   B. contrast.
   C. addition.
   D. comparison.

> Behaviors that do not signal deception (sentences 11–13) are contrasted with behaviors that may signal deception (sentences 4–10).

> See sentences 1, 3, and 14. In addition, words such as *often* (sentences 3, 5, and 7), *more likely* (sentence 6), *tend to* (sentence 9), and *prone to* (sentence 10) show that the cues are not guaranteed indicators of lying.

_A_ 5. On the basis of this passage, we can infer that
   A. there are certain cues which tend to indicate whether or not a person is lying, but they're not foolproof.
   B. most liars are eventually found out.
   C. liars have no feelings of guilt over their behavior.
   D. fidgeting and frequent blinking are sure signs that a person is lying.

_D_ 6. The author would probably agree with which of the following statements?
   A. Lying is no big deal since everyone does it.
   B. Most politicians are liars.
   C. People should never lie.
   D. Liars tend to exhibit certain behaviors.

> See sentences 3–10. Answers A, B, and C are not mentioned.

_D_ 7. The author's tone is mainly
   A. sympathetic and tolerant.
   B. scornful and superior.
   C. solemn and objective.
   D. informal but instructive.

_C_ 8. What is the best title for the selection?
   A. We All Lie
   B. Foolproof Methods of Lie Detection
   C. Lie Detection: An Inexact Science
   D. How Detectives Obtain the Truth

Item 7: The informality is suggested by the mention of Grandma's tasteless cake (sentence 2) and the use of contractions such as *It's* and *someone's* (sentence 1), *they're* (sentence 10), and *don't* (sentence 13) throughout the selection. The instructive tone is set by the information the author presents about behaviors that can suggest whether or not someone is lying.

Item 8: See the comment on question 5. Answer A is incorrect because nothing is said about who does or does not lie. Answer B is incorrect because the passage emphasizes that the cues are not foolproof. Answer D is incorrect because the passage says nothing about detectives.

COMBINED SKILLS: Mastery Test 13

Read the passage below. Then write the letter of the best answer to each question that follows.

[1]According to a recent survey by the travel company Expedia.com, a third of employed U.S. adults don't use all of their allotted vacation time; they feel too much job pressure. [2]And their allotted time isn't much to begin with: on average, fourteen days. [3]Contrast that with the average number of paid vacation days allotted to employees in some other industrialized nations: seventeen in Australia, nineteen in Canada, twenty-four in the United Kingdom, twenty-seven in Germany, and thirty-nine in France. [4]In fact, about a fourth of U.S. employees don't receive *any* paid vacation time. [5]In addition, many Americans who do take vacation days continue to work via cell phones and computers. [6]Approximately a fourth of U.S. vacationers check their business voicemail or e-mail while on "vacation." [7]Also, it's standard for U.S. employers to require a year on the job before granting two weeks of vacation. [8]Finally, the United States is the only leading industrialized nation that doesn't legally require any minimum vacation time. [9]Canada and Japan require at least two weeks of paid vacation, China at least three, and all the other leading industrialized countries at least four. [10]Going without vacations leads to stress, resentment, depression, and burnout, which reduce job performance and impair health. [11]U.S. companies that have implemented mandatory vacations of at least three weeks have seen increased productivity and profits. [12]For these reasons, U.S. law should mandate minimum vacation times.

_C_ 1. In the first sentence, the word *allotted* means
      A. required.
      B. surrendered.   Sentences 2 and 3 suggest that the passage is
      C. permitted.   discussing permitted vacation days.
      D. demanded.

_B_ 2. In contrast to many other industrialized nations, the United States

See sentence 8.   A. requires that employers grant their employees two weeks of paid vacation.
      B. doesn't legally require any minimum vacation time.
      C. recommends but doesn't require that employees receive paid vacation time.
      D. requires that employers grant their employees three weeks of paid vacation.

_D_ 3. Many Americans don't use all their allotted vacation time because

See sentence 1.   A. they fear that their employers will penalize them if they do.
      B. they enjoy working.
      C. it's now so easy to work from home via cell phones and computers.
      D. they feel too much job pressure.

Sentences 3 and ___C___ 4. This selection mainly
9 present
information about   A. lists reasons why Americans receive little paid vacation.
vacations in other countries   B. defines the term *paid vacation* and provides examples of paid
that contrasts with the   vacations in other countries.
information about vacations   C. contrasts how much paid vacation workers in other industrialized
in the U.S. The word   countries receive with how little American workers receive.
Contrast in sentence 3   D. compares attitudes toward work of Europeans and Americans.
is a clue.

    ___A___ 5. The author suggests that

See sentences 5–6. Answer   A. even while many American workers are on vacation, they're still
B is incorrect because the   working.
author does not indicate   B. workers in other nations receive too much paid vacation.
this opinion. Answer C is   C. productivity would suffer if American workers received more paid
contradicted by sentence 11.   vacation time.
Answer D is not discussed   D. Americans work long hours, but the quality of the work they
in the passage.   perform is poor.

    ___B___ 6. The writer's main purpose in writing this selection is to

    A. predict whether American workers would take time out for longer
        paid vacations if these were offered to them.
    B. persuade readers that the United States should require employers to
        provide minimum vacation time.
    C. entertain readers with amusing stories about how Americans
        continue to work when they're supposed to be vacationing.
    D. inform readers about differences in the amount of vacation time
        workers in industrialized countries receive.

    ___B___ 7. Sentence 12 expresses

    A. a fact.
    B. an opinion.

    ___D___ 8. The main idea of the selection is expressed in

    A. sentence 1.
    B. sentence 2.
    C. sentence 8.
    D. sentence 12.

    Item 6: The selection makes no predictions and does not try to entertain us.
        Answer D does not cover the last two sentences. Sentences 1–9 show
        that the U.S. is out of step with the rest of the industrialized world.
        Sentence 10 shows the problems that can result from the U.S. system.
        Sentence 11 shows the advantages of changing the U.S. system.
        And in sentence 12, the word *should* signals the author's purpose: to
        persuade us.

    Item 7: The word *should* signals that this is an opinion.

    Item 8: Answer A introduces the topic of allotted vacation time. Answers B
        and C are major details.

COMBINED SKILLS: Mastery Test 14

Read the passage below. Then write the letter of the best answer to each question that follows.

¹We all know deserts are dry places, but just what is meant by the term *dry*? ²That is, how much rain defines the boundary between humid and dry regions? ³Sometimes it is defined by a single rainfall figure, for example, twenty-five centimeters (ten inches) of precipitation per year. ⁴(*Rainfall* refers to the quantity of water that falls in the form of rain, snow, etc. in an area in a given amount of time.) ⁵However, the concept of dryness is a relative one that refers to any situation in which a water deficiency exists. ⁶Thus, climatologists define *dry climate* as one in which yearly precipitation is less than the potential loss of water by evaporation. ⁷Dryness, then, is related not only to total annual rainfall but also to evaporation. ⁸Evaporation, in turn, greatly depends upon temperature. ⁹As temperatures climb, potential evaporation also increases. ¹⁰Fifteen to twenty-five centimeters of precipitation can support forests in northern Scandinavia, where evaporation into the cool, humid air is slight and a surplus of water remains in the soil. ¹¹However, the same amount of rain falling on New Mexico supports only a sparse vegetative cover because evaporation into the hot, dry air is great. ¹²So clearly no specific amount of precipitation can serve as a universal boundary for dry climates.

___C___ 1. In sentence 3, the word *precipitation* means
    A. weather conditions.
    B. humidity in the air.
    C. water that falls to the earth in any form.
    D. dry places.

If ten inches of precipitation is a "rainfall figure," precipitation must be water that falls to the earth. Sentence 4, which mentions rainfall, rain, and snow, suggests that the water can fall in any form.

___B___ 2. Scientists who study weather consider a dry climate to be one in which
    A. ten inches of water fall each year.
    B. potential evaporation is greater than the rainfall.
    C. there is no rainfall at all.
    D. it gets very hot.

See sentence 6.

___C___ 3. The higher the temperature is,
    A. the greater the rainfall.
    B. the smaller the rainfall.
    C. the greater the potential evaporation.
    D. the smaller the potential evaporation.

See sentence 9.

___A___ 4. In the discussion in the passage, temperature is
    A. a cause.   *See sentences 8–9. Cause:* rising temperatures.
    B. an effect.   *Effect:* increased evaporation.

___C___ 5. The relationship between sentences 10 and 11 is one of
    A. time.   The amount of vegetation supported by fifteen to
    B. comparison.   twenty-five centimeters of precipitation in a cool
                            climate is contrasted with the amount of vegetation
    C. contrast.   supported by that much precipitation in a hot climate.
    D. cause and effect.   The word *However* signals the contrast.

___A___ 6. The main purpose of the passage is to
    A. explain the relationships between dryness, evaporation, and temperature.
    B. persuade us that a hot, dry climate is better for people than a cool, humid one.
    C. entertain us with vivid descriptions of life in a dry climate.
    D. predict that in the future, more of the Earth will become a desert.

___C___ 7. The author implies that one reason evaporation in northern Scandinavian forests is slight is that
    A. the rainfall is low there.
    B. there is no rainfall there.
    C. the air there is cool.
    D. a heavy ground cover prevents the moisture from evaporating.

___B___ 8. Which sentence best expresses the main idea of the selection?
    A. When temperatures are lower, there is less evaporation.
    B. A dry climate is one in which the rainfall is less than the potential evaporation, which depends on temperature.
    C. Evaporation in a northern forest is slight in comparison with the evaporation in a desert region like that of New Mexico.
    D. Rainfall is the amount of water that falls to earth as rain, snow, sleet, and hail.

Item 6: Nothing in the passage attempts to persuade or entertain us. The passage makes no predictions for the future. The passage explains the relationship of the three elements in a straightforward manner.

Item 7: Sentence 10 says that "evaporation into cool, humid air is slight."

Item 8: Answer A covers only sentences 8–11. Answer C covers only sentences 10–11. Answer D covers only sentence 4.

COMBINED SKILLS: Mastery Test 15

Read the passage below. Then write the letter of the best answer to each question that follows.

[1]It's Friday afternoon, and you have almost survived another week of classes. [2]You are just looking forward dreamily to the weekend when the English instructor says: "For Monday you will turn in a five-hundred-word composition on college football."

[3]Well, that puts a good big hole in the weekend. [4]You don't have any strong views on college football one way or the other. [5]You get rather excited during the season and go to all the home games and find it rather more fun than not. [6]On the other hand, the class has been reading Robert Hutchins in the anthology and perhaps Shaw's "Eighty-Yard Run," and from the class discussion you have got the idea that the instructor thinks college football is for the birds. [7]You are no fool, you. [8]You can figure out what side to take.

[9]After dinner you sit down at the computer that you got for high-school graduation. [10]You might as well get it over with and enjoy Saturday and Sunday. [11]Five hundred words is about two double-spaced pages with normal margins. [12]You open a new document, think up a title, and you're off:

Why College Football Should Be Abolished

[13]College football should be abolished because it's bad for the school and also bad for the players. [14]The players are so busy practicing that they don't have any time for their studies.

[15]This, you feel, is a mighty good start. [16]The only trouble is that it's only thirty-two words. [17]You still have four hundred and sixty-eight to go, and you've pretty well exhausted the subject. [18]It comes to you that you do your best thinking in the morning, so you shut down the computer and go to the movies. [19]But the next morning you have to do your washing and some math problems, and in the afternoon you go to the game. [20]The English instructor turns up too, and you wonder if you've taken the right side after all. [21]Saturday night you have a date, and Sunday morning you have to go to church. [22](You shouldn't let English assignments interfere with your religion.) [23]What with one thing and another, it's ten o'clock Sunday night before you sit down at the computer again.

_____C_____ 1. In sentence 17, the word *exhausted* means

    A. created.

    B. researched.

    C. completely covered.

    D. forgotten.

Sentences 15–17 imply that the student has no other thoughts and has therefore completely covered the subject. Answer A is incorrect because the English instructor created the subject. Answer B is incorrect because there is no evidence that the student did any research. Answer D is incorrect because a student who had forgotten the subject would not be planning to write a paper on it the next morning.

_B_ 2. The relationship between the first part of sentence 18 (before the comma) to sentence 19 is one of

A. cause and effect.

B. contrast.

C. comparison.

D. addition.

The intended action (writing the paper in the morning) is contrasted with the actual action (doing wash and math problems). The word *But* signals the contrast relationship.

_A_ 3. The overall pattern of organization is

A. time order.

B. list of items.

C. definition and example.

D. comparison.

The passage presents in order the student's actions from Friday afternoon through Sunday night. See the underlined words that signal the pattern.

_C_ 4. The author's tone can be described as

A. angry and worried.

B. encouraging and respectful.

C. humorous and sarcastic.

D. ambivalent and bewildered.

The informal style, as well as phrases such as "almost survived another week of classes" and "You are no fool, you," create a humorous tone. Sarcasm can be detected in sentence 22.

_B_ 5. To make his points, the author has chosen to use a

A. factual anecdote.

B. fictional anecdote.

The fictional "you" represents the typical student.

_A_ 6. The author suggests that the student

See sentences 18–23.

A. is more skilled at putting things off than at writing compositions.

B. would miss a party in order to attend church on Sunday.

C. actually enjoys writing compositions.

D. should have found out his instructor's view on football before writing the composition.

_D_ 7. The author implies in the second paragraph that the student

See sentences 6–8.

A. agrees with Robert Hutchins's views on football.

B. has no interest in football at all.

C. has paid no attention to class discussions.

D. feels his composition should defend the instructor's point of view.

_B_ 8. Which sentence best expresses the main idea of the passage?

The student spent neither time nor thought, thereby coming up with no composition.

A. College football should not be abolished.

B. A college composition assignment requires time and thought to complete.

C. English instructors should not assign homework for the weekends, when students have little available time.

D. Composition assignments should be based on class reading assignments and discussion.

COMBINED SKILLS: Mastery Test 16

Read the passage below. Then write the letter of the best answer to each question that follows.

[1]Why do American schools fail to create lifetime readers? [2]There are two basic and related "facts of life" that parents and educators seem to ignore. [3]The first fact is that human beings are pleasure-centered. [4]We will voluntarily do over and over that which brings us pleasure. [5]For example, we go to the restaurants we like, order the foods we like, listen to the radio stations that play the music we like, and visit the relatives we like. [6]Conversely, we avoid the restaurants, foods, music, and relatives we dislike.

[7]What does this pleasure principle have to do with reading? [8]Children love stories, so every time we read to a child at home or at school, we send a "pleasure" message to the child's brain. [9]You could even call it a commercial, conditioning the child to associate books and print with pleasure. [10]However, all too often, parents don't read to their children; and, to make matters worse, schools send "unpleasure" messages about reading. [11]Endless hours of worksheets, intensive phonics instruction, and seemingly unconnected test questions can be—to a child—tedious or boring, threatening, and meaningless. [12]If a child seldom experiences the "pleasures" of reading at home and meets only the "unpleasures" at school, then the natural reaction will be avoidance.

[13]The second basic fact is that reading is an accrued skill. [14]In other words, reading is like riding a bicycle, driving a car, or sewing: in order to get better at it, you must do it. [15]And the more you do it, the better you get at it. [16]The last twenty-five years of reading research confirms this simple formula. [17]Regardless of sex, race, nationality, or socioeconomic background, the students who read the most are the ones who read the best, achieve the most, and stay in school the longest. [18]In contrast, those who don't read much cannot get better at it. [19]And most Americans (children and adults) don't read much, and therefore aren't very good at it.

[20]Why don't Americans read much? [21]The reason is that a lack of "pleasure" messages in the home, coupled with the large number of "unpleasure" messages about reading they received throughout their school years, nullify any attraction a book might offer. [22]They avoid books and print the same way a cat avoids a rocking chair.

_B_   1. In sentence 6, the word *conversely* means
     A. in addition.
     B. in contrast.
     C. as a result.
     D. next.

Sentences 5 and 6 contrast our attraction to the things we like to do with our avoidance of the things we do not like to do.

_D_ 2. The author feels that children are encouraged to read by
   A. doing worksheets.   See sentences 8–9.
   B. riding a bicycle.
   C. having phonics instruction.
   D. being read to.

_A_ 3. Sentence 12 expresses a relationship of
   A. cause and effect.   *Cause:* lack of "pleasures" and too
   B. comparison.   many "unpleasures." *Effect:* avoidance.
   C. contrast.   The words *If . . . then* signal the relationship.
   D. addition.

All of the details _C_ 4. The passage discusses
in sentences 7–19 tell how   A. stages of reading education.
parents and educators fail   B. a list of methods for teaching reading to children.
to create healthy readers.   C. the causes of Americans' not becoming skillful, lifetime readers.
In addition, see sentences   D. a definition of the phrase *lifetime readers* with examples.
1–2 and 20–22.

_A_ 5. Sentences 16 and 17 state
   A. a fact.   This fact can be confirmed by examining the
   B. an opinion.   documentation of the reading research that has
                           been published in the past twenty-five years.

_A_ 6. The author's tone can be described as   The writer analyzes the reasons
   A. critical and analytical.   Americans do not read well or much, making
   B. joyful and optimistic.   critical remarks about how parents neglect
   C. tolerant and amused.   to introduce their children to the pleasures of
   D. pleading and hopeful.   reading and about how educators often make
                                        reading an unpleasant experience.

A cat purposely
stays away from   _B_ 7. Sentence 22 implies that most Americans
a rocking chair to avoid   A. carelessly seek out books and print.
getting its tail mashed.   B. purposely stay away from books and print.
In the same way, the simile   C. have no opinion about books and print.
suggests, most Americans   D. are often harmed by books and print.
purposely avoid books and
print.
              _A_ 8. Which sentence best states the main idea of the passage?
   A. Most Americans don't read much or well because parents and
      educators often fail to make reading a pleasant experience.
   B. Reading to children sends a message to them to associate books and
      print with pleasure.
   C. People, being pleasure-centered, will voluntarily avoid activities
      they dislike and repeatedly do activities that bring them pleasure.
   D. Twenty-five years of reading research has shown that the students
      who read the most are those that read the best.

              Answer B covers only sentences 8–9. Answer C covers only
              sentences 3–6. Answer D covers only sentences 16–17.

COMBINED SKILLS: Mastery Test 17

Read the passage below. Then write the letter of the best answer to each question that follows.

[1]The power of advertising to influence public attitudes and behaviors is well-illustrated by how diamonds have been "sold" to the public. [2]In 1938, some three-quarters of all diamonds mined in South Africa, the world's leading producer, were sold for engagement rings in the United States. [3]Most of these stones, however, were smaller and of poorer quality than those bought in Europe, where diamonds were purchased mostly by the aristocracy. [4]In addition, the diamonds that Americans purchased had an average price of only $80. [5]It was at this time that a South African diamond executive from the De Beers company engaged a New York advertising agency, N.W. Ayer, to prepare a plan for creating a new image for diamonds among Americans. [6]After researching the declining market for diamonds in the United States, the ad agency came up with a plan that stressed the need to strengthen the association in the public's mind of diamonds with romance. [7]Since young men bought over 90% of engagement rings, it would be crucial to impress on them the idea that diamonds were a gift of love: the larger and finer the diamond, the greater the expression of love. [8]Similarly, young women had to be encouraged to view diamonds as an integral part of any romantic courtship. [9]To accomplish this, movie stars, those shining examples of romance for the mass audience, were given diamonds to use as their symbols of indestructible love. [10]Magazine stories were written which stressed the size of diamonds that celebrities presented to their loved ones, and photographs conspicuously showed the glittering stone on the hand of a well-known woman. [11]Even the British royal family was enlisted to wear diamonds rather than other jewels. [12]Finally, the advertising agency came up with the slogan "A Diamond Is Forever," now considered to be the most recognized advertising slogan ever. [13]The advertising campaign succeeded in spectacular fashion. [14]By the end of the 1950s, the retail sales of diamonds had increased by over 50%, and a diamond ring was considered by virtually everyone, a necessity to engagements.

_B_   1. In sentence 8, the word *integral* means
   A. minor.
   B. necessary.
   C. inexpensive.
   D. extra.

In the same way that men needed to be convinced that "diamonds were a gift of love," women needed to be convinced that diamonds were a necessary part of courtship. And sentence 14 notes that "a diamond ring was considered a necessity to engagements."

_D_   2. In the late 1930s,

See sentences 2 and 4.

   A. diamond sales in the United States increased by 50%.
   B. most diamonds were purchased by American movie stars and European aristocrats.
   C. few young men bought their fiancées diamond engagement rings.
   D. the diamonds Americans purchased had an average price of only $80.

_C_ 3. The De Beers Company wanted to

See sentences 7
("larger and finer")
and 10 ("stressed the
size of diamonds").

    A. become the world's sole exporter of diamonds.

    B. encourage Americans to purchase many inexpensive diamonds.

    C. encourage Americans to purchase larger and finer diamonds.

    D. limit the amount of diamonds that could be exported by South Africa.

_D_ 4. Sentence 3 expresses a relationship of

    A. cause and effect.

    B. comparison.

    C. illustration.

    D. contrast.

The size and quality of diamonds bought in America is contrasted with the size and quality of those bought in Europe. The word *however* signals the contrast.

Item 5:
The sentences list
three ways diamonds
were "sold"—
they were
given to movie stars,
magazine stories and
photographs emphasized
celebrities' diamonds,
and the British royal
family was seen wearing
diamonds.

_A_ 5. Sentences 9–12

    A. list ways that diamonds were "sold" to the public.

    B. contrast European attitudes toward diamonds with American attitudes.

    C. compare men's attitudes toward diamonds with women's.

    D. present a series of steps in time order.

_B_ 6. The passage suggests that

See sentences 1, 5,
and 9–12.

    A. it was entirely natural for Americans to think of diamonds as a necessity to engagements.

    B. the American public has been cleverly manipulated into spending money on expensive diamonds.

    C. Americans would be better off if they spent their money on luxury goods other than diamonds.

    D. only movie stars and other wealthy people really believe that "A Diamond Is Forever."

_A_ 7. Sentence 14 is a statement of

    A. fact.

    B. opinion.

This information can be confirmed by checking the figures of retail sales of diamonds in the U.S. and by researching the attitudes of Americans about the relationship of diamonds and engagements in the 1950s.

_B_ 8. Which is the most appropriate title for the passage?

    A. Diamonds Aren't Forever

    B. How Diamonds Have Been Sold to the Public

    C. A Brief History of De Beers Diamonds

    D. Advertising in Action

Answer A is not supported. Answer C is too broad because the passage covers only the way in which De Beers increased its sale of diamonds in the U.S. Answer D is too broad because the passage is about only one specific advertising campaign, not advertising in general.

COMBINED SKILLS: Mastery Test 18

Read the passage below. Then write the letter of the best answer to each question that follows.

¹The Hawthorne experiment was conducted in the late 1920s and early 1930s. ²The management of Western Electric's Hawthorne plant, located near Chicago, wanted to find out if environmental factors, such as lighting, could affect workers' productivity and morale. ³A team of social scientists experimented with a small group of employees who were set apart from their coworkers. ⁴The environmental conditions of this group's work area were controlled, and the subjects themselves were closely observed. ⁵To the great surprise of the researchers, the productivity of these workers increased in response to any change in their environmental conditions. ⁶The rate of work increased even when the changes (such as a sharp decrease in the level of light in the workplace) seemed unlikely to have such an effect.

⁷It was concluded that the presence of the observers had caused the workers in the experimental group to feel special. ⁸As a result, the employees came to know and trust one another, and they developed a strong belief in the importance of their job. ⁹The researchers believed that this, not the changes in the work environment, accounted for the increased productivity.

¹⁰A later reanalysis of the study data challenged the Hawthorne conclusions on the grounds that the changes in patterns of human relations, considered so important by the original researchers, were never measured. ¹¹However, even if the original conclusions must be revised, they nonetheless raise a problem for social scientists: Research subjects who know they are being studied can change their behavior. ¹²Throughout the social sciences, this phenomenon has come to be called the Hawthorne effect.

_____C_____ 1. In sentences 2 and 5, the word *productivity* means
    A. attendance.   C. rate of work.
    B. human relations.   D. health.

"Rate of work" in sentence 6 is a synonym for *productivity*.

Item 2:
Cause: presence of observers. *Effect:* employees came to know and trust one another, developing a strong belief in the importance of their job. The words *As a result* and *accounted for* signal the cause and effect pattern.

_____D_____ 2. The pattern of organization of the second paragraph is
    A. list of items.   C. definition and example.
    B. time order.   D. cause and effect.

_____C_____ 3. The author implies that a sharp decrease in light increased workers' output because the workers
    A. experienced less eyestrain.
    B. had to pay more attention to what they were doing.
    C. knew they were being observed, and this motivated them.
    D. in the experiment were paid more than other workers.

In sentence 9, the pronoun *this* refers to the employees' beliefs (stated in sentences 7 and 8) that they were special, that they could trust each other, and that their jobs were important.

_C_ 4. Employers might conclude from the Hawthorne experiment that they should

See sentences 7–9.

  A. keep plant lighting low.
  B. constantly change environmental conditions.
  C. consistently let workers know that their work is important.
  D. keep social scientists away from their workers.

_A_ 5. The Hawthorne experiment suggests that

See sentences 7–9.

  A. workers' attitudes are more important than their environment.
  B. social scientists are good workers.
  C. productivity in electric plants tends to be low.
  D. even those Hawthorne workers who were not in the experiment improved their productivity.

_B_ 6. The Hawthorne effect is a problem for social scientists because

See sentence 11.

  A. researchers usually do not measure the changes in human relations among workers.
  B. the results of a study will be questionable if the subjects are aware that they are being observed.
  C. the Hawthorne research was done too long ago, when working conditions were quite different.
  D. the group of employees who were studied was small.

_A_ 7. The author's main purpose is to

  A. explain the Hawthorne effect.
  B. prove the importance of research.
  C. amuse with a surprising experiment.
  D. suggest ideas for future research.

Answers B and D are not addressed in the passage. Answer C is not correct because the passage has no humorous or amusing wording.

_C_ 8. Which sentence best expresses the main idea of the passage?

Answer A covers only sentence 1. Answer B covers only sentence 2. Answer D refers only to sentence 10, and it misstates the point made in that sentence.

  A. The famous Hawthorne experiment took place in the late 1920s and early 1930s.
  B. The Hawthorne experiment took place because the management of an electric plant wanted to find out the impact of environmental factors on workers.
  C. An experiment revealed the fact, known as the Hawthorne effect, that research subjects may behave differently if they know they are being studied.
  D. A reanalysis of data from an experiment at an electrical plant showed that the researchers were careless about how they conducted their study.

COMBINED SKILLS: Mastery Test 19

Read the passage below. Then write the letter of the best answer to each question that follows.

[1]Although teenage pregnancy and birthrates in the United States dropped dramatically during the 1990s, they remain many times higher than in other industrialized countries, where adolescents begin sexual activity just as early or earlier. [2]Teenage birthrates in recent years have been nearly five times as high in the United States as in Denmark, Finland, France, Germany, Italy, and Spain and twelve times as high as in Japan. [3]Experts disagree about why the U.S. rates are so high. [4]Some observers point to such factors as the reduced stigma on unwed motherhood, media glorification of sex, the lack of a clear message that sex and parenthood are for adults, the influence of childhood sexual abuse, and the failure of parents to communicate with children. [5]Contrasts with the European experience suggest the importance of other factors as well. [6]First of all, Europe's industrialized countries have provided universal, comprehensive sex education for a much longer time than the United States. [7]Comprehensive programs encourage young teenagers to delay intercourse but also aim to improve contraceptive use among sexually active adolescents. [8]Such programs include education about sexuality and acquisition of skills for making responsible sexual decisions and communicating with partners. [9]They provide information about risks and consequences of teenage pregnancy, about birth control methods, and about where to get medical and contraceptive help. [10]Secondly, European countries also provide access to reproductive services. [11]Contraceptives are provided free to adolescents in Britain, France, and Sweden. [12]Sweden showed a fivefold reduction in the teenage birth rate following the introduction of birth control education, free access to contraceptives, and free abortion on demand. [13]Indeed, U.S. teens who use contraception in their first sexual experience are much less likely to bear a child by age 20. [14]In the United States, the provision and content of sex education programs is a political issue. [15]Some critics claim that community- and school-based sex education leads to more or earlier sexual activity, even though evidence shows otherwise.

_B_ 1. In sentence 7, the word *comprehensive* means

    A. limited.   C. costly.

    B. complete.   D. immoral.

> Sentences 8–9 list the things that comprehensive programs include—education, acquisition of skills, information about a wide variety of topics. This list suggests that it is a complete program.

_D_ 2. Other industrialized countries have teenage pregnancy and birth rates that are

    A. about the same as those of the United States.

    B. much higher than those of the United States.

    C. slightly lower than those of the United States.

    D. much lower than those of the United States.

> See sentence 2. If the birthrates in the U.S. have been "nearly five times higher," then other industrialized countries must have rates that are much lower.

_____A_____ 3. Some critics of sex education programs believe that sex education

See sentence 15.

    A. leads to more or earlier sexual activity.

    B. is ineffective in reducing teen pregnancy.

    C. effectively reduces teen pregnancy but leads to increased rates of sexually transmitted diseases.

    D. has no effect on teens' sexual behavior.

_____C_____ 4. All of the following have been given as reasons for America's high rate of teenage pregnancy *except*

Answers A, B, and D are all stated in sentence 4.

    A. media glorification of sex.

    B. the influence of childhood sexual abuse.

    C. widespread availability of condoms.

    D. the failure of parents to communicate with their children.

_____A_____ 5. This selection mainly

Answer B is incorrect because the passage only implies attitudes of Europeans toward sexuality by describing the measures they take. Answer C is not supported. Answer D covers only sentences 7–9.

    A. lists possible reasons why European countries have lower teenage pregnancy and birth rates than the United States.

    B. compares sex education programs in the U.S. to those in Europe.

    C. presents a series of measures, in the order in which they were adopted, that some European countries have employed to reduce their rates of teen pregnancy.

    D. defines the term *comprehensive sex education* and provides examples of it.

_____A_____ 6. The author's main purpose is to

    A. inform.   C. entertain.

    B. persuade.   D. predict.

The passage presents possible factors that may explain the differences between U.S. and European teenage birthrates. There is no direct attempt to persuade us; persuasion is only hinted at through the more successful outcomes of the European approach.

_____D_____ 7. On the whole, the tone of this passage is

    A. defensive.   C. uncertain.

    B. outraged.   D. straightforward.

The author gives a simple, unemotional presentation of the information.

_____C_____ 8. The passage suggests that

See sentence 15. Judging by the outcomes of European programs, answer C is a logical conclusion. Answer A is contradicted by the European experience. There is no evidence to support answer B. Answer D is incorrect because the author makes no judgments about morality or immorality.

    A. sexual activity among American teenagers would rise dramatically if more teens were provided with community- and school-based sex education.

    B. teenage pregnancy and birth rates will continue to drop dramatically even if American teens are not provided with comprehensive sex education and free access to contraceptives.

    C. teenage pregnancy rates in the United States could be reduced if the United States provided universal sex education, free access to contraceptives, and abortion of demand.

    D. it is immoral to provide teenagers with free access to contraceptives and abortion on demand.

COMBINED SKILLS: Mastery Test 20

Read the passage below. Then write the letter of the best answer to each question that follows.

¹Imagine being on a treadmill, wearing a face mask connected to oxygen-measuring equipment. ²You are walking at a leisurely pace, at the slowest setting, so your oxygen consumption is fairly low. ³As the speed of the treadmill increases, your metabolism increases, and as a result, your oxygen consumption goes up as well. ⁴Your muscle cells are using the extra oxygen to break down carbohydrates, which they use for fuel, and turn them into energy, so their metabolism is said to be aerobic (with air). ⁵You are now jogging along at a comfortable speed, still supplying ample oxygen to your muscle cells, so your exercise is still aerobic. ⁶As you increase your speed, your oxygen consumption will continue to rise, but at some point, it will stop rising. ⁷That is because your heart and lungs have reached their maximum capacity for supplying oxygen to the muscles via the bloodstream. ⁸But you can still run a lot faster. ⁹Your speed keeps increasing and eventually you are running as fast as you can, but your oxygen consumption has not changed. ¹⁰Your muscle cells can keep on firing without getting the extra oxygen they need because they are able to break down carbohydrates without using oxygen. ¹¹This is called anaerobic (without air) metabolism. ¹²Sprinters, who run at top speed, perform most of their hundred-meter race anaerobically; in contrast, long-distance runners, who have time to vary their speed, perform most of their event aerobically.

¹³Anaerobic metabolism is far less efficient than aerobic metabolism but is capable of generating very high quantities of energy for short periods of time. ¹⁴It also generates lactic acid as a byproduct. ¹⁵This accumulates in the muscles and is associated with muscle fatigue and general exhaustion. ¹⁶That is why sprinting cannot be kept up for very long. ¹⁷After sprinting, the lactic acid that has accumulated in the muscles has to be broken down, and this requires oxygen, which explains why we puff and pant after a hard run.

_A_ 1. The body's energy is usually obtained through the breakdown of
   A. carbohydrates.   See sentence 4.
   B. lactic acid.
   C. the bloodstream.
   D. oxygen.

_C_ 2. When you run, your body begins anaerobic metabolism
   A. as you begin to pick up speed.
   B. after sprinting is completed.
   C. when your heart and lungs cannot supply sufficient oxygen.
   D. when the lactic acid in your muscles must be broken down.

Sentences 10–11 explain that *anaerobic* means "without air."
Sentence 7 mentions the heart and lungs as suppliers of oxygen.

_A_ 3. Aerobic metabolism
   A. is more efficient than anaerobic metabolism.
   B. breaks down carbohydrates without oxygen.
   C. generates lactic acid.
   D. happens for only brief periods.

See sentence 13. If anaerobic metabolism is "far less efficient than aerobic metabolism," then aerobic metabolism must be more efficient than anaerobic metabolism.

_C_ 4. The main overall patterns of organization of the passage are cause and effect and
   A. list of items.
   B. comparison.
   C. contrast.

The passage explains how aerobic metabolism is different from anaerobic metabolism. The words *but* and *in contrast* signal the contrast pattern.

_A_ 5. The purpose of this passage is to
   A. inform us about what happens to our bodies during walking, running, and sprinting.
   B. persuade us that we need to exercise regularly to keep our metabolisms going.
   C. entertain us with a vivid and detailed account of how our bodies work.

All of the details give information on how our bodies function during these activities. No details attempt to persuade or entertain us.

_D_ 6. We can infer that when we feel we are out of breath, we are low on
   A. lactic acid.
   B. carbohydrates.
   C. muscle cells.
   D. oxygen.

See sentence 17.

Item 7:
There is no support for answer A. Answer B is incorrect because the passage does not mention a reserve of carbohydrates. Details in sentences 12–17 show that answer D is incorrect.

_C_ 7. The passage implies that during sprinting,
   A. there is a dangerous strain on the heart.
   B. the body's reserve of carbohydrates increases.
   C. the body breaks down carbohydrates both with and without oxygen.
   D. the body needs less energy than usual.

_A_ 8. Which statement best expresses the main idea of the passage?
   A. Walking, jogging, and sprinting create different energy demands on the human body and also consume different amounts of oxygen.
   B. Running at top speed cannot be kept up nearly as long as jogging because of the different ways that energy is supplied to the muscles.
   C. Muscle cells can keep on firing in the absence of oxygen because they are able to break down carbohydrates for short periods.
   D. When lactic acid accumulates in someone's muscles, the person experiences muscle fatigue and general exhaustion.

Answer B covers only sentences 9–10. Answer C covers only sentences 10 and 13. Answer D covers only sentences 14–15.

Appendixes

Pronunciation Guide

Each word in Chapter 1, "Vocabulary in Context," is followed by information in parentheses that shows you how to pronounce the word. (There are also pronunciations for the vocabulary items that follow the readings in Parts One and Two.) The guide below and on the next page explains how to use that information.

Long Vowel Sounds

ā	pay
ē	she
ī	hi
ō	go
oo̅	cool
yoo̅	use

Short Vowel Sounds

ă	hat
ĕ	ten
ĭ	sit
ŏ	lot
oŏ	look
ŭ	up
yoŏ	cure

Other Vowel Sounds

â	care
ä	card
îr	here
ô	all
oi	oil
ou	out
ûr	fur
ə	ago, item, easily, gallop, circus

Consonant Sounds

b	big
d	do
f	fall
g	dog
h	he

Consonant Sounds

j	jump
k	kiss
l	let
m	meet
n	no
p	put
r	red
s	sell
t	top
v	have
w	way
y	yes
z	zero
ch	church
sh	dish
th	then
th	thick
zh	usual

Note that each pronunciation symbol above is paired with a common word that shows the sound of the symbol. For example, the symbol ā has the sound of the *a* in the common word *pay*. The symbol ă has the sound of the *a* in the common word *hat*. The symbol ə, which looks like an upside-down *e* and is known as the schwa, has the unaccented sound in the common word *ago*. It sounds like the "uh" a speaker often says when hesitating.

Accent marks are small black marks that tell you which syllable to emphasize as you say a word. A bold accent mark (′) shows which syllable should be stressed. A lighter accent mark (′) in some words indicates a secondary stress. Syllables without an accent mark are unstressed.

Writing Assignments

To the Instructor: Before assigning any of the following topics, you might want to go over with your students the guidelines that appear below and on the next page.

A Brief Guide to Effective Writing

Here in a nutshell is what you need to do to write effectively.

Step 1: Explore Your Topic through Informal Writing

To begin with, explore the topic that you want to write about or that you have been assigned to write about. You can examine your topic through **informal writing**, which usually means one of three things.

First, you can **freewrite** about your topic for at least ten minutes. In other words, write, for ten minutes, whatever comes into your head about your subject. Write without stopping and without worrying at all about spelling or grammar or the like. Simply get down on paper all the information about the topic that occurs to you.

A second thing you can do is to **make a list of ideas and details** that could go into your paper. Simply pile these items up, one after another, like a shopping list, without worrying about putting them in any special order. Try to accumulate as many details as you can think of.

A third way to explore your topic is to **write down a series of questions and answers** about it. Your questions can start with words like *what, why, how, when,* and *where.*

Getting your thoughts and ideas down on paper will help you think more about your topic. With some raw material to look at, you are now in a better position to decide on just how to proceed.

Step 2: Plan Your Paper with an Informal Outline

After exploring your topic, plan your paper, using an informal outline. Do two things:

- **Decide on and write out the main point of your paper.** It is often a good idea to begin your paragraph with this point, which is known as the *topic sentence*. If you are writing an essay of several paragraphs, you will probably want to include your main point somewhere in your first paragraph. In a paper of several paragraphs, the main point is called the *central point*, or *thesis*.

- **List the supporting reasons, examples, or other details that back up your point.** In many cases, you should have at least two or three items of support.

Step 3: Use Transitions

Once your outline is worked out, you will have a clear "road map" for writing your paper. As you write the early drafts of your paper, use **transitions** to introduce each of the separate supporting items (reasons, examples, or other details) you present to back up your point. For instance, you might introduce your first supporting item with the transitional words *first of all*. You might begin your second supporting item with words such as *another reason* or *another example*. And you might indicate your final supporting detail with such words as *last of all* or *a final reason*.

Step 4: Edit and Proofread Your Paper

After you have a solid draft, edit and proofread the paper. To evaluate your paper, ask yourself these questions:

1 Is the paper **unified**? Does all the material in the paper truly support the opening point?

2 Is the paper **well supported**? Is there plenty of specific evidence to back up the opening point?

3 Is the paper **clearly organized**? Does the material proceed in a way that makes sense? Do transitions help connect ideas?

4 Is the paper **well written**? When the paper is read aloud, do the sentences flow smoothly and clearly? Has the paper been checked carefully for grammar, punctuation, and spelling mistakes?

Writing Assignments for the Twenty Readings

Note: The discussion questions accompanying the twenty readings can also make good topics for writing. Some of the writing assignments here are based on these questions.

Part One Readings

Night Watch

1. Imagine that you are the son of the old man in the story. The day after your father died, you arrived and heard the story of the other Marine who had been with him in his last hours. How do you think you would feel about the situation? Would you feel primarily grateful, sad, angry, regretful, confused, or something else? Write a paragraph that describes what you think your reaction might be. If your response would be a mix of several emotions, say so. Along with stating your feelings, tell why you feel as you do.

2. The young Marine stayed by the old man's bedside, he said, because "I figured he really needed me." Tell in a paragraph about a time you felt needed. Who was it who needed you, and in what way? How did you respond to that person? Did you feel able to give the person what he or she wanted from you? Was feeling needed a pleasant experience, or did it seem like a burden? Here's a sample topic sentence for this paragraph: "Once my older brother really needed my help, and it felt very good to be able to help him."

3. It's not uncommon to see people reach out to help their loved ones. But the final paragraph of this article states that "in a uniquely human way . . . there are people who care what happens to their fellow human beings"—in other words, they care about people to whom they have no particular obligation. Think of experiences you have had, or heard about, in which people went out of their way to assist someone they do not know well, if at all. Write an essay that tells the stories of two or three such incidents. You might conclude your essay by talking about what, if anything, the "givers" in such situations gain by their actions.

Here's to Your Health

1. Few people go through life without being exposed to the negative effects of alcohol. In a paragraph, describe an unpleasant or dangerous incident you have been aware of, or experienced yourself, in which alcohol played a part. Who was involved? What happened? In what way did alcohol contribute to the situation? How did the incident end?

2. The advertising and sale of cigarettes are topics of much debate. There are already some legal restrictions in place—cigarettes are no longer advertised on television, they are not to be sold to minors, and warning labels on cigarettes inform consumers of health risks associated with smoking. In your opinion, are such restrictions needed or helpful? Should more restrictions be imposed on the tobacco industry, or should cigarettes be advertised and sold like any other product? Write a paragraph that explains your opinions about how or if cigarettes should be regulated and why.

3. As this article shows, alcohol is advertised as something that makes people more successful, sexier, healthier, and happier. The abuse of alcohol, however, often has quite the opposite effect. Write an essay in which you describe what alcohol advertisements would look like if they showed the negative side of drinking. What images would you choose to include in such advertisements? You might organize your essay by addressing several of the positive "myths" about alcohol mentioned in the article and describing an ad that would contradict each myth.

Child-Rearing Styles

1. Near the end of the article, the author lists six recommendations to parents who want to raise "competent, socially responsible, independent children." Choose one of those six recommendations and write a paragraph that demonstrates how it was (or was not) practiced in your own home. Illustrate the paragraph with examples from your childhood. Conclude by stating how you were positively or negatively affected by those examples.

2. Reread the author's descriptions of the three parenting styles: authoritative, authoritarian, and permissive. Think of a parent you know who is a good example of one of those three styles. Then write a paragraph that describes how that person interacts with his or her child. Provide one or more examples that demonstrate the adult's approach to parenting. You might try using some dialogue to emphasize a point or two. In conclusion, comment on how you think the parent's style is affecting the child.

3. It is not uncommon to hear parents say of their children, "I don't understand—we raised them all just the same, and yet they've turned out so differently." On the basis of your own experience growing up and your observations of other families, write an essay that comments on several possible explanations for why siblings develop different—sometimes dramatically different—personalities. Provide vivid real-life examples to illustrate your points. A possible central point for this essay might be: "Inherited personality, different parental treatment, and birth order account for many of the differences between siblings."

Rowing the Bus

1. Logan writes, "In each school, in each classroom, there is a George with a stricken face." Think of a person who filled the role of George in one of your classes. In a paragraph, describe why he or she was the target of teasing, and what form that teasing took. Include a description of your own thoughts and actions regarding the student who was teased.

2. Fearing that his life would be made miserable, the author decided to stop being friends with George. How do you feel about that decision? Do you think it was cruel? Understandable? Were there other options Logan might have tried? Write a paragraph in which you explain what you think of Logan's decision and why. Suggest at least one other way he could have acted, and tell what you think the consequences might have been.

3. In this essay, Logan provides many vivid descriptions of incidents in which bullies attack other students. Reread those descriptions and consider what they teach you about the nature of bullies and bullying. Then write an essay that supports the following main idea: "Evidence in 'Rowing the Bus' suggests that most bullies share certain characteristics." Mention two or three such characteristics, and provide evidence from the essay that illustrates how they are present in acts of bullying. In your concluding paragraph, you might write about what these characteristics tell us about bullies.

Wonder in the Air

1. In explaining why he refused at first to encourage his daughter's belief in Santa Claus, Gammage states that he wanted to be able to answer his daughter's questions about China "from an established position of truth-telling." Do you think Jin Yu will later doubt her father because he "lied" to her about Santa Claus? Or won't it make a difference? Write a paragraph which explains your thinking.

2. Write a paragraph that supports one of the following main ideas: "I believe that parents should encourage their children to believe in Santa Claus, the Easter Bunny, and the tooth fairy" or "I believe that it is important for parents to discourage their children's belief in Santa Claus, the Easter Bunny, and the tooth fairy." Explain your thinking, giving specific examples from your life experiences as well as from Gammage's observations in the article.

3. Although Gammage and his wife originally decided that "no lies" would be their one firm parental rule, they eventually come to realize that this rule is not realistic. What do you think are two or three good (and realistic) parental rules? Write an essay in which you state and then discuss each rule. Be sure to explain why you think each rule would benefit both parents and children.

Students in Shock

1. Students face a good deal of pressure in their new environment, as this essay shows. But they are not the only ones susceptible to "shock." Anyone in a demanding new situation can experience depression, frustration, and hopelessness. For example, someone who is new to a job, to a neighborhood, to marriage, or to parenthood might experience his or her own brand of shock. Write a paragraph that explores the possible causes of shock in a person facing a specific situation. You may choose one of the situations listed here, or another that occurs to you. Suggest ways the person might reduce the pressure he or she feels.

2. When you experience stress, what helps you to relax? Write a paragraph that describes your own favorite stress-reduction technique. Is it exercising, talking with a friend, taking a bath, playing golf, punching a pillow? You might begin with a vivid description of how stress affects you, then contrast that with a description of how your favorite technique changes your mood. Explain in detail how you go about using the technique.

3. Stress, anxiety, depression, burnout—these words are common parts of our modern vocabulary. What do you think are some of the main sources of this widespread stress? Write an essay that describes several common causes of stress. You could use as your central point a sentence similar to this: "There are three common reasons why people today are so stressed out." For each cause of stress you mention, provide specific ways in which it affects people. Add interest to your essay by using examples from the lives of people you know or have observed.

Gender Inequality in Health Care and in the Workplace

1. From your own observations, what group is the most openly discriminated against in the U.S. today? Members of a certain gender? People of a certain sexual orientation? Members of a particular ethnic, social, or religious group? Write a paragraph in which you state your conclusion and back it up by describing at least one incident of discrimination that you have witnessed.

2. Have you (or has anyone you know) been treated unfairly in school or in the workplace? Describe what happened. What do you think was the reason behind the unfair treatment? How did you (or the other victim) respond? Your topic sentence should explain in a nutshell what occurred. For example, "I once saw a merchant cheat my uncle because he did not speak enough English to complain."

3. All in all, do you think it's preferable to be a man or a woman in today's society? Write an essay in which you defend your choice. Select several points that support your point of view and develop them fully. Your thesis statement might be something like this: "In today's world, there are three very definite advantages to being a man."

The Scholarship Jacket

1. Marta remembers herself at 14 as, "Pencil thin, not a curve anywhere, I was called 'Beanpole' and 'String Bean,' and I knew that's what I looked like." Write a paragraph in which you describe yourself at a particular age. You may choose to focus on your appearance or on internal qualities. Here are a couple of sample topic sentences: "The summer I was twelve, I was in a bad mood nearly all of the time." "I went through a growth spurt when I was 15 that left me feeling as gangly and awkward as a baby giraffe."

2. Marta stresses again and again how important the scholarship jacket was to her and how hard she worked to win it. Write a paragraph about something you worked hard to achieve when you were younger. How long did you work toward that goal? How did you feel when you finally succeeded? Or, as an alternative, write about not achieving the goal. How did you cope with the disappointment? What lesson, if any, did you learn from the experience?

3. One reason Marta wanted the scholarship jacket so much is that she did not have the chance to participate in school sports. She wanted to make a name for herself somehow, and being a fine scholar was the way that she chose. In your high school, what were (or are) a few ways that people could become well-known? Those ways might be positive, such as being a top scholar or musician, or less so, such as being a class troublemaker. Write an essay in which you identify three categories of well-known students in your school, and describe the kind of people who belong in each category.

In Praise of the F Word

1. Has someone you know (or have you) received an F for a course? Write a paragraph describing what happened. What led to the poor performance? What effect did that experience have? Was failing a motivation to work harder? What were the effects, positive and negative, of receiving the failing grade?

2. This article concerns one way of motivating students—the threat of failure. Thinking back on your own classroom experience, what would you say are some other effective ways of motivating students to do their best? Write a paragraph that describes one other method teachers and instructors can use to motivate their students. Provide examples of times you have seen this method put into practice and how effective it seems to be.

3. Sherry believes that giving students F's when they deserve to fail would encourage them to take more responsibility for their performance. Most people agree that individuals truly overcome a problem only when they take responsibility for it, rather than expecting it to magically disappear or to be solved by someone else. In an essay, describe two or three people you know (you might be one) who have accepted responsibility for dealing with a difficult problem. The problems could be an unhappy marriage, an issue at work or school, or a crisis like substance abuse. How did the people demonstrate their willingness to take responsibility for their problems? What action did each take? How was the situation changed by what they did?

Gambling—A Dangerous Game

1. Volkmer begins his essay by describing a situation where he is asked to "rescue" a college classmate from a difficult situation. Although Volkmer is angry at his friend's request, he decides to help him anyway. Write a paragraph about a time when you were asked to bail a friend out of a tough situation. What was the situation? Did you have any misgivings about helping this friend? Specifically, what did you do? Looking back on the situation, would you have done anything differently? Explain.

2. In the article, Volkmer details the enormous growth of the casino industry in the past thirty years. Why do you think so many people are drawn to casinos? What is it in human nature that makes casinos so appealing? Write a paragraph that explains why growing numbers of our population seem to find the casino experience irresistible.

3. The author's friend Tom compares attempts to restrict gambling to "putting toothpaste back in the tube," implying that it's virtually impossible. But imagine that you are a citizen of a country which has never legalized gambling. Given the opportunity, would you vote to legalize gambling in your country? Or would you vote to keep it illegal? Write an essay which provides two or three reasons for your decision. You may use evidence provided in Volkmer's article, observations based on your life experiences, and evidence gathered from other sources (for example, you could go on the Internet and Google "reasons for gambling" and "reasons against gambling").

Part Two Readings

The Yellow Ribbon

1. Vingo's wife had to decide whether to forgive Vingo and welcome him back into her life. Think of a time when you had to decide whether or not to forgive someone. Write a paragraph that describes that situation. Begin by explaining who the other person was and what your relationship had been like. Then describe what he or she did to hurt or offend you and how you felt about what happened. Continue by explaining how you made the decision whether or not to forgive the person. End your paragraph by saying how you feel about your decision now.

2. In "The Yellow Ribbon," Hamill provides various clues to Vingo's character. His body language, his conversation with his fellow passengers, what he has to say about his past and his family, and his attitude as the bus nears his hometown all contribute to the reader's opinion of what kind of man he is. Write a paragraph that supports the following topic sentence: "Details in the story suggest that Vingo is a decent man who deserves the yellow ribbons." Find specific evidence in the story to back up that statement.

3. Vingo had to wait in suspense to discover something important about his future. Most people have had the experience of waiting a long time (or what seemed like a long time) to find out something important. Such situations might have involved a job, pregnancy, romance, health, or school. Write an essay about a situation in which you (or someone you know) had to wait for something. Tell the story a little at a time, as Hamill does, in order to keep the reader in suspense until the end. Begin by explaining what was being waited for and why it was important. Continue by describing the wait and the emotions experienced as time went by. Use time transitions (see page 184) to help the reader follow your story. Finish by telling how the wait finally ended and how you (or the person you are writing about) felt once it was over.

The Certainty of Fear

1. As Kendall states at the end of her essay, being aware of life's fears can help keep them from adversely affecting our lives. Write a paragraph about a time in your life when you recognized and overcame one of your fears. How old were you at the time? What did you fear? What steps did you take to overcome this fear? Did anyone help you along the way? Explain.

2. According to Kendall, adolescents' fear of being scorned by the "audience" can lead to such risky behaviors as getting into a car with an intoxicated driver, going on shoplifting expeditions, and so forth. Write a paragraph about a time in your life when you "went along with the crowd" and later wished you hadn't. In writing your paragraph, be sure to describe in detail the situation you were involved in, what you were thinking at the time, and the outcome of the situation. In looking back on it, how could you have acted differently?

3. Kendall discusses a television ad featuring an elderly woman saying, "Help! I've fallen and I can't get up." This example suggests that advertisers are well aware of "the certainty of fear." Write an essay which discusses three other ads that play upon people's fears. For example, you might devote one paragraph to discussing an ad that plays upon the adolescent fear of being conspicuous. In the next paragraph, you might discuss an ad which plays upon middle-aged fears of aging. Finally, you could discuss another ad which plays upon the fears of the elderly. You might conclude by stating whether you believe each of these ads presents a realistic picture of certain people's fears—or whether the ads exaggerate those fears.

Shame

1. When have you, like Gregory, regretted the way you acted in a particular situation? Perhaps you didn't speak up when someone was being teased, or perhaps you spoke harshly to someone because you were in a bad mood. Write a paragraph that describes the situation and how you acted. Conclude by explaining why you feel you acted wrongly and what you wish you had done instead.

2. Teachers are powerful figures in the lives of children. At times, because of impatience, poor judgment, a misunderstanding, anger—or some other reason—a teacher may hurt a student's feelings. Write a paragraph about a situation you experienced (or observed) in which you believe a teacher acted inappropriately and made a student feel bad. Be sure to explain not only what the teacher did but also how the student was affected.

3. A dictionary defines a word by briefly explaining its meaning. In this article, Dick Gregory defines the word *shame* in a different manner. He describes two incidents in his life in which shame played a central part. Write an essay in which you define a powerful word by narrating one or more events. Some words to consider include *gratitude, fear, jealousy, pride, joy, anger, kindness,* and *disappointment*. Your central point might be stated something like this: "Two incidents that happened ten years apart taught me the real meaning of _____." Focus on those parts of the incidents that illustrate the meaning of the word. Your essay will be more powerful if you, like Gregory, include significant bits of description and dialogue.

The Bystander Effect

1. This article suggests that people act quite differently when they are alone and when they're in a group, or in public. Write a paragraph that contrasts your own behavior when you're alone and when you're in a specific public setting. Examples of public settings might be a party, football game, dance, family gathering, or workplace. The tone of your paragraph could be serious or humorous. Provide lively examples of your behavior to illustrate your points.

2. "The Bystander Effect" is filled with anecdotes of people who stood back when help was needed, preferring to wait for someone else to act. Think of an individual who has acted in the opposite way, someone who perceived a need and quickly offered assistance. The situation might have involved an emergency like the ones mentioned in the article, or it might have concerned a more long-term need, such as an illness or a financial problem. Be specific in describing what the need was and how the individual reacted. Conclude by stating how the situation might have turned out if the individual had not helped.

3. Barkin defines *moral diffusion* as "the lessening of a sense of individual responsibility when someone is a member of a group." Drawing upon your own experience and knowledge of the world, write an essay that gives two examples of moral diffusion at work. For each example, describe what group is involved, how group members decline to take individual responsibility, and what happens as a result. Examples you might use include soldiers who commit war crimes and then say they were "just following orders," students who allow a classmate to be harassed because they don't want to get involved, or neighborhood people who let a park become overrun with trash because it's not their job to pick it up.

"Let's Roll."

1. It is nearly impossible to predict how one will behave in a frightening, unexpected situation. Write a paragraph about a time you suddenly found yourself in a scary situation. Perhaps, for example, you were being bullied, or you found yourself looking on while another student was being physically or verbally harassed. How did you respond? Looking back, are you surprised by your reaction? Do you wish you had done anything differently?

2. The terrorist attacks of September 11, 2001, made the day an unforgettable one for most Americans. Where were you when you first heard about the attacks? What was your first reaction? In looking back at that day, what is your most powerful memory? Write a paragraph about your personal response to that day. Here is a sample topic sentence: "When I think about September 11, I remember the many acts of kindness I saw New Yorkers perform for one another."

3. When the passengers on Flight 93 realized they were likely to die, many of them tried to contact their loved ones to say goodbye. If you knew your life was ending soon, who are two or three people you would want to talk to? What would you want to say to them? Write an essay in which you explain whom you would talk to, why you would choose these people, and what you would want to tell them.

Coping with Nervousness

1. What makes you nervous? What is something you occasionally—or often— need to do that makes your mouth go dry and your knees knock? Write a paragraph, in a serious or humorous vein, about a situation that makes you nervous and how you react to it. Some topics to consider include speaking in public, asking someone for a date, and applying for a job. Provide lots of vivid details so the reader can see and feel your nervousness.

2. Imagine that you were required to give a "how-to" speech on a process that you are very familiar with. What would you choose to talk about? Write a paragraph in which you state your topic and then give clear, step-by-step instructions on how to complete the process. Use time transitions (see page 184) to make your instructions easy to follow.

3. Verderber suggests that people who can master their nervousness, rather than allowing it to control them, will enjoy a sense of accomplishment. Think of a problem that you have faced and overcome. It might be a particular fear, like the one described in the article. Or you may have conquered a problem with a difficult person, overcome a bad habit, or figured out a solution to a problem in your life. Write an essay that explains, first, what problem existed and how it affected you; second, how you decided to deal with the problem; and finally, what happened as a result of your actions and how you felt about what you'd done.

Compliance Techniques: Getting People to Say Yes

1. Why do you think that compliance techniques are so often effective? What do they appeal to in the mind of the consumer that is lacking in the more straightforward approach of simply making a product available to those who want to buy it? Write a paragraph that explains a few reasons you think people are so easily influenced by compliance techniques.

2. Have you ever agreed to perform a service or to buy something and then later felt you had been persuaded by a clever, manipulative, or deceptive sales technique? Write a paragraph that describes the process that you and the seller engaged in. Use time transitions (page 184) to make the sequence of events clear to the reader. Explain how you believe you were manipulated into the agreement or purchase.

3. Think of a product you might want to sell or a service you might want people to agree to perform. Write an essay that tells how you could accomplish your goal by using three of these four compliance techniques: the foot-in-the-door, the door-in-the-face, the low-ball, and the that's-not-all techniques. Give a detailed explanation of the steps you would follow in each case. In conclusion, state which technique you believe would work best and why.

Lizzie Borden

1. Based on the information presented in the article, write a paragraph that supports one of the following main ideas: "I believe that Lizzie Borden was guilty of the murder of her parents" or "I think there is reason to doubt that Lizzie Borden killed her parents." Explain your thinking, backing up your opinions with evidence from the text.

2. Think of a time you were wrongly suspected of doing something bad. It might have involved anything from breaking a dish when you were a child to committing a crime. Write a paragraph describing that experience. Tell what you were suspected of and what (if any) evidence pointed to you. Were you able to prove you were innocent? How did you feel about being a target of suspicion?

3. The author suggests that a stereotype existing in Lizzie's day had a very specific effect—that she was found innocent of murder because of it. What are some stereotypes that exist today? How are people of certain ethnic groups, genders, sexual preferences, or economic groups stereotyped? Write an essay in which you explain how you believe certain groups are stereotyped. What effects might occur because people believe those stereotypes?

Nonverbal Communication

1. Write a paragraph that describes a time when you were made uncomfortable by another person's nonverbal communication. Tell where the incident occurred, who else was there, and what the relationship was between you and the person whose communication disturbed you. Then describe specifically what the other person did that made you uncomfortable and how you responded. You may also want to refer to the article and describe what kind of personal space was violated by this person's behavior.

2. As you may know, the "personal space zones" described in the article are not the same worldwide. For example, people from some Middle Eastern countries are accustomed to standing close together as they talk, even if they do not know one another well. On the basis of your reading of this article and your knowledge of human nature, how do you think a person from such a country might be perceived in America? How might an American visiting such a country be viewed? Write a paragraph that describes how people from the two cultures might judge one another based on their nonverbal communication.

3. Think of some people you see often but do not know well—perhaps people like store owners, your mail carrier, school secretaries, a bus driver, or a new neighbor. On the basis of their nonverbal communication, what do these people seem to be like? Write an essay in which you introduce each person and tell what impression you have formed of him or her. Be as specific and descriptive as possible as you tell about these people's nonverbal behavior and what it seems to say about them.

The Power Within

1. The author mentions Mahatma Gandhi, Robert Kennedy, and Dr. Martin Luther King—leaders who many people find inspirational. Write a paragraph about a person (he or she need not be famous) who inspires you. In writing your paragraph, be sure to describe what this person does or has done that is inspiring, as well as what you would like to accomplish by following this person's example.

2. Write a paragraph about a person you know (it could be you) who has shown a determination to succeed despite an "unequal playing field" or other obstacles in life. Describe the challenges the person has had to face. Then explain what he or she has done to overcome the challenges.

3. In "The Power Within," the author details six "escape routes" that students take to avoid studying. Write an essay in which you describe several escape routes that you or your peers are most likely to take. After presenting examples and details of each escape route, explain what must be done in each case to *not* escape in that way.

Limited Answer Key

An important note: To strengthen your reading skills, you must do more than simply find out which of your answers are right and which are wrong. You also need to figure out (with the help of this book, the teacher, or other students) *why* you missed the questions you did. By using each of your wrong answers as a learning opportunity, you will strengthen your understanding of the skills. You will also prepare yourself for the review and mastery tests in Part I, the reading comprehension questions in Part II, and the combined-skills tests in Part III, for which answers are not given here.

Answers to the Practices in Part One

1 Vocabulary in Context

Practice 1: Examples

1. Examples: *I couldn't find my car keys, I dropped a bowl of soup, my computer crashed twice;* A
2. Examples: *the TV is talking to them, others can steal their thoughts;* C
3. Example: *the giant land tortoise can live several hundred years;* B
4. Examples: *going to town concerts and ball games, visiting neighborhood friends, playing board games;* A
5. Examples: *gardening, chat groups on the Internet;* A
6. Example: *picking up the language and customs of their new home;* A
7. Examples: *financial help, free medical care;* C
8. Examples: *learning, reasoning, thinking, language;* B
9. Examples: *the phones were constantly ringing, people were running back and forth, several offices were being painted;* B
10. Examples: *accepting a bribe from a customer, stealing from an employer;* C

Practice 2: Synonyms

1. embarrasses
2. examine
3. practical
4. confusing
5. overlook
6. necessary
7. opponents
8. arrival
9. charitable
10. customary

Practice 3: Antonyms

1. Antonym: *long;* A
2. Antonym: *financial loss;* B
3. Antonym: *openly;* B
4. Antonym: *plainly;* B
5. Antonym: *active;* A
6. Antonym: *clear;* C
7. Antonym: *benefit;* B
8. Antonym: *increase in value;* B
9. Antonym: *careless;* C
10. Antonym: *weak;* C

Practice 4: General Sense

1. B
2. C
3. A
4. B
5. C
6. A
7. C
8. B
9. C
10. B

2   Main Ideas

Practice 1

1. S
   S
   G
   S

2. S
   S
   S
   G

3. S
   G
   S
   S

4. S
   S
   S
   G

5. S
   S
   S
   G

6. S
   S
   G
   S

7. S
   G
   S
   S

8. S
   G
   S
   S

9. G
   S
   S
   S

10. S
    S
    G
    S

Practice 2

Answers will vary.

Practice 3

1. P
   S
   S
   S

2. S
   S
   P
   S

3. S
   S
   S
   P

4. P
   S
   S
   S

5. S
   P
   S
   S

Practice 4

1. S
   S
   P
   S

2. P
   S
   S
   S

3. S
   P
   S
   S

4. S
   S
   S
   P

5. S
   P
   S
   S

Practice 5

Group 1
   A. SD
   B. SD
   C. MI
   D. T

Group 2
   A. MI
   B. SD
   C. SD
   D. T

Group 3
   A. T
   B. SD
   C. SD
   D. MI

Group 4
   A. MI
   B. SD
   C. SD
   D. T

Group 5
   A. MI
   B. SD
   C. T
   D. SD

Practice 6 *(Wording of topics may vary)*

1. *Topic:* Stories
   Main idea: Sentence 1

2. *Topic:* ESP
   Main idea: Sentence 2

3. *Topic:* Hospices vs. hospitals
   Main idea: Sentence 2

4. *Topic:* Driving (*or* Poor attitudes about driving)
   Main idea: Sentence 10

5. *Topic:* Dark chocolate (*or* Health benefits of dark chocolate)
   Main idea: Sentence 1

Practice 7

1. 1
2. 3
3. 2
4. 5
5. 1

3 Supporting Details

Practice 1 *(Wording of answers may vary)*

A. **Main idea:** Parents can take several steps to discourage TV watching and encourage reading.

1. Have only one TV set, and place it in the family room.
2. Connect reading with eating.
3. Don't put a TV set in a child's bedroom.

B. **Main idea:** Colleges of the early nineteenth century were distinctly different from today's schools.

1. Students were mostly white males.
   Minor details: College was considered a final polishing for upper-class gentlemen.

2. All students had to take the same courses.
   Minor details: They studied ancient languages, literature, natural science, mathematics, and political and moral philosophy.

3. Colleges were small.
   Minor details: Most had only a few dozen students, three or four professors, and three or four tutors.

4. Student life was more regulated.
   Minor details: Strict curfews determined when students had to turn off lights, and attendance at religious services was required.

Practice 2 *(Wording of answers may vary)*

A. Introduce yourself
   Refer to physical setting
   Ask a complimentary question
   Seek direct information

B. **Major detail:** Smaller labor force
   Minor detail: Milking machines use only one operator.

   Major detail: Higher milk output
   Minor detail: American cows give 7.5 times more milk than Brazilian cows.

Practice 3

   A. C
   B. B

Practice 4 *(Wording of answers may vary.)*

A. Passive listening—trying to make sense out of a speaker's remarks without being able to interact with the speaker
Example—Students listen to an instructor's lecture without having the chance to ask questions.

B. Self-serving bias—the practice of judging ourselves leniently
Example—When *he* lashes out angrily, we say he's moody. When *we* lash out angrily, we say we're under pressure.

4 Implied Main Ideas

Practice 1

Paragraph 1
1. D
2. B

Paragraph 2
3. D
4. A

Paragraph 3
5. C
6. B

Practice 2

1. C
2. D
3. B

Practice 3 *(Wording of answers may vary.)*

1. *Topic:* Reasons for lying
   Implied main idea: People tell lies for several reasons.

2. *Topic:* Being an only child
   Implied main idea: Being an only child has its drawbacks.

3. *Topic:* Opposition to capital punishment
   Implied main idea: People oppose the death penalty for different reasons.

Practice 4

1. C
2. B

5 Relationships I

Practice 1 *(Answers may vary.)*

1. also
2. For one thing
3. In addition
4. First
5. Third

Practice 2 *(Answers may vary.)*

1. After
2. Then
3. during
4. before
5. while

Practice 3 *(Wording of answers may vary.)*

A. Main idea: For several reasons, pork was America's most popular meat a hundred years ago.
1. Pigs grew quickly.
2. Pigs required little attention.
3. Pigs could be preserved cheaply.

B. Main idea: . . . aging process.
1. Our bodies simply wear out.
3. Our body chemistry loses its delicate balance.
4. Our bodies, with age, reject some of their own tissues.

Practice 4 *(Wording of answers may vary.)*

Main idea: The 1960s were a time of profound events in America.
1. 1963—assassination of President Kennedy
2. 1965—urban riots in black ghettos
3. 1968—protests against increasing American presence in Vietnam

Practice 5 *(Wording of answers may vary.)*

Main idea: People pass through three stages in reacting to unemployment.
1. Shock followed by relief
2. Strong effort to find a new job
3. Self-doubt and anxiety if no job is found

Practice 6 *(Wording of answers may vary.)*

Main idea: Taking certain steps will help you remember your dreams.
2. Put a pen and notebook near your bed.
3. Turn off your alarm so you can wake up gradually.
4. Write down the dream immediately.

Practice 7

1. B	6. A
2. A	7. A
3. A	8. B
4. B	9. A
5. B	10. B

6 Relationships II

Practice 1 *(Answers may vary.)*

1. For instance
2. for example
3. such as
4. including
5. illustration

Practice 2 *(Wording of answers may vary.)*

A. Shaping; *definition—1; example 1—2; example 2—10*
B. Irony—saying one thing but meaning another
   Example—To end the famine in Ireland, Swift suggests the Irish should raise babies to be eaten.

Practice 3 *(Answers may vary.)*

1. Similarly
2. Just like
3. in the same way
4. as
5. Just as

Practice 4 *(Answers may vary.)*

1. however
2. Although
3. but
4. despite
5. In contrast

Practice 5 *(Wording of answers may vary.)*

A. Contrast: Japanese employment practices and U.S. employment practices

B. Contrast: school and home

| Public discipline in school | Private scolding at home |
| Much competition in school | Minimal competition at home |

Practice 6 *(Answers may vary.)*

1. Because
2. as a result
3. so
4. Since
5. Therefore

Practice 7 *(Wording of answers may vary.)*

A. *Cause:* Chronic stress
   Effect: Painful muscle tension
   Effect: Weakening of body's immune system
   Effect: Psychological disorders

B. **Main idea** *(the effect):* There are several reasons people daydream.
   Major supporting details (the causes):
   1. To tolerate boring jobs
   2. To endure deprivation
   3. To discharge hostile feelings
   4. To plan for the future

Practice 8

1. A	6. B
2. C	7. C
3. B	8. A
4. C	9. C
5. A	10. B

7 Inferences

Practice 1

A. 1. C
   2. B
   3. C
   4. B

B. 5. C
   6. B
   7. A
   8. C

C. 9. B
  10. A
  11. B
  12. B

Practice 2

A. 3, 4, 6
B. 1, 4, 6
C. 1, 4, 6

Practice 3

1. B, Simile
2. C, Simile
3. B, Metaphor
4. C, Metaphor
5. C, Metaphor

Practice 4

1. B	6. B
2. B	7. A
3. C	8. A
4. C	9. C
5. A	10. B

Steps in Reading a Graph or Table

- *Title of graph:* Changes in U.S. Workforce, 1900–2010
- *Source of graph: Statistical Abstract 2005*; James M. Henslin, 2007
- *Span of years covered:* 1900–2010
- *Types of work covered:* White-collar, blue-collar, and farming

Practice 5

2, 5, 6

8 Purpose and Tone

Practice 1

1. P	6. E
2. I	7. P
3. P	8. I
4. I	9. E
5. E	10. I

Practice 2

1. B
2. C
3. A

Practice 3

1. D
2. B
3. A
4. C
5. E

Practice 4

A. 1. admiring	B. 6. straightforward
2. sympathetic	7. sarcastic
3. critical	8. threatening
4. objective	9. self-pitying
5. ironic	10. sympathetic

Practice 5

1. J
2. C
3. A
4. D
5. F

Practice 6

1. B
2. A
3. B
4. A
5. B

9 Argument

Practice 1

1. A. S
   B. P

2. A. S
   B. P

3. A. S
   B. P
   C. S

4. A. P
   B. S
   C. S

5. A. S
   B. P
   C. S

6. A. S
   B. P
   C. S

7. A. S
   B. P
   C. S

8. A. S
   B. P
   C. S
   D. S

9. A. S
   B. S
   C. P
   D. S

10. A. S
    B. S
    C. S
    D. P

Practice 2

1. A, C, F
2. C, E, F
3. A, C, F
4. B, D, E

Practice 3

1. B
2. B
3. B
4. C

Practice 4

1. C
2. A
3. B
4. D

10 Critical Reading

Practice 1

1. O
2. F
3. F+O
4. F
5. O
6. F
7. F+O
8. F
9. O
10. F

Detecting Propaganda

- *Bandwagon:* 2
- *Testimonial:* 2
- *Transfer:* 1
- *Plain Folks:* 2
- *Name Calling:* 2
- *Glittering Generalities:* 1

Practice 2

1. E
2. B
3. A
4. F
5. D
6. B
7. E
8. C
9. D
10. F

Fallacies That Ignore the Issue

- *Circular Reasoning:* 1
- *Personal Attack:* 1
- *Straw Man:* 1

Fallacies That Oversimplify the Issue

- *False Cause:* 1
- *False Comparison:* 2
- *Either-Or:* 2

Practice 3

A. 1. C
   2. B
   3. A
   4. C
   5. A

B. 6. A
   7. C
   8. B
   9. C
  10. A

Acknowledgments

Barkin, Dorothy. "The Bystander Effect." Copyright © 1991 by Trend Publications. Reprinted by permission.

Barry, Dave. Selections on pp. 324 and 358. Reprinted by permission.

Breslau, Karen, Eleanor Clift, and Evan Thomas. "Let's Roll." Originally published as "The Real Story of Flight 93." From *Newsweek*, December 3, 2001. Copyright © 2001 by Newsweek, Inc. All rights reserved. Used by permission.

Dunayer, Joan. "Here's to Your Health." Reprinted by permission.

Ellerbee, Linda. Excerpt from *Move On* on p. 312. Reprinted by permission of The Putnam Publishing Group. Copyright © 1991 by Linda Ellerbee.

Gammage, Jeff. "Wonder in the Air." Originally published as "Yes, Jin Yu, There Is Wonder in the Air." From the *Philadelphia Inquirer*, December 30, 2006. Used with permission of the *Philadelphia Inquirer*. Copyrighted 2007. All rights reserved.

Grasha, Anthony F. "Nonverbal Communication," from *Practical Applications of Psychology*, 3rd ed., pp. 248–250. Copyright © 1987 by Anthony F. Grasha. Reprinted by permission of Pearson Education, Inc., Upper Saddle River, NJ.

Gregory, Dick. "Shame," from *Nigger: An Autobiography* by Dick Gregory. Copyright © 1964 by Dick Gregory Enterprises, Inc. Used by permission of Dutton, a division of Penguin Putnam Inc.

Hamill, Pete. "The Yellow Ribbon." Copyright © 1971 by Pete Hamill. Reprinted by permission of International Creative Management, Inc.

Henslin, James M. "Gender Inequality in Health Care and in the Workplace," and table on page 293 from *Essentials of Sociology: A Down-to-Earth Approach*, 7th ed., pp. 267–270 and 308. Published by Allyn and Bacon, Boston, MA. Copyright © 2007 by Pearson Education. Reprinted by permission of the publisher.

Kellmayer, John. "Students in Shock." Reprinted by permission.

Kendall, Audra. "The Certainty of Fear." Reprinted by permission of the author.

Landers, Ann. "College Student Deplores the Drinking Around Her." Permission granted by Ann Landers/Creators Syndicate.

Lamott, Anne. Excerpt on p. 268. Copyright © 1994 by Anne Lamott. Published by Anchor Books.

Logan, Paul. "Rowing the Bus." Reprinted by permission.

Martin, James Kirby, et al. "Lizzie Borden," from *America and Its People*, 2nd ed. Copyright © 1993 by James Kirby Martin, Randy Roberts, Steven Mintz, Linda O. McMurry, and James H. Jones. Reprinted by permission of Pearson Education, Inc.

McGowan, Christopher. Excerpt on p. 590 from *The Raptor and the Lamb*. Copyright © 1977 by Christopher McGowan. Published by Henry Holt.

Orwell, George, Excerpt on pp. 287–288 from "A Hanging," in *Shooting an Elephant and Other Essays* by George Orwell. Copyright © 1950 by Sonia Brownell Orwell and renewed 1978 by Sonia Pitt-Rivers. Reprinted by permission of Harcourt, Inc.

Papalia, Diane E., and Sally Wendkos Olds. "How Parents' Child-Rearing Styles Affect Their Children," from *Psychology*, 2nd ed. Copyright © 1988 by McGraw-Hill, Inc. Reprinted by permission of The McGraw-Hill Companies.

Popkin, Roy. "Night Watch." Originally appeared in *The National Observer*. Reprinted by permission of Dow Jones & Company, Inc. Copyright © 1964 by Dow Jones & Company, Inc. All rights reserved worldwide. Also reprinted with permission from the September 1965 *Reader's Digest*.

Rhodes, Richard. Excerpt on p. 318 from *A Hole in the World*. Copyright © 1990 by Richard Rhodes. Published by Simon and Schuster.

Roberts, Paul. Excerpt on p. 580 adapted from "How to Say Nothing in 500 Words." From *Understanding English* by Paul Roberts. Copyright © 1958 by Paul Roberts.

Roker, Al. Excerpt #10 on p. 356 adapted from *Don't Make Me Stop This Car*. Copyright © 2000 by Al Roker. Published by Scribner.

Salinas, Marta. "The Scholarship Jacket," from *Nosotras: Latina Literature Today*, edited by Maria del Carmen Boza, Beverly Silva, and Carmen Valle. Copyright © 1986 by Bilingual Press/Editorial Bilingue, Arizona State University, Tempe, AZ. Reprinted by permission.

Sherry, Mary. "In Praise of the F Word." Used with the permission of Mary Sherry.

Taylor, Shelley E., Letitia Anne Peplau, and David O. Sears. "Compliance Techniques," from *Social Psychology*, 8th ed., pp. 217–219. Copyright © 1994 by Prentice-Hall. Reprinted by permission of Pearson Education, Inc., Upper Saddle River, NJ.

Trelease, Jim. Excerpts on pages 143, 169, and 582 adapted from *The Read-Aloud Handbook*. Copyright © 2001 by Jim Trelease. Published by Penguin Books.

Verderber, Rudolph E. "Presenting Your Speech," from *Communicate!* 7th ed. Copyright © 1993. Reprinted with permission of Wadsworth, a division of Thomson Learning: www.thomsonrights.com.

Volkmer, Jon. "Gambling—A Dangerous Game." Reprinted by permission of the author.

Index